D1173963

WORDSWORTH
and
The Recluse

KENNETH R. JOHNSTON

Yale University Press
New Haven and London

Published with the assistance of the Frederick W. Hilles
Publication Fund.

Copyright © 1984 by Yale University.
All rights reserved.
This book may not be reproduced, in whole
or in part, in any form (beyond that
copying permitted by Sections 107 and 108
of the U.S. Copyright Law and except by
reviewers for the public press), without
written permission from the publishers.

Designed by James J. Johnson
and set in Sabon Roman type.
Printed in the United States of America by
Edwards Brothers Inc., Ann Arbor, Michigan.

Library of Congress Cataloging in Publication Data

Johnston, Kenneth R.
   Wordsworth and The recluse.

   Includes bibliographical references and index.
   1. Wordsworth, William, 1770–1850. Recluse.
2. Wordsworth, William, 1770–1850. Recluse—Criticism,
Textual.   3. Philosophy in literature.   4. Self in
literature.   I. Title.
PR5865.J63   1984   821'.7   83-19713
ISBN 0-300-03108-4

*The paper in this book meets the guidelines for
permanence and durability of the Committee on
Production Guidelines for Book Longevity of
the Council on Library Resources.*

10 9 8 7 6 5 4 3 2 1

For Ilinca
and the happy band encircling,
KATE, LUCAS, MATTHEW, THEODORE

"On Man, on Nature, and on Human Life,
Musing in solitude, . . .

. . . .
                —may these sounds
Have their authentic comment. . . ."
                Wordsworth, "Prospectus" to *The Recluse*

The history of the unfinished *Recluse* is the history of Wordsworth's poetic life. . . . It represents, in fact, the persistent purpose of his life, to exhibit Man as a being formed for a happy and noble life, and capable in all conditions of realizing his destined end. . . . The result of any study of the history of *The Recluse* project must be to qualify considerably the conception of Wordsworth as a man of clear inflexible purpose, of steady, happy, self-satisfied industry, calmed and strengthened by the influence of Nature to pursue his aims with something of the self-absorption and indifference of Nature's own procedure.

           William Minto, "Wordsworth's Great Failure," in
           The Nineteenth Century, September, 1889

The fragment means more to us—since it demands more of us—than the whole. The mutilations are what we find the most provocative and beautiful.
           Wright Morris, *The Territory Ahead*

Contents

Preface   xi

Acknowledgments   xxv

Abbreviations   xxix

PART ONE: The First *Recluse* and the
First *Prelude*, 1797–1799

1   The First *Recluse*, 1797–1798   3
2   The First *Prelude*, 1798–1799   53

PART TWO: *The Recluse* and *The Prelude*, 1800–1806

3   "Home at Grasmere" in 1800   81
4   Building Up a Work That Should Endure:
    The Construction of the 1805 *Prelude*   100
5   *The Prelude* of 1805: A Reading in *The Recluse*   119
    The First Home: The Poet in His Poem   123
    The First Residence: Education   132
    The Second Residence: Civilization   158
    The Third Residence: Revolution   173
    The Final Home: Imagination   194
6   "Home at Grasmere" in 1806   217

PART THREE: *The Recluse* and *The Excursion*, 1808–1814

7   New Beginnings: The *Recluse* Poems of 1808   237
8   The Reckless Recluse: The Solitary (*The Excursion*, Books
    II–IV)   263
9   The Graveyard Recluse (*The Excursion*, Books V–IX)   285

Epilogue
10   *The Recluse* and *Biographia Literaria*, 1814–1815   333

Notes   363

Index   393

Preface

I

During the years in which he wrote his greatest poems, William Wordsworth was working on another poem, *The Recluse*, which he conceived to
be far greater in scope and value than all his other works. When he published the second part of it, *The Excursion*, in 1814, he likened *The Recluse*'s proposed three-part structure to "the body of a gothic church." *The
Prelude*, the long poem on "the growth of my own mind," was to be a
fourth part, an "ante-chapel" to this cathedral, and all "his minor Pieces
. . . when they shall be properly arranged, will be found by the attentive
Reader to have such connection with the main Work as may give them
claim to be likened to the little cells, oratories, and sepulchral recesses, ordinarily included in those edifices" (Preface to *The Excursion*). Thus *The
Excursion*, the longest poem by which Wordsworth was known to his contemporaries, represented less than a third of the epic plan he had in view,
while *The Prelude*, his posthumously published (1850) masterpiece, was
but an introduction to the grand edifice on which he hoped to base his poetic reputation. And all the shorter poems which, from first to last, have
guaranteed his place among the genius-poets of the English language—
"Tintern Abbey," "Michael," the Immortality Ode, "Resolution and Independence"—were relegated to subsidiary, occasional relations to *The Recluse*, as indeed they were in his mind when he composed them.

   This book is the story of that poem, and the first of its conclusions is
that *The Recluse* exists, not as an unrealized idea, but as a coherent
though incomplete body of interrelated texts, comprising nearly twenty
thousand lines of poetry susceptible of constructive reading. Since Words-

worth never published any other part of *The Recluse* but *The Excursion*
during his lifetime, his efforts to complete it have come to be regarded as
his "great failure" by scholars who have observed that he continued to
talk about it as a lively possibility—or onerous duty—until the last decade of his life, counterpointed by realistic comments from friends and relatives who doubted that it would ever be done. Furthermore, since *The
Prelude* is a much better poem than *The Excursion,* the conclusion has often been drawn that the remaining parts of *The Recluse* are not to be regretted, and that Wordsworth was badly misled in trying to write them—
partly by his huge creative egoism, partly by Coleridge's unending dream
of a great modern philosophical poem.

   Yet close attention to the large number of texts attributable to the
project discovers a poem more substantial and more valuable than critical
tradition has allowed, and a greater realization of their dreams than either
Wordsworth or Coleridge admitted: significant forms of an immense work
offering descriptive and meditative "views" of Man, Nature, and Human
Life, which was to have displaced outmoded religious epics (and perhaps
religious scriptures themselves) with persuasive representations of a humanistic philosophy integrating psychological, scientific, and sociopolitical
truths into epistemological—or at least imaginative—coherence. Though I
have doubtless erred occasionally on the side of excessive sympathy in in-
terpreting it, my conclusion is firm that an epic poem intended as the secular successor to Milton's theodicies, and whose extant sections are longer
than *Paradise Lost* and *Paradise Regained* combined, including *The Prelude, The Excursion,* "The Ruined Cottage," "Home at Grasmere," and
several other poems, cannot be dismissed in the illusion that it does not exist or by the misjudgment that it is simply a failure, but deserves full critical consideration in its own right.

   In attempting this task of interpretive reconstruction, I have tried to
avoid two equal but opposite temptations. On the one hand, I have es-
chewed much speculation on what *The Recluse* "might have been," either
as a formally complete poem or a logically systematic philosophy, preferring instead to see what aesthetic conclusions may be deduced from the
considerable number of its extant texts. Since this temptation was one often indulged by Wordsworth and Coleridge themselves, frequently as an
excuse for not finishing the poem, avoiding it has meant subordinating
their statements about the poem to the extant texts, many of which are
quite different from what might be deduced from the two poets' stated intentions at any given time. On the other hand, I have also tried to avoid
the temptation of claiming too much for *The Recluse,* recognizing that it is

after all a fragment, albeit a very large one. If it is not a nonexistent failed idea, still it is not quite an undiscovered diamond in the rough. Nonetheless, it can be read and interpreted satisfactorily in much the same way we read *The Canterbury Tales* and *The Faerie Queene*, and I believe its intention and much of its realization entitles it to membership in the company of these and other incomplete masterpieces in English, such as *An Essay on Man* and *Don Juan*. Like all of these long poems, the problem of *The Recluse* is not its incompleteness—neither its lack of conclusion nor the putative content of its missing parts—but the quality and interrelation of its existing texts. On this standard, its ratio of good, bad, and indifferent poetry can stand fair comparison with any of its rivals. As a peculiarly Romantic epic, *The Recluse* shares the fragmented fate of Byron's masterwork, and for the same general reason: an unresolved and probably unresolvable tension between its subjective, artistic motivations and its objective, social intentions. In this respect, the experience of reading it is also analogous to other ostensibly complete Romantic epics, Blake's *Jerusalem*, Shelley's *Prometheus Unbound,* Whitman's *Leaves of Grass*, and, preeminently, Goethe's *Faust*, each of which presents the same authorial history of long and difficult composition, and the same great challenge to readers to discover its coherence and integrity. I find the analogy to *Faust* particularly illuminating, even if it makes *The Recluse* pale by comparison, especially the tense relation between *Faust*'s coherent first part and its much more problematic second part, comparable to *The Prelude*'s autobiographically coherent "ante-chapel" leading into the "gothic church" of *The Recluse*—which, like *Faust* II, is supposed to turn the individual story out into sociocultural significance. If we knew that, even in its present form, Goethe considered *Faust* incomplete—and his satisfaction with what he was finally able to achieve was by no means unqualified—the stakes of readership and reputation would be quite similar to those existing for *The Recluse*.

I support my first general conclusion—that *The Recluse* lives—by demonstrating that it may be read, presenting the body of interpretation in this book, not by describing the order and contents of its constituent parts. I do some of the latter, to set each part in its biographical and historical context, but this work has already been largely accomplished by John Alban Finch, recently supplemented by Beth Darlington and Jonathan Wordsworth, and an experiment in scholarly critical interpretation is more congenial to my talents and interests. I hypothesized at first a yield merely of curious bits and pieces of unincarnate poetry, but quickly began to recognize recurrent patterns in *The Recluse*'s development. Though such pat-

terns are inevitably generated to some extent by my own interpretive energies, I am content to leave their persuasiveness and usefulness to the
judgment of my readers, for they constitute my second general conclusion:
that Wordsworth first made starts upon *The Recluse* that ended in fragmented failure; that he recoiled, second, in direct reaction to his perceived
failure, into autobiographical poetry of the sort associated with and exem-
plified by *The Prelude*; and that these recoils evidently restored him, for he
returned, third, to complete some larger or smaller portion of *The Recluse*.
This three-part pattern is repeated three times with slight variations in the
history of *The Recluse*'s active composition, corresponding to the three
parts of the present study: the First *Recluse* and the First *Prelude*,
1797–99; *The Recluse* and *The Prelude*, 1800–06; *The Recluse* and *The
Excursion*, 1808–14.

Deeper examination of these patterns led to my third general conclusion: that Wordsworth's central creative problem in pushing *The Recluse*
to completion was not simply Coleridge's failure to supply the philosophy
on which it was to be based (though this was indeed the form of the con-
tractual expectation shared by both men), but Wordsworth's own difficulty in accommodating his genius to the third of *The Recluse*'s announced
themes, "On Man, on Nature, and on Human Life"—that is, to society
and history. This difficulty has two dimensions, which a close study of the
extant *Recluse* texts clarifies.

First, as a "philosophical" poem, *The Recluse* is more moral than
metaphysical, more psychological and political than ontological and epistemological. Its philosophical assertions are everywhere crossed by its author's self-consciousness, a fact that seems much less unphilosophical in
the late twentieth century than it did in the late eighteenth century. Both
Wordsworth and Coleridge still conceived of philosophy as a logically integrated system of metaphysical articulations about the universe rather
than the human-centered programs of psychology, history, or language
that have become modern refinements of traditional philosophy, even
though both were crucially involved in the widespread cultural debates
through which this transformation occurred. It is an oversimplification,
but a useful one, to say that Wordsworth and Coleridge were in the process of writing a new kind of poetry while still in thrall to an older conception of philosophy. They were pioneers in that "breaking the crust of conventions" which John Dewey later set forth as philosophy's necessary new
agenda, seeking to become what Richard Rorty has recently defined as *edi-
fying* philosophers, for whom knowledge is a field of force (in W. V.
Quine's metaphor), even though their functional model was still that of the

great *systematic* philosophers, for whom it is an architectonic structure (*Philosophy and the Mirror of Nature* [New York: Oxford University Press, 1979], pp. 181, 369–79). In this perspective on philosophy, Wordsworth's difficulty with "Human Life" is exactly pertinent, since in it the problematic sociohistorical status of the creative interchanges between Man and Nature are more interesting than the abstract accuracy of the human mind as "mirror" of Nature. And, to identify the human faculty which both understands and affects these interchanges, Wordsworth and Coleridge, like most other post-Kantian Idealists of their time, celebrated the creative Imagination.

Second, Wordsworth's particular difficulty in this necessary turn toward Human Life appears, after close study of *The Recluse*, not simply as another glaring instance of what is often glibly assumed to be his antipathy to most human beings other than himself. Rather, the difficulty can be seen to arise precisely because of his earnest determination to turn his poetry *in* that direction, whatever his constitutional prejudices. The failure remains, but to be understood for crucially different reasons than those, like Matthew Arnold's, which criticize Wordsworth for turning his face "from half of human fate" ("Stanzas in Memory of the Author of *Obermann*"). The clearest, most contemporary, least after-the-fact statement of *The Recluse*'s intentions, which Wordsworth kept always before him, was Coleridge's suggestion that it should be addressed to idealistic intellectuals who had become cynical and disaffected by the course of the French Revolution (including the reactionary counterrevolution)—that it should, in effect, encourage the best minds of their generation to believe there was still reason to hope that the best efforts of human creativity could realize themselves in this world. Each of Wordsworth's three major efforts to complete *The Recluse* is marked by his determination to give "authentic comment" to human suffering, and each resulted in profound threats to his poetic vocation and identity, forcing him to grapple with questions of the good of poetry in the face of widespread human suffering—or, what amounts to the obverse of the same thing, in response to sweeping claims made for the possibility of universal human freedom and perfectibility.

Since *The Prelude* convincingly displays the Wordsworthian "egotistical sublime," readers have easily inferred that he is more himself there than he would have been in the outward-looking, socially responsible *Recluse*, especially when the often ponderous *Excursion* is taken to exemplify his poetry of social concern, and that his failure to complete the entire *Recluse* is a particular instance of the general failure of Romantic imaginations to turn away from contemplative enjoyment of their own powers toward the social generalizations they often imply but rarely manifest. Since a widespread tenet of modern critical faith is that an artist must necessarily fail when he tries to turn his genius toward social and historical effect, it has become common to assume that Wordsworth created *The Prelude* almost in despite of *The Recluse*, with *The Excursion* cited as confirmatory negative evidence. However, my argument shows the reverse to be true; it is neither accurate nor useful, after examining the evidence, to say that Wordsworth created *The Prelude*, the quintessentially Romantic masterpiece of self-reflection, accidentally while in pursuit of a goal somehow unsuited to his talents or less typically Romantic in its representation of imagination in social forms. Without the ideal of *The Recluse*, there was no need for *The Prelude*, and by studying *The Prelude*, large as it is, in the still larger context of *The Recluse*, we may see that it is less purely self-reflective than is often supposed, and that its self-reflection arises from and occurs within a framework of accommodating Imagination to the "residences" of Human Life. In similar fashion, it may be possible to revive more of *The Excursion* if we can view its nine thousand lines as but a subsidiary movement in the larger progress of *The Recluse*. Contrary to Ernest de Selincourt's judgment, a "constructive plan" and a "poetic form" do emerge from study of *The Recluse*, even if they are not coterminous with the "system of philosophy" Wordsworth and Coleridge felt was needed for its completion ("Introduction," *The Prelude* [Oxford: Clarendon Press, 1959], xxxix).

II

It may appear that this study is in advance of its object, since there is no book entitled *The Recluse* which a reader can pick up and read. But, although the notion that *The Recluse* can be read is a novel one, and requires surrounding oneself with several books, some available only from major university libraries, most of the poems I analyze have been read by most serious students of Wordsworth. Reading *The Recluse* at present is, to adapt Wordsworth's own metaphor, an archaeological project, uncovering the buried, ruined outlines of an immense but only partly constructed cathedral, and causing a realignment of the bearings of the smaller finished structures still standing around and above it. Since the object sought is not ineluctably there, especially not with the full-formed unities that have until very recently governed assumptions about the proper object of literary study, some methodological cautions and caveats are necessary, and may be aided by a provisional outline of the large fragment in front of which we are standing.

Approximate Plan and Chronology of *The Recluse*

The Recluse ("the body of a gothic church")

The Prelude or ("ante-chapel" "portico")	Part I	Part II	Part III
(13 books in 1805; 14 in 1850)	Book I: "Home at Grasmere" Book II?: "The Tuft of Primroses" (remainder never written)	*The Excursion* (9 books)	(Never written)

1797–99	The First Drafts: "The Ruined Cottage," "The Old Cumberland Beggar," "The Discharged Veteran," and "A Night-Piece"	1,300 lines
1798–99	The Two-Part *Prelude*	1,000 lines
1800	The Beginning of "Home at Grasmere"	500 lines
1800–02	"Prospectus" to *The Recluse*	100 lines
1803–05	Main Composition of *The Prelude*	8,000 lines
1806	Completion of "Home at Grasmere"	400 lines
1808	"The Tuft of Primroses," "To the Clouds," and "St. Paul's"	700 lines
1809–12	*The Excursion*, Books II–IV	3,200 lines
1812–14	*The Excursion*, Books V–IX	4,700 lines

NOTE: Line totals are very approximate, and some dates are almost equally so; more exact information is given in the notes to each chapter. "The Ruined Cottage" became Book I ("The Wanderer") of *The Excursion*; "The Discharged Veteran" concludes Book IV of *The Prelude*; the two-part *Prelude* forms the bulk of Books I and II of the finished *Prelude*; the placement of "The Tuft of Primroses" is conjectural.

Although all of the texts I analyze were intended at one time or another as parts of *The Recluse*, it is doubtful that all of them ever existed simultaneously in Wordsworth's mind as equal constituents. Thus, though I interpret all extant *Recluse* texts in their literary and chronological sequence, as if they constituted a single, stable poem, the shifting nature of their development requires that they be read with an awareness of their accumulative and diminishing forces. As Goethe said, "One cannot get to know works of art and of nature as finished products; one must grasp them as they come into being in order to understand them to some extent" (cited by John Gearey, *Goethe's "Faust": The Making of Part I* [New Haven: Yale University Press, 1981], p. iii). This very Romantic, organic view of grasping ends by understanding origins is highly useful in understanding fragments that never were finished. Yet it provides no stable method, and though the various extant parts of *The Recluse* were often implicitly or explicitly changing in their relation to each other, I have enforced a fictional chronological stability upon them, lest my interpretation become a juggling act, tossing new textual barbells in and out as time passes, an act beyond my skill and most readers' patience. For purposes of clarity, I have accepted Wordsworth's description of *The Recluse* as a three-part poem, with *The Prelude*, as "ante-chapel," constituting a fourth. Though not published until 1814 in the preface to *The Excursion*, this description is the most useful one for making sense of the extant *Recluse* texts and of other textual relations among them suggested during their seventeen-year gestation. Accepting this division does not mean, however, that I fully accept Wordsworth's characterization of any of the parts: that the first and third were to "consist chiefly of meditations in the Author's own person," that the second was "designed to refer more to passing events, and to an existing state of things," or that the "ante-chapel" has that relation to the other three parts or is essentially a review of "how far Nature and Education had qualified him for such employment." Quite apart from the fact that Wordsworth's description imposes his own fictional chronology on the order of *The Recluse*'s parts, I do not accept his internal characterization of each part because it will be a large part of my argument to show the dramatic tensions that recur as he tries repeatedly to shift from "meditations in [his] own person" to "passing events, and to an existing state of things."

Texts of widely varying status present themselves in such a study: some composed and published for *The Recluse* (*The Excursion*); some gradually incorporated into it but published posthumously by Wordworth's design (*The Prelude*); some composed for it but published posthumously by others ("Home at Grasmere"). Some were composed for *The Recluse*, but were published independently without reference to it ("To the Clouds"), while others changed in form and conception as a result of being moved into or out of the *Recluse* project ("The Ruined Cottage"). Others were not completed, but were clearly part of the project ("The Tuft of Primroses"), while the completeness or incompleteness of others is a matter of interpretation, often clarified by reference to the part they play in *The Recluse* ("St. Paul's"). Many of these poems changed over the years, sometimes in manuscript, sometimes in published revisions, and their changes were frequently a function of being included or excluded from *The Recluse*. All of the poems I discuss have a clearly demonstrable or strongly inferential relation to the *Recluse* project. I have excluded two which fall outside the period of Wordsworth's serious, active work on it ("Composed When a Probability Existed of Our Being Obliged to Quit Rydal Mount as a Residence," 1826; "On the Power of Sound," 1828). I have also avoided the relativizing temptation to consider almost any blank verse poem or fragment (e.g., "Nutting") as a likely candidate for *The Recluse*. Certain fragments, like "Incipient Madness" and "Argument for Suicide," were evidently intended for, but later excluded from, *The Recluse*, but the peculiar half-life of texts intended for a poem that itself was never fully realized makes them susceptible of interpretation within this study. Finally, Coleridge's *Biographia Literaria*, a text which I consider part of the *Recluse* project, if not Wordsworth's part, must be considered, if only tentatively, in an epilogue.

Facing such a welter of textual instability, one obviously proceeds with caution. Some readers may doubt whether formalist methods can be applied to this collection of texts, but all should recognize that mine is intended primarily as a formalist study, demonstrating the varying degrees of functional coherence and connection in the texts under consideration. It is, moreover, a formalism which assumes that biographical, textual, and historical information can shed light on our understanding of literary texts, including the assumption that a writer says what he means and means what he says—but not that his saying and his meaning are mutually coterminous. These assumptions, once ordinary, are nowadays so hotly contested as to constitute for some readers a contradiction in terms, even though they still describe the operational mode of most literary scholars and teachers. My formalism has sometimes taken aid and comfort from nonliterary formalisms, such as psychoanalytic criticism, which are themselves no unitary fields of practice. And some of my insights would not have come to me had I not been passingly familiar with still more compre-

hensive formalisms, such as phenomenology, structuralism, and the radically language-centered method, or attitude, of interpretation currently
known as deconstruction. The latter's concept of *aporia*, or self-exposing
"gaps" in texts, as formulated by Paul de Man, is congenial to my analysis
of fragments that are self-evidently gapped, though to train the heavy rhetorical artillery of deconstructionism upon literary fragments would be like
shooting fish in a barrel. Still, the question of whether a text can be constituted, if not unified, by its failures, is central to my reading of *The Recluse*
and establishes the pattern and dramatic interest of its three stages of development in reference to Wordsworth's determination to give Human Life
its "authentic comment." I do not by these remarks seek to remove myself
from the possibility of error and correction, but rather to acknowledge my
incomplete or inconsistent use of various interpretive methods. I aim to
elucidate a poem, not to exemplify a theory. If the charge is insufficient
methodological rigor, I can plead guilty in advance; but I must also confess
that I am not theoretically innocent.

III

Though I have intended only to interpret the developing shape of *The Recluse*, one of my results has been to provide notes toward a comprehensive
critical biography of Wordsworth. William Minto initiated the possibility
of critical study of *The Recluse* nearly a hundred years ago, with his insights that "the history of the unfinished *Recluse* is the history of Wordsworth's poetic life," and that Wordsworth achieved a grand unity of effect
for his oeuvre by "localizing" himself in the Lake Country while doggedly
maintaining that his purpose in doing so was to write a philosophical masterwork. That Wordsworth *is* "The Recluse," as well as the author of *The
Recluse*, is sufficiently indicated by his explanation of his title: "It may be
proper to state whence the poem . . . derives its Title of THE RECLUSE.
—Several years ago . . . the Author retired to his native mountains, with
the hope of being able to construct a literary Work that might live . . . a
philosophical Poem, containing views of Man, Nature, and Society; and to
be entitled, The Recluse; as having for its principal subject the sensations
and opinions of a poet living in retirement" (Preface to *The Excursion*).
What this might mean is clearer once we have looked closely into the shadowy recesses of *The Recluse*, as into Wordsworth's dream image of himself. Since Wordsworth's sense of himself is already known to be enormous, to recognize that it is even larger than generally supposed will not
be an entirely heartening experience for some readers. But though the en-

larged image does not contradict what we already know, it does extend
further than is usually realized in the direction of Human Life, or society;
indeed, the stages of *The Recluse*'s life follow with remarkable consistency
the pattern of Wordsworth's political development as described by Carl
Woodring in *Politics in English Romantic Poetry.*

Going further, it now seems possible to say that *The Recluse* was
Wordsworth's self-creating fiction; almost all of his greatest poetry was
written with direct or indirect reference to this poetic ideal of himself. This
could be put more strongly: that *The Recluse* made Wordsworth the poet
he is, even though he could not make *The Recluse*. After he abandoned the
idea in 1815 — by returning it, in effect, to Coleridge — he wrote much less
of the same great poetry, while Coleridge, having retrieved his idea, went
on to the second great stage of his career as philosopher of culture. Thus
Wordsworth's "great failure" is not *The Recluse* in any simple sense.
Though his decline in creativity parallels its fortunes, the failure was giving
up trying rather than not fully completing it. He was in fact writing and
completing poems intended for *The Recluse* during almost every year of its
active existence; during the same period he wrote the other poems, not directly intended for it, on which his reputation has come to be based. Even
though in his view many of these other poems were merely work-in-
progress, they reflected, as such, precisely the condition beyond which *The
Recluse* could not advance if it was to continue its usefulness to him.

Though much has been included, much has been omitted which
would be needed to fill out this critical biographical outline. Principally, I
regret my relative paucity of reference to the rest of Wordsworth's major
poetry. *The Recluse* background having been illumined, the better-known
shorter poems should be replaced in the foreground. Publishing exigencies
have necessitated my dropping one such chapter, relating *The Recluse* of
1797–98 to Wordsworth's other work of the same period, where the difference between his two main kinds of poems in *Lyrical Ballads* — lovely
lyrics celebrating relations between his mind and Nature, and stark ballads
about suffering humanity — can be seen as a direct reflection of his contemporaneous compositional difficulties on *The Recluse*: the difficulty of
integrating his aesthetic appreciation of nature with a socially responsible
poetry. Similarly, the 1800 volume of *Lyrical Ballads*, with its ambivalent
emphases on *homecoming pairs* would correlate very closely with Wordsworth's *Recluse* work of 1800, "Home at Grasmere." And the great preface of 1800 may be seen as constituting a prose version of the "Prospectus" to *The Recluse* at least as meaningfully as it forms an introduction to
that collection of smaller poems, where the discrepancy between its grand

claims and the simplicity of many of those poems has been an endless source of readerly bewilderment and critical controversy. Similar recontextualizing should also be done for Wordsworth's two other major collections during the *Recluse* years, the *Poems, in Two Volumes* of 1807 and the *Poems* of 1815, but I have limited myself to consideration of their prefaces, which in their original form carefully place the poems in those collections in the context of *The Recluse*, just as the 1814 preface to *The Excursion* likens all Wordsworth's shorter works to the "little cells, oratories, and sepulchral recesses" of its "gothic church."

Directions that such recontextualizing might take are suggested by two books that came to hand while my manuscript was being edited, David Pirie's *Wordsworth: The Poetry of Grandeur and of Tenderness* (London: Methuen, 1982) and Jonathan Wordsworth's *William Wordsworth: The Borders of Vision*. Both try to hold in fruitful solution tensions in Wordsworth's poetry that are usually simplified, resolved, or set in contradiction, just as I try to show how, in *The Recluse*, the poet's glory in nature and his own creativity is enriched by his determination to look and speak upon "Human Life." Jonathan Wordsworth provides, in addition, an epilogue on *The Recluse* that valuably complements my study, further expanding Finch's and Darlington's information about the circumstances of its composition, excellently filling in the background of its millenarian and necessarian impulses, and pointing out the strains occasioned by Wordsworth's attempts to combine his early, brief acceptance of pantheism with his later views of a more individually active human imagination. He also demonstrates clearly for the first time Cowper's influence on early models of *The Recluse*, as well as finely tracing Wordsworth's Miltonic echoes throughout. However, our approaches to the poem are also complementary in other more dialectical, not to say contradictory, ways, as suggested by his epilogue's title: "The Light That Never Was." By concentrating on the abstract systems of philosophy, politics, and religion that were to inform *The Recluse*, he follows—indeed, may be said to complete—traditional lines of investigation which find reasons for the poem's incompletion in the author's insufficient articulation of its structuring systems. Our objects are thus as different as our methods, since I demonstrate by intrinsic formal analysis the orders of meaning that do exist within and among the various *Recluse* texts, showing how in certain complete and justifiable senses it was written, rather than explaining by external reference how and why it was not.

I would, finally, have liked to develop further the implications of the gothic metaphor for the shape of Wordsworth's oeuvre. The image is sometimes understood to point toward a seamless (and therefore unachieved) unity, but the various revivals of Gothicism by 1815 make it likely that Wordsworth—who now appears as a pioneer in recognizing their serious intellectual possibilities—intended to convey an image of unity-in-diversity, of different styles and structures accreted over long periods of time from common materials by anonymous workmen. Nor is the subsequent and final image he adopted for his oeuvre, likening it to the body, emotions, and life-stages of a person, necessarily a scaling-down or shift in his intentions. Both are organic images. The ruins of great cathedrals figure importantly throughout his life and works, not only in the cornerstone of *The Recluse*, but at Tintern Abbey, the Grand Chartreuse, Bolton Priory, the retreats of Saints Basil and Gregory in Asia Minor, the Grasmere rectory where some of *The Recluse* was written, and even Stonehenge and other temples of other dispensations. Goethe also used the Gothic figure to describe *Faust*, and its usefulness for Wordsworth's entire oeuvre is enriched by his constant struggle, clearly evident in *The Recluse*, between wholeness and fragmentation. The struggle is apparent not only in the physical state of the *Recluse* texts themselves, but in their recurrent image patterns of ruined cottages and ruined dwellers, of unsatisfactory "Residences" and worthy "Inmates," of homes planned, built, and destroyed, and of the grave itself as terminal or memorial. The Romantic archetype for all such images is the sensitive traveler (real or mental) standing alone amid the ruins of a departed civilization, wild with surmise at the possibilities they suggest to his new secular spirit, yet nearly crazed by the enormity of his thoughts and the task they imply, a cultural borderer wandering between two worlds. This situation recurs crucially for both Wordsworth and Coleridge in writing (or writing about) *The Recluse*. Coleridge thought the destruction and fall of Jerusalem "the only fit subject remaining for an epic poem" (see Elinor Shaffer, *"Kubla Khan" and "The Fall of Jerusalem,"* Cambridge University Press, 1975); Wordsworth's extant epic repeatedly challenges itself in metaphors of the ruined edifices of English Christianity yet projects New Jerusalems that are neither religious nor liberal, but the despotic Oriental metropolises to which, in the very frenzy of his democratic humanism, he consistently likened the new worlds of his imagination.

The Gothic pattern is also useful in reviewing Wordsworth's reputation. Though he continues to inspire or provoke more study than any of his contemporaries, it is remarkable that he should so often be addressed, from Shelley and Keats through Browning and Arnold to Trilling and Hartman, in a framework of disappointed expectations. The name of this framework, more often than not, turns out to be *The Recluse*, the ultimate superwork of the Romantic imagination in English, which failed to deliver all that it promised. Carefully nurturing the image of himself as *the* Poet of Nature, Wordsworth's greatest imaginative achievement may have been his success in identifying his literary works with almost the whole of our given external world, or reality, and connecting his bizarre originality to the normal, the usual, and the commonplace. Scaling this "giant" down to human size has been the business of Wordsworth criticism ever since Coleridge began it in the *Biographia Literaria*, provoked by the need to rectify Wordsworth's claims for *The Recluse*. One cannot study Wordsworth for long without becoming aware of *The Recluse*'s looming shadow, and I have noticed, along the way of my investigations, certain patterns of critical rhetoric whereby any number of assertions are passingly substantiated by reference to its "failure," so that it functions, in its apparent absence, as an invisible subfloor or resonating vacuum chamber wherein Wordsworth's declining creativity, or religious or political conservatism, or prosyness or simplicity or egoism or Miltonism, or whatnot, may be more forcefully asserted. I do not say that all these assertions are wrong, but I hope by the present study to have enabled them to be made more meaningfully.

Many things remain to be said to integrate these general observations with various existing views of the relation of the self to nature and to society in Wordsworth's poetry. These issues, moreover, are not only important to understanding Wordsworth, but emanate directly from him down through the history of post-Romantic modern poetry, especially as it turns upon questions of the value and function of art (and criticism) in technologized mass democracies. In a sense, "the FIRST GREAT PHILOSOPHICAL POEM" (as Coleridge always headlined *The Recluse*) was not a discrete poem at all, but a germ of the modern secular ideal of the entire canon of imaginative literature constituting a scripture wherein we read and build our minds. Thus regarded, these texts have stimulated a massive growth of educational and interpretive institutions around themselves, a stimulus traceable in the English-speaking world to no source more important than Coleridge's ideas of cultural criticism. Wordsworth received some of these ideas from his friend as directives toward *The Recluse*, while Coleridge derived some of them in turn from *The Recluse*, especially the conception of the *clerisy*, or secular clergy, which in diverse forms will include most readers of this book. These issues are, however, far beyond the scope of the present study, and I have been content to let their implications speak glancingly for themselves as I pursue the path of my main task, reading *The Recluse*.

Acknowledgments

In a book often concerned with the relation of creative imagination to social institutions, it is a pleasure to record my indebtedness to the two institutions whose material aid has helped bring it to fruition. Indiana University has generously supported my work with grants-in-aid over several
years, successive chairmen of its Department of English—Donald J. Gray,
Kenneth Gros Louis, Paul Strohm, and Mary Burgan—have responded to
my requests for teaching assignments with warm personal understanding,
and my scholarly needs have been excellently accommodated by the resources of its libraries, particularly those under the care of Anthony W.
Shipps, English Liaison Librarian, and William Cagle, Director of the Lilly
Rare Book Library. Second, I am grateful to the National Endowment
for the Humanities, whose Summer Stipend in 1978 and Fellowship for Independent Research in 1979–80 allowed me to integrate the various parts
of this study into a whole. I would be remiss if I did not also acknowledge
a third debt of a semi-institutional nature to Richard and Sylvia Wordsworth, Directors of the Wordsworth Summer Conference in Grasmere;
their kind invitations and stimulating hospitality in 1972 and 1982 allowed me to present for public discussion the work which, in the event,
formed the beginning and ending of this book.

On the front of this whole study is written my obligation to Harold
Bloom and Geoffrey Hartman, who, early and late, teacher and mentor,
have led me forward in my way by intellectual prowess and spiritual example. They are present in this book more pervasively than any direct citation can acknowledge, yet I must rely on their friendship and skill in critical dialectics for appreciation and understanding of the often considerable
difference between my conclusions and theirs (which are not, of course,

identical with each other) on Wordsworth, Romanticism, and the goals
and methods of literary study.

My debts to the traditions of Wordsworth scholarship will be evident
throughout, but I wish to thank initially those intrepid explorers who have
preceded me in the shadowy paths of *The Recluse*. Foremost among these
is John Alban Finch, whose unpublished 1964 Cornell University dissertation, "Wordsworth, Coleridge, and 'The Recluse,' 1798–1814," might well
have obviated the need for my book if Finch had not died heroically
rescuing students from a fire in 1967. My study stands upon Finch's shoul-
ders, enabling me to do what he was not able to, critically interpret *The
Recluse*'s extant texts, by virtue of what he has done: given the first detailed account of its textual and biographical circumstances of composition, especially in its early stages. Finch's primary interpretive interest,
Wordsworth's debt to Milton in his epic plan and language, is, moreover,
persuasive enough for me to feel free to refer to it only in passing, since
close consideration of such an important issue would result in another and
quite different study. Like all Wordsworthians, I am in the debt of the edi-
torial labors of Ernest de Selincourt and Helen Darbishire, but like only
the most recent scholars am I in a position to reappreciate their work in
the new light cast upon Wordsworth's texts by the Cornell University Press
editions of the earliest form of his poems, directed by Stephen Parrish. I
have profited particularly from the illumination which this new work has
cast upon the relation of early poems to the *Recluse* project in the editions
by James Butler (*The Ruined Cottage*), Beth Darlington (*Home at Grasmere*), and Joseph Kishel (*Late Poems for "The Recluse"*). To these editors, as well as to Wordsworth's modern biographer, Mary Moorman, and
his definitive chronicler, Mark Reed, the extent of my gratitude is qualified
only by my sense of the utter reliance I have placed upon their facts.

Turning to more personal debts, I thank Morris Dickstein, David Erdman, Henry Remak, Michael Rosenblum, and Stuart Sperry for frequent
help in time of need; Jared Curtis, Jerome Christensen, Linda David, Sybil
Eakin, Ellen Graham and Barbara Folsom of Yale University Press, Karen
Hanson, Jeffrey Huntsman, J. Hillis Miller, Paul Strohm, and, last but
most, Carl Woodring for reading parts of the manuscript and commenting
frankly upon them; and others who have shown that the words "professional colleague" can still signify encouraging yet critical good friendship:
Michael Cooke, Alan Grob, Frank Jordan, Peter Manning, Gene Ruoff,
and Gordon Thomas. Only Elizabeth Silins can know how much the early
stages of this project owe to her encouragement; for my first training in
literary study I shall always be grateful to Henriette C. K. Naeseth and

Dorothy Parkander of Augustana College (Illinois). I appreciate the endurance of graduate students in three seminars between 1978 and 1982 dealing with aspects of this study, and to three in particular—Karl Johnson, Richard Matlak, and Sara Suleri—who have become my teachers in turn.

In thanking the editors of professional journals for permission to reprint material, I single out Marilyn Gaull of *The Wordsworth Circle* as first among equals, for to her I owe a debt far greater than that of republication rights for portions of "Wordsworth's Reckless Recluse" (1978). Her encouragement and decisions in my favor got this project off the ground into reality. I also thank the editors of *Studies in Romanticism* for permission to reprint parts of "'Home at Grasmere': Reclusive Song" (1975) in chapters 3 and 6, of *ELH* for the parts of "Wordsworth's Last Beginning: *The Recluse* in 1808" (1976) which appear in chapter 7, and of *PMLA* for "Wordsworth and *The Recluse*: The University of Imagination" (1982), an overview of my argument which is embedded throughout the present work.

Drafting these pages on what would have been my father's eighty-first birthday, I offer to him and to my mother, public-school teachers of music and literature who fulfilled ideals like those envisioned in *The Recluse*, the thanks which can never be commensurate to the gift. Finally, this book's cause from first to last and without end is acknowledged in its dedication to my wife.

Abbreviations

Borders	Jonathan Wordsworth, *William Wordsworth: The Borders of Vision*. Oxford: Clarendon Press, 1982.
BL, I, II	*Biographia Literaria*, ed. James Engell and W. Jackson Bate. 2 vols. Princeton: Princeton University Press, 1983.
Butler	James Butler, ed., *"The Ruined Cottage" and "The Pedlar,"* by William Wordsworth. Ithaca, N.Y.: Cornell University Press, 1979.
BWS	*Bicentenary Wordsworth Studies in Memory of John Alban Finch*, ed. Jonathan Wordsworth. Ithaca, N.Y.: Cornell University Press, 1970.
CEY	Mark Reed, *Wordsworth: The Chronology of the Early Years, 1770–1799*. Cambridge: Harvard University Press, 1967.
CMY	Mark Reed, *Wordsworth: Chronology of the Middle Years, 1800–1815*. Cambridge: Harvard University Press, 1975.
Darlington	Beth Darlington, ed., *"Home at Grasmere": Part First, Book First, of "The Recluse,"* by William Wordsworth. Ithaca, N.Y.: Cornell University Press, 1977.
Douglas	Wallace W. Douglas, *Wordsworth: The Construction of a Personality*. Kent, Ohio: The Kent State University Press, 1968.
Finch	John Alban Finch, "Wordsworth, Coleridge, and 'The Recluse,' 1798–1814." Ph.D. dissertation, Cornell University, 1964.
Friedman	Michael Friedman, *The Making of a Tory Human-*

	ist: William Wordsworth and the Idea of Community. New York: Columbia University Press, 1979.
Hartman	Geoffrey Hartman, *Wordsworth's Poetry, 1787–1814.* New Haven: Yale University Press, 1964, 1971.
HG	"Home at Grasmere" (see Darlington).
LEY	*The Letters of William and Dorothy Wordsworth: The Early Years, 1787–1805,* ed. Ernest de Selincourt, rev. Chester Shaver. Oxford: Clarendon Press, 1967.
LMY I	*The Letters of William and Dorothy Wordsworth: The Middle Years, Part I, 1806–1811,* ed. Ernest de Selincourt, rev. Mary Moorman. Oxford: Clarendon Press, 1969.
LMY II	*The Letters of William and Dorothy Wordsworth: The Middle Years, Part II, 1812–1820,* ed. Ernest de Selincourt, rev. Mary Moorman and Alan G. Hill. Oxford: Clarendon Press, 1970.
LSTC (I–VI)	*Collected Letters of Samuel Taylor Coleridge,* ed. Earl Leslie Griggs. 6 vols. Oxford: Clarendon Press, 1956–71.
Lindenberger	Herbert Lindenberger, *On Wordsworth's "Prelude."* Princeton: Princeton University Press, 1963.
McFarland	Thomas McFarland, *Romanticism and the Forms of Ruin: Wordsworth, Coleridge, and Modalities of Fragmentation.* Princeton: Princeton University Press, 1980.
Memoirs	Christopher Wordsworth, *Memoirs of William Wordsworth.* 2 vols. London: Moxon, 1851.
M. I., M. II.	Mary Moorman, *William Wordsworth.* Vol. I, *The Early Years, 1770–1803.* Oxford: Clarendon Press, 1957; *William Wordsworth.* Vol. II, *The Later Years, 1803–1850.* Oxford: Clarendon Press, 1965.
MH	Jonathan Wordsworth, *The Music of Humanity: A Critical Study of Wordsworth's "Ruined Cottage."* London: Thomas Nelson and Sons, 1969.
NS	M. H. Abrams, *Natural Supernaturalism: Tradition and Revolution in Romantic Literature.* New York: W. W. Norton & Co., 1971.
NSTC	*The Notebooks of Samuel Taylor Coleridge,* ed. Kathleen Coburn. 3 vols. New York: Bollingen Foundation and Pantheon Books, 1957–73.

Onorato | Richard Onorato, *The Character of the Poet: Wordsworth in "The Prelude."* Princeton: Princeton University Press, 1971.

Parrish | Stephen Parrish, ed., *"The Prelude," 1798–1799,* by William Wordsworth. Ithaca, N.Y.: Cornell University Press, 1977.

Potts | Abbie Findlay Potts, *Wordsworth's "Prelude": A Study of Its Literary Form.* Ithaca, N.Y.: Cornell University Press, 1953.

Prelude | William Wordsworth, *The Prelude: or, Growth of a Poet's Mind,* ed. Ernest de Selincourt, rev. Helen Darbishire. Oxford: Clarendon Press, 1959.

Prose (I–III) | *The Prose Works of William Wordsworth,* ed. W. J. B. Owen and Jane Worthington Smyser. 3 vols. Oxford: Clarendon Press, 1974.

PW (I–V) | *The Poetical Works of William Wordsworth,* ed. Ernest de Selincourt and Helen Darbishire. 5 vols. Oxford: Clarendon Press, 1940–49.

Sheats | Paul D. Sheats, *The Making of Wordsworth's Poetry, 1785–1798.* Cambridge, Mass.: Harvard University Press, 1973.

TP | "The Tuft of Primroses"

TT (I–II) | *Specimens of the Table Talk of Samuel Taylor Coleridge,* ed. Henry Nelson Coleridge. 2 vols. London: John Murray, 1835.

WAG | Jonathan Wordsworth, M. H. Abrams, and Stephen Gill, eds., *"The Prelude": 1799, 1805, 1850.* New York: W. W. Norton & Co., 1979.

Wordsworth & Gill | Jonathan Wordsworth and Stephen Gill, "The Two-Part *Prelude* of 1798–99," *JEGP* 72 (1973): 503–25.

WS | Karl Johnson, *The Written Spirit: Thematic and Rhetorical Structure in Wordsworth's "The Prelude."* Salzburg: Institut für Englische Sprache und Literatur, 1978.

PART ONE

The First *Recluse* and the First *Prelude*, 1797–1799

1

The First *Recluse*, 1797–1798

Why is it we feel
So little for each other, but for this,
That we with nature have no sympathy,
Or with such things as have no power to hold
Articulate language?
And never for each other shall we feel
As we may feel, till we have sympathy
With nature in her forms inanimate,
With objects such as have no power to hold
Articulate language. In all forms of things
There is a mind.

PW, V.340

The Recluse was not heralded with trumpets. Its first notice rises out of the same mix of large projects and small prospects that characterized all Wordsworth's correspondence with his old college friends in the 1790s. After he and Coleridge met utter defeat in their concerted assault on the London stage in December 1797 (with *The Borderers* and *Osorio*), he abandoned dramatic blank verse and spent the next three months composing blank verse narratives. By early March of 1798 he had accomplished enough to mention *The Recluse* to two Cambridge friends, an item of good news amid his usual complaints of boredom and inactivity. On March 6 he reported to James Tobin:

> I have written 1300 lines of a poem in which I contrive to convey most of the knowledge of which I am possessed. My object is to give pictures of Nature, Man, and Society. Indeed I know not any thing which will not come within the scope of my plan. [*LEY*, 212]

Except that this is a poem, and is actually partly composed, its omnibus quality resembles a liberal journal, to have been called *The Philanthropist*,

NOTE: Epigraphs for each chapter are from *PW*, V, appendix B: "Fragments of blank verse akin to *The Prelude* and *The Excursion*, written at a time when Wordsworth was contemplating *The Recluse*, or working at *The Ruined Cottage* and *The Pedlar*."

which Wordsworth had proposed starting in detailed correspondence with William Mathews between 1792 and 1794.[1] Like that project, *The Recluse* assumes the didactic stance of prevailing Neoclassical models and is romantic only in its exaggerated scope, as if the young Alexander Pope were proposing *An Essay on Man*, his magnum opus, as his first serious publication rather than *An Essay on Criticism*. To a degree, this is exactly what Wordsworth is doing, and it accounts in part for his failure to complete the project. Yet Pope's neoclassical decorum cannot be used to whip Wordsworth's romantic excess. The original plans for *An Essay on Man* envisioned a work at least four times larger than the poem we have, topically as comprehensive as Wordsworth's: "having proposed to write some pieces on Human Life and Manners . . . I thought it more satisfying to begin with considering *Man* in the abstract, his *Nature* and his *State*."[2] In both cases and many others that could be adduced, such as Whitman's *Leaves of Grass*, young genius projects a world-encompassing artwork as a function of its own self-recognition. Similar projections are characteristic of fools and madmen; hence the corollary motivation for a continuous fluctuation between attention to the world and to the artistic self: fluctuations, in Wordsworth's case, between *The Recluse* and *The Prelude*.

A second letter, to James Losh on March 11, is similarly relaxed. Losh, like Tobin (like Mathews, like Wordsworth, like Coleridge), had been trying to do something in a literary way, having recently become a contributor to another friend's new enterprise, *The Œconomist or Englishman's Magazine*. Like Wordsworth's proposed *Philanthropist*, this "cheap monthly for the enlightenment of the masses" (*LEY*, 214*n*) was liberal-reformist in slant, "a quiet, indeed, a very safe, little journal."[3] But Wordsworth has not yet seen it, because he has been "tolerably industrious within the last few weeks. I have written 1300 lines of a poem which I hope to make of considerable utility; its title will be *The Recluse or views of Nature, Man, and Society*" (*LEY*, 214). Given the gentlemanly assumptions governing these letters, Wordsworth does not want to appear too enthusiastically hard-working, yet to have written 1,300 lines in a few weeks was a huge achievement for him, even though it was more like two months, and even if most of them were additions to "The Ruined Cottage," composed a year earlier.[4] He must have been somehow aware that these 1,300 lines were the first poetry he had written which can be called "major" without qualification: this is *The Recluse*'s first claim to fame. But, to Losh, its "considerable utility" probably only balanced *The Œconomist*'s sense of social responsibility.

Scholarly discussion of *The Recluse* has made much of these two let-

ters of March 1798, and with good reason: there is no further mention of
The Recluse by name for six years in the Wordsworth correspondence, until he is deep into composition of *The Prelude* and justifying time spent on
it as an "appendix" to *The Recluse* (*LEY*, 440). It is mentioned in Coleridge's letters during the interim, and we may be sure it loomed large in
their private conversations, but nothing substantial enough was produced
to warrant sharing the news with friends who might wonder, with a not
altogether uncompetitive interest, what Wordsworth was up to. Although
the letters to Tobin and Losh imply hundreds of more lines forthcoming
("my eloquence, speaking with modesty, will be carried off . . . for at least
a year and a half to come . . . into my poem," *LEY*, 212), the 1,300 lines
announced then constitute nearly the sum total of what was to be written
of *The Recluse*, except for revisions, for the next two years.

The 1,300 lines of poetry which Wordsworth called *The Recluse* in
March of 1798 constitute four poems, all subsequently published in revised form.[5] First, longest, and most important is "The Ruined Cottage,"
composed in the spring and summer of 1797, before Wordsworth and
Coleridge were living in close quarters, and before Wordsworth had got
from Coleridge any substantial ideas about a philosophic masterpoem. Indeed, Coleridge's hearing this bleak tale of the ruining of Margaret and her
cottage by economic hardship and mental stress may have stimulated him
to propose such a project to Wordsworth. Once settled at Alfoxden,
Wordsworth extensively revised and extended it until, by March 1798, it
contained about 900 lines.[6] It continued to be revised over the years, expanding or contracting material about its internal narrator, the Pedlar, until it was published as Book One of *The Excursion* in 1814, with Margaret's story put in the mouth of the Wanderer, a generic type of the
Pedlar. The second poem is "The Old Cumberland Beggar," which may
have existed as a sketch even earlier than "The Ruined Cottage,"[7] but was
finished in 1797, then expanded with discursive political commentary in
1798. An "overflow" of 20 lines was published in the 1798 *Lyrical Ballads* as "Old Man Traveling; Animal Tranquility and Decay, A Sketch,"
and the remainder, with the main title, in the second edition of 1800. Together, they make up just over 200 lines. The remaining two *Recluse*
poems were composed in January and February of 1798. "A Night Piece"
is a visionary skyscape of two dozen lines, closely based on Dorothy's
journal entry of January 25, 1798. Its claim to be one of the first *Recluse*
poems is weakest on external grounds, but internally it is consistent with
the other three in style, mood, and theme.[8] It was first published in

Wordsworth's collected poems of 1815. Finally, there is Wordsworth's description of his encounter with a sickly discharged veteran on a deserted highway late at night. Containing slightly less than 200 lines in its original manuscript version,[9] it appears at about half this length as the concluding episode of Book IV in the 1805 *Prelude* and did not appear in print until its posthumous publication in 1850.

In length, these four poems add up almost exactly to the 1,300 lines Wordsworth mentioned to Tobin and Losh. More important, they have several elements in common to justify his speaking of them as a single unit. Although they do not in their extant versions form a continuous narrative, each of them is a coherent poem. They are all blank verse narratives with strong meditative overtones, and can easily be imagined as a connected set of "pictures" or "views" of Man, Nature, and Society. Moreover, they all follow the rudimentary plot which Wordsworth, left to his own devices at this time, could hardly vary: walking along a road, he meets somebody who tells him his or her life-story. Since these life-stories have little plot themselves, other than the wearing facts of life's constant losses (of love, family, welfare, faith, hope, and sanity), the true plot of the first *Recluse* poems, as of many of the lyrical ballads Wordsworth composed subsequently in 1798, becomes the effort of an external narrator to respond adequately to a tale he's been told and now retells.

The thematic unity of the four poems arises from their characters and settings, as interpreted by this narrator-observer. Except for "A Night-Piece," they are about the poorest, most miserable people in England in the 1790s. The deranged war widow, the disabled discharged veteran, and the infirm, ancient beggar are living victims of the social disruption war with France caused in a domestic economy already stretched thin by the double pressure of imperial expansion and technological innovation. Traditional communities at home and abroad were being eroded by the force of industrialism in the one and imperialism in the other. To write about the victims of these processes, especially after the spectre of revolutionary terror had raised its head in France, while having invested oneself in the same system, as Wordsworth had, in his brother John's potentially lucrative voyages for the East India Company,[10] constituted a strong and potentially contradictory political statement. Wordsworth was not unique in writing about such subjects, yet his treatment of them differs from most other contemporary artists' depiction of similar material, whether with sentimental regret in the tradition of Goldsmith's *The Deserted Village* (1770), unsentimental realism like Crabbe's *The Village* (1783), liberal humanitarianism such as Langhorne's *The Country Justice* (1777) and much of Cowper, or radical agitation propaganda like Joseph Fawcett's *The Art of War* (1795).[11] Wordsworth's treatment also differed from another attitude toward human suffering, not much represented in the art of the period but the very staple of received opinion in such matters, the laissez-faire view that suffering, however unfortunate, is inevitable, eternal, or otherwise necessary in the scheme of things. This view was not the sole property of selfish rich people but could also be found in such works as Godwin's *Enquiry concerning Political Justice* (1793) and Malthus's *Essay on the Principle of Population* (1798). Wordsworth entertains elements of all these attitudes in the first *Recluse* poems, sometimes pursuing them to pathological extremes, as he tried to clarify his own mind about his suffering subjects.

He closely observes the suffering caused by social forces beyond the control of ordinary people, particularly as it affects their mental condition as both cause and effect of their inability or unwillingness to cope with consequences. In "The Ruined Cottage," bad harvests throw Margaret's husband out of work,[12] then unemployment drives him to enlist for the government's bounty of three pounds, leaving Margaret to wonder forever if he will return, while the rest of her life (cottage, children, sanity) slips away almost without her noticing. The discharged veteran has been permanently disabled by malarial fever from his service in the West Indies, a service consisting largely of subduing the native population and suppressing rebellious slaves, and he has returned to his native land weakened in his will to care for himself, putting his trust instead "in the God of Heaven / And in the eye of him that passes me." The social threat to the old Cumberland beggar is not his poverty, but legislation aimed at removing mendicant nuisances from the public highways by placing them in workhouses. Although such a law would effectively prevent the beggar from reaching his goal in one version of the poem—the naval hospital at Falmouth where his son is dying—he can do no more for his son than he can for himself, and Wordsworth's impassioned opposition to the law rises because it would remove a source of humanizing charitable instincts from the local neighbors who help the beggar on his rounds. The progress of all three "views" of Man, Nature, and Society begins with a situation created by Society and works inward to observations on the mind of Man, set down in a world of Nature whose operations contrast, support, or otherwise illuminate what man has made of man.

In all four poems, the narrator or the characters travel along the public highway, and their need for shelter and security is the immediate motivation for the minimal action of the narrative. Even in the relatively static

"Ruined Cottage," where we observe the dereliction of shelter rather than the search for it, the Pedlar's seasonal rounds provide the time lapses during which Margaret and her home may plausibly be seen to decline and decay. These settings—the open road, the houseless plain—where the physical need for shelter is raised to metaphysical proportions (Is man at home on earth?), are the same Wordsworth had used in *Salisbury Plain* (1793–95) and *The Borderers* (1796–97), and the first *Recluse* poems are direct advances from these in Wordsworth's wedding of scene, action, and theme. But material facts contribute as much as philosophy and poetics to his new work. He himself had been wandering—touring, more accurately—the highways and byways of England in the mid-1790s, and had had plenty of opportunity to see the "shoals of artisans" and other poor folk cast adrift by economic and military dislocations. He was deeply affected by what he saw, even though his inherited social assumptions sometimes led him to observe these poor people as creatures not fully human. But are they fully human, and if so, are we?

These were the questions Wordsworth was beginning to invest with feeling informed by Coleridge's philosophical conversation. Much as he loved wandering, he loved homecoming more, and these poems beat with the pulse of this dialectical pressure. The idea of being together with Dorothy in "our little cottage" had been the controlling fantasy of both their lives in the early nineties and appears as a symbolic focus of hope in many of his early poems.[13] Even after they ended their long separation, the sight of other broken homes evoked special pathos in Dorothy's journals and William's poems. At Racedown, in Dorset, they had seen English poverty at its worst, the huts of the peasants, Dorothy reported, "shapeless structures (I can almost say) of wood and clay, indeed they are not at all beyond what might be expected in savage life" (*LEY*, 162). Throughout the history of *The Recluse*, the image of a "happy band" secure in a snug cottage, perhaps derived from Edmund Burke's "little platoon," will appear as a symbolic contrast and partial resolution to dislocated lives and ruined cottages in the world at large, with strongly regressive psychological and political undertones.[14]

Yet for all the stark representation of human suffering in these poems, a right attitude toward it is by no means taken for granted. Indeed, exploring a proper attitude is in large part the point of all of them—a point easily overlooked by modern readers informed by more than a century of official social liberalism, ready to grant plausibility to the philosophical ramblings of picturesque pedlars, and insufficiently experienced in the phenomena of widespread beggary to appreciate how easily feelings of disgust and aversion arise toward it. The need of a proper attitude is the narrator's problem in each poem. A markedly aesthetic or poetical young person, he moves from an initially mistaken or inadequate response to suffering to one more deeply informed by a recognition of the human *being* present in the sufferer. His final attitude, though shifted from prior aversion or senti-mental pity, is not the conventional liberal assumption that "something should be done" for, about, or to the sufferers. Although charity is as-sumed to be good (not without difficulty, in the case of the veteran), the poems nevertheless indicate that it is insufficient or beside the point. The narrator represents the normal state of human being relative to the abnor-mal sufferer; he is able to offer some assistance. But whatever he does, the poems offer the corollary that little can be done: Margaret is inconsolable, the veteran is preeminently careless of himself, and the old beggar is be-yond self-reflection of any sort. They represent extremes of the human condition, for which *nothing can be done*, and therefore threaten the nor-mal, ordinary narrator. The normal is not enough. Anger, fear, and impa-tience are part of the narrator's response, further provoked by suggestions that none of the sufferers would help themselves even if they could. The narrator's increasing mental stress thus becomes a mirroring correlative of the sufferer's condition, whether it is fear (as in his first reaction to the vet-eran) or helpless pity (as in his penultimate response to the tale of Mar-garet). These moments of mutual pain raise in turn the question of who is suffering, and how, leading on to the question of the aesthetic observer's responsibility for what he sees, which is a version of Wordsworth's cre-ative problem: How is it possible to write *poems* about these subjects? This question is expressed in all the poems by the ambivalent relation be-tween each teller and his tale, is overtly anticipated in manuscript frag-ments leading toward them, and subsequently is enacted in Wordsworth's ambivalence toward his own epic project, the relation of the poet of *The Prelude* to the poem of *The Recluse*.

ENTER COLERIDGE.

So far, we have been considering what the 1,300 lines written by early March 1798 made of *The Recluse*. Now it is time to turn the question round to ask what *The Recluse* made of these poems, or what made Wordsworth call these poems *The Recluse* in the first of its several exis-tences? There is no mystery as to the largest part of the answer. It is Coleridge and philosophy. Wordsworth's first acquaintance with Cole-ridge in 1795 had grown into intimate friendship and admiring love, overflowingly reciprocated. Since July of 1797, their creative union had begun to bear fruit; Coleridge already dreamed of a huge philosophical master-poem, Wordsworth was writing and reworking these poems at that time; therefore they became that masterwork, *The Recluse*. Wordsworth's imagination, more absorbent than egotistical in 1797–98, soaked up the flood of ideas, interests, projects, and speculations springing from the fountainhead of Coleridge's active mind and voracious reading. Coleridge devoured philosophical speculation the way ordinary people read fiction, and in late 1796 he had cataloged his main interests as follows: "Metaphysics, & Poetry, & 'Facts of mind'—(i.e. Accounts of all the strange phantasms that ever possessed your philosophy-dreamers from Tauth [Thoth], the Egyptian to Taylor, the English Pagan,) are my darling Studies" (*LSTC*, I.260). Coleridge's interest in exploring the nature of mind by means of poetry was not unique among intellectuals of the late eighteenth century—in fact it was an intellectual fashion of the times—but it would hardly have been possible for Wordsworth to fall into a more enthusiastic vortex of speculation, and certainly not one as ready as Coleridge to abandon his own plans in Wordsworth's favor. Like their later definitions of poetry and symbolism, their literary relationship in 1797–98 was a wedding of the Coleridgean ideal and the Wordsworthian real; Wordsworth was to realize what Coleridge thought.

Coleridge's influences on *The Recluse* can be roughly divided into poetry and philosophy: on the one hand, plans for a poetical form and style; on the other, the thought and theme which was to inform them. Left begging was the open question of the story or plot in which they were to be embodied.

Coleridge and the Form of The Recluse

As early as April of 1797, and probably well before that, Coleridge was meditating "a gigantic poem on a Miltonic scale in which all modern scientific and historical knowledge" might be contained.[15]

> I should not think of devoting less than 20 years to an Epic Poem. Ten to collect materials and warm my mind with universal science. I would be a tolerable Mathematician, I would thoroughly know Mechanics, Hydrostatics, Optics, and Astronomy, Botany, Metallurgy, Fossilism, Chemistry, Geology, Anatomy, Medicine—then the *mind of man*—then the *minds of men*—in all Travels, Voyages and Histories. So I would spend ten years—the next five to the composition of the poem—and the five last to the correction of it.

So I would write haply not unhearing of that divine and rightly-whisper-
ing Voice, which speaks to mighty minds of predestinated Garlands,
starry and unwithering. [*LSTC*, I.320–21]

"Religious Musings" had been one start in this direction, especially its second part, which Wordsworth particularly admired when he read it in
1796, singling out two grand apocalyptic passages as "worth all the
rest."[16] By 1798, these ideas had temporarily coalesced around a poem to
be called *The Brook*, in which Coleridge, by descriptively following the
course of his "dear gutter of Stowey" from its source in the hills down
through villages, past towns and cities, and out to sea, hoped to find
"equal freedom for description, incident and impassioned reflections on
men, nature and society" (M. I.363). This seems to be a natural source for
Wordsworth's phrase, "Nature, Man, and Society," but before awarding
Coleridge all originality in the conception of *The Recluse* (always keeping
in mind that Wordsworth wrote the nearly 20,000 lines of which it actually consists), we should note that John Thelwall, author of *The Peripatetic; or, Sketches of the Heart, of Nature and Society* (1793), had visited
Coleridge in Nether Stowey in August 1797, a semifugitive from government agents in London, to talk about further composition in the same
vein; this was when Coleridge was first contemplating *The Brook* and after he had heard Wordsworth read "The Ruined Cottage" in June (*LEY*,
189).[17]

     These details, though immediately applicable, are too particular to de-
termine influences accurately. We must ask more generally who, among
the bright young authors of the late 1790s, was *not* contemplating an epic
poem with some combination of the same elements? The words *Nature
Man*, and *Society*, signify Everything, the favorite subject of enthusiastic
young writers. Only God is left out. Many epic dreams of the day were religious, but the *topoi* of projects like Thelwall's, Coleridge's, and Wordsworth's were not supernatural or mythological, but secular and modern,
reflecting the enlightened advances their age was heir to. Their framework
of justification would not be that of *Paradise Lost*: this is the significance
of Coleridge's claiming *The Recluse*, some years later, as "the first and
finest philosophical poem" in English—it would not be religious (*LSTC*,
II.1034). (It is also the context in which Coleridge cited Wordsworth's ap-
proval of his own religious poetry to the atheistic Thelwall, as that of "a
Republican and at least a Semi-atheist" [*LSTC*, I.127].) The traditional
epic poem was dying out in English, but in efflorescence, not atrophy, and

the literary landscape of the time is strewn with huge carcasses of religious, patriotic, and scientific poems like so many dinosaurs caught in an evolutionary storm of sensibility.[18] The idea of replacing Milton was present in many of these ambitions, including Coleridge's for Wordsworth, and the literature of the preceding century seemed to offer a clear field, since the epic achievements of English Neoclassicism had been predominantly mock epics, and the latter half of the eighteenth century was soggy with imitations of Milton that are nine parts enthusiasm, one part hard work, and no part genius. Classical models still controlled humanistic curricula, so the idea of a poet's progress from lyric to epic was built into everyone's thinking about literature; it was as common as the idea of The Great American Novel, with the same ratio of brilliance to dullness. Add to this the pervasive sense of scientific enlightenment from superstition, plus political idealism stirred by the American and French revolutions, and you have a climate, circa 1798, in which the writing of rejuvenative epic poems would occur almost inevitably to anyone contemplating a literary career. In retrospect, we can see that the Romantics lyricized and personalized the epic, but they did not recognize their intention aforethought, and the twin stories of *The Recluse* and *The Prelude* are, along with those of Byron's *Childe Harold* and *Don Juan*, the primary documentation of this process in English.

Coleridge was the main conduit by which most of this reached Wordsworth, as knowledge if not as power. Wordsworth knew almost as much as Coleridge about poetry but was propelled into the mainstream of contemporary literary activity by Coleridge's enthusiasm. When he took over from Coleridge, via Thelwall, the idea of a masterly epic poem simultaneously defining and creating a new spirit of the age, he was taking what Coleridge freely offered. Coleridge's fine critical insight, as well as his entrepreneurial shrewdness, sensed that Wordsworth was more suited to the task in every way. He overestimated Wordsworth's ability to generate ideas systematically, but he overestimated himself in the same way. For Wordsworth, making *The Recluse* his own was part of his comprehensive wish to please Coleridge during this first bloom of their love. There is no evidence of Wordsworth entertaining any plans for epic poetry before his close association with Coleridge, and he could hardly have embarked on a project so like Coleridge's without Coleridge's knowledge, assent, and active encouragement.[19] Coleridge thought that the plan of *The Brook* offered a degree of unity that recent English epic ventures lacked, citing Cowper's *The Task* as a case in point. This, plus the close proximity of Thelwall's *The Peripatetic*, indicates that Wordsworth was not being led,

initially, into a vast nebulous scheme,[20] but one close to current conceptions of loco-descriptive-meditative poetry that would allow him to ar-
range "pictures" or "views" of Nature, Man, and Society in a didactic
framework of enlightened, liberal slant.

The word *recluse* does not at first seem a promising choice for a poem
intended to address "Human Life," but its connotations in the late eighteenth century were generally positive, signifying a desire to escape from
evil urban influences, to which the poets of Sensibility, like Cowper in
"Retirement," added responsiveness to Nature.[21] As a sign of moral reaction to social ills, it was, however, quite different from "Philanthropist,"
the title of Wordsworth's earlier abortive literary project, which was in England virtually a Godwinian code-word by which ideologically committed
but nonactivist intellectuals indicated their more-than-patriotic "loyalty to
the welfare of mankind."[22] A recluse disengages himself from society both
physically and mentally, to get his philosophical long views in right perspective, and since Wordsworth knew personally Charlotte Smith, author
of *Ethelinde, or the Recluse of the Lake* (1790), which is set in the ruins of
a fictitious Grasmere Abbey, there is a good likelihood that this limp
Gothic narrative is the Ur-source of his epic's title. (In 1791, Smith gave
him letters of introduction to English radicals and Girondin leaders in
Paris [M. I.170–72].) Moreover, as her novel starts with an exploratory
visit to the Grasmere abbey by the domestic circle of a young gentleman
who has redeemed this part of his estate by a fortunate marriage—
approximately the family fantasy of the Wordsworth children—it also
makes its contribution to *The Recluse*'s controlling image of new life
reviving old institutions. A preference for a reclusive over a philanthropic
hero would have been natural for Wordsworth in 1798 as a way of distancing himself from his earlier enthusiasms for revolutionary projects,
and the appeal of quietist political theories may have been further reinforced by Godwin's popular *Caleb Williams* (1794), whose attractively
melancholy protagonist follows a "mode of living . . . in the utmost degree
recluse and solitary."

Readers who feel there must be more than this to the proposed form
of *The Recluse* may be experiencing in part what Wordsworth himself often felt, but though more specific descriptions follow in later years, this is
substantially all that can be derived from contemporary records other than
the first *Recluse* poems themselves. However, *The Peripatetic* has been un-
dervalued as an influence, probably because it is more prose than poetry
and mixes so much fustian and cliché with its radical political views. As
an *organizational* model it offered much that Wordsworth could and did

use. On the title page alone, in addition to the key phrase, *Sketches of the Heart, of Nature and Society,* he found: *A Series of Politico-Sentimental Journals, in Verse and Prose, of the Eccentric Excursions of Sylvanus Theophrastus, Supposed to be Written by Himself.* Throughout its three volumes, which are divided into short descriptions, incidents, and meditations, are many subheadings which, though conventional, would have both stimulated and reflected Wordsworth's particular interests. Among characters and natural objects, to cite only the most obvious, are: The Beggar, The Old Sailor (who speaks with "modest indifference . . . a serious tint to the whole of his conversation"),[23] The Road, The Cottages, The Sky, The Cavern, The Monastery, The Village Church, The Gipsy, and The Maniac (a graveside mourner like Martha Ray or Ruth). Among assorted themes, the philosophical: "Appropriation of Time," "Visions of Philosophy," "A Problem for the Metaphysicians"; the political: "Effervescences of Political Enthusiasm"; the psychological: "Traits of Singularity," "Painful Recollections," "Wanderings of Despair," "A Digression for Parents and Preceptors"; and the aesthetic: "Topographical Digressions," "Sketches of Picturesque Sublimity," "Picturesque Beauties." I stress these similarities because it is an important part of my argument that much of the difficulty of *The Recluse* was not writing it but organizing it. To these may be added the various odes, epistles, and epitaphs Thelwall scatters throughout, his narrative device of stories within stories, his frequent topic of social and political abuses, the peripatetic metaphor itself (it opens, like *The Prelude,* with a walk out from a city, "enjoying the enfranchisement of vision from dull captivity of brick walls"),[24] and, not least, "The Friend: A Character." Some of these also have relevance to *The Excursion,* not only "A Romantic Excursion," but also "The Wanderer," and many of the subheadings devoted to him: "Progress of Infantile Attachments," "Traits of Parental Tyranny," "The Calm of Desperation," "Estimates of Duty," and "A Melancholy Interview." Many such headings could be affixed with no impropriety and considerable gain in organizational clarity to long passages in both *The Prelude* and *The Excursion.*

But influences upon a poem that did not fully come into existence are less important than what does exist. Wordsworth's representations of suffering poor people in the first *Recluse* poems do not fit easily into any conventional scheme of politics, nor most available literary categories. So too, *The Recluse* was from the outset informed by philosophic considerations which enriched, complicated, and probably doomed its ultimate completion—at least insofar as "philosophy" signified, for Wordsworth, metaphysical elaboration and systematic consistency.

Coleridge and the Philosophy of the First Recluse *Poems*

Because *The Recluse* was described by its creators as a philosophic poem, and because it was never completed, the assumption is often made that its philosophy was incomplete, inadequate, or misunderstood. Wordsworth and Coleridge themselves assumed a complete metaphysical system constructed by Coleridge which Wordsworth would use or illustrate in presenting "views" of Man, Nature, and Society. Thomas McFarland has argued that *The Recluse* could not be written as a true philosophic poem because its thematic triad omitted God.[25] This is true from the standpoint of traditional metaphysics, but Coleridge was, at least occasionally in 1798, envisioning a comprehensive system independent of orthodox religion—a secularism that Wordsworth would have tended to accentuate. However, the assumptions of both men regarding *logical consistency* became all the stronger the less the poem was written. The more grandly philosophical the conception became, to justify necessary delays for adequate intellectual preparation, the more difficult it became to meet the higher expectations which the assumption created. But the assumption that *The Recluse* is incomplete because its philosophy was incomplete is unwarranted, unless we expect from philosophy an account of existence persuasively applicable to all facts and accidents of human life, or imagine that a coherent philosophy will necessarily produce an artistically unified poem. In fact, the philosophy of *The Recluse*, like that of *The Prelude*, is as complete as any artwork's, in the sense of reflecting a recognizable form of metaphysical and moral inquiry; indeed, compared with most other major poems (especially in English), its problem is rather too much philosophy than too little, giving rise to expectations that it cannot satisfy.

The philosophy informing *The Recluse* shifts, during the three main stages of its active compositional existence (corresponding to the three parts of the present study), from an initial phase in which human mental consciousness is presented in strongly ambivalent tension with its sociophysical contexts (have the minds of Margaret, the Old Cumberland Beggar, and the Discharged Veteran endured through or been obliterated by their experiences?); through a dialectically contrary stage in which, in the form of the artist's creative imagination, it acts as if radically independent of material limitation (the increasingly transcendental way in which Imagination is treated during the course of the 1805 *Prelude*); to a tertiary compromise between acts of mind and their necessary containment and conservation in the social, educational, and religious institutions of human civilization. As thesis, antithesis, and synthesis, some version of this process is also enacted within each of the three stages, in Wordsworth's daring but fragmented starts upon *The Recluse*, followed by a recoil—more complete but more personal—into his *Prelude*-mode, concluding with a return to and modified completion of some part of *The Recluse*. But, just as there is no evidence beyond prevailing cultural fashion of Wordsworth's planning an epic poem before he met Coleridge, there is surprisingly little (relative to the enormous critical literature devoted to Wordsworth's philosophies) for the philosophic system(s) *The Recluse* was to assume.[26] Coleridge by 1798 was beginning to see the need to abandon his fascination with the apparent sophistication of David Hartley's associationism, and was moving toward his lifelong reaction against it—various forms of religious transcendentalism that implied some degree of innate, independent human mental power, whether of free will or secondary imagination. Wordsworth's position is summarized contrastingly by Alan Grob: "The author of *The Recluse* was far more inclined in 1798 to the belief that the mind was the product of the senses than to the conviction held by Coleridge . . . that 'the senses were living growths and developments of the mind and spirit.'"[27] However, I find no evidence of this implicit disagreement in their recorded contemporaneous statements about *The Recluse*, where the working situation is consistently one of Wordsworth's respectful and eager attendance upon Coleridge for a set of notes or other direct indication of a philosophical outline to support his "pictures of Nature, Man, and Society."

In trying to state accurately the philosophy of the poem that both men would later (Coleridge rather more stridently, but also more privately, than Wordsworth) insistently characterize as "philosophical," we come to a junction between two different kinds of studies that might be made of it: one on philosophical outlines and backgrounds, the other—the road I have chosen—on poetical foregrounds, aiming to arrive at an understanding of *The Recluse* and its philosophy intrinsically, not by means of what was said, or might be said, about it. Thus, while accepting Grob's statement of the situation in 1798, I note (as he does) that his quotation of Coleridge comes from the letter of 1815 in which, as a postmortem on *The Excursion*, he gave the fullest statement we have of what *The Recluse* should have been (*LSTC*, IV.574–75); and I may here assert my personal caveat against trying to state too firmly the philosophical positions of young men who, at any given moment, were far more interested in getting their works published than in preserving their ideological purity.

The generally operative form of *The Recluse*'s philosophy through all three of its major phases can be clearly stated if we keep in mind, on the key issue of the status of human consciousness, its tendency not to gradual modifications but precisely to radically dialectical reversals. It is a version of Kantian idealism as modified by Schelling and other contemporary German philosophers whom Coleridge in turn sought to modify, affected, on the one hand, by his knowledge of Berkeley's still more radical idealism and the Platonic and Neoplatonic traditions, and, on the other, by his always more respectful awareness of the contrary traditions of British empiricism, of which Hartley's efforts to realize moral ideas in the accumulation of random associations of "vibratiuncles" in the brain was the most significant contemporary British form.[28] The principal features of this philosophy, as discussed by Coleridge and Wordsworth, are well known in Wordsworth's works, where his shifts in emphasis or inconsistencies in formulation have been meticulously charted.[29] It posits a real, vital relation (analogy, similarity, or identity, by turns) between the structures of the physical world and the structures of the human mind, a relation which can point, in one direction, to their common transcendental basis in a metaphysical First Principle or God, and, in the other, toward an understanding and inducement toward positive moral action among human beings, based on the sense of loving mutuality felt between sensitive individual minds and external nature. The operative human power in the system is an innate, intuitive, or otherwise tacit understanding of its various interlinkages, which Wordsworth and Coleridge, following many other continental Idealists, called Imagination, struggling constantly to maintain its relations with both the natural-material and spiritual-transcendental poles of the system without letting it be subsumed by either.

As formulated, this is not a decidable proposition, and is necessarily subject to radical reversals. As soon as the smallest degree of independent existence is accorded human consciousness (e.g., in free will or imaginative creativity), the way is open toward philosophical equivalents of the demonstrability of the existence of God—the real existence of something Else, or Other, or, perhaps, Like—as in the parallel case of *external* consciousnesses, intelligent life on other planets, or Artificial Intelligence in computers. But in traversing this familiarly scarred philosophical landscape, it is more important to keep respectfully in mind its fundamental contraries—Realism or Materialism—than to chart the small internal variations worked out by Coleridge and Wordsworth. They were part of a tiny philosophical avant-garde which had sprung up a century earlier in reaction against the alienating implications of Descartes's new philosophy: a dead earth inhabited by powerful but groundless ghosts. Cartesian materialist assumptions have continued to be the predominant molder of our modern world, a process which began first and most strongly in the British

Industrial Revolution. In a world where questions of whether mind may be said to exist in machines, related to questions of whether it has any existence independent of nature (the brain's electrochemicals) or culture (language), have become more important than whether the mind may be said to exist in external nature, the efforts of Romantic Idealists to preserve a humanizing connection between mind and nature seem sentimental. Yet insofar as such questions are intellectual forms of man's increasingly tangible ability to divorce himself destructively from his given universe, they point toward the same large task Coleridge set for Wordsworth when he proposed *The Recluse* as the poem to make these connections manifest.

This sketch of Wordsworth's Romantic philosophy is reduced from an extensive scholarly tradition which has sought, with far more precision, to demonstrate what he meant by saying,

> One impulse from a vernal wood
> May teach you more of man;
> Or moral evil and of good
> Than all the sages can.   ["The Tables Turned," 21–24]

My purpose in presenting the sketch is to suggest that it is not the incompleteness of Wordsworth's and Coleridge's philosophy that left *The Recluse* incomplete, but its *indemonstrability*, both as system and as story. (Which "impulse"? How will we recognize it?) The intuitive power of mind in this system cannot be logically demonstrated to or by mind except through prior participation—that is, by the exercise of free will in belief, which Coleridge found so necessary yet so bedeviling to his labors on the question in *Biographia Literaria*. Like *The Prelude*, Coleridge's autobiography of the growth of his mind is an attempt to demonstrate the real existence, operation, and benevolence of Imagination in a personal case history. Wordsworth's task in *The Recluse* was, roughly speaking, to show this power at work more generally, in Man, Nature, and Society; his effective problem would have been, not to present a single convincing proof but to avoid monotony: his poem would tend to show Imagination's operation, effects, benefits, thwartings, and consequences over and over again. Given Wordsworth's dependence on Coleridge for rationalizing schemes, there would be, in default of the latter, a tendency for *The Recluse* to turn at every critical point into *The Prelude*, and this is more or less exactly what does happen throughout the chronology of its composition. Imagination does not "create" reality in this version of Idealist philosophy but is the agent of man's right apprehension of it, and thus, as the entrée to understanding, cannot be demonstrated to man as *Spectator ab extra*, the position which Coleridge, idealizing Wordsworth's strong independence of mind, later assigned him as bard of *The Recluse*: "Wordsworth should assume the station of a man in mental repose, one whose principles were made up, and so prepared to deliver upon authority a system of philosophy" (*TT*, II.70). The operative question for the first *Recluse* poems is thus not what their philosophy is, but how is it represented.

THE PHILOSOPHICAL PEDLAR

Returning to the first *Recluse* poems, we immediately recognize that their primary philosophical impulse is moral, not metaphysical,[30] and that the proper operative question is not what is the relation of Mind to Nature in them, but what, in Wordsworth's presentation of Margaret, the discharged veteran, and the old Cumberland beggar, can be seen as constituting philosophical "views of Nature, Man, *and Society* . . . of considerable utility"? In opposition to the atomistic tendency of Cartesian thought, Wordsworth's triad resembles traditional religious formulations of man's relationship to God, the universe, and himself; yet the philosophic problem of the first *Recluse* poems emerges in their tendency—which Wordsworth simultaneously introduces and seeks to overcome—to portray human beings as radically separated from each other in what should be the communality of Human Life. Since versions of "The Ruined Cottage" and "The Old Cumberland Beggar" antedate Wordsworth's first mention of *The Recluse*, the question of how *The Recluse* conception affected these poems philosophically can be answered in part by comparing their original form with that of March 1798. Changes in "The Old Cumberland Beggar" mostly concern the political application of moral philosophy, but the alterations in "The Ruined Cottage" provide clear evidence of what the idea of *The Recluse* meant to Wordsworth in composition. Between January and March of 1798 he added several hundred lines to it, almost all concerned with the character of the Pedlar who tells Margaret's tale to the young narrator. They are largely devoted to describing the Pedlar's special sensitivity, since childhood, to natural phenomena as sympathetic to human consciousness.

> While yet a child, and long before his time
> He had perceiv'd the presence and the power
> Of greatness, and deep feelings had impress'd
> Great objects on his mind with portraiture
> And colour so distinct that on his mind

> They lay like substances and almost seem'd
> To haunt the bodily sense.   [MS E, 130–36][31]

Such passages represent the defeat of dualism: the external world is "great," not little, as it appears to Cartesian man; the similes of connection—"so," "like," "almost seem'd"—mount up rhetorically until we soon forget they are figurative. Many of these passages were subsequently transported directly into *The Prelude*, since they derive from Wordsworth's imaginative reconstitution of his own childhood, as he much later testified: "I am here called upon freely to acknowledge that the character I have represented in his person [The Pedlar] is chiefly an idea of what I fancied my own character might have become in his circumstances."[32] Wordsworth had written lines anticipating these earlier, in his additions to *Descriptive Sketches* in 1794, but they are more remarkable as versions of the pervasive fictions of natural sentiment which imbued English poetry as the eighteenth century wore on than as evidence that Coleridge was not the source of "Wordsworth's ideas on the life of Nature."[33] Constant conversation with Coleridge returned him to these sentiments as realities, reinforced by the kind of pantheistic poetry Coleridge was already writing:

> 'Tis the sublime of man,
> Our noontide Majesty, to know ourselves
> Parts and proportions of one wond'rous whole:
> This fraternizes man, this constitutes
> Our charities and bearings. But 'tis God
> Diffus'd thro' all, that doth make all one whole.
> ["Religious Musings" (1796), ll. 141–46]

Coleridge still wrote schematically, and Wordsworth was ready to take help for his schema wherever he could find it: within a few days of the letters announcing the birth of *The Recluse*, he asked a friend to send a copy of Erasmus Darwin's *Zoonomia; or, The Laws of Organic Life*, one of the most literal of many contemporary popularizations of the idea of an organic relationship between Mind and Nature (*LEY*, 198–99).

For *The Recluse*, the purpose of these additions to "The Ruined Cottage" was to invest the Pedlar with philosophic—that is, metaphysical—authority that would make him a plausible interpreter of Margaret's sufferings. Without such interpretive authority, her suffering raised too negatively questions of the worth of human life, as in the stark conclusion of the poem in its original form of 1797: "and here she died, / Last human tenant of these ruined walls!" In early 1797, Wordsworth was of a mood to let these implications speak for themselves, but a year later, fired by

Coleridge with the idea of a comprehensive philosophic poem, the naked-
ness of the human condition thus represented required commentary.
Hence, as Dorothy wrote Mary Hutchinson at the same time William was
writing Tobin and Losh, "The Pedlar's character now makes a very, certainly the *most*, considerable part of the poem" (*LEY*, 199).

There is in fact no mention in 1798 of *The Recluse*'s being a philosophical poem, but its "views" of Nature, Man, and Society present sociocultural criticisms that obviously tend toward philosophically informed
politics. Thus, as in a traditional philosophic system, the Pedlar's metaphysical authority, based on his youthful receptivity to the "One Life" in
nature and man, keeps his mature "mind in a just equipoize of love" (MS
B, *app. crit.*, p. 179, l.24), enabling him to understand the suffering caused
between man and man, so unlike the "unutterable love" he felt between
himself and Nature's "great objects." His "way-wandering business" is
very useful to his creator, for it enables him to roam about, "unclouded by
the cares of ordinary life," in what for Wordsworth amounts to a species
of lifelong, walking *generalization*:

> Time had condensed the rose upon his cheek
> But had not tamed his eye which under brows
> Of hoary gray had meanings which it brought
> From years of youth which, like a [being] made
> Of many beings he had wondrous skill
> To blend with meanings of the years to come
> Human or such as lie beyond the grave
>
> [MS B, p. 187, ll. 10–17][34]

This represents general truth or authority, not by logical demonstration,
but by implying that the Pedlar, in the length and range of his experience,
metaphorically multiplied ("like a being made of many beings"), has actually seen enough to make his statements universally applicable. His experience is further hinted to be a general human possibility—not a philosophy, strictly speaking, but what a philosophy based on imagination will
enable us to *do*:

> By contemplating these forms
> In the relations which they bear to man
> We shall discover what a power is theirs
> To stimulate our minds, & multiply
> The spiritual presences of absent things
> Then weariness shall cease. We shall acquire
> The [   ] habit by which sense is made
> Subservient still to moral purposes

A vital essence, & a saving power
Nor shall we meet an object but may read
Some sweet & tender lesson to our minds
Of human suffering or of human joy.
All things shall speak of a man & we shall read
Our duties in all forms & general laws
And local accidents shall tend alike
To quicken & to rouze & give the will
And power which by a [   ] chain of good
Shall link us to our kind. No naked hearts
No naked minds shall then be left to mourn
The burthen of existence.   [MS B, pp. 263–65]

Of whence come those naked hearts and minds to be roused dutifully from
the burden of existence I shall speak in a moment. For the present, it is
enough to see that Wordsworth represents the Pedlar relating to human
life imaginatively (that is, multiplying "the spiritual presences of absent
things") by virtue of his pure connection to Nature. He makes sure at the
same time that no bad vibrations or contaminations come through in the
other direction:

He walked
Among the [   ] haunts of vulgar men
Unstained; the talisman of constant thought
And kind sensations in a gentle heart
Preserv'd him; every shew of vice to him
Was a remembrancer of what he knew,
Or a fresh seed of wisdom, or produced
That tender interest which the virtuous feel
Among the wicked, which when truly felt
May bring the bad man nearer to the good,
But innocent of evil, cannot sink
The good man to the bad.   [MS B, p. 179, ll. 5–16]

This remarkable philosophic one-way street, down which comes only good
and never bad goes up, ensures that the Pedlar's comments on life will retain inviolate his original pure relation to Nature. Besides seeing philosophy made simple in these sequences, we also see Wordsworth coming to
terms with his newly sensed responsibility to address the evils of his
time—a sense that does not, assuredly, derive only from his friendship
with Coleridge, but, coupled with his own "way-wandering business" of
1791–95, was now being focused by Coleridge on the possibility of writing a poem that would deal with those evils in a grandly comprehensive

philosophic scheme. He represents the Pedlar as seeing what he had seen
and understanding it:

> In his various roun[ds]
> He had observ'd the progress and decay
> Of many minds, of minds & bodies too
> The history of many families
> And how they prosper'd, how they lived in peace
> And happiness and how they were o'erthrown
> By passion or mischance or such misrule
> ~~Of government~~
> Among [   ] and masters of the earth
> As makes the nations groan.   [MS B, pp. 183, 187]

The boldness of the phrase "the progress and decay . . . of minds & bod-
ies," like "naked hearts" and "naked minds," takes one's breath away
from the simplicity of its representation. This is what the Pedlar sees and
understands in Margaret's tale, where passion, mischance, and misrule all
play a part, and where simple grammatical copulae suggest cruel cause and
effect: "how they lived in peace and happiness and how they were
o'erthrown."

Since the artistic motivation for making the Pedlar a philosophical
character is to give plausibility to his interpretation of Margaret's suffering, it is remarkable that Wordsworth puts great stress on the fact that the
Pedlar's special relationship to Nature began without the mediation of any
human element and has no basis in any attribute of human consciousness
or thought, such as predication, conceptualization, or articulation. It is,
very literally, "unutterable love," and the knowledge it gives him is potent
precisely because it is untainted by the passions that distort human relations. This severe separation may seem paradoxical, but logically
Wordsworth's strategy is correct, because it represents the Pedlar's interpretations of society as rising from a context outside of, and larger than,
human relations. Like other redeemers of human alienation, he assumes a
vantage point above human nature which enables him to interpret it in
ways unavailable to those enmeshed in its physical sufferings and mental
contradictions.

The key passage describes the Pedlar's experience of "unutterable
love" while tending sheep on the mountainside "ere his ninth year." The
heavily underlined point of the passage is not simply the Pedlar's powerful
experiences of love, nor their source or content, but their unutterability. It
is a "visitation from the living God," and almost everything Wordsworth
says about it stresses what *cannot* be said:

He did not feel the God: he felt his works
Thought was not. In enjoyment it expired
Such hour by prayer or praise was unprofaned
He neither prayed, nor offered thanks or praise
His mind was a thanksgiving to the power
That made him . . .
. . . .
Ah! *then* how beautiful, how bright appeared
The written promise; he had early learned
To reverence the volume which displays
The mystery, the life which cannot die
But in the mountains did he feel his faith
There did he see the writing—All things there
Looked immortality, revolving life
And greatness still revolving, infinite;
There littleness was not, the least of things
Seemed infinite, and there his spirit shaped
Her prospects nor did he believe—he saw
What wonder then if his being th[us] became
Sublime and apprehensive . . .
                [MS B, pp. 157, 159; Wordsworth's underlining]

The experience, though unutterable, was not unreadable ("written promise
. . . volume . . . see the writing"), and in another passage developed from
his Alfoxden notebook, Wordsworth stresses the Pedlar's power of interpretation based on his hearing "the ghostly language of the ancient earth,"
which, though again "inarticulate," prepares him for the more difficult interchanges of human language by virtue of its freedom from human taint.
This passage separates the Pedlar from human passion as insistently as the
preceding one did from human articulation.

                Not useless do I deem
These quiet sympathies with things that hold
An inarticulate language for the man
Once taught to love such objects as excite
No morbid passions no disquietude
No vengeance and no hatred needs must feel
The joy of that pure principle of love
So deeply that unsatisfied with aught
Less pure and exquisite he cannot chuse
But seek for objects of a kindred love
In fellow-natures and a kindred joy
Accordingly he by degrees perceives
His feelings of aversion softened down

A holy tenderness pervade his frame
His sanity of reason not impaired
Say rather all his thoughts now flowing clear
From a clear fountain flowing he looks round
He seeks for good and finds the good he seeks
Till execration and contempt are things
He only knows by name and if he hears
From other mouth the language which they speak
He is compassionate and has no thought
No feeling which can overcome his love
[MS D, *app. crit.*, pp. 372–73, ll. 1–23][35]

This passage is remarkable in two directions. One is the extreme aversion toward humankind which it assumes as a starting point, and the other is the nearly automatic operation of the faith and love toward which it accelerates. The Pedlar's authority as an interpreter of human suffering entails a great deal of prior insulation from its effects, effects which strongly complicate the reactions of the narrators of the other *Recluse* poems. He overcomes a striking amount of "passion . . . vengeance and . . . hatred" in listening to earth's "inarticulate language." Love of nature leads to love of man by softening down "feelings of aversion" toward humanity that are presented as the original condition of the man who learns to love from passionless—that is, nonhuman, nonlinguistic—nature. "He could afford to suffer / With them whom he saw suffer" because "he had no [painful] pressure from within" and was "unclouded by the cares / Of ordinary life" (MS B, *app. crit.*, p. 183, ll. 1–2, 13–16). The idea that we all participate in human suffering has become so current in modern social sentiments that it is easy to forget the fears—"coward fears," as Wordsworth unflinchingly calls them—such fellow-feeling must overcome, fears for oneself, for preserving "sanity of reason not impaired," and, not least, for earning one's own living.

These are all fears that the young poetical narrator of "The Ruined Cottage" must overcome, via the interpretive agency of the Pedlar. The fragmentary beginnings of the Pedlar passages in the Alfoxden notebook provide a nearly prose topic sentence for the detailed psychological examination which follows:

Why is it we feel
So little for each other but for this
That we with nature have no sympathy
Or with such idle objects as have no power to hold
Articulate language.   [Butler, p. 15]

Lack of feeling for others is the base condition, like the Pedlar's "feelings of aversion." Another draft pushes this negative cause–effect sequence (we feel so little for each other because we have no sympathy for natural—i.e., prelinguistic—objects) toward a more positive prospect:

> And never for each other shall we feel
> As we may feel till we have sympathy
> With nature in her forms inanimate
> With objects such as have no power to hold
> Articulate language. In all forms of things
> There is a mind.   [Butler, p. 15]

But, evidently, it speaks a different language than ours. Yet its incommunicability somehow rushes into a plenum of human communication. From these negative starting points, these naked origins, this moral vacuum created by morbidity, disquietude, vengeance, hatred, aversion, execration, and contempt, Wordsworth accelerates his Pedlar to a fullness of articulate human knowledge ("All things shall speak of man") that is its structural corollary, its binary opposite. Love and faith suddenly become the inevitable conditions of life. The Pedlar will urge his young auditor to "rise from this oblivious sleep, these fretful dreams / Of feverish nothingness," till "all things . . . live in us," every day "enlarge our sphere of pleasure & of pain," our senses and our intellect "each to each supply a mutual aid . . . forms & feelings acting thus, & thus / Reacting" until:

> . . . each be multiplied
> With a variety that *knows no end*
> Thus deeply drinking in the soul of things
> We shall be wise *perforce*, and we shall move
> From *strict necessity* along the path
> Of order and of good. *Whate'er* we see
> *Whate'er* we feel by agency direct
> *Or* indirect shall tend to free *and* nurse
> Our faculties *and* raise to loftier height
> Our intellectual soul.   [MS D, *app. crit.*, p. 374; italics added]

Thus Wordsworth urges himself, since both the Pedlar and the young narrator are versions of himself, to come to terms (words) with his feelings toward human suffering, as he grappled with the new necessity of writing a comprehensive philosophic poem about it. The point of all this is not to show how loveless or unloving Wordsworth might recently have felt, nor to present his message of love as the overcompensations of an unfeeling monster, nor to explain it as the displacement of Godwinian Necessity, psychologized in order to be socialized, nor to illustrate his appropriation of Coleridge's pantheism. Rather, we want to see the radical character of Wordsworth's exploration of the nature of man, his quest for "naked" hearts and minds stripped of accidental qualities in the philosophical sense and thus made into acceptable subjects for poetry. Behind these philosophic additions to the Pedlar's character, stimulated by his conversations with Coleridge, lie still more radical passages, written during the previous three or four years, which show Wordsworth exploring other options of response to human suffering, plumbing beneath "coward fears" and aversion to hatred and murder. Only from these extremely negative, inhuman origins can we fully appreciate the feelings of love with which the Pedlar interprets Margaret's story and the reason for their rising from the "unutterable" and "inarticulate" language of love in Nature.

ANTICIPATIONS AND REFLECTIONS OF *THE RECLUSE*

The ambivalent attitudes of the narrators of the first *Recluse* poems are anticipated in Wordsworth's work immediately preceding them (*Salisbury Plain*, 1793–95, and *The Borderers*, 1796–97) and are reflected in the poems he composed immediately afterward, in March–May 1798, the bulk of his contribution to *Lyrical Ballads*, where the question of narrators' relations to their tale has been a constant element in all subsequent critical interpretation (for example, "The Thorn," "The Idiot Boy," "The Mad Mother"). This ambivalence involves both the identity of the narrator (to what extent is he Wordsworth?) and whether he is merely telling a story or implicating himself in it. In a large sense, it is the origin of the dialectical intertwining between *The Recluse* and *The Prelude*, as Wordsworth tries to decide if he can tell a story or if he must *be* his story. Many readers are impatient with such scruples, but Wordsworth had reason to doubt the motives of both narrators and audiences, especially when, as in "The Ruined Cottage," one version of himself is telling the story to another.

Narrative plausibility was more than a merely technical problem regarding literary and social conventions available to Wordsworth for representing suffering poor people and intending their words and situations to be taken with full, tragic significance. James Averill places Wordsworth's treatment of such characters persuasively in the context of eighteenth-century theory and practice of tragic and sentimental drama; psychoanalytic critics see much less conscious control in the powerful ambivalence these characters release.[36] In following the psychological path toward Wordsworth's unconscious motivations, I nevertheless agree with Averill's implied thesis that Wordsworth was using available means to solve practi-

cal problems—how to write poems—and would go further to suggest that
he connected these problems with the still larger ones of shaping the nature of reality and seeking to save the world. Picturesque pedlars are no
problem for modern audiences, but disabled, disaffected, discharged veterans can be, and if we imagine these stories coming from truck drivers or
traveling salesmen we reappreciate Wordsworth's dilemma. Yet he does
not write primarily to help his characters or even to create sympathy for
them; he wants, rather, to speak through them from an abnormal perspective that will enlighten normal conceptions of reality.[37] He is not sure
how to feel about the suffering his characters bespeak. He feels sorry for
them, he feels desperately helpless, he feels almost sick; their suffering up-
sets his mental balance. He is also angry, at the causes of their suffering,
sometimes at the sufferers themselves, perhaps even hating their vulnerability. He empathizes with them completely, then recoils and tries to cast
them out of his sight, ignoring them, wishing them dead, murdered. The
theme of these early poems is presented as a rudimentary plot. Why don't
these people go home? They have no home. What is it like to be homeless?
The question implicates the narrator, too, for we find it possible to ask, on
suggestions given by the poems, What is he doing out there on the open
road? Doesn't *he* have a home? Does poetry require such exposure?

In the early versions of *Salisbury Plain* the narrator is a first-person
"traveller," as Wordsworth had been in his momentous crossing of the
plain in 1793. This "traveller" is given unspecified psychological correlatives for his presence on the plain:

> Though I had seen
> Worse storms, no stranger to such nights as these,
> Yet I had fears from which a life like mine
> Might long have rested . . .   [*PW*, I.293.23–26]

Nearly a third of the original poem is a highly overdetermined narration
which bounces this traveler from one false hope of relief to another,
shocked by flashes of lightning, terrified by supernatural or subconscious
voices. Through the traveler's fears should not be linked literally to
Wordsworth's, it would be equally unwise to remove them altogether from
his experience and explain them as gothicisms he was exploring from
purely stylistic motives. Literary conventions and personal needs exist in a
richer mixture, and Wordsworth had a considerable range of mental stress
on which to rest his empathy for such wayfarers. He had failed to establish
his worldly independence on respectable terms, he had failed to provide
for his intended wife and their child, and he had failed to write the poems

he felt capable of. His personal failures were in turn connected with a still larger failure: the hopes of his young intellectual generation for spiritual renovation from the French Revolution, complicated in Wordsworth's case by his temporary identification of this hope with his growing awareness of his own creative powers.

In *The Borderers*, critical tact is also necessary in assessing the degree of identification between Wordsworth and the play's hero (Marmaduke) and villain (Oswald), yet ambivalence stands out starkly in the basic point of the dramatic action: will Marmaduke save old Baron Herbert and his daughter Idonea, or will he destroy them? Wordsworth tries to sustain this radically absurdist choice through five acts, mainly of heated argument between the naive, idealistic Marmaduke and the cynical Oswald. Entrances and exits, scene and act changes, are almost entirely dictated by the necessity of putting these two corollary characters in one situation or another where they are perfectly poised to kill—or save—their potential victims, preferably alone on a road at night, ideally in heavy storm. This action of the drama is directly anticipated in the "Fragment of a 'Gothic' Tale," where a young man conducts an old blind sailor (Baron Herbert is also blind) through a stormy night to the dungeon of a ruined castle: to safety, the old man thinks; to murder, the young man intends. As in *The Borderers* itself, we are never sure whether we are at the promising beginning or the desperate end of things. In a bald prefiguration of his recurrent *Recluse* situation—human potential amid gothic ruins—Wordsworth draws the contradiction between the sufferer's expectations and the putative helper's intentions as tightly as possible. When the old man, in an ecstasy of gratitude, promises to make the young man his heir, his very words become emblems of the young man's opposing motive:

> His hopes the youth to fatal dreams had lent
> And from that hour had laboured with the curse
> Of evil thoughts, nor had the least event
> Not owned a meaning monstrous and perverse;
> And now these latter words were words of blood
> And all the man had said but served to nurse
> Purpose most foul with most unnatural food.

> [*PW*, I.290.134–40]

The "Gothic Tale" breaks off—becomes a "Fragment"—when its coupled oppositions of love versus hate reach their inevitable absurd impasse, the young man falling down in a fit from the same subterranean rumblings that awaken the old man from the sleep in which the young man intended to murder him.[38]

To deny completely Wordsworth's emotional involvement in these grotesque situations would be as difficult as to prove it. But it is impossible to deny his powerful imaginative empathy for situations in which poor, old, suffering humanity is in mortal danger from the very persons who seem best placed to aid it; the pattern is too clearly repeated and leads too clearly to the position of the narrators in the first *Recluse* poems. Further evidences of this deep ambivalence are present in the preface to *The Borderers*, an introductory essay on the plausibility of unmotivated evil, devoted to a defense of the character of Oswald (or Rivers, as he was originally named). Possible identifications with Wordsworth spring out from the first sentences:

> Let us suppose a young man of great intellectual powers yet without any solid principles of genuine benevolence. His master passions are pride and the love of distinction. He had deeply imbibed a spirit of enterprise in a tumultuous age. He goes into the world and is betrayed into a great crime.—That influence on which all his happiness is built immediately deserts him. His talents are robbed of their weight, his exertions are unavailing, and he quits the world in disgust, with strong misanthropic feelings. [*PW*, I.345]

That Wordsworth's "great crime" might be the abandonment of Annette and Caroline, into which he was "betrayed" by the declaration of war between England and France, and that the "influence" which then "deserts" him is his uncles' withdrawal of the curacy they had promised him, are all likely possibilities for biographical speculation, as is the connection between frustration of genius and dangerous morbidity. But for the present purpose, it is more important to note that Wordsworth's explanation of Oswald's motivation is based on a psychological principle of *reversal* which totally inverts his ideas of good and evil, normal and abnormal. His "pleasure and his consolation [is] to hunt out whatever is bad in actions usually esteemed virtuous," and vice versa. He seeks to recover "his original importance and . . . powers" through evil actions rather than good, since evil actions usually have immediate results, "good actions being for the most part in their nature silent and regularly progressive." His penchant for reversals manifests itself in his attempted psychological seduction of "an amiable young man" (Marmaduke) into the same kind of crime into which he was betrayed. Suffering victims become objective correlatives of his own internal feelings. If we protest that this is no motive, Wordsworth assures us we are wrong: "to make the non-existence of a common motive itself a motive to action is a practice which we are never so prone to attribute exclusively to madmen as when we forget ourselves.

Our love of the marvelous is not confined to external things. There is no object on which it settles with more delight than on our own minds" (*PW*, I.347). This is not to say that society is mad, but that much of what is considered mad is in fact quite normal. Oswald is not necessarily mad, though "his pride . . . borders even on madness." This is the principal border crossed for exploration in the play,[39] and Wordsworth's further explorations in this direction are apparent in other fragments leading still more directly to the *Recluse* poems via poetical narrators' temptation to cross the thin line between love and hatred when faced with irremediable suffering.

The mood and style of Oswald's speeches can be found in "Argument for Suicide,"[40] which appears in manuscripts containing the "Old Man Travelling" lines of "The Old Cumberland Beggar" and a version of some lines from "The Ruined Cottage," called "Incipient Madness." If "Argument for Suicide" is Wordsworth's title, it encompasses a number of possibilities as to *whose* argument it is.

> Send this man to the mine, this to the battle,
> Famish an aged beggar at your gates,
> And let him die by inches—but for worlds
> Lift not your hand against him—Live, live on,
> As if this earth owned neither steel nor arsenic,   5
> A rope, a river, or a standing pool.
> Live, if you dread the pains of hell, or think
> Your corpse would quarrel with a stake—alas
> Has misery then no friend?—if you would die
> By license, call the dropsy and the stone   10
> And let them end you—strange it is;
> And most fantastic are the magic circles
> Drawn round the thing called life—till we have learned
> To prize it less, we ne'er shall learn to prize
> The things worth living for.—   15
> [*PW*, I.316]

As an argument for suicide, this is strangely roundabout. It is not a suicide's meditative farewell note; rather, it is the modest proposal of a very distanced observer, wondering if suicide might not be the best answer to widespread conditions of human misery. The opening lines are against one kind of social euthanasia relative to another: better to let sufferers die in the mines or in war than to kill them outright. This grotesque argument arises in response to a still more grotesque presumed alternative, the statement and implied counterstatement recalling the rigorous reversal of social norms in *The Borderers*. Only in the fourth line is the sufferer addressed directly, warned of eternal damnation as if the murder contemplated in the opening lines had been his idea. Lines 9–11 begin the transition to the sestet of this macabre quasi-sonnet, invoking fatal illness as misery's only acceptable "friend," another redundant circularity akin to the sharp paradoxes in the " 'Gothic' Fragment" and *The Borderers*, where the savior may turn out to be the slayer. The concluding moral generalizes the paradox appropriately to the world the poem invokes, saying that until we can learn to prize human life *less*—to see that murder and suicide are viable alternatives to the terrible conditions people find themselves forced into—we shall never learn "the things worth living for." The sonnet is a demystification of suicide on its surface but a demystification of ordinary moral conceptions of life at a deeper level, trying to show the unreality ("fantastic," "magic") of prohibitions against willfully ending life when set against certain unstated conditions of "misery."

"Argument for Suicide" may be said to arise from "coward fears" like those the Pedlar had to overcome before "he could afford to suffer / With them whom he saw suffer." Its logic also connects with the nearly automatic spiritual process that moved him from aversion and contempt for mankind to unquestioning, inevitable faith and love. The two arguments are mirror images of each other. The Pedlar tries to convince his young auditor in more palatable terms that conventional attitudes toward suffering, like conventional attitudes toward suicide, do not get at the heart of the matter. The desire to kill a suffering fellow being arises from a very deep appreciation of life—and an arrogant one. Under guise of wishing to put the sufferer out of his misery, it may mask a need to remove a threat to one's sanity, either from an excess of empathy or from a sense of guilt at one's own well-being—exacerbated in Wordsworth's case by his enormous pleasure in his supreme human gift of imaginative creativity. The question for the excessively sensitive narrators of "The Ruined Cottage" and "The Discharged Soldier" might be: How can I be a poet in the face of such suffering? Its dialectical underside would be: Why should I love or care for anybody?[41] The heroic answer Wordsworth gives, almost despite himself, is: By making such suffering the very stuff of my poetry, forcing myself to come to terms with the least loveable human creatures, old beggars, disabled veterans, deranged widows, fugitive sailors, female vagrants, mad mothers, idiot boys, and all their like.

These difficult questions and answers come still closer to "The Ruined Cottage" in the fragment called "Incipient Madness," which describes the mental state of a visitor to a ruined hut very like Margaret's cottage.[42] Butler takes pains to separate the fragment's bizarre description of mental imbalance from the calmer poetry of 1797–98: "its gothicism no doubt helped inspire *The Ruined Cottage* but does not fit with the more simple story the poem later became. Wordsworth's work on *The Ruined Cottage* increasingly focused on the unbalanced minds of Robert and Margaret; the teller of the tale, confronted with the ruin that reminds him of their tragedy, remains sane and calm."[43] This is true, but leaves open two questions: (1) How do descriptions of insanity help "inspire" determinedly sane poems? and (2) How does the teller of the tale of Margaret—whether the narrator or the Pedlar or both—remain sane and calm in the face of great temptations to abandon his mind to grief? Wordsworth's attention in "The Ruined Cottage" is equally on the unbalanced minds of Margaret and Robert and the balanced minds of the Pedlar and the narrator, and focuses most closely on the possibility of "contagion" between them, a fear at the root of the ambivalence of teller to tale in all the first *Recluse* poems.

"Incipient Madness" opens on the familiar scene of all these poems: "I cross'd the dreary moor." But this speaker is not seeking physical shelter; instead, he seeks psychic companionship. His "mood," "settled temper," "grief," and "sickly heart"—all unspecified as to cause—fasten compulsively on "a broken pane which glitter'd in the moon / And seemed akin to life" (6–7). He returns to the hut "many a long month" to look at "this speck of glass" and assuage the feelings of emptiness he feels without it. Initially, he knows he is sick, creating mental "food . . . where it is not" (10–11). But "one gloomy evening," driven thither as usual for his ration, he hears the "dull clanking" of a poor man's horse inside the hut. Though he seems to know perfectly well the source of the sound, he flees in a panic like that of the overly sensitive would-be murderer in the " 'Gothic' Fragment." The rest of the poem represents the further incipience of madness, if not its full onset:

> Three weeks
> O'erhung by the same bramble's dusky shade
> On this green bank a glow worm hung its light
> And then was seen no more. Within the thorn
> Whose flowery head half hides those ruined pales,   40
> [Three] seasons did a blackbird build his nest
> [And] then he disappear'd. On the green top
> [Of th]at tall ash a linnet perch'd himself
> And sang a pleasant melancholy song
> Two summers and then vanish'd. I alone   45
> Remained: the winds of heaven remained—with them

> My heart claimed fellowship and with the beams
> Of dawn and of the setting sun that seemed
> To live and linger on the mouldering walls.   [Butler, pp. 468–69]

Three weeks, three seasons, and two summers the glowworm and birds attached themselves to the cottage; the narrator intones his continued presence like the victory of a weird Ishmael: "I alone remained." He earlier told us, with clear awareness of his "strange incontinence," that he had been coming "many a long month" to see the glass, but only indirectly do we realize that he has been in a covert competition with the birds for three years! His "fellowship" with the incorporeal natural presences at the end—wind and sunlight—sounds reassuring in its echo of so many similar lines throughout Wordsworth's poetry, but in this poem it is the confirmation of his pathology. His sense of life has been reduced to reflected light, from the pane of glass glittering in the moonlight to "the setting sun that seemed / To live and linger on the mouldering walls." One would not want to claim this speaker is the Pedlar or the narrator of "The Ruined Cottage," let alone Wordsworth, yet they all share an obsessive fixation on a ruin for reassuring signs of life.[44]

These early poems and fragments enforce the close connection, for Wordsworth, between mental instability brought on by unmerited suffering, and by the observation and narration of such suffering, equally "unmerited," occurring as it does by chance along the highways of life. They link Wordsworth's narrative uncertainties illuminatingly to his uncertainties about philosophic consolations or answers. If the only help is reflected light, that does not seem to be enough. Yet the Pedlar in "The Ruined Cottage" will derive much comfort from some spear-grass "by mist and silent rain-drops silver'd o'er," and the philosophical insight Wordsworth added to the Pedlar's childhood experience often came from reflections of heavenly light:

> Oh! then what soul was his! when on the tops
> Of the high mountains he beheld the sun
> Rise up and bathe the world in light. He looked,
> The Ocean and the earth beneath him lay
> In gladness and deep joy. The clouds were touched
> And in their *silent* faces did he *read*
> *Unutterable* love.   [MS B, pp. 155, 157; italics added]

Both here and in similar passages repositioned into *The Prelude*, such experiences are pointedly defended as "not useless," not idle, not—in contrast to conventional late-eighteenth-century attitudes about solitude—

insane, not "incipient madness" but its opposite, deep insight and understanding of the human condition. Like the Pedlar as a boy, the protagonist
of "Incipient Madness" seeks life and relationship without "an appropriate human centre";[45] he obviously has not found it wherever he wanders
out *from*, to his nightly rendezvous with the moonlight. But the sense of
love that comes to the Pedlar without any human articulation does not follow for him; instead, any other creature, horse, bird, or bug, becomes a
hated rival for Nature's reflective favors.

In many respects, "Incipient Madness" and other verses leading to the
first *Recluse* poems are Wordsworth inside out, the poet examining negatively themes that in positive form will become his trademark. As in *Lyrical Ballads*, he looks at what is normal from a contrary direction, as an
experiment in interpretation. In connecting these fragments to the humanitarian intentions of *The Recluse*, I am not trying to turn Wordsworth on
his head, to suggest that his later formulation, "love of nature leads to love
of man," derives from hatred of mankind. Wordsworth himself turns his
head round. As he says of Oswald, "such a mind cannot but discover some
truths," and he tries to see what they might be, carrying out his metaphysical, psychological, and moral speculations in the integrity of verse rather
than in systematic syllogisms. His knowledge of the states of mind he argues against is often buried so deeply as to be laughable to worldly readers
who never bother to question prevailing assumptions. Of course, he sometimes goes too far. But equally of course, the nature of his investigations
requires going too far: how else discover what is enough? "Enough! or
Too much," said Blake, an eccentric of equal power for whom the "Prospectus" of *The Recluse* was too much. There is doubtless an element of
psychic compensation in Wordsworth's movement from narrators who feel
threatened by suffering humanity to those who understand it. But such a
movement may be the most normal of all human responses to suffering,
and the compensation does not imply the anteriority or "truth" of either
response. To use terms from structuralist psychoanalysis, points of origin
are absences or reversals (like Nature's "inarticulate language"), which
conscious assertions attempt to cover, neither successfully nor hypocriti-
cally; the other is "always already" present.[46] To speak more simply, by
seeing feelings of hate and fear associated with the philosophy of natural
sympathy and humanitarian love which Wordsworth gave to the Pedlar
under Coleridge's influence, we can say he knew whereof he spoke, and
that much of the power of the poetry arises from, even if it is not identical
with, this knowledge.

FEAR AND PITY: *THE RECLUSE*'S TRAGIC FIGURES

The first *Recluse* poems are finally successful because the deep ambivalence of their narrator is justified by the fearful or pitiable qualities of the characters whose story he tells. Margaret, the veteran, and the old Cumberland beggar are not tragic figures, as they have made no fateful choice to cause their suffering nor do they have any significant recognition of its causes. Each of the poems is a scene of tragic recognition for the narrator rather than the sufferers. The tragedy is the human condition, circa 1795, brought about by the absence of meaningful choices, represented by the passive refusal or inability of the characters to help themselves, an inarticulate response to society's impersonal actions against them: war, economic dislocation, and other government pressures (impressment, enlistment incentives, residential enclosure of social undesirables, stringent parish relief rates, and so on). The emotions they inspire are not exact mirrorings of their objective condition in the narrator's subjectivity, since he has personal difficulties of his own in coming to terms with suffering—mainly his prior wish to indulge in escapist aesthetic fantasies, delightful wanderings through the landscape compared to which, for Wordsworth, writing poetry was only the *next* best thing. These motivations do not obtrude upon our interest at first reading, since Wordsworth knew that a tale's rebound upon its teller is likely to annoy most readers' expectations, just as his own expectation of *The Recluse* made the self-conscious *Prelude* seem a distraction. Therefore, the fear or pity inspired by the *Recluse* sufferers must originate convincingly in the poet's representation of their condition, if the deep reactions they cause are to be aesthetically plausible.

If we imagine the first four *Recluse* poems as a single work, "A Night-Piece" provides a natural prologue to the other three, for it portrays a night-wanderer undergoing a change in attitude, but without the dangerous catalyst of a suffering object.

> The sky is overspread
> With a close veil of one continuous cloud
> All whitened by the moon, that just appears,
> A dim-seen orb, yet chequers not the ground
> With any shadow—plant, or tower, or tree.   5
> At last a pleasant instantaneous light
> Startles the musing man whose eyes are bent
> To earth. He looks around, the clouds are split
> Asunder, and above his head he views
> The clear moon & the glory of the heavens.   10
> There in a black-blue vault she sails along

Followed by multitudes of stars, that small,
And bright, & sharp along the gloomy vault
Drive as she drives. How fast they wheel away!
Yet vanish not! The wind is in the trees;   15
But they are silent. Still they roll along
Immeasurably distant, and the vault
Built round by those white clouds, enormous clouds,
Still deepens its interminable depth.
At length the vision closes, & the mind   20
Not undisturbed by the deep joy it feels,
Which slowly settles into peaceful calm,
Is left to muse upon the solemn scene.   [*BWS*, p. 431][47]

A nearly pure visionary narrative, it only suggests that the character's final musing is more meaningful—deeper—than his initial one. The published version of 1815 (*PW*.II.208) confirms these hints by making the man "pensive," "lonesome," and "unobserving," and the previsionary landscape "dull," "contracted," and "feeble." He has perceived a greater depth in the nature of things than the veiled appearances he originally mused upon, like the narrators of "The Ruined Cottage" and "The Discharged Soldier." The suggestiveness of the scene is heightened by several subtle touches which become characteristic of Wordsworth's more fully developed visions. Normal visual phenomena are presented as spectacular paradoxes: "How fast they wheel away! Yet vanish not!" An imaginary contrast is established between the effect of wind on earth and in outer space: "The wind is in the trees; But they [the moon and stars] are silent." Effects of unity-in-multiplicity and finite-motion versus infinite-stasis are conveyed by puns ("*Still* they roll along") and linguistic denomination disguised as physical predication ("the vault . . . still *deepens* its interminable depth"). The effect of the spectacle on a delicate sensibility is both acknowledged and checked by the double negative, "not undisturbed," which modulates emotional "joy" into thoughtful "calm," and turns the formerly monotonous landscape "solemn," seeming to transform a third-person character into a first-person narrating "mind" between the beginning and end of the piece. "A Night-Piece" anticipates the other 1798 *Recluse* poems in its human observer's receiving a depth of insight directly from Nature which in the others is negotiated, through Nature, into the life of Man.

Stark Fear: The Discharged Veteran

The discharged soldier appears like a human form of abstract personifications of Fear in late-eighteenth-century poetry. No one could be blamed for hanging back from his gaunt spectacle, least of all a poetical young man night-wandering in search of the peculiar sensations of a public road emptied of its daytime humanity. He is an "uncouth shape,"

> A foot above man's common measure tall,
> And lank, and upright. There was in his form
> A meagre stiffness. You might almost think
> That his bones wounded him. His legs were long,
> So long and shapeless that I looked at them
> Forgetful of the body they sustained.
> His arms were long & lean; his hands were bare;
> His visage, wasted though it seem'd, was large
> In feature; his cheeks sunken; and his mouth
> Shewed ghastly in the moonlight.   [*BWS*, p. 434, ll. 42–51]

At about the same time he wrote these lines, Wordsworth was describing the Pedlar's boyish fondness for "preternatural tale / Romance of giants, chronicle of fiends," read in "a straggling volume torn & incomplete,"

> Profuse in garniture of wooden cuts
> Strange & uncouth, dire faces, figures dire
> Sharp kneed, sharp-elbowed & lean-ankled too
> With long & ghostly shanks forms which once seen
> Could never be forgotten.   [Butler, p. 165]

Scary emblems from a child's book become thematic horrors in "The Discharged Soldier," particularly the idea of a body threatening to be cut apart by the sharpness of its own suffering. The wounds the veteran's bones seem to inflict on him parallel his alienation from society; he is cut from both directions: "a man cut off / From all his kind, and more than half detached / From his own nature" (58–60). Wordsworth elaborates all that "appertained to solitude" in his appearance ("no attendant, neither dog, nor staff, nor knapsack") until the accumulating negations raise an irrational but understandable need in the narrator for any humanizing detail whatsoever: "I think / If but a glove had dangled in his hand / It would have made him more akin to man" (65–67). An exaggerated challenge to human recognition faces the narrator, whose personal affinity for solitude is similarly exaggerated in the opposite direction; he loves "the public way when for the night, / Deserted in its silence, it assumes / A character of deeper quietness / Than pathless solitude" (2–5). The idea of this narrator coming to the aid of this human spectre is as dramatically absurd as the situation in the pre-*Recluse* fragments where the protagonist may either help or murder the person in his care. Structurally, the two situations are complementary; the narrator's fanciful terrors mirror the soldier's terrible appearance.

   The polarity is intensified by the soldier's refusal to help himself and
the lack of available help in the immediate social context. Though "hard
by a village stood," the narrator knows no help is forthcoming from that
avenue: "all were gone to rest . . . / . . . every silent window to the
moon / Shone with a yellow glitter (106–09). These glittering panes are
not, like the one in "Incipient Madness," signs of life however queer, but
the realistic contrary: human indifference and coldness. They must retrace
their steps back through a wood to a laborer's cottage: "He will not murmur should we break his rest" (113). Finally, the terror the veteran inspires is compounded by the fear he feels, a detail revised out of these
verses in *The Prelude*. Asked why he didn't seek "rest at inn or cottage,"
he explains,

> ". . . the village mastiff fretted me,
> And every second moment rang a peal
> Felt at my very heart. There was no noise,
> Nor any foot abroad—I do not know
> What ail'd him, but it seemed as if the dog
> Were howling to the murmur of the stream."   [131–36]

He seems not to consider that the dog might be barking at him, though
earlier the narrator had noted the mastiff's continual barking in conjunction with the soldier's "scarce audible" moans. He is not indifferent to human feeling; his fear of humans makes him fearful to humans. This emotion, like the narrator's initial "mingled sense of fear and sorrow"
(Wordsworth echoing Aristotle), is only negative, but is replaced at the end
(passing through "mild indifference") by a "reviving interest" in normal
human relations. This revival parallels the narrator's, who, having given
up the pleasant "self-possession" (34) of his original indulgence in "peace
and solitude," and having overcome his "heart's specious cowardice"
upon seeing the veteran, now turns his companion over to the kindly laborer, gives up his nocturnal rambling, and seeks "with quiet heart my distant home." Tragedy is averted, at least circumvented, and the drama ends
with the conjunction of peace and domesticity characteristic of so many
Wordsworthian endings, but only after extreme threats of terror and alienation. Such threats are usually muted or elided in Wordsworth's later
verse,[48] causing some readers to underestimate the cost of his natural religion, but in the first *Recluse* poems they are clearly visible.

Moving Pathos: The Old Cumberland Beggar

   All three of the first *Recluse* characters are beggars. Or, if only they
would beg, they could survive, and the deep unease they inspire would
subside. Begging is recommended to the discharged soldier, and his re-

sponse shows that beggary is beneath him, but not its effects: "My trust is in the God of heaven, / And in the eye of him that passes me." The regarding eye of the passing narrator[49] is enlarged during the course of "The Old Cumberland Beggar" into an "eye of Nature" which sees far deeper into the beggar's state than liberal, civic-spirited legislators who feel they must *do* something about it. These "statesmen," with their Poor Laws and workhouses, are public, generalized forms of the normal but limited human attitudes challenged by the inability or refusal of the three *Recluse* characters to help themselves.

The old Cumberland beggar does not inspire fear like the discharged soldier, nor heart-stopping pity like Margaret. Instead, he causes impatience, and the narrator's task is to calm our impatience by illustrating the beggar's moral value, to make us patient as the beggar makes his parishioners patient. The impatient reaction against him—the well-intentioned, brisk desire to sweep the streets clean of beggars for the public good—is the most acceptable reaction of the normal world to any of the first *Recluse* characters, because it is the official action of a nation toward an entire subset of the population, "the class of Beggars, to which the Old Man here described belongs" (Wordsworth's headnote). Wordsworth uses slow motion as his controlling metaphor to describe the beggar's salutary effect upon society. He is a slow-speed figure moving through the fast-paced frames of ordinary busy life, and his inertia retards hurrying humanity, almost against its will, into moral reflection and humanizing acts of charity:

> So helpless in appearance, that for him
> The sauntering Horseman throws not with a slack
> And careless hand his alms upon the ground,
> But stops,—that he may safely lodge the coin
> Within the old Man's hat; nor quits him so,
> But still, when he has given his horse the rein,
> Watches the aged Beggar with a look
> Sidelong, and half-reverted.   [*PW*, IV.234.25–32]

Like Wordsworth leaving the discharged veteran, the horseman looks back—reflects—upon the object of his charity, no longer a "careless" saunterer but a considerate human being. Similarly, the toll-gate keeper, the proverbially rude post-boy, the "slow-paced" waggoner, "Boys and girls, / The vacant and the busy . . . all pass him by" (63–65), but, so the metaphor creeps, slowed down by this beggar's minimum into taking notice and care of him. His regular progress outlasts—slows down—the eroding effects of time itself: "The kindly mood in hearts which lapse of years . . . make[s] slow to feel" (92–94).

But if the beggar retards the world to charity, his uncanny slow motion threatens to break into awful comic grotesquerie, as in similar poems like "Simon Lee." We had better not laugh! One smile and Wordsworth's pathetic touches are ruined. Yet his flirtation with humor here, like the touches of horror in "The Discharged Soldier," raises radically the question of just how deep our supposedly normal good instincts lie. The beggar shares the veteran's physical disintegration as well as his alienation from common humanity. He cannot control his "palsied hand," which, attempting to protect his crumbs, is "baffled still," and sweeps them away toward the waiting birds. His eyes too move independently, both of his physical body and his mental consciousness:

> On the ground
> His eyes are turned, and, as he moves along,
> *They* move along the ground; and, evermore,
> Instead of common and habitual sight . . .
> . . . .
> . . . one little span of earth
> Is all his prospect . . .
> . . . his eyes for ever on the ground,
> . . . seeing still,
> And seldom knowing that he sees, some straw,
> Some scattered leaf, or marks. . . .   [45–55; Wordsworth's italics]

Like a monstrous perversion of Emerson's "transparent eyeball," the beggar's eyes seem to roll along by themselves, not seeing the world which is the world of all of us, but random marks, disconnected percepts. In the Alfoxden notebook, where "The Old Cumberland Beggar" originated along with "The Discharged Soldier" and some of the additions to "The Ruined Cottage," the connection between his physically disintegral quality and its social corollary is explicit: "Dismantled as he is of limbs to act / Almost of sense to feel . . . / . . . His very name forgotten among those / By whom he lives. . . (*PW*, IV. 236–37, *app. crit.*).

Like the veteran, the beggar represents an extreme challenge to human recognition, yet his movement through the parish stitches it together into human community. This humanizing effect of the nearly nonhuman recalls the Pedlar's moral education by emphatically nonhuman, nonverbal nature, and there are "some" in the poem who gain the same benefit from the beggar:

> Some there are,
> By their good works exalted, lofty minds,
> And meditative, authors of delight
> And happiness, which to the end of time

> Will live, and spread, and kindle: even such minds
> In childhood, from this solitary Being,
> Or from like wanderer, haply have received
> (A thing more precious far than all that books
> Or the solicitudes of love can do!)
> That first mild touch of sympathy and thought,
> In which they found their kindred with a world
> Where want and sorrow were.   [105–16]

We easily recognize this "author" as that of the "Prospectus" and the Snowdon vision, whose healing message of the marriage of mind and nature is curiously based on, and thrust out from, radical disjunctions: "authors" whose sources lie deeper than any books or moral exhortation, "exalted, lofty" doers of good deeds whose original "kindred" are evidently not of this world at all, and who require special human mediators to overcome the deep moral shock of entering "a world where want and sorrow" are. This transit, or leap, from individual creativity to social responsibility is described over and over again in the history of *The Recluse*, in its dialectical dance with Wordsworth's *Prelude*-movements.

"The Old Cumberland Beggar"'s return to human community is much more comprehensive than "The Discharged Soldier"'s, since the beggar's humanizing retardations of society are the basic metaphor of the entire poem and are taken more literally and put more hortatively. The necessary transformation is finally focused in the eye, the organ which in the beggar is disembodied almost beyond human recognizance. On the premise that even the "meanest . . . most vile and brute, . . . dullest or most noxious" of creatures have a use, Wordsworth challenges "Statesmen" to say how

> . . . can aught—that ever owned
> The heaven-regarding *eye* and front sublime
> Which man is born to—sink, howe'er depressed,
> So low as to be scorned without a sin;
> Without offense to God cast out of *view*.   [80–84; italics added]

Again the beggar reverses us into morality: he who has eyes to see, let him *be seen*. The beggar is a moving, pathetic corollary to moral injunction. He no longer regards heaven at all; he but half perceives and nothing creates; yet he binds disparate selfish beings into human community, and the eyes by which he is seen become more important than his eyes which see not, a process finally generalized, in conclusion, to metaphysical proportions: "As in the eye of Nature he has lived, / So in the eye of Nature let him die!" (196–97). To feel that this is a heartless moral is as inappropriate a response to the poem's terms as the statemen's sanitary liberalism; neither response will solve the problem of poor, old, suffering humanity. Wordsworth's placing the beggar's life and death in the "eye" of nature is the symbolic culmination of all the eyes which have regarded him during the course of the poem, humanized and moralized even against their will, "sidelong, and half-reverted."

Sensual Pity: The Tale of Margaret

The tale of Margaret in "The Ruined Cottage" engenders a sense of tragic pity greater than the fear raised by the discharged soldier or the pathos stirred by the old Cumberland beggar. It is so strong it stimulates an almost prurient interest, flirting with sensationalism as "The Old Cumberland Beggar" flirts with comedy. The question of a proper response to Margaret's tale has always been the central issue dividing critics' assessment of the poem: whether Wordsworth improved or damaged it by adding the Pedlar's philosophic interpretation to soften his tale's effect upon his young interlocutor. The question is properly critical, for its answer depends not on the Pedlar nor the young narrator but on the reader. Margaret's decline, her increasingly irrational hopes for her husband's return, manifested in her growing neglect of her children, house, garden, and herself, is presented with a repetitive relentlessness that is literally fascinating. The suspense of the poem hangs on the Pedlar's recurring visits and the reader's anticipations of new signs of physical and mental decay, which are carefully delayed then artfully satisfied. Many powerful critics, from Coleridge and Lamb to F. R. Leavis and Jonathan Wordsworth, have responded to the poem's naked power, proclaiming it one of the finest narratives in the language. They have, for the most part, disliked his addition of the Pedlar's philosophical backgrounding.[50] But Wordsworth was a powerful critic too and knew that he would have few such readers as Coleridge or Leavis, who could see without coaching the tragedy of Margaret's tale. He was right to add the mediating buffer of the Pedlar's philosophy, not simply because Margaret's tale is so painful, but because it is so sensationally effective, enjoyable to read, and easy to take in the wrong way—and because he made it that way.

The Pedlar is aware of his story's potential sensationalism. After he has given its essential outline (Part I), he will not continue until he has clarified the issue.

> "It were a wantonness, and would demand
> Severe reproof, if we were men whose hearts
> Could hold vain dalliance with the misery
> Even of the dead, contented thence to draw

> A momentary pleasure never marked
> By reason, barren of all future good."   (MS B, 280–85)[51]

This caution comes in response to the narrator's begging "that for my sake / He would resume his story" (278–79). At first, the story had not much effect on him, because he saw in the Pedlar's face "such easy chearfulness, a look so mild / That for a little time it stole away / All recollection, and that simple tale / Passed from my mind like a forgotten sound" (259–62). The apparent discrepancy between suffering and "easy cheerfulness" is philosophically based, learned by the Pedlar from Nature's special dispensation, but it does not "take" on the narrator immediately. He is unable to interpret its significance, first misses the point altogether, then goes to the opposite extreme and overreacts. Wordsworth's late additions to the poem include not only the Pedlar's philosophic interpretation but also a delineation of the narrator's helpless, unmanned response:

> I turned aside in weakness, nor had power
> To thank him for the tale which he had told.
> I stood, and leaning o'er the garden-gate
> Reviewed that Woman's suff'rings, and it seemed
> To comfort me while with a brother's love
> I blessed her in the impotence of grief.   [MS D, 495–500]

Similar sexual or romantic undertones are present in an early version of *Salisbury Plain*, and seem equally inappropriate. After the Traveller and the Female Vagrant have spent the night together in the "lonely Spital" on the plain, telling each other the story of their lives, she begins to regard him with a domestic sympathy, and he recognizes the charms that had once made her "the prime of Keswick's plain," particularly her breasts, which he views with an eroticized naturalism that seems uniquely Wordsworthian:

> Like swans, twin swans, that on some secret brink
> Of Derwent's stream, when south winds hardly blow,
> 'Mid Derwent's water-lillies swell and sink
> In union, rose her sister breasts of snow,
> (Fair emblem of two lovers' hearts that know
> No separate impulse), or like infants played,
> Like infants, strangers yet to pain and woe,
> Unwearied Hope to tend their motions made
> Long Vigils, and Delight her cheek between them laid.
>
> [PW.I 105, *app. crit.*]

Of these highly overdetermined breasts, one must say that their creator has mused more on their moral significance than their physical capabilities, or feels constrained to present the latter under cover of the former.

Whence rises this sexual element in response to suffering? Wordsworth is dealing with the issue of proper responses to *stories* of suffering, not only of suffering per se; this, as much as the events of Margaret's life, is what "The Ruined Cottage" is about. The potential sensationalism of such stories is the very stuff of modern journalism, and Wordsworth was one of the first major literary figures in English to foresee the impact of mass journalism on the fabric of society, in competition with the supposed humanizing effect of serious literature. In the preface to *Lyrical Ballads* he dedicated himself to enlarging mankind's capability "of being excited without the application of gross and violent stimulants," believing that this capability is the most important criterion by which "one being is elevated above another"—namely, a standard of humanity which is a valid hierarchical principle in democracy. To be dedicated to this "service" is the best thing a writer can be, "especially . . . at the present day [when] a multitude of causes, unknown to former times, are now acting with a combined force to blunt the discriminating forces of the mind, and, unfitting it for all voluntary exertion, to reduce it to a state of almost savage torpor." These causes were, primarily, "the great national events which are daily taking place, and the increasing accumulation of men in cities," but Wordsworth links their erosive power to the devaluation of literary classics by "the literature and theatrical exhibitions of the country," which were driving Shakespeare and Milton into neglect in favor of "frantic novels, sickly and stupid German Tragedies, and deluges of idle and extravagant stories in verse." Considering that "The Ruined Cottage" is partly based on a fragment by Goethe, that parts of it contributed to or derived from sentimental tales by both Lamb and Southey, and that its focus on an unprotected, exposed female is the very stuff of the "frantic novels" and sentimental drama and opera of the time,[52] the Pedlar's "severe reproof" against sensationalism anticipates the argument of the preface. But as the poem's own sensational potential is so great, the question remains whether it is part of the solution or part of the problem, a deeply humanizing narrative or part of that "degrading thirst after outrageous stimulation" which the *Lyrical Ballads'* preface scorned?

The Pedlar's story stimulates deep emotion where no human connection exists at all. The young narrator is *not* Margaret's "brother" (l. 498); she is, after all, dead; what's he to her or she to him? Just as the Pedlar's "look so mild" initially made the tale pass from his mind "like a forgotten sound," so his overreaction also responds to the Pedlar's. The old man is not the unfeeling stoic some readers see in him; his philosophy does not insulate him, and all versions of the poem contain moments when he is nearly overcome.[53] The very questions which end the story *he* means to tell (Part I) imply its effect:

> "Why should a tear be in an old Man's eye?
> Why should we thus with an untoward mind
> And in the weakness of humanity
> From natural wisdom turn our hearts away,
> To natural comfort shut our eyes and ears,
> And feeding on disquiet thus disturb
> [The calm] of Nature with our restless thoughts?"   [250–56]

Because we do, that's why. Human vulnerability is the only answer to these questions, as to those at the end of Blake's *Book of Thel*, another Romantic inquiry into the nature of human suffering that uses the metaphor of female sexuality. The tear in the old man's eye is as much an answer to his questions as the need for a natural philosophy they arouse. The apparent lack of connection between emotion and "wisdom" is, dialectically, the strongest reason for believing in its existence, at least for the young Wordsworth, who put the same questions negatively in the notebook jottings from which the Pedlar's "natural wisdom" sprang: "Why is it we feel / So little for each other but for this / That we with nature have no sympathy / Or with such idle objects as have no power to hold / Articulate language." But the sensational pathos of Margaret's tale arises from language that is highly articulated, not from a neutral sociological report on the condition of the poor, nor from the narrator's direct observation. The Pedlar apologizes that his tale is "scarcely palpable / To him who does not think" (294–95); but he is overly modest, if not downright duplicitous, since his telling makes all too palpable the pathos of broken attachments, stimulating the narrator's "impotence of grief" toward an unknown woman he now feels he loves like a brother. While Margaret seems like a sister to him, she gave to the Pedlar "a daughter's welcome . . . and I loved her / As my own child" (149–50). Indeed, the extreme pathos of Margaret's isolation can be measured in direct contrast with the wealth of human relations she solicits: "no one came / But he was welcome, no one went away / But that it seemed she loved him" (155–57). Harmless enough, on everybody's part. But the immediately succeeding lines hit the reader with a contrast so stark that their pathos surely blinds him to Wordsworth's continuation and intensification of the preceding rhetoric of romance and domesticity:

> "But that it seemed she loved him. She is dead
> The worm is *on her cheek*, and this poor hut,
> *Stripped of its outward garb* of household flowers,
> Of rose and jasmine, *offers* to the wind
> *A cold bare wall* whose earthy *top* is *tricked*
> With weeds and rank spear-grass. She is dead,
> And nettles rot and adders sun themselves
> *Where we have sat together while she nursed*
> Her infant *at her bosom*." [157–65; italics added]

What is this? a reader less sentimentally inclined than the narrator might ask. More than a brutal juxtaposition,[54] this forcing together of associations is almost unfairly overpowering, images of death usurping the place of earthly lovers to whom, in deathly displacement, Margaret and her surrogate cottage seem to offer themselves.

Pathos, sexually reinforced, makes Margaret a more dangerous object of suffering to the weak narrator than the ghastly veteran. I do not mean that Wordsworth is presenting an unconscious motivation for Margaret's fall, as if she flirted with the disaster that ultimately befell her. Rather, we see here one of the central means by which the narrator is set up for his penultimate response, that of inappropriate impotence. The narrative is radically overdetermined, a vestige of the shockingly inappropriate—but shockingly attractive—responses to suffering which Wordsworth explored in "Argument for Suicide" and "Incipient Madness." Similarly inappropriate responses are residual in "The Ruined Cottage," and the narrator must be educated away from them by the Pedlar, which is to say that Wordsworth's philosophic nature must educate his naively responsive nature. This passage calls all human love and relationship into question, the Pedlar's fatherly feelings toward Margaret as well as the emotions felt by any passerby whom Margaret welcomes. It gives special point to the diction in which the Pedlar warned the narrator against taking her tale the wrong way: "wantonness . . . vain dalliance . . . momentary pleasure . . . barren of all future good." Few have been disposed to see pornographic possibilities in the tale of Margaret, yet Wordsworth has the Pedlar acknowledge the inappropriateness of his language: "You will forgive me, Sir, / I feel I play the truant with my tale" (170–71). Truant from what? From its moral intention, and toward its sensational possibilities? From its instruction, and toward its uncensored prurience? Perhaps the truancy is toward all suggestions of improper—that is, humanly unfounded—relationships with Margaret, for the next line introduces the character who restores propriety to the tragedy: "She had a husband, an industrious man, / Sober and steady" (172–73).

Much of the pathos of the story attaches to this husband, Robert, particularly regarding his love for their children compared to hers. The eldest is apprenticed away for its own good by the parish authority, an act whose wisdom seems confirmed by the subsequent death of the youngest, which seems to effect Margaret not at all in comparison with her passion for Robert. The passion of Margaret is so great that it could be the title of the poem, and it explains the overflow of love with which she greets all comers ever after. All of Part II is governed by Margaret's questioning passersby about Robert; everything else is secondary.[55] She becomes like the "woman wailing for her demon lover" in "Kubla Khan" naturalized into an ordinary English landscape. Such are the interests that stimulate the narrator to "beg" the Pedlar to continue: "In my own despite / I thought of that poor woman as of one / Whom I had known and loved" (264–66). In his own despite, maybe, but we have at least a glimmer of whence such attractions have come into his mind.

The Pedlar accedes to his plea by describing the scene that will be repeated throughout Part II. On his next visit, he walked in expecting his usual welcome, but received the only greeting Margaret will ever give:

> "Oh Sir!
> I cannot *tell* how she pronounced my name:
> With fervent love and with a face of grief
> Unutterably helpless and a look
> That seemed to cling upon me, she inquired
> If I had seen her husband." [311–16; Wordsworth's italics]

This human scene parallels the Pedlar's recognition of "unutterable love" in nature as a boy, with the same paradoxical insistence upon love without human articulation ("tell" emphatically conjoined to, yet negated from, nominalization) displaced into meaningful looks: Margaret's facial, not verbal, expression becomes her physical embrace. This scene is repeated four times in Part II, each climax managed with cinematic sureness: the Pedlar comes to the cottage, seems at first to see it unchanged, then gradually notices signs of neglect and decay, and finally meets Margaret and confirms his suspicions. The connection between the ruining of the cottage and Margaret's decline is the poem's master effect, but besides the crescendo of pathos as the Pedlar returns each time and notes anticipations of tragedy, there is an accompanying increase in Margaret's unnaturalness, parallel to Wordsworth's presentation of the discharged soldier and the old Cumberland beggar as monstrous, disintegrating figures. By his second visit, Margaret's grief has given her an undesired immortality: "my tears / Have flowed as if my body were not such / As others are, and I could never die" (408–10). Like the old beggar's eyes, her tears have an independent life. Her sighs also are perceived like the dismantled, alienated physical oddities of the beggar and the veteran: "still she sighed, / But yet no motion of the breast was seen, / No heaving of the heart . . . sighs came on my ear; / I knew not how and hardly whence they came" (422–26). Wordsworth was fascinated by the spiritual possibilities of disembodied sounds (like poetry) and had a genius for phrasing them, as in *The Prelude*'s "steps almost as silent as the turf they trod." But the suggestion of higher power they convey in "The Ruined Cottage" is demonic and destructive. On his third visit, the Pedlar finds these sighs contagious: "Her infant babe / Had from its mother caught the trick of grief / And sighed among its playthings" (448–50). The possibility of emotional contagion is apt, for the narrator catches something from the story that the Pedlar, having induced, must finally exorcise. The baby's contagion is also literal, for it dies of neglect, and on the Pedlar's final visit the increasing abnormality of Margaret's love is implicit in the uneasy contrast between her half-line report, "that her little babe was dead" (475), and her reiterated compulsion: she "begged / That wheresoe'er I went I still would ask / For him whom she had lost" (480–82).

Like the old soldier and the beggar, Margaret might have maintained herself better, even if it meant begging, but again Wordsworth stresses the displacement of self-preservation: she regards normal life with "careless stillness which a thinking mind / Gives to an idle matter." (421–22), and begs only for the useless or the impossible: she loves to distraction. Hartman sees a quality of insatiable imagination in such longings,[56] but Wordsworth does not reveal them unawares; having released such desires into the poem, he seeks also to show the means of correcting or curbing them. In the Pedlar's hearsay report of her last days, her pathetic distraction is complete: she rises to look for Robert if even a dog passes by, "and evermore her eye / Was busy in the distance, shaping things / Which made her heart beat quick" (491–93). Her emotional beggary increases, importuning with "fond inquiry" not only people she knows, but any "man whose garments shewed the Soldier's red," and ultimately complete strangers with no shred of plausible connection to Robert:

> "And when a stranger horseman came . . .
> . . . [she] in his face look[ed] wistfully,
> Most happy if from aught discovered there

> Of tender feelings she might dare repeat
> The same sad question."   [508–12]

This is Margaret's end: promiscuously she seeks tenderness just to ask her question, possibly no longer caring for the answer. This is Margaret, from whom "no one went away / But that it seemed she loved him," now seeking any excuse to put the love-question that will expose her situation. She, "reckless," and her cottage, "reft," die together in "this wretched spot," "endeared"—but also bewitched—by "one torturing hope" (525).

Such powerfully manipulated pathos fully justifies the narrator's ambivalent "impotence of grief." Though strong readers have wished to reject Wordsworth's addition of the Pedlar's philosophic interpretation, it seems to me that the power he unleashes makes it obligatory for him to restrain it. DeQuincey's reaction, that Margaret is guilty of "criminal self-indulgence . . . sloth, and the habit of gadding abroad,"[57] is hardly the answer, but DeQuincey was no fool, and was, besides, a master of psychologically manipulative suspense tales. He reacted to something in the tale of Margaret which calls not for a moral judgment but an aesthetic one: that Margaret's inability to cope—however little one is disposed to disapprove it—is presented to us in ways that are far from neutral, establishing factitious relations between her and the narrator which, effectively but extremely, raise questions of normal versus abnormal responses to human suffering. In this light, the Pedlar's final advice, added in subsequent revisions, to see dead Margaret in nature's dispensation, calm and beautiful, is certainly no more exaggerated than the sensuality with which her suffering has been represented. The "image of tranquility" that he saw in some wet weeds and spear-grass on a later visit, after Margaret was dead, provided what he needed even then, and still does: respite from "the uneasy thoughts which filled my mind," so that

> "all the grief
> The passing shews of being leave behind,
> Appeared an idle dream that could not live
> Where meditation was."   [MS D, 521–24]

The image of weeds and spear-grass is one of several ways in which Wordsworth rounds off "The Ruined Cottage" by returning to its beginning.[58] At the outset, they are "matted" and "rank" (117, 162); in the end, they are "by mist and silent raindrops silver'd o'er" (D, 515). But in a poem where landscape description is pressed so heavily into the service of morality, the important question is, who sees them differently, and how? The outsetting narrator sees no meaning in them, but he has not yet been initiated into the Pedlar's natural mysteries: " 'I see around me . . . things which you cannot see' " (129–30). The main purpose of the poem's strange beginning is to show the exacerbated, misdirected, perhaps paranoid[59] sensibility of this narrator, who walks across a "bare wide Common" in a frenzy of discomfort, jealous of a figment of his own imagination (a "dreaming man" he imagines looking out on the scene from shady comfort), who flings himself down in full sunlight even with shade in sight, and is annoyed by the "murmurs" of the "the insect host" and the "tedious noise" of bursting gorse seeds (juniper berries) as if personally insulted by boring company (1–25). All this is an exaggerated presentation of the "idle dream" in which we often live, making ourselves miserable to no purpose and calling it reality.

But if we lived with "meditation," saith the Pedlar, such "passing shews of being" literally "could not live." The narrator must learn, as Wordsworth had been learning, what is idle and what is not, what is mere dreaming and what real meditation, what aesthetic escapism and what serious art. For there *is* a "dreaming man" lying in the shade even though the narrator does not know it: the Pedlar, but he is meditating, not dreaming, and by the end of the story he has instructed the narrator in the difference. At the end, after telling and hearing of Margaret's tale, they join company in a fellowship of human normality: "we left the shade / And ere the stars were visible attained / A rustic inn, our evening resting-place" (D, 536–38). This fellowship has been established at risk, by a narrative excursion into threatening abnormality and psychic disintegration. Their move to a "rustic inn" parallels the last line of "The Discharged Soldier," "Then sought with quiet heart my distant home." Better a rustic inn than a ruined cottage, obviously, but the narrator now appreciates the commonsense difference with "thought" or "meditation."

In all three poems, the suffering characters have posed a threat to the narrators that cannot be dealt with by a normal human reaction. The beggar could be taken care of—perhaps better—if he went to a poorhouse; the veteran could beg, and Margaret could too, or spin, or garden—but none of them will do these things. True, a world without poverty or war would largely solve these problems; but these are not the problems as Wordsworth creates them. These figures threaten their narrators' assumptions about normal human responsiveness and caring. Why and how should we care for each other at all? Wordsworth's representation of an answer derives its authority from his radical researches, more psychological than philosophical, into negative, abnormal responses—rejection,

blame, murder, exploitation, even enjoyment—in the pre-*Recluse* fragments. These negative possibilities are vestigially but powerfully present in
"The Ruined Cottage," "The Old Cumberland Beggar," and "The Discharged Veteran," and Wordsworth's redirecting their dangerous power
back into normal human community is the triumph of the first *Recluse*
poems.

2

The First *Prelude*, 1798–1799

Yet once again do I behold the forms
Of these huge mountains, and yet once again,
Standing beneath these elms, I hear thy voice,
Beloved Derwent, that peculiar voice
Heard in the stillness of the evening air,
Half-heard and half-created.

PW, V.340

If the first *Recluse* poems owe much of their existence to Coleridge's presence in 1797–98, the first *Prelude* poetry owes its existence to Coleridge's absence from Wordsworth in 1798–99. The plan of exporting their "little colony" of literary journalists from England to Germany to increase their stock of language and philosophy worked out rather badly for the Wordsworths and caused a major shift in *The Recluse*'s development (*LEY*, 213). They separated from Coleridge a few weeks after their arrival in Hamburg (September 18, 1798), and the separation lasted a full year except for one day in Göttingen in April. Coleridge went to Ratzeburg, a fashionable intellectual enclave near Hamburg, while the Wordsworths traveled south to the small town of Goslar, near the Harz mountains, between Hannover and Göttingen (M. I.411–12). The separation left Wordsworth without his friend's "cheering voice" to spur on *The Recluse*, but this failure for *The Recluse* was the making of *The Prelude*. Deprived of Coleridge's company, which was his principal object in any event, Wordsworth was thrown back upon himself. He was isolated in a small provincial town in a foreign country, without books because Goslar had no library, unwilling to apply himself to learning the language, deprived of company by social and financial constraints, and, finally, frozen in by one of the coldest winters of the century. In his own fin de siècle malaise, Wordsworth found himself in the sort of enforced exile that has stimulated many writers, from Ovid to Joyce, to creative self-preservation. Rarely have home thoughts from abroad resulted in such a magnificent creation of a literary personality as Wordsworth's reconstruction of himself from recollections of his early childhood.

It did not seem so at the time, but his deprivation of Coleridge's company was the beginning of Wordsworth's independence from him,[1] signaled by the first of a series of alterations in his conception of *The Recluse*. Principally, it led to the intuition that "the first great modern philosophic poem" must include the full examination and conscious presence of the personality of its author, an intuition that nearly every subsequent philosophical test of truth-value has corroborated. Yet even as an intuition, Wordsworth's composition of the biographical fragments that led to *The Prelude* had no very clear goal as to the kind of poem they might lead to, and still less of their relation to *The Recluse*.[2] After three months, Wordsworth sent Coleridge a progress report: "As I had no books I have been obliged to write in self-defense" (*LEY*, 236). His cause–effect logic reveals the different assumptions of *The Recluse* and *The Prelude*, which he would spend the next fifteen years trying to reconcile. As a "philosophic" poem, *The Recluse* depended on external, objective knowledge and assumed a course of reading from which the author could, as Coleridge said later, "deliver upon authority a system of philosophy" (*TT*, II, 70). Coleridge's twenty-year plan for producing an epic poem, with its heavy emphasis on "universal science" and outward-looking assumptions about "the *mind of man*—then the *minds of men*—in all Travels, Voyages and Histories" (*LSTC*, I. 320–21), must often have been recounted to Wordsworth. Coleridge's constant presence had reassured Wordsworth of the possible existence of a metaphysical framework to contain such knowledge, but without Coleridge he was forced to grapple single-mindedly with fundamental questions of the relation of knowledge to will. A great act was required of him, but he was not sure what it was or how to do it; small wonder that some of the early *Prelude* passages sound like Hamlet's soliloquies, especially its famous abrupt opening, "Was it for this?" There are plenty of reasons for the ad hoc, defaultive quality of *The Prelude*'s beginnings, but this one is crucial. Although it was a distraction from *The Recluse*, and in part an apology to Coleridge for being so distracted, as well as an expression of creative self-doubt,[3] *The Prelude* also begins, in this fortunate fall of coincidences, as an inquiry into the status of the power of human subjectivity vis-à-vis a sense of public responsibility toward all objective knowledge of the world. Wordsworth continued to dabble in scientific writings[4] and was always glad to indulge his passion for books of travel and discovery, but the nearly twenty years he spent on *his* epic poem were far more taken up with self-definition as a necessary corollary to book-learning. Paradoxically but appropriately, Coleridge's long curricula of the knowledge requisite to epics led Wordsworth—in Coleridge's absence—to consider the nature of the self as a structural counterbalance to the whole of human civilization. The "egotistical sublime" arose to meet a corollary challenge of epistemological sublimity.

Initially, Wordsworth's writing in self-defense consisted of approximately 250 lines of recollections of some half-dozen exciting childhood experiences, which make up about half of Part I of the two-part *Prelude* of 1798–99 as now reconstituted.[5] He had begun writing autobiographical recollections in early 1798, to supply the Pedlar with the profundity of natural insight necessary to interpret Margaret's suffering. But what he had attributed to the Pedlar he now applied directly to himself, as a way toward understanding his own suffering at being unable to raise the grand poetic edifice on which he believed his greatness would be founded. "Was it for this?" signifies, among other things, What has my life so far been for? Is it a ruin, or can it be a foundation? He hopes that Coleridge will sympathetically agree with him, "less aptly skilled than many are," about the difficulty of comprehending the infinity of causes contributing to the healthful development of a powerful mind. Left to his own devices, he accomplishes several things in a verse epistle whose structure very much resembles the lines addressed to Dorothy above Tintern Abbey, based on the same dialectic between disappointment experienced in the adult social world and restoration imagined in nature's eternal perspectives.

First, the 1798–99 *Prelude* reassured Wordsworth about the sources of his imaginative power, despite recurrent doubts about what seems "vain" and "idle" in his life so far—namely, almost all of his adult life.[6] It begins with a reiterated hanging question, "Was it for this?" and there is ample antecedent for that unspecified "this" in Wordsworth's immediate life context. Yet the depression of the opening sentence is but a launching pad into the poem's marvelous confidence, as Wordsworth asserts his mind's pure fitness for higher callings despite its experience of the corrupting world; he pushes off from the "vulgar" works of man into quasi-transcendental justifications of his fitness to correct human vulgarity. He had been reading Burns's "Ode to Despondency," which contrasts the "bustling strife" of the "sons of busy life" with a situation very like his own, "unfitted with an aim" (M. I.420–21), and the dialectical force of the contrast appealed to him. The "fretful dwellings of mankind" (i.13) are partly a conventional image of the corrupt city versus the pure countryside, but additionally they represent an unhappy definition of maturity against which Wordsworth defends his sense of creative maturity as something better. Worldliness seems almost by definition harsh and hostile.[7] His determination to defend his state of mind by distinguishing it from what the world understands as maturity—principally the ability to maintain oneself independently—is the over-arching intention of the first *Prelude*.

Second, the means of this justification are represented as quasi-supernatural beings whom Wordsworth credits with having kept him pure among "the mean and vulgar works of man." Especially in its earliest composed sections, the 1799 *Prelude* places the boy Wordsworth in eternal perspectives, where "the sky seemed not a sky of earth," and the earth is peopled by "huge and mighty forms that do not live like living men." But, though grounded in "eternal things" by his early exposure to nature's "high objects," Wordsworth is not very certain about the nature of Nature or the value of his attachment to it. Progressively more abstract, philosophical, and theological revisions greatly altered Nature's appearance in *The Prelude* by the time of its posthumous publication in 1850. In 1799, "high objects" sometimes signify no more than high things, like mountains. For his spiritual vocabulary, Wordsworth utilizes obviously fictional, provisional terms from fairy tales and folklore ("Genii of the springs," "Familiars of the lakes"): the "Godkins" and "Goddesslings" that Coleridge would scoff at.[8] Such patently artificial diction is of a piece with Wordsworth's manifest uncertainty about the analytic task he had undertaken, for which post-Freudian readers will hardly fault him. He picked up from Coleridge, and pursued in his own independent and powerful way, what was to become the characteristically nineteenth-century philosophic project of explaining the ends of things by researching their genetic origins.[9] Wordsworth did not take his researches into his past fully seriously; he hoped only to fetch "reproaches from my former years" to spur him on "to honorable toil"—*The Recluse*. He readily admits he may simply be indulging himself, "feeling, as I fear, / The weakness of a human love for days / Disowned by memory" (i.443–45). He is not altogether sure whether his self analysis is regressive or progressive, whether it tends toward "manhood now mature" (a pointed redundancy) or is a symptom of unmanly weakness for which he must beg Coleridge's indulgence.

This doubt, however, is largely rhetorical and arises from the poem's being addressed to Coleridge as, first, a respected master in mental analysis, and, second, the originator of the project for a world-redeeming poem that would deal out comprehensive views on Man, Nature, and Society from an assumed base of unquestioned self-knowledge. He is finally triumphantly confident that his mind's base in nature is neither regressive nor insane. The trouble lies with the world, not with him, as it would for generations of Romantic writers who made this perception the ground of their artistic confidence. At the end of the poem Wordsworth incorporates one of Coleridge's cheering letters to describe the world's depressed condition: "these times of fear, / This melancholy waste of hopes o'erthrown . . . when good men / On every side fall off we know not how" (ii.478–82). He thus attaches the particular depression of English intellectuals' hopes for the French Revolution to what, elsewhere in the poem, is simply the generality of what adults must do all the time, especially in cities—accept workaday assumptions about worthwhile work, and perhaps thereby fall into the selfishness, envy, and jealousy from which Wordsworth has managed to hold himself free. This transfer is largely accomplished in the Second Part, where growth toward social consciousness is grafted onto the more emotional childhood experiences described in the First Part. To see clearly how this important shift occurs, we must take a comprehensive look at the first *Prelude*'s "unity of argument" (i.253), which is as novel in its poetics as it is in psychology.

The first *Prelude*, like its later forms, is at once convincing and confusing. That Wordsworth is not sure of himself, of his past accomplishments, or of what he is accomplishing in this poem, is as necessary to the poem's progress and unity as the fact that he *is* confident of the value of his life's experiences, and of their promise for his poetry to come. As a category of interpretation, confusion is of dubious repute; hence critics' tendency with all versions of *The Prelude* to stress Wordsworth's convictions and allow only the confusions that he admits to. The 1799 version is, as Stephen Parrish claims, "coherent and thematically rounded," and may well have, as its modern discoverer, J. R. MacGillivray, avers, "a much more unified theme and a much stronger sense of formal structure than . . . the poem completed first in 1805 and published in 1850."[10] Abbie F. Potts divined some of its internal similarities to contemporary models like Beattie's *The Minstrel* from fragmentary manuscript evidence, and the most useful view of its status as an independently interpretable poem is that of Wordsworth, Abrams, and Gill: that it was "for the time complete—hence the rounding off, and the faircopies—and . . . was in the event not continued, but taken apart and redistributed, in the construction of 1805."[11] But like so many other Wordsworth texts, the 1799 *Prelude* is also an enactment of the poet's search for a unifying faith that love of nature leads to love of man, the implied sequence of *The Recluse*'s themes, and it negotiates some stages more surely than others. Wordsworth's uncertainties are not, however, simple flaws in aesthetic perfection, but often the sources of his poem's dramatic tension and persuasive sincerity.

Wordsworth, Abrams, and Gill see the two-part development of the 1799 *Prelude* as resulting from Wordsworth's determination to answer the question, "What was the link between such [childhood] experiences and his adult creativity?"[12] Many readers have traditionally been willing to accept Wordsworth's love of nature at face value; others have been content with Wordsworth as poet of "man's unconquerable mind." More recently, critics have interpreted the former as a cover, defense, or displacement of the latter—which in turn is often redefined as Wordsworth's own particular creative mind. But in the 1799 *Prelude* and throughout the compositional history of *The Recluse* we can see that none of these positions was sufficient for Wordsworth, that he was determined, for better or worse, to push beyond relating mind and nature to some position defending the social responsibility of his work as not "idle." Yet countering the poem's general movement from Part One's emphasis on natural phenomena to Part Two's emphasis on human social forms is a subsidiary movement within each part from external to internal considerations, provoked by the poet's uncertainty that he was proceeding in the right way.

FIRST PART (464 lines)

1–198: Seasonal Organization (external events): three subsidiary units, alternating episode and commentary.
 a. 1–80: Summer swimming, autumn poaching, spring bird-nesting, concluding with: "The mind of man is fashioned and built up"
 b. 81–141: Boat-stealing, concluding with: "Ah! not in vain, ye Beings of the hills!"
 c. 142–98: Winter ice skating, concluding with: "Ye Powers of earth! ye Genii of the springs!"
198–258: Mid-Point Conflict: Wordsworth argues with himself about the usefulness of continuing his preceding mode of presentation, because, though "not useless," yet "much is overlooked." Therefore, rejecting "delicate fears" about spoiling the unity of its argument, he shifts to "such effects as cannot here / Be regularly classed" (255–58), after he has recapitulated his entire seasonal scheme, with summer races, winter card-playing, autumn fishing, and spring kite-flying (198–248).
258–442: Emotional Organization (internal events): based on the conventional neoclassical aesthetic categories of The Sublime and The Beautiful, addressed, respectively, to the human emotions of Fear and Joy.

258–374: The Ministry of Fear ("spots of time"):
    a. The Drowned Man of Esthwaite (258–87)
    b. The Murderer's Grave (288–330)
    c. Waiting for the Horses at Christmas (330–74)
375–442: The Ministry of Beauty: generalized pleasurable sights, forming "The bond of union betwixt life and joy."
442–64: Conclusion: Apology, plea for indulgence, and self-defence to Coleridge.

SECOND PART (514 lines)

1–236: Social Organization (external events)
    1–31: Introduction: farewell to "woods and fields," welcome to "the town in which we dwelt a small domain."
    31–53: Village center: "a gray stone of native rock . . . gone to build a smart assembly room."
    53–214: Boat races to the islands, school-time picnics, livery horses ridden to Furness Abbey, Coniston Hall, and the White Lion Inn, formerly "a hut . . . more worthy of a poet's love."
    215–36: Conclusion: Nationalization and domestication of sun and moon, because they seemed to appertain "by a peculiar right / To thee and thy grey huts, my native vale."
237–67: Mid-Point Conflict: As in Part One, Wordsworth argues with himself, not about the usefulness of continuing his mode of presentation, but what amounts to the same thing, the difficulty of pursuing his next stage, the growth of consciousness ("nature . . . now at length . . . sought for her own sake"). He again advances by advising himself of the folly of paying too much attention to mechanical unities: "Who shall parcel out his intellect by geometric rules?"
267–464: Psychological Organization (internal events)
"Bless'd the infant Babe," and all that flows from its security upon its mother's breast: the building up of personality, "an inmate of this *active* universe," and integration into society: "solitude / More active even than 'best society,' / Society made sweet as solitude" (343–46).
465–514: Conclusion: Celebration, reaffirmation, and incorporation of Coleridge into their newly defined task, whereby living "with thyself and for thyself" becomes the means of providing "blessing to mankind."

In such an outline, one cannot fail to notice the relative balance and proportion Wordsworth maintains. Like the two parts themselves, the two halves within each part are roughly equal in length. In Part One, the three seasonal episodes and commentaries are in fair proportion, as are the three "spots of time." If the lines devoted to Fear outnumber those given to Joy almost two to one, that is as Wordsworth intends it; for in differentiating nature's "gentle" and "severe" ministrations, he identifies his experiences primarily with the latter: "of their school was I" (80). The same proportions are evident in Part Two; the biggest change is from the seasonal to a social mode of organization, in the boys' sports and vacation activities, and the local buildings with which they were associated—institutionally determined time and space.

The addresses to Coleridge at the end of each part are especially noteworthy in their differences from each other. At the end of Part One, Wordsworth pleads defensively for Coleridge's indulgent understanding of his fondness for "recollected hours [of] infancy." But at the end of Part Two, Wordsworth, now surer of this mind's attachment to the powers of earth (and back in England and about to go to live in the Lake Country), takes Coleridge's own words into his mouth (from Coleridge's letter of September 10, 1799) and makes the poem he is concluding a prospective answer to the sociohistorical problems which Coleridge suggested he address in *The Recluse*. As an extended conversation poem,[13] the two-part *Prelude* is essentially a love poem, written to the beloved under the pressure of their first separation and accomplishing one of the most usual of courtship rituals: taking the beloved back to one's own home, offering oneself in one's entirety, not only as he had been known to Coleridge (from Racedown to Germany), but also as he had been before they met, showing the whole life for him to love. This attempted seduction of Coleridge is evident throughout the poem, subtly transmuted from personal to social grounds. Although Coleridge had been the dominant partner at the outset of the friendship, the balance of power began to shift during and after the German sojourn; we can observe the change occurring in the conclusions of the two parts of the 1798–99 *Prelude*. Words and actions lie very close together there.

Coleridge may have been given the two-part *Prelude* on the instant it was completed—a traveling gift, as he and Wordsworth set out on the walking tour to the Lake Country in November 1799 (see chapter 3). One purpose of this trip was to introduce Coleridge to the region's beauties, to entice him to live there. The end of the 1799 *Prelude* seeks self-actualization, to close the separation which occasioned its agonized beginnings. Not only its conclusions, but its entire structure seek to establish actual biographical fact as an imaginative reality, to change life materially by the power of art. This transforming power is best seen in the poem's own turning points, its midpoint conflicts and its point of departure, as well as its points of termination.

STRONG REVERSALS: MIDDLES, BEGINNINGS, AND ENDINGS

The whole poem proceeds according to an inside-out rhetoric, a series of not-this-but-that constructions, which give Wordsworth the power of launching off from his own denials, his commonest mode of argument.[14] This rhetorical strategy supports the redefinition of maturity he seeks to establish: *not* the world's definitions of adult behavior, *but* the special one that he has discovered. It also moves his address to Coleridge, during the course of the poem, from that of suppliant to that of partner, with overtones of the lordly commander. The fulcrum of this rhetoric is most obvious in each part's midpoint conflict, where Wordsworth pivots from a content-centered mode of presentation (seasonal in Part One, social in Two) to one stressing process (aesthetic-emotional in One, analytic-psychological in Two). Wordsworth announces his need for transition so boldly as to weaken his argument's authority, in classical decorum. But as a now-familiar Romantic strategy, such openness increases our sense of the author's sincerity and allows him to retain the value of his assertions even as, without bringing them to conclusion, it gives him energy to launch off on a new tack.

Obvious in the two midpoint conflicts, this reversing rhetoric is more problematic in the hanging question with which the two-part *Prelude* begins: "Was it for this . . . ?"[15] No doubt Coleridge had a clear sense of what "this" referred to—all the difficulties of the past year, with particular reference to Wordsworth's failure to make progress on *The Recluse*— and could fit the text into the immediate context of actions and decisions Wordsworth was taking in real life. Yet the question is not so obscure that it prevents us from advancing into the poem. As a literary convention, its conversational gambit is not far removed from the openings of verse epistles and dialogues ("Shut, shut the door, good John! fatigu'd I said, / Tye up the knocker, say I'm sick, I'm dead"), and, as a tonal modulation of the formal structure outlined above, Wordsworth's partial repetitions and variations of the question ("For this didst thou," " 'twas," "It was"), along with his understated provisional answers ("*Not uselessly* employed, / I might pursue this theme"), draw us into the poem as if we were overhearing a man trying to convince himself of something and only gradually achieving the courage of his convictions (*"palpable* access / Of knowledge," ii.335–36).[16] The open-beginning quality of this question (as contrasted with open-ended) is disguised, but not removed, by the nearly three hundred lines which Wordsworth set down in front of it in 1805. If anything, these lines increase the anguish of the question: the difficulty of writing this poem (*The Prelude*), heightened by an uncertain sense of its relevance to a still greater poem (*The Recluse*), to which all this self-questioning is prelusive. On the other hand, the referent of "this" is specified, in great detail, by all the information the 1805 version adds *after* the two parts written in 1798–99: that is, the whole history of self-doubts and unfulfilling experiences Wordsworth had had to overcome since leaving home for Cambridge in 1787—the precise point at which the poem resumes in 1804 (Book III: "Residence at Cambridge") and runs on through thirteen books, ending at Alfoxden and the time of his departure for Germany, when *The Recluse* was to be composed—and *The Prelude* was begun instead. All versions of *The Prelude* end at the point of *The Recluse*'s beginning; *The Recluse* could begin any time *The Prelude* could be considered finished. This is the essential reason *The Prelude* never was completed, or never left alone *as* complete. Contrariwise, it is the same reason *The Recluse* was not completed; but that Wordsworth could accomplish so much of it in the face of so powerful a mechanism for never beginning it is one of his greatest compositional achievements, not his "great failure."

Speculation about the substantive antecedent of "this" should not, however, distract us from the ways in which Wordsworth glosses it over and makes us forget it. Even considered by itself, the opening question is a rhetorical one that generates its own answer: "'Was it for this' . . . that Nature nurtured me? No, it was not for this, but for something else, which I am in process of doing . . . writing this poem and thereby launching myself into heroic imaginative endeavor." The reversal pushes off from something unspecified; but more rigorously considered, the question implies a disconnection which is then converted into a tautology. Was it [my early life] for this [my present state of confusion] that [my early life was what it was—or what I am now about to describe it as having been]? Was my early life for my present life? Yes or No? Yes! Despite all feelings of dislocation, my early life and my present life are massively, naturally interconnected.[17] Finch and Parrish both note the presence of an answer—"Ah, not in vain"—to the repeated opening question.[18] This phrase completes the rhetorical formula, but it does not enter the text until line 130, after several dramatic boyhood incidents have intervened, making us further forget that their urgency derives from their being answers to a very large, unspecified, and therefore dangerous question. Too close a connection between these answers (boyhood confidence) and that question (adult despair) might render the answers ridiculous (regressive or irrelevant) and release the damaging force of the question.

The rhetoric of reversal present in its middles and beginnings is also strongly operative in this *Prelude*'s endings, both within each part's conclusion and between Part One's apologetic close and Part Two's triumphant one. In the paragraph ending the First Part (442–64), Wordsworth fears he is displaying only the "weakness of a human love for days / Disowned by memory" (444–45). But in a neat, brief specimen of ring-construction, he converts fear to hope, via the agency of Coleridge's sympathy, which allows him to continue, following this sequence: fear$_1$→sympathy→hope→sympathy→fear$_2$. The paragraph's center rests on a hope which is in the present perfect of its own discourse:

> *Meanwhile* my hope has been that I might fetch
> Reproaches from my former years, whose power
> May spur me on, in manhood now mature,
> To honourable toil.   [450–53; italics added]

No sooner offered than withdrawn ("Yet, should it be / That this is but an impotent desire," 453–54), his hope falls back on Coleridge's sympathy, but not, now, for failing "honourable toil," but as a license to continue his recollections without fear.

> [Nor] . . . need I dread from thee
> Harsh judgements if I am so loth to quit
> Those recollected hours that have the charm
> Of visionary things, and lovely forms
> And sweet sensations that throw back our life
> And make our infancy a visible scene
> On which the sun is shining?—   [458–64]

This is indeed the language of "a human love." The rich Shakespearean ambiguity of the phrase, "throw back our life," besides being a literal statement of what Wordsworth is doing with his present adult existence, also carries connotations of covers thrown back to reveal the body of the beloved, a nearly helpless erotic fascination with his childhood which certainly threatens that his wish for "honourable toil . . . in manhood now mature" may "be an impotent desire."

At the end of the Second Part, the address to Coleridge proceeds by still more daring reversals. It, too, begins with ready acknowledgment of possible weakness, not simply in Wordsworth's fondness for talking about his childhood, but also in the faith in nature's beneficence with which he has undergirded it. Yet the conditional *if* of "If this be error" (465) rapidly slides from his possible impiety to his certain ingratitude, "*if* I should fail with grateful voice / To speak of you, ye mountains!" (469–70), and leads firmly to his powerful conviction that his faith in nature is just what the sickly times require: "*if* in these times of fear, / This melancholy waste of hopes o'erthrown . . . I yet . . . retain / A more than Roman confidence . . . the gift is yours, / Ye Mountains!" (478–92 passim). The reversal from doubt to confidence which pivots on the shifting *if* is made all the more daring by the fact that the ten lines beginning, "if in these times of fear," are a direct paraphrase of Coleridge's letter of September 10, 1799, written to spur Wordsworth on to *The Recluse*, with additional suggestions as to whom it should be addressed.

> I wish you would write a poem . . . addressed to those who, in conse-
> quence of the complete failure of the French Revolution, have thrown up
> all hopes of the amelioration of mankind, and are sinking into an almost
> epicurean selfishness, disguising it under the titles of domestic attachment
> and contempt for visionary *philosophes*. It would do great good, and
> might form part of *The Recluse*. . . . [*LSTC*, I. 527]

Coleridge's own words thus become a further defense of the preparatory poem addressed to him in lieu of *The Recluse*. But Wordsworth is not finished yet. Though the number of disillusioned intellectual radicals who might be thus addressed was substantial in England in late 1799, one may legitimately wonder to what extent Coleridge was hinting that Wordsworth was among them. Wordsworth's use of the letter suggests that he was aware of a possible implication, since all his energies were now devoted to establishing permanently his "domestic attachments" with Dorothy, and with the Coleridge family too, if possible. He avoids Coleridge's indirect charge by turning it into part of his project, reverses it by redefining it.

The poem's final hail and farewell tightens the screws on Coleridge's complicity by a process of incorporation from which it is impossible for him to dissent. A great decade is about to begin, but Wordsworth must first close off, actually and poetically, a lost decade of doubt and confusion. The human condition he seeks to address has been defined by Coleridge's own words, and if he objects, even by so much as the "silent language" (502) of a loveless look, he is consigned to being part of the problem ("contempt, the insinuated scoff of coward tongues") rather than part of the solution. Coleridge must have felt the overdetermination by which Wordsworth's last blessing, like his prayer for Dorothy at the end of "Tintern Abbey," rebounds toward its giver:

> For thou hast sought
> The truth in solitude, and thou art one,
> The most intense of Nature's worshippers,
> In many things my brother, chiefly here
> In this my deep devotion.   [505–09]

The grammar of the sentence has been altered by the more imperious logic of creative need. Coleridge's brotherhood with Wordsworth should be based on *his* deep devotion—"thy deep devotion," to parallel Coleridge's seeking truth in solitude and the intensity of his nature worship. "My" makes sense, but at the cost of construing Wordsworth's "deep devotion," not toward Nature but toward Coleridge. The possibility is not unlikely. With Wordsworth inserted in Coleridge's lexical pronoun slot, the reference of "here" to "this" floats free—not the first demonstrative adjective to come unstuck in this poem—and the "devotion" to which it may attach is not Coleridge's faith, but Wordsworth's poem, *The Prelude* of 1799 as a devotional act.

THE TWO-PART MOVEMENT OF THE 1799 *PRELUDE*

Like its beginning, middles, and endings, each part of the 1799 *Prelude* reverses itself yet maintains a connection with what remains behind. This is what, in a very much larger sense, Wordsworth was seeking to do with all his earlier life: reverse its tendency by creatively distancing it, in order to accept it as the veritable basis of his art. In the First Part, he moves from natural events to supernatural metaphors in six seasonal episodes. This progression is paralleled in the second half of the First Part by his movement, in the Fear and Joy episodes, from "ordinary sights" to "visionary dreariness" by utilizing non sequitur as a rhetorical strategy. Since no one knows the *sequitur* from natural to transcendental experience, Wordsworth's genius is revealed at its best trying—seeming—to close the gap.

In the Second Part, connections are more prominent than gaps: between the boys and their society in the first half, and between the stages of individual psychic development in the second. The recent publication of an accurate text of the 1799 version makes it possible to recognize clearly for the first time the social patterns of the first half of Part Two, which in turn makes possible a more comprehensive understanding of the second half. Book II of the finished *Prelude* (1805 or 1850) has always been harder to appreciate than Book I, as its woolly amateur psychologizing raises more commonsensical human questions than the grand transcendental periods of Book I. Mary Moorman makes the best defense: "[it] consists of very intricate and complicated descriptions of the origins and growth of consciousness from infancy to adolescence . . . and an attempt to draw from [descriptions of actual states and feelings in boyhood] some conclusions on the nature of the essential spirit or being of man" (M. I. 445). The new edition allows us to clarify that intricate complexity, by showing that the second half of the Second Part of the 1799 *Prelude* is in large part a metaphorical extension of the actual buildings and social activities described in the first half, in an attempt to give poetic plausibility to an account of the construction of personality.

Overall, the entire movement of the first *Prelude* provides an illuminating contrast to the typical structure of the first *Recluse* poems of 1797–98. The buildings and persons in those poems, shown in the process of erosion back into natural, nonmental forms, appear at a structurally opposite extreme here; they are weak and their habitations ruined or nonexistent, whereas the Wordsworth of the first *Prelude* is strong, and his homes are many, and full—even when ruined, like Furness Abbey, they interchange life-energies with the exuberant boys. In the first *Recluse* poems, lost or abandoned home-seekers are observed by a narrator who moves from an initial position of escapist sentimentality to a final understanding of the need for integration within human communities. In the 1799 *Prelude*, the movement is from Wordsworth's solitary, free-spirited relation to nature in the First Part to the socially determined relations suggested in the Second. In the psychology of Wordsworth's creativity, a crucial dialectic exists between the first *Recluse* and the first *Prelude*. He recoils from those minds *in extremis* to his own mind *in excelsis*; rebounding from mind's affliction with "animal tranquility and decay," he soars toward godlike independence of material limitations. But he ends, as he will always seek to end *The Recluse*, by linking that flight to "Human Life." Ultimately, his determination to reach that end will be the cause of his failure to finish it.

First Part

Accepting Coleridge's high valuation of his talents but lacking his friend's present assurances, Wordsworth in Germany in late 1798 had to make himself believe that the joys of his childhood were not insignificant, not "in vain," but importantly related to his expanding creative powers.

He gave his early pleasures stature by placing them in transcendental perspective, yet scrupulously respected their ordinariness. The first half of
Part One records six discrete episodes: summer swimming, autumn poaching, spring bird-nesting, summer boat-stealing, winter ice skating, and a
concluding medley (card playing, fishing, and kite-flying) in which the first
incident provides the dominant note. The first and last of these six episodes frame the natural-to-transcendental movement implied in the middle
four with an intermediate step: they place the boy Wordsworth in a heroic
position, far above or beyond his native region but still on earth, short of
godlike vision. In the first, Wordsworth raises his eyes from a description
of himself running and splashing in the Derwent to the mountains in the
background, and with a single word, *bronzed*, attaches the four-year-old
boy to their sunset splendor. He had been a "naked Boy . . . bask[ing] in
the sun," and as the mountains "were bronzed with a deep radiance, [he]
stood alone, / A naked Savage in the thunder shower" (16–26). He and
they were bronzed together; the little boy becomes an impressive savage.
In the last, the childrens' cardplaying in the cottage is suddenly interrupted by the sound of ice splitting on the lake outside, "imitative
some / Of wolves that howl along the Bothnic main" (232–33). But the interruption also implies a connection. The mock heroic description of the
worn cards—

> Queens gleaming through their splendour's last decay,
> Knaves wrapt in one assimilating gloom,
> And Kings indignant at the shame incurr'd
> By royal visages—   [222–25]

more than gratuitous charm or arch ideology,[19] is an anticipation of real
heroism heard and imagined ("imitative some") outside. The ice "sank
down" (230) like the kings and queens, the frost rages like the villain
knaves, "bitterly with keen and silent tooth" (227), and the whole ensem-
ble evokes a northern drama along the Gulf of Bothnia, of wolves snap-
ping at a regal sleigh. Small touches, but complementing their southern polar opposite, the "naked Savage in the thunder shower."

Between these two framing hints of heroic significance are the four
better-known incidents, each heightened by an element of disobedience:
poaching birds from others' traps, snatching eggs from ravens' nests, using
a shepherd's boat without asking, and staying out late skating. Psychological guilt adds a dimension not present in the framing episodes, a perpetua-
tion of the actual event into an aftereffect of "unknown modes of being."
The boy's "hurrying" and "scudding" from trap to trap continues, after he
has robbed someone else's trap, as

> Low breathings coming after me, and sounds
> Of undistinguishable motion, steps
> Almost as silent as the turf they trod.   [47–49]

His conscience pursues him in his own tracks, as a separate, ghostly being. The boat-borrowing episode is the most developed instance of Wordsworth's escalation of natural event into supernatural suggestiveness by repetition in a higher key. The "huge and mighty forms" which moved through his dreams after he guiltily returned the boat recapitulate the apparent motion of the mountain peak that suddenly loomed above his horizon as he rowed out into the lake: "the huge cliff . . . like a living thing, / Strode after me" (111–14). Its "measured motion" returns in dream as the "huge and mighty forms, that do not live / Like living men, moved slowly through my mind" (127–28). The actual event already participated in the peculiar slow-motion with which the dream interpretation invests it; the boat moved "just like a man who walks with stately step / Though bent on speed" (89–90), matching his "steady view" on the horizon's ridge. "Do not live like living men" continues the uncanny but unspeakable quality (are they dead? deathless?) of "sounds of undistinguishable motion." Something is experienced, but is unadaptable to human language: "strange utterance."[20] Finally, in the ice-skating episode, once envisioned as "the conclusion of a poem of which the beginning is not yet written" (*LEY*, 238)—the standard condition of *The Prelude*, inverse to that of *The Recluse*—Wordsworth experiences his alienation transcendentally, "even as if the earth had rolled / With visible motion her diurnal round" (181–82), when he suddenly stops short on his skates, exaggerating by counteraction the optical illusion of the banks' passing by. His representation of the calming of this wintry sensation rounds off his interconnection of them all—"Till all was tranquil as a *summer* sea" (185; italics added)—the seasonal simile conveying the year-in, year-out, continuity of his special development.[21]

Such natural supernaturalism is reinforced in the second half of Part One, dealing with the internal, emotional impact of experiences of terror and joy. Wordsworth here transfers whole passages from the Pedlar's fictional biography to his own, but he puts more emphasis on his experience of Nature's sublimity, playing down the second stage in the Pedlar's philosophical education, the "lesson deep of love."[22] Instead of expanding natural images into supernatural dimensions, Wordsworth employs non sequitur to suggest the "visionary dreariness" which invested ordinary sights for him in childhood. Yet the events of the three original "spots of time" are not random; all involve death: the drowned man in Esthwaite Lake, the murderer's grave, and Wordsworth's own father's death in 1783. But, as "tragic facts" which rose up abruptly to pierce the tissue of ordinary existence, they are presented as "archetypes" to which "in following years" he attached "far other feelings" (282–87). The presence of death heightens the meaning of these scenes as did guilt in the earlier seasonal episodes. Wordsworth stresses the emotional impact of the scenes by emphasizing the lack of logical connection between them and the feelings they produced, a fact often overlooked by readers determined to find connections between the events and their emotions.[23] He pointedly eschews description of the "visionary dreariness" that invested the landscape when he came running back to the high road from seeing a murderer's grave:

> It was in truth
> An ordinary sight but I should need
> Colours and words that are unknown to man
> To paint the visionary dreariness
> Which . . .
> Did, at that time, invest the naked pool,
> The beacon on the lonely eminence,
> The woman and her garments vexed and tossed . . .   [319–26]

"Colours and words that are unknown to man" recall the negatively described "huge and mighty forms that do not live like living men." But without any linking explanation (such as the personification of the huge cliff) the emotional impact disengages and enlarges itself, and he can only repeat its elements: pool, beacon, and woman. Seeing a pile of clothes by the lakeshore, the boy stands "half an hour" to see if anyone claims them, but his considerable patience for ordinary explanation is disappointed ("no one owned them") and apparently mocked by nature's obscure contentment:

> . . . the calm lake
> Grew dark with all the shadows on its breast,
> And now and then a leaping fish disturbed
> The breathless stillness.   [271–74]

When the drowned man bobs up amid the search parties next day, the contrast, the lack of significant explanation between fact and context, is marked: "At length the dead man 'mid that beauteous scene / Of trees, and hills, and water, bolt upright / Rose with his ghastly face" (277–79). As in his startled sight of the Discharged Veteran, Wordsworth's imagination is released by a strong experience of discontinuity, though nature may have warned him by signs he could not read (that darkly shadowed lake, the disturbing fish). Finally, in the third "spot," waiting for the horses to take him and his brothers home from school for Christmas vacation, the bleak landscape precedes rather than follows the death-event, but is interpreted retrospectively as a prelude to his "chastisment" for excessive eagerness. The non sequitur of childish faith—that God was directly punishing him for his eagerness by taking his father—is acknowledged to be "trite reflections of morality," but the scene recurs to him not for this reason (which in adult terms is no reason at all) but for the power of the apparent interconnections with which he as a boy invested it. Such appearances remain with the man-poet as an "archetype" of human imaginative expectation, of our ability, however illogical, to go beyond ourselves, thus reinforcing the natural-to-supernatural movements of the first half of Part One. Both movements together strengthen Wordsworth's intuition that his boyhood experiences—and more importantly his recollecting and writing them—are not "useless" or "in vain" but are connected to higher levels of meaning and are thus a worthy preparation for the great poem he had promised Coleridge.

Second Part

As the First Part rhetorically negotiates gaps between ordinary and extraordinary existence, the Second Part tries to establish connections, but with an undertone of the difficulty of maintaining them. Written almost entirely at Sockburn-on-Tees, the Hutchinson family farm where William and Dorothy found refuge from their German misadventures (M. I.437), its smoother composition belies the increased obscurity of Wordsworth's argument. Coleridge increased Wordsworth's sense of the burden of his "great work," by renewing his urging toward *The Recluse* as soon as he returned from Germany, linking Wordsworth's promised achievement in poetry to his own in metaphysics, and announcing a resolve to "publish nothing with my name till my Great Work."[24] Was this a stimulus or a deterrent? In all their extant early correspondence about *The Recluse*, Coleridge says surprisingly little about its content but very much about its size and magnificence—and the lordly ease with which he imagines Wordsworth proceeding on his way. Equally remarkable is the literalness of Wordsworth's expectation of philosophic and organizational formulae from Coleridge, exactly what he did not get, in the letters that have survived. Under the circumstances, Wordsworth's determination to describe clearly the growth of his mind to the "one / More deeply read in thy own thought" (ii.250–51) is admirable. Of course, he hoped for just such a close reading in return, to assure him of the value of his own thoughts.

At one point, Part Two itself was to have been the "loftier song" toward which Part One's childhood recollections led.[25] That Wordsworth intended its first half (1–236) to have a social emphasis is evident from some lines he added, then later canceled. Having "retraced the way . . . when I first began / To love the woods and fields" in Part One, he now turns to his boyhood games and sports, centering them in that "rustic spot / The town in which we dwelt a small domain" (ii.7/8; *app. crit.*). This introductory hint, plus the presence of the lines on Coniston Hall (140–78; removed in 1805), make the social message of Part Two clear. In a connected series of adventures in man-made structures or times (e.g., recesses, holidays, and the "school-time" of Book II's eventual title), Wordsworth credits their function in developing his mind as he did the spirits associated with lakes, mountains, and hills in Part One. "A grey stone / Of native rock, left midway in the square" marks the "centre of these joys," though now "split and gone to build / A smart assembly-room" (31–37)—as Wordsworth discovered when he returned to Hawkshead for the first time in ten years, on his walking tour with Coleridge (M. I.449–50). His return involved some new construction, as well as some recognition, of his own old foundations. The authenticating presence of old building materials under new, far from being mere picturesque detail, is integral to the metaphors of growth to which Wordsworth will adapt his descriptions of buildings in the second half of Part Two. The new must be accepted—"let the fiddle scream / And be ye happy!" he says magnanimously to the "smart assembly-room"—as part of the process of adapting his genius to the actual forms of human life. Authenticity pertains especially to buildings in ruined or "original" form, like the terminus of their boat races, an "island where remained / An old stone table and one mouldered cave, / A hermit's history" (61–63). The hermit's history, like the "old dame" who sat by the grey stone for sixty years selling her wares, is an appropriately aged human accompaniment to these ancient organic structures, as is "the old man who had sate / A later lingerer" (11–12), watching the boys at their evening play. Most important among them is the goal of their long, wild horseback rides: "a Structure famed / Beyond its neighbourhood, the antique walls / Of a large Abbey with its fractured arch" (107–09). This is Furness Abbey, in whose "sequestered ruin" he says he "could have made / My dwelling-place" (114, 128–29). Despite his adolescent boisterousness, he still heard the voice of the spirit of nature ("the invisible bird [that] / Sang to itself . . . in the nave / Of the old church"), but now mediated through human structures, including the rules and forms of the games, races, and contests themselves.

Some of these buildings have religious associations, which, though in ruins, make them susceptible of a new, secular inspiration; others have traditional social origins needed in a new political dispensation; together they anticipate the "residential" structure by which Wordsworth will organize the longer *Prelude* of 1805, and the fundamental image of *The Recluse*: free yet vulnerable spirits gaining strength from ancient ruins. Coniston Hall (140–78) is "old," "grotesque and beautiful," a "neglected mansion-house," where Wordsworth says he first realized, at age fourteen, that these "fair scenes" would be important to him till death. His imagined dying there is of a piece with his imagined "dwelling-place" in Furness Abbey; he is making vows till-death-do-us-part. Its "cool piazza" and gloomy "cloister" are not literal, but metaphors for its trees, stretching their branches out over the boys in the boats, thus linking natural form to human function, actually manifested in the generosity of the Hall's current residents, who gave the boys "fresh butter, tea-kettle, and earthen-ware, / And chafing-dish" (152–53). Finally, the value of their bowling at the "splendid" inn is underwritten by the fact that,

> In ancient times, or ere the Hall was built
> On the large island, had the dwelling been
> More worthy of a poet's love, a hut
> Proud of its one bright fire and sycamore shade.   [186–89]

The poet's vanished "rhymes," in contrast to the "large gold characters / On the blue-frosted sign-board [that] had usurped / The place of the old Lion in contempt / And mockery of the rustic painter's hand" (190–94), are a picturesque gesture, but they do not make the hut any less a house, only one more fit for poetry, and Wordsworth grants the new inn its due with the same condescending magnanimity he vouchsafed the "smart assembly-room": "Yet to this hour the spot to me is dear / With all its foolish pomp" (195–96).[26] The value of his love for all these ordinary social activities and public places is spiritually guaranteed in a summarizing valedictory address to the sun and moon which nationalizes and domesticates them, thus counterpointing his metaphoric naturalizing, aging, and seasoning of the valley's human structures. He does not love the sun and moon for their usual, adult symbolism ("as a pledge and surety of my earthy life") but in a specifically provincial way, "To patriotic and domestic love / Analogous," because they shine on these places: "thee and thy grey huts, my native vale" (229–36). The last conjunction signifies a careful differentiation: his object of worship is the totality of the natural form *and* its humanly defining features.

Throughout the first half of Part Two, Wordsworth accompanies his naturalizing of human structures with a determination to accept unpleasant human emotions, the jealousy and meaningless frivolity he generally associated with cities, but which realism demands he must also acknowledge in Grasmere and Hawkshead. He can be generous toward the "smart assembly room that perked and flared" and the "foolish pomp" of the "splendid" inn, because he knows the deeper truth lying underneath them, the grey stone of native rock and the old poet's hut. Similarly, in the boys' boat and horse races, "disappointment could be none, / Uneasiness, or pain, or jealousy; / We rested in the shade all pleased alike, / Conquered and conqueror" (63–67). "In such a race, so ended"—that is, at the hermit's cave or Furness Abbey—squabbling adolescents behave like a teenage company of saints. The virtue of Coniston Hall lies precisely in its being "neglected," not pretentious, not upstarting like the nouveaux riches whom Wordsworth saw beginning to use the Lake District as a pleasure ground. Adult consciousness of the world is not necessarily wise; this object lesson, implicit in Wordsworth's lordly condescension in the first half of Part Two, must be faced directly in the second, where his subject becomes his own growth into consciousness, separating him from his integral, inchoate relations with nature before puberty.

In the Second Part's midpoint conflict (237–67), Wordsworth protests the difficulty of continuing in metaphors of the geographic forms he has been describing: "who shall parcel out / His intellecl by geometric rules, / Split like a province into round and square?" (242–44). His irritable self-doubt springs naturally from the fact that the "province" of his discussion can no longer be closely identified with Westmorland, because he must attempt what is always a heuristic fiction, the description of how consciousness is built upon invisible foundations, and, furthermore, distinguish his maturing consciousness from what the world usually understands as maturity. He was well aware that proposing a solution from "the permanent objects of nature" would only create another problem (of mindless escapism) unless it could be shown to replace the unhappy definitions of maturity that society usually offers ("the fretful dwellings of mankind"). Thus the second half of Part Two (267–464) represents Wordsworth's most conscious effort, to date, to negotiate the most difficult transition in his work, from love of nature to love of mankind. In Book II of the longer *Prelude*, these lines have caused many readers impatience, because Wordsworth abandons the apparently simple, sequential, episodic structure of his poem. Readers in this frame of mind are prepared to listen to anything about William Wordsworth and are put off when he fails to assume their interest in him. But this was not an assumption Wordsworth could make in late 1799, when precisely at issue was the value, if any, of his interest in himself.

Nonetheless, Wordsworth shares such impatience, as he writes-reads himself, querulously cogitating whether narrative per se is the appropriate form for the representation of mental growth. It is almost the only mode he knows, yet "how shall I trace the history, where seek / The origin of what I then have felt?" (395–96). The point of origin is by definition unknowable: "Hard task to analyse a soul in which . . . each most obvious and particular thought . . . in the words of reason deeply weighed, / Hath no beginning" (262–67). How can he tell a story that has no beginning? "Was it for this . . . ?" He maintains the possibility of lucidly understanding such a subject by rhetorical use of Coleridge as his ideal reader, to whom "the unity of all has been revealed," as contrasted with simple mechanical psychologists who can "class the cabinet / Of their sensations and in voluble phrase / Run through the history and birth of each" (258–60).[27]

The famous metaphor of the "infant Babe . . . upon his Mother's breast" helps him start out with the unconscious in the arms of the conscious. Following Coleridge following the German Idealists, he will argue that sensations thus received and organized are not different in kind from artistic creativity: "Such verily is the first / Poetic spirit of our human life" (305–06). But this metaphor breaks down as soon as its recapitulation of general human mental growth reaches the point of self-consciousness his own autobiography has reached.

> Yet is a path
> More difficult before me, and I fear
> That in its broken windings we shall need
> The Chamois' sinews and the Eagle's wing:
> For now a trouble came into my mind
> From obscure causes. I was left alone
> Seeking this visible world, nor knowing why:
> The props of my affection were removed
> And yet the building stood as if sustained
> By its own spirit.   [317–26]

He is lost on the path of his own poem's understanding of his development, as he will be lost repeatedly in longer versions of *The Prelude*, most notably on the actual mountain paths of the Simplon Pass and Mount Snowdon. But before him, on the metaphoric "broken windings" of his path, stands an equally metaphoric "building" of consciousness, and he

rushes into it to get through the impasse of his argument. Linking up with
the several actual buildings described in the first half, he recycles them,
metaphorically, as analogues to the construction of his personality, to
show that he, William Wordsworth, like every infant in every mother's
arms, is "an inmate of this *active* universe" (294). Anything that has been
built is, implicitly, social; and so, the "props" or scaffolding of unconscious participation in nature removed, his now-knowing is recognized as
an improvement over his not-knowing-he-knew-it earlier: "palpable access / Of knowledge" (335–36). The process is summarized in the terms of
a social dialectic:

> Hence life, and change, and beauty, solitude
> More active even than "best society,"
> Society made sweet as solitude
> By silent inobtrusive sympathies . . .   [343–46]

Yet his pleasure brings also consciousness of his difference from others;
what pleases him they do not even see: "difference / Perceived in things
where to the common eye / No difference is" (348–50). Consciousness
separates him from both the body of nature and the body of men, and
both separations must be overcome. The allusion to *Paradise Lost* (344)
authorizes what is happening to him as more, not less, humanizing than
what usually happens to men: their souls are subdued "by the regular action of the world" (410), but Wordsworth experiences a reciprocity between Culture and Nature that goes Milton one better, since "society
made sweet as solitude" was no idea of his.

   Wordsworth tries to clarify this meaning through nearly a hundred
lines of mysterious exempla which come perilously close to acknowledging
that no one can understand it. Recalling a "passionately loved . . . Friend"
(John Fleming) with whom he used to walk, he speculates

> with heart how full
> Will he peruse these lines, this page, perhaps
> A blank to other men, for many years
> Have since flowed in between us, and, our minds
> Both silent to each other, at this time
> We live as if those hours had never been.   [383–88]

How full will Fleming's heart be? One possible retort to this rhetorical formula is, "not full at all," following Wordsworth's unexpected development of it from Fleming's presumably interested perusal to their silent,
uncommunicating minds. Each of his efforts to see a straightforward development from the society of boys in the first half of the Second Part to

the society of men in the second half is defeated, as here, by Wordsworth's *singularity of expression*—and then is suddenly located exactly there, in his artistic sensibility:

> I still had loved
> The exercise and produce of a toil
> Than analytic industry to me
> More pleasing, and whose character, I deem,
> Is more poetic, as resembling more
> Creative agency: I mean to speak
> Of that interminable building reared
> By observation of affinities
> In objects where no brotherhood exists
> To common minds.   [426–35]

"Interminable" is a wonderfully Wordsworthian adjective for mixing the huge magnitude of his subject with a pun upon his difficulty in putting it into words while maintaining its social utility, like the Pedlar's "unutterable love." This endless, undefinable building, like the earlier "building" of his own spirit (325) now provides an intratextual social metaphor for his soul's

> obscure sense
> Of possible sublimity to which
> With growing faculties she doth aspire,
> With faculties still growing, feeling still
> That whatsoever point they gain, they still
> Have something to pursue.   [366–71]

Unendingness becomes an answer to the problem of inarticulate, unconscious origins; the problem of not being able to tell his story's beginning may be solved by refusing to admit it ever ends—a solution good for continuing *The Prelude* but fatal to starting *The Recluse*.

In the deeper "brotherhood" of this higher society of metaphor-makers, Wordsworth finds confirmation of the value of "the common range of visible things" he described in Part Two's first half. He grew up, therefore, *more* socially aware, not less, than others: his infant creativity not "supressed . . . by uniform control of after years" (307), "by the regular action of the world . . . unsubdued" (410–11), his "plastic power . . . at war / With general tendency" (411–15), seeing wholes where others see only fragments—"from *excess* / Of the great social principle of life / Coercing all things into sympathy" (437–39; italics added). This benignly dictatorial coercion signals Wordsworth's confidence that he is ready to conclude his argument. He ends with an escalating rhetoric of

pantheistic unification similar to "Tintern Abbey" and the Pedlar's cre-
scendoes of love rising from original lovelessness. "I felt the sentiment of
being spread / O'er all that moves, and all that seemeth still, / O'er all that
... liveth to the heart ... all ... all ... for in all things / I saw one life and
felt that it was joy" (450–60). This Wordsworth believed. But we honor
that belief by noting that its metaphysical paeans are motivated from specific social and personal situations. In the 1799 *Prelude*, these include his
feeling of having been cast out from his true adult identity, "amid the fretful dwellings of mankind," which he has tried to recover, first, by substituting for them the joyful dwellings of his boyhood, and, second, by attaching these dwellings metaphorically to the growth of soul which, "in
the words of reason deeply weighed, / Hath no beginning." As in the
agonized motivations of the Pedlar's biography, the height of Wordsworth's declarations of faith must be measured by the depth of his feelings
of isolation, and the value of his call to poetry by his intense depression in
"trivial occupations and the round / Of ordinary intercourse" (i.291–92).

As we have already seen, Wordsworth's coercion of "all things into
sympathy" continues into the poem's conclusion (465–514), where the
principal thing coerced is Coleridge himself and his latest suggestions for
The Recluse. They were now, in late 1799, reunited for the first time since
separating in Hamburg in September 1798. Wordsworth hoped to reestablish in Grasmere the "little colony" of Alfoxden which inspired him to
produce the first *Recluse* poems, but which, scattered abroad, had produced only this strange hybrid poem on the growth of his mind. Coleridge
had come rushing to Sockburn, alarmed by Wordsworth's reports of severe ill health. The day after his arrival, the ailing poet was suddenly cured
and embarked immediately upon a strenuous winter walking tour. The
conclusion of the poem asserts to Coleridge that they have reached "the
self-same bourne" (499) of thought, and he is whisked off to its objective
correlative in reality. Though the tour did not immediately result in Coleridge's establishment in the Lakes, he is sent off to his new job in London
with a farewell that gives a highly determined set of directions on how he
should live his life there from his disciple who now, after a year's separation, speaks for all the world like a master:

> Fare thee well!
> Health and the quiet of a healthful mind
> Attend thee! seeking oft the haunts of men
> But yet more often living with thyself
> And for thyself, so haply shall thy days
> Be many and a blessing to mankind.—   [509–14]

Sincerely given, the blessing rebounds upon its bestower because of its peculiar congruity with everything he has said about his own paradoxical
progress—leaving "the haunts of men" to become "a blessing to mankind" via the unusual route of "living with thyself / And for thyself"—in
this preparatory poem for "a poem which I hope to make of considerable
utility; its title will be *The Recluse or views of Nature, Man and Society*"
(*LEY,* 214).

PART TWO

The Recluse and *The Prelude,* 1800–1806

3

"Home at Grasmere" in 1800

A mighty vale,
Fresh as the freshest field, scoop'd out, and green
As is the greenest billow of the sea:
The multitude of little rocky hills,
Rocky or green, that do like islands rise
From the flat meadow lonely there—
Embowering mountains, and the dome of Heaven
And waters in the midst, a second Heaven

PW, V.347

The identification of William Wordsworth with the English Lake District is so elemental a fact of literary history that one easily forgets there was a time when the fact had to be created in competition with other available options. Despite the fine biographical and poetical inevitability of the Wordsworths' move to Grasmere, the principals in the case were by no means sure of destiny's direction. In their correspondence of 1798–99, the question of where to settle (closely linked to questions of what to do) is indeed preeminent; but by far the most important variable was how to remain close to Coleridge. Grasmere and the Lakes entered into the decision belatedly, as an entertaining diversion. Once their dissatisfaction with Germany had set in (December 1798), Dorothy wrote to Coleridge that they should all explore together "every nook of that romantic country" the following summer, "wherever we finally settle" (*LEY*, 241). Coleridge, during the whole year, held out for the south as being better for Wordsworth because it was nearer the intellectual company he felt Wordsworth needed more than books. In July he reported with disappointment that Wordsworth "renounces Alfoxden altogether," but William and Dorothy's letters indicate no clear alternative except for "William's wish to be near a good library, and if possible in a pleasant country" (*LEY*, 266).

These domestic decisions are important poetically as well as biographically because they help to explain the peculiarly aggressive vehemence of Wordsworth's joy in the portions of "Home at Grasmere" written in the

spring of 1800 as a fresh start on *The Recluse*. There is undoubtedly creative psychological significance in the curious fact that almost all major
segments of *The Recluse* were undertaken when the Wordsworths had just
completed, or were just beginning to contemplate, a move to a new
home—and, moreover, that this occurred with each of the residences they
occupied from Alfoxden on. That this is more than mere coincidence is
strongly suggested by one of the poet's few post-1815 efforts to work on
his masterpiece, "Composed When a Probability Existed of Our Being
Obliged to Quit Rydal Mount as a Residence," 1826 (*PW*, IV.381–87), a
meditation of over two hundred lines in which *The Recluse*'s frequent discrepancy between grand themes and small occasions is especially marked.
In 1800, the Wordsworths were not returning home to Grasmere but going to Grasmere *as if* it were home, a situation "conducive to a self-
conscious awareness of himself as an observer," not to the recapture of
an "indigenous" childhood.[1] Their seven-month stay with the Hutchinson
family at Sockburn had shown them brothers and sisters reunited as a
happy, independent family of adults, a potent image because of their own
painful childhood memories of being scattered abroad after the death of
their father in 1783 (M. I.438). They had also been living for four years in
what seemed to their elder relations a state of semivagabondage and were
very eager to stop it.[2] The question of Wordsworth's career—indeed, of
his profession—was crucial in deciding where to go from the temporary
hospitality of the Hutchinson farm. Careers were not to be made in Grasmere; not the least of Wordsworth's imaginative achievements was his establishment of a national literary reputation from so remote a provincial
spot. Cowper and Collins and others may have suggested models, but they
were gentlemanly recluses on church, university, or family sinecures, and
in any case they did not plan to save the world with their poetry. The November walking tour was not the summer vacation jaunt Dorothy had proposed but an effort to interest Coleridge in the North; yet it also had the
effect of allowing Wordsworth to see the Lakes with newly approving
eyes—Coleridge's. His letter back to Dorothy at Sockburn concentrates on
Coleridge's responses—"Coleridge enchanted with Grasmere and Rydal"
(*LEY*, 271)—and Coleridge's enthusiasm catalyzes his own: "Coleridge
was much struck with Grasmere and its neighbourhood and I have much
to say to you, you will think my plan a mad one, but I have thought
of building a house by the Lake side . . ." (*LEY*, 271–72). Barely a
month before the great move "home" to Grasmere, the idea struck its
proposer as "mad," as it surely must have seemed to his relatives and to
received ideas of how and where a not-so-young man of uncertain promise

would establish his independence in the world. Nor was the author of "The Mad Mother," "Incipient Madness," and other lyrics of the psychopathology of everyday life likely to use the word with sophisticated frivolity.

William and Dorothy's return in December of 1799 was full of wonder and loving observation. They were returning, brother and sister, aged twenty-nine and twenty-seven, to the general neighborhood of their childhood, reentering after long absence a childhood dream. The reestablishment of their feelings for this landscape was inextricably tied up with the re-formation of their family. Their brother John's behavior upon arriving for a visit to the new household in January is expressive of the powerful emotions underlying these changes. From the inn, he twice walked up to the door of William and Dorothy's cottage, put his hand on the latch, and twice walked away. Finally, he sent word from the inn to warn them (M. I.471). He was struggling with a terrific ambivalence of joy and sorrow as he anticipated entering the first household they had had, as a Wordsworth family, since their father's death nearly twenty years earlier. The return to childhood memories entailed a wrenching of adjustments to adult life that had been made with great precocious sacrifice; they were trying to return to simpler, more usual, or normal relationships that had been interrupted or postponed. The reunion with John was soon followed by the reestablishment of other old ties broken by the German misadventure, culminating with Coleridge's return in April for a visit, which by June had become a new residence. The James Loshes, once invited to join the "little colony" in Germany, came to greet the new couple during the extended housewarming of 1800; Losh was another ex-radical who had tempered revolutionary enthusiasm with domestic bliss, and (like Wordsworth and Coleridge themselves) was one of the disillusioned intellectuals whose fading idealism Coleridge proposed The Recluse to revive. The re-formation of their family led naturally to thoughts of family growth by marriage and children, for which the Loshes and other friends offered plenty of models.[3] For a period of a year or two it was not clear who would marry whom, but the two Hutchinson sisters, Mary and Sara, were eligible, and the two Wordsworth brothers, William and John, were interested. The entire milieu was one of young people entering optimistically into adulthood. Mrs. Coleridge bore a son soon after her arrival, and her husband promptly named him Derwent, after the river that Wordsworth had invoked at the beginning of "the poem to Coleridge." Other identifications of themselves with the place would soon follow, in "Poems on the Naming of Places"; although their controlling fiction suggests that they build on childhood associations, their operative model is the sophisticated pastoral one of literary young adults concocting emblems for themselves in the wild.[4]

Moorman's claim that William had established "familiar and affectionate" relations with Grasmere by the end of the summer of 1800 (M. I.463) is certainly true but also suggests that it was a project involving conscious effort. Coleridge's picture of them all dancing around a bonfire on Grasmere island that summer is a fit image of the childlike joy indulged in by these young adults, and of the sense of recovered innocence that imbues Wordsworth's return to *The Recluse* in "Home at Grasmere": "I lay and saw the woods, and the mountains, and lake all trembling, and as it were *idealized* through the subtle smoke . . . and the Image of the Bonfire, and of us that danced round it—ruddy laughing faces in the twilight—the Image of this in a Lake smooth as that Sea to whose waves the Son of God had said, '*Peace*'" (M. I.477–78). His friend's resumption of their idealized master-poem would continue to manifest the same predilection for picturing the lifeworks of this "happy band" in divine images and analogies.

Both Wordsworth and Coleridge later associated the start of *The Recluse* with the year 1800 rather than with the 1,300 lines Wordsworth had announced in 1798.[5] As a return to *The Recluse*, "Home at Grasmere" is indeed more like a new beginning than a continuation; such radical freshness was to become characteristic of each resumption of the project. Each new start has much more in common with other work Wordsworth was doing at the moment than with the most recent prior state of *The Recluse*. This is not surprising to common sense, but it illumines the unstable, ad hoc nature of the philosophy on which the poem was to have been founded. "Home at Grasmere" thus resembles the 1798–99 *Prelude* far more than it does *The Recluse* of 1797–98.[6] Its extremity of joy is from a different world than the extreme suffering of Margaret, the old Cumberland beggar, and the discharged veteran. In his determined efforts to finish "Home at Grasmere" in 1806, Wordsworth inserted specimens of decrepitly enduring mankind to reassert his epic's socially responsive intentions, but the 1800 portions of "Home at Grasmere" are a direct continuation of the moods and scenes of the 1799 *Prelude,* from whose composition they are separated only by the very similar "Poems on the Naming of Places," in which the Wordsworth entourage claimed Grasmere valley by naming its striking features after themselves, like latter-day Adams and Eves. "Home at Grasmere" brings the 1799 *Prelude* into the present tense, installing Wordsworth in propria persona, age twenty-nine, amid the scenes the first *Prelude* had described up to his age seventeen.

However, "Home at Grasmere" is even less straightforward autobiography than *The Prelude*. Lionel Stevenson acutely views it as a transition from autobiography to something else, once Wordsworth's autobiographical record had reached the present and no longer offered a convenient formula for composition; perhaps the "topographical unity of an isolated region" would offer a spatial coordinate to extend the temporal one, pressing landscape into the service of biography.[7] It opens with a "spot of time" which shows him gazing on the valley during a boyhood ramble, experiencing in a visionary moment some distinctly unboyish thoughts:

> "What happy fortune were it here to live!
> And if I thought of dying, if a thought
> Of mortal separation could come in
> With paradise before me, here to die."   [9–12][8]

The recently composed "spots of time" in the 1799 *Prelude* had shown "the imaginative power" acting upon ordinary sight; this compositional moment of March 1800 shows imagination sharing its power with a more extraordinary place. In moving from *The Prelude* in 1799 to "Home at Grasmere" in 1800, Wordsworth skipped, as it were, his intervening awful decade, from Cambridge to Sockburn. At this point, a biographical record was not his intention. But he would not be able to complete "Home at Grasmere" until he gave that decade its full due in his greatest poem, *The Prelude* of 1805. Only then could the promise of *The Recluse* be once more assayed.

His sense of returning to Grasmere as if in response to a *vocation* is adumbrated in some lines he incorporated from the poem he wrote on Hart-Leap Well, a notable local sight he and Dorothy had passed in their December march on Grasmere (M. I.454). These lines identify a millennial moment of newly established right relations between Man and Nature with the Wordsworths' advent in Grasmere:

> Among the records of that doleful place . . .
> . . . .
>   . . . we found
> A promise and an earnest that we twain,
> A pair seceding from the common world,
> Might in that hallowed spot to which our steps
> Were tending, in that individual nook,
> Might even thus early for ourselves secure,
> And in the midst of these unhappy times,

> A portion of the blessedness which love
> And knowledge will, we trust, hereafter give
> To all the Vales of earth and all mankind.
>
> [MS B, 241, 247–56; PW ii.514]

Attuned to the inarticulate lore of "grey-headed Shepherds," they can appreciate the almost supernatural powers that attend upon conscious home-comers and interpret the meaning of the wounded hart's bleeding out its life at the wellsprings of its birthplace. In "awful trance," Wordsworth sees "the Vision of humanity and of God / The Mourner, God the Sufferer, when the heart / Of his poor Creatures suffers wrongfully" (243–46). But "Home at Grasmere" falters when this vision tries to shift the referent of "poor creatures" from animals to men.

Although "Home at Grasmere" deserves to be read as a complete poem, that has been done elsewhere,[9] and the present context requires that it be separated out into its two main compositional eras, 1800 and 1806, in order to appreciate how the break between them manifests Wordsworth's difficulty in turning *The Recluse* toward human life—and how much of the structure of the great *Prelude* of 1805 is determined by the necessity to heal the breach human suffering causes here. If we consider the five hundred-odd lines of "Home at Grasmere" written in 1800 as a unit,[10] we discover a Romantic Ode to Joy written in one of the highest keys ever attempted. No small part of Wordsworth's achievement in these lines, incomplete and unbalanced as they are, is his avoidance of the outright hysteria to which such odes were prey, like some of the youthful effusions of Shelley and Keats. This Ode to Joy launches itself, moreover, by its own design, over the brink into the depths of its counterpoint, the Ode to Dejection, as in such dialectically mature works as Keats's "Ode to Melancholy." Wordsworth "breaks Joy's grape against his palate fine," and then hangs his poem up, defeated, among the "shadowy trophies" of the goddess Melancholy. Unlike the conventional pastoral poet who writes himself into his landscape as a refuge from wordly pain and corruption, Wordsworth writes himself out of it, as he gradually, reluctantly, recognizes the social responsibility he is shirking.[11] Beyond its repeated "braving" of Milton—"paradise before me" tops *Paradise Lost*'s "the earth was all before them"[12]—it courts resemblance to Milton's biblical sources, especially the thanksgiving Psalms and the *Song of Songs,* with the striking variation that the body of the beloved is not the expectant community but the receptive landscape: "Embrace me then, ye Hills, and close me in" (129).

These lines effuse the eager anticipation of a man rubbing his hands together before a satisfying piece of work. There is not a risk Wordsworth fears to take, literary or psychological. This is the place, and he is in it.

> What Being . . . since the birth of Man
> Had ever more abundant cause to speak
> Thanks . . . ?
> . . . .
> The boon is absolute . . .
>   . . . among the bowers
> Of blissful Eden this was neither given
> Nor could be given. . . .   [117–25]

Better than Eden, Grasmere provokes expressions of paradise consciously regained, suited to Coleridge's vision of *The Recluse* as a philosophic displacement of *Paradise Lost*. Both self and world seem born again, and Wordsworth feels his experience to be archetypal:

> The unappropriated bliss hath found
> An owner, and that owner I am he.
> The Lord of this enjoyment is on Earth
> And in my breast.   [85–88]

All his past life has led to this place and these moments. The sign of true miracle is how easy it turned out to be:

> And did it cost so much, and did it ask
> Such length of discipline, and could it seem
> An act of courage, and the thing itself
> A conquest? Shame that this was ever so. . . .   [64–67]

This open rhetorical question is like a rebuttal to the hanging question of the 1799 *Prelude,* "Was it for this . . . ?" The discipline, courage, and conquest lay not in his disappointed efforts to break successfully into print in London, but in his rejection of London's terms in favor of his own. Everything becomes easy if seen in the right light—seen, that is, not as a regressive retreat to "that romantic country" of childhood memory, but as a mature choice which supersedes the false values of the world with a higher calling.

The 1800 segments of "Home at Grasmere" advance by a series of rhetorical leaps and bounds, excited verse paragraphs each ending in exclamations more sweeping than the last. These rhetorical periods are more oratorical than narrative or descriptive in form, like the "prolusions" which both Milton and Wordsworth knew at Cambridge as compositional models in Latin. After the opening "spot of time" (1–43) there is a thematic introduction (44–170), followed by a general biographical perspec-

tive (171–215), the specific biographical context of the December walk to
Grasmere (216–77), and the immediate confirmation of their expectations
in the coming of spring, celebrated in the winter birds' riotous pleasure in
the new warm weather (277–321). To this point, the poem works toward
identification with the very moment of its composition—toward saying,
here am I, writing this poem.[13] If all its linguistic peculiarities were generalized into a single compressed sentence, they would collapse all tenses
into one: "Once upon a time I am living happily ever after." It bursts into,
and eventually through, its moment of inspiration. Every aspect of its
structure and language strives toward self-identification. Everything about
it is circular: its arguments tautological, its syntax redundant and repeti-
tious, its imagery full of rounded reflections which reinforce the circling
tensions of its structure. Proofs are presented ostensively, not argued: "For
Proof behold this Valley and behold / Yon Cottage, where with me my
Emma dwells" (97–98). It is nothing if not internally coherent, since it virtually implodes itself. All these traits taken together make it an absurdist
or fabulist text, in the technical sense; this, of course, was not Wordsworth's intention but the dramatic result of his radical literalism. Its absurdism is a function of its modes of presentation, not its contents, which
are familiarly Wordsworthian but juxtaposed in extreme patterns, half car-
icature, half sublime allegory: baroquely plain, simply rococo. Its favorite
images are themselves images: things seen in reflection.[14] Wordsworth's
description of the joyous birds wheeling "in wanton repetition" is apt for
the style of the whole poem and a fit culmination of the poem's upbeat
movement, as Grasmere mirrors their heavenly motion:

> Behold them, how they shape,
> Orb after orb, their course, still round and round,
> Above the area of the Lake, their own
> Adopted region, girding it about
> In wanton repetition, yet therewith—
> With that large circle evermore renewed—
> Hundreds of curves and circlets, high and low,
> Backwards and forwards, progress intricate,
> As if one spirit was in all and swayed
> Their indefatigable flight.   [292–301]

"As if" is a suspect simile, and "adopted region" may point to troubling
questions of true origin, but the vigor of Wordsworth's style does not allow such problems to emerge into conscious discourse to challenge the
wide claims he makes for Grasmere:

> A Centre, come from wheresoe'er you will,
> A Whole without dependence or defect,
> Made for itself and happy in itself,
> Perfect Contentment, Unity entire.   [167–70]

Rather, these effusive prolusions run into trouble at the level of literal description. It comes as no surprise to any level-headed reader that this dizzying, surreal absurdism cannot be long sustained, that the denomination of the first wild day of March 1800 as an imaginative entity—new century, new career, new revolutionary agenda—should falter in the face of real time. But it came as an untoward shock to Wordsworth, and we can see it in the poem. At the very height of his "O altitudo!" Wordsworth looks down, sees death, poverty, and evil, and plunges to ground, not to resume the poem for over five years. Just when he seems to be parsing his poem off the page of the landscape, he reads something he doesn't like:

> But two are missing—two, a lonely pair
> Of milk-white Swans. Ah, why are they not here?
> These above all, ah, why are they not here
> To share in this day's pleasure?   [322–25]

The repetitions, the reiterated gasp, the insistent questioning, all show the poem's intrinsic characteristics imploding in upon it. And the reason is as honestly presented as the ecstasy: he and Dorothy have identified themselves with these two swans to an extraordinary extent:

> From afar
> They came, like Emma and myself, to live
> Together here in peace and solitude,
> Choosing this Valley, they who had the choice
> Of the whole world.
> . . . .
> . . . to us
> They were more dear than may be well believed,
>
> . . . .
> . . . their state so much resembled ours;
> They also having chosen this abode;
> They strangers, and we strangers; they a pair,
> And we a solitary pair like them.
> They should not have departed . . .
> . . . .
> Shall we behold them yet another year
> Surviving, they for us and we for them,
> And neither pair be broken?
>   [325–29, 333–34, 338–42, 348–50]

The poem's extreme symbolism rebounds upon the narrating observer. Finch notes interesting parallels between Wordsworth's description of the missing swans and Milton's account of Satan's rebellion,[15] but rebelliousness in this instance attaches not to the objects described but the describing subject (Wordsworth), a characteristic example of the poem's tendency to deconstruct its own structural principles. If the swans are gone, just like that, with no explanation or meaning, what does it signify for the fate of another "solitary pair" coming into this valley?[16]

Wordsworth has pitched his claims for the special qualities of Grasmere so high that this ridiculous literalism threatens to spoil it. In the sequence of The Recluse's development, he has sailed off the top of the axis of vision, just as in the 1,300 lines written by March 1798 he came close to bottoming out on the axis of things, where mental power dwindles to a mere feature of physical existence, subject to "animal decay." He goes immediately on the defensive, and the bulk of the remaining lines composed in 1800 show him back-pedaling furiously to restore the damage he has done. But it is no good; he ultimately backs himself into a corner, out of the poem, and breaks it off.

The extremes to which he goes to explain the swans' absence are the best guarantee of the sincerity of the joy which preceded his discovery of it. Given the situation, it is not surprising that "Home at Grasmere"'s subversion of normal language becomes most radical in the hundred-odd lines in which the poet tries to rectify the damage a gap in reality has wreaked upon the fabric of his literalistic art. His first conjecture is that the swans may have been shot by Grasmere "dalesmen," but this leads to an even worse crisis, lack of moral confidence in Grasmere's residents. He apologizes both to the place and to his own poem for "harbouring this thought": "Recall, my song, the ungenerous thought; forgive, / Thrice favoured Region, the conjecture harsh."[17] His determination to make amends leads beyond this reflexive hypostasis of his own text to a surreal identification of language with place, in which moral predication of any sort becomes redundant.

> Ah! if I wished to follow where the sight
> Of all that is before my eyes, the voice
> Which is as a presiding Spirit here
> Would lead me, I should say unto myself,
> They who are dwellers in this holy place
> Must needs themselves be hallowed. They require
> No benediction from the Stranger's lips,
> For they are blessed already. None would give

> The greeting "peace be with you" unto them,
> For peace they have; it cannot but be theirs.   [362–71]

This curious apology implies that all apologies are unnecessary because morally irrelevant. The unsubtle repetition of cognate forms as predicates ("holy / hallowed," "benediction / blessed," "peace / peace") risks the charge of illogic only to flaunt the irrelevance of logic to the tautological self-sufficiency of the situation. Grasmere is placed once more beyond the realm of ordinary discourse. Partly, of course, he is simply seeking to avoid the presumption of bestowing upon the dalesmen virtues they already have in surplus. But a deeper impulse is at work (after all, they may indeed have killed the swans): to deny that anything need be predicated of Grasmere because it is literally self-validating. To say that people who dwell in a holy place are themselves holy is a form of predication. But to deny they need benediction, which presumably all people can benefit from, is to move toward asserting that anyone who does not fully share their special condition cannot possibly predicate anything of them. The rest of the passage moves further in the same direction, claiming Grasmerians need nothing because they have "charity beyond the bounds of charity" (375). In denying the efficacy of strangers' benedictions of the dalesmen, Wordsworth is denying the power of "performative verbs" to perform "speech acts" upon them.[18] In a speech-act, to say is to do (for example the "I do" of marriage); it is thus one of the most powerfully self-sufficient uses of language, and its redundant uselessness in Wordsworth's Grasmere further highlights the radical uniqueness he attributes to the place.

The effort of each succeeding verse paragraph to correct the overstated extremes of its precedessor leads further and further away from the missing swans and the real fact they imply, that Grasmere is not *necessarily* congenial to solitary pairs who choose it. Wordsworth stoutly avers that he and Dorothy did not come hither "betrayed by tenderness of mind" (398); they were well aware that accusations of romantic sentimentalism would be leveled at them. As evidence that they know men are not angels, he cites the profane language he has heard the shepherds utter. This bit of social realism is important for the poet who will in a few months write the most famous manifesto in English defending ordinary language for art (Preface to *Lyrical Ballads*), and is introduced by a belated attempt to unravel his own tautologies. They did not expect to find "in midst of *so much loveliness / Love, perfect love*, of *so much majesty / A like majestic* frame of mind in those / Who here abide, the *persons* like the *place*" (401–04; italics added). But even in denial, the tautological redundancies suggest residual longings for affirmation. He who has heard the human voice in harmony with nature's power has, he insists, heard "that voice, the same, the very same":

> Debased and under prophanation, made
> An organ for the sounds articulate
> Of ribaldry and blasphemy and wrath
> . . . .
> The common creature of the brotherhood,
> But little differing from man elsewhere
> For *selfishness* and *envy* and *revenge*,
> . . . .
> *Flattery* and *double-dealing*, *strife* and *wrong*.

> [424–26, 434–38; italics added]

The bearing of this evidence is clearer in the context of *The Recluse*'s development. From the 1799 *Prelude*, as well as the 1798 *Lyrical Ballads*, we recognize Wordsworth's peculiarly intense yet narrow characterizations of human evil ("greetings where no kindness is, nor all / The dreary intercourse of daily life"). He is not saved from being "betrayed by tenderness of mind" because he can stand to hear profanity; he is not so dainty. Rather, to have heard profane language and recognized the human weakness it implies is for Wordsworth to have heard language as it is used in cities, especially under conditions of competitive work. His not being "betrayed by tenderness of mind" here closely parallels his faith in "Tintern Abbey" that "Nature never did betray the heart that loved her," with the immediate proof provided there against "evil tongues, rash judgment [and] the sneers of selfish men." Wordsworth generalizes these narrowly particular abuses of language under conditions of ambitious competition into a morally corrupt condition for so-called normal, "worldly" language, against which he defines his vocation-cum-location as a restoration to real normal health. There is a quality of courageous naiveté in these assertions that resembles the admission of another famous self-biographer, Henry Adams, that his education did not attain to comprehending Wordsworth until he was thirty; neither, in a sense, did Wordsworth's.

But this evidence has introduced a complication into the argument which proves insuperable and soon breaks off his composition of "Home at Grasmere" in 1800. Other human beings have been recognized, and *The Recluse*'s theme of "Human Life" once again disrupts the Man–Nature bonding Wordsworth celebrates, because of his extremely unguarded defense of Grasmere's moral significance. He tries desperately to assert that Grasmere's dalesmen could not be swearing, wrathful, selfish, envious beings (or shoot swans) for the usual external reasons—that is, because they are poor, hungry, or ill-clothed—since "Labour here preserves / His rosy

face . . . extreme penury is here unknown . . . they who want are not too
great a weight / For those who can relieve" (440–48). But the strain of
this special pleading is too much, for reasons closer to the springs of
Wordsworth's genius than his "rentier's" view of Grasmere,[19] and the
poem breaks off, at the interesting words, "so here there is . . ." (457). The
conjunction is meant to complete a moral or human simile drawn from the
geographic form of the valley: "*as* these lofty barriers break the force / Of
winds—this deep vale *as* it doth in part / Conceal us from the storm—*so*
here there is. . . ."[20] But nothing follows; there is no moral counterforce
equivalent to Nature's forms. Instead, there is only a brief coda, which will
in fact become the predicating guarantee, in a variety of forms, of all subsequent *Recluse* fragments. It is the image of the one spiritually creative
community Wordsworth can vouch for and actually could complete the interrupted simile:

> And if this
> Were not, we have enough within ourselves,
> Enough to fill the present day with joy
> And overspread the future years with hope—
> Our beautiful and quiet home, enriched
> Already with a Stranger whom we love
> Deeply, a Stranger of our Father's house,
> A never-resting Pilgrim of the Sea,
> Who finds at last an hour to his content
> Beneath our roof; and others whom we love
> Will seek us also, Sisters of our hearts,
> And one, like them, a Brother of our hearts,
> Philosopher and Poet, in whose sight
> These mountains will rejoice with open joy.
> Such is our wealth: O Vale of Peace, we are
> And must be, with God's will, a happy band!   [859–74]

The necessary social dimension which has been raised in "Home at Grasmere" by Wordsworth's fantastically literal effort to save his own unifying
symbols, the two swans, is finally put in terms of an extended family. This
is as far as Wordsworth's social vision could extend with confidence in
1800. Resuming the poem in 1806, he will try specifically to generalize
Grasmere's joy through a series of tales of men and animals intended to
prove "that solitude is not where these things are," to show that this
happy band in this valley is not as naive as Rasselas and his friends in their
Happy Valley in Abyssinia, and that "Home at Grasmere" is more than a
domesticated Oriental tale of self-indulgent escapism. In the interim, in the

introduction to the 1805 *Prelude*, he will insert, between the "glad Preamble" of late 1799 (so close in spirit to "Home at Grasmere") and the abrupt, "Was-it-for-this?" beginning of the two-part *Prelude*, a series of possible epic subjects, all of which deal with historical or mythic versions of his own "happy band," followers of an unjustly expelled leader who flee, usually to the north, only to return in body or in spirit after years of creative exile to wreak their just revenge on the corrupt, tasteless civilizations to the south which cast them out (chapter 5).

But in the 1800 portions of "Home at Grasmere," the identification of the master-poem with the master's life was too quick and insufficiently mediated. Wordsworth still conceived writing about himself and about Man, Nature, and Human Life as separate tasks, and he thought he had just finished with himself in the two-part *Prelude* of 1799. The first sequence of *Recluse* compositions, with its depressed vision of human conditions, had pushed him into investigations of his own mental condition (the two-part *Prelude*) in order to raise his sights back to the work at hand. Now, after this second sequence, he is again forced to return to his own mind because his new start has soared too high. Having cast himself and Dorothy as Adam and Eve in a new Eden, the strain of saving the whole world *from this place* has quickly proved to be too much. Wordsworth's return to his "*Prelude*-movement" within *The Recluse* is, therefore, not simply a second rebound back to investigations of his own mind, but to investigations of the growth of mind in terms of the *places* in which it found—or did not find—itself at home as it did at Grasmere. Thus the 1805 *Prelude*, which he began haltingly in late 1803, begins as a "residential" elaboration of both the social faith evident in Part Two of the 1799 *Prelude*, and of the social impasse which "Home at Grasmere" reached in 1800.

THE GREAT PROSPECTUS

Between abandoning "Home at Grasmere" in about March 1800 and resuming *The Prelude* in full swing by March 1804, Wordsworth worked on two other texts important to *The Recluse*'s history: a revision of "The Ruined Cottage" into "The Pedlar," and the famous "Prospectus" of *The Recluse*, eventually published in the preface to *The Excursion* (1814). The result of his efforts on the first of these may be summarized by one of Dorothy's pained journal entries: "Disaster Pedlar."[21] This was the most intense of several efforts over the years to separate the character of the Pedlar from the tale of Margaret,[22] efforts which we can see, in the

Recluse-context, as attempts to adjudicate between the claims of the narrative character and the authorial character, and as enactments of Wordsworth's dilemma in relating his story, *The Recluse*, to its teller, *The Prelude*: were they to be joined or separated? Butler's summary of these changes indicates their congruence with Wordsworth's other work during the three years between the interruption of "Home at Grasmere" and the resumption of *The Prelude*: [they] "change *The Pedlar* from a philosophic exposition to a character sketch which resembles some of the *Lyrical Ballads* and the poems of 1802 in which Wordsworth returned to portrayals of character."[23] Besides adding many personal details to give the Pedlar's folk-wisdom biographical (rather than philosophical) plausibility, Wordsworth's most interesting change was the temporary insertion of a little girl precisely into the lines which establish a special relationship between the poem's aesthetic young narrator and the Pedlar, thereby distancing two characters who were both essentially versions of himself and preventing the Pedlar's interest in the young man (as a boy) from collapsing into a virtual identity that would destroy the usefulness of their conversation as a framework of conversion ("And for myself / He loved me, out of many rosy Boys / Singled out me, as he in sport would say / For my grave looks, too thoughtful for my years").[24] The little girl, by contrast, cannot believe the wise old Pedlar could ever have been the ragged little poor boy he says he was, cannot believe the child could be father to the man—an appropriately challenging audience for a Wordsworthian conversion poem. But this little girl did not stay in the poem long, for the Pedlar's finding "a kindred heart to his" in the young narrator guarantees that his history will be heard aright, in much the same way Wordsworth could rely on Coleridge's correct audition of *The Prelude*.

But in the stirring lines of the "Prospectus," all doubts and displacements between tale and teller are overridden by the most sustained grandeur Wordsworth ever achieved. Despite their prospective function, they speak so wonderfully of the relationships imagined between *The Recluse*'s universal themes—"On Man, on Nature, and on Human Life"—that we hardly require anything to follow from them. As a prayer for inspiration, the "Prospectus" constitutes an act of faith that ennobles itself. Much of its splendor derives from Wordsworth's successful appropriation of Milton's idiom to his own concerns, a humanistic "counter-cry" to Coleridge's "Religious Musings."[25] Beyond this, the structure, theme, and movement of the "Prospectus" bear rhetorical comparison with two other texts that are similarly prospective yet self-sufficing, the Lord's Prayer and the Apostles' Creed, which the boy Wordsworth would have read every

Sunday on facing pages of the *Book of Common Prayer*. Like the former, it moves from a redefined heaven ("the mind of Man") through the fullness of earthly beauty to the social world of trespasses, temptations, and evil: "the tribes / And fellowships of men" (1017–18). Yet the structure of the "Prospectus" lines is exactly homologous to a text even closer to hand: the portions of "Home at Grasmere" itself that Wordsworth had just completed,[26] which also move, as we have seen, from an initial state of radically Edenic self-consciousness ("This solitude is mine; the distant thought / Is fetched out of the heaven *in which it was*," 83–84; italics added), to an extremely unguarded celebration of full interchange between human consciousness and earthly beauty, which fetches up abruptly on the simplest contradiction in its metaphoric terms (the two missing swans), and then descends helplessly into successively inadequate efforts to come to terms with human evil. The structure of the "Prospectus" recapitulates that of "Home at Grasmere," but succeeds in making a coherent poetic statement where "Home at Grasmere" fails, by praying for inspiration rather than essaying its realization, and by transmuting the simple places and persons of Westmorland into the highest possible levels of mythological significance. Ultimately, Wordsworth will complete "Home at Grasmere" by attaching these prospective lines to it as a conclusion.

Whether considered as a conclusion or a prospectus, the "Prospectus" is, like "Home at Grasmere" itself, preeminently a definition of poetic inspiration in terms of the *places* which nurture it and which it must in turn minister to. Indeed, it simply elaborates, as poetical regions, the three basic terms of *The Recluse* announced in its opening line: "On Man, on Nature, and on Human Life." The "mind of Man" displaces the Christian "Heaven of heavens" and "darkest Pit of the profoundest Hell" with the heaven and hell of human consciousness (976–90). Second, the "living home" of Nature's beauty is a constant invitation to a daily promised land: "An hourly Neighbour" (991–1001). After these two passages Wordsworth inserted, in 1805 or 1806, the lines (1002–14) celebrating the "great consummation" of the wedding of "the individual Mind" and "the external world," a connection that has come to seem so quintessentially Wordsworthian that it deflects us from his original determined turn to the third region of his song, Human Life, which follows immediately after the first two in the earlier versions of the "Prospectus":

> Such [pleasant haunts] foregoing, if I oft
> Must turn elsewhere, and travel near the tribes
> And fellowships of men, and see ill sights
> Of passions ravenous from each other's rage,

> Must hear humanity in fields and groves
> Pipe solitary anguish, or must hang
> Brooding above the fierce confederate storm
> Of Sorrow, barricadoed evermore
> Within the walls of cities—may these sounds
> Have their authentic comment, that even these
> Hearing, I be not heartless or forlorn!   [1015–25]

If the lines about passing Jehovah "unalarmed" into "the mind of Man" are brave (though even Blake found them crazily blasphemous) and those on Nature's Beauty greatly promising, Wordsworth in his Human Life triad achieves an acuity of insight that is as shockingly compressed as the other two are grandly expansive. All forms of human suffering are swiftly included—mutual, solitary, and social-historical. The perverse way in which human emotions feed upon the frustration, not the satisfaction, of others' emotions is breath-takingly stated in a half-dozen words ("passions ravenous from each other's rage"),[27] then generalized into a vision of human life as a self-contained siege *against itself* ("confederate storm") that recalls, for sheer paradoxical power, Blake's "mind-forg'd manacles." In between these two images, the anguish of the individual mind is put in terms of a sad pastoral (ll. 1019–20), whose "fields and groves" are ill-matched with the "paradise and groves Elysian" that Wordsworth has, just ten lines earlier, promised will be "the growth of common day." So much does the human factor complicate Wordsworth's vision, that all of the biblical, Exodus imagery in the "Prospectus" comes together in it. Instead of following "Beauty . . . pitch[ing] her tents before me," he is side-tracked from the Promised Land, traveling "near the tribes and fellowships of men," those Moabites or Philistines of alienation, a veritable Confederation of the Cities of the Plain of Sorrow.[28]

Wordsworth's reluctance to make this detour is matched only by his determination to complete it: "if I oft / Must turn elsewhere . . . may these sounds / Have their authentic comment, that even these / Hearing, I be not heartless or forlorn!" Yet for all the acute analytic power of the "Human Life" lines, we must ask if they are not too unremittingly negative, just as the "Mind of Man" section is too expansively grandiose, and the natural beauty section too confidently tempting? The question, whether addressed to the "Prospectus," to "Home at Grasmere," or to most of Wordsworth's poetry, reveals that *The Recluse*'s presumptive relations between Man, Nature, and Human Life were skewed in a way that predetermined Wordsworth's failure to keep them balanced. He could not see Human Life wedded to Man and Nature as he could imagine them wedded to each

other. Jonathan Wordsworth and Stephen Gill assert that the objective poetry implied by "Human Life" was simply impossible for Wordsworth;[29]
this has been the criticism of Wordsworth's egotism from the beginning.
Yet at each stage of *The Recluse*'s development we see that Wordsworth's
failure was not simply in turning his eyes "from half of human fate," as
Arnold gibed,[30] but turning *toward* "the tribes and fellowships of men"
with a determination to make an "authentic comment" that was immediately undercut by his representation of general human experience in the
terms of his own painful individual experiences. His determination not to
neglect Human Life spelled the doom of his *Recluse,* but also gave it its fit-
ful glory.

Wordworth's own experience also provided the way out of the dilemma that the "Prospectus" lines reached. Invoking a "prophetic Spirit"
like the Holy Spirit that concludes the Apostles' and Nicene creeds, and
that was associated by Milton and tradition with poetic inspiration and
the final redemption of mankind in a New Jerusalem, he gets himself back
on track for the Promised Land via his own poetry:

> Come, thou prophetic Spirit, Soul of Man,
> Thou human Soul of the wide earth that hast
> A metropolitan Temple in the hearts
> Of mighty Poets . . .   [1026–29]

He comes in from the Wilderness to a Holy See of Imagination that both
rescues and completes the Exodus imagery of the "Prospectus" lines. But
whereas Milton's spirit prefers "Before all Temples th'upright heart and
pure" (*P.L.* I.18), Wordsworth's is not only humanized but localized in
hearts of genius rather than virtue.[31] When these lines were published
in 1814, the "metropolitan Temple" resonated with the "gothic church"
to which Wordsworth then compared his entire oeuvre. In MS D, the
"metropolitan Temple" of poetry contrasts directly with the "vacant commerce" of the man "by the vast Metropolis immured . . . where numbers
overwhelm humanity" (595–99). Considering Grasmere as a "strategic retreat" from the public world, Finch compares Wordsworth's replacement
of politics by imagination to the biblical prophets' denunciations of the
sinful cities from the spiritual purity of the desert.[32] This redemption of
the sinful city is also, as I argue in the next two chapters, the fundamental
pattern of *The Prelude*'s search for satisfactory "residences" for Imagination. The city of Human Life will finally be redeemed as a city of poetry.
And when Wordsworth prays that his "verse may live and be / Even as a
Light hung up in heaven to chear / Mankind in times to come!"

(1032–34), we may be sure, both from the imagistic development of the "Prospectus" and from the entire *Recluse*'s pattern of spiritual-edifices-humanistically-redeemed, that it is not just any Star in the sky, but one of very distinct house and lineage, hanging above a region which, though provincial, is confident of out-shining the nominal capital (Jerusalem or London) as a center for the world's admiration. Tracing the star's lineage will in fact be the next order of business: "with this / I blend more lowly matter . . . describe the mind and man / Contemplating, and who and what he was . . . when and where and how he lived" (1034–39).

Thus the "Prospectus" lines end, in context, not as a prospectus to *The Recluse* but to *The Prelude,* turning back from their universal scope to their person of origin. Their redemptive hope ("chear Mankind in times to come") is identical with that expressed at the end of the 1805 *Prelude,* but its realization first requires the full examination of "the mind and man contemplating." Wordsworth tried to keep the *Prelude–Recluse* relationship sequential, or one of cause and effect; but in tracing closely the history of their mutual development, we see how often and how easily this relationship collapsed into an identity. The crisis of the first *Recluse* poems was: how could this poetically immature narrator deal with those terrifying sufferers? Wordsworth's first response, in 1798, was to revise "The Ruined Cottage" to give the Pedlar plausible explanatory insights from his own biography; his second (in 1799), to begin the poem to Coleridge on the growth of his own mind. That, in substance, is exactly what happens again in the next stage of *The Recluse*'s development. Determined to give the storms of human sorrow their "authentic comment," "Home at Grasmere" breaks off in a crisis of confidence, which in the "Prospectus" lines is elided by promisory mythopoeic notes. In 1802, Wordsworth again returned to "The Ruined Cottage," tried to recast it as an independent poem, "The Pedlar," abandoned the effort after great pain, and then, slowly in 1803 and massively by 1804, dropped his pedlar guise and again returned to the poem to Coleridge, *The Prelude.*

4

Building Up a Work That Should Endure: The Construction of the 1805 *Prelude*

Thou issuest from a fissure in the rock
Compact into one individual stream,
A small short stream not longer than the blade
Of a child's coral, then, upon the face
Of the steep crag diffused, thou dost flow down
Wide, weak and glimmering, and so thin withal
Thy course is like the brushing of a breeze
Upon a calm smooth lake. A few bold drops
Are there, these regularly starting forth
Strike somewhere on the rocks and stones beneath
And are thy voice, for thou wert silent else.

PW, V.342

THE PRELUDE'S RELATION TO THE RECLUSE

In the fluctuating history of the *Recluse* project, the thirteen-book, 8,500-line poem completed in May of 1805, now known as *The Prelude*, is evidently Wordsworth's major movement into subjective exploration of his own genius. But, in the powerfully dialectical polarities of the intertwined *Recluse-Prelude*, this subjective movement proceeds very largely in terms of Wordsworth's representation of his mind's accommodation to "residences" of Human Life, as they are called in the central recurrent word of the poem's subtitles ("Residence in Cambridge . . . London . . . France . . . and French Revolution"). This representation of self in terms of the public world (often oversimplified as a problem of two unrelated "voices" in the poem)[1] mirrors Wordsworth's double bind in his work on "Home at Grasmere" in 1800. There, setting out to write Book First of Part First of *The Recluse*, his address to the poem's public, philosophic topics proceeded increasingly in terms of his own private experience, until he broke it off, evidently recognizing his lack of success in turning from himself to the world at large. If it is true that Wordsworth said he gave "twelve hours' thought to the conditions and prospects of society, for one to poetry,"² the force of this truth for *The Recluse* lies in our recognition that the two subjects were not separate but ratios of each other which Wordsworth struggled to integrate.

The long poem "on the growth of my own mind" completed in 1805 is assigned to *The Recluse* project more closely than the version of 1799. The earlier version had been a progress report in a private verse epistle between friends. But renewed composition of the poem "on my own early life" led to renewed speculation about its purpose, steadily moving in the direction of tying it more closely to *The Recluse*. Initially, the two poems appear as completely discrete works; the poem on his life would have no published connection to *The Recluse* "during my lifetime" (*LEY,* 454). More often, the personal poem is described as "tributary" or preparatory to the other, gradually shifting to a forward position from Coleridge's earlier image of it as a "tail-piece." By the time it was finished in May 1805, it was "considered as a sort of portico to the Recluse, part of the same building" (*LEY,* 594), the images Wordsworth would use publicly to describe their relation in the preface to *The Excursion* (1814). It thus became what it is properly entitled: a prelude. But whether this prelude is connected to *The Recluse* so as to constitute "part of the same building" remains moot, not simply because *The Recluse* is incomplete, but because its incompletion is so closely involved with Wordsworth's decision to push "the poem to Coleridge" to a further stage of completion, thereby changing its nature.³ As directives to an unfinished masterwork, these statements about *The Recluse* must be used provisionally, since Wordsworth and Coleridge changed their conception of it continually during their lifetimes; but between them it was clear that Wordsworth's poem on his own life was not *The Recluse*, whatever their relation might finally be. Nonetheless, the 1805 *Prelude* is integral to *The Recluse* project in a way that neither the 1799 nor 1850 versions could be; the former is too early for the idea of attachment to have occurred, while the latter is too late—by the 1840s Wordsworth was admitting that *The Recluse* would never be finished.

If *The Recluse* had even half-fulfilled its conceivers' dreams, we might now read *The Prelude* as we read Goethe's *Dichtung und Warheit,* a great artist's creation of a backdrop for his greater works. For nearly a century after its publication, this was the dominant mode of reading it. But *The Prelude* will not stay in the background; even while using *The Recluse* as a convenient teleological fiction, it keeps thrusting itself into the foreground, blocking out the larger work which was to be its justification. Since this usurping power was precisely its creative force for Wordsworth, he could not consciously admit it, which accounts not only for his inability to title it and his reluctance to publish it, but also for his difficulty in composing and organizing it.

Wordsworth's return to concentrated composition of "the poem to Coleridge" was halting and inconstant, not the result of any single decision. Between 1799 and 1804 he tinkered with the two-part version, polishing and adding a bit here and there.[4] But in late 1803 he received a strong stimulus to return to it in the news that Coleridge was leaving England for Sicily and Malta.[5] Both men interpreted Coleridge's imminent departure as a reason for increased effort on *The Recluse,* acting on their belief that it could only be written while they were together. Coleridge's urgings typically take the form of very emotional, suggestively metaphoric descriptions of how he felt about *The Recluse,* or about Wordsworth writing it:

> I rejoice . . . with a deep & true Joy, that he has at length yielded to my urgent and repeated—almost unremitting—requests & remonstrances—& will go on with the Recluse exclusively. —A Great Work, in which he will sail; on an Open Ocean, & a steady wind; unfretted by short tacks, reefing, & hawling & disentangling the ropes—great work . . . that is his natural Element. The having been out of it has been his Disease—to return to it is the specific Remedy, both Remedy and Health. It is what Food is to Famine. . . . I have seen enough positively to give me feelings of hostility towards the Plan of several of the Poems in the L. Ballads: and I really consider it a misfortune that Wordsworth ever deserted his former Mountain Track to wander in Lower valleys. . . . [LSTC, ii.1013]

> . . . devoting himself to his great work—grandly imprisoning while it deifies his Attention & Feelings within the sacred Circle & Temple Walls of great Objects & elevated Conceptions. [NSTC, i.1546 (21.266); October, 1803]

One assumes that Coleridge was more specific in conversation, but his written comments over the years consistently deal more in metaphors of the size of the poem and its author ("the Giant Wordsworth, God love him"), than in careful philosophic statements about its contents. Such metaphoric cheers were doubtless exciting to Wordsworth (particularly the self-fulfillment metaphor of the poem as *deifying* temple), but also must have been unsettling, giving him so little to go on. Coleridge's heroic urgings are structurally complemented by Wordsworth's very literal and extremely anxious expectations of detailed help: "I am very anxious to

have your notes for the Recluse. I cannot say how much importance I attach to this, if it should please God that I survive you, I should reproach
myself for ever in writing the work if I had neglected to procure this help"
(6 March 1804; *LEY*, 452). This implies that *The Recluse* could go forward without Coleridge, but a follow-up letter is more nakedly demanding:

> Your last letter but one informing us of your late attack was the
> severest shock to me, I think, I have ever received . . . I will not speak of
> other thoughts that passed through me; but I cannot help saying I would
> gladly have given 3 fourths of my possessions for your letter on The Re-
> cluse at that time. I cannot say what a load it would be to me, should I
> survive you and you die without this memorial left behind. Do for heav-
> en's sake, put this out of the reach of accident immediately. [29 March
> 1804; *LEY*, 464]

One must be wary of overinterpreting these statements; nevertheless,
Wordsworth is saying either something silly—that he would prefer Coleridge's *Recluse*-notes to news of his illness—or something very complex—that he would like to be securely *in possession* of the notes whenever
he does receive bad news about his friend's health. In both letters, the
powerful Wordsworthian phrase, "I cannot say,"[6] is connected to
thoughts of Coleridge's death, and to simultaneous thoughts of Wordsworth's workload without him. The suggestion that the life of the poem
was more important than the life of the man is simply the truth of the two
poets' estimate of the value of their masterwork. In both mens' letters the
unspoken assumption is that whatever the other has (Coleridge: philosophic notes; Wordsworth: poetic power) is (1) absolutely necessary to
The Recluse and (2) relatively easy for him to supply to his friend. Yet
Wordsworth's implication of a set of notes hastily jotted down to explain
The Recluse's philosophy touches the very nerve-end of the near failure of
Coleridge's entire philosophic career, while Coleridge's metaphors of "the
Giant Wordsworth" and his world-striding poem point up by contrast
Wordsworth's shaky sense of the ultimate value of his poetic achievement.

Between these extreme expressions of confidence and need, strictly
complementary yet missing each other by miles, little was actually being
accomplished. Despite Coleridge's confidence, Dorothy wrote in November
of 1803 that William "has not yet done any thing of importance at his
great work" (*LEY*, 421). In the event, what he recommended writing was
The Prelude, not *The Recluse,* thus repeating the pattern of 1798–99 in
Germany, when he was left alone to explore the development of his own
mind in the absence of the mind to whom "the unity of all has been re-

veal'd," which was to be reflected in *The Recluse*'s system. This neat arrangement, writing *The Prelude* while Coleridge was away from *The Recluse*, was small comfort to Wordsworth if it occurred to him, for it meant taking up "the poem to Coleridge" as an admission of his inability to go on with *The Recluse* by himself. Moreover, the poem on his life continued to have the same function it had had in 1799: an assurance to Coleridge of Wordsworth's fitness to write the great philosophic poem they conceived together.

WORDSWORTH'S DECONSTRUCTION OF THE 1799 *PRELUDE*

If Coleridge's impending departure was the main external motivation for resuming "the poem to Coleridge," a primary internal motivation was, of course, the existence of its 1799 version. Although regarded as "for the time complete,"[7] it remained attractively available, an autobiographical frame filled with an account to age seventeen of a poet now twice that age. The possibility of doubling the account to fill out the frame was obvious, even though it may have presented itself, initially, as a temptation to be resisted on grounds of self-indulgence, unpublishability, or, mainly, diversion from *The Recluse*.

The first difficulty of writing the 1805 *Prelude*, therefore, was deciding to extend and alter the 1799 version. The two-part *Prelude* had been very difficult to compose, but for all its provisionality was nevertheless a tightly organized and consistently sustained composition, *especially in its conclusiveness*. The 1799 version, if we look at it as if no other *Prelude* existed, does not necessarily present an open-ended autobiographical framework. It needs some opening lines to make it formally complete, but it certainly does not lack a sense of an ending. It concludes satisfyingly with an elevated hail and farewell to Coleridge and an elaborate generalization linking Wordsworth's powers to the spiritual crisis of the age which *The Recluse* was intended to address: the cynicism spreading among the best minds of their generation because of the failures of the Revolution. The completeness of the 1799 conclusion is especially clear in comparison with the narrative opening of Book III, "Residence at Cambridge," the point at which the 1805 version is grafted on. The 1799 version ends with the high philosophic rhetoric of "Tintern Abbey:" "with my best conjectures I would trace / The progress of our being" (ii.268–69); this dignity attaches both to the mature speaker and to the wisdom and stature of the seventeen-year-old boy. But beginning with Book III, and for most of the ensuing poem, the speaker's tone toward that growing boy is much more distanced, by turns condescending, satiric, maturely realistic, or fondly self-indulgent. As a preparatory poem, the 1799 version is sufficient; the origins and current status of the poet's mental health are adequately reported out, and the main work could begin. If there were a completed *Recluse,* and the two-part *Prelude* were attached to it either as a preface or an appendix, no one would feel that it was incomplete for failing to trace the poet's life up to the very moment when composition on *The Recluse* began.

But, once having decided to return to "the poem to Coleridge," Wordsworth had the problem of what we may provisionally call deconstructing his earlier version: that is, to read it interpretively with a view toward exposing its underlying structural principles, and particularly to isolate points of apparent rhetorical strength that could be re-converted into passages, or gaps, of original conceptual weakness. Only then could he begin to dismantle it. His problem was both poetical and autobiographical. He had to make himself appear less fully developed in order to give plausibility to the long narrative to follow, and also to make the *poem* appear less solid for the same reason. He accomplished this by two principal means: removing the powerful "spots of time" from Part One of 1799 and the lines on Coniston Hall from Part Two. By removing the "spots of time" (as well as by his subsequent uses of them), Wordsworth shows clear recognition of their conclusive character. They are his clinching representations of the mind's power to "see into the life of things," and although several vivid representations of childhood spiritual experiences remain in Book I, removing the "spots of time" pulled the plug of power from *1799*'s representation of Wordsworth's early intimations of imagination in nature. Wordsworth's shifts in the function of the "spots of time" are represented in small by his successive changes in the adjective used to describe their "virtue": in 1799, it is "fructifying"; in early 1805 drafts, "vivifying"; in 1805 (and 1850), "renovating." Each change lessens the connotations of imagination's invulnerability,[8] correlative to the "spots'" relocation in a constantly changing poem: from a power of *growth* in the two-part version, to a power of *living* in the initial stages of 1805, to a power of *restoration* in its final stages, as the overall movement of his poem became clearer to Wordsworth: from expectation to impairment to renovation.

The removal of the forty lines on Coniston Hall from Part Two effectively dismantles the social sequence of the 1799 version and truncates the development that it portrays: how Wordsworth grew from Nature's nur-

ture (Part One) into consciousness of "Human Life" (Part Two). Without
the Coniston Hall sequence, Part Two (i.e., Book II of 1805, as it then became) centers more on the animal spirits of the teenagers' games than on
their social setting. If the displacement of the "spots of time" allows
Wordsworth to expand and vary his representations of mental vision in ordinary sight by delaying his strongest statement thereof, the removal of the
Coniston Hall lines, disconnecting Part Two's social sequence, gives him
leeway to stretch out and develop the central thematic problem of *The Prelude* as it bears upon *The Recluse*: how to represent his mind's accommodations to the "residences" of Human Life. All his subsequent residences
build upon the social sequence first established, but then dismantled, in
Part Two of the 1799 version. The main difference, of course, is that in his
later residences—Cambridge, London, and France—Wordsworth's accommodations are largely unsatisfactory, whereas in *1799* he lives in the
"small domain" of the Lake District villages as comfortably as he lives
amid Nature's presences in Part One.

THE FIVE-BOOK *PRELUDE* OF JANUARY-MARCH 1804

By making him appear less powerfully insightful and less socially mature,
Wordsworth's dismantling of the 1799 *Prelude* made his autobiographical
representation of the growth of his mind more realistic. An autobiography
was not, however, what he was clearly set on writing. Although *The Prelude* is one of the most autobiographical works in English literature, none
of its versions is *an* autobiography, and a great deal of confusion
arises—about both the poem and the poet's life—if any version is read as
literal autobiography. Since much of *The Prelude* recounts how Wordsworth did not, after all, move out into public Human Life, but came back
home to the Lakes (and, he argues, to a higher conception of his life's
work than society had been able to provide him), his thematic problem in
dealing with Human Life correlates, in the expanding composition of the
poem, with the dilemma he raises in the Introduction: the lack of a "steady
choice" of "time, place, and manners" other than his own, suggesting that
the autobiographical mode was, initially, as much a cause of blockage as it
was of advancement. As suggested by the evident reasons for his failure to
complete "Home at Grasmere" in 1800, Wordsworth's problem was to
generalize persuasively beyond his own experience to the world at large. It
was what Coleridge, sure of his man, had repeatedly said Wordsworth
must do: "I prophesy immortality to his *Recluse,* as the first and finest

philosophical Poem, if only it be (as it undoubtedly will be) a Faithful Transcript of his own most august & innocent Life, of his own habitual Feelings & Modes of seeing and hearing" (*LSTC*, i.1034). Notwithstanding that such descriptions of *The Recluse* seem to denote *The Prelude* as well, Wordsworth, for all his putative egotism, was less convinced of the sufficiency of this argument than Coleridge.

Therefore, in his first full resumption of "the poem to Coleridge" in early 1804, before deciding to describe his own "time, place, and manners" as "a theme single and of determined bounds," he assayed to transpose the two-part poem of 1799 into a five-book poem organized on the theme of "Books and Nature," or nurture and nature, education and environment. This would make his life appear normative by presenting it in the familiar classical genre of the young poet's education, resurgently popular in such widely varying late-eighteenth-century forms as Beattie's *The Minstrel*, Collins's "Ode on the Poetical Character," and Blake's *Milton*.[9] Wordsworth's five-book contribution to this genre would have rounded off the 1799 version not by chronological expansion but by thematic control. It would have complemented *1799*'s emphasis on Nature with acknowledgment of the gifts of civilization and culture through formal education. The 1799 version pictures a powerfully spiritual young man, but if we did not already know he was William Wordsworth we might suppose him destined to become a philosopher, moralist, or priest, for all the poem tells us about the extent of his hopes for his poetry. But in the five-book version we would recognize a poetical education and the start of the young poet's realization of his promise by enunciating his characteristic themes, as Pope did in his *Essay on Criticism*. In this sense, the five-book plan represents the most fully developed stage of *The Prelude* as an actual, plausible prelude or portico to *The Recluse*.

This five-part *Prelude*, as reconstituted by textual scholars, would have contained Books I-III largely as we now know them, a Book IV containing most of the present Books IV *and* V, and a fifth concluding book that would have opened with the ascent of Snowdon and closed with the "spots of time."[10] Between this fifth book's introduction and conclusion there would have been some description of Wordsworth's imaginative impairment but no mention of the French Revolution, only some description of domestic tribulations. Thus the five-book *Prelude* would have had a mighty finale, but the reader would have wondered why all the rhetorical power of Snowdon and the "spots of time" was necessary when the only crises needing to be overcome were, on the evidence offered in five books, the speaker's disaffection with college and contemporary educational theories, some rather far-fetched fears about the perishability of books, and an overstated distaste for the claims of domestic life on a poet's time.

As provisionally reconstructed by Jonathan Wordsworth and Stephen Gill, the middle section of this fifth book gives an abstract of the impairments of imagination which Wordsworth felt interfered with his progress. The absence of any mention of the French Revolution is most striking, especially in contrast to Wordsworth's complaints about domestic cares which, functionally, must play the same role as the revolutionary books in the finished 1805 *Prelude*. He laments

> The unremitting warfare from the first
> Waged with this faculty [Imagination], its various foes
> Which for the most continue to increase
> With growing life and burthens which it brings
> Of petty duties and degrading cares,
> Labour and penury, disease and grief,
> Which to one object chain the impoverished mind
> Enfeebled and [?], vexing strife
> At home, and want of pleasure and repose,
> And all that eats away the genial spirits,
> May be fit matter for another song;
> Nor less the misery brought into the world
> By degradation of this power misplaced
> And misemployed [?where] [???]
> Blind [?], ambition obvious,
> And all the superstitions of this life,
> A mournful catalogue.[11]

Although Jonathan Wordsworth says this account of "the degradation of social life" is more appropriate to *The Recluse*,[12] its main burden is self-pity, and is not likely to provide "fit matter for another song" that anyone would want to read for very long. Wordsworth's care to keep his imagination safe from being "misplaced and misemployed," bears more particularly on *The-Prelude*-as-prelude-to-*The-Recluse*, since it signifies in part Wordsworth's determination, under Coleridge's urging, to write only the greatest poetry he is capable of producing, and to resist the easy temptation of shorter poems. The *misplacement* and *misemployment* of imagination in social contexts are also the effective motive forces—as "degrading cares"—of *The Prelude*'s residential structure. In these lines' "warfare" imagery, we see imagination beset by internal distractions and ringed round by enemies without, which Wordsworth developed in a series of "living pictures" intended to connect this passage about imagination's "unremitting warfare" to the Snowdon vision. They all concentrate on moments of profound stillness at the heart of great agitation, in which heroic explorers (Columbus, Mungo Park) are shown at the very instant they move into a startlingly new, incomprehensible reality, whether of discovery, recovery from disaster, or the certain imminence of death and destruction.[13] The bearing of these images would have been obscure in the five-book *Prelude,* though it is easy enough to see, from the vantage of the thirteen-book version, that these explorers are metaphors for Wordsworth, ringed round with fatal dangers as he supposed his imaginatively heroic probes into the mind of Man terribly frustrated by "petty duties and degrading cares" and "all the superstitions [worldly success] of this life."

But though these apocalyptic moments culminate in "my restorations," their metaphorical force does not correspond to any concomitantly impressive image in the text of Wordsworth's danger or impairment; "petty cares" and "blind ambition" are not enough, are indeed ridiculously discrepant. Though the five-book *Prelude* "was within easy striking distance of completion" by early March 1804, these discrepancies indicate that the distance was only quantitatively short. Wordsworth dismantled his five-book poem very suddenly and quickly, sometime between circa 10 March and 18 March. It may well be that his precipitancy resulted from dissatisfaction at having left out much biographical material and his unwillingness to move on to the central philosophic message of *The Recluse.*[14] But these reasons, besides being opposite sides of the same coin (finish-*The Prelude*-as-a-way-of-not-starting-*The-Recluse*), can be elaborated in terms of what we see happening at the end of the five-book poem. Or rather, what we do not see. For Wordsworth certainly had a concomitantly impressive image of his own life to match against those of Columbus, Park, Gilbert, and Dampier: it was his experience of the French Revolution and his sense of his imagination's betrayal by it.[15] Writing about this would launch him into a much different poem, far beyond the five-book frame of "Books and Nature," and he was unsure about his ability to represent his imagination's rescue from revolution. The "engulphment" which threatens his metaphoric explorers is also a frequent peril to imagination in *The Prelude,* and the Revolution and finishing the poem are equal sources of it, in content and form, roughly speaking. If we phrase Wordsworth's dilemma as that of maintaining a balance between truthfulness to imagination's impairment and confidence in its restoration, his uncertainty at representing this process was part and parcel of his uncertainty of maintaining it within himself: namely, of being sure that his "restorations" were real, actual, true, permanent, substantial—in a word, *philo-*

sophically or *metaphysically* certain. Thus the reason for suddenly dismantling this poem, all-but-ready to send off with Coleridge, was his need to
keep on writing to Coleridge, because only then could he believe that his
writing was being read philosophically, by the one to whom "the unity of
all has been revealed."[16] By sending Coleridge an obviously incomplete
poem, Wordsworth effectively guaranteed that his work would continue to
make philosophic sense—that such sense would be made of it by its primary reader—even if (and especially because) it was not the "philosophic"
poem itself. He accomplished this by removing all of the original fifth
book with its heavy rhetorical artillery, and sending Coleridge something
much more like the present Books I-V—something obviously open-ended.
Coleridge was going away, and Wordsworth would, in effect, continue
writing him the verse epistle of 1798–99. But for this short-term gain in
philosophic readership he would pay a heavy price, for in taking his narrative into revolutionary France he was changing not only its biographical
limits but also abandoning the manageable theme of "Books and Nature"
and setting himself up for a sharp confrontation between his ongoing
poem and its intended sequel, *The Recluse.*

COMPOSITION OF THE 1805 *PRELUDE*

The actual ensuing order of Wordsworth's final composition of *The Prelude* is significantly different from the order of the finished poem. After
Coleridge's departure, he went straight on with what is now Book VI,
summarizing his Cambridge experience and describing his final summer
vacation, the walking tour of 1790 through republican France, the Alps,
and the Italian lakes. Then he continued immediately with his further experience of France and the Revolution in 1791–92, composing what are
now Book IX and the first half of Book X by late April of 1804.[17] This
brought his story up to his return to England in October 1792, when he
experienced the shock of Britain's declaration of war on France and the
dismaying news of the Reign of Terror. He broke off work during the
summer of 1804 amid descriptions of the increasing complications that external events were bringing to his first joyous response to the Revolution:
"a sense / Of treachery and desertion in the place / The holiest that I knew
of, my own soul" (X.379–81). He had, however, done little to explore the
internal crisis these events caused or to indicate how his imaginative impairment was restored.

    He resumed work in the fall of 1804, most likely with what became the bulk of Book VIII, "Love of Nature Leading to Love of Mankind." This sentimental argument thus arises, in the chronology of composition, after his first indications of his imagination's temporary allegiance to, and betrayal by, the course of revolutionary events—and not, as he finally placed it, as a retrospective view of his residence in London (Book VII). But the final arrangement may have occurred to him almost immediately, for the writing of most of VII followed in November 1804. Manuscripts show some important exchanges of material between Books VII and VIII,[18] which suggest that Wordsworth prepared for VIII's conclusions by building them into VII's premises. The latter half of VII is much more critical of London than the first half, so we may opine that Wordsworth was intensifying his dissatisfaction with the city in order to steer this residential crisis into its soothing solution in VIII.

By the end of December he had substantially completed the remainder of Book X, fully admitting into the text the worst of his mental crises, his yielding up of "moral questions in despair" (X.901). To the end of this book he appended an imaginary correspondence with Coleridge, wishing him home again. For an image of the extent of his unhappiness, which was simultaneously biographical and compositional, he turned to the high point of his 1790 walking tour, which he had begun describing immediately after Coleridge's departure the preceding March: "the lordly Alps themselves, / . . . are not now / Since thy migration and departure, Friend, / The gladsome image in my memory / Which they were used to be" (X.991-96). Most of the completion of the poem belongs to late April and May of 1805 because all composition ceased after the first week of February, when news of John's drowning reached Grasmere.[19] Books VI-X were completed under the burden of Coleridge's temporary absence; Books XI-XIII, under the tragic weight of the loss of John. Probably as a result, they are constructed largely from material written earlier: the "spots of time" from the 1799 version, the North and West Country road-wanderings (XII) from their first drafting in Book VIII the preceding fall, and the ascent of Snowdon from its originally planned function as the conclusion of the five-book version.[20] By a certain fatality, all endings of *The Prelude* come together: in December 1804 Wordsworth was describing his deepest moral-imaginative crisis and reiterating his need for Coleridge's help; February brought news that, "O dear Friends! Death has come among us!" (*LSTC*, ii.1168), breaking up the community—the "happy band"—on which the creation of *The Recluse* was constantly founded; summer 1805 brought news that Coleridge was returning, just as the poem reached the point of recounting Wordsworth's first acquaintance

with him—"that summer [and] all which then we were," 1798 at Alfoxden, where *The Recluse* was conceived.

Composition on *The Prelude* did not stop in 1805, but its basic arrangement was established then. Although Wordsworth brought the 1799
version up to date, he did so in a highly selective manner that reveals an
overall pattern of imaginative impairment followed by restoration. This
pattern repeats itself in three stages, which can be called Innocence, Fall,
and Redemption at the highest level of cultural generalization.[21] It recurs
in the same sequence as the "spots of time": (1) an original expectation
(naive or misguided) is thwarted by (2) surprise or disappointment, resulting in (3a) a subsequent reinterpretation not only of the original expectation but, more importantly, (3b) of the power of the human mind to form
expectations and respond to unexpected variation.[22] It is a pattern stressing continuous mental growth over discontinuous gaps in reality. In his
composition and rearrangement of his poem in 1804–05, Wordsworth
shows how his original expectations of Cambridge, London, and the
French Revolution (Human Life) were, successively and with increasing
force, disappointed, and how he responded each time with an increasingly
higher estimation of his own moral and creative powers (The Mind of
Man). His relocation of Books VII–VIII between Books VI–IX–X (the
compositional sequence) is the most important organizational decision in
the establishment of this pattern. But all of *The Prelude*, we must remember, was in a sense an interruption of *The Recluse*, and by stretching out
his personal narrative in Books XI–XIII to the very moments when *The
Recluse* idea was hatched, Wordsworth brought himself back to the moment when the necessity of writing *The Prelude* was implanted.

THE FINAL PLAN OF THE 1805 *PRELUDE*

The doom of the five-book *Prelude* was dictated much less by Wordsworth's chronological extension of his poem into the material that became
Book VI, "Cambridge and the Alps," than by its thematic significance: the
French Revolution and his imagination's reaction to it. With the admission
of these two themes, Wordsworth transposed his exploration of his mental
powers into a higher key, and his development of them made *The Prelude*
the masterpiece of English Romanticism. Chronologically, all the material
in Book VI could have been included in the five-book plan, or in a briefly
entertained six-book plan which still presented a normative picture of the
growth of a poet's mind.[23] Even as it stands the poem gives little sense of
a new beginning in Book VI, but rather, in its first third, of summary and

conclusion. However, once Wordsworth took his story beyond Cambridge, through his first direct experience of the French Revolution, and into the Alps and his belated discovery of Imagination as a humanly infinite power, he put his poem on a course that could not be contained by any of the forms he had employed thus far: conversation poem, verse epistle, educational epyllion, or *Künstlerroman*.

This new development is clearly announced in the titles of Books IX–XII: "Residence in France," "Residence in France and French Revolution," "Imagination, How Impaired and Restored." The two preceding books, composed after the main French sequence and inserted into it later, "Residence in London," and "Retrospect: Love of Nature Leading to Love of Mankind," could still have been accommodated in a more conventionally autobiographical or generic description of a poet's development, capping his growth with a move to the big city, his discovery of its wonders and subsequent disenchantment with its corruption, and final retirement to the country, virtue, and poetry. Such a generic plan goes back to Latin models by Virgil, Ovid, and Juvenal, and was essentially the form of contemporary models like Cowper's *The Task*. As a plan, it closely resembles the image Coleridge gave in old age of what Wordsworth was to have done in *The Recluse*:

> he was to describe the pastoral and other states of society, assuming
> something of the Juvenalian spirit as he approached the high civilization
> of cities and towns, and opening a melancholy picture of the present state
> of degeneracy and vice; thence he was to infer . . . the . . . necessity for the
> whole state of man and society being subject to, and illustrative of, a re-
> demptive process in operation. [*TT*, ii.71; 21 July 1832]

Coleridge's omission of any reference to the French Revolution, even at that late date, is remarkable and underscores the difficulties Wordsworth faced. Once the fatal hints of Revolution and Imagination had been dropped in Book VI, the structural function of Books VII and VIII becomes, not to cap a thematic sequence, Nature→Books→Civilization (Nature, Man, and Human Life as conventionally understood), but to *postpone* the appearance of crisis in the poem by intervening between the speaker's educational experience and his shattering experience of revolution. This function is achieved with a nice sense of widening spheres that has some chronological accuracy, since Wordsworth did go to London for four months after leaving Cambridge in 1791; but the thematic function of the placement of the two urban books is much more important than its biographical plausibility, since neither Wordsworth's brief residence in 1791 nor his trips in and out of London between 1792 and 1795 can account for the nearly 20 percent of the entire poem he devotes to his "residence" there. This high percentage of urban theme is dictated as a counterbalance to Wordsworth's elaboration of the Revolution and Imagination themes, which constitute nearly 40 percent of the entire poem, and nearly half of the poem composed in 1804–05.

The French Revolution jolted *The Prelude*—as it jolted much of the world—out of all normative, conventional schemes of understanding life's experiences. Wordsworth gave memorable notice to its uniqueness: "a stride at once into another region" (X.240), "The man to come parted as by a gulph, / From him who had been" (XI.60). Far less than Cambridge and London could the French Revolution be a "residence," though Wordsworth moved for a time on the fringes of those English radical circles which thought it might be. As Geoffrey Hartman has said in an only slightly different connection, "Apocalypse is not habitable,"[24] and this is as true for the "residence" of Revolution in *The Prelude* as it was for Englishmen in Paris after August 1792. Wordsworth's inclusion of the French Revolution plunged his poem into the real history of his time, yet it did so, paradoxically, with an event that could not be contained in any normative historical framework available to him. To be sure, his accounts of his childhood, his university, and his capital also contain real historical elements, but they are essentially similar to the histories of most Western childhoods, universities, and cities, and thereby provided his poem (in its five-book form) with universality. The French Revolution, however, had no substantial precedents (though Wordsworth makes allusions to the fall of Rome and the destruction of Sodom and Gomorrah); yet precisely because of its universalistic ideology, it fixed Wordsworth's poem in a unique time and place. Like an exponential rather than an arithmetic factor, its inclusion thus raised the complicated reverberations of Self and Human Life in *The Prelude* to a radically higher power.

Wordsworth's development of the theme of Imagination was closely linked to his experience of the Revolution, but it was a continuing mystery for him to say how. Indeed, the crisis of the poem arises from his difficulty in understanding this linkage. Although it is generally accepted that Romantic writers displaced their initial faith in revolutionary redemption from public to private artistic realms, this broad academic consensus should not obscure the fact that the process of displacement was managed with varying degrees of success by various artists, and that in every case the difficulties of the process appear in significant tensions within their works. Although the resumption of *The Prelude* in 1804 was, in the total history of *The Recluse*, a return by Wordsworth to his subjective self, his

exploration of Imagination as a humanly infinite power represents a
marked intensification and transcendentalization of that subjectivity; it is
the heart of the heart of his matter, the center of his movement toward a
more mysterious conception of human creativity, paralleled in his exactly
contemporaneous completion of the "Ode: Intimations of Immortality
from Recollections of Early Childhood." In this movement, the revelation
of Imagination's power in his 1804 description of his 1790 crossing of the
Simplon Pass is crucial, but in the present context we must ask: would the
Simplon revelation have occurred without the immediately preceding experience of revolution? The question has the same double signification as the
two events—namely, to what extent did Wordsworth's 1790 experience of
Revolution affect his 1790 vision of Imagination? And, to what extent did
his 1804 *description* of his first experience of revolutionary enthusiasm
trigger his 1804 *discovery-via-description* of Imagination's power?[25]

Like the inclusion of the French Revolution, the new, transcendental
emphasis on Imagination as a specific power of mind knocked the poem
out of any normative scheme but in a contrary direction. The Revolution
plunged *The Prelude* into history, but with a unique event that could not
be accommodated to a normative scheme of human growth or history.
Conversely, the revelation of Imagination lifted the poem out of history,
out of time and space altogether, and placed its hero in a realm of mental
infinity: "our home / Is with infinitude, and only there" (VI.538–39); yet
it does so, paradoxically, by concentrating on his individual uniqueness.
Moreover, like France-in-Revolution, this "home" was equally inhospita-
ble for normal poetic life (however temptingly attractive), especially for the
poetic stance imagined for the creator of *The Recluse*: "the station of a
man in mental repose, one whose principles were made up, and so prepared to deliver upon authority a system of philosophy" (*TT*, II.70). Like
revolution, Imagination accelerated *The Prelude* far beyond "Books and
Nature," and placed Wordsworth's psychology of mind in categories that
were at once unique and infinite. Before Book VI, Wordsworth had discussed his imaginative development as part of his overall mental growth,
but imagination was subordinated to the whole of human mentality, especially its moral component, virtue. But after Book VI's apostrophe to
Imagination, and especially in the books devoted to it by title (XI–XII),
Imagination begins to gain the upper hand among Wordsworth's mental
powers, until at the end it seems the best, most comprehensive name for
them all:

> This love more intellectual cannot be
> Without Imagination, which, in truth,

Is but another name for absolute strength
And clearest insight, amplitude of mind,
And reason in her most exalted mood.   [XIII.166–70]

Some readers have deplored Imagination's usurpation of powers in Wordsworth's mental state, but we should recognize that its radical force in the
1805 *Prelude* arises as a means of accommodating, or coming to terms
with, revolution's parallel usurpation of human powers.

   If we were to subject the titles of *1805*'s thirteen books to a kind of
algebraic factoring, removing all their specific "residences" and organizational pointers (like "Introduction" and "Continued"), we would be left
with the following table of elements from which to deduce the poem's
"manners":

   Books
   Love of Nature Leading to Love of Mankind
   French Revolution
   Imagination, How Impaired and Restored

To historical hindsight, this short list presents an abstract of the cultural
transition from Enlightenment rationality, through various eighteenth-century compromises with benevolent emotion and sentiment (roughly,
Shaftesbury through Wesley), to the humanistic crisis of Revolution and
the Romantic retrenchment in Imagination. It also shows the poem's
"manners" as a matter of process: educational, moral, political, and creative. The participial, Becoming (existence over essence) nature of a poem
thus subtitled appears as a "leading to," a "how." These sequences describe the process by which Imagination is restored to the grounds of its
education, and to a positive metaphysics engendering positive morality following an impairment (a word applied specifically to processes or functions in English, not to objects) occasioned by the challenge of historical
events. The sense of crisis overcome is evident not only in the movement
from "Impaired" to "Restored," but also in the "leading" from Nature to
Mankind, implying a prior antipathy or neutrality toward the latter. Revolution interrupts this "leading to" but is itself integrated into the subsequent *restoration,* another process word, with appropriate political overtones.

   This paradoxical combination of Revolution and Imagination, each
with its own internal paradox, or dynamic, tended mightily to make *The
Prelude* supplant whatever the proposed *Recluse* might say more philosophically "on Man, on Nature, and on Human Life." At its conclusion,
Wordsworth placed his and Coleridge's future imaginative work (preemi-

nently *The Recluse*) as triangulating acts of mediation between Mind and Nature, on the one hand, and the *relation* of Mind and Nature to Human Life, on the other. The former is sufficiently paradoxical: "Prophets of Nature, we . . . may . . . instruct them [mankind] how the mind of man becomes / A thousand times more beautiful than the earth / On which he dwells" (XIII.435–41). But the latter is necessarily conditional, and finally impossible. The poem's concluding paragraph is rife with its difficulties, which only a too single-minded concentration on the "typically" Wordsworthian Mind-Nature relation allows us to ignore. The teachability or redeemability of men is severely qualified in the paragraph's opening ("though too weak to tread the ways of truth, / This Age fall back to old idolatry," XIII.431–32), doubtfully alluded to in the comparatives and conditionals of the main statement—

> . . . we shall *still*
> *Find solace* in the knowledge which we have,
> Bless'd with true happiness if we *may* be
> United helpers forward of a day
> Of *firmer* trust, joint-labourers in a work
> (*Should Providence such grace to us vouchsafe*)
> Of their redemption, *surely yet to come*—   [425–31]

and awkwardly interrupts even the poem's last words with a reiteration of the huge difficulty of the task:

> . . . the mind of man becomes
> A thousand times more beautiful than the earth
> On which he dwells, above this Frame of things
> (Which, 'mid all revolutions in the hopes
> And fears of men, doth still remain unchanged)
> In beauty exalted, as it is itself
> Of substance and of fabric more divine.

> [446–52; all italics added]

The permanence of the physical universe seems to anchor the divine beauty of the human mind, but only by a blurring immersion in "all revolutions" which are, willy-nilly, the very source, force, and constitutive essence of humanity's exaltation. But throughout the passage one revolution has been substituted for another: for the "old idolatry," the new faith in mind's mastery of its earthly frame, founded on the works of Coleridge and Wordsworth.

Thus *The Prelude* existentially presents a gigantic prospectus which, like the actual "Prospectus," is sufficiently millennial. Although Wordsworth continued for a while to look to Coleridge for the systematic demonstration of these truths, nearly two centuries of philosophy have only slowly begun to accomplish the task. Wordsworth thought that in *The Prelude* he had defended Imagination only in personal terms; Coleridge felt the same way about his *Biographia Literaria*. But both works imply much more than the first person. All that was lacking was the recognition that placement of the human person at the center was the new condition of philosophy, not metaphysical elaboration—a recognition which was dawning in Germany in the philosophic generations extending from Hegel to Fichte to Feuerbach to Marx, Kierkegaard, Nietzsche, and Freud.

5

The Prelude of 1805:
A Reading in *The Recluse*

where truth
Like some fair fabric in romantic glory
Built by the charm of sounds and symphonies
Uplifts her fair proportions at the call
Of pleasure her best minister.

PW, V.342

The challenge that Revolution and Imagination pose for *The Prelude*'s organization echoes throughout the poem. The reconciliation of these two forces—the fundamental identities of *The Recluse*'s objective-subjective dialectic— was for Wordsworth a task equal in magnitude to the composition of all the individual lines, and has been felt to be so by almost every serious reader of the poem. Thus his modern biographer generalizes the problems of Book VI's composition: "such irregularity of composition is characteristic of the whole of *The Prelude,* whose present text took its final shape only after numberless reshufflings and remouldings" (M. II.14); John Jones notes "the difficulties of the immensely complex character of the poem's forward movement," concluding that "much of *The Prelude* is mere joinery, and often none too neat"; and Herbert Lindenberger, the foremost student of the poem as a single work of art, marvels that the depressed, introspective tone of its introduction did not disintegrate the poem in the process of composition, or leave it a series of inspired fragments.[1] Recent textual scholarship confirms that its process of composition evidently *was* a continuous series of disintegrations and reintegrations. But however inscrutably unanalytic Wordsworth's method, its result was a masterpiece of architectonics—not of generalizations following from particulars, which Coleridge's aid would presumably have provided, but of artistic proportions. Wordsworth extended the challenge to his readers to appreciate this quality of the poem, though none of his editors before 1979 saw fit to print it:

. . . he who deigns to mark with care
By what rules governed, with what end in view,
This Work proceeds, *he* will not wish for more.[2]

The challenge reverberates in each book of the poem, and in the larger "residential" units they comprise. There are obviously three such units—Cambridge, London, and France—but each includes more than the one book so titled, and each contains its own intermediate resolution, as does each book within it. Each new residence initiates a crisis that is partially resolved before the next residence is established. The first new biographical and compositional unit, Books III–VI, includes Wordsworth's own university experience and larger questions of the mind's "residence" in any structure of education. The second unit, Books VII–VIII, composed third for the most part and only nominally second in biographical sequence, considers, more than just London, the city as apex of the nation's cultural history, the focus and formation of provincial tastes. Just as the first unit stresses educational process over educational product, so Wordsworth finds conventional views of the city insufficient and reorients the center toward the circumference (from London to the Lakes). The third unit, Books IX–X, concerns not simply his residence in France but the Revolution as Imagination-in-action. The first two units, as we have seen, derive from potentially normative schemes of mental growth: man in general, universally the same in all times and places. The third unit, however, considers the possibility of existentially altering the essence of what is given, changing human nature. The impossibility of reaching this utopia or earthly paradise through revolution impairs Wordsworth's imagination, leading to the third unit's resolution (and the poem's): imagination's restoration in Books XI–XIII.

In each book within each unit, there is a crisis both of content and of structure. The former concerns the actual situation Wordsworth encountered in each residence: college foolishness, city spectacle, revolutionary enthusiasm and terror. But each book also enacts a drama of composition. Wordsworth's open presentation of his crises threatens the structure of each book, endangering the likelihood of its concluding in a unified, artistically satisfying manner. (Hence the warm, harmonic tones of all the final lines in the "residential" books.) These dangers are apparent in the text; they are of the same color as the rhetorical fragmentation devices in "Tintern Abbey." Wordsworth's surmounting of each structural crisis is of a piece with his reported triumph over the content crisis, and it is moot to say which has priority. For example, the threatening possibility that he wasted his mind at Cambridge is overcome, not only by his simple biographical assertion at age thirty-four that, on balance, his university experience wasn't so bad after all, but also by his construction of alternate, ideal universities where his mind would not have been in peril then, and is not now, by virtue of his imagination's ability to build such schools. Each book is simultaneously stage and goal, process and product. In this sense, "all" of *The Prelude* can be read in any one of its books. While it is theoretically possible that any part of an organic whole may contain the whole, holographically, this feature is more marked in *The Prelude* than in any of the major canonical poems among which it stands—*The Faerie Queene, Paradise Lost,* or *Leaves of Grass*; and in none of these is so large a message—that the human mind grows well in this world—so fully recapitulated as in each part of *The Prelude*.

The mode of structural resolution varies from book to book. It may be an idealized image, like the alternative universities in Book III or Michel Beaupuy in IX; a special argument such as the "Blest infant Babe" in II; a rhetorical assertion (like most of Book VIII); an indulged fantasy (the dream of the Arab-Quixote in Book V); a visionary peak (Simplon, Snowdon); or an admonitory contrast, such as the figure of Vaudracour in Book IX, Robespierre in Book X, or Bartholomew Fair in Book VII. Overall, the "spots of time" provide the most frequent pattern of resolution, repeating in localized sequences what they do cumulatively in each of the last three books. The position and number of each structural resolution varies from book to book, and is not a discrete symbol but an integral part of each book's entire texture.

Such an overview of *The Prelude*'s structure will be familiar to experienced readers of the poem, though opinions vary as to Wordsworth's degree of success. Some books' and units' resolutions are more persuasive than others, and Wordsworth did not completely cover the seams where various versions or stages of the poem were joined together, or where he moved from one unit to the next: the startling shift in tone between II and III, the sense of repetition as VI follows V (the thirteen-book poem taking off from the five-book plan), the special pleading of VIII after VII (where an argument—"Love of Nature Leading to Love of Mankind"— compositionally provoked by the unique spectre of revolutionary terror is organizationally applied to the universal problem of urban corruption), and finally, the murky connections among XI–XIII, which are hard to see because Wordsworth abandons his narrative framework. Like Milton, he uses invocations (usually to Coleridge-as-Muse) to announce new divisions, and they occur according to this plan, at VII, IX, and (as the beginning of the end) at XI. The resolution of the whole poem may be seen in the Snowdon description—event, interpretation, and generalization all in one, leading to a conclusion that depends upon yet another completion, "building up a work that should endure": *The Recluse* as validation of *The Prelude*.

To say that Wordsworth reenacts each of his life's crises in the structure of his poem may, to some readers, presuppose the poet's ignorance of craft, while to others it will imply an anachronistic sophistication in modern discontinuous forms. But in demonstrating the 1805 *Prelude*'s thirteen-times-repeated temptation to destroy its own texture, I intend to address neither of these alternatives, nor the looseness of the 1805 version relative to 1850, nor the general Romantic predilection for open-ended fragments and inconclusive preludes.[3] Still less do I wish to engage the methodological polemics newly swirling around the old question of the nature and extent of the gap between an author's intention and his expression. But in trying to elucidate a poem rather than a theory, I am sailing a hermeneutical strait between the Scylla of intentional authorial presence and the Charybdis of abstract linguistic structure—and, worse, landing occasionaly to take succor from each. But, whether Wordsworth or his words' worth is its source, I see in *The Prelude* a sequence of repeated poetic triumphs achieved by successive courtings of disaster.

Wordsworth's compositional crises are, furthermore, crises in which the reader must participate to some extent. The sensation of losing one's way that occurs in reading almost every book of *The Prelude* is not limited to uninitiated readers; it properly accompanies every rereading of the poem. The author, too, seems to get lost repeatedly: "My drift I fear is scarcely obvious." This is not (for the most part) an aesthetic flaw, nor one resolvable by unconvincing tautologies (for example, that Wordsworth was writing a confusing poem about his confusions). Rather, it is an experience that both poet and reader must resolve, each in his own way. Sometimes Wordsworth seeks a temporary resolution by invoking Coleridge as his ideal reader, implicitly challenging other readers to be so insightful. One could follow these observations into a reading of *The Prelude* on the model of Stanley Fish's interpretation of *Paradise Lost,* which demonstrates various ways in which Milton forces his reader to recapitulate Adam's experiences of temptation, fall, and redemption (*Surprised by Sin,* 1967). Only, in *The Prelude,* the effect would be one of being "surprised by Joy," as form enacts content and the reader participates in Wordsworth's repeated experiences of expectation, disappointment, and ultimate (though revised) recognition of the mind's creative powers.

These degrees of authorial and lectorial implication are part of the central dialectic of *The Prelude* in its relation to *The Recluse,* as the private, personal, subjective talk of the former echoes in the public, social, objective speech of the latter. Wordsworth's biographical and compositional crises are one and the same, given the burden of his poem: "I am the mind sufficient to this poem, for I have written the history of its growth *as the poem.*" And as *The Prelude* and *The Recluse* veer or waver unstably toward each other, so do the individual books within them, along the same private-to-public axis. Accepting these tensions rather than reducing them helps us to negotiate *The Prelude*'s "retrograde" progress,[4] which we can now see as an extension of the dialectical relation between the first *Recluse* and first *Prelude* poems, where pervasive social ills are—preposterously, unless we see these reasons for it—construed as personal mental threats.

Wordsworth's dramatization of this dialectical simultaneity begins at—and as—his new beginning, the preamble and introduction he placed in front of his altered 1799 version, leading up to and fitting into its open-ended question, "Was it for this?" and answering it with a new beginning. *The Prelude* is not only an open-ended work but something more difficult to conceive, a poem with an open-beginning, which enacts the creative challenge of origin-ality even as it strives for conclusively persuasive aesthetic form.

THE FIRST HOME: THE POET IN HIS POEM

Having excised the "spots of time" and the Coniston Hall lines from the 1799 *Prelude*, Wordsworth added two passages to provide a proper beginning for his poem, thereby creating Books I and II of the 1805 version. First, he set in place the "glad Preamble" (I.1–54), composed contemporaneously with the completion of the 1799 *Prelude* and his inception of "Home at Grasmere." Second, he composed the topical introduction (55–271) which complicates the optimistic mood of the preamble until, by stages, it becomes an appropriate antecedent to the question, "Was it for this?" from which *The Prelude* springs. The post-preamble (55–156) initiates this process of textual self-commentary which turns an enthusiastic mood to one of frustration, representing compositionally the whole biographical sequence of confidence and doubt that provoked Wordsworth's agonized questioning of himself. The introduction proper (157–271) then defines the poem to follow negatively, by extended differentiation from a variety of poems that it might be but is not. As usual in Wordsworth's processes of negative definition, that which is ruled out nevertheless reveals some of the deepest intentions of that which is inscribed.

I omit here any discussion of Book I beyond its "Introduction," or of Book II. Though they deserve recapitulation, their function in the 1805 *Prelude* is adequately treated by the discussion of Parts I and II of *1799* in chapter 2, in conjunction with that of chapter 4 on Wordsworth's "deconstruction" of the earlier version. In sum, they extend the feeling of being-at-home that Wordsworth established metapoetically in the "Introduction" into a real-life biographical mode. Though not without dramatic tension, their most critical issues were modulated by displacement into *The Prelude*'s enlarged structure.

Preamble

The sense of release with which the new *Prelude* opens is so great that, if we did not know it was a beginning, we might take it for an ending. It opens the poem in a mood of living happily ever after, very much like the portions of "Home at Grasmere" with which its composition is contemporaneous. It is morning, and a young hero sets out toward a destination he is sure he cannot miss even though he does not know what or where it is, escaped "from a house of bondage . . . yon City." It reads like an ending because it was composed at a time of ending, not only the conclusion of the 1799 *Prelude*, but the end of a whole decade (1791–1800) of wandering, vocational doubt, and creative uncertainty, closed by his decision to return with Dorothy to a cottage in their native region. But, as a birth ends a pregnancy, so the preamble, like this decisive moment in Wordsworth's life, is also manifestly a beginning, leading us to understand its mood of "happily ever after" as the confidence of a young hero setting out to seek his fortune. Since there is evidently a long story to follow, we may be disposed to read some of its expressions of boundless optimism with caution—a disposition in which the poet progressively encourages us.[5]

The outsetting force of the preamble derives both from what it leaves behind and what it aims toward. "Yon City" needs little identification as a narrative element. From the biblical allusion, "house of bondage," and its correlative "prison" metaphor we see that it is a place to be escaped from. Although the city can be identified plausibly as Bristol or Goslar or London,[6] the connotations of the passage point toward the most general typological interpretation, even beyond Odysseus or Aeneas leaving Troy, for it is the city of everyday life, the constraint of responsibilities other than those the speaker feels toward himself. A moralist could accuse the released "captive" of simply going on vacation, but Wordsworth elevates his mood as a dedication to a new kind of work, *his* work, more important than what the world expects of him. His elevation comes largely from Miltonic allusions, particularly "The earth is all before me" from *Paradise Lost*. Wordsworth here takes another ending, Adam and Eve setting out from the Garden of Eden, and attaches it to his beginning. But he is not fallen from grace. By conflating biblical allusions, he puts behind him not the Garden of Eden but the "house of bondage" and advances outward toward a promised land with much less trepidation than Adam and Eve set out toward the fallen world.

His progress toward his goal is as lightly inevitable as the city had been heavily constrictive: "I cannot miss my way." He underscores his certainty in ways that, later in the poem, we shall recognize as preparations for a coming fall (for instance, his exaggeration of his confidence in the triumph of the French Revolution at the beginning of Book X). To take happily as a guide "nothing better than a wandering cloud . . . or twig or any floating thing" is to emphasize confidence to the point of causing opposing notions to rise up in readers' minds. His confidence is directed toward finding a home, which is defined by the "chosen tasks" he will perform in it. No mention is made of his creative work until near the end of the preamble, when "a corresponding mild creative breeze" rises up in Wordsworth to greet the "welcome Messenger" from Nature and Heaven with which it opened. Wordsworth passes over without comment the fact that this first correspondence between inner and outer inspiration[7] does not result in a poem but in conflict: "A tempest, a redundant energy / Vexing its own creation" (46–47). However, such conflicts become the motive theme of the post-preamble and introduction, recurring three more times until, demanding more and more attention, they become the antecedent to the question "Was it for this?" that provokes, rather than inspires, the poem. The conflict is not simply the difficulty of creation, but arises in each case from the specific failure of the *automatic* sequence Wordsworth has posited between the *place* where he is going and the *work* which he expects to produce there, almost as if the place could do the work. The preamble, however, determined to be "glad," glosses over the conflict by seeing only "vernal promises" in the meeting of the two inspiring breezes, and ends by returning to its outsetting young hero as a knight-errant anticipating "prowess in an honorable field" because of his pure dedication to "the holy life of music and of verse" (52, 54). This light mixture of Arthurian with biblical images is a foretaste of many of *The Recluse*'s controlling intentions for English Christianity, refined by modern English poetry (i.e., Wordsworth's), for the redemptive good of the world.

Post-Preamble

The rest of *The Prelude*'s opening is a rhetorical interpretation of issues raised in the preamble, modulating its gladness into the strategic dejection of "Was it for this?" The post-preamble begins as a past-tense
gloss, addressed to Coleridge, on the preamble, extending its journey image in two stages, en route (55–115) and at home (116–156), both of
which manipulate the twin terms—place and work, home and poem—the
preamble introduced. Increasingly, Wordsworth shows himself becoming
aware that the right choice of home does not lead automatically to the
right choice of work, still less to its performance, until, in the final lines of
the Introduction he concludes with a far different journey image from that
with which he began:

> Unprofitably travelling toward the grave,
> Like a false Steward who hath much received
> And renders nothing back.   [269–71]

Here the controlling question "Was it for this?" is placed as an interruption—i.e., this is the grafting point at which the 1799 *Prelude* is attached—and the rest of the poem follows as a direct examination of the
dialectic between Wordsworth's mind and the places ("residences") in
which it expected so much, and received so little.

En route, the second check to Wordsworth's creative powers arises in
the two days' "pleasant loitering journey [that] brought me to my hermitage." Although he begins by reaffirming the preamble's dedicated calling,
"cloth'd in priestly robe," this holy moment is quickly gentled, "being not
unwilling now to give / A respite to this passion" (68–69). He rests. Most
of the post-preamble's lines about the journey are in fact about resting in
preparation for it, "sooth'd by a sense of touch / From the warm ground,
that balanced me, else lost / Entirely, seeing nought, nought hearing"
(89–91). This soothing of his poetic feelings lasts only as long as he presents himself at rest, however. When the journey resumes (95 ff.)—the
choice of home having been made and firmly linked again to "assurance of
some work / Of glory, there forthwith to be begun" (85–86)—the concomitant resumption of poetic composition again is frustrated, now more
forcefully:

>   my soul
> Did once again make trial of the strength
> Restored to her afresh; nor did she want
> Eolian visitations; but the harp
> Was soon defrauded, and the banded host
> Of harmony dispers'd in straggling sounds
> And, lastly, utter silence.   [101–07]

But this suggestion of sublime hopes betrayed is accepted in an accommodating mood of gentling high spirits, and he contents himself with a lesser role—"So like a Peasant I pursued my road"—than that of knight, prophet, or priest which had promised himself in the preamble.

Once home, the same sequence of expectation, frustration, and accommodation is repeated. The place meets all his expectations, is "happiness entire,"[8] but the corresponding hope, "with a frame of outward life [to] fix in a visible home . . . those phantoms of conceit" (128–30), is discouraged as speedily as it arises. The poem which has opened on a morning scene of limitless expectations, prolonged through an afternoon and evening of gentle confidence, now first raises the possibility of a false dawn: "gleams of light / Flash often from the East, then disappear / And mock me with a sky that ripens not / Into a steady morning" (134–37). As before, he tries to put off this third failure with accommodating acceptance, "to yield up / Those lofty hopes awhile for present gifts / Of humbler industry" (142–44). But he can no longer extemporize; even his "meditative mind"—Wordsworth's characteristic presentation of his best self—now gives in to "less quiet instincts" and "passion" rather than accepting its duty (150–56). "Though no distress be near him but his own / Unmanageable thoughts" (148–49), the poet will at last give in to them, and thus the *theme* of the Introduction is broached, that the author doesn't know what to write about, in marked contrast to the overt burden of its *narrative*.

Introduction

In his thematic introduction proper (157–271), Wordsworth explores the assumption of place-leading-to-work which has been his reason for confidence. Is he in fact capable of performing the work he feels dedicated to, when all signs of promise so far have been frustrated? The problem is not his mental, spiritual, or imaginative powers, which are summarily approved (160–68), but the putative poem's needs: "Time, place, and manners; these I seek" (169). The condition of fullness which was for the poet-as-man a happy one—"The earth is all before me . . . I cannot miss my way"—is for his poem a liability: "Time, place, and manners . . . I find in plenteous store; but nowhere such / As may be singled out with steady choice" (169–71). The mode of achievement he proposes duplicates his own homecoming, anticipates the epic subjects he will consider in greatest detail, and ultimately becomes one of the strongest images in the subsequent development of *The Recluse*. He seeks some

> . . . little Band of yet remember'd names
> Whom I, in perfect confidence, might hope

> To summon back from lonesome banishment
> And make them inmates in the hearts of men
> Now living, or to live in times to come.   [172–76]

This "little Band" is the literary form of Grasmere's "happy band," the body that would *em*body the music that has been escaping him ("the banded host / Of harmony dispers'd in straggling sounds," 105–06). Its efficient power is striking: it would find its home in his poem, which would thus in turn achieve the home Wordsworth and Coleridge destined for *The Recluse*: poetic immortality. Though apparently an escapist, a recluse is a homebody par excellence, for he is his home.

The longest section of the introduction (177–238) is a listing of five categories of poems Wordsworth entertains as possible subject matter, a list often glossed over by commentators simply because it is a list and does not contain, after all, the poem Wordsworth finally did write. But it consists of more than mere topics, describing in dramatic projection the figurative action of the poem to come. The first two categories are Wordsworth's homage proposed and challenge declined to Milton and Spenser, the only two poets whom, in the confidence of later life, he considered as rivals and competitors (M. I.100–01). Together, they present the same sequence of sublime expectation (Milton) followed by gentle accommodation (Spenser) which has been operative in the introduction thus far, but has proved to be, as here, a "mistaking vainly" (177).

The third category (185–219) is by far the longest and most important, framed by the word *stern* in its opening and closing lines ("Sometimes, more sternly mov'd, I would relate . . . Of independence and stern liberty," 185, 219), a word typically used by Wordsworth to denote both political themes and the nature of Imagination, as in his crossing the Simplon Pass in "something of stern mood" (VI.489). In this group are six subtopics, all concerned in one way or another with the avenging return of an outcast hero and his band of loyal followers (e.g., Mithridates-Odin, Sertorious, Gustavus I of Sweden), bringing destructive justice to the corrupt civilizations which have cast them out. They are concrete forms of the mode of existence Wordsworth has imagined for the effect of his own poem ("little Band[s] of yet remember'd names . . . summon[ed] back from lonesome banishment," 170–72), summoned by time or the justice of their cause rather than the poet's power, but working, as he hoped to, "in perfect confidence." They are republican, reformist, or separatist heroes, returning home with great, inevitable force, public forms of the private condition in which Wordsworth represented himself in his outsetting preamble, escaping from immurement with a force that cannot help but carry him / them home. All have been banished, literally or figuratively, or somehow restrained from action, and their force gains irresistible strength from their enforced inactivity, which transforms it into a spiritual force more powerful than its original political form, like a poetry that might affect Human Life. The catalog advances progressively closer to Wordsworth's time and place, circling northward through Europe from the Roman Empire, past exploits of the Age of Discovery in Spain and France, picking up associations of Protestant individual nationalism versus Catholic hierarchical imperialism along the way, and finally devolves upon the story of William Wallace, with which Wordsworth had first become impressed on his tour of Scotland in 1803, the year before the introduction was composed, and which he had added to the Pedlar's repertoire to give him more biographical plausibility (M. I.609; *PW*, V.515). In comparison with the heroic explorers he had used as metaphors for himself in the five-book plan, these libertarian heroes point up his changing conception of *The Prelude*. Whereas the explorers were single over-reachers upon whom some hugely sublime event was about to devolve (the discovery of new worlds—America or death), these avengers have all dramatically altered the structure of the existing corrupt old world ("That Odin, Father of Race, by whom / Perish'd the Roman Empire," I.188–89), by virtue of collecting their powers in reclusive meditation. If the explorers expressed Wordsworth's sense of discovery as he pressed his normative theme of "Books and Nature" to its limits, the avengers are buried allusions to his sense of triumph at having admitted the great contemporary apocalyptic political theme of liberty and justice for all into his poem, and having transformed its implications of worldwide power into the very stuff of his own creative imagination.

However, since he did not write any of these possible poems, and since the triumph of *The Prelude* would still require validation by a completed *Recluse,* it is appropriate that the catalog ends so close to home, with Wallace, who was, of course, finally defeated. Wordsworth therefore celebrates not his actual deeds but their memorials, the persistence of his name as a sign of triumph in his native place:

> How Wallace fought for Scotland, left the name
> Of Wallace to be found like a wild flower,
> All over his dear Country, left the deeds
> Of Wallace, like a family of Ghosts,
> To people the steep rocks and river banks,
> Her natural sanctuaries, with a local soul
> Of independence and stern liberty.   [213–29]

William Wallace's works have filled his home, a grand idea has been localized, like *The Recluse's* goal of high meanings in ordinary language. The
dialectic of place and work operating in *The Prelude's* introduction has
here made the two nearly interchangeable. William Wordsworth must do
the same; his work must become his place, the Lake District, and his place
his work, *The Recluse*. As approaches to Human Life, the "time, place,
and manners" of the third category share a final characteristic: their action
describes a plot whose denouement is decisive, destructive, vengeful triumph. No attention is given to what happened after their victories, to any
subsequent building up of a good society; even Wallace's memories are
"like a family of Ghosts." Given Wordsworth's pride, egotism, and enormous sense of imaginative power, it is not unlikely that he at times fanta-
sized his eventual triumph as a poet in similar terms, blasting unapprecia-
tive London circles and Scottish journals with his poetic vindication. And
if we seek a mythic type of these heroes' actions, the homecomings of
Odysseus and Aeneas are similarly instructive. But, as Wordsworth linked
his imagination benignly to Nature, so he must turn it beneficially toward
Human Life, and these topics, however emotionally satisfying, would not
easily lodge themselves, or him, as "inmates in the hearts of men / Now
living, or to live in times to come."[9]

The fourth (220–28) and fifth (228–38) categories of possible subjects are linked in theme and in the reason Wordsworth gives for their failure of achievement. The fourth, "some Tale from my own heart," would
be *"Lofty,* with interchange of *gentler* things," and the fifth would be
"some *philosophic* Song / Of Truth that cherishes our *daily* life." Like the
song of Wallace, they would combine the sublime and the ordinary, in the
interchange between "holy services" and "gentler happiness" (63, 73)
which has motivated the entire introduction. But, in a mirroring contrast
to the delayed denouements of the third category, these two kinds of
poems leap up too immediately to their proposed ends, they become
"lofty," "immortal," and "Orphean" too soon, without the necessary in-
cubation time of brooding meditation and spiritual transformation, leading to "deadening admonitions" (225), "awful burthen" (235), and no
poem. The required parturition will be the function of *The Prelude,* leading to *The Recluse,* and indeed the fourth and fifth categories describe either poem well enough.

In the conclusion of his introduction (238–71), Wordsworth presents
himself as living without recognizing it—therefore dangerously—in a condition like that of his banished heroes. He is "a mockery of the brother-

hood of vice and virtue," and his confusion of motives betrays him in a false garment, "serving often for a cloak / To a more subtle selfishness" (246–47), a far cry from his earlier priestly robes. His functions are locked up in "blank reserve," guarded by "an over-anxious eye / That with a false activity beats off / Simplicity and self-presented truth" (248–52). This psychological imprisonment, where he is "baffled," "recreant," "interdict," is equivalent to the suffering exile of his avenging heroes but leads only to the grave, because there is no truth, no inspiration, in him: wearing false garments, engaged in "false activity," he is "like a false steward." Not only would anything be better than this, *nothing* would be better—sheer vacuum—and it is from this condition of self-banished hopes that, inquiring "Was it for this?," he launches into his sure triumph, *The Prelude,* almost as if in revenge upon himself for doubting his powers.[10]

The *Prelude* of 1799 thus reappears as the sure praise of a place, "My 'sweet Birthplace,'" for naturally producing its work, William Wordsworth, who will now be presented *as* the work, "giving me, / Among the fretful dwellings of mankind, / A knowledge . . . of the calm / That Nature breathes among the hills and groves" (282–85). He was not, of course, "among" those fretful dwellings as a boy; rather, he has just left them, generalized as "yon City," where he has been "immured" in false exile since moving into the first of the residences (Cambridge) around which the 1805 *Prelude* is now structured. By a series of small domiciliar additions to the open beginning of *1799*, Wordsworth connects the introduction's theme of self-validating homecomings to the narrative content of his own autobiography: he runs "abroad in wantonness . . . from my Mother's hut," steals eggs "where the Mother Bird had built her lodge," adds a special hymn of praise to the "lowly Cottages" of the district (I.525–33),[11] and makes himself a "Playmate" of the river Derwent by virtue of their mutual identification with his home: "When, having left his Mountains, to the Towers / Of Cockermouth that beauteous River came, / Behind my Father's House he pass'd, close by, / Along the margin of our Terrace Walk" (286–89). Rejoined in the poem as they had been in life, together they become natural partners in the central river metaphor that winds throughout *The Prelude,* passing by the "residences" of Human Life with the same inevitability which characterized Wordsworth's wishful catalog of avenging heroes, toward a worldwide rescue of equal magnitude: "Though men return to servitude as fast / As the tide ebbs . . . / By Nations sink together," Wordsworth and his other, mental, partner will be "joint-labourers in a work . . . of their redemption, surely yet to come" (XIII.433–41)

THE FIRST RESIDENCE: EDUCATION

Books III–VI are the first major step in the process that is the essence of the 1805 *Prelude*: Wordsworth's representation of his mind's accommodation to the realities of Human Life, or Society. They concentrate on the structures, physical and mental, by which society seeks to guide and control mental development, dramatizing the mixed results for Wordsworth's sense of uniqueness. Books I and II, though partly titled "School-Time," do not represent any time spent in school, only recesses and vacations. Moreover, the unified development of the two-part *Prelude* of 1799 was, as we have seen, dismantled for attachment to the 1805 version, particularly the societal structures of Part II, which are now subordinated to a new plan running from Cambridge through London to France. In the first, strictly educational part of this plan, Wordsworth's main problem is to balance his mind's tendency to be unprofitably housed in such residential structures, whether from their inherent inadequacy or because of his own willfulness or irresolution, with an acknowledgment of the positive value his genius owes to them.

Book III: "Residence at Cambridge"

Between the end of Book II and the beginning of Book III, a shift in authorial tone is immediately noticeable and has a significance greater than the fact that they were composed some years apart. In III, the author's attitude toward himself as a college freshman is distanced to the point of condescension, compared with the wise seventeen-year-old of Book II, who felt "the sentiment of Being" (II.420) everywhere. Wordsworth characterizes his effort to take a more objective view of his growth in wider circumstances of Human Life as a wish "to pen down / A satire on myself" (IV.54–55). The earliest drafts toward Book III, dating from December 1801, are contemporaneous with Wordsworth's analogous efforts to rework *The Pedlar* in the direction of plausible objectivity,[12] both motivated by the quintessentially educational challenge to *The Recluse*'s claims: How can one so simple be so wise?

In Book III, collegiate foolishness—unthinking social entertainments and equally mindless academic competition—breaks out into open crisis twice, threatening the structure of the book. The first of these corresponds almost exactly to Wordsworth's work on the book in 1801, and to probable reasons for breaking off further composition till 1804. It occurs when his satiric yet indulgent portrait of himself as a dizzy freshman caught up in the whirl of the opening school year ("I was the Dreamer, they the

Dream") pushes on into honest reappraisal—"things they were which then / I did not love, nor do I love them now" (69–70)—and breaks out into clear alienation: "a strangeness in my mind, / A feeling I was not for that hour, / Nor for that place" (79–81). This sudden emergence of crisis, so unlike Books I and II in its sense of *displacement*,[13] yet so like most of the long poem to follow, provokes questions that lift Wordsworth out of his narrative into thematic considerations that are simultaneous with the moment of composition: "Wherefore be cast down? / Why should I grieve?" (81–82) These are versions of the questions that impel "Tintern Abbey" ("If this be but a vain belief"), and give birth to *The Prelude*— the "Was it for this?" that Wordsworth dared not answer affirmatively lest his uncertainty about his project and his powers immobilize both. Here again he rejects his questions rather than answering them, with a strong reassertion of his theme of mental integrity (81–194). The sheer fact that this *is* his theme assures him that he need not "grieve" or be "cast down" for whatever was lost in his years of mental residence at Cambridge. Harking back to the elevated rhetoric of the end of Book II, in words originally intended to refer to the Pedlar, he insists that he was "a chosen Son," "look'd for universal things," that everything he saw "respired with inward meaning," concluding with a direct address to Coleridge (168–94) that all "This is, in truth, heroic argument . . . Of Genius, Power, / Creation and Divinity itself." That this is addressed to Coleridge is doubly significant. It is the first address to the Friend-Reader in the newly expanding *Prelude,* and it represents the place *and means* of Wordsworth's resuming the poem in 1804, fitting *The Prelude* into the new context which he and Coleridge had established for it by then: that it would be either a preface or appendix to the now consciously postponed *Recluse,* equally "heroic," and necessary to complete before the masterwork could begin. Second, it "solves" the problem of mental alienation, into which Wordsworth's satiric, objective narrative has led him, by appealing to Coleridge's corrective philosophical interpretation, thus reinvoking the dialogical context out of which *The Recluse* sprang.

Book III's second crisis arises in Wordsworth's attempt to assign meaning to his total Cambridge experience. Emboldened by the force of his "heroic" assertion to Coleridge, he had been enabled to return to his narrative: "Enough: for now into a populous Plain / We must descend.— A Traveller I am, / And all my Tale is of myself" (195–97). This impetus to autobiography-as-travel-literature carried him through the largest part of Book III (195–375), a catalogue of "the novel show" of Cambridge, happy youths in august surroundings that affected them but little. This goes on well enough until he tries to summarize it conclusively, when he finds he had caught the Cambridge contagion: "my life became / A floating island, an amphibious thing" (339–40). The first crisis was of alienation, "a strangeness" within and without; the second crisis is of too close identification with the miscellaneous randomness all around him. Contemplating his mind's "spungy texture"—hardly the stuff of "Genius, Power, Creation and Divinity itself"—he wonders who is to blame. Looking for a "lodging" for the fault, and partly willing to find it in himself, he yet avers he would have been a better student had the university been a better school. Thus the resolution (375–491) of this second crisis is accomplished not as an appeal to Coleridge to guarantee the quality of Wordsworth's mind, but in terms of an idealized "image of a Place" better suited than Cambridge to house sensitive growing minds. These are three different universities, past, present, and future, all characterized by qualities of *correspondence* between mind and place that make them alma maters akin to Mother Nature of Books I and II.

> Toil and pains
> In this recess which I have bodied forth
> Should spread from heart to heart; stately groves,
> Majestic edifices, should not want
> A corresponding dignity within.   [388–91]

Wordsworth proposes no curriculum; he sees in these ideal images what he seeks in Human Life throughout *The Recluse*: an integral community constituted by integrated personalities, mental "toil and pains" connecting through strong emotions to reflect all that is "stately" in nature and "majestic" in civilization. To explain this dialectical operation, Wordsworth makes one of his odd but deep shifts to preverbal analogues:

> . . . the whole place should wear a stamp of awe;
> A habitation sober and demure
> For ruminating creatures, a domain
> For quiet things to wander in, a haunt
> In which the Heron might delight to feed
> By the shy rivers, and the Pelican
> Upon the cypress spire in lonely thought
> Might sit and sun himself.   [447–54]

A fullness of human communication is expressed in images of silent animals in an equally silent landscape. Since it is very hard for Wordsworth to imagine real students suited to this ideal place, he looks back to olden

times for human figures who could truly find this university a home away
from home:

> . . . when Boys and Youths,
> The growth of ragged villages and huts,
> Forsook their homes . . . errant in the quest
> Of Patron, famous School or friendly Nook,
> Where, pension'd, they in shelter might sit down.   [477–81]

The heroes of this ideal university are some of those reformist "Lovers of
truth" whose enlightenment is represented as the result of their hardy cooperation with Nature: "Bucer, Erasmus, or Melancthon read / Before the
doors or windows of their Cells / By moonshine, through mere lack of
taper light" (488–91).[14]

Having constituted by these ideal images a place more suited to mental residence than his actual Cambridge University, Wordsworth regains
the feeling of his argument's persuasiveness and proceeds to end Book III
with a compromise: the university is "a midway residence" between childhood and adulthood (554) or, alternatively, "midway betwixt life and
books" (613). The commonsense appearance of this compromise should
not lead us to overlook its strange rhetorical power (especially of the second alternative) nor underestimate the difficulty Wordsworth had arriving
at it, given his extraordinarily high estimate of the powers of the human
mind, and his very low estimate of the places in which it must lodge
itself—or, more accurately, his extreme sensitivity to the power places
have to woo the mind away from itself. Nevertheless, the compromise delivers Book III's necessary quota of insights into "what pertains to human
life" (531) for this young man "hitherto . . . in my own mind remote from
human life" (544), gazing now for the first time upon "the surfaces of artificial life / And manners" (590–91). His insights into his grotesque pro-
fessors and misguided peers are not very deep; they return us to the
public, satiric mode of Book III's beginning, a catalogue of abstract personifications from an academic *Pilgrim's Progress*:[15] "here was Labour,"
"Hope / That never set the pains against the prize," Idleness, Shame, Fear,
Pleasure, Honour, Dignity, Submission, Decency, "And blind Authority,
beating with his staff / The Child that might have led him" (630–43). This
highly problematic tableau suggests that the real university remains a
"gaudy Congress" with a still-fatal power in a poem on the growth of a
poet's mind: "The head turns round, and cannot right itself" (663). But
the ideal universities he has imagined in place of the real one underwrite

his mind's investment in it—"Whence profit may be drawn in times to come" (668)—and he is safely delivered: "the tenth [month] return'd me to my native hills again."

Book IV: "Summer Vacation"

Book IV thus opens on a note of restoration strongly countering the alienation movement which opens Book III,[16] continuing the return of the homecoming freshman over the hills, across the lake, and snug into his bed in Ann Tyson's cottage. This narrative restoration is extended into an account of his poetry-composing walks around his old stamping grounds (84–180) thematically generalized into visions of how "Life pervades the undecaying mind" (155). Wordsworth has followed the pattern opening Book III (narrative plus generalization) to make essentially the same point: that his desire to write poetry connotes mental health, not madness (IV.118–20), or, as he had maintained to Coleridge, that this poem *about* such desires is itself, "in truth, heroic argument" (III.182). But when he attempts, in the characteristic movement of the 1805 *Prelude*, to extend his private visions to Human Life, and show "a dawning, even as of another sense, / A human-heartedness about my love" (224–25), the introduction of the *Recluse* theme again endangers the progress of *The Prelude*. Although he found "a freshness . . . at this time / In human Life" (181–82), such a discovery does not bear generalization any more plausibly than did Cambridge's miscellany. This is not because Wordsworth disliked his fellow man or loved man in general more than man in particular.[17] Rather, the specifically poetical problem Wordsworth faced was to show the compatibility between the growth of his individual imagination and its useful responsiveness to Human Life. It is one thing for a returning collegian to notice differences back home—babies grown, elders gone, some girls prettier, others plainer. He would be dull indeed not to see them. But when he attempts to generalize from this purely accidental "truth" to "human-heartedness" as a definite stage of his mental growth, he reflects that memory "cannot part / The shadow from the substance" (254–55) and admits that the general condition of Cambridge still holds him: "there was an inner falling-off" (270). As a boy, before going to college, he was "given up / To Nature and to Books" (281–82) but now has made "a poor exchange / For Books and Nature" (305–06): the dancing parties, trivial conversations, and exciting but aimless flirtations of a vacationing undergraduate vying with his old pals. If pursued too far, either in life or as narrative descriptions lacking a conclusive point, such activities would turn "Summer Vacation" into as big a waste as the university term itself. Therefore, "in chastisement of . . . regrets [for] / That vague heartless chace / Of trivial pleasures" (314, 304–05), Wordsworth places the Dawn Dedication and his encounter with the Discharged Veteran as the conclusion to Book IV, solving its structural crisis by showing his "Conformity as just as that of old / To the end and written spirit of God's works, / Whether held forth in Nature [the Dawn Dedication] or in Man [the Discharged Veteran]" (357–59).[18]

The dedication at dawn is to a life of the spirit; the encounter with the discharged veteran assures that this spiritual commitment will not turn away from social responsibility. Both passages follow the pattern of the "spots of time": unexpected revelation leading to revised interpretation of the mind's power. Returning home early one morning from the "promiscuous rout" and "unaim'd prattle" of a dance, Wordsworth sees a "magnificent" dawn, which he presents in careful painterly fashion, moving from background to foreground to integrate images of human life with nature's ordered hierarchies.[19]

> The Sea was laughing at a distance; all
> The solid Mountains were as bright as clouds,
> Grain-tinctured, drench'd in empyrean light;
> And, in the meadows and the lower grounds,
> Was all the sweetness of a common dawn,
> Dews, vapours, and the melody of birds,
> And Labourers going forth into the fields.   [333–39]

Although the dawn strikes Wordsworth more forcefully by contrast to the dance, the dance also prepares us for the dawn, its "gaiety and mirth" echoed in the "laughing" sea, its "glittering tapers" absorbed in the mountains' "empyrean light," the "din" of its instruments modulated in the "melody" of the birds.[20] The dawn contains, not rejects, the dance. Some critics see the laborers as more part of the natural cycle than the dancers,[21] but this is to out-Wordsworth Wordsworth. The dancers are having fun, the laborers are going to work, but Wordsworth is prim enough without our drawing an invidious distinction between them that he does not. The "chastisement" contained in this "memory of one particular hour" begins with the dance as necessary prelude to the dawn. In cultural perspective, the landscape alone seems most "Wordsworthian," but full interpretation of the 1805 *Prelude* as a "leading to" *The Recluse* requires that we understand the function of the dancers and the laborers framing the landscape description as part of Wordsworth's effort to blend his spiritual dedication with his growing "human-heartedness."

His encounter with the discharged veteran depends equally upon the force of contrast, between his attitude before the incident as qualified by his attitude afterward. As in the version of 1798, this unexpected meeting is preceded by a description of one of his nighttime rambles in search of feelings diametrically different from those associated with running into unhappy wretches in need of help: the piquant sense of solitude on a deserted public road. If critics have been too quick to see the image of Wordsworth dancing as an impropriety in need of correction, they have been equally hasty in accepting the image of him nightwalking as exactly what is to be expected of our nature poet. Wordsworth takes considerable pains to elaborate his state of mind before the encounter, mixing hints of weakness with notes of pleasant enjoyment: "receiving in my own despite / Amusement" (376–77), "an exhausted mind, worn out by toil, / And all unworthy of the deeper joy / Which waits on distant prospect" (381–83). His mental images "rose / As from some distant region of my soul / And came along like dreams" (393–95). Such pleasures are surely not all bad, any more than the pleasures of dancing, but like silly sociability this dreamy self-indulgence must, for the prospective author of *The Recluse,* be corrected in a larger dispensation. Into his pleasant reverie comes the waking nightmare of an extremely grotesque figure: "A man more meagre, as it seem'd to me, / Was never seen abroad by night or day" (408–09).[22] Gradually and fearfully approached, the soldier reports his life's experience with "stately indifference." The boy, for his part, may be peculiar in his taste for dark roadways, but he is no fool when it comes to social realities. He knows the village "hard by" will give them no comfort, so he takes the veteran to the forest cottage of a laborer who "will not murmur should we break his rest." The veteran, "with a reviving interest . . . thank'd me." The human interest of both parties has been revived; they have established a kind of community, in the exchange of blessing in their parting gestures.[23] The soldier is safely housed, but so is Wordsworth; abandoning his artificial ramble along the nighttime road, he goes where he belongs: "Then sought with quiet heart my distant home" (504).

Wordsworth is also home free compositionally, having overcome the threatened aimlessness of his "human-heartedness" by employing two extended images which balance Nature and Human Life with satisfying dramatic contrast.[24] Furthermore, each contains internally the tensions they balance against each other: the social dance and the naturally thought-provoking dawn, the purely aesthetic enjoyment of an empty road and the sturdy humanitarianism shown to suffering vagrants on it, by young poets equally vagrant.

Book V: "Books"

Even allowing him a thematic interruption of narrative sequence, Wordsworth says so few of the things we expect him to say about books that many readers despair at Book V. But Wordsworth's unusual view of books is not surprising in light of his dislike of normal, "bookish" conceptions of the writer's function. Within the democratic overtures of the preface to *Lyrical Ballads* lies an ideal of poetry requiring a conversion of readers' sense of the world. Poetry at this level is knowledge, and true reading or writing an epistemological act of the highest significance. Book V is thus "a poetic essay on education" (M. II.11) with a difference. Rather than celebrate the *contents* of books, the *process* of reading and writing weighs more heavily on his mind, causing Book V to move in reverse, from a rhetorical lament for the frailty of books (and poets), to a shrill attack on wrong-headed theories of education (of readers), through Wordsworth's own childhood reading, to a conclusion in which the internal dynamism of language transforms the apparent frailty of books and reading into a strength like Nature's.[25]

The shift from Book IV's Discharged Veteran to Book V's opening lament for the frailty of books is abrupt, but was even more so in the five-book plan, where they followed without interruption. This suggests that, for Wordsworth, the perishability of books and the real suffering of mankind had a transitive connection, parallel to the function of *The Prelude* as a "leading to" *The Recluse* which would confirm the wisdom of his decision to become a poet. A sudden shift from an image of suffering humanity to the recondite worries of poets about the fragility of their craft is characteristic of the binding polarities we have already seen in *The Recluse*'s development. The "residential" aspect of this theme is expressed in Wordsworth's conclusion to his opening lament:

> Oh! why hath not the mind
> Some element to stamp her image on
> In nature somewhat nearer to her own?
> Why, gifted with such powers to send abroad
> Her spirit, must it lodge in shrines so frail?   [44–48]

The power of the mind is not in question, but the strength of any medium or home in which it tries to find lodging. Wordsworth is not implying that the creative mind's launching itself "abroad" has the same importance as the discharged veteran's weak wanderings, but that, ideally, poetry needs a place as safe and sound as his young benefactor finds for him.

Wordsworth returns this dilemma to seminarrative form in the famous dream of the Arab-Quixote (49–165), whom he meets racing across
a desert to save Poetry and Mathematics (represented by a shell and a
stone) from apocalyptic destruction, "the fleet waters of the drowning
world." The power of this story should not lead us to forget the smiling
disclaimer with which Wordsworth introduces it, that worrying too much
about such things is "in plain truth . . . going far to seek disquietude."
Admitting that the emotions of poets are relatively special, when they hold
in their hands some "poor earthly casket of immortal verse," the more
comprehensive question raised by the dream of the Arab-Quixote is the
weakness of all education, all efforts of human civilization to stamp the
mind's image on nature. To take literally Wordsworth's fear for the destruction of books in a natural apocalypse is to undercut the dream's significance. Reversal and doubling are essential to the interpretation of
dreams, especially Wordsworth's dreams about his love of poetry and his
wish for it to do good in the world. The primary formal characteristic of
the dream is a sense of total separation and conflict between human consciousness and natural physical existence.[26] Critics who find this split
based in Wordsworth's psychology (his repressed resentment at his parents' early death) or in his politics (his anguish at the course of the French
Revolution) rightly sense its radically dialectical function.[27] The most
completely dialectical interpretation is Geoffrey Hartman's reading of the
sea as figuring Wordsworth's ambivalent fear/desire that Imagination
might triumph over Nature, or the world, destructively.[28] Though this
may seem too bold a reversal of the dream's terms, it is the best interpretation of the dream's power, if it is understood within the dream's immediate context—varieties of human suffering—and Wordsworth's immediately following attack upon misguided theories of education.

For the dream is preeminently a *vocation,* a story about the proper
choice of one's life's work. This is emphatically the point of the famous
dreams of Descartes from which Wordsworth derived it,[29] but is amply
clear in Wordsworth's own comment upon it: "Enow there are on earth to
take in charge / Their wives, their Children, and their virgin Loves . . . that
I, methinks, / Could share that Maniac's anxiousness, could go / Upon like
errand" (153–61). Simply put, Wordsworth's love for poetry is closely accompanied by a feeling of its frailty (its unproductiveness, its selfishness),
and this feeling, rebounding from his helpless love, results in a fantasy of
heroically saving it from apocalyptic destruction, which is nearly indistinguishable from fantasies of Imagination's vengeful triumph over the real
world. We saw in the earliest *Recluse* poems suggestions that Words-

worth's undoubted sympathy for poor suffering human beings could on occasion erupt as hatred for them. The theme of world-revenge for imagination is, moreover, exactly the stuff of the possible epic subjects he entertains in *The Prelude*'s "Introduction." It is not easy for art to be socially responsible, nor to prove that it is. By the end of Book V, Wordsworth will transpose this fantasy image to a quasi-philosophic argument that the linguistic power of literary art is a natural force, thus alleviating his fears of its uselessness by allying it with the power which, in the latent content of the dream, he imagines destroying it—or being destroyed by it.

Validating his decision to be a book-writer required of Wordsworth a demonstration of the social utility of books: that is, a defensible theory of education. As in Book V's opening movements, he presented his own theory antithetically. His only overt praise of books (166–222) is dominated by his sense of the obviousness of what he's saying, and he cannot discuss educational theory except by a long lambasting (223–388) of modern theories whose primary fault is their undervaluing of precisely his mode of learning and writing: *in*direction. Wordsworth satirizes educational theories which presume to press adult categories of useful knowledge directly into the memory of malleable children: the human mind seeking to "stamp her image" misguidedly. He concentrates on the monstrous product of such theories—"no Child, / But a dwarf Man" (294–95)—who emerges as one of several types of the Lost Son in *The Prelude*, foils to its "chosen Son." This prodigy holds the whole world in his head, but his "Ensigns of . . . Empire" (328) are alien because unnatural, and the workings of his mind are represented as those of a decaying, oppressive institution—a prison, not a residence, to say nothing of a home:

> His discourse moves slow,
> Massy and ponderous as a prison door,
> Tremendously emboss'd with terms of art;
> Rank growth of propositions overruns
> The Stripling's brain; the path in which he treads
> Is chok'd with grammars.   [320–25]

From the frailty of books, the argument has advanced to the frailty—the sheer wrong-headedness—of supposedly enlightened theories of public education.

Wordsworth seeks to destroy this falsely impressive institution by introducing the Boy of Winander, a disguised version of himself, who counters the Child Prodigy with illustrations of the value of surprise and indirection in any full theory of education—the unaccountable in man's dealing with nature which cannot be controlled, only given room to work. The boy is linked to nature by his "mimic hootings to the silent owls" across the lake, but his best education begins in those moments when the owls fail to respond:

> And when it chanced
> That pauses of deep silence mock'd his skill,
> Then sometimes, in that silence, while he hung
> Listening, a gentle shock of mild surprize
> Has carried far into his heart the voice
> Of mountain torrents; or the visible scene
> Would enter unawares into his mind
> With all its solemn imagery, its rocks,
> Its woods, and that uncertain Heaven, receiv'd
> Into the bosom of the steady Lake.   [404–13]

This mode of mental appropriation of reality is clearly contrary to the Infant Prodigy's,[30] and Wordsworth sanctifies it with a "full half-hour" of silent meditation over the boy's grave. That the boy should be represented as dead is odd but important, as are most of Wordsworth's many oddities. Such experiences with nature can only be William Wordsworth's, and the poet's graveside meditation on the dead form of his youthful imagination parallels his opening meditation on the apocalyptic destruction of the basic forms of human thought, with the same inherent ambivalence, that this death somehow represents a triumph for imagination. The fact that the boy is dead provides a species of generalization for his example, since the church which overlooks his grave, "forgetful of this boy," still sees "a race of real children" whose random, noisy movements between "books and nature" give Wordsworth the conclusion he demands of any educational theory: "Knowledge not purchas'd with the loss of power!" (449). Similarly, the Boy of Winander's "unaware" appropriation of the world is preceded and followed by Wordsworth's homage to books of fantasy and fairy tales, whose dominant characteristic, in contrast to the chokingly predictable "grammars" of the Infant Prodigy, is precisely that anything might happen in them.

But a big problem still faces the poet: to present an ideal of education that can confront at an appropriate level of seriousness the apocalyptic fancifulness of his dream of the Arab-Quixote. Book V has many indications of the difficulties he experienced with his argument ("My drift hath scarcely, / I fear, been obvious," 290–91), which may be schematized as a movement from fanciful statements about books and education to imaginatively serious ones:

Fancy	Fancy	Imagination	Imagination
The Dream of the Arab-Quixote	The Satiric Attack on the Infant Prodigy	The Boy of Winander and Wordsworth's Childhood Reading	"the great Nature that exists in works / Of mighty Poets"

His direct assertion that reading in "the Forest of Romance" prepared him for such untoward experiences as seeing the Drowned Man of Esthwaite bob "bolt upright . . . 'mid that beauteous scene . . . with his ghastly face" (470–72) is true and sincere but ungeneralizable because of its uniqueness. We don't read fairy tales to prepare for everyday life. Yet Wordsworth, whose sense of the magical in the ordinary was so profound as to seem ridiculous on occasion, bases his defense on mystery. To give point to his opening meditation and dream about the frailty of books he must connect the spirit of books with that "living Presence" of human rejuvenation which he believes would "still subsist / Victorious" (33–34) after any natural catastrophe. He does this by allying the mind's powers of mediation with man's bodily, im-mediate powers of action, following a route from the inarticulable truth of fiction to the reality of language considered as a natural phenomenon. Nowadays we might expect the argument to run in the other direction, but in either case a gap must be leaped.

As a poet, Wordsworth stakes his claim on the attractions of stories and story-telling, which, however useless, have in the present context the necessary staying power: "these, will live till man shall be no more" (529). They feed "dumb yearnings, hidden appetites" which we retain from childhood (530). He will not guess "what this tells of Being past, / Nor what it augurs of the life to come" (534–35), but avers that it supports us on the "isthmus which we cross / In progress from our native continent / To earth and human life" (560–62). This progress toward human life exactly parallels the advance of *The Prelude* toward *The Recluse*'s complicating third term. Mankind's general progress of accommodation to reality is matched in Wordsworth's experience by his progress in reading, until, at about age thirteen, he discovered "the charm / Of words in tuneful order, found them sweet / For *their own sakes*, a passion and a power" (577–79). Wordsworth does not use italics lightly; like the nine other instances in the 1805 *Prelude*,[31] this phrase points to a mind-turning revelation, which we may connect with the elemental truth of the Arab's shell, the grammar of poetry.

Wordsworth makes it still more important by linking it to the positive aspects of man's insatiable desire: "That wish for something loftier . . . /

Than is the common aspect . . . / Of human life" (599–601). The word *something* is characteristic of Wordsworth's language for imagination's action, its "something evermore about to be" from Book VI, its "obscure sense of . . . something to pursue" from Book II. And he drives home his point by adapting precisely that passage from Book II, thus following his rare but important italics with still rarer and still more important self-quotation, successfully concluding the argument of Book V by rhetorically attaching a quality of immortality to language via Nature, overcoming the book's initial nightmare of a second Deluge drowning "all the meditations of mankind" with a discovery of "the great Nature that exists in works / Of mighty Poets" (618–19). Placed side by side, the two passages seem to blur into each other.

Book II.324–32	Book V.619–26
[I]	
Have felt whate'er there is of *power* in *sound*	*Visionary Power*
To breathe an elevated mood, by *form*	Attends upon *the motion of the winds*
Or image unprofaned; and I would stand,	Embodied in *the mystery of words.*
Beneath some rock, listening to sounds that are)	There *darkness makes abode,* and all the host
The ghostly language of the ancient earth,	Of *shadowy things* do work their changes there,
Or *make their dim abode in distant winds.*	As in a mansion like *their proper home*;
Thence did I drink the *visionary power.*	Even *forms and substances* are circumfus'd
I deem not profitless those fleeting moods	By that transparent veil with light *divine.*
Of *shadowy exultation.* . . .	[Italics added]
[Italics added]	

In Book II, he heard natural sounds as language from which he drank visionary power. In Book V, language's visionary power is figured as a domesticated natural phenomenon ("abode," "proper home") which divinizes actual natural phenomena ("forms and substances"). In the first passage, Wordsworth uses language as a metaphor to describe his youthful experiences of nature. In the second, the general character of all language is described in metaphors whose vehicle is grounded in the tenor of the first passage, nearly two thousand lines previous. In both cases, the strategy is the same: confirming his appropriation of public, adult reality by allying it to inarticulate childhood experience. Natural winds (perhaps breath) and human words abide powerfully together in an indistinguishable darkness which is their "proper home." Their companionship refutes the now somewhat hysterical-seeming cry from Book V's opening lament: "Why must [the mind] lodge in shrines so frail?" Mind does not lodge in "poor earthly casket[s] of immortal Verse," but in language, and therefore in nature, and therefore in that "great Nature that exists in works / Of mighty Poets." The quasi-logical sequence resolves the paradoxical irony ("caskets/immortal") of the earlier line. In Book II, Wordsworth heard a pure, nonreferential language ("by form or image unprofaned"); in Book V, the referentiality of language is equally unprofane ("forms and substances are circumfus'd . . . with light divine"), and this claim is expanded for specifically poetic language:

> And through the turnings intricate of Verse,
> Present themselves as objects recognis'd,
> In flashes, and with a glory scarce their own.   [627–29]

If we ask whence that glory, or how we recognize "objects" in language, or whether the "flashes" are more splendid than they are distressingly brief, no specific answer will be forthcoming but will lie in that same powerful recognition scene to which Wordsworth's soul attained in Book II's "fleeting moods of shadowy exultation":

> Remembering how she felt, but what she felt
> Remembering not, retains an obscure sense
> Of possible sublimity, to which
> With growing faculties she doth aspire,
> With faculties still growing, feeling still
> That whatsoever point they gain, they still
> Have something to pursue.   [II.335–41]

Although both passages can be read transcendentally, it is hard to say finally whether they tend upward or downward, whether the glory of the object-world precedes or follows the sublimity of language, though "visionary power" is clearly anterior to both. However, unless we expect this preparatory poem of 1805 to provide definitive answers about the status of language and fictiveness relative to each other and to natural objects, we can say that Book V ends by meeting the terms it has set for itself, by finding an appropriate residence for Wordsworth's imagination in books and education—not as he finds them in the world, but as he has redefined them for his own purposes.

Book VI: "Cambridge and the Alps"

Though Book VI concludes the first of *The Prelude*'s main "residential" units, it simultaneously opens the next ones. Wordsworth's decision to go beyond an account of his formal education fundamentally altered the normative schemes of poetical autobiography he had used through the first five books, because his last college vacation was spent partly in France in the summer of 1790 during the celebrations of the first anniversary of the fall of the Bastille. By giving an account of the French Revolution, no matter how idiosyncratic, Wordsworth places his poem in history, yet the unique nature of those historical events, combined with the extreme nature of his imaginative reaction to them, precluded using them in a typological fashion, as for example Voltaire used the Lisbon earthquake of 1755. Like *Candide* and *Rasselas, The Prelude* through its first five and a half books uses the biographical mode partly to criticize various intellectual excesses of late-eighteenth-century Europe. But its advent into the Revolution, and its revelation of its author's imagination's deep implication in revolutionary ideals, makes it, from the viewpoint of a Voltaire or a Samuel Johnson, part of the problem rather than the solution. Instead, like Rousseau's *Emile,* it broaches the possibility of "human nature . . . born again," with the concomitant problem for old human nature of recognizing its new self aright, and the specific problem for Wordsworth of accommodating his understanding of his own mental growth to this new definition of humanity. Wrestling with these problems embroils Wordsworth in most of the rest of his poem, and his conclusion, that human nature is *not* being born again, leads him, like the best minds of his generation, to seek some other principle of human reformation to escape postrevolutionary cynicism and despair. He could not say of Revolution and Imagination what he had said of Books, that their importance is "already written in the hearts of all that breathe." By launching into the French Revolution, his poem accelerates from Books and Nature into History and Infinity, and becomes a far richer and more complicated work of art, nowhere more so than in its redoubled efforts to integrate Human Life into the fruitful transactions it records between the mind of its creator and external nature.

Cambridge Revisited

Despite Book VI's vast implications for the subsequent course of *The Prelude,* its first half is a summary conclusion of the poem's first residential sequence, relatively free of the structural crises which mark the preceding books in the unit. Wordsworth rounds off the meaning of his college career by giving both himself and Cambridge a better report than in Book

III, distancing them from each other: "I was detached . . . and wish'd to be a lodger in that house / Of Letters, and no more" (29, 32–33). He makes his point by constructing three ideal images that sum up his humanistic, scientific, and social profit from Cambridge: a lovely ash tree (90–109) beneath which he had visions "of human Forms and superhuman Powers" equaling all those that exist in "the hemisphere of magic fiction"; a tribute to geometry, the study of which (135–87) opened up for him, "with Indian awe and wonder," a sense of connections between "the frame / And laws of Nature . . . and paramount endowment in the mind"; and, most important, a redemption of the social aspect of his Cambridge years through an elaborate fantasy (246–331) of the steadying effect he might have had on Coleridge had they been together at Cambridge.

His imaginative vision beneath the ash tree and his homage to geometry not only idealize his literary ambitions and his respect for science, they also re-present the same two entities figured by the shell and the stone in Book V's dream of the Arab, suggestively affirming that Wordsworth has overcome that fanciful crisis in the waking, normal life of his ongoing poem. Yet, as in the dream, he is strikingly alone in both of these ideal moments. Except in the most general way, citing a quantity of "'good-natured lounging,'"[32] he does not say anything about his relations with his peers, his social life. This omission is not true biographically, for Wordsworth had good college friends and kept up relations with several of them all his life. The importance of the omission is thematic, for it requires of Wordsworth some plausible summation of the social benefits of college, parallel to what he has said of his literary and scientific growth.

He achieves this in the identifying hallmark of all conclusive moments of *The Recluse*, early or late: he turns to praise Coleridge, Dorothy, and Mary as his ideal image of human community. The appearance of some or all of these people anywhere in *The Recluse* (sometimes including John Wordsworth and Sara Hutchinson) invariably brings with it a feeling of conclusion. Though Wordsworth is in fact beginning a new stage of composition, probably having started Book VI with the lines to Coleridge in heartfelt dejection at his recent departure (M. II.12), these lines could well have served as an end to the poem, had he decided to let it stand as a five- or six-book work in the genre of poetical education. As a conclusion, they would have summarized the social aspect of Wordsworth's education by reference to people who were not at Cambridge with him. But what if Coleridge had been? The disproportionate extent (246–331) of Wordsworth's indulged fantasy about being at college with his friend is explicable as a function of his difficulty in coming to terms with the "Human

Life" dimension of residence at Cambridge. Without any condescension, Wordsworth simply speculates how much better it would have been for *Coleridge* had he had the benefits of Wordsworth's "maturer age" to calm his intellectual, theological, and political enthusiasm. This has a modicum of biographical plausibility, for whereas Wordsworth's university career was undistinguished, Coleridge's was disastrous. Nonetheless, it reflects the nature of their relations in 1804 more closely than what they might have been in 1789–91, especially when we remember that when they first met, Coleridge was the one with solid adult achievements, Wordsworth the aimless failure. But, even if we allow Wordsworth a solid personality and Coleridge a volatile one, the one context in which Wordsworth's Big Brother fantasy is not plausible is the context of the 1805 *Prelude* itself. It is hard to imagine the feckless, mind-wandering collegian of Book III calming anybody, as he swerves unsteadily between silly social engagements and lonely night walks that made him seem daft. But Wordsworth's fantasy has a rhetorical function more important than its lack of plot consistency: it presents a saving fiction of a unity of Mind and Nature which Coleridge and he might have established at Cambridge, with great advantage to easing their subsequent troubles in making their way in Human Life or society. Coleridge is described in the tropes of disembodied intellect he stimulated in everyone who knew him:

> Thy subtle speculations, toils abstruse
> Among the Schoolmen, and platonic forms
> Of wild ideal pageantry, shap'd out
> From things well-match'd, or ill, and words for things,
> The self-created sustenance of a mind
> Debarr'd from Nature's living images,
> Compell'd to be a life unto itself,   [308–14]

while Wordsworth appears as the very soul of organic Nature on a fine summer's day:

> . . . my maturer age,
> And temperature less willing to be mov'd,
> My calmer habits and more steady voice
> Would with an influence benign have sooth'd
> Or chas'd away the airy wretchedness
> That batten'd on thy youth.   [321–26]

Combined, these mental forms and natural strengths were to produce *The Recluse*; but they hadn't, certainly not in 1791, only fitfully since 1797, and now again unlikely to do so in 1804 because of Coleridge's absence.

Still, with this conflation of what they might have done, set against their knowledge of what they actually had done, Wordsworth is able to leave his account of Cambridge with the suggestion of an ideal student, one Wordsridge or Coleworth, who might have done more with what was provided there.

If they had met then, things would be different now, but he wandered, Coleridge wandered, and now his poem wanders too, as it might not if they had met earlier, or if Coleridge had not left him alone again: "Far art Thou wander'd now in search of health" (249). This present fact stimulates past reflection: "I, too, have been a Wanderer!" (261). And, following his fantasy of their combined personalities, Wordsworth recalls, "A passing word erewhile did lightly touch / On wanderings of my own; and now to these / My Poem leads me with an easier mind" (332–34). These verbal connections are not accidental; at the end of his long account of his 1790 walking tour, he again intertwines self-wandering and poem-wandering: "But here I must break off, and quit at once, / Though loth, the record of these wanderings, / A theme which may seduce me else beyond / All reasonable bounds" (658–61). The truth of this applies to much more than the mere length of the poem. For, having wandered off to France from an imaginary moment when he and Coleridge were one and the same person, he has wandered into the critical complications of his imagination's allegiance to revolutionary ideals, and his unseemly haste to drop their thematic ramifications indicates that it is already too late. By the end of Book VI, the poem on the growth of his mind has already entered the era in which his imagination was indeed seduced "beyond all reasonable bounds," suffering the damage from which he was just beginning to recover when he met Coleridge, and for which Coleridge proposed *The Recluse* as a generation-wide remedy.

Wordsworth Abroad

In his twenties, Wordsworth loved wandering more than anything else, even poetry. His 1790 walking tour had been "an open slight to college cares and study," but in the economy of imagination his investment of that summer paid dividends for the rest of his life. Reverential references to it abound in his and his sister's correspondence, and their tour in 1820 over the same ground was conducted like a pilgrimage to a holy land.[33] His account of the tour in the second half of Book VI divides into three geographical sections, France, Switzerland, and Italy. In the middle of the middle of these, describing his accidental crossing of the Alps in the Simplon Pass, he breaks out in the very moment of composition into a

paean of praise to Imagination which takes him into a fourth region beyond geography: Infinity, or The Sublime. The obvious importance of
these lines has tended to make them dominate interpretations not only of
Book VI but of all The Prelude and of much of Wordsworth's total oeuvre,
especially since Geoffrey Hartman's landmark study of 1964, though the
philosophic centrality of this passage was first recognized with modern
critical insight by A. C. Bradley in his Glasgow lectures of the 1890s.[34]
Hartman's interpretation is a culmination of a line of Wordsworth criticism which has rescued the poet from the easy misunderstanding that, as a
"nature poet," he is a sort of hedge- or mountain-moralist. But criticism
proceeds dialectically. As the Bradley-Hartman line of Idealist interpretation has rescued the poet's words from a pervasive cultural confusion with
their natural referents, so more recent interpretations have tried to incorporate the radical implications of this view (i.e., that Wordsworth's consciousness of his imagination must separate him from nature) back into the
texture of the verse. Such interpretations share with Wordsworth the task
of integrating Imagination not only with the body of Nature but also with
the body of his poem; in the sequence of Recluse poems, this implies his
necessary accommodation of poetic inspiration to ordinary forms of human life.

A good example of such revisionism is Mark Reed's identification of a
pattern of expectation-confusion-clarification in Wordsworth's account of
the Alpine tour.[35] All three sections are marked by initially positive movements of high enthusiasm and rapid progress, followed by slow, confused
movements of disappointment and loss, resulting in an attempted resolution or synthesis. (The second and third of these movements are delayed in
the France passage until Books IX–X—which, however, follow immediately in compositional sequence—becoming the rationale for most of the
rest of the poem.) In all three, practical traveling questions of where to go
and where to stay are interwoven with a heightened poetic significance:
whither does Imagination lead and where does it dwell? In each section
Wordsworth makes specific reference to the immaturity of his aesthetic responses in 1790, compared with his present understanding of what he saw
and felt then. From a poseur of fashionable late-eighteenth-century melancholy, he has grown into a mature poet whose "tones of learned Art and
Nature mix'd / May frame enduring language" (604–05). Finally, all three
sections of the tour present idealized images of human activity in fruitful
cooperation with scenes of perfect natural beauty. These idealizations are,
however, equally affected by the overall movement from thesis to antithesis to synthesis; neither the people nor the places are always adequate to

his imagination—and vice versa. Although Wordsworth says he went mainly for the scenery ("Nature then was sovereign in my heart," 346), he admits that the times promised added attractions ("France standing on the top of golden hours, / And human nature seeming born again," 353–54), and the primary significance of all three scenes of the tour derives from his interweaving of these two emphases.

Sheer chance landed Wordsworth and Robert Jones in Calais on the evening of July 13, 1790, to awake next morning to France celebrating its first anniversary of liberty; but Wordsworth makes the most of it. In less than a hundred lines (355–425), he achieves one of European literature's marvelous representations of the ecstasy which greeted the bourgeois phase of the French Revolution. He extends the Bastille Day celebrations as a metaphor for his entire trip across France, so that the whole journey seems like a march of triumph or revolutionary waltz in double time. Every topographical detail joins in the great parade, from the typically French "Elms . . . in files . . . on the stately roads" (371–72) to the most generalized landscape: "Enchanting show / Those woods, and farms, and orchards did present . . . / Reach after reach, procession without end / Of deep and stately Vales" (387–91). He particularly singles out his memory of eating and dancing out of doors at night. These moments, splendid to any tourist, were especially so to Wordsworth, for he presents them as a disruption of normal orders of human activity into a higher synthesis. Consider the importance of his placement of the opening word in these lines:

> Unhous'd, beneath the Evening Star we saw
> Dances of Liberty, and, in late hours
> Of darkness, dances in the open air.   [380–82]

The conjunctive clause adds nothing, only apposition; the dances simply went on and on, but the redundant inside-out motion (from "unhous'd" to "open air") makes them seem to belong outside, blessed first by the star and then by the air itself. Indeed, Wordsworth seems to have spent the whole time outdoors; human life in general had moved outside, at large, into a more primitive relation to nature. This archaic feeling persists in Wordsworth's seemingly facetious simile for their reception: "Guests welcome almost as the Angels were / To Abraham of old" (403–04). Yet his extravagance is borne out at each level of interpretation. They were received like angels because they "bore a name / Honour'd in France, the name of Englishmen" (409–10). Besides carrying the reputation of British

liberty, the comparison between *les anglais* and *les anges* would occur easily to this literary descendant of the Angles, who would return to revolutionary France the following year on the thin pretext of seeking to improve
his French. Thematically, their being welcomed as angels resonates with
one of the most domestic holy scenes in the Bible, Abraham hurrying to
offer refreshment to three strange men who appeared outside his tent in
the heat of the day. These angels came to tell him that Sarah would bear a
son, and "Abraham shall become a great and mighty nation" (Genesis 18).
Wordsworth feels a similar birth of nationhood in France, and his egotistical imagination describes his reception as similar to that of God's angels
announcing a chosen son who shall make it come true. Finally, the hyperbolic simile is biographically plausible, as Wordsworth experiences every
young traveler's gratification at being received abroad with more importance than he ever had been at home. In England, he was a cause of
growing concern to his family: what was William going to do with his life?
In France, he didn't have to do anything; it was enough to be—an Englishman. The sense of spiritual significance bestowed by his place of birth
reverberated deeply in Wordsworth's response to these scenes of revolutionary joy. "Human nature seeming born again," and welcoming *him*.
His sense of great possibilities is submerged in his slighting reference to his
youthful imagination: " 'Twas sweet at such a time, with such delights /
On every side, in prime of youthful strength, / To feed a Poet's tender melancholy" (375–77). In 1790, the sweetness arose from bizarre contrast between his weak imagination and those mighty events; yet "youthful
strength" conveys a sense of latency, and its reference floats ambiguously
between his powers and those of revolutionary France, suggesting that
they may partake of each other.

A similarly unsteady relation between imagination and place divides
Wordsworth's account of his walk through Switzerland, between the actual country and a country of the mind, The Sublime. In Switzerland
proper (426–86), he and Jones continue their extremely rapid progress
("fast as clouds are chang'd in Heaven") across a landscape that appears,
like reborn France, as the perfection of man's cooperation with nature,
where human communities grow like natural organisms: "naked huts,
wood-built, and sown like tents / Or Indian cabins over the fresh lawns"
(450–51). Their disappointment with Mont Blanc might have warned
them they were investing too much hope in sheer landscape, but the Vale
of Chamounix seemed to "reconcile [them] to realities" (461). These "realities" are presented as yet a further integration of Man and Nature (owing

to the proximity of the glacier to human habitations) in a community of typological equals:

> The Eagle soareth in the element;
> There doth the Reaper bind the yellow sheaf,
> The Maiden spread the haycock in the sun,
> While Winter like a tamed Lion walks
> Descending from the mountains to make sport
> Among the cottages by beds of flowers.   [463–68]

Wordsworth is in too "unripe state / Of intellect and heart" (470–71) to sense that these ideal combinations are too good to be true. He emphasizes his aesthetic attitudinizing ("Dejection taken up for pleasure's sake") as the sign of his immaturity, stressing, as in the French section, its grotesque contrast with its objects: "the willow wreath, / Even among those solitudes sublime, / . . . Did sweeten many a meditative hour" (VI.483–84, 487).

To contrast these indulgences of Fancy, the Simplon crossing (488–580) introduces the "deep and genuine sadness" of the deeper strata of Imagination. But it is crossed, in turn, by a vision of Imagination cut off from any natural hierarchy.[36] In marked contrast to his earlier representations of their fantastic rate of progress, Wordsworth's description of their unwitting ascent is slow and difficult, with an almost microscopic attention to detail (501–11). Their conversation with a peasant perpetuates the confusion on a linguistic level; their imaginations' unwillingness to accept his information contributes as much to the misunderstanding as their difficulty in speaking his language. Both physical and linguistic strains lead to the same unlooked-for result: *that we had cross'd the Alps* (524).

Here Wordsworth placed the apostrophe to Imagination as a present-tense interruption of his narration.[37] Like the narrative ascent, it too moves slowly and confusedly at first, but accelerates surely in meter, metaphor, and theme until it outstrips even the amazing speed of his physical journey and launches him into infinity. Imagination rises "like an unfather'd vapour" to blur the "eye and progress of my Song," but the eye, abandoning its conscious quest for poetical sensations,[38] then clears and recognizes the new soul-region around it in a peculiarly impacted self-reflection: "to my Soul I say / I recognise thy glory" (531–32). Overcoming the bodily eye is the way toward seeing what else is around him: "when the light of sense / Goes out in flashes that have shewn to us / The invisible world" (534–36). Careful commentators have noted the potentially general nature of this process ("to us"),[39] which seems to counter radically idealistic interpretations like Hartman's. However, any human relation established between finite and infinite is logically nil, and to say that the former "leads to" the latter is like trying to answer childish questions about the biggest number in the world, or how high is up. There must be a gap, which Wordsworth stresses by representing the *process* as a *place* that is not Alpine but domestic. In such "visitings," such "usurpation," such goings-out,

> . . . doth Greatness make *abode*.
> There *harbours* whether we be young or old.
> Our destiny, our nature, and our *home*
> Is with infinitude, and only there   [536–39; italics added][40]

The exclusivity is surprising, but not the development of the metaphor which seeks to make it general: "The mind beneath such banners militant / Thinks not of spoils or trophies" (543–44). Wordsworth's suggestion that the mind in full power marches like a splendid archaic autocracy or oriental despotism is repeated (despite his republican sympathies) many times in *The Prelude,* as in the "more than Indian awe" he felt for the laws of mathematics (IV.142), the "promise scarce earthly" of *The Arabian Nights* (V.491), or his credulity of "golden Cities ten months' journey deep / Among Tartarian wilds" (VII.87–88) in thinking about London.

He returns from this heavenly empire to his poem gradually. Having glimpsed Imagination's "abode" in infinity, his disappointment at having missed the whole point of his trip—namely, sublime *scenery,* which now seems oxymoronic—is "soon *dis*lodg'd" (551; italics added) as he and Jones experience the natural sublimity they had hoped for, in the Ravine of Gondo. The more usual Wordsworthian economy of vision reestablishes a proper relation between mind and nature: false expectation, disappointed, is recompensed by vision in surplus. Expressive of the new relation, "the brook and road were fellow-travellers," gradually returning the two human fellow travelers to the trip they wanted. Gondo compensates for Simplon as Chamounix compensated for Mont Blanc, but in a sterner mood, with elements of terror, that nonetheless reconcile opposites in a progression that leads back to what might be called *usable* infinitude. Woods, waterfalls, and rocks

> Were all like workings of one mind, the features
> Of the same face, blossoms upon one tree,
> Characters of the great Apocalypse,
> The types and symbols of Eternity,
> Of first and last, and midst, and without end.   [568–72]

Mental infinity, the sense of "something evermore about to be," has been read back into the face of God or book of Nature, the visible world seen in its invisible aspect as Wordsworth's mind subsides from its "flashes" of alienating visionary insight.

Yet Wordsworth is not apotheosized; he travels on. The odd coda to the entire Simplon-Gondo experience, their lodging for the night in an Alpine "Inn or Hospital" (573–80), implies that, in addition to vision and its natural complements, there is also ordinary life, not very well suited to either. How easy it would have been for him to excise these lines if they had been irrelevant travel detail:

> A dreary Mansion, large beyond all need,
> With high and spacious rooms, deafen'd and stunn'd
> By noise of waters, making innocent Sleep
> Lie melancholy among weary bones.　　　　　　　　[577–80]

This house is unsuited to both the infinity of Wordsworth's mind and the finitude of his body; "Apocalypse is not habitable."[41] The apocalyptic voices of the Ravine of Gondo are here distorted by preposterous human dimensions, and the splendid imperial abode of Imagination assumes the aspect of a charnel house, as bodily needs are not met: "making innocent Sleep / Lie melancholy among weary bones." The first disappointment was crossing the Alps unaware; the last is having glimpsed eternity but continuing to live on earth. The accommodation of Imagination is a constant struggle, for rarely are the residences of Human Life suited to it. The Simplon crossing is qualified, not undercut, by the "Alpine House" coda. But when Wordsworth and Dorothy returned to these scenes in their pilgrimage of 1820, he, besides having trouble finding where he had lost his way before, refused to enter this house.[42]

Wordsworth represents the same ordering of experience in his tour of the Italian lakes (581–657): pleasing generality followed by specific disappointment and the need for subsequent reinterpretation. Nature now tutors him with The Beautiful, not The Sublime, but again the force of her lesson depends on contrast. Initially, Italy appears like a picture postcard of Nature's splendors ("Como, thou, a treasure by the earth / Kept to itself, a darling bosom'd up / In Abyssinian privacy," 590–92), wonderfully intertwined with human society: "pathways roof'd with vines / Winding from house to house, from town to town, / Sole link that binds them to each other" (595–97). Such links seem fragile as well as beautiful, and a certain amount of suspicion attaches to any darling kept so private, but these hints do not interrupt Wordsworth's regular touring pace ("motion without pause") until, as in France and Switzerland, he broaches the topic of differences between his "undisciplin'd" sensibility of 1790 and his "learned . . . tones" of 1804 (600, 604). Until, that is, he essays an imaginative interpretation. He elevates the moral benefits of natural beauty as high as possible ("whose power is sweet . . . almost might I dare to say, / As virtue is, or goodness . . . Or gentlest visitations of pure thought / When God . . . is thank'd / Religiously," 609–15), but an experience of "sterner character" falls athwart this extreme generalization, just as "something of stern mood" crossed his "gilded" poetical fantasies in Switzerland.

Outside the town of Gravedona, he records an experience as confused and labored as the Simplon crossing. Unused to the Italian system of clock chimes, they arise at 1:45 A.M. rather than 4:00 A.M., and are soon foiled in their dogged English tourists' quest for scenic effects. They had hoped to "behold the scene / In its most deep repose" (628–29), but instead they endure a waking nightmare worthy of "The Rime of the Ancient Mariner": "the sullen water underneath, / On which a dull red image of the moon, / Lay bedded, changing oftentimes its form / Like an uneasy snake" (635–38). They are betrayed not only by social misinterpretation (the Italian clocks) but also by Nature herself. Thinking they could follow "the Water's edge / As hitherto, and with as plain a track / To be our guide" (626–28), they are instead "lost, bewilder'd," as in their very similar failure to understand that the brook and road were "fellow-travellers" in the Simplon Pass. As with the incident of the Alpine spital, we must ask why Wordsworth included this one. Like the clocks that keep chiming throughout it, it is "unintelligible" yet somehow admonitory to Wordsworth's pat assignment of virtuous meaning to the beautiful landscape. There is no imaginative compensation, as for Mont Blanc or Simplon. Instead, this experience seems to parody the earlier ones. In the nighttime insects' "noise like that of noon," there is no reconciliation like Gondo's "darkness and the light." The joyous eating and drinking out of doors, "unhous'd," in France is now changed for a continuation of the discomforts of Saint John's Spital.

> On the rock we lay
> And wished to sleep but could not, for the stings
> Of insects, which with *noise like that of noon*
> Fill'd all the woods; *the cry of unknown birds,*
> The mountains, *more by darkness visible*
> And their own size, *than any outward light,*

> *The breathless wilderness* of clouds, the clock
> That told with *unintelligible voice*
> *The widely-parted hours, the noise of streams*
> And sometimes rustling motions nigh at hand
> Which did not leave us free from personal fear,
> And lastly *the withdrawing Moon*, that set
> Before us, *while she was still high in heaven*
>
> [641–53; italics added]

The accumulation of cadences and the juxtaposition of opposites almost lead one to expect to hear next, "Were all like workings of one mind. . . ." But not so; no mind is at work in the scene except Wordsworth's, and he has taken pains to intensify the experience's meaninglessness. Emotional affect appears as physical distortion ("the widely-parted hours" are no further apart than ever), and physical fact as optical illusion (the moon sets on "high" because it goes behind the mountains, no surprise to an English Laker). Instead of eternity, there is only stark, unsatisfying contrast: "these were our food" (654) on a night on Lake Como, which only two days before had been that "same delicious Lake" (657).

Throughout his walking tour, Wordsworth reveals himself to have been confused in his relation to Nature by interventions of human life: the Italian clocks, like the Swiss muleteers and the dancing French republicans, have misled him. His misinterpretations of signs, which he emphasizes by referring to the immaturity of his imagination in each episode, can be interpreted as a chastisement of his lust for controlled excitement,[43] represented by his apparent failure to sleep anywhere. Dancing at night in France, lying awake in the Alpine spital or outside Gravedona, he finds no place in which to recollect his emotions in tranquility. The final disappointment is yet to come, as the full meaning of those French *carmagnoles* winds out through most of the rest of *The Prelude*. When he says he "must break off" his account of his wanderings lest they "seduce [him] beyond all reasonable bounds" (660–61), he acknowledges what has already happened, randomly and uniquely, in each episode, but will soon recur (immediately, in composition) with terrifyingly massive consistency: the seduction of his imagination by the wizardry of revolutionary ideologies.

But he concludes Book VI satisfactorily (658–705) by making a fundamental readjustment of his epic triad of Man, Nature, and Human Life. Though he began his tour in allegiance to Nature, "then . . . sovereign in my heart" (346), he ends by rebelliously insisting he was no "mean pensioner / On outward forms" (667–68). Instead, he says that he worships

Nature only as the sensations it gives flow "into a kindred stream" of moral emotions associated with the Sublime ("grandeur") and the Beautiful ("tenderness"). This is so important that he implies it could be the title of his poem: "On the front / Of this whole Song is written" (669–70). Yet the confluence of these two streams is "circuitous," and becomes more so when he makes his farewell to the public scenes he has witnessed, of "human nature seeming born again." He stresses the limitations of his powers of political analysis ("A Stripling, scarcely of the household then / Of social life," 693–94) because he knows, at age thirty-four, what every mature reader of the poem will know, that the heady optimism which was then "the common language of all eyes" soon degenerated into Babel. But determined to end the book positively, he makes a virtue of his inexperience—"I needed not that joy" (700)—and reasserts the self-sufficiency of insights into infinity ("the ever-living Universe," 701) which have provided Book VI's peak experiences. Though this lends assurance "as constant as the grass upon the fields" (705) with which to end the book, it lays a covert but enormous weight upon his mind that will soon break down as he continues to explore his imagination's involvement with revolution. For, if the ecstasies of human life (however misguided) are not necessary to him, or are desperately naturalized into "a Blackbird's whistle in a vernal grove" (for "the fife of War" stirring the Swiss and Belgians to follow the French example), and if Nature's "outward forms" are reverenced only as they feed the "kindred stream" of Mind, then his experiences in the Alps carry meaning only as they are addressed to, are proper to, his mind. This would be the apocalyptic self-sufficiency of Imagination which Hartman discerns in Wordsworth: Nature and Human Life are radically subordinated to it. But this is an inequality of powers which will require fundamental readjustment as *The Prelude* continues, if it is to lead to a proper balance between the three estates of *The Recluse*.

THE SECOND RESIDENCE: CIVILIZATION

Wordsworth wrote almost all of Books VII and VIII after Books IX and X, but placed them earlier in his final arrangement.[44] Putting London before Paris was a good idea, for though he resided there for only four months after leaving Cambridge—which he stretches to "a year thus spent" (IX.31) to give it proportional plausibility—this order allows his poem to move with greater inevitability from the university's "midway residence" into thematic consideration of the capital city as apex of the nation's life and representative peak of human civilization before broaching the possibility of revolutionary change in human nature and Human Life. Nevertheless, Wordsworth's organizational strategy nearly backfires, because the city is both far better and far worse than he had imagined. The onward structure of *The Prelude* is again determined by the discrepancy between his expectations and reality, and the interpretation he places on the difference. On the one hand, London's wonderful spectacles threaten to detach his eyes from his imagination and make him a mere observer of the passing parade. Yet as the pinnacle of British civilization the city shocks him with sights of human degradation that sharply contrast with its tempting splendors. Wordsworth tries in Book VII to reconcile these opposing pressures but fails; in order to proceed, he allows the city to destroy itself (Bartholomew Fair), freeing him to approach it more comprehensively in Book VIII.

Book VII: "Residence in London"

The seventh book opens expansively upon urban pleasures, gradually narrows to a complex core of mixed feelings surrounding the story of Mary of Buttermere, then expands outward again in increasingly vehement criticism of London that finally explodes in the hellish image of Bartholomew Fair. Since the second part of the book was composed separately from the first, its negative views are the likely result of Wordsworth's making up his mind about the bearing of the lines he composed first[45]— largely, it would seem, as he came to feel that Book VIII's argument ("Love of Nature leading to Love of Mankind") was inadequate to follow (as it did in the order of composition) the revolutionary crises recorded in the first half of Book X. At the center of VII's transitional core, where enjoyment turns to criticism, is a powerfully obscure figure of imaginative death, as Wordsworth moves by free association from Mary of Buttermere, to her hypothetical dead son, to a prostitute's lovely child seen amidst the city's squalor, to an imaginary confrontation between them at Mary's son's Lake Country grave, in which we cannot but feel that the only real person present is William Wordsworth, contemplating two versions of London's effect upon his imagination: death by antagonistic destruction or by seductive corruption.

In the first third of Book VII, Wordsworth indulges himself in the city's distractions, and his indulgence very much includes the pleasure of reliving that time by writing about it: "Shall I give way, / Copying the impressions of the memory . . . idly . . . as the mood / Inclines me, here describe, for pastime's sake / Some portion of that motley imagery, / A vivid pleasure of my Youth" (145–51). Some grouchy critics, accepting Wordsworth too much at his doctrinal word, have devalued Book VII in Nature's currency. But this is not the case with fresh first readers, such as college students of approximately Wordsworth's age at the time. All these twenty-year-olds are ready and eager to get to the big city and savor its delights, footloose and fancy-free: "to have a house / It was enough (what matter for a home?)" (76–77). They are also ready to read Book VII as uncritically as Wordsworth started out reading London, and are equally confused by the sense of imaginative danger that grows upon him. One has to be very somber not to be caught up in Wordsworth's rapid catalogues of city sights, moving so quickly back and forth between stage shows and street scenes that we, like him, begin to lose the distinction between them and are no more prepared than he to see any danger in the fun of a man's being rendered invisible simply by having "the word / INVISIBLE flame . . . forth upon his chest" (309). The possibility that anonymous urban pleasures turn all too easily into the alienation of Invisible Man surfaces only later, when Wordsworth sees in a blind beggar's life story, written "upon his Chest . . . a type, / Or emblem, of the utmost that we know, / Both of ourselves and of the universe" (612, 617–19). Although Wordsworth's London is partly indebted to Johnson's and Dryden's and the Juvenalian model behind them, he is not satirizing the city at the outset, and his joy at sheer description falters only when he begins to seek some standard of value to give it point. Book VII describes "Human Life" on a broader scale than "Residence at Cambridge," but here, as there, Wordsworth's standard is individual integrity, and when he finds this standard violated, as in the story of Mary of Buttermere, he is forced to turn to more judgmental perspectives upon London.

Amid his description of other stage shows, Wordsworth includes the dramatized version of the story of Mary Robinson of Buttermere, seduced and abandoned by a heartless adventurer.[46] That Wordsworth should be disturbed by the city's jaded taste for making entertainment out of rural tragedy is not surprising. What is surprising is that he himself lays down this difficulty in the path of his poem's progress. He could not have seen *The Beauty of Buttermere* in any of his London stays in the 1790s because it was not produced until 1803. Indeed, he may never have seen it; he inserts it as an urban item that happened to be in his mind at the time he was composing Book VII. Yet this casual anachronism leads to much more problematical developments.[47] The first peculiarity of Wordsworth's account of Mary of Buttermere is his deeply empathetic attraction to her, almost to the point of identification. (He dismisses the play itself in a half dozen lines.) As with Margaret, Wordsworth attaches himself to Mary like

a sister, for they shared a common mother, the River Cocker, which ran
from his home in Cockermouth to hers on Buttermere: "For we were
nursed, as almost might be said, / On the same mountains" (341–42). He
is evidently plumbing below the depths of casual acquaintance: "these last
words utter'd," Mary's image rises up to impede him "in that way which I
must tread," his argument. The "daring Brotherhood" of hack playwrights
have sinned in making a melodrama of Mary's tragedy, "too holy theme
for such a place" (316–17). Like the interruption of Imagination in Book
VI, this discrepancy between place and meaning involves Wordsworth in a
thematic crisis, forcing him to come to grips with the sickly imaginative
uses to which the city's insatiable demand for distraction puts real, common, everyday catastrophes. How should the poet of Human Life make
something different of Mary's suffering from what his nation's capital
makes of it?

Wordsworth begins his answer by shifting his view from Mary as a
sister to her as a mother, even, by obscure suggestions, as something like
his own mother.[48] He imagines Mary and "her new-born Infant . . .
sleep[ing] in earth . . . in quietness, without anxiety . . . beneath [a] little
rock-like Pile" (353–57). This tableau restores morality at a high price,
for the scene is more sentimental than even the "daring Brotherhood"
would try to get away with. But Wordsworth, ever one of the most un-
earthly poets in the language, pushes on from this cold immortality to still
stranger modes of being, imagining a prostitute's bastard son looking
"With envy on thy nameless Babe that sleeps / . . . undisturb'd!" (410–11).
Better dead than ruined. Yet even this queer scene is more plausible, in the
literature of moral platitude, than Wordsworth's long preparation for it,
deeply meditating the spiritual significance of the prostitute's "lovely
Boy": "A sort of Alien scatter'd from the clouds / . . . / Among the wretched
and the falsely gay, / Like one of those who walk'd with hair unsinged /
Amid the fiery furnace" (377, 396–98). Although the literal incarnation of
urban evil, the boy is represented as radically, grotesquely preserved from
all the complications of maturation that have begun to cause his author
difficulty:

> He hath since
> Appear'd to me oft–times as if embalm'd
> By Nature; through some special privilege,
> Stopp'd at the growth he had; destined to live,
> To be, to have been, come and go, a Child
> And nothing more, no partner in the years
> That bear us forward to distress and guilt,

> Pain and abasement, beauty in such excess
> Adorn'd him in that miserable place.   [398–406]

This child's "special privilege" of eternal youthful beauty is very like his poet's pride of childlike perceptual power, and we may well believe Wordsworth's testimony: "So have I though of him a thousand times, / And seldom otherwise" (407–08; italics added). When he places him, in conclusion, at the grave of Mary's "nameless Child," we feel, as in the very similar account of the Boy of Winander, that one aspect of Wordsworth is paying homage to another, deeply envying something lost in London.

He has been trying to rectify the "daring Brotherhood's" profane treatment of Mary with his own brand of sublimity, but the very private bearing of these memorial tableaux of Lost Sons has taken Wordsworth far afield. He tries to return his argument to general applicability by citing the profound effect produced upon him when he first heard "The voice of Woman utter blasphemy" (417). Even making allowances for the inaptness of this to Mary's story, Wordsworth's expression of it remains difficult to credit:

> a barrier seem'd at once
> Thrown in, that from humanity divorced
> The human Form, splitting the race of Man
> In twain, yet leaving the same outward shape.   [423–26]

This is apocalyptic language, of the sort he will apply to the French Revolution ("The Man to come parted as by a gulph, / From him who had been," XI.59–60). It makes the distinction between abstract Human Life and real human beings surreally diagrammatic. And because so much is predicated upon so little, it leaves him precisely nowhere in his efforts to reach a general statement about the life of mankind in the cities of high civilization. He allows that he gradually got used to "such spectacles," but, "in truth / The sorrow of the passion stopp'd me here" (433–34), and "here" seems to be right at that word on the page. Defeated in his efforts to find a meaning for the life of imagination in cities, he abandons all pretense of poetic unity: "I quit this painful theme" (435).

Compulsion motivates the poem's attempts to depart from this point of unresolved crisis. True, "enough is said / To shew what thoughts must often have been mine / At theatres, which then were my delight" (435–37). But too much has been said for us to accept any very orderly connection between his "thoughts" and his "delight": they have unraveled in his oddly self-implicating account of *The Beauty of Buttermere*. Wordsworth resumes cataloguing "living Figures on the Stage" (444), but his enjoyment is expressed in dangerous imagery for *The Prelude*: "the mind / Turn'd this way, that way!" (469–70). He is trying to move back responsibly to the real world, but the trope of all-the-world's-a-stage suits him less well than all-the-stage-is-a-world, and he displays with perfect clarity the regressive pleasures of sheer irresponsible spectatorship in an image of sitting in "a Country-Playhouse," cozily heightening his enjoyment of the security of fiction by contrasting it with outer reality: "having caught, / In summer, through the fractur'd wall, a glimpse / Of daylight, at the thought of where I was / I gladden'd more than if I had beheld / Before me some bright Cavern of Romance" (481–85). A preference for artifice seems natural in an account of a poet's mind, but Wordsworth is trying to make his poetry come to grips with reality and is unequal to the task. He feels "the imaginative Power / Languish within" him as he thinks of the "more lofty Themes" he should be dealing with (498–99, 495), and even his usual saving proviso, that this residential crisis was not so bad after all, admits, in its striking figure—"yet all this / Pass'd not beyond the suburbs of my mind" (505–06)—his failure to find a capital home in the real city, to establish there that "metropolitan Temple in the heart of mighty Poets" of which the "Prospectus" boasted.

In self-defense, he raises the possibility, as in Cambridge, that the residence was inadequate to his mind. The remainder of Book VII becomes increasingly satirical at London's expense. The standard for his satire is mainly the violence done to language by prating orators (516–42) and mincing preachers (543–65), the fops of State and Church. Again, this seems natural for a poet, but Wordsworth is not a purist for language's sake. Rather, the inability of language to convey deep human reality (in the city) overwhelms him, like the frailty of books in V. His sight of a blind beggar with his life story on his placard is the prime "type" or "emblem" of the crippling challenge London delivers to Wordsworth's imagination: "on the shape of the unmoving man, / His fixèd face and sightless eyes, I look'd / As if admonish'd from another world" (620–22). Quite unlike his mind's earlier giddy turning, "this way, that way" (470), this admonishment comes from a world where, presumably, language is full of, and identical with, life itself. Despite his superficial similarity to other Wordsworthian solitaries, the Blind Beggar is not a positive image; his sightless eyes and "written paper" on his chest represent the extreme frailty of correspondences between Language and Human Life. But he is a very powerful image as an interpretive device, and provides Wordsworth a way to conclude Book VII. The beggar is Wordsworth's main effort to em-

body the "one feeling . . . which belong'd / To this great City, by exclusive
right . . . [that] the face of every one / That passes by me is a mystery"
(592–93, 596–97). Yet even this image is, he admits, "chiefly [one of]
such structures as the mind / Builds for itself" (624–25). When he looks
for actual correlative evidence, "full-form'd" and given by the city itself,
he describes only nighttime streets in winter, "When the great tide of human life stands still" (630). We recognize this as Wordsworth's usual way
of dealing with the city by naturalizing it and removing human beings
from view. But even this strategy does not work. As in the episode of the
Discharged Veteran, the appearance of natural peace turns into human
pain:

> at late hours
> Of winter evenings when unwholesome rains
> Are falling hard, with people yet astir,
> The feeble salutation from the voice
> Of some unhappy Woman, now and then
> Heard as we pass; when no one looks about,
> Nothing is listen'd to.   [635–41]

Not even by Wordsworth. Human sound is "nothing"; a "salutation"
(beggary or prostitution) is as alienating as the sight of the blind beggar's
face. The beggar's admonition is confirmed, not denied, by plain external
evidences. When Wordsworth says these sights are, "I fear, / . . . falsely
catalogu'd," he directly acknowledges the inadequacies of his argument,
for such sights tend to show the opposite of what he wished to suggest, a
sense of massive unity somehow persisting below all the strangeness of
London's faces.

In reaction, he throws himself into the arms of the city's temptations,
and with a maniac glee proceeds to destroy the fabric of his argument by
embracing the spectacle of London with all the passion he can muster, exacerbated by his inability to come to terms with it. His description of Bartholomew Fair as "a type not false / Of what the mighty City is itself"
(695–96) thus breaks out as reckless bravado, almost jeering at his earlier
solemn "type, / Or emblem, of the utmost that we know, / Both of ourselves and of the universe" (617–19). If even the quiet, impressive scenes
he has tried to present are "falsely catalogu'd" because of the inevitable in-
trusion of "unhappy" Human Life,

> What say you then,
> To times, when half the City shall break out
> Full of one passion, vengeance, rage, or fear,
> To executions, to a Street on fire,
> Mobs, riots, or rejoicings?   [644–48]

The description of Bartholomew Fair is splendid poetry, but bought at a high price. Wordsworth gives up his imagination to an almost porno-graphic orgy of spectacular details, the pornography less in the content than in the act of description, its sheer self-indulgence. "What say you then"; how do you like *this*? "What a hell / For eyes and ears! what anar-chy and din / Barbarian and infernal!" (658–60). So many things are thrown together, good and bad, "All moveables of wonder from all parts . . . All freaks of Nature, all Promethean thoughts / Of Man" (679, 688–89), that all distinctions between spectators and performers, abnor-mal and normal, are lost, as in Book VII's benignly distracted opening, but here more nearly abandoned:

> All jumbled up together to make up
> This Parliament of Monsters. Tents and Booths
> Meanwhile, as if the whole were one vast Mill,
> Are vomiting, receiving, on all sides,
> Men, Women, three-years' Children, Babes in Arms.   [690–94]

In short, Human Life. The presence of babies in this conclusion, besides emphasizing the difficulty of maintaining normative standards in London, also links back to the many spots throughout the book where images of a boy-child have highlighted the city's threatening imaginative force.

From this rout none can be saved, or see it otherwise, "except a Strag-gler here and there" (697). On this exception, William Wordsworth makes his exit from London and Book VII, harking back to his initial presenta-tion of himself as a "vagrant . . . casual Dweller . . . transient visitant" (60–61, 74). The way to conclude the book is to separate himself ("The Spirit of Nature was upon me here," 735) from the city, now radically car-icatured in the hell of Bartholomew Fair. We may take his word for it, or we may not, when he ends in "Composure and ennobling Harmony" (740). But this concluding line, whatever it refers to in Wordsworth's bio-graphical mental state, sits so ill with what has occurred in Book VII that another poetical effort must be made to show what this book has mani-festly *not* shown, "Love of Nature leading to Love of Mankind"—the subtitle of Book VIII. The "retrospective" function of Book VIII is, in the poetic event, a long backing-up for another run at London, which returns to occupy the book's last quarter.

Book VIII: "Retrospect—Love of Nature Leading to Love of Mankind"

Book VIII is a favorite whipping boy of Wordsworth's detractors be-cause it seems to expose the weak link in his faith: if only mankind were more like the country shepherds I knew in my youth, it would be easier to love. But, though the book is weak, this is not the precise form of its weakness. Wordsworth fails to sustain his argument not because of dubious evidence (country people are more virtuous than others) or false premises (country people are representative of mankind), but because he is strongly tempted to abandon it altogether. In full retreat from the hellish image of Bartholomew Fair, he rushes back to the Lake Country, and his impetus nearly bursts through any real places whatsoever. He does not seek to prove that shepherds are more virtuous than city dwellers, but that they present "more of an imaginative form . . . spiritual almost / As those of Books" (417–19). Each time he sets himself to assert the valuable humanity of real shepherds, he pushes off from a putative rejection of the shepherds of literary pastoral, yet each rejection becomes a fondly regretful farewell to something dearly loved—the image of Human Life, not in Westmorland, and certainly not in London, but in Books. Again we might ask, what could be more natural for a poet? But Wordsworth, as author of *The Recluse*, seeks to be the poet of reality, casting out all merely literary conventions. His "hard" and "soft" pastorals can be reconciled in the strict algebra of contemporary theories of the Sublime and the Beautiful, but his "hard" shepherds are not as tough as he implies, while his "soft" ones remain a lot more attractive than he wants to let on.[49]

Since Book VIII depends so heavily on a shaky argument, I once again ask the reader's indulgence for the oversimplification of an outline.

I.   Prologue (1–61): Helvellyn Fair (contrasting Bartholomew Fair)
II. Main Argument (62–510): Love of Nature Leading to Love of Mankind
   A. The People (62–119): "Love human to the Creature in himself"
   B. The Place (119–221): "Beauteous the domain"
      1. Arcadian Images (122–43 + 159–65 + 183–203 = 50 lines)
      2. The Lake Country (144–58 + 166–82 + 205–21 = 50 lines)
   C. "The Matron's Tale" (222–311), or A Lost Son Found
      (An illustrative "proof" of the power of local stories "to make imagination restless")
   D. Recapitulation (312–471): Lake Country Shepherds vs. Classical Models
      1. Arcadian Images (312–53 = 42 lines)
      2. The Lake Country (353–428 = 76 lines)
   E. Apology for excessive schematization of his moral and psychological development (472–510).
III. Transition (511–640): First stirrings of Fancy and Imagination in response to images of Human Life

IV. Return to Public World (641–870)
    A. Cambridge (641–77): "present actual superficial life"
    B. London (678–870): "Preceptress stern!"

The reason for the high proportion of lines Wordsworth gives to literary or "spiritual" shepherds is clear: he must return to face London as his "preceptress stern," strengthened by an infusion of images of men of "rocks and precipices . . . that seize / The heart with firmer grasp" (354–55). Like many preventive inoculations, this one has habit-forming side effects. Though Book VIII is intended, like Book VI, to resolve one of *The Prelude*'s residential crises, it also contains, like VI, a crisis implicit in the terms of its own resolution. The shepherds of literary pastoral constantly tempt Wordsworth away from Lake Country actuality (which, of course, is highly sentimentalized itself, reminding us that he was not a shepherd), just as in Book VI his compositional discovery of Imagination's "abode" in the realms of infinity made it all the harder for the narrative traveler, William Wordsworth, to spend the subsequent night in a "dreary Mansion" in the real mountains.

    Helvellyn Fair is sweet, like its "sweet Lass of the Valley," and much to be preferred to London's streets of prostitution, yet its very innocence provokes in Wordsworth a thought akin to Gray's "Ode on a Distant Prospect of Eton College" ("where ignorance is bliss, / 'Tis folly to be wise"):

> How little They, they and their doings seem,
> Their herds and flocks about them, they themselves,
> And all that they can further or obstruct!
> Through utter weakness pitiably dear
> As tender Infants are: and yet how great!   [50–54]

The last assertion does not quite come off, even in the long perspective of "Old Helvellyn, conscious of the stir"; these are microscopic people. And though we soon see shepherds who work like men but walk like angels ("Emerging from the silvery vapours, lo! / A Shepherd and his Dog!" 94–95), we also feel Wordsworth's longing for the literary swains and vales to which he prefers these supposedly real ones. In an initial stage of composition, Book VIII opened with the lines that now begin Book II of *The Excursion* ("In days of yore how fortunately fared / The Minstrel!"), and manuscript variants draw the parallel between poets and other workmen directly ("his Harp still pendent at his side / Familiarly as now our Labourers wear / Their Satchels when they plod to distant fields," *PW*, V.41n.).[50] This passage develops a safe-poet image ("protected . . . by vir-

tue of that sacred instrument") that is exactly analogous to the safe place
that Helvellyn Fair represents in *The Prelude*'s progress, following the dangers to imagination represented by the city and, still more revealing in the
compositional sequence (VI, IX, X, VIII, VII), following the dangers presented by revolution, against which poetry is figured as a perennial safe
conduct: "Opening from land to land an easy way / By melody, and by the
charm of verse" (*Ex.* II.17−18).

From the very first time Wordsworth seeks to compare the Lakes, not
to London but to Books, the counter-pull of the imaginary is obvious:

> Beauteous the domain
> Where to the sense of beauty first my heart
> Was open'd, tract more exquisitely fair
> *Than* is that Paradise of ten thousand Trees,
> Or Gehol's famous Gardens, in a Clime
> Chosen from widest Empire, for delight
> Of the Tartarian Dynasty composed;
> . . . .
> Scene link'd to scene, an evergrowing change,
> Soft, grand, or gay! with Palaces and Domes
> Of Pleasure spangled over, shady Dells
> For Eastern Monasteries, sunny Mounds
> With Temples crested, Bridges, Gondolas,
> Rocks, Dens, and Groves of foliage taught to melt
> Into each other their obsequious hues
> Going and gone again, in subtile chace,
> Too fine to be pursued. . . .   [119−25, 129−37; italics added]

But he continues to pursue it for several more lines. Given the comparative
in the paragraph's topic sentence, we may well ask where we are, or where
he is, by the time it reaches its conclusion. His beloved travel books are
obvious sources for such passages, but their significance lies in Wordsworth's fascination with them, a fixation upon the imaginary which, moreover, exactly parallels his earlier expressions of wonder about London:

> There was a time when whatsoe'er is feign'd
> Of airy Palaces, and Gardens built
> By Genii of Romance, or hath in grave
> Authentic History been set forth of Rome,
> Alcairo, Babylon, or Persepolis,
> Or given upon report by Pilgrim-Friars
> Of golden Cities ten months' journey deep
> Among Tartarian wilds, fell short, far short,
> Of that which I in my simpleness believed
> And thought of London   [VII.81−90]

Each time he tries to blend "common haunts" (Nature) and "ordinary human interests" (Human Life), "each with the other's help" (170), he finds they need some additional help. The marriage of Mind and Nature requires a priest; this priest derives his authority from literature; he describes their wedded bliss in corollary negatives— "Not such as in Arcadian Fastnesses . . . ancient Poets sing"—that ravel out into a miniature history of the pastoral (185–203) which ends by hinting that his authority is validated not by unmediated nature but by vestiges of this artificial tradition persisting almost into his own lifetime: "True it is, / That I had heard (what he [Spenser] perhaps had seen) / Of Maids at sunrise bringing in from far / Their May-bush, and along the Streets, in flocks, / Parading with a Song of taunting Rhymes" (191–95). But, setting aside at last these *Recluse*-ideals of poetry-in-the-streets to get down to the business at hand, a breath of profoundly real loss escapes through his conventional sigh: "This, alas! / Was but a dream; the times had scatter'd all" (203–04).

To prove his point about the spiritual values of real dalesmen, Wordsworth tells a story—his usual way of clinching arguments, as *The Prelude* itself is a story proving-out *The Recluse*'s system. The "Matron's Tale" (222–311) ostensibly shows that tragic beauty can arise even from "the unluxuriant produce of a life / Intent on little but substantial needs" (208–09). Yet the real question is how this story could make "imagination restless" in anyone.[51] A father and son go out looking for a lost sheep and are separated. The son then finds the sheep in a dangerous river spot, immediately causes its death, puts his own life in peril, and is rescued only by his father's nearly miraculous following of a hunch ("not knowing why, as oftentimes / Long afterwards he has been heard to say," 299–300). We can recognize this as a story of a Lost Son Found and appreciate its power to make Wordsworth's imagination restless. It complements his vague but deep involvement with Mary of Buttermere's dead child and the prostitute's "lovely Boy" in Book VII, and reverberates with other accounts of lost sons sprinkled throughout *The Prelude,* counterpoints to its calling of a "chosen Son." But, as a proof of the spiritual stature of Lake Country Man, the Matron's Tale shares in the weakness of the "fair proofs" Wordsworth used to complete "Home at Grasmere" in 1806 and *The Excursion* in 1812–14: they all derive, as Coleridge noted, from convictions so firmly "self-established" that they give "to certain Thoughts and Expressions a depth and force which they had not for readers in general" (*LSTC*, IV.573). However, it suffices to return him to his argument as though a proof had been produced. His only direct defense of actual shepherds' work (354–428) manages to convey such an agreeable way of life ("hard labour interchang'd / With that majestic indolence so dear / To native Man," 388–90), that he can confidently end by insulting anyone who would disagree with him:

> Call ye these appearances
> Which I beheld of Shepherds in my youth,
> This sanctity of Nature given to Man
> A shadow, a delusion, ye who are fed
> By the dead letter, not the spirit of things,
> Whose truth is not a motion or a shape
> Instinct with vital functions, but a Block
> Or waxen Image which yourselves have made,
> And ye adore.   [428–36]

Such confidence is not rhetorically argumentative at all, nor can it very well be called defensive; it is, rather, supremely self-sufficient, as gods compared to idols, in the poetic manner Keats acutely ascribed to Wordsworth: "poetry that has a palpable design upon us—and if we do not agree, seems to put its hand in its breeches pocket."[52]

Once Wordsworth has assumed this self-satisfied posture, he unconcernedly allows all sorts of provisos (472–510) that seriously weaken the force of his argument. His very inconclusiveness makes it unnecessary, he says, that he should speak of farmers, quarry workers, fishermen, or miners—as if adding these categories of rural labor to shepherding would constitute a logical generalization. Instead, having dismissed anyone who dares think his shepherds are delusive "appearances," he proceeds with a self-indulgent account of the steps by which "that first poetic Faculty [Fancy] / Of plain imagination and severe / . . . came among those shapes of human life / . . . And Nature and her objects beautified / These fictions ["the notions and the images of books"], as in some sort in their turn / They burnish'd her" (511–12, 520, 523–25). Of all the examples that follow, silly as they are, we can immediately say, in contrast to his roundabout ways of talking about shepherds, that we at last hear a man talking about something he knows about. The ghosts attached to yew trees, "the tragic super-tragic," the soapy exaggeration of widows' sorrows, the "wild obliquities" attributed to drooping plants, the gleaming water drops which seemed "to have some meaning which I could not find" (but readily supplied)—in all this long catalogue (525–623) we truly recognize his claims: "the shapes / Of wilful fancy grafted upon feelings / Of the imagination" (583–85). The only surprise is when we realize that this is the road back to London. His theme is to "retrace the way that led me on / Through Nature to the love of Human Kind" (587–88), and it now becomes evident, as he begins to negotiate this transitive passage of his argument, that it is not the hard life of real shepherds that seized his "heart with firmer grasp," but the imaginative, "spiritual" stimulation they provided, in their close, dialectical, now-this-now-that proximity to the exaggerated fictions of pastoral convention. This is what gives him confidence to say, without blinking an eye at his paradox, that he "at all times had *a real solid world / Of images* about me; did not pine / As one in cities bred might do" (604–06; italics added).

The basis of Wordsworth's return to London is his new insight into the imaginative greatness looming beneath the city's superficial spectacles: as W. J. B. Owen has persuasively demonstrated, London-the-Sublime.[53] This is the real, poetic function of Book VIII's "retrospect." Its implied summary of his whole life and poem to this point is hurriedly and imprecisely disposed of (624–64). Originally composed as a response to his descriptions of his French experiences, its structure is redetermined by Wordsworth's knowledge that he must return to London Re-imagined, and indeed the city at the end of Book VIII is hardly recognizable as the same one at the end of Book VII. This new London is stern, impressive, and historical, whereas the other London had been exciting, frantic, and above all, immediate.

> London! to thee I willingly return.
> Erewhile my Verse play'd only with the flowers
> Enwrought upon thy mantle; satisfied
> With this amusement, and a simple look
> Of child-like inquisition   [679–83]

In London, the human mind has stamped its image on its element with a vengeance, and Wordsworth's return to it breathes strength because the city is a seat of power ("Power growing with the weight," 706) and he is nakedly power-hungry: "I sought not then / Knowledge; but craved for power, and power I found / In all things" (754–56). Rather than try to learn from London, he will try to imitate it, for however much is wasted at this apex of civilization there is always more to come, and its inexhaustibility is finally an image of the cultural edifice he wants *The Recluse* to be, the imperial center of an imperious imagination:

> [I] afterwards continu'd to be mov'd
> In presence of that vast Metropolis,
> The Fountain of my Country's destiny
> And of the destiny of Earth itself,
> That great Emporium, Chronicle at once
> And Burial-place of passions, and their home
> Imperial and *chief living residence*.   [745–51; italics added]

He goes on for dozens of lines which, were they given us to read out of context, we would be sure were about no place but Imagination, so close is his identification with this newly accommodating residence, a "vast Abiding-place / Of human Creatures" (837–38) that supports by sheer magnitude his much-needed conclusion that "here imagination also found / An element that pleas'd her, tried her strength, / . . . And the result was elevating thoughts / Of human Nature" (797–98, 801–02).

But though Wordsworth's imagination is best able to deal with London when he conceives it as an equal to his genius,[54] he cannot very well erect his "metropolitan Temple" there. He knows he still has to face the already composed books on the French Revolution. By placing Book VIII after VII, Wordsworth played his Grasmere card against London, and had no real place left to set against his experiences in Paris, Blois, and Orléans; no place, that is, but Imagination itself, which supplies the title and theme of *The Prelude*'s three concluding books. Thus his return to London-as-Sublime must be qualified by predetermined images of "union or communion"—images of Nature's mode of existence, like the "corresponding dignity" of the idealized universities of Book III—and "individual sights / Of courage, and integrity, and truth" (839–40), lest he seem foolishly to pretend he had single-mindedly usurped the nation's capital in an imaginative coup d'etat that nobody noticed. Of these sights, the "brawny Artificer" holding his "sickly babe" in the sunlight is chief, a "counterview" (along with the Lost Son Found of the Matron's Tale) to both the blind beggar and the two lost sons of Book VII.

> He held the Child, and, bending over it,
> As if he were afraid both of the sun
> And of the air which he had come to seek,
> He eyed it with unutterable love.   [856–59]

The moment's precariousness, caught in the father's awkward posture, balances on Wordsworth's self-quotation (always his strongest rhetorical figure)—"unutterable love"—from his account of the Pedlar's spiritual growth in "The Ruined Cottage," one of his surest statements of faith in the beneficence of man's relations with nature. But the Pedlar was looking at clouds, not at a sick child in a polluted city. "Human kind / And . . . the good and ill of human life" (862–63) represent continued dangers to love in London, but Wordsworth is in no position to explore, or "utter," his meaning further. He has achieved his second residence's resolution, and must be done. Though Book VIII's subtitle is "Love of Nature Leading to Love of Mankind," its last lines so severely qualify all its claims that the process of argument seems not even to have begun:

                              but no,
          My Fellow beings still were unto me
          Far less than she [Nature] was, though the scale of love
          Were filling fast, 'twas light, as yet, compared
          With that in which her mighty objects lay.   [866–70]

The figure implies that a day is coming when Love of Man and Love of Nature will be balanced. But the "scale of love" was filling too fast, and overflows in blood and terror as Wordsworth moves into *The Prelude*'s third residence, France and the French Revolution. The destructive flood of revolutionary ideals of love and brotherhood produces a reign of terror in the poem as well as in Paris, threatening to engulf even Nature's "mighty objects." With this great fear in mind, Wordsworth proceeds extremely cautiously into Books IX and X.

THE THIRD RESIDENCE: REVOLUTION

Shrewd analysts of Wordsworth's development have argued that his writings about his experience of the French Revolution are the efficient cause of the entire *Prelude*, that they doom *The Recluse* and damage *The Prelude* by including material in the latter that belongs to the former, or that they anticipate his recognition of the apocalyptic character of his own imagination.[55] These views are not entirely irreconcilable. We certainly find ourselves, in Books IX and X, in a much different poem than the one we began, though not so different from the parts dealing with Cambridge and London. If we took out all these residential crises, we would have a poem that more resembles the cultural monument Wordsworth has become: Books I–II and XI–XIII, a five-book *Prelude* of Nature and Imagination without any mediating social structures whatever. But *The Recluse* was to be addressed to idealists disillusioned by the course of the Revolution, and Wordsworth's preparatory poem could not very well exclude his own participation in that wide experience of disillusionment. Nor can his experience of the Revolution be elided into a mere foreshadowing of his own developing faith in imagination. Rather, the crisis of the Revolution, as represented in *The Prelude*, arises from Wordsworth's identification of his own feelings of creative power with the Revolution's, not as an analogue but as a direct possibility of imaginative action transforming the world. His subsequent imaginative development, along with the course of historical events in Europe, had shown him that he must disengage himself from the Revolution. Enthusiasm followed by withdrawal is also characteristic of his experiences in Cambridge and London, but here the stakes are proportionately much higher.

We recall that composition of Book VI was followed immediately by Wordsworth's elaboration of his further, postgraduate experience in France in 1791–92, comprising all the particulars of his personal involvement in specific historical events from his arrival in Paris in November 1791 until his learning of the death of Robespierre in the late summer of 1794. But he did not begin composing the second half of Book X (1850 Book XI), dealing with the difficult psychological dimensions of his response to the Revolution, until he first attempted Book VIII's convoluted argument about "Love of Nature Leading to Love of Mankind" as his initial response to revolution, only to readjust it by a complicated set of maneuvers to the London-crises of the subsequently composed Book VII. This left him, in very late 1804, still facing the terrific internal dimensions of his revolutionary crisis, which he then wrote about in lines (X.568–1039) that, in the event, became his last sustained, original narrative composition in *The Prelude*, since Books XI–XIII were largely made up from material written earlier. In this sequence of compositional events, starting with his poetic crossings of revolutionary France and the sublime Alps in Book VI, Wordsworth began to recognize that adjusting Imagination to its "residence" in the world was the primary process by which he would become the fit author of *The Recluse*, which was to perform a similar task for all mankind, and that the worst crisis, his imagination's temporary but deep allegiance to the Revolution, worked retroactively to make such adjustments, sequentially rearranged, the main business of *The Prelude*. Having played his Grasmere card against London, there was nothing left to do but make Imagination the full antagonist of the Revolution, not because they were so different, but because, in his experience and the experience of the best minds of his generation, they had seemed so promisingly similar.

The process of this accommodation is represented in Books IX–X as the familiar three-part "spot of time" structure: expectation (IX), disappointment (Xa.1–567), and revaluation (Xb.568–1039).[56] It is somewhat obscured by Wordsworth's poor decision in 1805 not to retain the last stage as a separate Book XI—a decision, however, that had the considerable merit, for him, of further submerging the seriousness of the crisis. The revolutionary books put in dramatic form the elemental question that Wordsworth is constantly dealing with: what good is poetry, or how is one justified in becoming a poet? Following Kant, Wordsworth believed that the perfection of human community requires acting as well as telling.[57] Books IX–X record the process by which he determined that the most ennobling actions available to him in his young maturity were in fact not noble, and that what he did instead—write poetry—was more noble, as an exercise of the human faculty that alone justifiably raises one human being above another. Each stage of their three-part sequence is marked by a symbolic tension between two characters: Beaupuy and Vaudracour in IX, Wordsworth and Robespierre in Xa, Wordsworth and Coleridge in Xb. Each of these tensions reflects dialectically unstable strains within Wordsworth's understanding of his poetry's relation to human life. In Book IX, an excessively idealized portrait of revolutionary promise (Beaupuy) is set over against an excessively weak image of allegiance to tradition (Vaudracour); in Xa, a fantastically negative image of revolutionary excess (Robespierre) is pitted against and "defeated" by a fantasy image of Wordsworth himself as a putative revolutionary leader who retains respect for tradition through nature and poetry; in Xb, this fantasy scenario breaks down as Wordsworth finds he has insufficient arguments to make his case, and turns toward Coleridge-in-Sicily for an image of the philosophic mind that will save him from the reign of terror in his own mind. These three stages of revolutionary crisis thus prepare, at a deep level of signification, for the three stages of Imagination's restoration in *The Prelude's* last three books: by Nature (XI), for Human Life (XII), and in the Mind of Man (XIII).

Book IX: "Residence in France"

The difference between the titles of Books IX and X is significant; only the latter adds "and French Revolution." Although Wordsworth in Book IX is inevitably in the Revolution, the book works hard to show him not in it. As the beginning of a new residential unit, Book IX's prologue promises to "start afresh" with the poet's "impulse to precipitate my Verse" (9–10), but the impulse is not precipitous after all, and the book continues the "motions retrograde" that Wordsworth says are past, moving him very slowly and carefully toward the "devouring sea" of his revolutionary crisis. This holding-off from revolution is emphasized in his visit to the ruins of the Bastille "in the guise / Of an Enthusiast, yet, in honest truth . . . I look'd for something that I could not find, / Affecting more emotion than I felt" (66–67, 70–71). Turning this contrast the other way round, he says he preferred Le Brun's sentimental painting of Mary Magdalene ("fair face / And rueful, with its ever-flowing tears," 78–79) to what he stared at in the streets: "Hawkers and Haranguers, hubbub wild! / And hissing Factionists with ardent eyes, / . . . Builders and Subverters, every face / That hope or apprehension could put on" (56–60). He usefully continues his London role of observing outsider, for revolutionary Paris is like a Bartholomew Fair every day. Book IX is less about William Wordsworth than any book in *The Prelude*, and more about the effects of the Revolution as he saw them in others—particularly, as in the examples just cited, in their faces.

This attention is divided between three major foci: the Royalist officers at Blois, the republican general Michel de Beaupuy, and Vaudracour, the hero (in a manner of speaking) of the sentimental romance with which Book IX ended in 1805. Beaupuy is an ideal image mediating between the reactionary zeal of the Royalist officers and Vaudracour's insufficient revolutionary energy. In Beaupuy, Wordsworth blends enthusiasm for the new with respect for the old. His handsome face and figure are signs of his ability to keep body and soul together under the pressure of the times. By contrast, the face of the chief Royalist officer is "ravage[d] out of season" by the daily news from Paris:

> His temper was quite master'd by the times,
> And they had blighted him, had eat away
> The beauty of his person, doing wrong
> Alike to body and to mind . . .
>
> . . . .
> Disarm'd his voice, and fann'd his yellow cheek
> Into a thousand colours . . .   [146–49, 159–60]

Such details anticipate not only Beaupuy's fair face and mien, but also Vaudracour's "savage outside" and "imbecile mind." Further, this special emphasis on faces is linked directly to the compositional drama of the book, Wordsworth's effort to contain the Revolution in words:

>   oft said I then,
> And not then only, "what a mockery this
> Of history, the past and that to come!
>
> . . . .
> Oh! laughter for the Page that would reflect
> To future times the face of what now is!"   [169–71, 176–77]

Many external factors help to hold him off from the conflict—his youth, his foreignness, his natural republicanism—but most useful of all is his ability to hold things off from himself for maximum perspective and impact:

> Even files of Strangers merely, seen but once,
> And for a moment . . .
>
> . . . .
>   . . . here and there a face

> Or person singled out among the rest,
>
> Yet still a Stranger and belov'd as such   [280–81, 283–85]

In these unknown faces, he sees "arguments from Heaven" (288), as they reflect his own favorite role of "Stranger" ("Straggler," in London), never more than now in need of the name Coleridge applied to it, *spectator ab extra*.

Thus protected, he enters into Book IX's main conflict, a symbolic contest between the effects of custom and revolution as seen in the face of two protagonists, Beaupuy and Vaudracour. Like other ideal images in *The Prelude* (Book III's universities, Book VIII's shepherds), Beaupuy's ideality consists of his reconciliation of opposites, his ability (as portrayed by Wordsworth) to establish *correspondence*, or continuity, between the old and the new. He is at once like a chivalric knight of "old Romance or Tale," walking through "the events / Of that great change . . . / As through a Book" (304–06), and a "Patriot, thence rejected by the rest / . . . with an oriental loathing" (295–96). Over and over Wordsworth's account approaches the condition of oxymoron, creating Beaupuy, Knight of the Revolution, Champion of the Republic. He is meek yet heroic, highborn "but unto the poor / . . . in service bound" (309–10). In both appearance and action, he presents the image of revolutionary patriotism as the very imitation of Christ: "Injuries / Made *him* more gracious, and his nature then / Did breathe its sweetness out most sensibly / As aromatic flowers on alpine turf / When foot hath crush'd them" (300–04). Granting that no other man except Coleridge ever had such a positively admirable effect upon Wordsworth as Beaupuy,[58] we may see in this representation of him, filtered back through several years of Coleridge's influence, a stress upon Beaupuy's power to unify the contraries of existence—at the fever pitch of revolution—into a symbol of universal man in a particular place. Beaupuy is a "spot of time" personified, a Coleridge at arms.

This ideal activism becomes veritable in Wordsworth's description of their long conversations. Topically introduced as "discourse about the end [purpose] / Of civil government" (328–29), they quickly shift to more congenial slants. "The miseries of royal Courts" are, in their view, not oppression or debauchery but hypocrisy; for revolutionary politics they substitute reform of courtly manners. When they do get to actual changes in forms of government, they concentrate on the lightning speed with which change can occur, especially when "single Spirits . . . catch the flame from Heaven / . . . Triumphant over every obstacle / Of custom, language, Country, love and hate" (375, 379–80). Such idealism makes Girondism look downright hardheaded, and as a representation of the way in which single

imaginations can generalize themselves into social effect, has far less to do
with real politics than with Wordsworth's fascination, announced in *The
Prelude*'s introduction, with single, solitary avengers of justice returning
from exile to alter the course of decadent history. The conversations themselves are given heroic exemplars—"Such conversation under Attic
shades / Did Dion hold with Plato, ripen'd thus / For a Deliverer's glorious
task" (414–16)—tied to talks with Coleridge (396–400), and all pointed
toward the same *Recluse*-goal: "philosophic war / Led by Philosophers"
(422–23). Under influence of the romantically "solemn region" in which
they took place, heroic deliverance soon becomes the conversations' whole
theme, and discourses of civil government become fantasies of rescuing
damsels in distress. "Often in such place / From earnest dialogues I slipp'd
in thought / And let remembrance steal to other times" (444–46):

> It was Angelica thundering through the woods
> Upon her Palfrey, or that gentler Maid
> Erminia, fugitive as fair as She.   [453–55]

Or he hears the roar of "boisterous merriment" more sinister:

> Of Satyrs in some viewless glade, with dance
> Rejoicing o'er a Female in the midst,
> A mortal Beauty, their unhappy Thrall.   [461–63]

Once again, the rescue—or perhaps the ruin—of a helpless woman enters
powerfully into Wordsworth's imagination. Residual guilt for having left
Annette can hardly account for all these appearances, from Margaret to
Mary of Buttermere to Mary Magdalene. They are subsumed under the
larger category of what Imagination can do to alleviate human suffering,
the threatened women that "chosen Sons" might save. Coming in sight of
ruined chapels, ancient chateaux, and "that rural Castle" where Francis I
"a Lady lodg'd / . . . bound to him / In chains of mutual passion" (484–
87), he is led back through history from purely literary fictions to an actual
damsel in distress, "a hunger-bitten Girl," whom Beaupuy, evidently startling the poet from his reveries, points out in agitation: " 'Tis against
that / Which we are fighting' " (518–19).

This return to reality via the Revolution's early promise of eradicating
poverty leads to another damsel in distress, Vaudracour's Julia, whose
story is a thematic prelude to *The Recluse*'s argument that the Revolution
failed partly because bright young spirits failed to respond to it adequately.
Wordsworth introduces the story by citing several specific legal reforms
which might have saved such languid, hunger-bitten girls: (1) abolishing
legalized exclusion from political action; (2) popular representative legisla-

ture; (3) writs of habeas corpus instead of lettres de cachet; and (4) the right to a fair and open trial before one's accusers. Each of these legal recourses has a bearing in turn upon Vaudracour and Julia's dilemma; any one of them might have saved their story from tragedy, and all of them would have assured it. Perhaps. For, even though Vaudracour is falsely arrested, held incommunicado, and denied a fair trial, his continuing inability to disobey his father hints that the paternal powers of society are not easily resisted. Wordsworth presents their "tragic Tale" in lieu "Of other matters which detained us oft / In thought or conversation, public acts, / And public persons" (544–46). When the argument requires a proof, he tells a story, like the Matron's Tale in Book VIII; but, again, it is difficult to see why this self-confessedly *un*singular tale is "haply worth memorial" (551–52). As with the Matron's Tale, Wordsworth subsequently decided Vaudracour and Julia's story was too obscure and excised it from *The Prelude*; but posterity has for the last sixty years seen it as his disguised representation of his love affair with Annette Vallon. It would be foolish to deny the presence of memories of Annette in a story which begins, "Oh! happy time of youthful Lovers!" (555). But it is equally foolish to imagine that Wordsworth is here covertly, still less unconsciously, representing his youthful indiscretion in a poem whose primary audience and tireless recopiers were his wife, his sister, and his sister-in-law, to all of whom the events were very well known.

Nevertheless, historical research and constructive reading can press out of the story's unpromising presentation the kind of significance Wordsworth probably meant it to have. His literary source was Helen Maria Williams's *Letters from France*, fleshed out with similar accounts heard orally[59] and of course influenced by the parallels in his own experience. Like Wordsworth's story, Williams's letters are in the genre of a tract for the times, showing in greatly sentimental detail one of the most interesting aspects of the Revolution to popular readers: how its reforms aided star-crossed lovers in distress, especially those who were already the staple of romantic fiction, the members of differing social classes. Wordsworth had gone to France with a letter of introduction to Williams, whose work he greatly admired (his first published poem was addressed to her),[60] and we should not underestimate his enthusiasm for writings about France which so closely matched his own early attitude toward it: "'Living in France at present,' she said, 'appears to me somewhat like living in a region of romance'" (M. I.175–76).

But unlike Williams's story, which races along in the best tradition of popular thrillers, Wordsworth's is boring, repetitive, and obscure, all too lifelike and uncrafted. This is because he has made two signal changes in the story as Williams tells it: her hero is really heroic, leaping from fifty-foot walls at great peril to life and limb; and her story has a happy ending, the wedded lovers celebrating a Bastille Day by dancing round a Liberty tree with the young man's former tenants, the very image of the world (or at least considerable property) well lost for love. The central difficulty of Wordsworth's story, by contrast, which points to its very different significance, is the flawed, ambivalent character of Vaudracour, who does not act consistently, flares up heroically only to recoil submissively, and fritters away his many opportunities in an aimless series of comings and goings, hidings and findings, arrests and releases, all caused by the "will of One" (his father) whom he dreams of reforming by sympathy but fears to rebel against by force. Vaudracour is a gradualist; he believes his father's heart will soften at the sight of a grandson. But the old man is too hard for him, refuses to see him, to sanction his marriage, even to disinherit him and set him free. The cautionary element in Wordsworth's tale, unlike Helen Williams's, is that Vaudracour is driven mad by his failure to resist parental power, even when "the voice of Freedom" resounding throughout France could have roused him to "public hope, / Or personal memory of his own deep wrongs" (930–32). This is what the story was introduced to exemplify (542–54) but loses sight of in its unremittingly dialectical manner of presentation.

Richard Onorato finds in the story evidence of Wordsworth's unconscious grievance against his father for leaving him alone after his mother's death, and attributes its exasperating quality to the fact that its unrealized conflict—passion versus authority—was Wordsworth's own: that Wordsworth felt he had failed, like Vaudracour, to grasp a moment of huge social upheaval to achieve his own success.[61] But given the evidence that Wordsworth was taking a "good" story and turning it into a "bad" one, his motivations cannot have been quite so unconscious, nor can we easily say he failed to resolve his conflicts. The story remains exasperating, but in the developing context of the *Recluse* project, we can see it as a self-admonitory instance of another one of *The Prelude*'s lost sons failing to take the initiative to rescue another of its damsels in distress, representing in its final line the defeat from which *The Prelude* ever fends off its "chosen Son": "His days he wasted, an imbecile mind" (934).

Book X: "Residence in France and French Revolution"

Wordsworth versus Robespierre

Wordsworth further delays the appearance of such threats to his own mind by presenting the Revolution's external crises before their internal effect on him. Book X was originally composed as two books corresponding to these two themes but almost immediately combined into one, and subsequently redivided into Books X and XI of the 1850 version.[62] The two halves of Book X in the 1805 version (1–567 and 568–1039) thus offer markedly different perspectives on the Revolution. Although the first half refers to its worst historical events (the September Massacres, the Reign of Terror, the onset of world war), it ends in a moment of great triumph, Wordsworth's imaginary victory over the revolutionary arch-fiend, Maximilian Robespierre. This half of Book X is a well-made psychodrama pitting Wordsworth against Robespierre for the championship of the Revolution's ideals. Deeply rooted in Wordsworth's psychology,[63] this fantasy-action is clearly apparent in the text's three well-proportioned acts: (1) Wordsworth in Paris, or "Denunciation of the Crimes of Maximilian Robespierre" (1–189); (2) Wordsworth in London, "victim" of both the Terror and Counter-Revolution (189–440); and (3) The Death of Robespierre (441–567).

In the first act, Wordsworth presents his brief stay in Paris en route home as the meditations of "an insignificant Stranger" (the same role he took in Cambridge and London) on the phenomena of reaction and recoil in nature and human life. He spins his meditations around the actual evidences that the Revolution was turning violently against both its enemies and against itself: "Hawkers in the crowd / Bawling, *Denunciation of the crimes / Of Maximilian Robespierre*" (86–88). Robespierre is the human center of Wordsworth's brooding upon reaction, the focus of which is what single individuals can do to bring it about, or must helplessly suffer in its consequences. Historically, Robespierre's antagonist is his fellow Jacobin, Louvet, who "walked *singly* through the avenue / And took his station in the Tribune, saying, / 'I, Robespierre, accuse thee!'" (98–100; italics added). Thematically, Wordsworth's fascination with the effect of single individuals on world events continues from his conversations with Beaupuy, and more generally from the motivation of *The Prelude* as an examination of the author of the world-affecting *Recluse*, written in place of a series of epics all dealing with heroes who seem to have defeated whole corrupt civilizations in single combat. His fixation upon individual power is paralleled by his attention to what mathematicians call "catastrophe theory": the precise instant when one course of events suddenly reverses itself into another. He imagines the Battle of Valmy, where the revolutionary troops first stopped the advance of the monarchical Allies (September 20, 1792), as "the last punctual spot" where "a race of victims" recoiled upon their foolishly overconfident pursuers (17–18). Thinking how Robespierre and Louvet's struggle for control of "the capital City . . . would soon / To the remotest corners of the land" be felt (108–11), he generalizes, as in his sublimation of London in Book VIII, to the analogous power of central imaginations: "Inly I revolv'd / How much the destiny of man had still / Hung upon single persons" (137–39). He wishes—simply fantasizes—that people like himself ("every soul / Matured to live in plainness and in truth," 120–21) would rise up to save France from dishonor. His fantasies include oddly poetic practicalities, that "the gift of tongues might fall" upon such souls (cf. IX's "single Spirits . . . Triumphant over every obstacle / Of custom, language, Country"), and his self-deprecating concern for his lack "of eloquence even in my native speech" (133) suggests an imaginative desire to cut a figure as a revolutionary leader. This points toward the imaginary power struggle that Onorato has noted between Wordsworth and Robespierre—his unnatural brother, the extreme form of his repressed desires, and foil to Beaupuy as their ideal form.[64] Inevitably, such thoughts lead him again to high-minded, solitary avengers of justice and the "truth" that they know,

> . . . visible to Philosophers of old,
> Men who, to business of the world untrain'd,
> Liv'd in the Shade, . . . to Harmodius known
> And his Compeer Aristogiton, known
> To Butus, that tyrannic Power is weak   [164–68]

Though he deflects such thoughts as "trite . . . commonplaces" for schoolboys, they come, "Yet, with a revelation's liveliness," and we recognize in these philosophical Sicilian avengers further types of the epic heroes he would have written about if he had not written about himself. They appeared in his conversations with Beaupuy and will appear again at the end of Book X for Coleridge's benefit in Sicily, avengers whose cause justified their conspiracies and assassinations, closely associated with Wordsworth's ideas of the force of his poetry's effect on the world. The "ten shameful years" since 1793 have not "annull'd [his] creed," "that the virtue of one paramount mind / Would have abash'd those impious crests" (179–81), and the first half of Book X shows, ten years later, one mind doing just that, at least in poetry. His return to England is presented as the salvation of a poet who might have died in "common cause" with those who tried to stem the tide of terror, "a poor mistaken and bewilder'd offering, . . . A Poet only to myself, to Men / Useless" (196, 200–01). This saving of a poet useful to mankind is crucial to structure of the drama of the first half of Book X, for it is specifically as an anointed poet that Wordsworth triumphs over Robespierre at its conclusion.

The theme of the power of individual reaction clearly set forth, the

second act of Book X's psychodrama (189–440) introduces the dramatic
complication, a classic tragic dilemma in which our protagonist is torn
from both sides, by England's war and France's terror, and becomes in
imagination a victim of both. The hero is set up for his fall by hubris, his
naive faith in the Revolution's success, portrayed as an exaggerated confidence which made him careless of agitations against the slave trade—
"superfluous pains," they seemed, for slavery would fall with all other social evils "if France prosper'd" (223–27). Wordsworth's presentation of
himself as foolish for rhetorical effect is a regular feature of the 1805 *Prelude*'s residential structure (cf. especially Books III and VII). Thus when
England and France declare war upon each other, the scene is set for the
real revolution of the poem to begin:

> No shock
> Given to my moral nature had I known
> Down to that very moment; neither lapse
> Nor turn of sentiment that might be nam'd
> A revolution, save at this one time,
> All else was progress on the self-same path
> On which with a diversity of pace
> I had been travelling; this a stride at once
> Into another region.   [234–42]

"That very moment . . . at this one time . . . at once": as in the "last punctual spot" at which the French turned to rout the Allies, Wordsworth now
finds himself involved in a catastrophic moment of *re*volution. Like many
idealistic young activists, he is caught unprepared for the moment when
thought is transformed into action, and people begin to be killed in the service of ideas. From being "an insignificant Stranger" in Paris, he turns into
something worse in England, "an uninvited Guest" in the dearest scene he
can imagine, a country congregation offering up prayers for English boys
beneath "a Village Steeple," while he sits apart, feeding "on the day of
vengeance yet to come" (266–75).

The historical fact that England's reaction against the Revolutionary
government precipitated Wordsworth's revolution should not, however,
blind us to his equally self-dramatized involvement in France's Terror:

> I scarcely had one night of quiet sleep
> Such ghastly visions had I of despair
> And tyranny, and implements of death,
> And long orations which in dreams I pleaded
> Before unjust Tribunals, with a voice
> Labouring, a brain confounded, and a sense
> Of treachery and desertion in the place
> The holiest that I knew of, my own soul.   [374–81]

This confounding of his brain links back to his mental instability in *The Prelude*'s earlier residences ("The head turns round, and cannot right itself," III.663; "the mind turn'd this way, that way!" VII.470), now connected to a horrible correlative in reality, the insatiable thirst of the guillotine ("Head after head, and never heads enough / For those that bade them fall," 336–37), obscurely but powerfully blamed on the failure of *his* eloquence: voice labored, brain confounded, soul betrayed. Without discounting evidences of Wordsworth's direct experiences of revolutionary politics compiled by David Erdman and E. P. Thompson, we can say that his poem about such experiences shows the representatives of evil prospering (in these bad dreams of France as in his earlier Parisian fantasies) because of the failure of ordered language to control social reality—a tragic flaw in a poetry that would speak with philosophical authority on man, on nature, and especially on human life.

This is the nadir of Human Life in *The Prelude*. In the face of such holocaustic events, what reverence or worship is possible toward Man, "In single or in social eminence" (390)? Wordsworth's constitutional distaste for the pettiness and spitefulness of ordinary political work ("all unfit for tumult or intrigue," 134) seems apocalyptically confirmed, and the way is certainly open for him to retire from public life, even from thinking about it, as did many of his generation, to whom Coleridge thought *The Recluse* might be addressed and "do great good." But the central drama of *The Recluse* is Wordsworth's determination to turn his imagination *toward* Human Life, however unwillingly, and here he finds an answer to his dilemma by assuming the mantle of "the ancient Prophets . . . when they denounced / On Town and Cities, wallowing in the abyss / Of their offences" (402–06). It is indeed a "different ritual for this after worship" of mankind, but it is still a form of worship—and, more to his point, an effective form of language. Its "wild blasts of music" are attuned to a kind of natural inevitability that Wordsworth, like many others, accepted as an explanation for the Terror:

> . . . it was a reservoir of guilt
> And ignorance, fill'd up from age to age,
> That could no longer hold its loathsome charge,
> But burst and spread in deluge through the Land.   [437–40]

The Old Testament leitmotifs remind us that Wordsworth is following a theodical pattern that began when he was received in France as "welcome almost as the Angels were / To Abraham of old" (VI. 403–04).[65] The reintroduced redemptive pattern also continues its tension between affirmation of the chosen nation or people and implicit recognition of its true prophet or messiah—Wordsworth, not Robespierre.

In denouement of the crisis between revolution and reaction comes the third act of Book X's psychodrama, a carefully managed set-piece (441–567) presenting the impact of another single moment, Wordsworth's participation in the end of the Terror by virtue of the special place and way in which he heard of Robespierre's death. Robespierre is reintroduced into the story by a peculiarly back-handed rhetorical strategy. Beginning one of his characteristic provisos that things were not actually as bad as he has presented them, in the form of a reassuring epic simile ("as the desart hath green spots, the sea / Small islands in the midst of stormy waves," 441–42), Wordsworth recalls his 1790 walking tour, "when first I travers'd France, / A youthful pilgrim." The memory of this "glad time" is not, however, one of those "green spots" which buoyed him up. Quite the contrary of the paragraph's topic sentence, the pleasant memory suddenly mocks him because he also recalls that he walked through "the Town of Arras, place from which / Issued that Robespierre, who afterwards / Wielded the sceptre of the atheist crew" (456–58). Instead of respite, he finds further mental anguish, heavily dramatized:

> As Lear reproach'd the winds, I could almost
> Have quarrel'd with that blameless spectacle
> For being yet an image in my mind
> To mock me under such a strange reverse.   [463–66]

The paragraph's very movement has described a "strange reverse," since the verb tense ("could . . . have quarrel'd") refers less sensibly to 1790, or any time thereafter when he thought of Arras, than to the beginning of the paragraph itself, when he set out to present a reassuring image but is foiled in the very moments of composition by its opposite ("For being *yet* an image in my mind / To mock me"). Nonetheless, the famous walking tour has again presented him with what he wants, "an image in my mind," which he now proceeds to purge in Book X's catharsis: "few happier moments have been mine / . . . than that when first I heard / That this foul Tribe of Moloch was o'erthrown, / And their chief Regent levell'd with the dust" (467–70).

But we are held off from this "moment" of reversal—parallel to the first act's "last punctual spot" and the second's "very moment"—by an elaborate preparation of the stage and the protagonist's frame of mind that makes the Death of Robespierre as climactically important as the Crossing of the Simplon, the Climbing of Snowdon, or other "spots of time" in which expectation meets reversal and causes mighty reinterpretation.[66] Crossing Leven estuary on a beautiful day, the clouds seem like "Creatures . . . met / In Consistory, . . . / Or crown of burning Seraphs" (481–83) —angels to Robespierre's "Tribe of Moloch"—whose holiness is underwritten, so to speak, in a curiously familiar way: "Underneath this show / Lay, as I knew, the nest of pastoral vales / Among whose happy fields I had grown up" (484–86). Hawkshead is thus set over against Arras.

But what is the source of Wordsworth's power against Robespierre's? It derives from his seeing the scene "with a fancy more alive on this account": that he had that very morning, he attests, visited the grave of William Taylor, the schoolmaster who first encouraged him to write poetry, and whose deathbed words to Wordsworth, " 'my head will soon lie low,' " now monumentalized to an epitaph, "a fragment from the Elegy of Gray" (500–02), give a personal, powerful, poetic riposte to Robespierre's crimes—"Head after head, and never heads enough." This schoolmaster's love for "one not destitute / Of promise," confirms the wisdom of Wordsworth's retreat from France (else "a Poet only to myself, to Men / Useless," 200–01), now victorious over the Terror on his own terms, fulfilling "the kind hope" (513) which Taylor had in him. To confirm this strange concatenation of personalized landscape emblems, Wordsworth details two otherwise incidental presences in the scene before him: first, "a fragment . . . / . . . of what had been / A Romish Chapel, where in ancient times / Masses were said at the hour which suited those / Who crossed the Sands with ebb of morning tide" (519–23). This "still Ruin" sanctifies our present, secular interpreter of the tides of human life, and Nature confirms him with a second symbolism: "the great Sea meanwhile / Was at safe distance, far retired" (529–30), sacramentally signaling the coming end of floods that earlier "burst and spread in deluge through the Land" (France). A traveler "chancing" to pass, Wordsworth "carelessly" asks the news, and "he replied / In the familiar language of the day / That, *Robespierre was dead*" (533–36). The italicized phrase fulfills the omen of the title being hawked about the streets on Wordsworth's first morning in Paris, "*Denunciation of the crimes / Of Maximilian Robespierre*" (87–88), and is, along with the revelation in Book VI, "*that we had cross'd the Alps*," the only complete statement so emphasized in the entire poem.[67]

Wordsworth underscores this dramatically internalized representation of a public event with his still more potent form of verbal stress: self-quotation. First, an internally quoted "Hymn of triumph"— " 'Come now ye golden times' " (542)—answers in heightened archaic diction and theme

(the cleansing of the Augean stables) the voice he heard (his own) prophe-
sying in his nightmare in Book X's first act: " 'Sleep no more' " (77). The
ambiguous reference to the Labors of Hercules also completes his revised
understanding of this stage of the Revolution's development from the earlier image of "The Herculean Commonwealth [which] put forth her arms /
And throttled with an infant Godhead's might / The snakes about her cra-
dle" (363–65). But Robespierre is not Hercules; he and his cohorts "by
the might / Of their own helper [Rivers of Blood] have been swept away"
(549–50). Who, then, is the demigod? The end of revolutionary terror and
reactionary war are compressed by these allusions into a moment's imagination, as Wordsworth continues across the tidal sands, framing "schemes
. . . more calmly, when and how / The madding Factions might be
tranquillised, / And, . . . / The mighty renovation would proceed"
(554–57)—as though he were in charge of it, now that his arch-rival has
been removed. The suggestion that he has imaginatively usurped Robespierre's place is confirmed by a final self-quotation, not of what he said
then, but of what he has already said much earlier in the poem, in Book
II's description of his boyish crew's breakneck rides across the same sands,
to and from Furness Abbey. The italicized words are picked up variously
from II.110–44, merging with a stunning inevitability to the final word-
for-word quotation (of II.144) in the last line:

> I pursued my way,
> Along that very Shore which I had skimm'd
> In former times, when, *spurring* from *the Vale*
> *Of Nightshade*, and *St. Mary's mouldering* Fane,
> And *the Stone Abbot*, after *circuit made*
> *In wantonness of heart, a joyous Crew*
> Of School-boys, hastening to their distant *home*,
> Along the margin of the *moonlight Sea*,
> *We beat with thundering hoofs the level Sand.*
>
> [559–67; italics added]

The drama has effectively rounded upon itself, closing off Book X's theme
of reaction and recoil in triumph over the Terror of France and the terror
of its author. Moreover, since this is effectively the end of the narrative
line in the poem, the historical forward movement of *The Prelude* stops
with this moment of Wordsworth's imagined victory over Robespierre, the
"thundering hoofs" of the "joyous Crew / Of School-boys" signifying the
rout of "the atheist crew . . . foul Tribe of Moloch"—one small band of
virtuous avengers victorious over the most devilish destroyers of civilization known to Wordsworth's times.

The Inner Power Struggle

The first half of Book X showed what could happen "when reason
. . . is not sequester'd"—not kept in a place safely consecrated from
contaminating general intercourse (O.E.D.). The second half (568–1039)
represents the same theme internally, but in reverse: what happens when
reason, in the guise of "wild theories" of human perfection, is cut loose
from feelings, giving rise to the cultural condition that Wordsworth and
Coleridge were most devoted to correcting by an improved philosophy. To
sever value from fact is to cut off heart from head, and Wordsworth represents himself as threatened by intellectual guillotines, a victim of mental
forms of revolutionary terrorism. The movement of Xb follows the same
overall pattern as Xa (since they describe the same crisis), from initial euphoria through increasingly critical complications to release and resolution; but the denouement is much less convincing, because an ideological
crisis is resolved in personal terms. As in Wordsworth's other crisis poems,
especially "Tintern Abbey," the resolution of Book X is projected onto
other persons, Dorothy and Coleridge, lifted out of the narrative time of
the poem (1795–96) and set down into the time of composition (1804).
He cannot find terms of resolution within the crisis itself—as in Xa he had
found a "different ritual" for worshipping mankind by prophetically de-
nouncing it. All Wordsworth could find by himself in his mental crisis was
the sterile therapy of mathematics, like the "abstruse research" that was
Coleridge's "sole resource, only plan . . . to steal / From my own nature all
the natural man." In both theme and composition, the second half of Book
X is Wordsworth's Dejection Ode. Like Coleridge's ode, and like the other
books (VI and VIII) that conclude stages of *The Prelude*'s residential crisis
structure, Book X's hard-earned resolution raises further questions which
spill over into the next unit. The revolutionary crisis being the worst in the
poem, its spillover is the largest, leading to the categorical examinations of
the final books: "Imagination, How Impaired and Restored." Although
the final books are titled "Imagination," Mary Moorman has well said
that they constitute Wordsworth's "reflections on the French Revolution"
(M. I.220); their new topic is in large part dictated by Wordsworth's need
to strengthen the shaky resolution he achieves in Xb.

The end of the Terror returns him to a state of obviously exaggerated
confidence, as he sets himself up for his fall: "to the ultimate repose of
things / I look'd with unabated confidence" (580–81). He "never
dreamt / That transmigration could be undergone" (599–600) by France's
revolutionary idealism or, worse, by his own. To explain his confidence he
recapitulates his knowledge of human nature in terms that are, if anything,

more idealized than Book VIII's. He approached "the Shield / Of human nature from the golden side" (663–64), and felt, even if he did not understand, all that was "Benevolent in small societies, / And great in large ones" (670–71). Like France's, his understanding was not "sequester'd," and just when he thought his principles were safe from external reversals, he found they were "Lodged only at the Sanctuary's [Reason's] door, / Not safe within its bosom" (678–79). His is a "noviciate mind," and in this context the famous paean to revolutionary enthusiasm, "Bliss was it in that dawn to be alive, / But to be young was very heaven" (690–728), appears as rhetorical hyperbole—sincere, but preparing for the fall, the novice-knight deluded in his quest by mirage castles. The whole passage rings with echoes from the "Prospectus" ("Not in Utopia, subterraneous Fields, / Or some secreted Island, Heaven knows where," 724–25), but it is too good to be true, and Reason is clearly not herself: "Reason seem'd the most to assert her rights / When most intent on making of herself / A prime Enchanter" (698–700). This "residence" is not a home because it came to him too easily:

> Why should I not confess that earth was then
> To me what an inheritance new-fallen
> Seems, when the first time visited, to one
> Who thither comes to find in it his home?
> He walks about and looks upon the place
> With cordial transport, moulds it, and remoulds,
> And is half pleased with things that are amiss,
> 'Twill be such joy to see them disappear.   [729–36]

In his examination of the moral "revolution" which ended this euphoria, Wordsworth does not use the language of turmoil which he used at the analogous point in the active, external first half of Book X. Instead, infected with "wild theories [that] were afloat" (775)—Godwin's necessarianism and other extreme visions of millennium—he enters into a mental landscape marked by images of dryness and disease, as vacant as his hopes had been over full. His mind goes "elsewhere," and his "understanding's natural growth" is stopped by the course of events; separated from his healthy natural sentiments, his opinions "in heat / Of contest . . . / Grow into consequence, till," like moulds or parasites, "round my mind / They clung, as if they were the life of it" (802–05). Trying to "abstract the hopes of man / Out of his feelings," he steps into the "tempting region" of a moral vacuum chamber: "where passions . . . work / And never hear the sound of their own names" (808–14), where growth is corruption because it is discontinuous: "transition by such means / As did not lie in nature"

(843–44). This is the world of the mind of Oswald, the vengeful rationali-
zer of *The Borderers*, from which Wordsworth lifted the arrogant lines celebrating "the light of circumstances, flash'd / Upon an independent intellect" (829–30).[68] He dissects to murder; negative imagery of disease and
corruption becomes even more negative language of pitiless cure and
heartless examination: "I took the knife in hand . . . / . . . to probe / The
living body of society / . . . I push'd without remorse" (873–77). He is a
mad social scientist, Madame LaFarge become Dr. Strangelove, and his knife
inevitably turns against him as Robespierre's did. In the first half of Book
X, France was a "goaded Land wax'd mad" (313); here, Wordsworth's
"mind was both let loose, / Let loose and goaded" (863–64). As in the
first half, he dreamed himself a victim of the Terror, "brain confounded,"
the dream now becomes a waking nightmare and the earlier trial scene is
repeated in *The Prelude*'s great last judgment:

> Thus I fared,
> Dragging all passions, notions, shapes of faith,
> Like culprits to the bar, suspiciously
> Calling the mind to establish in plain day
> Her titles and her honours, now believing,
> Now disbelieving, endlessly perplex'd
> With impulse, motive, right and wrong, the ground
> Of moral obligation, what the rule
> And what the sanction, till, demanding *proof*,
> And seeking it in everything, I lost
> All feeling of conviction, and, in fine,
> Sick, wearied out with contrarieties,
> Yielded up moral questions in despair.   [889–901]

The brilliantly conceived legal rhetoric shows his mind as bailiff, prosecu-
tor, jury, judge, and legislature all at once. The Romantic poet's dream of
becoming the world's acknowledged legislator turns into nightmare, as
art's powerful powerlessness tries to meet the world's rigorous standards
of logical proof and the even less forgiving tests of ideological purity.
Overburdened, he abandons all relations of Human Life to Poetry, and
"turn'd toward mathematics, and their clear / And solid evidence"
(904–05).

      This crisis is the most severe in the poem, but not because of Words-
worth's despair over the course of the Revolution: taken by itself, this is an
unlikely source of crisis for a personality so egotistical and so reserved.
Rather, it is a crisis precisely because his personal reserve had issued forth
and attached his hopes, imaginatively grand and actually slender as they

were, to the Revolution's promises. The Revolution had seemed to be Imagination in action, but despite the "wild theories" he spun round it to save it ideologically if not practically, it turned out to be "a work of false imagination." Wordsworth cannot turn to prophetic denunciation of mankind's errors, for they are now his own. Even if he does denounce himself, no recourse or corrective punishment will follow. His earlier dreams of the Terror were of "unjust Tribunals," but in this rationalist nightmare of "dragging all passions . . . to the bar," the crisis is not injustice but the absence of any standard whatever. In this dilemma he needs mercy, not justice, and he receives it by turning to Dorothy and Coleridge; the Old Testament drama of due vengeance in the first half of Book X becomes a New Testament passion play in the second. Without even placing a period (no more the "last punctual spots" of the first half's catastrophic logic), he turns, in mid-line and mid-sentence, down and out at Racedown in 1795–96, to imagining Coleridge's aid:

> Turn'd toward mathematics, and their clear
> And solid evidence—Ah! then it was
> That Thou, most precious Friend! about this time
> First known to me . . .   [904–07]

And to Dorothy's real presence: "the belovèd Woman in whose sight / Those days were pass'd" (909–10). Immediately, their reappearance in the poem produces an image modifying the seriousness of his sickness: "for, though impair'd and chang'd / Much, as it seem'd, I was no further chang'd / Than as a clouded, not a waning moon" (916–18). This is not a strong image of restoration. Why a random change (clouded/clear) should be preferable to a regular one (waxing/waning) is not obvious, except for the far-fetched explanation that the moon is normally darkened for shorter periods by clouds than by its monthly cycle. Rhetorically, however, the purpose of the image is to reintroduce Book X's theme of action and reaction, now with the difference that Wordsworth's return "again to open day" (924) is confirmed by present events—of December 1804, the time of composition. Napoleon has called in the pope to crown him emperor: according to Book X's logic of past events, when things get so bad how can they help but get better? This negative dialectic turns Book X's former images of great and powerful returns (earthquakes, tides, seasons) into disgusting and absurd annoyances:

> . . . we see the dog
> Returning to his vomit, when the sun
> That rose in splendour, was alive, and moved

> In exultation among living clouds
> Hath put his function and his glory off,
> And, turned into a gewgaw, a machine,
> Sets like an opera phantom.   [935–41]

Unlike this mechanical sun, Wordsworth's clouded moon, even at its darkest, was still alive and natural; Robespierre represented a real threat, but the Napoleon of 1804 is disposed of as a joke.

Without in the least doubting the reality of Dorothy's restoration of her depressed brother, we may say that for readers not necessarily disposed to grant them the roles into which literary tradition has sympathetically cast them, this resolution of crisis is too abrupt and personal to be persuasive, in light of the depth and power with which Wordsworth created the crisis in the first place. The image of the clouded moon is sentimental naturalism; the image of passions dragged to the bar of reason's remorseless judgment is universal human experience. This critical judgment upon Book X is, moreover, Wordsworth's own, for he closes the book with a hundred-line coda addressed to Coleridge in Sicily, in which the resolution of the crisis is continued in other terms, and the crisis is extended from the despair of the 1790s to the causes of unhappiness in 1804: missing Coleridge, not progressing on *The Recluse*, still awaiting Coleridge's notes, while Coleridge's return is delayed by the dangerous movements of that same operatic phantom, Napoleon Bonaparte.[69]

These hundred lines (941–1039) could easily be dismissed as a digression wherein the poem unsteadily reverts to a private verse epistle. But they contribute to Wordsworth's resolution of his crisis—a large part of which is to conclude Book X effectively—by projecting onto Coleridge and Sicily some of the same issues the book has raised. Wordsworth generalizes his grief for the loss of France's promising new civilization into what he imagines as Coleridge's much greater grief among the ruins of a far greater civilization: "Where Etna looketh down on Syracuse, / The city of Timoleon! Living God! / How are the Mighty prostrated!" (950–52). Timoleon is another driver-out of tyrants of the special type that Wordsworth admired: those who come from afar to save the central city, as Timoleon came from Corinth to rout not only the tyrant Dionysius but all the Carthaginians for good measure.[70] Wordsworth then moves below the rise and fall of civilizations to the imaginative principle he sees underlying this movement, as he did in London: "There is / One great Society alone on earth, / The noble Living and the noble Dead: / Thy consolation shall be there" (968–71; cf. VIII.678–836). This restoration-via-Coleridge continues as Sicily's "dull / Sirocco air of . . . degeneracy" becomes for

Coleridge "a healthful breeze" (974–76), whereby Coleridge's physical condition harks back to Wordsworth's earlier images of his own moral sickness. Wordsworth empathizes with Coleridge to the extent of making him, in 1804, what he himself was in 1794, "a lonely wanderer," and puts his hopes for Coleridge's recovery and return in the highest terms *The Prelude* offers its author: now Coleridge is gone, Wordsworth's recollections of his 1790 walking tour among "the lordly Alps . . . are not now . . . The gladsome image in my memory / Which they were used to be" (991–96). This is the second time in Book X that Wordsworth's image of that memorable tour has been spoiled, first by Robespierre's uncanny presence in it, now by Coleridge's absence from it, though gone "to kindred scenes, / On errand, at a time how different!" (996–97). Compositional time and historical time are once again strongly intermixed. In 1790, France was "standing on the top of golden hours" and "the name of Englishmen [was] honour'd in France" (VI.353, 410), but England is the "last spot of earth where Freedom *now* / Stands single in her only sanctuary" (IX.982–83; italics added). Undertaking to describe those scenes in France was the act which moved *The Prelude* beyond the boundaries of a poem on the normative growth of a poet's mind, into the crisis, at once political and transcendental (Revolution and Imagination), which he has barely survived, and he pays Coleridge homage for being more able to integrate them imaginatively than he was, or is: "a heart more ripe / For all divine enjoyment, with the soul / Which Nature gives to Poets, now by thought / Matur'd, and in the summer of its strength" (998–1001). This strategic use of Coleridge very closely parallels Wordsworth's use of Coleridge's letter about *The Recluse* as a device for concluding Book I. Finally, Sicily's Greek heroes are invoked yet again, as earlier in Books IX and X and Book I's introduction, as images of the successful transformation of imaginative or philosophic thought into action: Empedocles, Archimedes, Theocritus, and, singled out, "divine Comates," who foiled his "tyrant lord" by staying alive on the honey brought to him by bees: "Because [he], blessed Man! had lips / Wet with the Muse's Nectar" (1023–28).

In such imagined correspondences between imagination and nature Wordsworth tries to comfort himself over the temporary loss of the friend who saved him in 1796, and in so doing rescues the tenth book of his 1804 poem from its crisis of "yield[ing] up moral questions in despair." Having projected himself out onto Coleridge, he now brings Coleridge back home by converting his loneliness for Coleridge into Coleridge's loneliness for him. Coleridge shall not be "an Exile," nor "a Captive, pining for his home," "but a Visitant . . . a gladsome Votary" to Sicily's shrines of imagination, such as "pastoral Arethuse" (1033–38). Only the two books of the 1805 *Prelude* devoted to "Residence in France and French Revolution" end with negative final lines: "His days he wasted, an imbecile mind" (IX.934) and "not a Captive, pining for his home" (X.1039). Both refer to crises Wordsworth has avoided or overcome by substituting another person in his place: Vaudracour's failure to rise to the Revolution's promise, and Coleridge's hoped-for return to complete the cure of Wordsworth's rising to it too far and too fast. The name of the cure, very like its patient's condition, was to be *The Recluse*.

THE FINAL HOME: IMAGINATION

The last three books of *The Prelude* develop the symptoms and cures of Wordsworth's final "residential" crisis, his imagination's involvement in the French Revolution. Though catalyzed by political events, the roots of his crisis lay in a sensibility in love with its growing sense of creative power, simultaneously dejected by its inability to realize its power successfully. Hazlitt's famous statement, that it was a misfortune for any man of genius to have been born in the last quarter of the eighteenth century, should not be taken to mean that the fault lay entirely with the times; the congruence of personal genius with social possibility led fatefully to the sense of enormous opportunities *missed* which was for Hazlitt "the spirit of the age."[71] This profound despair Wordsworth felt he had narrowly escaped, and the last three books are his "reflections on the French Revolution" (M. I.220–21), in which he traces the organic roots of his imagination's health—as Burke had traced the origins of social health—in its uninterrupted traditional associations.

His restoration came in three stages, one for each of the concluding books: in the context of his love for Nature (XI), in his relations toward Society or Human Life (XII), and finally in his understanding of Mind's action upon reality (XIII). Each of the three focuses around a visionary episode of conclusive power that overrides obscurities in his argument: in XI, the two original "spots of time"; in XII, his visions of primitive man on Salisbury Plain; and in XIII, the unexpected revelation of the moonscape on top of Mount Snowdon. Powerful as they are, they gain persuasiveness by being placed in contexts in which Wordsworth had already qualified the extent of his crisis. The "spots of time" and Salisbury Plain visions conclude their respective books, are anything but self-explanatory, and tend to silence objections rather than answer them. The Snowdon vision, in contrast, opens Book XIII and is, if anything, overelaborated, leading into *The Prelude*'s "Conclusion" proper (the second half of XIII) with the effect of an argument systematically explained, even though, as many readers have observed, what has been explained is Wordsworth's own image or emblem, and the mode of his explanation is essentially literary criticism, not philosophic argument.

Book XI: "Imagination, How Impaired and Restored"

The prologue of Book XI announces the beginning of the end: "Long time hath Man's unhappiness and guilt / Detain'd us . . . Not with these began / Our Song, and not with these our Song must end" (1–2, 7–8). This is a different sort of invocation than the new residential themes announced in Books VII and IX. Though "Man's unhappiness and guilt" marked Wordsworth's residence in London and France, the reference to the beginning and ending of his song indicates that he is now finishing with all degrees of unhappiness and guilt present in all his "residences," and returning to the mood of joy with which the entire poem began. The prologue further establishes an anticipatory image of balanced relationship between the three terms of Wordsworth's epic project—Man, Nature, and Human Life—invoking

> . . . ye Groves, whose ministry it is
> To interpose the covert of your shades,
> Even as a sleep, betwixt the heart of man
> And the uneasy world, 'twixt man himself,
> Not seldom, and his own unquiet heart.   [15–19]

Though the idea of sleep is not a promising one for imaginative restoration, Wordsworth begins describing his three stages of restoration with this "covert" ministry of Nature, to reestablish the unselfconscious "ground of being" (Tillich) on which human activity, social and mental, rests. Estrangement, followed by reunification, becomes the ground of a new human being: the "unselfconscious self-consciousness" of post-Romantic theory.[72]

Book XI's conclusion is that Wordsworth's mind remained in a basically right relation with nature despite its temporary impairment (a carefully chosen word) by "wild theories" of rational perfectionism. Spilling over from politics to aesthetics, the empirical, proof-seeking impulse of such theories made sensory evidence his only test of truth, but the "spots of time" will show how his mind remained "lord and master . . . outward sense . . . the obedient servant." At the beginning of XI he is still "upon

the barren sea" (55) of the arid, abstract imagery of Book X, and reason is
still disguised as a "prime Enchanter" (X.700), dealing in "Spells" (XI.49),
"charm" (83), "Idols" (127), and causing him to act, like a sorcerer's ap-
prentice, against himself:

> . . . as by simple waving of a wand
> The wizard instantaneously dissolves
> Palace or grove, even so did I unsoul
> As readily by syllogistic words
> Some charm of Logic, ever within reach,
> Those mysteries of passion which have made,
> And shall continue evermore to make,
> (In spite of all that Reason hath perform'd
> And shall perform to exalt and to refine)
> One brotherhood of all the human race.   [79–88]

As in Book X's last judgment, Wordsworth's method destroys ("unsouls")
his object, universal brotherhood. Such rational magic makes short work
of History (60–67) and Poetry (68–73) — "Can aught be more ignoble
than the man / Whom they describe" — as sources of positive images for
social reconstruction. But for Wordsworth the crisis of the infection comes
in the rationalizing fever it introduced in his first allegiance, to Nature. He
still loved nature, but as a connoisseur, making her an object of conscious
scrutiny and losing sight of her soul, under domination of "a strong infection of the age, / . . . Unworthily, disliking here, and there / Liking, by
rules of mimic art" (156, 153–54). This is the contemporary fashion of
Picturesque theory and practice, a predominantly conservative custom,
linked for Wordsworth, as for very few other people, to radical social theory, moving from love of nature to love of mankind.

Although the "spots of time" are clearly at an extreme of *un*consciousness from such mincing judgments, the dominance of mind in them
must be distinguished from the dominance of mere rationality in Picturesque cultivation of proper views, which is a false usurpation, since reason
places itself at the disposal of external scenes, accepting the eye's dominance over the mind. Establishing this transition from lower to higher Reason would indeed be "a worthy theme / For philosophic Verse" (132–33),
but one that Wordsworth is ill equipped to develop. Instead, he prepares
for the "spots of time"'s refutation of his rationalistic errors by two preparatory steps, neither conclusive but both tending to lessen our sense of the
depth of his crisis, thus allowing the spots to work more freely. He first
proposes a sort of democratic theory of relations between the senses,
noting how "Nature studiously . . . thwart[s] / This tyranny . . . / In which

the eye was master of the heart" (179–80, 172), by making all the senses
"subservient in their turn / To the great ends of Liberty and Power"
(183–84). He wisely leaves this physiological system of checks and balances ("all the senses each / To counteract the other and themselves,"
180–81) as "abstruser argument . . . matter for another Song," but whatever it might mean, it represents the sort of "wild theory," dear to the
hearts of many Romantics (as in Goethe's *Optics*), that sensory experience
might innately carry humanized significance ("the great ends of Liberty
and Power") beyond its merely abstract, physical categories of operation.
Second (199–223), Wordsworth presents Mary Hutchinson as evidence of
a person who remained uncontaminated by the mental excesses to which
he was driven (the same use to which Coleridge put Sara Hutchinson in
"Dejection: An Ode"): "far less did critic rules . . . Perplex her mind . . .
For she was Nature's inmate" and Nature itself "should have had / An in-
timation" of her feelings (203, 205, 214, 219–20).[73] The hyperbolic
praise is sincere, but its function in the argument is to provide Wordsworth with grounds to continue: "Even like this Maid before I was call'd
forth / From the retirement of my native hills / I lov'd whate'er I saw
. . . / And afterwards, when through the gorgeous Alps / Roaming, I carried with me the same heart" (224–26, 241–42). Because of his early
Cumberland connection to Nature, reinforced by the generalizing effect of
the Alpine tour (from hills to mountains), the "degradation" of false taste
"aggravated by the times" did not impair him irreparably: he "shook the
habit off / . . . and again / In Nature's presence stood . . . / A sensitive, and
creative Soul" (254–57). Thus, internal evidence (the mutually successive
revolutions of the senses), supported by the external evidence of Mary's
freedom from rationalistic taint, brings Wordsworth to his first statement
of imagination's restoration to power, a benevolent dictatorship of mind
over sense.

   The "spots of time" now enter the structure of *The Prelude* for the
third time, not as evidence of spontaneous *nourishment* as in the 1799 version, nor as a conclusion of his "vivifying" education by Nature and
Books rounding off the five-book plan, but as the first of three stages of a
cure or "renovation" of an imagination seriously impaired by a "strong infection" contracted from wild political theories.[74] Wordsworth is clearly
aware that he is plunging deeper into the roots of human consciousness
than in *1799*'s childhood recollections or the five-book plan's normative
educational scheme. Images of depth and mystery abound, thickening the
originally spare narrative. As in the Simplon crossing and the Snowdon
climbing, unexpected alteration in mental categories of explanation results

in a vastly heightened reappraisal of the mind's grasp of the world, arising
from such ordinary incidents as a five-year-old boy's pride at riding like a
grown-up, or the same boy's intense anticipation, at age thirteen, of going
home from school for Christmas vacation. Wordsworth subtly repeats
each scene's details, once as they were presented to his eye, and then, in a
finer tone, as they were seen in the mind's eye. When the five-year-old
rider came back up on the high road after being separated from his father's
servant, he saw

> A naked Pool that lay beneath the hills,
> The Beacon on the summit, and more near,
> A Girl who bore a Pitcher on her head
> And seem'd with difficult steps to force her way
> Against the blowing wind.   [304–08]

Seen in the mind's "visionary dreariness," the scene is the same, but different—"somewhat changed," as Shelley urbanely says of a similar moment
of human transformation in *Prometheus Unbound* (IV.71):

> . . . the naked Pool,
> The Beacon on the lonely Eminence,
> The Woman, and her garments vex'd and toss'd
> By the strong wind.   [313–16]

To express the difference would require "words that are unknown to
man" (310); human words can point to it, but it can be felt, in recollection
of similar moments in our own lives ("if but once we have been strong"),
and one should be wary of making too much of the fact that, in the transition from sight to vision, the summit has become a "lonely Eminence," the
"Girl" a "Woman," the "blowing" wind a "strong" one, or that her difficulty in walking has been transferred to the vexing and tossing of her
garments.

In the Waiting for the Horses, loss and death also characterize the intervention which forces mind to change its mind into a scene of visionary
power. In the first "spot," the boy was separated from his father's manser-
vant and saw a rude roadside memorial of a wife-murderer's execution
site; in the second, he is separated from his father by death, and his recollection of waiting for the horses to take him home to "my Father's House"
changes accordingly.

> . . . 'twas a day
> Stormy, and rough, and wild, and on the grass
> I sate, half-shelter'd by a naked wall;
> Upon my right hand was a single sheep,

> A whistling hawthorn on my left, and there,
> With those Companions at my side, I watch'd,
> Straining my eyes intensely, as the mist
> Gave intermitting prospect of the wood
> And plain beneath.   [356–64]

Re-imagining the scene after his father's death ten days later, it is one line shorter but several times more powerful:

> And afterwards, the wind and sleety rain
> And all the business of the elements,
> The single sheep, and the one blasted tree,
> And the bleak music of that old stone wall,
> The noise of wood and water, and the mist
> Which on the line of each of those two Roads
> Advanced in such indisputable shapes . . .   [376–82]

—"All these were spectacles" from which he drank "as at a fountain" (383–85). Slightly more abstracted or generalized in each case, slightly more ominous or suggestive, the naked power of the repeated scene in each "spot" is *informed* with power, unlike the "barren sea" of the rationalized world in Wordsworth's ideological fall, from which power— "soul"—had been *abstracted*. It may be that appreciation of these differences requires more sympathy with an author than he has reason to expect from strangers, but clearly it is a power Wordsworth felt constantly, as he expressed it in the Lucy poem: "Oh! the difference to me!"[75] Arbitrary changes in external circumstance—the boy goes riding but is lost at the grave of a wife-murderer, he goes home but loses his father—change the world's appearance; it is either a truism or a revelation. But Wordsworth's emphasis in Book XI is how the world changes under dominance of the mind's changes, not through the barren, endless logical succession of "wild theories" and "minute analysis," but by a power that is not felt until accidentally revealed; then what the eye sees is transformed, independent of the eye, altering its ground of empirical evidence.

Book XII: "Same Subject (Continued)"

The key sections of Books XI and XIII—the "spots of time" and the ascent of Snowdon—had first been used as the conclusion of the five-book plan of "Books and Nature." The necessity for Book XII, however, arose directly from Wordsworth's later composition of his experience of the French Revolution. Although XII deals with the "Same Subject"—the impairment and restoration of his imagination—it is now "Continued" with reference to Human Life and the hopes for a qualitative change in human nature which the Revolution raised and then dashed. Such a theme could not be accommodated to what one might learn from "Books and Nature." Books might speak of it, but Wordsworth had seen the idea in action, so XII presents what he learned on "the lonely roads [which] / Were schools to me," where he "daily read / . . . the passions of mankind" (XII.163–65); this lifelike reading of human psychology restores perspective to the idea of "human nature seeming born again" which he first entertained on the "public . . . stately roads" of France (VI.354, 364, 372).

In XII as in XI, the causes of imaginative impairment are the separation of reason from feeling and common human circumstance. Restoration similarly requires the reintroduction of "soul" into Wordsworth's attitudes, but toward mankind rather than external nature. The "wild theories" of revolution promised a "Man to come parted as by a gulph, / From him who had been" (XI.59–60), but when Wordsworth asks one of his profound simple questions, "Why is this glorious Creature to be found / One only in ten thousand?" (XII.90–91), his aimless, homeless wanderings in England between 1791 and 1795 become field trips upon the highways and byways of life, researches among actual men to see if the ratio is not already much higher than futurists and other ideologues suppose.[76] His conclusion is that ideal man already exists—grinding poverty and ignorance aside—did we but recognize him. His hypotheses about the imaginative worth of common man are rarely more unguarded than in the middle section of Book XII, where he seeks "pure" specimens of mankind, unadorned by social privilege, natural gifts (of language, for example), or indeed anything at all, even outward dress and comely appearance. Rarely also is his need for philosophical or logical correction more evident, of the sort Coleridge could and did supply in his critique of the *Lyrical Ballads*' similar theory of common language. Significantly, these portions of XII were originally intended for Book VIII,[77] where Wordsworth's effort to come to grips with the unnerving spectacle of social man in London led him into similar extremes of idealized faith and untenable logic. Connecting epistemology to sociology, he descends the class ladder to ever simpler specimens "among the *natural abodes* of men" (107; italics added), until he comes near to preferring those "least practis'd in the strife of phrase" (as though all philosophy were so much sophistry), who hardly speak at all ("Words are but under-agents in their souls," 272), reaching the democratically heartening and romantically absurd conclusion that men's outer appearances are all equally valuable indices of their inner worth, "if we have eyes to see" (283).

Where do we get such eyes? Exactly at this point of romantic democratic sentimentality, "the genius of the Poet" (294) will enter in, with this particular poet's imprimatur of truth, a visionary scene: his peculiar experiences on Salisbury Plain (312–53). We reach this point where vision supererogates reason, where imagination spontaneously restores itself, by following Wordsworth, "wandering on from day to day," along the public roads where he "saw into the depth of human souls, / Souls that appear to have no depth at all / To vulgar eyes (166–68). Between these "vulgar eyes" and the critical conditional of "*if* we have eyes to see," Wordsworth tries to strip away all supposedly factitious distinctions of depth and surface in Human Life, revealing its universal glory by "the genius of the Poet"—his own, which he then offers to the history of Poetry as his distinctive contribution and exemplar for all future poets. His search for unaccommodated man on "unappropriated earth,"[78] however illogical, is still the strongest example in English of the desire to put literature into contact with unconditioned human reality, unmediated by literary convention or religious piety. He quickly jettisons ordinary understandings of culture and civilization (as he did History and Poetry in XI), being "convinced at heart / How little that to which alone we give / The name of education hath to do / With real feeling and just sense" (168–71). Hearing "a tale of honour . . . From mouths of lowly men and of obscure" (182–83), he is further convinced of the class-bound error that "strong affections" and "love" require "retirement, leisure, language purified" (185, 189). This is hardly an error that democratic revolutionaries are likely to be guilty of, but Wordsworth's aim is not to disprove revolutionary promise, but the alienating force of any "wild theories" whatever, from radical justifications for terror to the reactionary complacency of Godwinian necessarianism. Books are cast out because of the frequently mistaken intentions of both authors and readers, "looking for their fame / To judgments of the wealthy Few" (207–08). When literature qua literature is seen as part of the same system of "outside marks by which / Society had parted man from man" (217–18), it must be rejected out of hand rather than discriminatingly reformed. At this point, the polemical fat is in the fire and Wordsworth unstoppably en route to his most fervid statements of faith in the innate democracy of imagination, soon driven below the level of "men adroit in speech" to his powerful native speakers, silent philosophers conversing in "the language of the heavens" (270), whose examples lead him on to

> Convictions still more strong than heretofore
> Not only that the inner frame is good,
> . . . but that no less

> Nature through all conditions hath a power
> To consecrate, if we have eyes to see,
> The outside of her creatures, and to breathe
> Grandeur upon the very humblest face
> Of human life.   [279–86]

This is a conclusion such as Emerson reached in his enthusiastic essay, *Nature*, that all "disagreeable appearances, swine, spiders, snakes, pests, madhouses, prisons, enemies, [will] vanish," once "we come to look at the world with new eyes," bringing "the axis of vision" into coincidence with "the axis of things." Like Emerson and many another Romantic prophet, Wordsworth asserts his faith that "the genius of the Poet hence / May boldly make his way among mankind / Wherever Nature leads" (294–96), without observing that his appropriation of a new subject matter comes into conflict with his rebuke to "men adroit / In speech and for communication with the world / Accomplish'd" (255–57). For the poet is certainly such an adroit speaker, even (perhaps especially) the poet who does not want to be one, but "a man speaking to men, bringing with him everywhere relationship and love" (Preface to *Lyrical Ballads*). Wordsworth, in his enthusiasm, has skipped over the fact that the fault of other adroit writers—the successful poets and powerful reviewers in London—is not their accomplished language but the vanity with which they employ it: "Most active when they are most eloquent / And elevated most when most admired" (258–59). He has made an accidental, secondary quality of a medium of social communication an intrinsic, primary quality of the linguistic phenomenon itself, mirroring his basic assumption in Book XII that essential man means man stripped of all "accidents" of dress, station, education, appearance, and, most important for democratic poets, language. This is not circular argument, but an uncircling, centrifugal one, akin to other passages in *The Recluse* where words like *unutterable, unintelligible, interminable,* and *untaught* are paradoxically enlisted in Wordsworth's search for a truth-speaking poetry, referring to the power released in language (or felt in the nature of things) by the authority of genius, while simultaneously raising it far above ordinary speech with adjectives reflecting a layman's naive faith in what philosophy can do, or say. In spinning outward, this argument spins out of control; but just here, leaping over all inconsistencies, Wordsworth makes his stand, calling to his "Dearest Friend" for trust that he speaks "in a mighty scheme of truth" when he claims his "peculiar dower, a sense / . . . to perceive / Something unseen before" (302–05): his vision of the imaginative worth of all men, to be validated by his greatest hope

> that a work of mine,
> Proceeding from the depth of untaught things,
> Enduring and creative, might become
> A power like one of Nature's.   [309–12]

This naturalization of his imagination parallels and completes the series of accommodations of human power to natural force worked upon books and language in Book V, upon London and urban civilization in Book VIII, and upon revolutionary violence and despair in Book X.

As proof, Wordsworth offers an account of his visionary experience on Salisbury Plain in the late summer of 1793, the details of which are almost entirely unknown, but which were as crucial in his imaginative development as the crossing of the Simplon or the ascent of Snowdon.[79] Like Book XI's "spots of time," the Salisbury Plain visions conclude an unstable argument with a leap of faith into mystery that can be neither totally explicated nor lightly ignored. There are three visions, slightly separated by content and mode of appearance. First, "overcome" by solitude, he "had a reverie and saw the past," ancient Britons in their military might:

> The voice of spears was heard, the rattling spear
> Shaken by arms of mighty bone, in strength
> Long moulder'd of barbaric majesty.   [324–26]

Second, he calls "upon the darkness; and it took"

> All objects from my sight; and lo! again
> The desart [*sic*] visible by dismal flames!
> It is the sacrificial Altar, fed
> With living men, how deep the groans, the voice
> Of those in the gigantic wicker thrills
> Throughout the region far and near, pervades
> The monumental hillocks; and the pomp
> Is for both worlds, the living and the dead.   [329–36]

Third, "at other moments," less intense, "gently charm'd . . . with an antiquarian's dream," he imagines Druids giving instruction from Stonehenge's "mystery of shapes":

> And saw the bearded Teachers, with white wands
> Uplifted, pointing to the starry sky
> Alternately, and Plain below, while breath
> Of music seem'd to guide them, and the Waste
> Was chear'd with stillness and a pleasant sound.   [349–53]

The immediate question, in the context of Book XII's argument, is what these three visions of ancient power, pomp, and wisdom have to do with the poor silent men among whom Wordsworth's ambulatory researches have taken him, the singing of whose praises he claims as his own "peculiar dower" in the "mighty scheme of truth" in which "Poets, even as Prophets," are connected?

The easiest part of the answer is to see Wordsworth's vision as an example of Romantic primitivism, a validation of his claim by historical essence: the poet hath stood "By Nature's side among the men of old, / And so shall stand forever" (297–98). But Wordsworth introduces his vision of ancient warriors, priests, and sages not as a defense of the worth of the simple, wordless, essential men he met upon the public roads of mid-1790 England, but as evidence, "once above all," of his conviction that his poetry *about* such men constitutes his peculiar claim to genius. Thus the proper interpretive question is: what does Wordsworth have in common with these ancient warriors, priests, and sages? The answer is another of *The Prelude*'s associations of Imagination with eternity via the intermediation of death, or thoughts about death, and another defense of its philosophical merits by means of the emotional process it recapitulates rather than the logical system it assumes, desires, and simultaneously doubts.[80] The "mighty bone" of the ancient Britons represents earthly physical power. The "bearded Teachers" patiently demonstrate correspondences between heaven and earth, representing "their knowledge of the heavens" in earthly forms and images. But how do we get from power to knowledge, that important Romantic question, reiterated in Yeats's "Leda and the Swan": "Did she put on his [Zeus's] knowledge with his power?" The connecting link, clearly marked as the deepest and darkest of the three visions, is Wordsworth's sight of a threshold initiation scene in which "living men" are about to be fed into another world, like the doomed explorers in the five-book *Prelude*, "and the pomp / Is for both worlds, the living and the dead." This is no time for liberal squeamishness about human progress, still less for objections of taste at Wordsworth's simplistic representation. He neither blinks nor mollifies the horror—"how deep the groans." But why does "the voice / Of those in the gigantic wicker *thrill* . . . / Throughout the region"? For whom does it thrill? He who has ears to hear, let him hear. Or, in his earlier visual formula, "*if* we have eyes to see," we will see possible connections between finite and infinite human nature, in ancient human sacrifice or on modern "lonely roads which were schools to me."

Imagination is connected to Human Life through prehistorical images, as it was connected to London by Wordsworth's historical "sense of what had been here done, and suffer'd here / Through ages" (VIII.781–83). He backs away from any explanation of his conclusive images (reserving all interpretations for the Snowdon image to follow immediately), disarmingly relegating them to what "may be view'd / Or fancied, in the obscurities of time" (354–55) and to Coleridge's indulgence. Coleridge was the first non-Wordsworthian source for Wordsworth's faith in his peculiar genius, and Coleridge first made this claim when he read, in 1796, "some imperfect verse / Which in that lonesome journey was composed," *Adventures upon Salisbury Plain*. Wordsworth now repeats Coleridge's claim to confirm his own estimate of his powers:

> . . . Friend, [who said]
> That . . . then I must have exercised
> Upon the vulgar forms of present things
> And actual world of our familiar days,
> A higher power, have caught from them a tone,
> An image, and a character, by books
> Not hitherto reflected.   [356–65]

Books, hitherto cast out in the extremes of Book XII's argument, are now redeemed, at least Wordsworthian books, which can see "into the depth of human souls, / Souls that appear to have no depth at all / To vulgar eyes" (166–68).

Wordsworth caps Coleridge's estimate by a further judgment of his own worth, which develops this metaphor of deep-seeing, in language that constitutes a sort of philosophical conceit, suggesting an apparently metaphysical justification for his democratic genius.

> I remember well
> That in life's every-day appearances
> I seem'd about this period to have sight
> Of a new world, a world, too, that was fit
> To be transmitted and made visible
> To other eyes, as having for its base
> That whence our dignity originates,
> That which both gives it being and maintains
> A balance, an ennobling interchange
> Of action from within and from without,
> The excellence, pure spirit, and best power
> Both of the object seen, and eye that sees.   [368–79]

In this passage, an infinite regression of terms recoils from extinction at the last instant into an infinite "interchange," paralleling the masterful imagery of depth and mystery Wordsworth added to *1799*'s "spots of time"

in adapting them to Book XI and reflecting his contemporaneous composition of the Intimations Ode.[81] He moves backward from "every-day appearances" to "a new world," then to that world's "base," which is in turn
the self-sufficient equivalent of human worth, or "whence" it arises: its
very essence ("being") *and* also its principle of resistance—or balance, or
self-definition—over against the external world, making the "interchange"
between the two "ennobling," rather than, say, crippling or annihilating
because of nature's superior strength. The "base . . . whence our dignity
originates" is apparently also the base of the object-world, or, if not its actual, physical basis, then of its qualities of "excellence" and purity:
namely, qualities of human meaning. Undeniably a rhetorical sleight-of-
hand occurs when Wordsworth inserts the phrase "and from without,"
not to mention the slippery pronoun references throughout. This is dizzying rhetoric troping logical language, not radical philosophic idealism.
"Action . . . from without" may hark back to "life's every-day appearances," as his earlier claim to "have exercised / *Upon* the vulgar forms of
. . . things . . . a higher power" segued invisibly into his having "caught
from them a tone, / . . . by books / Not hitherto reflected" (360–65), but
any effort to hold apart things that are being so powerfully forced together
will not yield a consistent philosophic definition beyond Wordsworth's
overweening desire to assert his imagination's restoration on the basis of
his unique vision of the worth of common man, seen as part of an "ennobling interchange" between the "being" of mind and of nature. His defense of this conclusive statement spills over, as elsewhere in *The Prelude*,
from the end of one book to the beginning of another, becoming the intention of his elaborate explanation of his vision atop Snowdon, which came
to him, as Book XIII begins by informing us, "in one of these excursions"
(XIII.1), the road-wanderings which Book XII has presented as his postgraduate school in Human Life, and which Book XIII will extend into the
final haunt and region of Wordsworth's song, the Mind of Man.

Book XIII: "Conclusion"

Book XIII concludes *The Prelude* in two stages; the first (1–210), the
vision from Mount Snowdon in Wales and Wordsworth's elaborate interpretation of it, completes the three stages of imaginative restoration begun
in Book XI; the second (269–452) is the summary and conclusion of the
poem as a whole. The two endings are interrelated by means of a transitional bridge (211–68) of thanksgiving addressed to Dorothy and Coleridge, characteristic of every conclusive moment in *The Recluse's* history,
and here crucially linking Wordsworth's paramount resolution-image

(Snowdon) of the Mind of Man to the preparatory poem defending the mental development of the man who has such visions—who sees, interprets, and re-presents them poetically.

Imagination on Snowdon: Snowdon's "perfect image of a mighty Mind" gives evidence of Wordsworth's specifically mental recovery from revolutionary impairment, as the "spots of time" evinced his imagination's recovery of its relations with Nature, and the Salisbury Plain visions, its restoration to Human Life. Snowdon is the poem's fullest elaboration of its "spots of time" representation of mental growth: expectation, followed by surprise, leading to reinterpretation of mental powers, and, here more than anywhere else, to metaphysical generalization and social application. It is like a completed oil painting for which all the earlier "spots" have been preparatory sketches. The structural significance of his attribution of the Snowdon vision to "one of these excursions" that produced the Salisbury Plain visions is underscored by our knowledge that it did not occur, biographically, on one of Wordsworth's excursions of 1793–94 after his residence in France, but in 1791, when, with his 1790 Alpine companion, Robert Jones, he was again wandering in search of scenes of natural sublimity: "to see the sun / Rise from the top of Snowdon."[82] But, relocated in imaginary time, Snowdon functions as a contemporary, personal version of the "ennobling interchange" represented mythohistorically by the Druids' wands pointing back and forth between the stars and Stonehenge. Wordsworth inserts himself in place of the Druids, directing our attention to moon, cloudscape, and the "fracture in the vapour" — his archetypal scene of imaginative process. This rhetorical strategy of substituting himself in propria persona at critical junctures in a vast cultural continuum was implicit in his Adamic enthusiasm in "Home at Grasmere," and in the parallels he suggested between his own poetically outcast situation and the high-minded avengers of liberty he entertained as likely epic subjects in *The Prelude*'s "Introduction." It will be made explicit in his account of his wish to save the abbey of the Grand Chartreuse from revolutionary destruction in "The Tuft of Primroses" (1808). Such cultural egotism, substituting the individual imagination for vanishing social tradition, is the central point of *The Prelude* as "antechapel" to *The Recluse*'s secular "gothic church." By presenting Snowdon as the conclusion of *The Prelude*'s final sequence of restorations, Wordsworth makes it the necessary elaboration of the "ennobling interchange" between "the object seen, and eye that sees" with which Book XII ended, and the goal of the "dim uncertain ways" he found himself traveling, "in quest of highest truth," in Book XI's "spots of time."

Taking more than a hundred lines to interpret his own image, he clarifies the terse explanations offered in XI and XII, but by means of the same rhetoric of philosophic conceit that powerfully blurs inexplicable connections in a rising, three-stage sequence: (1) event, (2) interpretation, (3) generalization.

The actual physical description of the Snowdon event (1–65) is a passage of unparalleled clarity in Wordsworth's work. Hiking up to see the special sublimity of a mountain sunrise, he is surprised to find himself in the midst of a splendid moonscape, of three distinctly emblematic parts. The sky is all brilliant, sharp definition: "The Moon stood naked in the Heavens" (41). The earth presents a mixture of real and apparent features: mists extend out from his feet like a "huge Sea" that also appears, in the distance, like a landscape ("headlands, tongues, and promontory shapes"), through which the actual landscape is intermittently visible: "A hundred hills their dusky backs upheaved" (45). Below this, "the sea," emphatically "the real Sea" (49), though invisible, sends up a "homeless voice of waters" through a gap in the mists—and in "that dark deep thoroughfare had Nature lodg'd / The Soul, the Imagination of the whole" (64–65). As in the Simplon Pass and the Gondo ravine, a pass, path, or thoroughfare—a medium of physical progress—is transmuted into a home, abode, or lodging for an "*un*father'd vapour" or "home*less* voice," in an effort to image an ongoing mental process within the normally static mode of philosophical definitions. As a pictorial representation, this is a clear Romantic-Idealist view of that aspect of human mentality—Imagination, "Reason in her most exalted mood"—which operates between, partakes of both, and thereby binds, the object world of sense perception and the subject world of consciousness and spiritual awareness, which are otherwise divided from each other into endlessly alternating roles of conqueror and victim: consciousness and civilization defeated by death, nature constantly violated as a mere body of resource. Hence the mixed quality of the middle mind/landscape: mist, ocean, "headlands" (indeed!), hills, and "dusky backs" all together, pointedly spread out, as Wordsworth three times emphasizes, at his "very feet" (36, 44, 54). Defending this view of reality was Coleridge's justification for his life's work and his definition of Wordsworth's *Recluse*: "He was to treat man as man . . . in contact with external nature, and informing the senses from the mind, and not compounding a mind out of the senses . . . thence he was to infer and reveal the proof of, and necessity for, the whole state of man and society being subject to, and illustrative of, a redemptive process in operation, showing how this idea reconciled all the anomalies, and promised future glory and restoration . . ." (*TT*, II.70–71).

This is also how Wordsworth interprets the scene in his "meditation" after it passes away (66–119). Its representation of the operation of human imagination is clearly the most important feature for him; only six lines are *not* given to variations on the theme of "higher minds . . . build-[ing] up greatest things / From least suggestions" in "express resemblance" to the operation of some higher "Power." And in those six lines he draws the *meta*physical dimensions of the scene in his most impressive idiom of philosophic rhetoric:

> . . . it appear'd to me
> The perfect image of mighty Mind,
> Of one that feeds upon infinity,
> That is exalted by an under-presence,
> The sense of God, or whatsoe'er is dim
> Or vast in its own being—   [68–73]

Like his sonorous "somethings," the grand "whatsoe'er" of these lines will not yield a definite meaning; their complex syntax refers comprehensively up, down, inward, and outward simultaneously, and even Wordsworth's subsidiary clarification, that the scene represents "above all / One function of such mind" (its giving-and-taking creativity), ambiguously suggests both a natural representation of a mental function and a mental version of a natural one. But these blurrings serve to get him to his sure ground, his description of the workings of "the glorious faculty / Which higher minds bear with them as their own" (89–90). The persuasiveness of Snowdon as an image of imagination's state of mind in the world has not fundamentally diminished since 1805, particularly as a humanistic-humanitarian model of the moral self-sufficiency of such "higher minds." They "need not extraordinary calls / To rouze them, in a world of life they live, / By sensible impressions not enthrall'd / . . . / Hence chearfulness in every act of life / Hence truth in moral judgements and delight / That fails not in the external universe" (101–03, 117–19): sound minds in a sound world in sound relations with human life.

Having elaborated the Snowdon vision into an emblem of the mind's self-sufficiency by virtue of "dim and vast" transcendental resemblances, Wordsworth's third step is to generalize this power to others (120–210). This becomes, instead, a particularization of the sort common throughout *The Prelude*. His opening rhetorical question ("Oh! who is he that hath . . . / Preserved . . . this freedom in himself?") turns out not to require the expected rhetorical negative (e.g., "very few, if any"), but to be an *oyez!* seeking a witness and affidavit that is immediately forthcoming: "Witness, ye Solitudes! . . . that, howsoe'er misled, / I never . . . / Did tamper with

myself from private aims / . . . in place of that / Which is divine and true"
(122–43 passim). The "perfect image of a mighty Mind" thus devolves
upon "a meditative, oft a suffering Man" determined to hold himself off
from "private aims . . . selfish passions . . . mean cares and low pursuits."
As in "Tintern Abbey," this laudable behavior is, in the immediate context, evidence from a relatively narrow range of morality, used to support
extremely large claims: Wordsworth attesting that his own mind's restoration is a philosophic possibility for the general Mind of Man. His spiritual
integrity, which by itself might be indistinguishable from "selfish passions," is guaranteed by love: "This love more intellectual cannot
be / Without Imagination, which, in truth, / Is but another name for . . .
reason in her most exalted mood" (166–70). The interrelations of love,
reason, and imagination in this statement are as insusceptible of definitional priorities as the relation between Nature and Imagination in the initial Snowdon event. Wordsworth combines all three in one last river-image
that encapsulates the entire movement of *The Prelude* as its author's effort
to accommodate his imagination to benign views of Human Life: following "this faculty" from the "blind cavern" of its preconscious origins
(Book I) "to light . . . Among the ways of Nature" (II, and parts of IV and
VI), then "Lost sight of . . . bewilder'd and engulph'd" in Cambridge, London, and France, then greeted "as it rose once more / With *strength*, reflecting in its *solemn* breast / The works of man and face of human life"
(179–81)—adverb and adjective indicating the revised, deep-structure
view of Human Life in Books VIII and XII—

> And lastly, from its progress have we drawn
> The feeling of life endless, the great thought
> By which we live, Infinity and God.   [182–84]

At this moment, *The Prelude* is precisely up-to-date; what has "lastly"
occurred, the interpretation of the Snowdon vision, is here at the end of its
taking-place. The entire interpretation turns upon imaginative love of others; human community is the ultimate goal of all, but rising from an invisible point of individual origin, "far / From any reach of outward fellowship" (195–96): "Here must thou be, O Man! / Strength to thyself; no
Helper hast thou here; / Here keepest thou thy individual state: / No other
can divide with thee this work" (188–91). The man-in-general who
achieves this paradox has realized the ideal of "feeling intellect"
(205)—like the particular man just summarized in his river-image—and
has achieved the goal, the "station of a man in mental repose, one whose
principles were made up," from which Coleridge said Wordsworth might
write *The Recluse* (*TT*, II.70).

Just at this point of insistence upon the necessarily individual origins
of social love, Wordsworth turns to the little community, Dorothy and
Coleridge, which helped him preserve love in himself (211–68). The
movement to another human being at the conclusion of an escalating series
of complicated philosophic assertions, characteristic of "Tintern Abbey"
and "Dejection" and many other Romantic odes, is also a regular feature
of *The Recluse*'s several conclusive moments. Although Wordsworth's
statement of the operation of imaginative love is more concrete than his
nod in the direction of its "dim and vast" metaphysics, it too has reached a
point of discontinuous progression, where selfishness transmutes to self-
lessness, identical to the paradox of the Pedlar's rapid moral development
from human aversion to "unutterable love." Dorothy and Coleridge are
represented as gentling Wordsworth's native tendency to excessive self-
sufficiency, above all his love of "that beauty, which, as Milton sings, /
Hath terror in it" (225–26), which tended to keep him locked in his "individual state" without bothering to reach out to others. Coleridge tones
down Wordsworth's philosophic fascination with "the life / Of all things
and [their] mighty unity" (253–54) by interposing "thoughts / Of man
and his concerns, such as become / A human Creature, be he who he
may! / Poet, or destined for a humbler name" (257–60). The end result is
that

> . . . God and Man divided, as they ought,
> Between them the great system of the world
> Where Man is sphered, and which God animates.   [266–68]

It is a little hard to realize that these lines are not a religious or philosophical generalization but a description of the relative disposition of things in
William Wordsworth's mind—the implication being that, without Coleridge's intervention, he would have been content to stay with God, that is,
to view reality from a godlike perspective. Overcoming this temptation is
necessary if *The Prelude* is to lead on to *The Recluse*, if the poet's epyllion
is to lead to the great redemptive epic "Of man and his concerns
. . . be he who he may!"

The Postlude to *The Prelude:* A tendency to begin speed-reading *The
Prelude* at about this point is nearly irresistible, as though its last two
hundred lines were a hodgepodge of philosophical second thoughts. Wordsworth himself was the first reader to feel the tendency, and he resisted it
by a series of false endings functionally paralleling *The Prelude*'s effective
false starts, but also manifesting the disequilibrium of ending that afflicts
all of the *Recluse* segments in the face of getting on with the project. As

the first half of Book XIII concludes *The Prelude* thematically, the second half (269–452) concludes it structurally, leading out of the poem in inverse order to Book I's lead-ins:

Book I	Book XIII
Glad Preamble: "I cannot miss my way."	Preliminary Conclusion: Topics not done justice.
Post-Preamble: Cautions upon opening confidence.	Pre-Postlude: Qualifications upon closing confidence: "All gratulant if rightly understood."
Introduction: Poetic qualifications and alternative epic subjects.	Prospective Postlude: "redemption surely yet to come."

Preliminary Conclusion (269–367). Throughout his concluding stages, Wordsworth no sooner approaches the functional end of his poem—"our object from the first / . . . to make me capable / Of building up a work that should endure" (274, 277–78)—than he recoils to reiterate his *Prelude*-mode, "that marvellous world / As studied first in my own heart" (308–09). More than a simple longing to keep writing about himself, each of these recoils concerns something he might have said about himself in relation to Human Life. The three main topics under "much hath been omitted" (279)—Fancy, Public School, and Raisley Calvert —could hardly seem more miscellaneous; yet within each of them Wordsworth finds grounds that prepared him to be the poet of *The Recluse*. Fancy, largely neglected in favor of "the main essential Power, / Imagination" (289–90), might have been traced "by elaborate research" to her maturity, showing how we "in the Rivers and the Groves behold / . . . forms and definite appearances / Of human life" (295, 300–01), leading to public responsibility: "life among the passions of mankind / . . . the infinite varieties and shades / Of individual character" (310–13).

This process of fanciful maturation leads next to his gratitude for having been "the pupil of a public School" (316), because it prepared him for "the shock / Of various tempers . . . conflicting passions" (318–19). His words for these conflicts are strong—*forced, hardy, shock, mysteries, endure*—bespeaking a very delicate sensibility for whom the ordinary business of Human Life was almost unbearably sordid, yet which his conception of his masterwork determined him to face. His homage to public education is itself a fanciful fiction—that "when call'd / To take a station among Men, the step / Was easier" (325–27)—for few steps could have been less certain, few stations more ephemeral, than Wordsworth's after college. But the internal benefits of school's "timely exercise" are more true to life, for they confirmed his natural tendency toward the condition of *spectator ab extra*: "to keep / In wholesome separation the two natures, / The one that feels, the other that observes" (329–31).

Finally, to confirm the humane value of his spiritual separation from ordinary life, his expression of thanks for Raisley Calvert's bequest comes in a paragraph (332–67) minimizing the "three years" (late 1792–late 1795) between his "unwilling" withdrawal from France and his settling at Racedown as requiring "less regard / To time and place" in his "Story" —precisely the years (and books) of critical mixture between Imagination and Revolution which fundamentally established *The Prelude*'s complex thematic structure. Calvert's bequest converted a vocational dilemma into a mission. During these years Wordsworth "led an undomestic Wanderer's life . . . roam'd about from place to place" (343, 347). But this condition, which neither Wordsworth nor any of his friends or relations regarded with promising favor, Raisley Calvert is represented as having seen with a dying man's clairvoyance: "He deem'd that my pursuits and labors lay / Apart from all that leads to wealth, or even / Perhaps to necessary mainte- nance" (362–64). Which is to say that Calvert "deem'd" Wordsworth's "pursuits" should be exactly what they already were, confirming him fi- nancially in the spiritual worth of his wandering life: "By a Bequest suffi- cient for my needs / Enable me to pause for choice, *and walk / At large and unrestrain'd* . . . / By mortal cares" (357–60; italics added). Such a walk is preeminently the mood of *The Prelude*'s opening—"Now I am free, en- franchis'd and at large" (I.9); the poem now corroborates the life. Calvert was a sort of heavenly messenger ("Himself no Poet, yet / Far less a com- mon Spirit of the world," 360–61), and by fulfilling the promise that Calvert saw, Wordsworth has become more than just a poet—a dedicated spirit, a humanist, a man living for other men, avoiding the "hazard to the finer sense" (365) of the need to earn a living. His attention to each of the three main topics *The Prelude* has neglected represents their Human Life–value in ways similar to the redemptive retreat from public life of the cast-out heroes which he said in *The Prelude*'s "Introduction" he would most like to write about. In his way, he has. Mithridates, Sertorius, DeGourges, Gustavus, Wallace, and their followers all nursed the justice of their cause in solitude until they could descend in triumph on the civiliza- tions which offended them; Wordsworth, secret adept in social Fancy, publicly schooled in private reserve, is finally rewarded by Calvert's be- quest and his imaginative onslaught released: "He clear'd a passage for me, and the stream / Flow'd in the bent of Nature" (366–67). The man walked free, and his poem flowed after him; *The Prelude*'s dominant im-

age for the narrative of its hero's life (walking, wandering) and its dominant image for its own progress (a river or stream) here join forces.

Pre-Postlude (367–427). Slighted topics noted, *The Prelude* again approaches its appointed end: "I have other tasks" (370). Each of its four final paragraphs swerves from initial acceptance of the *Recluse*-task to further justifications of *The Prelude*, thus paralleling the outsetting
confidence of the preamble and post-preamble with qualified expressions
of conclusive hope. In the first paragraph, the provocative question of the
poem's beginning—"Was it for this?"—reappears with its burden of
guilt: "I said unto the life which I had lived, / Where art thou? Hear I not a
voice from thee / Which 'tis reproach to hear?" (375–77). "Thee" is not,
in this unique case, Coleridge, but his own life, which reassuringly answers
his doubtful question with a world-scope image of its significance: "Anon
I rose / As if on wings, and saw beneath me stretch'd / Vast prospect of the
world which I had been / And was" (377–80). As throughout the final
books' restoration of his imagination, this world-view ends in social responsibility: "often with more plaintive voice / Attemper'd to the sorrows
of the earth" (382–83). The second concluding paragraph also begins by
looking forward ("Whether to me shall be allotted life / . . . / Sufficient to
excuse me . . . / For having given this Record of myself," 386–89), but
ends by looking backward to a more satisfying time, the summer of 1798,
when Wordsworth and Coleridge composed most of *Lyrical Ballads*.
"When thou dost to that summer turn thy thoughts, / And hast before thee
all which then we were" (404–05; italics added), these curiously substan-
tialized sights of past times and achievements will make Coleridge feel
"that the history of a Poet's mind / Is labour not unworthy of regard"
(408–09). The third paragraph also justifies "the last and later portions"
of *The Prelude* by stretching a connective tissue between those past times
"wherein we first / Together wanton'd in wild Poesy" (413–14) and
Coleridge's now expected return from Sicily and Malta, spanning the grief
of John's death and Coleridge's ill-health, unhappiness, and long absence.
Coleridge's going abroad was the reason for the resumption of *The Prelude*; now he is returning, it can be ended, and *The Recluse* resumed.

Postlude (428–52). Coleridge's understanding, memory, and anticipated pleasure are each in turn the fulcrum on which justification for *The
Prelude* turns in the first three of its final four paragraphs. In the fourth, a
postlude which becomes a preamble for *The Recluse*, the justification is
Coleridge's future work, to which Wordsworth gradually adds his own
contribution. Again the paragraph begins by looking forward, but this
time it does not look back, except in a revision that only Coleridge might

be expected to recognize: "a few short years of useful life, / And all will be complete, thy race be run, / Thy monument of glory will be raised" (428–30). This conventional wish might or might not recall to Coleridge's mind the only other conclusion of the poem he knew (never having seen a proper conclusion to the five-book version): "so haply shall thy days / Be many, and a blessing to mankind" (*1799*, ii.513–14). But he could hardly fail to recognize Wordsworth's generalized re-revision of his letter of September 1799, which had provided the material for *1799*'s conclusion and was still the most detailed contemporary statement—on paper—of *The Recluse*'s intentions:[83]

1799, ii.478–82, 485–88	XIII.431–36
. . . if in these times of fear,	
This melancholy waste of hopes o'erthrown,	Then, though, too weak to tread the ways of truth,
If, 'mid indifference and apathy	This Age fall back to old idolatry,
And wicked exultation, when good men	Though men return to servitude as fast
On every side fall off we know not how	As the tide ebbs, to ignominy and shame
. . . .	By Nations sink together, we shall still
Yet mingled, not unwillingly, with sneers	Find solace in the knowledge which we have . . .
On visionary minds, if in this time	
Of dereliction and dismay, I yet	
Despair not of our nature . . .	

Besides invoking the authority of Coleridge's own statement, Wordsworth is again invoking what we have seen to be the strongest authority operating in *The Prelude*, his own words, now ventriloquized by deep allusion to his former quotation of his friend. Ostensibly, this all still refers to Coleridge's race for glory, but the plural person has emerged: "*we* shall . . . Find solace," be blessed, "sanctified by reason and by truth," in building *The Recluse*:

> United helpers forward of a day
> Of firmer trust, joint-labourers in a work
> (Should Providence such grace to us vouchsafe)
> Of their redemption, surely yet to come.   [438–41]

I have already commented upon the counterpoint of confident assertion and doubtful qualification in this paragraph (chap. 4); we can now see that it conveys meaning by the same combination of buried figuration and philosophical rhetoric which characterizes each of the key passages in *The*

Prelude's concluding movement: Book XI's "spots of time," Book XII's Salisbury Plain visions, and Book XIII's Snowdon emblem. As "Prophets of Nature," Wordsworth and Coleridge will address their "age" and its "Nations":

> Instruct them how the mind of man becomes
> A thousand times more beautiful than the earth
> On which he dwells, above this Frame of things
> (Which, 'mid all revolutions in the hopes
> And fears of men, doth still remain unchanged)
> In beauty exalted, as it is itself
> Of substance and of fabric more divine.   [446-52]

These final words of *The Prelude* parallel the Snowdon vision, but as an image of creation, not a natural emblem, of truths which both seek to inculcate. At bottom, always enduring, is "this Frame of things." Exalted above it to the thousandth power is "the mind of man," which achieves its Becoming beauty in the mixed, painful process of "revolutions in the hopes and fears of men"—akin to Snowdon's "deep dark thoroughfare" containing "the Imagination of the whole." These revolutions of hope and fear are the refining process of spiritualization by which the mind's "substance" and "fabric" are realized as "more divine." The figure here is not a mountain landscape, real or metaphoric, but something like a beautiful tent—stretched on, yet above, the "Frame of things" in which man "dwells"—the beautiful, ever-changing, always vulnerable fabric of human creativity, a construction endlessly in process, as Snowdon showed the mixed, beautiful, insubstantial middle state of earth through which "the homeless voice of waters" rose toward clear, naked heaven. The "monument of glory" which Wordsworth and Coleridge will be "joint-labourers" in raising is, similarly, a "race" to be run (429), nowhere but "'*mid* all revolutions in the hopes / And fears of men," just as Nature "*lodg'd*" the imaginative essence of the Snowdon vision in "that deep dark thoroughfare." In this tent or dome—oracular, instructive, loving, and inspiring —would sit a double-natured person, part godlike poet, part philosopher-friend, half Wordsworth, half Coleridge: the Recluse.

6

"Home at Grasmere" in 1806

these populous slopes
With all their groves and with their murmurous woods,
Giving a curious feeling to the mind
Of peopled solitude.

PW, V.341

Wordsworth finished the thirteen-book *Prelude* in May 1805. The occasion was neither a happy nor a conclusive one; he expressed his dissatisfaction with what he had achieved to Beaumont:

> I have the pleasure to say that I finished my Poem about a fortnight ago, I had looked forward to the day as a most happy one . . . but it was not a happy day for me I was dejected on many accounts; when I looked back upon the performance it seemed to have a dead weight about it, the reality so far short of the expectation; it was the first long labour that I had finished, and the doubt whether I should ever live to write the Recluse and the sense which I had of this Poem being so far below what I seem'd capable of executing, depressed me much. . . . [*LEY*, 594]

Grief over John's death underlay much of this depression, for *The Prelude* had finally been completed as a surrogate for the poetic memorial Wordsworth wished to erect to his brother, which was swept away in a "torrent" of emotions he could not master (*LEY*, 586). But if the end of *The Prelude*'s composition was marked by tragedy and disappointment, Wordsworth was correspondingly eager to get on with *The Recluse*. In his letter to Beaumont, he cemented *The Prelude* to *The Recluse* with a metaphor much stronger than the "tail-piece" or "appendix" he and Coleridge had spoken of earlier: "This work may be considered as a sort of portico to the Recluse, part the same building, which I hope to be able erelong to begin with, in earnest" (*LEY*, 594). By December he was already hard at work on his usual precomposition exercises: reading voraciously while Dorothy and Mary recopied portions of the manuscripts already written (*LEY*, 607, 617; *CMY*, 292, 309–10). There is an appropriate symbolism in the fact that the first record of actual new work on *The Recluse* dates from Christmas Day, 1805 (*LEY*, 664), and that the finished poem resulting from the effort was the one begun six years earlier in spontaneous homage to the moments when they first found themselves home at Grasmere.

But, even as the sixth anniversary of their homecoming was celebrated with special ceremony during the holidays (*LEY*, 659), Wordsworth's return to *The Recluse* was again associated with thoughts of a new home and a newly reconstituted imaginative community. Dove Cottage was too small; William and Mary were expecting their third child in June 1806; in November Wordsworth had determined to buy "a spot [Broad How] he prefers above all others that he has seen for building a home" (*CMY*, 309).[1] In early March they received word that Coleridge was en route home (*CMY*, 315). Coleridge's presence or absence was the crucial external variable in *The Recluse*'s progress. Dorothy had wisely observed at Christmastime that "I do not think [William] will be able to do much more [than read] till we have heard of Coleridge" (*LEY*, 664). Wordsworth was spurred with a desire to present his homecoming friend not only with the preparatory poem which had grown to such "an alarming length!" (*LEY*, 586) in his absence, but also with something completed on the main work. He spent over a month in London in the spring, waiting for Coleridge (*CMY*, 317–23); there his domestic thoughts were affected by home-thoughts of much larger scope, which are also reflected in the visions of a nonpoliticized natural democracy in the 1806 sections of "Home at Grasmere." With his friends Scott and Humphry Davy, he attended dinner parties where his republicanism was commented upon (*CMY*, 318), reminding him of Scott's revelation the previous summer that Lord Somerville had set the spy on him and Coleridge in 1797, and still regarded him and Southey as Jacobins at heart (*CMY*, 296). He met again his early political hero, Fox, at the brilliant gatherings of Regency intellectuals hosted by Fox's nephew, Lord Holland, just emerging as leader of a new generation of Whigs. Pitt's death in January complicated the Opposition's sense of the political direction of the world war even more than Nelson's the preceding October (which William and Mary had been stunned to receive just as they were inspecting Broad How; *CMY*, 304, M. II.63–64), while Napoleon's brilliant victories at Austerlitz and Jena forced Austria and Prussia out of the coalition against him, leaving England as the world's last best hope of stopping the advance of imperialist revolution. At the same time, but in much different surroundings, Wordsworth dined with Godwin, his old radical intellectual mentor of the mid-1790s, now a disappointed and discredited man, walking evidence to Wordsworth of the dangers of excessively stated hopes for the reformation of society by human justice.

He was called home by the imminence of Mary's delivery (Thomas

Wordsworth was born June 15), and the main period of 1806 composition on "Home at Grasmere" followed, between June and September. Although identification of the lines composed for, or transferred to, "Home at Grasmere" in 1806 remains somewhat conjectural, the completed poem could certainly have been ready for presentation or recitation to Coleridge when the two friends finally met again in October of that year. But what a changed man Wordsworth discovered, occasioning what great sea-changes in the conception and progress of *The Recluse*, will be considered in chapter 7 as bearing more upon another new beginning of the masterwork, rather than the hopeful first-stage conclusion represented by the completion of "Home at Grasmere" in 1806.

The portions of "Home at Grasmere" most likely composed in 1806 (ll. 458–859 of MS B, plus a bridge passage, lines 875–958, leading to the "Prospectus"-as-conclusion)[2] present a remarkably coherent yet fantastically literal response to the problems that had stopped Wordsworth's composition on the poem in 1800, which were in turn specific forms of his basic dilemma in writing *The Recluse*: the need to generalize persuasively beyond his own experience. This was necessary not only to achieve the systematic quality required of a philosophic poem, but also, as he now felt increasingly, to represent a social view of imaginative democracy that steered clear of dangerously individualistic political implications that might arise from insisting too radically on his unique imaginative powers. He wanted to write a poem that was, like him, Jacobin *at heart* but still able to articulate quite different persuasions of mind and will. The 1800 portions of the poem had left both Wordsworth and Grasmere in too exposed a position as manifestations of the independent power of human creativity to make a redemptive difference in the world. The early manuscript broke off at the words, "so here there is. . . ." But there had been nothing to justify his special claims for Grasmere's potency. His claims had become extravagant because of his overreaction to the material fact that "two [were] missing," the two swans with which he and Dorothy so strongly identified themselves. This had to be forced down as an objection to Grasmere's perfection—because Grasmere, in this context, was not an actual place but, even more than an imaginative idealization,[3] a sort of philosopher's stone (or valley) intended to provide foundation for a vast structure of philosophic assurances about human life.

The new portions composed in 1806 speak directly to this dilemma, in Wordsworth's efforts to generalize the validity of his claims beyond himself and his place to other persons in other places. Of the four hundred

narrative lines most certainly written in 1806, nearly three-quarters are devoted to stories of Grasmere creatures (plants and animals as well as humans) other than William Wordsworth. In them, we recognize Wordsworth's characteristic trope of generalization in *The Recluse*: story-telling
to achieve a sense of logical force by rhetorical multiplication. This function of the stories is underscored by their placement in the poem: two separate groups of stories are followed by passages of quasi-logical language
that, as in the very similar strategy of "Tintern Abbey," effectively give the
appearance of clinching a conclusion. Compared with the ecstatic, erratic
oratorical leaps and bounds of the 1800 portions, the 1806 portions of
"Home at Grasmere" proceed according to a much tighter argumentative
structure—though, as we shall see, their logical appearance is also deeply
affected by the circular fantasticality of the lines written in 1800.

"HOME AT GRASMERE," 1806 (MS B)

[Connective passage to 1800 portions: ll. 458–68]
  I. Grasmere Stories (Human): ll. 469–645
  II. Argumentative Deductions from Stories
      Internal Objection (ll. 620–31): "Is there not / An art . . . / That shall
        be . . . the acknowledged voice of life?"
      Internal Rejection (ll. 646–92): "No, we are not alone; we do not
        stand, / . . . here misplaced and desolate."
      First Conclusion (ll. 693–719): "Fair *proof* of this . . . / Already have
        I seen."
  III. Grasmere Stories (Animal): ll. 720–806 (domestic, 720–52; wild, 753–
        806)
  IV. Argumentative Deductions from Stories
      Rejection of Inapplicable External Standards (ll. 807–18): "solitude is
        not / Where these things are."
      Redefinition of External Standards (ll. 818–28): "Society is here."
      Second Conclusion (ll. 829–59) "Dismissing *therefore* all Arca-
        dian dreams."
["Happy band" passage from 1800: ll. 859–74]
  V. Bridge Passage to "Prospectus": ll. 875–958
      Adult (or *Recluse*) Application (ll. 875–909): "'tis not to enjoy
        . . . / That we exist; no, something must be done."
      Child (or *Prelude*) Application (ll. 910–52): "While yet an innocent
        little-one. . . ."
      Third Conclusion (ll. 953–58): "*Then* farewell to the Warrior's deeds
        . . . A Voice shall speak, and what will be the Theme?"
["Prospectus" Conclusion, composed ca. 1800, ll. 959–1048: "On Man,
  On Nature, and on human Life."]

The first Grasmere folktales clearly exemplify the dialectical movement of Wordsworth's imagination, in *The Recluse*, between private needs and public responsibilities. Abandoning the painful extremities to which he had been driven in 1800, to show that "I shrink not from the evil in disgust" (432), he resumes in 1806 with the houses of Grasmere—the stories each cottage could tell in support of his claims for the valley's special qualities. In the overall context of *The Recluse*, the 1806 return to "Home at Grasmere" by means of human and animal tales, shifting from the personal ecstasy of the 1800 portions, exactly parallels the movement of the two-part *Prelude* of 1799, from a first part of wild natural spontaneity to a second part which attempts to contain that spontaneity in more permanent social forms. But the stories are odd as generalizations about the special mental power of Grasmere because they are so nearly pointless, or require so much special pleading and reading to discern their purpose. This is partly because they all concern death and men's creative energy in overcoming—or even causing—death and grief. But connections between death and imagination are familiar to readers of Wordsworth's poetry, and the real peculiarity of these stories lies less in their contents than in their obscure manner of reaching their conclusions. Akin to the circular imagery, tautological arguments, negative denominations ("'Tis (but I cannot name it)," 161), subverted oxymorons ("Unity entire," 170), and other linguistic abnormalities of the 1800 lines, these stories proceed to denouement by a narrative syntax that strives toward a grammatical condition beyond predication.

Their paradoxical quality is clear in the first one (469–532), in which a local farmer commits adultery with the family maid, lets his farm go to ruin out of remorse, and finally dies of it. This certainly suggests that "the old / Substantial virtues have a firmer tone [here] / Than in the base and ordinary world," but rather more so than is either plausible or desirable. Yet the force of the adulterer's example is carried more by Wordsworth's syntax than by the events reported, since the farmer possesses that peculiarly Grasmerian quality of self-containment which enables him to execute himself for his own sins: "himself / Was his own world" (515–16), "he died of his own grief, / He could not bear the weight of his own shame" (531–32). Mere clichés in standard public English, these have special literal power in Wordsworth's Grasmere, where the guilty die of their own grief through supremely organic mental processes that require no outward mediation—social, political, or religious. If this were generalized into political terms, the 1806 Grasmere of Wordsworth's *Recluse* would be one of constant nonviolent moral revolution.

The second tale balances the adulterous husband's sin with a charm-
ing picture of a widower whose six blooming daughters reconcile him to
his loss by transforming their house from an indistinguishable piece of
"native Rock" to a highly crafted human artifact, a "play thing and a
pride," with walls "curious for shape or hue," a "mimic Bird's-nest" in a
bush, and other cutely humanized features of house and garden. These are
nice things, but we do not imagine how they might speak to the widower
words *other* than those "which might be a prelude to a Tale / Of sorrow
and dejection" (539–40), until we recognize that, like the adulterer's mor-
tally substantial grief, the daughters' arts and crafts are more fantastico-
literal evidence that "the old / Substantial virtues have a firmer tone" in
Grasmere—they have more substance as virtue because they tend toward
actual, concrete, material existence; they are visible pieces, so to speak, of
substance as a philosophic concept.

Human emotions are similarly displaced into natural growth in the final tale (607–45) about a couple who, "in their prime of wedlock,"
planted a grove of fir trees to shelter their sheep. The old woman, now a
widow, tells Wordsworth that the grove is "just six weeks younger than
her eldest Boy" (613), and the word *younger* reinforces other suggestions
that children, sheep, and trees were all equally dependents of the pair. But
the grove is "now flourishing while they / No longer flourish; he entirely
gone, / She withering in her loneliness" (640–42); the reversal of the organic metaphor suggests that they are being supplanted by their own
sowing. At best, the banality of such phrasing suggests that old folks don't
die in Grasmere, they just fade away—jokes that Wordsworth courts by
insisting on mind–nature parallels that defend Grasmere by transforming
its ordinariness into phenomena more suited to a fairy-tale kingdom.

Such objections occurred simultaneously to Wordsworth; few poems
give more insight into their creator's acts of reading in the very act of
composition. (He never brought "Home at Grasmere" to a state he considered publishable.)[4] He interrupts himself to ask precisely the pertinent
questions of these stories whose conclusions leave us looking round for
point, predicate, and poetry. "Is there not / An art, a music, and a stream
of words / That shall be life, the acknowledged voice of life?" (620–22). Is
there an art that is not art, but life? If there were, we would certainly allow
the priority of Wordsworth's claim to it among all other poets. The difficulty of such an ideal is not that it is so hard to find, but that it is, for
Wordsworth, so temptingly and readily available: "Or must we seek these
things where man is not?" (631). Writing poetry of picturesque, sentimental, descriptive views was something he was good at and enjoyed doing,

and bulks large enough in his collected works to provide much of the basis of his reputation with posterity. But this would never do for *The Recluse*, of which "Home at Grasmere" was now in the process of being made Book First, Part First, principally by means of accommodating Wordsworth's naturally escapist aesthetic imagination to responsible views of Human Life. Thus, though he concludes the old shepherd couple's story with the admission that capturing its moral significance may be "a task above my skill," yet his "silent mind" listens to and loves the old woman, and thereby "honours[s] humankind" (643–45); we must take it on faith, not in words.

The defense of this claim that follows (646–92) is intended to prove the human moral value, not simply of Grasmere, but of educated and ambitious poets retiring to remote valleys to live and work. Contrary to the public urban world's assumptions about provincial life, Wordsworth insists that "matter for a thought" (662) exists as abundantly in Grasmere as in London. Although Wordsworth in 1806 was not exactly a famous poet, he was certainly a controversial one, by dint of his strenuous prefaces to the new editions of *Lyrical Ballads* in 1800 and 1802 insisting on the superior moral value of unrefined language, and their concomitant implication of the superior human value of common, uneducated life. Since the quality of Wordsworth's poetry has to a large degree proved his contemporary critics wrong and has seemed to validate the consistency of his theories about it, we tend to assume his heroic confidence toward the poetry and the life he was leading; but this was by no means the case in medias res. "Home at Grasmere" exemplifies his uncertainties, as in the heavy accumulation of negatives with which he rejects the charge of selfish escapism: "No, we are not alone; we do not stand, / My Emma, here misplaced and desolate, / Loving what no one cares for but ourselves" (646–48). He must prove that human life in outlying districts is recognizably human, that he and his entourage are not bestowing "unprofitable kindliness . . . / On Objects unaccustomed to the gifts / Of feeling" (651–53), in contrast to the accepted view that true humanism is achieved by cultivation of the arts of high culture. He clinches his strong assertions of the human value of "untutored Shepherds" with a "Fair proof" whose manner is perfectly consistent, not with logic, but with the special circularity that invests every aspect of "Home at Grasmere's" structure.

> Fair proof of this, Newcomer though I be,
> Already have I seen; the inward frame [of human emotions],
> Though slowly opening, opens every day.
> Nor am I less delighted with the show

As it unfolds itself, now here, now there,
Than is the passing Traveller, when his way
Lies through some region then first trod by him
(Say this fair Valley's self), when low-hung mists
Break up and are beginning to recede.
How pleased he is to hear the murmuring stream,
The many Voices, from he knows not where,
To have about him, which way e'er he goes,
Something on every side concealed from view,
In every quarter some thing visible,
Half seen or wholly, lost and found again—
Alternate progress and impediment,
And yet a growing prospect in the main.   [693–709]

As a "proof" in the ordinary sense, this is hardly intelligible. There is
no premise (about what constitutes the basic worth of human beings), no
marshaling of evidence, and no conclusion drawn. Almost the entire passage is taken up with the description of a mountain valley, and more especially with the sensory processes by which an outside observer becomes
aware of it. We are, of course, familiar with the conclusive force of such
"proofs" elsewhere in Wordsworth's poetry: the Simplon crossing and the
Snowdon climbing also record the process of "how" his soul came to its
feeling of conviction, rather than "what" those convictions were. MS D replaces "this fair Valley's self" with "some Helvetian Dell," bringing the
passage into even closer proximity to Wordsworth's most important visionary moments.[5] However, compared with the Simplon and Snowdon
visions, this is visionary gradualism. In the Simplon Pass, he was "lost . . .
without a struggle"; but the humane vapors of Grasmere are ones in which
one finds, not loses, oneself, because of the social, philosophic require-
ments of *The Recluse* as distinct from the personal, imaginative goals of
The Prelude. What sprang into his mind in the peak *Prelude* moments was
an awareness of the infinite thirst of his own imaginative powers. Here,
however, the subject is the minds of all men, about which he is less sure,
with respect both to powers and progress. Hence there is no hint of apocalyptic breakthrough; the mists hardly part at all in parting; there is no
rending of the veil.[6] Like a cyclical or spiral vision of human progress, it is
"alternate progress and impediment"; knowing and not-knowing the direction of human progress alternate easily in a single, continuous, back
and forth, but ultimately progressive vision. If his confidence in human nature in Grasmere is occasionally shaken, he assures himself that it will continue to grow without damaging gaps. Thus the "ungenerous thought" of

"mortal separation" first raised by the particular evidence of the missing swans in 1800 has been overcome by a fabulous "Fair proof" that caps Wordsworth's generalized evidence of other human beings' experience in Grasmere, with which he resumed *The Recluse* in 1806.

The second large movement of the 1806 portion of "Home at Grasmere" proceeds like the first, from a group of putative generalizations by Wordsworth beyond his own experience to an appearance of logical deduction drawn from this evidence. The animal stories or emblems of lines 720–806 are intended as corollaries to the three human folktales of lines 469–645; as the human stories showed how *natural* human beings could be, the animal emblems show how very *human* Nature is, in Grasmere. Wordsworth says he quickly "inscribe[d] upon my heart" (724) his new acquaintances, the horse that carried a paralytic man, the ass that bore a crippled miner, the specific thrush, wren, or robin associated with each cottage, and so on, up to "Helvellyn's Eagles . . . ancient Hold" and "The Owl that gives the name to Owlet-crag" (739, 742). But by far the most important item in this new catalog of proofs that the Wordsworths "are not alone" in Grasmere—that their educated humanism is reciprocated by the inherent human qualities of the dalesmen—is Wordsworth's final image, the flock of spring birds (753–806). These are the same birds among whom he noticed, in his pell-mell progress through the lines written in 1800, that "two are missing," and got his poem into insuperable trouble because of his heavy identification of Dorothy and himself with the two swans. They had opened a crack toward imaginative death and isolation in the progress of *The Recluse* into which the entire *Prelude* of 1805 was thrust. Wordsworth now heals the remaining scar by a significant change in metaphor, from 1800's image of the birds as wild, free dancers in air, to 1806's dwellers in "a settled residence," or, at the very least, homecoming strangers. Whereas in 1800 the birds' circular unity-in-motion had been purely aesthetic, it is now described by analogy to the human community Wordsworth seeks to establish:

> Whether in large communities ye dwell
> From year to year, not shunning man's abode,
> A settled residence, or be from far,
> Wild creatures, and of many homes, that come
> The gift of winds, and whom the winds again
> Take from us at your pleasure—yet shall ye
> Not want for this, your own subordinate place,
> According to your claim, an underplace
> In my affections.   [758–66]

The dialectical motion of Wordsworth's thought on solitude versus community is particularly notable in his unique definition of wildness as, not homeless, but "of many homes": pertaining to homes, like his accommodation of his imagination to Grasmere. Although the birds are still wild, he is reluctant to accord them the unqualified restlessness of 1800 (e.g., "As if they scorned both resting-place and rest," l. 314). He now worries the question of restlessness versus settledness in a way that closely resembles the visionary gradualism of his preceding "Fair proof," very much determined by the *Recluse–Prelude* dialectic of social imagination versus private creativity: "see them now at rest, / Yet not at rest . . . / They cannot rest" (768–70):

> Incapable although they be of rest,
> And in their fashion very rioters,
> There is a stillness, and they seem to make
> Calm revelry in that their calm abode.   [799–802]

Pursued this far, such dialectical images degenerate, as metaphors for social versus individual uses of imagination, into inscrutable paradox, and it is much easier to say that Wordsworth is simply describing birds than to realize he is playing out tensions between his intended masterwork and his unintended one.

Thus Wordsworth's second attempt in 1806 to generalize to beings other than himself has succeeded, not by logic, but by illogic dressed up in the guise of logic (circular imagery, circular argument, circular vision), to enable him to reject external standards of judgment which would regard his removal to Grasmere as an escape from the public world of poetical careers and, more threatening, from the public responsibilities of his poetical masterwork. However, Wordsworth is well aware that metaphors are at best analogies to the ideal of human community he seeks to establish. Although after the first three human stories he violently rejected charges of personal selfishness in "seceding" to Grasmere (l. 249), he now goes further and rejects the very standards on which such judgments are based— that is, the standards of the city, of the public world—so that his move to the country may be seen not as an apolitical act but, on the contrary, as a secession, or civil division, of the highest political significance and idealism.[7] He first reverses the charges by an extravagant imputation of real loneliness—alienation, as we would say—to the city-dweller:

> Then boldly say that solitude is not
> Where these things are: he truly is alone,
> He of the multitude, whose eyes are doomed

> To hold a vacant commerce day by day
> With that which he can neither know nor love—
> Dead things, to him thrice dead—   [807–12]

The city is by now three times worse than the country, in Wordsworth's excited negative hyperbole, but "worse than this . . . / and worse than all," the man of the crowd holds vacant commerce with "swarms of life . . . / His fellow men," and what should be a concentration of humane imaginative possibilities is to him "no more / Than to the Forest Hermit are the leaves" of the trees, and finally, "far less, / Far less" than that (813–17).

The counteraction is an equally vehement appropriation of political language to Grasmere, equivalent to *Prelude* VIII's preemption of London's "home Imperial . . . chief living residence," an emphatic redefinition and consolidation of Grasmere's powers to true civic *oneness*, in diametric opposition to the extrapolating powers of alienation in the ordinary city:

> Society is here:
> The true community, the noblest Frame
> Of many into one incorporate;
> That must be looked for here; paternal sway,
> One Household under God for high and low,
> One family and one mansion; to themselves
> Appropriate and divided from the world
> As if it were a cave, a multitude
> Human and brute, possessors undisturbed
> Of this recess, their legislative Hall,
> Their Temple, and their glorious dwelling-place.   [818–28]

Such exuberantly literal e pluribus unum allegiances ("of many into one") have long been understood as something specially unguarded in Wordsworth's canon, but they are entirely consistent with the overall development of *The Recluse* project.[8] It stands out in particular relief in these moments when Wordsworth attempts to cement the relationship of Mind to Nature by sociopolitical metaphors which—after two hundred years of politicized romanticism—seem inconsistent with our ideas of *both* primary terms, especially with received ideas of Wordsworth's understanding of them.

At the similar point in his first efforts in 1806 to redefine the places in which a truly humanistic poetry might arise, Wordsworth had asked in agony if there were "not / An art . . . / That shall be . . . the acknowledged voice of life?" (620–22). Now he is prepared to go further, in a second conclusion that extends his earlier "Fair proof" of humane value in Grasmere to the value of the poetry which might be written there, inspired by

it: "Dismissing *therefore* all Arcadian dreams . . . Give entrance to the sober truth" (829, 837). He sets his face resolutely toward a new poetry of
reality, if only he and his friends can come to share Grasmere's self-
validating self-sufficiency, by becoming "Inmates not unworthy of their
home, / . . . Dwellers of the Dwelling" (858–59): literally intellectuals akin
to Grasmere's heroes of ordinary life, the "rational and suffering" adulterer who "himself / Was his own world" (515–16), and the reconciled
widower who was "not gay . . . [but whose] whole House is filled with
gaiety" (605–06). As the moment to write this new kind of poetry—*The
Recluse*—approaches, such tautological identifications lead back to the
poet himself and the "happy band" around him, characteristic of all *Recluse*-endings. Exactly at this point (line 859) the continuity of the manuscript breaks off, and the "happy band" lines from 1800 (859–74) are
plugged in, celebrating the promise of that new beginning, overriding
Wordsworth's grief at the failure of "the present day's" joy to "overspread
the future years with hope," a complex allusion to John's death, Coleridge's absence, and *The Recluse*'s difficulties all at once. From having just
been constituted as the legislative and religious center of an imaginative
universe, the population of this Grasmerian commonwealth shrinks suddenly to seven (William, Mary, John, and Dorothy Wordsworth, Samuel
and Sara Coleridge, and Sara Hutchinson), and then precipitously to one,
Wordsworth himself, as the basic structural question of *The Recluse*
emerges explicitly, to be negotiated in a passage bridging from the poem
proper to the grand conclusion in reserve for it all ready: How does the
artistic, creative imagination exist for other people? Why bother?

The bridge passage (875–958) links the main body of "Home at
Grasmere," as composed in both 1800 and 1806, to the "Prospectus" lines.
It is the most miscellaneous part of the poem, composed of lines and passages which, as Jonathan Wordsworth has well suggested, are now con-
structively drawn together to build a way to a conclusion.[9] These lines
have a repetitive, time-marking quality that reveals, perhaps more than
any other part of this revealing poem, the dilemma of Wordsworth's work
on his masterpiece. The passage falls into two clearly different parts, one
of which (875–909), concerning mature responsibility and public achievement can be closely identified with *The Recluse*, while the other (910–33)
obviously deals with *Prelude*-like material, and concerns Wordsworth's
childish raptures over the idea of dangerous enterprises undertaken against
overwhelming odds. Thus the very structure of Wordsworth's bridge to his
conclusion manifests the conflicting tensions between public and private

verse which were both the intention and the dilemma of *The Recluse*: it seems to offer a way out, but then works like a drawbridge to pull him up short of his goal.

The passage begins with a stern summons to duty from Wordsworth's conscience: "'tis not to enjoy, for this alone / That we exist; no, something must be done" (875–76). These are the harshest words yet in a poem that has tried, with considerable difficulty, to convince itself that writing poetry is an acceptably mature vocation. But though he generously allows himself that "each Being has his office" (880), he is not sure what his duty is. Though he feels his creative genius burn brightly within him, he does not perceive in it any necessarily social intention:

> Why does this inward lustre fondly seek
> And gladly blend with outward fellowship?
> Why shine they round me thus, whom thus I love?
> Why do they teach me, whom I thus revere?
> Strange question, yet it answers not itself.   [888–92]

It is a strange question on any account, but especially strange to arise in the mind of a man who has just substituted Grasmere for London as an appropriately humane world-center on the basis of its "outward fellowship." It is finally an absurdly strange question, because it refuses to participate in the terms of Wordsworth's Grasmere myth by *answering itself*: the Grasmere, that is, where unfaithful husbands answer the question of their moral guilt by dying of it. Although Wordsworth is now resolutely home at Grasmere, no sooner does he take his stand there—as poet of *The Recluse* who knows that "something must be done"—than his imagination thrusts itself in and threatens to alienate him all over again. Even the place itself cannot give him an answer: "That humble Roof . . . / That calm fire side—it is not even in them, / . . . to furnish a reply" (893–95). More than a sentimental hyperbole, such an observation fits exactly with the circular, self-validating quality of the imaginative universe Wordsworth has tried to construct in Grasmere and now finds wanting. The place will not necessarily supply the poetry (cf. the similar rhetorical expectation operating in *The Prelude*'s preamble and post-preamble). The answer is not in Grasmere nor, by extension, in Nature—the answer, that is, to the relation between the inner joy of creative genius and its social usefulness. Like the earlier doubt that occurred to him—that the true art of life might have to be sought "where man is not"—Wordsworth here challenges himself to say if there is any reciprocity at all between the inspiration of genius and the lives of ordinary people.

The question has a close Romantic parallel in Goethe's *West-ostlicher Diwan* (1819): "Does a man live when others also live?" If Wordsworth had been able to answer such questions comprehensively, he might have become, according to Harold Bloom, "a greater poet than the one he became, a more externalized maker who would have had a subject beyond that of his own subjectivity."[10] This clearly applies to the Wordsworth of the "egotistical sublime," yet the questions themselves suggest that his subjective sublimity was not a matter of choice but of his unhappy inability to refuse it. Self-knowledge in terms of community, or vice versa, which will it be? Instead of choosing one term or the other and fully developing it, like later nineteenth-century thinkers (preeminently Freud and Marx), Wordsworth keeps choosing one and then the other, the spark of his imagination leaping back and forth across the gap throughout *The Recluse*'s life-history. He insists upon his "Something within, which yet is shared by none . . . / I would impart it; I would spread it wide, / Immortal in the world which is to come" (898, 901–02). Yet the reference of "immortal" is ambiguous; is it an adverb or an adjective? How can the poet's personal desire for immortality be separated from the value of divine gifts which he would generously "impart" to others? Such questions can lead in only one direction in *The Recluse*, and they do so again here: back to the *Prelude*-mode, as Wordsworth turns to what he is much more sure of than his message "of what in man is human or divine," namely, his medium and motive: that "I have felt" it to be so (908–09).

In lines that may overflow from either Part I of the 1799 *Prelude* or Book I of the 1805 *Prelude* (or both), or from very similar passages used to describe the Pedlar of "The Ruined Cottage,"[11] Wordsworth turns back to his sure ground and concludes the bridge passage with a miniature *Prelude*: "While yet an innocent little-one" (910 ff.). As in *The Prelude* itself, the innocence and "tender moods" of this little-one are quickly shunted off in favor of his "wild appetites and blind desires, / Motions of savage instinct" (913–14), with which he read the book of Nature according to the interpretation of his own fiercely independent imagination:

> Nothing at that time
> So welcome, no temptation half so dear
> As that which [urged] me to a daring feat.
> Deep pools, tall trees, black chasms, and dizzy crags—
> I loved to look in them, to stand and read
> Their looks forbidding, read and disobey,
> Sometimes in act, and evermore in thought.   [915–21]

These willful misreadings of Nature are linked to other, literal readings of similar intent:

> With impulses which only were by these
> Surpassed in strength, I heard of danger met
> Or sought with courage, enterprize forlorn,
> By one, sole keeper of his own intent,
> Or by a resolute few, who for the sake
> Of glory fronted multitudes in arms.
> Yea, to this day I swell with like desire;
> I cannot at this moment read a tale
> Of two brave Vessels matched in deadly fight
> And fighting to the death, but I am pleased
> More than a wise Man ought to be; I wish,
> I burn, I struggle, and in soul am there.   [922–33]

I believe that Wordsworth's present-tense elaboration (928–33) of his violent youthful reading habits may well reflect his devouring of accounts of Nelson's last moments at Trafalgar, subconsciously underlain by the family's deeply mingled pain and pride over John's bravery in going down with his ship, both of which had already come together during this same period in the "Character of a Happy Warrior" (M. II.44).[12] More generally, we recognize again in this passage the little band of courageous exiles and their heroic leader, the archetypal Wordsworth-circles of *Prelude* I's regretted epic heroes. His recent redefinition of Grasmere as legislative center of a new imaginative universe set over against London also reminds us that these outnumbered autodidacts were mostly northern men who wreak the revenge of the philosophic mind on the unjust and misunderstanding urban empires to the south from which they have been cast out. The reappearance of this "resolute few" is the repetition in mythopoeic or literary terms of the actual "happy band" of the Wordsworth circle, recapitulating in a higher key his excitement at the idea of imaginative triumph even as his mature judgment forces him to correct it: "I am pleased / More than a wise Man ought to be."

For the third time, in his 1806 composition and reconstruction of "Home at Grasmere," Wordsworth has brought himself to a need of conclusion. Now he must force himself to dismiss conventional epic dreams ("the Warrior's deeds . . . the heroic trumpet") and get down to the business at hand: *The Recluse*, a redemptive social poem for modern man, already disillusioned with the promise of human improvement by the failures and excesses of the French Revolution. The concluding verse para-

graphs of "Home at Grasmere" are remarkable in revealing the great difficulty Wordsworth had in harnessing himself to his task because of the
obvious strength of his "insatiable mind" (848) to *resist* the very poem
that his will or conscience was determined to fit it into. More clearly than
anywhere else in his poetry, Nature is here the agent of Imagination's chastisement: "me hath Nature tamed and bade me seek / For other agitations
or be calm" (934–35), and what Nature accomplished upon him unconsciously, now "hath Reason sanctioned" (942). This is the logic and sequence of "Ode to Duty" (1804) and "Peele Castle" (1805),[13] and not, in
the context of *The Recluse*, a lessening of imaginative confidence or loss of
imaginative energy so much as a determined reining in of his own energies,
in order to make, as the "Prospectus" will say, "authentic comment" upon
suffering social reality. Yet even Reason's sanctions, returning him to the
social purposes of poetry, define his new poetic "office" in analogues
which threaten to make us forget that it is supposed to be different than
the *Prelude*-mode:

> "Yet fear [says Reason] . . . no want
> Of aspirations which have been—of foes
> To wrestle with and victory to complete,
> Bounds to be leapt and darkness to explore.
> That which enflamed thy infant heart—the love,
> The longing, the contempt, the undaunted quest—
> These shall survive, though changed their office, these
> Shall live; it is not in their power to die."
>
> [945–52]

Clearly the potential excitement and ultimate stature of the enterprise fire
Wordsworth more than its contents. He speaks with the confidence, not of
a philosophic poet, but of an epic one—or, more accurately, an epic hero
whose quest is to complete the poem in which he acts. This violent metaphoric scene of supposedly rationalized and naturalized poetry-writing is
nearly indistinguishable from the "tale / Of two brave vessels matched in
deadly fight" a few lines earlier, and, together with Wordsworth's fond
"farewell to the Warrior's deeds," very possibly represents an *ave atque
vale* from Grasmere to Trafalgar, one prospective national hero opposed
to the disillusioning aftermath of the French Revolution saluting another
just killed in the same cause, mediated through his own relation to heroic
death by his brother, the "silent poet."

"Bounds to be leapt and darkness to explore" are also clear lead-ins
or cues to the "Prospectus," which now fits neatly into place in response

to nagging questions of what his great poem will be *about*: "A Voice shall speak, and what will be the Theme? / On Man, on Nature, and on human Life" (958–59). In the "Prospectus," considered as a conclusion to "Home at Grasmere," the theme of poetry written for the good of mankind is extended onto a culture-wide grid in the most elevated language available to an English poet. Even Nelson's heroic battles are left behind as Wordsworth tries to surpass Milton in a daringly humanistic redaction of *Paradise Lost*'s war in heaven:

> For I must tread on shadowy ground, must sink
> Deep, and, aloft ascending, breathe in worlds
> To which the Heaven of heavens is but a veil.
> All strength, all terror, single or in bands,
> That ever was put forth in personal forms—
> Jehovah, with his thunder, and the quire
> Of shouting angels and the empyreal throne—
> I pass them unalarmed. [977–84]

Wordsworth's exiled, reclusive hero here ventures into regions metaphysically more remote than any of his earlier prototypes and does not avenge his cause upon the powers that be (Christian civilization in all its cultural representations), but reduces them to insignificance by finding terrors beyond their ken—terrors which, indeed, reside precisely in his place of reclusion:

> The darkest Pit
> Of the profoundest Hell, chaos, night,
> Nor aught of ["blinder," MS D] vacancy scooped out
> By help of dreams can breed such fear and awe
> As fall upon us often when we look
> Into our minds, into the mind of Man. [984–89]

The "Prospectus," as we have already seen (chap. 3), opens up all three regions of Wordsworth's song—Man, Nature, and Human Life— with a dialectics of place / poetry so powerful that it tends to override, or flatten, all objections to the redefinitions of poet to place accomplished in the 1806 portions of "Home at Grasmere." The most difficult of these three regions for the Wordsworth of *The Recluse* is, of course, Human Life, which comes last with simple *authenticity* its goal (1024), in comparison to the grand sublimity of "the mind of Man" (989) and the peaceful beauty of "the green earth" (991). In 1806, Wordsworth added the lines about a "great consummation" between "the individual Mind" and "the external world" (1002–14).[14] Although providing an impressive quasi-philosophic image with which to greet the soon expected Coleridge, they express a resolution of Mind–Nature relations that is manifestly not extended to Human Life, except in an obscure parenthetical conjecture: "(And the progressive powers perhaps no less / Of the whole species)" (1007–08). The real presence and power of Human Life in the *Prelude–Recluse* dialectic are felt in the fact that his reluctant turn toward "the tribes and fellowships of men" is followed immediately by a return to and recasting of his muse. At the beginning of the "Prospectus" she was called "Urania" (975), but at the end of this credal statement she is identified in humanized superlatives of the Holy Ghost ("Thou human Soul of the wide earth"), more daring than Milton's Christianizing of his classical muse, and located in a city-center more specifically individual even than Wordsworth's imaginative urbanization of Grasmere Valley: "that hast / Thy metropolitan Temple in the hearts / Of mighty Poets" (1027–29). And the prayer's final petition seems correspondingly a prospectus for quite a different poem than the one spoken of earlier: "if with this / I blend more lowly matter—with the thing / Contemplated describe the mind and man / Contemplating, and who and what he was, / . . . when and where and how he lived, / With all his little realities of life— / Be not this labour useless" (1034–41). The relation of this poem to the intention of *The Recluse*, far from being dialectically reconciled, is nearly extraliterary: "may my life / Express the image of a better time, / More wise desires and simple manners" (1044–46).

Wordsworth, however, had already written this poem — *The Prelude* of 1805—and had reached the conclusion that the life of this "mind and man contemplating" was fit to teach the sinking nations (*Prel.* XIII.428–52). The next effort on "the thing contemplated"—*The Recluse*—was "The Tuft of Primroses" of 1808, which attempts to generalize the experience of this "transitory Being," not by local evidence and special logic as in the 1806 portions of "Home at Grasmere," but by using the ruined abbeys of Christian history as spiritual analogues to the "metropolitan Temple" in the heart of mighty modern secular poets. The necessary transfer of spiritual power occurs nevertheless at the same single point, the imagination of William Wordsworth, with the same result— that the little band at Dove Cottage is again faced with writing the poem of the new civilization, another "enterprize forlorn" of exiles against overwhelming odds. It was, however, the change in Coleridge as much as anything else that dictated this great shift in *The Recluse*'s frame of reference from quasi philosophy to quasi-ecclesiastical history, as Wordsworth tried to proceed on his way alone. This change opens the third and final stage of *The Recluse*'s history, extending from 1808 to 1815.

PART THREE

The Recluse and *The Excursion,*
1808–1814

7

New Beginnings: The *Recluse* Poems of 1808

As when, upon the smooth pacific deep
Dense fogs, to sight impervious, have withheld
A gallant vessel from some bold Emprize
Day after day deferred, till anxious hope
Yields to despair, if chance a sudden breeze
Spring up and dissipate the veil, all hearts
Throb at the change, and every sail is spread
To speed her course along the dazzling waves
For recompense of glorious conquest soon
To be achieved upon the astonish'd foe.

PW, V.346

Having finally completed "Home at Grasmere" in 1806, Wordsworth was eager to push beyond Book I of Part I of *The Recluse*. In August he told Sir George Beaumont he would "go on swimmingly" if only he might "have some conversation with [Coleridge] upon the subject" (*LMY*, I.64). Like earlier references to Coleridge's notes for *The Recluse*, such statements imply that Coleridge could supply the key words briefly and easily.[1] But when they finally met in October (*CMY*, 332), Coleridge's shocking appearance and unsteady behavior made clear his inability to help himself, let alone others. The recitation of *The Prelude* to its intended auditor in January 1807 should have inaugurated a new start for *The Recluse* but seemed instead to mark an ending. Throughout, it appeals for Coleridge's aid, but his response, "To William Wordsworth," clearly testifies to his sense of separation from their past shared inspiration ("the memory of that hour / Of thy communion with my nobler mind," 83–84), and abases his own earlier achievements before his friend's work, which is described in terms far higher than those of "prelude," "portico," "tail-piece," or "appendix" to another work. The next state of *The Recluse* is thus markedly different from what had gone before, partly as a result of Coleridge's inevitably diminished role in it, but also bound up with other alterations in Wordsworth's perception of the meaning of his life and work.

For the time being, in late 1806, it was clear that *The Recluse* would not "swim." While finishing "Home at Grasmere," Wordsworth had composed additional Lake Country narratives, but their bearing upon the great project was not clear.[2] They eventually ended up in the later books of *The Excursion*; Wordsworth had spoken of this "narrative" project in 1804 as one of his three remaining life-works, but its form and conception were indeterminate in 1806 and remained so at least until 1809—until, that is, Wordsworth had tried and failed the new direction of the *Recluse* poems of 1808.[3] Instead, he first took up the task of arranging his shorter poems and was occupied through the spring of 1807 with the publication of *Poems, in Two Volumes* (CMY, 338). This diversion of his creative energies repeated the pattern of 1798–1802, when he spent much time composing, revising, and rearranging new poems and prefaces for *Lyrical Ballads*, often against Coleridge's strong admonition that he was wasting his powers on small pieces. But the *Poems* of 1807 contain the major lyrics on which Wordsworth's reputation is securely founded, thus again suggesting the subconscious usefulness of *The Recluse* as a creative fiction: his dutiful commitment to his large public project freed his imagination to create shorter poems of more enduring value. This possibility is confirmed by the recent recovery of Wordsworth's canceled "Advertisement" to the 1807 *Poems*:

> The short Poems, of which these Volumes consist, were chiefly composed to refresh my mind during the progress of a work of length and labour, in which I have for some time been engaged; and to furnish me with employment when I had not resolution to apply myself to that work, or hope that I should proceed with it successfully. Having already, in the Volumes entitled Lyrical Ballads, offered to the World a considerable collection of short poems, I did not wish to add these to the number, till after the completion and publication of my larger work; but, as I cannot even guess when this will be, and as several of these Poems have been circulated in manuscript, I thought it better to send them forth at once.[4]

Along with similar statements in the prefaces of *The Excursion* (1814) and the *Poems* of 1815, entwining all his shorter works with the "system" of his one large project, this shows to what an extent Wordsworth's attachment to *The Recluse* was the heartbeat of his creative life. His use of the word *resolution*, for example, suggests that the great "Resolution and Independence," which first appeared in 1807, may also be a poem about the difficulty of writing *The Recluse*, avoiding "despondency and madness" (l. 49) without Coleridge's aid, and independent of his example.

The dialectical relation between small pieces and great work is an as-

pect of Wordsworth's increasing concern for his permanent literary reputation, which, in default of Coleridge and *The Recluse*, was expressed in the
growing intimacy of his friendship with the Beaumonts, on whose estate
the Wordsworths resided for over six months in the winter and spring of
1806–07 and where the first reading of *The Prelude* took place. The
Beaumonts are a proper symbol of Wordsworth's deliberate movement toward cultural conservatism—a direction endorsed by Coleridge. During
that winter at Coleorton, Dorothy drily announced that they had become
"regular churchgoers" (*LMY*, I.136), and this marks the first period since
his childhood that Wordsworth could be called a practicing Christian
(*CMY*, 337). To Sir George, Wordsworth expressed a distinction between
the "*People*," honest readers who would ultimately recognize Wordsworth's genius, and the "*Public*," debased creatures whose "state of mind
with respect to my Poems," he adds in a revealing comparison, is like that
of "the French . . . in respect to Shakespeare" (*LMY*, I.194–95). With
Lady Beaumont he was even less guarded, making appreciation of his kind
of poetry a synecdoche for living a truly human life: "Among nineteen out
of twenty . . . persons who live . . . in the broad light of the world" there
cannot be "any genuine enjoyment of Poetry," an "awful truth," because
to be "incapable of a feeling of Poetry in my sense of the word is to be
without love of human nature and reverence for God" (*LMY*, I.146). This
severe ratio is expressed in images of urban "worldlings" that will contribute importantly to the dramatic tension of *The Recluse* poems of 1808.
"The things which I have taken, whether from within or without,—what
have they to do with routs, dinners, morning calls, hurry from door to
door, from street to street, on foot or in Carriage; with Mr. Pitt or Mr.
Fox . . . with endless talking about things nobody cares anything for except as far as their own vanity is concerned . . . what have they to do (to
say all at once) with a life without love?" (*LMY*, I.145). Whether his genius escapes self-indictment for its own contrary vanity in such statements
is the polar, *Prelude*-tension of the 1808 poems, especially "The Tuft of
Primroses."

When the Wordsworth entourage returned home to Grasmere from
Coleorton in the summer of 1807, these immense differences between their
criteria of human value and the rest of the world's seemed to be corroborated by external evidence. Large stands of fir and ash trees, and
favoritely placed sycamores and other trees had been cut down all over the
valley, shorn from around the church and off the top of the encircling hills,
victims of two landlords' dispute over timbering rights (*LMY*, I.159).
More serious was the news of the death of Reverend Sympson, the curate,

and of his son-in-law, Reverend Dawson, who had briefly taken his place. The entire Sympson family, from grandfather to grandchild, was wiped out in the space of two years. Their demise, represented by the subsequent ruination of their cottage, figures largely in "The Tuft of Primroses," along with the general sense of life-cut-down conveyed by the loss of a beloved landscape. Coming home to Grasmere was not in 1807 what it had been in 1800. In July they visited the ruins of Bolton Abbey, which inspired (along with *The White Doe of Rylstone*) "The Force of Prayer, or, The Founding of Bolton Priory: A Tradition" (*PW*, IV.88–90), a poem whose "dark words" question rather than confirm the implied statement of its title: "whence can comfort spring / When Prayer is of no avail?" These combinations of images of natural destruction, human death, the ineffectuality of prayer, and the scarcity of humane feeling—all related to the foundation and endurance of spiritual institutions—form the leitmotifs of the 1808 *Recluse*.

These accumulating concerns began to spill over into *The Recluse* when Wordsworth returned to Grasmere in April of 1808, having gone posthaste to London in February at word that Coleridge was near death, nursing him day and night there, only to be called back by equally desperate accounts of Sara Hutchinson's condition. The first sign of a new synthesis is apparent in his letter to Beaumont about his experience in London:

> You will deem it strange, but really some of the imagery of London has since my return hither been more present to my mind, than that of this noble Vale. I will tell you how this happens to be.—I left Coleridge at 7 o'clock on Sunday morning; and walked towards the City in a very thoughtful and melancholy state of mind; I had passed through Temple Bar and by St Dunstan's, noticing nothing, and entirely occupied with my own thoughts, when looking up, I saw before me the avenue of Fleet street, silent, empty, and pure white, with a sprinkling of new-fallen snow, not a cart or Carriage to obstruct the view, no noise, only a few soundless and dusky foot-passengers, here and there; you remember the elegant curve of Ludgate Hill in which this avenue would terminate, and beyond and towering above it was the huge and majestic form of St Pauls, solemnised by a thin veil of falling snow. I cannot say how much I was affected at this unthought-of-sight, in such a place and what a blessing I felt there is in habits of exalted Imagination. My sorrow was controlled, and my uneasiness of mind not quieted and relieved altogether, seemed at once to receive the gift of an anchor of security. [*LMY*, I. 209]

The letter is a prose draft of "St. Paul's (see below), marking Wordsworth's amazement that he should see such an "unthought-of-sight, in such a place," and that his "habits of exalted Imagination" could present him with a vision in a place which he considered to be a loveless hell, especially, in the context of his earlier letters to the Beaumonts, as defined by its reception and appreciation of his poetry. The gates of inspiration had been unlocked, as is so often the case with this dialectical poet, by strong force of contrast. "To the Clouds" and "The Tuft of Primroses" quickly followed in rough drafts,[5] both also intimately involved in relating thought to the places in which it arises, and probing its possible metaphysical significance beyond its natural location. By late summer he had extensively reworked all three and arranged them in fair copies in a new notebook, probably in the order he conceived of them as the new beginning to *The Recluse*, which he then announced to competitively interested friends: "To the Clouds," "The Tuft of Primroses," and "St. Paul's."[6]

"TO THE CLOUDS"

If Wordsworth intended "To the Clouds" as a prologue to a new section of *The Recluse*, as Joseph Kishel suggests,[7] it was a wise choice, for as a poem (in its 1808 version) it comes to nothing but what might follow from it. Unimpressive as an example of what many consider the typically Wordsworthian inspiration by Nature, it is striking for the evidence it gives of the poet's keen awareness of the limitations of any simple contract between nature and human thought. It addresses itself to natural phenomena in portentous rhetoric ("Army of Clouds! ye wingèd Host in troops / Ascending," ll. 1–2)[8] yet fails to achieve significance because the poet cannot find any basis for his metaphoric comparison of human thoughts to passing clouds that might lead to a satisfactory general statement about the relation of man to nature. On the contrary, the fleeting speed of the clouds impresses upon him the insubstantiality of his thoughts; their splendor, the lowly insignificance of his earthly station. The poem ends in metaphoric confusion in 1808; when Wordsworth finally published it thirty-four years later, he did what was necessary to give the clouds and his thoughts a mutually satisfactory resting place: he "Lodged [them] in the bosom of eternal things" (l. 94).

But before he found a conclusion beyond the horizons of this world, Wordsworth developed a series of rhetorical challenges to the clouds, taking up more than half the poem, which are impressive for the expectation they raise that he will find an appropriate human answer or response to their high, magnificent motion. They are variously compared to a mighty army on the march, flocks of birds in "due migration," pilgrims in caravan, or the massed worshipers of some oriental deity. Each of these images of large movement has a logic or a goal that seems to anticipate its aptness to human thought, but when Wordsworth demands an answer, he gets none: "Speak, silent Creatures.—They are gone, are fled" (30). They have gone into a large "gloomy mass" of clouds that also becomes questionable in Wordsworth's metaphor: "the unapproachable abyss / . . . that hidden gulf from which they rose / To vanish" (35–37). This anticipates one of the central images of "The Tuft of Primroses"—"the gulf that renders nothing back"—that Wordsworth will try to bridge by suggesting an alliance between imagination and religion. In "To the Clouds," however, he shakes off the gulf's grim implications by a renewed series of metaphoric identifications between his soul and the "bosom of the firmament / O'er which [the clouds] move" (50–51). Though he insists bravely upon this correspondence ("An Image, a reflection palpable / Of [his soul's] capacious self," 1808.61–62), the resulting contrast with his actual life is as unsatisfactory as his comparison of his thoughts to the clouds: "A humble walk / Here is my body doomed to tread, this path, / A little hoary line and faintly traced" (53–55). To avoid this diminution, he turns to the special quality of his thoughts: "my words have wings" (59). Thus his specifically poetic power gives him confidence to launch his challenging questions a third time, not only to Nature but to all former poetic relations with her: "Where is the Orphean lyre or Druid Harp / To accompany the Song? the mountain Wind / Shall be our *hand* of music!" (1808.72–74). The use of a poetic project, or prospect, as a way of ending poems has by this time become a regular feature of *The Recluse*. Yet it is important to see that he ends this initial poem in his new work on *The Recluse* by leaving open (for thirty-four years) an ambivalence in his typical metaphor. Having linked his soul to the sky, his thoughts to the clouds, his craft to the winds, he appears to clinch his argument:

> . . . for our Song is of the Clouds,
> And the Wind loves them, and the gentle gales
> Love them . . .
> . . . and the Sun
> (That is the daily source of joyous thought,
> And type of man's far darting reason, he
> Who therefore was esteemed in ancient times
> The God of Verse, and stood before men's eyes
> A blazing intellectual Deity)
> Loves his own glory in their looks, the Sun
> Showers on that unsubstantial Brotherhood
> A Vison of beatitude and light.   [1808.77–79, 80–88]

But to what does the sun correspond in his preceding catalog of metaphors? The only possible answer is Wordsworth, understood as "a blazing
intellectual Deity." This is the truth, as both he and many readers since
have understood it, but he does not dare say so in the poem, so the parenthetical mythological note is a philosophic throwaway line. The actual
sun's loving the clouds falls as a pointless recommendation in a conclusion
that has not met its metaphoric contract with a human tenor but has only
continued to elaborate metaphoric vehicles.

We can, of course, accept in a general way that Wordsworth is saying
"Nature inspires Poetry," yet some such reading of the poem as I have presented anticipates his very similar difficulties in "The Tuft of Primroses."
The simple form of its difficulty lies in attempting to connect natural and
human processes by focusing too literally on phenomena of *movement*,
without distinguishing their human, mental, temporal forms from natural,
physical, spatial analogues. Yet as an invocation it might have done very
well; its "humble walk" nicely anticipates similar references to Wordsworth's life in "The Tuft of Primroses."[9] However, its unintentionally
ironic final image, "that unsubstantial Brotherhood," will emerge to complicate and ultimately to destroy Wordsworth's attempt to bring his major
Recluse poem of 1808 to closure, as he considers which brotherhoods of
imagination and spirit have *not* been too unsubstantial—too weakly
founded—to provide a ground of faith in the permanent significance of
the creations of the human mind, especially his.

"THE TUFT OF PRIMROSES"

In "The Tuft of Primroses," Wordsworth tries to break away from the
largely biographical material he had been reworking for *The Recluse* for
nearly ten years. Though he never assigned it a position in the project, it
looks as much like a new beginning as a sequel to "Home at Grasmere,"
Book I of Part I. Indeed, it tries to accomplish the same task as "Home at
Grasmere"—generalizing Wordsworth's imagination away from meditations on his own place and person—and ends by running into the same
problems, but by a vastly different route. It makes possible an inquiry into
the extent Wordsworth was aware of tensions lurking in his "high argument": "How exquisitely the individual Mind / (And the progressive powers perhaps no less / Of the whole species) to the external World / Is fit-
ted." These lines, which Wordsworth probably composed and added to
the "Prospectus" in 1806 when he was finishing "Home at Grasmere,"[10]
dangerously raise the philosophic stakes of his epic task. Not only do they
starkly oversimplify the relation of mind to nature, but, by the obscurely

Godwinian reference to the "progressive powers . . . of the whole species," they introduce the theme of "Human Life" as a kind of organic evolutionary history, for which the Wordsworthian diffidence of "perhaps no less" shrugs off much more historical evidence than it can bear. The lines were inserted in the "Prospectus" directly preceding Wordsworth's reluctant acceptance of his duty to "travel near the tribes / And fellowships of men," and the specific form this argument takes in "The Tuft of Primroses" is whether or not imagination flourishes more surely in rural solitude than in "the fierce confederate storm / Of Sorrow, barricadoed evermore / Within the walls of cities." This statement of the problem is not superficial or sentimental but a paradigm of the Romantic dilemma as it occurs in Wordsworth: how can individual genius live for and among ordinary people?

Although "The Tuft of Primroses" breaks off in mid-line, it has a recognizable thematic unity that eventually, like the address to the clouds, moves toward another point of departure, permitting us to see this as the ineluctable form of Wordsworth's *Recluse*. It advances in four clearly discernable emblematic stages.[11] In each of these, Wordsworth searched for a synthesis of individual consciousness and its awareness of history, seeking to bind up progress (or the future) and the sense of Otherness, as in "Tintern Abbey" he had balanced Past and Self. The first long movement (1–234)[12] weaves a tableau in which the perennial primroses and the newly exposed Grasmere chapel are juxtaposed in a chastened emblem of hope, in contrast to image patterns of the Sympson family's ruined cottage, Sara Hutchinson's illness, John Wordsworth's death, and Coleridge's fevered estrangement. The second long movement (235–465) moves gradually toward a quasi-historical generalization of the primrose-chapel emblem by means of a free poetic translation of the letters of Saint Basil of Caesarea (b. 329) urging Gregory of Nazianzen to quit the corrupt city and join him in his "delicious Pontic solitude," his hermitage in Asia Minor. A third short movement (466–569) brings this past up to the present with a bird's-eye view of the progress of Basil's monastic ideal across the centuries of Western Christendom, ending with Wordsworth's first drafting of his visit to the abbey of the Grand Chartreuse in 1790, when he thought he saw revolutionary troops coming to destroy it. This leads to a still shorter fourth movement (570–94)—coda-cum-prologue—in which he himself is back in the present, with his "female Votaries," and faced with the task, not simply of reconciling himself to losses in Grasmere and the Wordsworth circle, but of writing an "unwearied Song" that will somehow complete, extend, or replace the ecclesiastical history he has invoked. Wordsworth later wrote the sonnet sequence *Ecclesiastical Sketches* in preparation for a projected history of the Christian church. But this was not what he intended in 1808, nor was he prepared to offer the poem on his own life as a substitute. Some other story was implied, and he had not yet hit upon the idea of offering his complete oeuvre as a substitute cathedral, as he did when he published *The Excursion* in 1814.

Schematically, "The Tuft of Primroses" is like "To the Clouds," though its linking of natural phenomena and human thought is obscured by its long historical detour. It combines metaphor and metonymy through the architectural image of the "lowly Edifice" with which it ends. This, though not literally Dove Cottage or Allan Bank, is too much like one of Wordsworth's idealized home-residences to be anything else. The tuft of primroses is to the "lowly Edifice" as the edifice is to the ruined abbeys of France and England. The metonymic connection is simply, egotistically, sublime: Wordsworth's "lowly Edifice," Tintern Abbey, and the Grand Chartreuse are all dwellings of spiritual power. The metaphoric link between the primroses and the abbeys is harder to see, but it comes to this: they are both emblems of strength combined with beauty, and precursors of something greater to follow. The primroses come early and survive the shocks of late snow and frost; Basil's hermitage was one of Christianity's first physical plants. Both, in successively regenerated forms, remain fixed in place despite natural and human violence. The four moments in the poem in which primroses, hermitages, ruined abbeys, and lowly cottages are isolated in emblematic tableaux are the cruxes requiring interpretation. In them Wordsworth manifests the treatment of visionary insight which, it appears to me, is the imagistic signature of *The Recluse*. Unlike similar moments in *The Prelude*, these are strangely shrouded; they are veiled visions in which the impulse to a final, apocalyptic rendering of human and natural events is simultaneously invoked and drawn back. They are dramatically less tense than the Simplon or Snowdon visions, and philosophically more conservative, but Wordsworth achieves in them images of the consummation of mind and nature which are canonically unique and aesthetically valid.

The Argument from Primroses

The tuft of spring primroses is elevated to symbolic significance when Wordsworth invokes it as a counterimage to the ruined cottage of the Sympson family. In the opening lines of the poem, turgid with sentimental diction, the primroses are inadequate to the meaning Wordsworth seeks to give them, but after his unusual presentation of the Sympsons' story they command our attention. The Sympson cottage stands as an "image" (204) which Man has neglected and which, as a result, Nature is obliterating. This cause and effect sequence, unexceptional to most of us, is fraught with ambiguous possibilities for Wordsworth, given his philosophic commitments, and provides the first of several hints that "The Tuft of Primroses" was abandoned because of its tendency to become critical of Wordsworth's proposed "great consummation" between Mind and Nature.

We are prepared for the symbolic role the primroses will play when they are proposed (63 ff.) as minimal substitutes for the many large trees cut down in 1807. "Ah what a welcome!" he exclaims to return to Grasmere and see at a glance that the center has not held:

> I look'd a first glad look, and saw them not!
> Was it a dream? th'aerial grove, no more
> Right in the centre of the lovely Vale
> Suspended like a stationary cloud,
> Had vanish'd like a cloud—   [97–101]

A "look" is redundantly "look'd," an absence perceived—and the visual vacuum blinds him. "Saw them not!" He doubts his eyes, not the landscape. The emphatic banality of "right in the centre" underscores his shock. Syntax and imagery whirl centripetally, homing in on Grasmere; and death and absence are the counterweights giving the fly-wheel its motive power. Though the poem's affirmations are often sentimental, they are nevertheless the result of an unflinching dialectical process. The old center has vanished, only to expose a new one underneath:

> Now stands the Steeple naked and forlorn
> And from the Haven, the "last Central Home,"
> To which all change conducts the Thought, looks round
> Upon the changes of this peaceful Vale.   [128–31]

Change exposes a new focal point for meditations upon change. The church, thus changed—and possible change in the function of the Church is the imaginative fulcrum of the poem—can now see the valley more clearly, more humanistically.

Nothing the church "looks around" upon calls for "more regret" than the Sympsons' cottage. Like the steeple, it is now "laid open to the glare of Common day" (141): natural light is glaring and vulgar when it does not shine upon a fruitful interaction of human inventiveness and natural fecundity. From a human perspective, Wordsworth's determined refusal to mourn the death of the Sympsons is decidedly unpleasant. He stresses the gentleness of their passing: "a consummation . . . / Sweet, perfect, to be wish'd for" (156–57). The weak allusion to *Hamlet* may make us feel, with Blake, that Wordsworth's fitting of mind and nature is "exquisite" only from a nonhuman point of view. Although he can look on "their associate graves / With nothing but still thoughts,"

> It costs me something like a pain to feel
> That after them so many of their works
> Which round that Dwelling covertly preserved
> The History of their unambitious lives
> Have perish'd, and so soon!   [185–91]

Now they are gone, the Sympsons seem to have been an ideal instance of human communion with nature, in such details as the jasmine branch which the eldest daughter had trained to grow into her bedroom, "to pervade / The inside of her chamber with its sweet" (209–10). Although we may protest the discrepancy between his apparent valuation of a human family and a ruined cottage, he does not intend to undervalue human life but to express a greater loss: that of the image-making power. The daughter's bower is now "creeping into shapelessness, self lost / In the wild wood, like a neglected image / Or Fancy which hath ceased to be recalled" (203–05). Balancing on a fine line between conceptual subtlety and the bathos of a suburban gardener, Wordsworth is saying that Nature does not create for man an image of Self; though man may symbolize his presence in a natural image, that can also be lost forever in nature. As in his lament over the fragility of books in *Prelude* V, Wordsworth regrets that malleable nature does not long retain man's stamp. The conjunction here between shapelessness and the ambiguous little phrase, "self lost," has this same significance. An image lost is like a "fancy" *un*remembered, and for Wordsworth the fear that memory has stopped working lies very close to the fear that imagination is dead.

Thus his paradox rebounds against him, placing him in a double bind. Metaphysically, the danger of fitting the mind to nature is that the mind might be unfit to itself. The Sympsons' ruined cottage demonstrates, not that the mind becomes less than human in becoming more like nature, but that human energy seems meaninglessly wasted when, having transformed nature into a human image, the image of mutual identity is inexorably worn down by natural processes themselves. Common sense may boldly say "What do you expect?" to Wordsworth's private train of associations, but the terms of the poem have by this time clearly begun to move into the realm of myth. Nevertheless, the myth is inadequate, and Wordsworth recognizes the impasse he has reached. There is nothing to do but mourn: "I grieve to see . . . that a gulf / Hath swallowed them which renders nothing

back" (211, 214–15). The image of the gulf has famous antecedents in
Wordsworth's poetry: the "mind's abyss" in the Simplon Pass lines (1850),
and the "fixed, abysmal, gloomy breathing-place" on Snowdon (1850). Unlike these, but very like the "unapproachable abyss" of "To the Clouds,"
this gulf "renders nothing back." The presence of death is stronger in all
The Recluse fragments than in *The Prelude*. The gulf or abyss is essentially
the same metaphor in all instances, for there is undoubtedly a strong submerged link in Wordsworth's mind between Imagination and Death (or,
more broadly, the Eschaton or Apocalypse). But in *The Prelude* the linkage
is triumphant; the closer imagination comes to death, the closer it comes
to its own world "Of first and last, and midst, and without end" (*Prel.*
VI.572). In *The Recluse* fragments, especially the later ones, the linkage is
at once more obvious and less certain: there is simply no relief.

Yet the logic of the poem's intentions demands relief, so without
break or interruption in the lines, but with an almost total reversal in argument, Wordsworth at this very point swerves to describe — is indeed forced
to achieve — the emblem of consolation which is the first imaginative center of the poem.

> Meanwhile the little Primrose of the rock
> Remains, in sacred beauty, without taint
> Of injury or decay, lives to proclaim
> Her charter in the blaze of noon; salutes
> Not observed the Early Shepherd-Swain
> Or Labourer plodding at the accustomed hour
> Home to his distant hearth, and will be seen
> Long as the fullness of her bloom endures   [219–26]

All his comfort is asserted in this description, and it derives especially from
the mode in which the image appears. The primrose is now cast in universal terms, exposed yet secure, "not *un*observed" by anyone (contrasting
with the "neglected image . . . which hath ceased to be recalled"). The laborers' regard for it is, of course, utterly gratuitous; nothing can be predicated upon it; it is the pathetic fallacy in reverse. But the sheer baldness of
the claim provides an entrée into the special intensity of Wordsworth's
own vision of the primrose, as does the word *meanwhile*. In much the
same way that the apostrophe to Imagination burst upon him while he was
describing his Simplon Pass crossing, his deep need to articulate consolation breaks in upon his meditation on the Sympsons' ruined "image" and
pulls him back from the "gulf . . . which renders nothing back." "Meanwhile" is a compositional bridge, simple and desperate, from a vision of
the death of imagination to an emblem of its life, the tuft of primroses.

The peculiar visual balance at the end of the passage is a good example of Wordsworth's personal participation in the veiled vision of *The Recluse*.

> . . . as I myself
> Have often seen her, when the last lone Thrush
> Hath ceas'd his Vesper hymn, piercing the gloom
> Of Twilight with the vigor of a star;
> Or rather say, hung from the shadowy Rock
> Like the broad Moon, with lustre somewhat dimm'd
> Lovely and bright, and as the Moon secure.   [228–34]

The interior emendation, "or rather say," preserves his metaphor from going too far. The primrose's piercing "vigor" threatens to overpower Twilight, and a twi-light vision is precisely Wordsworth's goal. Others may see the primrose in the stark blaze of noon, but he will see her simultaneously bright and dim. All his word choices contribute to the effect: *broad* (not bright), *lustre* (not light), *somewhat* (not wholly). The flowers hang precipitously from the mountain rock, yet securely as the motion—or rather say, the station—of a planet, the characteristically suspended Wordsworthian moon, "hung / Midway between the hills, as if she knew / No other region" (*Prelude* II.198–200), somewhere between immanence and transcendence.

"Delicious Solitude": From Basil of Caesarea to Wordsworth of Grasmere

The second movement of the poem proceeds from the twilit emblem of the primrose to two concomitant images of *human* solitude: one individual (Basil in his hermitage) and one corporate (the ruined remnants of his monastic ideal). Although the primrose hangs secure, Wordsworth is not so naive as to pretend his symbol settles any real life-and-death issues. His fastening upon Saint Basil is therefore fortuitous yet ultimately catastrophic for the poem's development.[13] Since "The Tuft of Primroses" is a draft, Wordsworth does not closely control his levels of discourse as he wanders off, from the temporary symbolic resolution provided by the primroses into wishful thinking about "some wardenship of spirits pure" (249) that would guard places like Grasmere, and all that they represent for him: "to protect / Here, if here only, from despoil and wrong / All growth of nature and all frame of Art" (252–54). Writing randomly past forest wardens, bandits, and hermits, he hits on the idea that a holy place needs a body politic commensurate with its "frame" and enters the heart of his poem, over two hundred lines on Basil's "delicious Pontic solitude." Asking rhetorically what impulse drives the hermit to spend his life "fast

anchored" in the desert—as the primrose is anchored to its shadowy
rock—Wordsworth arrives at this answer:

> What but this
> The universal instinct of repose
> The longing for confirm'd tranquillity
> In small and great, in humble and sublime,
> The life where hope and memory are as one,
> Earth quiet and unchanged, the human soul
> Consistent in self-rule, and heaven revealed
> To meditation in that quietness.   [288–95]

This hermitic emblem is wrought up in the paradoxes characteristic of all
the major *Recluse* fragments. High and low, Sublime and Picturesque, Past
("memory") and Future ("hope"), all become as one. Space and time are
joined: presence is in the present. The last three lines, with their triple subject, Earth / Soul / Heaven, are artfully revealing. Mention of an "unchanged" earth, following so closely upon Wordsworth's meditation on
the Sympsons' cottage, shows one of the main impulses of *The Recluse* at
work: the longing for immortality in nature. The lines blend natural existence and supernatural revelation; for the hermit properly conceived, they
are comfortable partners, familiar alternatives. The constancy of the human soul is the mediating link between an eternal earth and an eternal
heaven, in monastic practice as in the syntax of the lines. The direct statement of the lines is that revelation comes *in*, not after or through, the natural scene, and the last specification, "that quietness," rounds the passage
back to "Earth quiet"—but it also becomes, by virtue of the ambiguity of
its antecedent reference, another quality of the human soul: "*that* quietness" (cf. "wise passivity"). Consistency and quiet are near allies in the
emerging faith of *The Recluse*. The self-ruled soul shares with unchanging
earth a quiet revelation that is as distinct from apocalyptic shock, on the
one hand, as it is from the shocks that flesh is heir to, on the other.

In his free translation of Basil's description of "the lineaments and image of that spot," Wordsworth added landscape details to make the place
in every sense a happy medium. Physically, it is a "secret place" situated in
the middle of its surroundings, like Kubla Khan's pleasure dome, on a
mount which is at a junction of hills, valleys, "fertile meadow-ground"
and the River Iris. Spiritually, the special attraction of the place is the combination of exercise and reflection which it demands if one is to maintain
the via media it promises. One can achieve pure visions of "that entire
beautitude in which / The Angels serve," but man's animal needs also deserve attention here:

> when thou must descend
> From the pure vision . . .
> . . . .
> . . . or when thou would'st assume
> The burthen and the seasonable yoke
> Befitting our frail nature, would'st be tamed
> By vigils, abstinence and prayer with tears,
> What place so fit?   [380–81, 385–89]

The paradox of Pontus is the paradox of Grasmere. Here, through hermitic discipline, man can realize his essential humanity, between animals
and angels. And yet, "not a human form is seen this way" (392): the double entendre here is unintentional but illuminating. "Home at Grasmere"
was much devoted to demonstrating the essential humanity of Grasmere;
"The Tuft of Primroses" abjures this argument and takes *The Recluse*'s
paradoxes further: that love of nature best leads to love of man where man
is not.

But even this objection is answered in context. The rhetoric of the
passage is hortatory and suasive because it is directed to Basil's friend
Nazianzus, who plays very much the role of Coleridge to Basil's Wordsworth. Basil writes Gregory that he has found, in fact, "purer fields / Than
those which Pagan superstition feigned" (350–51), and Gregory replies
in the vein of Coleridge (or Lamb) teasing Wordsworth, in images re-
fracted from the "Prospectus":

> . . . Nazianzen fashion'd a reply
> Ingenious and rhetorical, with taunts
> Of wit and gay good-humoured ridicule
> Directed both against the life itself
> And that strong passion for those fortunate Isles
> For the Arcadia of a golden dream   [424–29]

But eventually Nazianzen came, "and numbers more,"

> Men of all tempers, qualities, estates,
> Came with one spirit, like a troop of fowl
> That single or in clusters, at a sign
> Given by their leader, settle on the breast
> Of some broad pool, green field, or loftiest tree
> In harmony and undisturbed repose.   [435–40]

These images extend the transformation of the flock metaphor which
helped Wordsworth complete "Home at Grasmere." It appears here with
the strong suggestion that the spirit who orchestrates their movement is
Basil, or Wordsworth, both of whom are inspired by their sisters, Macrina

or Dorothy. In "Home at Grasmere" Wordsworth initially dismissed the golden isles as an escapist fantasy only to reclaim them, in the famous "Prospectus" lines, as the "simple produce of the common day." In "The Tuft of Primroses" this Arcadia is saved from fantasy by admitting the fact of death. Unlike those fields "which Pagan superstition feigned / For mansions of the happy dead," Pontus was found by Basil to be no fiction but an "Enduring Paradise" because these isles are "coverts serene of bless'd mortality" (355). What makes this solitude "delicious," then, is not that one can escape from thoughts of death in it, but that one can meditate upon them undistracted by the vicissitudes of life in society: the "civil faction" and "religious broils" of Athens, which sound exactly like what Wordsworth hated about London ("Sophists glorying in their snares, / Her Poets, and conflicting Orators," 300–02).[14] *Et in Arcadia ego . . . vixit.* This kind of meditation in nature quietly reveals heaven, not as an apocalyptic shock but as a natural part of an everyday discipline.

From Monuments of Revelation to Nature's Pure Religion

Thus, in two broad movements "The Tuft of Primroses" has set forth Wordsworth's *Recluse*-ideal in two images of calm beauty rooted in natural solitude: a spring flower and a hermitic discipline fifteen hundred years gone by. But he must still deal with the obvious question: What of the Human Present, that tense person? The next movement of the poem updates the poet's natural and religious symbolism, linking Basil's ideal to its surviving remnants in an immensely powerful rhetorical address. For sheer strength of language there is nothing else like it in the poem; yet it is, generically, a dirge:

> Fallen in a thousand vales the stately Towers
> And branching windows gorgeously array'd
> And aisles and roofs magnificent that thrill'd
> With halleluiahs, and the strong-ribb'd vaults
> Are crush'd; and buried under weeds and earth
> The cloistral avenues—   [466–71]

The verse is slightly rough but wholly magnificent; images of grandeur and immensity sustain the long conjunctive constructions. Wordsworth's redundancy is at its most effective stretch. We expect predication: fallen now, the stately towers are . . . what? But predication is here almost non-existent, the verb ("crush'd") nearly repeats the noun participle ("fallen"). Of course there is a literal grammatical sense: the towers fell, and were crushed. But what Wordsworth conveys of their present condition is that they are doubly ruined. The slight personification, "strong-ribb'd . . .

crush'd," suggests giants fallen back to earth. Given the catastrophic rhetorical weight of these lines, it is remarkable how astutely and swiftly
Wordsworth moves from them to an affirmation of something like natural
revelation. One aid, as his description proceeds from past to present, is
that it also moves from east to west, so he can build on the literal fact that
the monasteries of Britain suffered less damage in the Reformation and
English Revolution than the monasteries of the Loire and the Rhone suffered in the French Revolution (or damage less presently evident). As he
moves closer to home, the verb *buried* (470) resurrects itself: "the Piles
that rose / On British lawns" (474–75). *Piles* is a pivotal word because it
ambiguously denotes both edifice and ruin, and it gets him where he wants
to be: Tintern Abbey.

> . . . to this day beholds
> Her faded image in the depths of Wye;
> Of solemn port smitten but unsubdued
> She stands   [477–80]

An "image" has endured. This ancient but unsubdued image contrasts
with the "neglected image" of the Sympsons' cottage, soon forgotten and
run to shapelessness. There is a power and authority in the ideal of corporate discipline and meditation which, though the individual is there both
"forgetting and forgotten" (367), endures through centuries: "So cleave
they to the earth in monument / Of Revelation, nor in memory less / Of
nature's pure religion" (485–87).

It is just here, however, at its third climactic emblem, that "The Tuft
of Primroses" begins to run into insuperable difficulty, apparent in the
spotty condition of the manuscript from this point on. Having got his
poem into one of his imagination's most holy places, Wordsworth must
somehow make a transition from Christian remnants to "nature's pure religion." The earlier transition, from the primrose hanging securely on its
rock to Basil's mountain hermitage, was managed purely in metaphoric
terms. Wordsworth knew that neither a flower nor a history of departed
things would do for the image he sought, and he continued to feel, despite
The Prelude, that the image of his own life was too private and transitory.
Yet when he invokes "nature's pure religion" as a complement to Christian tradition and its meditative revelations, we find that the poem turns
inexorably toward its creator and hence to the impasse which breaks it
off:

> . . . nature's pure religion, as in line
> Uninterrupted it hath travelled down

> From the first man who heard a howling storm
> Or knew a troubled thought or vain desire,
> Or in the very sunshine of his joy
> Was saddened at a perishable bliss
> Or languish'd idly under fond regrets
> That would not be subdued . . .   [487–94]

Here the poem hits its thematic nadir, and the continuity of the manuscript breaks off upon it. Wordsworth subsequently wrote in, and then wisely crossed out, a wildly inappropriate swerve toward a more sunshiny band of reclusive avengers of public wrongs, Robin Hood and his Merry Men. His difficulty arises from the fact that the mythic "first man" in this broken passage is his real alter ego in the poem, his episcopal brother much more truly than Basil. But his "pure religion," though older than Basil's, has no signs of permanence, no "monument of Revelation" other than human thought and sensation; Tintern Abbey is "unsubdued," but so is human desire. Conceived in joy and pumped full of optimism, the poem keeps running up against despondency. The tendency is partly inherent in the locomeditative genre; many long descriptive paragraphs in Thomson, Akenside, and Cowper turn lugubriously toward mortality as the poet's invention falters in its simple task of bolstering the report of eye and ear. But generalized pious reflections always provided the poets of Sensibility with an acceptable way out of such metaphysical deadends, whereas for Wordsworth it is precisely the individual, not the general, that must provide the fulcrum for his upward movement if he is to "construct a literary Work that might live."

From the Grand Chartreuse to Dove Cottage

Wordsworth's mode of resolving this spiritual and compositional impasse has become a habit of modern literature: to preserve a connection with transcendental reality by treating Christianity as a stage in the evolution of human consciousness. The writer acknowledges that the age of faith has gone by, but—and this is a key difference between Romantic and Enlightenment demythologizing—he avers that we are inevitably connected to it by virtue of the organicism inherent in his fundamental evolutionary myth. When Wordsworth elects to see, in the ruined "monuments of Revelation," a species of imaginative energy, he anticipates Stephen Daedalus's rejection of the Eucharist: "I fear . . . the chemical action which would be set up in my soul by false homage to a symbol behind which are massed twenty centuries of authority and veneration."[15] Wordsworth seeks hope where Stephen fears traducement, but neither questions the reality of the power symbolized, and both are thus cogently part of a Romantic tradition.

Given the development of issues in the poem to this point, there is a fine inevitability in the fact that Wordsworth resumes his fractured narrative with the lines on the Grand Chartreuse, crying out dramatically against the revolutionary agents who come to destroy the monastery as a symbol of repression. His first recorded response to this event, in *Descriptive Sketches* of 1793, is, despite its hackneyed expression, one of the first instances of Western man beginning to have second thoughts about his transition from Enlightenment liberalism to Romantic radicalism. His reconception of the experience in "The Tuft of Primroses," eighteen years after the event, must be one of the first instances in poetry of the next stage: revolutionary hesitations turning toward a conservative, but still Romantic, theology of the sort proposed by Coleridge and elaborated by his Victorian heirs in the next generation. Just as Wordsworth's drafting of his Simplon vision fourteen years after the event signals a major shift toward transcendentalism in his conception of Imagination, so his recomposition of the Grand Chartreuse passage in 1808 indicates an extension of that transcendentalism from private vision to more permanent, corporate forms.

He was literally mistaken about the intentions of the revolutionary phalanx whose flashing arms he glimpsed, but the importance of the passage lies in his deeply imagined *what if?* He feels exposed to social alarums as the primrose was exposed to the glare of noon, and he seeks refuge in a refuge soon to be lost.

> "And is thy doom
> Pronounc'd . . .
> . . . .
> and are we twain [he and Robert Jones]
> The last, perchance the very last, of men
> Who shall be welcom'd here . . .
> . . . .
> . . . hark, those Voices! let us hide in gloom
> Profoundest of St. Bruno's wood—these sighs
> These whispers that pursue or meet me, whence
> [   ] are they but a common [   ]
> From the two Sister streams of Life and Death,
> Or are they by the parting Genius sent
> Unheard till now and to be heard no more?"
>
> [509–10, 514–16, 521–27]

Two emphases in these lines are unique to this version of the passage: (1) Wordsworth's melodramatic supposition that he may be the last man to

see the old order of Chartruese; and (2) his use of the "parting Genius,"
from Milton's Nativity Hymn, which is more than an auditory personification of the twin rivers Guif, yet less than the abstract personification ("Nature's voice") to which Wordsworth altered it in the *Prelude* VI version of
the lines. His stagey mysteriousness about the source or meaning of these
"sighs" and "whispers" makes the complication of alternatives rife in the
passage, but it seems to be an attempt to claim a new *parousia*—the passing of the genius of the place (which is to say, of Christianity generally) to
the one revolutionary man who can sympathize with the spiritual value inherent in the ancien régime of Consciousness.

The implication of the scene is sublimely egotistical: it is a miraculous
coincidence of the right man in the right place at the right time. The voice
he hears is unique; it comes close to being a voice that only he, William
Wordsworth, can hear and, still more amazing, that never can have been
heard by anyone before him. We can understand why it will soon be
"heard no more," but why should it have been "unheard till now"? Who
has *not heard* it? No Christians till this moment, not even the "blameless
priesthood" of the Carthusians? No, it seems rather to be a special voice
saved for eschatological emergency—an apocalyptic whisper indeed. Sent
by the "parting Genius," it is the literal *pass*word of the transition from institutional to existential religion which Wordsworth is seeking, the word
of which he alone may be the translator. The "sighs" are the imaginative
effluence of Christianity, heard by William Wordsworth and transmittable
by him to the new world creating itself on the ruin of the old. He is the
Last Man who can translate them into the creed of "nature's pure religion" as it came, *in*articulately, to "the first man who heard a howling
storm." The Revolution brought predictions of apocalypse from many
speakers less well qualified than Wordsworth, and nothing we know of his
high conception of the poet's calling dissuades us from believing that this
interpretation of the passage is too extreme.[16]

This is the most striking of many instances of *The Recluse*'s deep affinity for romanticized Arthurian lore, where ruined gothic abbeys are
haunted by magical beings, cursed abbots or disgraced knights who
through meditative penitence have become examples of transformed spiritual power, remnants at the end of one dispensation (ancient Christianity)
who may form the nucleus of small bands that could become the beginning
of another.[17] Though Wordsworth, like Milton, dutifully entertained such
subjects for his epic project ("some British theme, some old / Romantic
tale, by Milton left unsung," *Prelude* I.179–80), he usually approaches
them more indirectly, as in the nearly invisible transition between Stone-

henge at the end of *Prelude* XII and Snowdon at the beginning of Book XIII (from pre-Christianity to post-Christianity via the *wanderjahres* of William Wordsworth), or at Tintern Abbey (located, like most of these legends, in Wales), with whose "faded image" Wordsworth began the daring development that leads into his stanzas on the Grand Chartreuse—and, ultimately, to the "gothic" image for *The Recluse* itself.

In his elegiac apostrophe to the Chartreuse, Nature speaks out boldly and clearly in defense of her fading sister, Religion. Wordsworth begs the Revolution to spare the Chartreuse not only for the sake of the spirit in its "courts of mystery," but also for the sake of the spirit bodied forth in the natural landscape around it. As in the "Prospectus," he inserts the enduring power of human subjectivity (3) between heavenly (1) and natural (2) eternities:

> "Let it be redeem'd
> With all its blameless priesthood for the sake [1]
> Of Heaven-descended truth; and humbler claim [2]
> Of these majestic floods, my noblest boast,
> These shining cliffs, pure as their home, the sky,
> These forests unapproachable by death
> That shall endure as long as Man endures [3]
> To think, to hope, to worship and to feel;
> To struggle,—to be lost within himself
> In trepidation,—from the dim abyss
> To look with bodily eyes, and be consoled."   [559—69]

His insight into the Carthusian landscape is like that in the Ravine of Gondo ("woods decaying, never to be decay'd"), and there is also a good deal of "Tintern Abbey" in the passage, with its cliffs whose "home" is the sky. The theological issue is the same in all poems: where is the dwelling of the divine, and, more important, how will we humans know it? The Chartreuse will be a memorial to "Heaven-descended truth," but the new dispensation will not be from higher to lower, but from inner to outer.[18] Perhaps Christianity will continue to serve, for some. But its natural surroundings will be the boast of others who, "humbler" in person, know that nature will endure as long as man endures. Here, as in the "Prospectus" lines, the connection between the awesomeness of the Mind of Man and its equally awesome dependence on Nature is particularly clear and altogether stripped of the sentimentality which cloys the story of the Sympsons' cottage.

This subjectivity is what distinguishes the New Man from the Old, the inmate of Chartreuse. Logical symmetry would suggest that the approach-

ing revolutionary troops embody the New Man, but worshipful subjectivity is a low priority item at this stage in revolution, and it will have to be
preserved in silence and reclusion by a visionary Elect until its time is ripe.
This is the most literal epiphany in all of Wordsworth's poetry, and it
seems to have been simultaneously therapeutic and exhausting. He goes
on without a break after line 569: "Such repetition of that [   ] / My
thoughts demanded" (570–71). The lacuna is intriguing, not only for the
poem and for Wordsworth, but for all post-Romantic experience. That
what? Almost equally intriguing is the fact that he calls his statement a
"repetition," which can hardly refer to a literal repetition of the first version of these lines in *Descriptive Sketches*, so immense is their difference.
What has been repeated, contextually? An experience, an epiphany, or a
credo? All three, probably; they are the trinity of his deepest poetic processes. By analogy to the composition of the Simplon Pass lines, we may
guess that Wordsworth has totally repeated the Chartreuse experience by
recapturing in poetry thoughts and sensations that sprang upon him from
"hiding-places ten years deep."[19] More starkly than anywhere else in his
work, we see here that there is little or no middle ground between Wordsworth's transcendentalism and his naturalism. It is the elision of the mediating middle term—"that [   ]"—that often makes his logic susceptible
of easy misinterpretation, rather than the sublimity of his transcendentalism or the simplicity of his naturalism, taken by themselves.

Thus it is that he turns, within two lines, from the "dim abyss" in
the Alps to "a lonely Vale" where a "humbler task" awaits him, and
the "female Votaries" of the place. Though this place cannot literally be
Grasmere, because of its "olive-bowers" and "vineyard" (593–94), the
similarity to his other descriptions of idyllic cottages that provide head-
quarters for his imagination is too strong to be resisted, especially in light
of the fact that we can now recognize Wordsworth's turn to himself, his
home, and his small band of friends as a regular feature of almost all parts
of *The Recluse*. If he seems to be confusing his life's story with that of the
saints, this is precisely my point, except that I believe the confusion is deliberate as well as doomed. The religious terminology appropriate to the
Grand Chartreuse is carried over casually to his own new ministry. He begins it by yet another summing up, ticking off the main points of the poem
and redefining them in terms of his own mission. Grasmere is not like Basil's retreat or the Chartreuse, nor is his "lowly Edifice" sublime like the
ruined abbeys (574–83). The force of these negative truisms depends on
Wordsworth's prior assumption that it is possible to entertain these similarities in the first place. The simple fact that they are not similar is not

enough for him; they are not the same because they do not need to be! Consistent with his mode of progress throughout, Wordsworth shows rather than explains his reasons, in a last snapshot of the cottage which is carefully framed to project the same emblematic impact as the tuft of primroses.

> Them ["the gentle Beings"] a lowly Edifice
> Embraced by grounds that did not aim
> To overshadow but to screen and hide,
> Contented . . .   [588–91]

The cottage, though hidden, is not lost; neither does it stand out boldly in its landscape. Rather, it is manifested in-between: screened, or veiled. Though we have little more than the shorthand beginnings of an image to go on, it is fair to say that the cottage, as here represented, is twice symbolic: first in what it is (the place where the epic of the New Man will be written), and second in how it is described (embraced by nature but not in danger of being overrun like the Sympsons' cottage). It is pictured as bodying forth . . . itself. It is itself a symbol of the kind of symbolism we have seen Wordsworth intending for *The Recluse*.

There is, of course, too great a discrepancy between tenor and vehicle in his symbolism, as there was in "To the Clouds," jerking "The Tuft of Primroses" too abruptly from the Grand Chartreuse to Dove Cottage and forcing it to a conclusion at the expense of a sequel. It swerves recklessly from "the ghostliness of things" to "gentle Beings" who presumably speak "words which speak of nothing more than what we are." The heroics of the "Prospectus" are the right tone for the project, not the simple "realties" (as Wordsworth aptly misspelled them) of "Home at Grasmere" and "The Tuft of Primroses." Nevertheless, these two fragments reveal the compromise between Power and Humility that Wordsworth intended: "a certain Union of Tenderness and Imagination . . . which Union, as the highest species of poetry, and chiefly deserving that name, 'He was most proud to aspire to.'"[20] The institutional inclination of *The Recluse* assumes its most acute angle in "The Tuft of Primroses," only to be toppled at the last moment. It goes further toward imaginative establishmentarianism than "Home at Grasmere's" "legislative Hall," but the same questions of personal and cultural inspiration, intertwining with thoughts of death and destruction, rise again to break it off. The epic task is not rejected, only the terms in which it has been framed, as implying a magnitude of tradition unnecessary, offensive, or otherwise inconsistent with the "gentle Beings" who would undertake it. Wordsworth rejects his cultural parallels,

deconstructs his own poem, in order to make himself, again, personally responsible for the creation of a poem that would itself be a redeeming structure, and not a mere analogy. The forward motion of *The Recluse* is once
again baffled by the reiteration of the *Prelude*-mode, as the first *Recluse*
was by the first *Prelude*, and as Book I of Part I ("Home at Grasmere")
was by the massive interruption of the 1805 *Prelude*. The regularity of
these movements permits us to conceive "The Tuft of Primroses" as not
exactly a fragment, but rather the poetic form that Wordsworth's *Recluse*
project inevitably produced: like "Home at Grasmere" and *The Prelude*
and *The Excursion*, it ends at the point where the civilization-redeeming
task is handed over to the individual who intends it. Having raised up an
institutional structure of imagination from himself, and having razed it
again back down to himself, Wordsworth will now return (in 1809) to the
individual personality—not his own, but an only slightly displaced version
thereof: the Solitary. And the Solitary's mental condition is introduced
into *The Excursion* in exactly the same terms with which "The Tuft of
Primroses" ends: the ruined buildings of a destroyed civilization.

"ST. PAUL'S"

Wordsworth's placing his London vision of St. Paul's last in his 1808
notebook of *Recluse* poems was a decision as shrewd as making "To the
Clouds" a prologue. For, of the three poems written in 1808, "St. Paul's"
is the only one strong enough to stand on its own and speak for itself (*PW*,
IV.374–75). Although the letter containing its prose first draft was addressed to Beaumont, the poem became part of *The Recluse* by virtue of
Wordsworth's making its addressee Coleridge: "I parted from thee, Friend,
and took my way / Through the great City" (2–3). Along with the ex-
changes between Basil-Wordsworth and Gregory-Coleridge, "St. Paul's"
may be seen in part as Wordsworth's attempt to restart *The Recluse* by re-
establishing its original author-audience relation. His placement of "St.
Paul's" as postlude or coda to the 1808 *Recluse* poems also suggests some
of his ideas of the architectonics of his masterwork, in its very close similarities to the style and placement of "A Night-Piece" in the 1798 *Recluse*
poems.[21] It is easy to imagine that Wordsworth had "A Night-Piece" in
mind when he wrote "St. Paul's." The context of the nighttime walk, the
muted lighting effects, and the protagonist's subtle change in mood are all
similar, and the similarity between the heavenly "vault" of "A Night-
Piece" and the "Temple" of "St. Paul's" is especially striking. The fact that
one is a rural vision and the other urban, or that "A Night-Piece" focuses

on the open night sky while "St. Paul's" focuses on a cathedral, is less significant than the effectiveness of both poems in conveying deep emotional power with only a very minimal indication of what, if anything, has transpired in them. In the overall progress of *The Recluse* it is indeed noteworthy that Wordsworth concludes his new beginnings of 1808 with "a visionary scene" that is both quasi-urban and quasi-religious. But, whereas he falters in "The Tuft of Primroses" and "Home at Grasmere" by too blatantly admitting his need for philosophical explanation, "St. Paul's" as the postlude of the *Recluse* poems of 1808 succeeds by reducing all explanation to a minimum while yet forestalling self-parody. Its preliminary explanation—"how, by sudden gift / Gift of Imagination's holy power, / My Soul . . . received / An anchor of stability" (8–11)—links imagination to holiness by a traditional image of faith, yet the explanation is only slightly more explicit and traditional than that in "A Night-Piece." The presence of traditional religious topoi cannot in itself constitute an aesthetic flaw. Wordsworth's way of appropriating the city scene by naturalizing it is obvious; as in the Westminster Bridge sonnet, the street seems like a mountain valley, and the time of day (dawn) reduces human traffic to a minimum. The sleep of his senses ("eye / Downcast, ear sleeping, and feet masterless," 3–4) allows imagination freer access to his "conflicting thoughts," and though the elements of the vision are not as interesting as those in "A Night-Piece," the final climax is more impressive.

> And high above this winding length of street,
> This moveless and unpeopled avenue,
> Pure, silent, solemn, beautiful, was seen
> The huge majestic Temple of St. Paul
> In awful sequestration, through a veil,
> Through its own sacred veil of falling snow.   [23–28]

This is the paradigm of the veiled vision of *The Recluse*, and the religious connotations, or what I would prefer to call the connotations of *spiritual institution*, are clear. Like the occurrence of the vision itself, St. Paul's is *sequestered* in the midst of the city. The falling snow is "sacred" because of the temple visible through it, yet it also introduces a slight sense of movement into the otherwise insistently static scene. The efficient cause of the emotional impact of the experience is the sudden realization that, "It's snowing!" Both the letter and the poem make clear that there is snow on the ground, but the poem withholds the information that it is still (or again) snowing until the last two words, giving a small but significant sense of spontaneous, natural life to an experience that is made generally impressive by its religious focus.

A search for a philosophical guarantee of the products and processes of imagination by social generalization preoccupies Wordsworth during the entire last active phase of *The Recluse*'s development. Realizing from his 1808 poems that he was hitting too close to home, he turned in the next year to the creation of another character, the Solitary, whose biography is like an abstract of his own but whose valuation of it reads like a parodic attack upon everything that Wordsworth stood for. The Solitary's disaffection is partly symbolized by images of ruined civilization akin to "The Tuft of Primroses" and intensified by his failure to recognize the spiritual significance of the mountain landscapes around him. Abandoning *The Recluse* in 1808 with a postlude that illustrates "Imagination's holy power" to create visionary scenes "in such a place" as London, Wordsworth recommences it in 1809 with the hard test case of a man who cannot see them even in Nature's holy places.

8

The Reckless Recluse: The Solitary
(*The Excursion,* Books II–IV)

I lived without the knowledge that I lived
Then by those beauteous forms brought back again
To lose myself again as if my life
Did ebb and flow with a strange mystery.

PW, V.341

To move from Wordsworth's abortive new beginning of *The Recluse* in 1808 to the labors of 1809 that led ultimately to *The Excursion* is to travel between familiarly contiguous territories. Indeed, there are many more similarities between "The Tuft of Primroses" and the poetry that became Books II–IV of *The Excursion* than there are between Book I of *The Excursion* (originally composed in 1797) and all the books following it (mostly composed in 1809–14).[1] Passing from Book I to Book II, we move from a strong character (the Pedlar-Wanderer) and an affecting story ("The Ruined Cottage") to a weak character (the Solitary) with a life story whose affect is lessened by his self-pitying attachment to it. But the laments and dirges of the 1808 *Recluse* poems could well have been uttered by the Solitary, and in Book II's wistful opening praise for the minstrel's life of yore we recognize the universe of imaginative institutions which Wordsworth had begun to construct in "The Tuft of Primroses." Those old poets were "fortunate" because they were safely *at home* anywhere in the world:

> —beneath an abbey's roof
> One evening sumptuously lodged; the next,
> Humbly in a religious hospital;
> Or with some merry outlaws of the wood;
> Or haply shrouded in a hermit's cell.
> . . . .
> . . . protected from the sword of war
> By virtue of that sacred instrument
> His harp, suspended at the traveller's side. [II. 7–11, 13–15][2]

Following *The Recluse*'s difficult progress in "Home at Grasmere" in 1806 and "The Tuft of Primroses" in 1808, Wordsworth was an author in search of a character other than himself in order to establish some distance from the problems of sociopolitical generalization (or philosophy, construed as logical system) which dogged him in those poems. Instead of celebrating his own life as a promising image of a redeemed future (linked to past histories of redemption), he proceeded antithetically once more, writing about a character who stands foursquare against all that "Home at Grasmere" and "The Tuft of Primroses" had assumed, a persona who lives negligently, thinks cynically, and speaks sarcastically in the midst of the classically profound Wordsworthian landscape. As everyone has recognized, the Solitary represents aspects of Wordsworth's brooding personality, and his life story is a generalized version of Wordsworth's, fleshed out with historical and literary analogs.[3] His specific similarities and differences from the historical Wordsworth are, however, less noteworthy than the boldly caricatured relief into which his creator casts them.

The Solitary is the absolute perversion of the favorite Wordsworthian formula, Love of Nature leading to Love of Mankind. Utterly disgusted with mankind, he has retreated into rural nature not out of love but from a settled depression ("despondency") that he nurses with excruciatingly misanthropic care. In the theodicy implied by Wordsworth's epic, he is an impatient Job, a consciously parodic version of almost all the standard objections that can be raised to Wordsworth's nature-worship, nowhere more so than in the inversion he presents to Coleridge's prescription of the attitude Wordsworth had to assume to write *The Recluse*: "a man whose principles are made up, and prepared to deliver upon authority a system of philosophy." The Solitary's principled philosophy, based on the authority of his own life-experiences, is that human life is without meaning, that human efforts to give it meaning are pretentiously laughable, and that we are better off dead. Appropriately, he is first introduced into the poem by a funeral that is mistaken for his own.

Certain aspects of spiritual immaturity in the character of the young narrator of "The Ruined Cottage" are in effect transferred from him (as he becomes the Poet of *The Excursion*) to the Solitary, who thus appears as a person for whom the kind of wisdom dispensed by the Pedlar-Wanderer in Book I is unconvincing. "Correction" of his "despondency" is the mission the Wanderer and the Poet set out to accomplish, providing the motivating interest for most of the rest of *The Excursion*. In the sequence of *Recluse* fragments, we recognize Books II–IV as Wordsworth's swing back into the *Prelude*-mode of inner spiritual examination, from the foiled public impulse of "The Tuft of Primroses" and "St. Paul's." In addition, these books mark a correlative shift in the primary focus of the original *Recluse* fragments, from Margaret's sufferings in "The Ruined Cottage" as recast into Book I, to the Solitary's as reported in Books II and III: from primary exploration of intellectual, spiritual, and poetical responses to human suffering, to a secondary examination of the despondency (dejection, depression) that falls easily upon reflections about the inadequacy of almost all human responses to suffering. The Solitary has suffered as much as Margaret; indeed, to the extent that their loss of spouse and children is caused by the impingement of huge economic and political forces upon their lives, their sufferings are identical. But the Solitary is, like Wordsworth, an intellectual. Where Margaret pines, he complains. She does not think but fantasizes; he thinks and theorizes too much. Investing in the Solitary almost every personal, social, religious, and philosophic catastrophe that could possibly befall a character born, like himself, in the last quarter of the eighteenth century, Wordsworth establishes the formidable opponent whose redemption, as a possibility for his age, he sets out to accomplish in this next stage of work on *The Recluse*. Sometimes turgid in execution, though by no means consistently so, Wordsworth's conception of the Solitary is, in the progress of *The Recluse,* marvelously heroic. The Solitary is like a sarcastic Byronic hero suddenly stalking through the benignly paradisal Wordsworthian landscapes. Not content, like Byron, to represent magnificently the despair of his era, Wordsworth (like Goethe) takes the next, dangerously unattractive step: he tries to overcome it. That he did not succeed is obvious, but it is not simply a matter of his inability to write dramatic verse dialogs; rather, a worse but yet more noble fault, it is the enormity of the world-redeeming task he again takes on for *The Recluse,* the outlines of which we can recognize in Books II–IV of *The Excursion* as the ghost of Childe William's Pilgrimage.

That *The Recluse* had begun to be a different poem than it was in 1798 is not surprising; Wordsworth was a different poet by 1809. Coleridge was back in the Lake Country, living in Keswick, from September 1808 to October 1810. This fact alone is sufficient to explain Wordsworth's renewed efforts on *The Recluse*; the dates correspond very closely to the completion of work on "The Tuft of Primroses," on the one hand, and the end of the first intense period of work toward *The Excursion,* on the other. But Coleridge was deteriorating apace and brought far more trouble to Wordsworth at Grasmere than Gregory of Nazianzen did to Basil of Caesarea. There is no direct evidence of Coleridge's involvement in the 1809–10 work on the Solitary, except for the fact that the Solitary represents in a single character that whole generation of despondent idealists for whom Coleridge had suggested *The Recluse* in 1799: "those who, in consequence of the complete failure of the French Revolution, have thrown up all hopes of the amelioration of mankind, and are sinking into an epicurean selfishness, disguising it under the titles of domestic attachment and contempt for visionary *philosophes*" (*LSTC*, I.527). And in considering the Solitary as Wordsworth's antithetical projection of his own worst self, we should not rule out the possibility that the character also partly reflects the friend he saw going to ruin; Coleridge had also been a radical preacher in the 1790s, mightily attractive to Wordsworth.

Like the rest of the world during these years, Wordsworth was deeply concerned with the progress of Napoleon's "Continental System" across the old regimes of Europe. From late 1808 through the spring of 1809, he was heavily involved in writing the longest prose work he ever produced (*Prose*, I.216), *The Convention of Cintra*, an elaborately meditative explanation of why the pusillanimous English generals should not have provided safe escort and transport home to the marauding French armies they had defeated in Portugal. Coleridge, who knew whereof he spoke, said that Wordsworth's tract was "somewhat too much *idealized*," and seemed "almost a self-robbery from some great philosophical poem" (*LSTC*, III.214, 216). The tract transmutes the actual political situation in Spain and Portugal into a metaphoric pattern for humanity's rising above despondency to spiritual power,[4] exactly the pattern that Wordsworth began to develop for the Solitary immediately following its publication.

Equally important to the development of *The Excursion* at this time was Wordsworth's close involvement in one of the great progressive stages of English culture, the movement toward free public education, an enlightened citizenry beginning to be seen, in light of events on the Continent, as the best way to moral political behavior among nations. The establishment of a universal education system was still two generations away (M. II.178) because of the dilemma puzzling all thinkers on the topic at the time: whether a national educational system should be under the direct supervision of the established church or a secular institution informed only by the Christian humanitarian spirit of its leaders. Wordsworth supported the former position (the famous antidisestablishmentarianism), but his authoritarianism was tempered by his enthusiasm for Dr. Andrew Bell's nondirective pedagogical method of pupil-tutors (the "Lancastrian" system), described in *An Experiment in Education Made at the Asylum of Madras* (1797), which he first read in the summer of 1808 (*CMY*, 389). He was forced to make his private opinions on education public by the appearance in *The Friend* of a "Letter of Mathetes," written by two of his young Lake District admirers and visitors, John Wilson and Alexander Blair, aided and abetted by the irrepressible De Quincey. "Mathetes" is Greek for "learner," "pupil," or "disciple" (*Prose*, II.3), and these young men adjured Wordsworth to come forward as a teacher to the despondent youth of the era who had lost faith in progress because of the world's degeneracy. They identified a "Teacher . . . conspicuous above the multitude in superior power . . . [whose] annunciation of truths . . . seemed to speak in thunders . . . that mighty voice has not been poured out in vain . . . there are many, to whom the name of Wordsworth calls up the recollection of their weakness, and the consciousness of their strength" (*Prose*, II.33). It is to Wordsworth's credit that his "Reply to 'Mathetes'" does not swallow this bait, but urges upon his admirers something akin to Dr. Bell's pedagogy of imitation rather than direct inculcation of abstract truths. The best teacher, he said, preserves for his students the processes of his own education, presenting, like *The Prelude*, "an unbroken image of the winding, excursive, and often retrograde course along which his own intellect has passed" (*Prose*, II.22). Insofar as he must announce a plan, he says it will be best expressed "by that living Teacher of whom [Mathetes] speaks [i.e., Wordsworth himself] . . . when, in his character of Philosophical Poet, . . . he transfers, in the transport of imagination, the law of Moral to physical Natures, and, having contemplated, through the medium of that order, all modes of existence as subservient to one spirit, concludes his address to the power of Duty in the following words: 'To humbler functions, awful Power! . . . *The confidence of reason give; / And in the light of truth thy Bondsman let me live!*'" (*Prose*, II.22; Wordsworth's italics). Such transfers of imaginative power from moral to physical nature figure prominently in the "correction" of the Solitary's "despondency," who must be, in the essay's terms, "remanded to Nature" (*Prose*, II.16), in order to be, in the poem's word, "reconverted" to the world. Wilson and Blair represented, like Byron, Shelley, and Keats, disillusioned idealism in a mediated, second-generation form, and though their Byronic pose was put on for rhetorical purposes, it suggested to Wordsworth how the disaffection of his generation could spread, even as fashion, to others.

These personal, political concerns come together in the ongoing life of *The Recluse* in Books II–IV of *The Excursion*, as an examination of the values of living and acting in the public world of human life versus the attractions of escaping from it. Since the Solitary has opted for the latter in complete rejection of the former, the argument (of which Book IV is the central statement) seeks to demonstrate that living out of the world need not be an escapist retreat, but, on the contrary, can become the means to even greater public good than immediate activism. The Solitary is the right man in the right place at the right time, but he doesn't realize it. "It is enough for complacency and hope, that scattered and solitary minds are always laboring somewhere in the service of truth and virtue" (*Prose*, II.12). *The Excursion* is Wordsworth's overt identification of his solitude's "somewhere." Though derisively called a "Laker" by the reviews, and though his two earlier volumes (*Lyrical Ballads* and the *Poems* of 1807) contained many scenes of rural solitude, it was not until the publication of *The Excursion* in 1814 that he publicly affirmed the anthropological value of his imagination's location, principally by a dialectical examination of its easily misunderstood appearance of escapism, dramatized in the character of the Solitary.

BOOKS II AND III:
"THE SOLITARY" AND "DESPONDENCY"

All this comes to a focus in Book IV ("Despondency Corrected"), which Lamb considered the most valuable part of the entire poem, but preceded by the nearly two thousand lines of Books II and III, both of which contain accounts of the Solitary's life, once as told by the Wanderer to the Poet (II.138–315), and then again by the Solitary to the Wanderer and the Poet together (III.461–991). These two narrative accounts are set off, in each book, against non-narrative images, themes, and emblems, to establish a counterpoint of appropriate and inappropriate forms of reclusion from the public world. Though the Solitary, "dissevered from mankind" (II.732), is obviously wrong in the poem's scale of values, he is frequently called the "pale" or "shy" Recluse, thus apparently becoming the title character, or hero, of the whole magnum opus, but in sickly shape. It is therefore of the first importance for Wordsworth to present carefully the Solitary's transformation into a ruddy, forthright, and socially responsible recluse.

In Book II, the Solitary's story is played off against negative and positive emblems of human civilization. When the Wanderer and Poet enter his valley, the first man-made object they see—the first "stamp" of the human mind—is a miniature ruined city, "a proud show / Of baby-houses" (II.424–25) built by children with the Solitary's indulgent help. Out of it they fetch a damp copy of *Candide* (much to the Wanderer's disgust), which "had lent its help to raise / One of those petty structures" (II.435–36). The allegory is obvious: a ruined "petty" civilization foundered on "no better stay" than the caustic rationalism with which Voltaire punctured the benign necessitarianism of the eighteenth century, and which, in its more abstract Godwinian form, Wordsworth had temporarily embraced in his own moral despondency of the mid-1790s. Inside the Solitary's cottage, things are the same, only worse:

> What a wreck
> Had we about us! scattered was the floor,
> And, in like sort, chair, window-seat, and shelf,
> With books, maps, fossils, withered plants and flowers,
> And tufts of mountain moss. Mechanic tools
> Lay intermixed with scraps of paper, some
> Scribbled with verse: a broken angling-rod
> And shattered telescope, together linked
> By cobwebs, stood within a dusty nook;
> And instruments of music, some half-made,
> Some in disgrace, hung dangling from the walls.   [660–70]

Underneath the Solitary's messy housekeeping we are meant to see the decay of a highly civilized mind in its neglect of all the arts and sciences, his self-indulgent depression ruining all that makes man humane.

Countering these negative images of the worldwide implications of the Solitary's condition is evidence of his residual imaginative powers in his description of a heavenly city seen among the mountain vapours: ". . . a mighty city—boldly say / A wilderness of building . . . / . . . marvelous array / Of temple, palace, citadel, and huge / Fantastic pomp of structure without name" (II.835–36, 857–59). We recognize here the excitement of Wordsworth's imagination at its highest pitch, the splendors of imperial cities being his constant image of transport, whether it be in recognition of his own imaginative powers (*Prelude* VI), his description of Vaudracour's romantic joy (*Prelude* IX), his putative rejection of literary shepherds for real ones (*Prelude* VIII) or, especially, his joy of anticipation at the coming of this heavenly city in the French Revolution (*Prelude* X). The Solitary, too, like a more resilient Vaudracour, had once thought he saw such a city on earth: France's "voice of social transport reached even him! / He broke from his contracted bounds, repaired / To the great City, an emporium then / Of golden expectations" (II.214–17). But the urban rhetoric of his cloud-vision is also similar to that of "Home at Grasmere" and the "Prospectus," and for all its technicolor splendor contains the seed of their difficulties: it is a "structure without name." A sense of purpose in an individual's life should, ideally, provide the name or identity of its social structures; the plot of *The Prelude* is motivated by the difficulty of this process for Wordsworth in Cambridge, London, and Paris. In the ensuing discussions of *The Excursion,* the Wanderer makes much of the Solitary's visionary susceptibilities as represented by this vision. As the concluding set piece of Book II, it not only plays off against the failure of the French "emporium" to deliver on its golden promises, but also reinforces the book's opening set piece, the medieval minstrel at home in all levels and conditions of society by virtue of the "sacred instrument . . . suspended at [his] side." This ideal poet is a sort of imaginative vigilante, brought up to date in the Poet's urbane image of that "obscure Itinerant" (The Wanderer) "ranging through the tamer ground / Of these our unimaginative days" (II.22–24), a type of walking spiritual democracy, received everywhere with "the welcome of an Inmate from afar," dispensing folktales and family justice with equal ease, the very essence of what Wordsworth had wished in *The Prelude* his poetry might do: "summon back from lonesome banishment . . . inmates in the hearts of men" (*Prel.* I.174–75).

For Book III, Wordsworth composed and added later[5] a three times longer version of the Solitary's life, setting it over against the entire first half of the book, which is a long overture on the interpretation of images of human life. This overture is further divided into two parts (1–224 and 225–460). The first part expatiates on the shapes of the rocks in one of the Solitary's many hidden nooks. In its standing pillars and altarlike shapes the Wanderer sees "a chronicle . . . / Of purposes akin to those of Man" (89–90) and praises all recesses (including universities) that allow contemplation, "high above the misty air / And turbulence of . . . cities vast" (103–04). But the Solitary, who has long since named the rocks his "Pompey's pillar . . . Theban obelisk . . . and . . . Druid cromlech" (131–33), sees in their kinship to ruins of human civilization emblems "fraught rather with depression than delight" (156). In the second half of Book III's opening meditation, he scorns not only the Wanderer's optimistic parallels but the very exercise of such analogizing powers, opting for agnosticism: "I, without reluctance, could decline / All act of inquisition whence we rise, / And what, when breath hath ceased, we may become" (234–36). The Poet counters with one of his rare speeches, defending poetry's image-making power against Philosophy's "spiritless and dull" dreaming (340), because Poetry is "courteously employed / In framing models to improve the scheme / Of Man's existence, and recast the world" (335–37), while Philosophy simply escapes to "world-excluding groves" (347). But this description, which more accurately describes the intention of *The Recluse* than any of Wordsworth's best poetry, is brushed aside by the Solitary's stubborn defense of solitude for its own sake, in a revisionary adaptation of a long passage from "The Tuft of Primroses" (367–405). In 1808, this passage had introduced Basil's strategic retreat, which ultimately led out "o'er the vast regions of the western Church" (*TP,* 462). But the Solitary has a bleaker view of the history of Christianity and praises the contemplative life simply for its escape value, "though the wished-for end / By multitudes was missed, perhaps attained / By none" (406–08). Needless to say, he has overcome his own youthful indiscretions in the opposite direction, of demanding "from real life / The test of act and suffering" (417–18).

In both books' accounts of the Solitary's life, his search for faith in social action bulks much larger than his loss of it with the death of his wife and children. Wordsworth goes out of his way to invest himself in the Solitary's character, most bravely by the late addition of mention of the death of two children, following the stunning double blow of the deaths of Catherine and Thomas Wordsworth in 1812, and puts the Solitary's subsequent soul-searching in the same terms he had used for the impairment of his own imagination in *Prelude* X: "life was put / To inquisition, long and profitless!" (*Excursion* III.697–98). Placing the newly married Solitary in a parish in Devon with his bride, he summons up all the enthusiasm of his walks in the Quantock Hills with Dorothy and Coleridge in 1798, and a rejected manuscript passage has the Solitary's wife paint a picture, in the style of "Home at Grasmere," of their happy cottage as "Finished and fair as Paradise itself / Where the first Adam dwelt with sinless Eve" (549/550, *app. crit.*). In the context of the Solitary's despair, such joys are made to seem excessively confident, leading to the falls that Wordsworth had experienced both in life and in the poetry of *The Recluse* since 1800. Furthermore, the specific reasons for the Solitary's disillusion with revolution fall, like Wordsworth's in *The Prelude,* within an intense but strikingly narrow range of human evils. Though his hopes of what could be accomplished are as wide as possible ("The cause of Christ and civil liberty," II.221), his disillusion is expressed not in terms of grand philosophical or political opportunities lost, but in his inability to stick out the struggle with meanly motivated men:

> he forfeited
> All joy in human nature; was consumed,
> And vexed, and chafed, by levity and scorn,
> And fruitless indignation; galled by pride;
> Made desperate by contempt of men who throve
> Before his sight in power or fame, and won,
> Without desert, what he desired.   [II.296–302]

The indictment of egotism here is plain, making the Solitary's idealism suspect. As with Wordsworth and Beaupuy in Books IX-X of *The Prelude,* the press of unseemly emotions in a great cause bothers the Solitary more than the progress of the cause itself. Similarly, in Book III's redaction of this same story, the Solitary is "reconverted to the world" (III.734) in huge terms ("My soul diffused herself in wide embrace / Of institutions," 738–39) that dwindle rapidly by comparison to the reasons given for his recoil from it:

> How rapidly the zealots of the cause
> Disbanded—or in hostile ranks appeared;
> Some, tired of honest service; these, *outdone,*
> *Disgusted therefore,* or appalled, by aims
> Of fiercer zealots.   [770–74; italics added]

Wordsworth has accurately captured the essence of close political in-fighting, and rather than chide him (or the Solitary) for failing to stomach it, we should see in the Solitary's imaginative expanse of idealism, shrunk by the spectacle of human meanness, a portrait of a fame-motivated personality. The full extent of his emotions at the prospect of successfully manifesting himself in the world is hinted at in his suggestion that he thirsted for far more apocalyptic satisfactions:

> The tranquil shores
> Of Britain circumscribed me, else, perhaps
> I might have been entangled among deeds,
> Which, now, as infamous, I should abhor—
> Despise, as senseless: for my spirit relished
> Strangely the exasperation of that Land,
> Which turned an angry beak against the down
> Of her own breast; confounded into hope
> Of disencumbering thus her fretful wings.   [812–20]

Strange relish indeed, which is to say, curiously refreshing: would he have abhorred the Terror less had the Jacobins maintained their power and fame? Clearly this is a personality moved more by his images of things than by the work of realizing them in action, and it is precisely his imaginative, or emblematic, tendencies which the Wanderer sets to work on in Book IV, seeing in them the grounds for correcting his despondency, recognizing that the Solitary has imagination, not political skill, despite the fine figure he cut in the world as a handsome radical preacher.

BOOK IV: "DESPONDENCY CORRECTED"

Because he senses the Solitary's peculiar imaginative powers, the Wanderer begins with emblems, leading by stages that he and his creator seem almost unaware of to the most radical mythmaking in all of Wordsworth's poetry, set down in the middle of his most respectable and solemn public address to his countrymen. At the end of Book III, the Solitary had summarized his sorrowful biography: "languidly I look / Upon this visible fabric of the world" (ll. 962–63). Book IV seeks to energize this languor—his unwise passivity, his positive incapability. In the Wanderer's peroration near the end of Book IV, he pictures the "visible fabric of the world" as a veil enabling the imagination to transfigure the accidents of mortal life to moral good:

> Within the soul a faculty abides,
> That with interpositions, which would hide
> And darken, so can deal that they become
> Contingencies of pomp; and serve to exalt
> Her native brightness. As the ample moon,
> In the deep stillness of a summer even
> Rising behind a thick and lofty grove,
> Burns, like an unconsuming fire of light,
> In the green trees; and, kindling on all sides
> Their leafy umbrage, turns the dusky veil
> Into a substance glorious as her own,
> Yea, with her own incorporated, by power
> Capacious and serene. Like power abides
> In man's celestial spirit; virtue thus
> Sets forth and magnifies herself; thus feeds
> A calm, a beautiful, and silent fire,
> From the encumbrances of mortal life,
> From error, disappointment—nay, from guilt;
> And sometimes, so relenting justice wills,
> From palpable oppressions of despair.   [ll. 1058–77]

Lamb singled out this passage as "high poetry," and despite ornate diction Wordsworth's figure is aptly chosen and provides an emblem for the entire argument of Book IV. He has taken a traditional image of incarnation, immanence, or spiritual indwelling (e.g., The Burning Bush) and adapted it to psychologized landscape description by exploiting the visual ambiguities of the veil image: it conceals, reveals, and reveals-by-concealing. The result illustrates the special mode of human domination over natural contingency which *The Excursion* consistently projects. There is no vision here, no obliteration of common experience. The veil of flesh is not rent, it is incorporated (or "embodied," l. 1069 MS variant) with a source of spiritual energy. The irradiating source is called Virtue rather than Imagination, but this instance is one among many in the latter parts of Book IV where the Solitary is urged to inspire his seeing with an impulse from his soul called, alternatively, "virtue," "Imagination," "the imaginative will," or "the mind's *excursive* power." Virtue in this sense denotes both strength and goodness, and carries its own validating power; by transforming "the encumbrances of mortal life" into "contingencies of pomp," it operates imaginatively, supplying and receiving value simultaneously.

This passage is one that finally moves the skeptical Solitary. In it Wordsworth makes general application of the process of Imagination's dealing with "the encumbrances of mortal life." It moves slowly, by suffusion, and there are complementary possibilities of interpretation. Though we first see Virtue or Imagination shining through natural limitations (like Plato's Ideas through natural forms), the focal distance is primarily "the dusky veil" itself, wherein natural encumbrances take on significance by creating for the mind a reflected image of itself, "set forth and magnified." The first interpretation accurately describes the way landscapes most often appear in *The Excursion*, but the latter is an account of how they come to be that way. Throughout the poem, Nature is interposed as a covert or shade between the characters and their respective horizons: literally, as trees or clouds (e.g., the "finer distance" of the "impending covert" in the opening lines of Book I); figuratively, as the masks of God (the sunset concluding Book IX); or existentially, as in the distance the Solitary has put between himself and public view. Such imagery is especially dominant in the heart of Book IV, the Wanderer's relaxed amble into the origins of mythology which stirred the enthusiasm of Keats and Leigh Hunt. But we must first briefly notice how Book IV arrives at its peculiar endorsement of private mythmaking.

Providential Vision

In the first 331 lines of Book IV the power attributed to "man's celestial spirit" in the concluding passage on "the dusky veil" is assigned to the nearly mechanical operations of benign Providence: "Whose everlasting purposes embrace / All accidents, converting them to good" (16–17). Without the visual interest of the moon image, this assertion is simply a theological abstract—the flaw of all 331 lines. If Wordsworth meant these opening lines (added shortly before the poem's 1814 publication) to be a corrective buffer of orthodoxy against the pleasant mythopoeia later in the book, they more than serve the purpose. It is to the Solitary's credit that he receives them "less upraised in spirit than abashed" (l. 256). But the Wanderer is also an acute diagnostician of nervous states, as was Wordsworth, and he offers the opinion that the Solitary's problem lies not in his inability to accept the proffered recompense but in misunderstanding his own disease. Real despondency like the Solitary's does not make a person stop seeing "with bodily eyes" (l. 172). Rather, such despondency arises from trying to strain beyond what the bodily eye can see, from being too optimistic, too idealistic:

> . . . the innocent Sufferer often sees
> Too clearly; feels too vividly; and longs
> To realize the vision, with intense
> And over-constant yearning;—there—there lies
> The excess, by which the balance is destroyed.
> Too, too contracted are these walls of flesh.   [174–79]

The Solitary, if he were not Wordsworth's Job, could his Hamlet, driven to despair by the gap between human possibility and actuality, which his common sense nevertheless accepts. As Geoffrey Hartman has said, there is in such transcendental longings a power of imagination which in certain literalistic persons converts a belief in immortality to an actual longing for death.[6]

Lines of Sight, Lines of Being

Not until the Wanderer has elaborately treated all the possible sources of the Solitary's despondency does Book IV begin to take a more interesting turn, starting (at l. 332) with a passage originally composed for "Home at Grasmere" (*CMY,* 23). There are subtle differences between it and "Home at Grasmere" which indicate changes in emphasis in the development of *The Recluse* between 1806 and 1809. The Wanderer begins by proposing meditation on the Great Chain of Being as therapeutic mental exercise. But whereas in "Home at Grasmere" Wordsworth was fascinated with "the line invisible, the boundary lost / That parts the image from reality"—the indistinctness between thought and perception—in *The Excursion* the focus of meditation is precisely on separation, on lines and boundaries that demarcate one mode of being from another. The happy man should seek to find

>   where begins
> The union, the partition where, that makes
> Kind and degree, among all visible Beings;
> The constitutions, powers, and faculties,
> Which they inherit,—*cannot step beyond,*—
> And cannot fall beneath.   [335–40; italics added]

This states the Wanderer's intention but also allows an opening in the general argument of Book IV, into which the Poet thrusts a recommendation for a lower form of such speculations: the aptness of rural nature for contemplation and refreshment. The Poet does not say much in *The Excursion,* but here he is literally Wordsworth's mouthpiece, for this little transition that he is "tempted to interpose" gets Book IV off the track of traditional theology and onto a range of speculations more characteristically Wordsworthian, though it develops with emphases nearly unique in his work.

The Wanderer takes up the Poet's interruption, and in long alternating periods (ll. 351–610), each agreeing with the other, they extol the benefits of exercising mind and body in nature: "Be as a presence or a motion—one / Among the many there" (520–21). The mind's imaginings, giving shape to presences suggested by natural forms, are the focus of the famous passages on primitive mythopoeia which follow. The three discussants have arrived at this point by a special subsidiary route, far removed from the solid orthodoxy with which the Wanderer began. The Wanderer senses that in the Solitary they are faced with an extreme case. How can they lead him to love of man from love of nature if he does not even love nature? "A piteous lot it were to flee from Man— / Yet not rejoice in Nature" (575–76). If this is indeed the Solitary's condition, then the Wanderer's and Poet's recommendations of natural sights and sounds are pointless. So the Wanderer slips into a mood of condescending yet pleasant sympathy and begins to speak of a temporary indulgence the Solitary might allow himself in the amusements of superstition. The Wanderer here is like a kindly college chaplain agreeing halfheartedly to discuss esoteric religious therapies with students burned out by political radicalism. Such speculation in animism and spiritual correspondences can be allowed to men doubly despondent (i.e., despairing of their despair), if they "in due time / May issue thence" (594–95). But the imaginative bases of superstition are taken more and more seriously as the discussion goes along, and the rest of Book IV never does quite issue thence.[7]

Truth, he says, has "her pleasure-grounds . . . haunts of ease / And easy contemplation; gay parterres, / And labyrinthine walks" (588–90).

> If tired with systems, each in his degree
> Substantial, and all crumbling in their turn,
> Let him build systems of his own, and smile
> At the fond work, demolished with a touch;
> If unreligious, let him be at once,
> Among ten thousand innocents, enrolled
> A pupil in the many-chambered school,
> Where superstition weaves her airy dreams.   [603–10]

This Keatsian thought arrests him. Immediately, in the spirit of "Great God! I'd rather be a Pagan suckled in a creed outworn" (published 1807), he launches into the magnificent digression of Book IV, *The Excursion*'s excursus into mythology as an exercise of imaginative powers infinitely to be preferred to "the repetitions wearisome of sense, / Where soul is dead, and feeling hath no place" (620–21). The rest of Book IV is an argument against analytic positivism of the sort Wordsworth himself knew well from his own revolutionary crisis of the 1790s. Against the Solitary's "vacancy," the Wanderer pits the fullness of life available to the mind that sees in nature "Life continuous, Being unimpaired" (755), a form of imagination which, though wholly reliant on natural suggestion, meets nature on equal, consummate terms, neither engulfed nor overawed. Nor is it merely Fancy. In early editions of *The Excursion*, Wordsworth stated in Book IV's "Argument," "If the elevated imagination cannot be exerted—try the humbler fancy." But he removed this after 1820, and with good reason, for over and over again we hear in these lines that "the imaginative faculty was lord / Of observations natural" in ancient times, and could be still (707–08). This continues the thematic progression of *The Recluse* from 1806 to 1809, each new attempt presenting more radical, or reckless, linkings of human imaginings to natural processes.

The Wanderer begins with the Fall, and the startling mythopoeia of Romanticism appears: the Solitary's fall into despondency has its parallels in sacred histories. Personal psychology and theodicy are linked suggestively as Hegel had already and Nietzsche would later link them with full seriousness. Like original man, the Solitary has fallen from a state in which his senses seemed to have transcendent power, either for "actual visions" or visions "that in this sort / Have condescendingly been shadowed forth / . . . intuitions moral and divine" (643–46). Now fallen, man's permanent dilemma is to conceive and establish contact with his former mode of being, with things that are now, in his present condition, "Veiled, nor approachable by living Man."[8] The Wanderer aims only at recapturing the secondary, veiled power of original vision; "actual vision" is gone forever. This secondary state can be approximated by exercising imagination over sight: "eye distinguishes . . . soul creates" (833).

All the Solitary needs is the simple energy required to body forth a being like his own in nature, but within limits: "to bonds of sense / Yielding his soul, the Babylonian framed / For influence undefined a personal shape" (681–83). Book IV stresses the conservative paradox that by yielding to *bonds*—of sensory experience, natural limitation, ritual, and ordinary duty—man achieves not full freedom (an abstract fiction) but freedom from the harsher and crippling bondage of despondency and solipsism. As it was for the Babylonian, so also for the Chaldean shepherds,

> The imaginative faculty was lord
> Of mighty Nature, if 'twas ever meant
> That we should pry far off yet be unraised;
> That we should pore, and dwindle as we pore,
> Between the orbs of our apparent sphere
> And its invisible counterpart. . . .   [707–12]

The necessary existence of invisible planets gives the Chaldean an almost mathematical assurance of immortality because of the dialectic it opens up between the "apparent" and the "invisible." "Set rotation" thus parallels the Babylonian's "bonds of sense" and can be seen as an extension of similar mutable-immutable phrasing from "Home at Grasmere" ("From high to low, from low to high, yet still / Within the bound of this high Concave") and "The Tuft of Primroses" ("The longing for confirm'd tranquility / In small and great, in humble and sublime, / The life where hope and memory are as one"). Finally, when the "lively Grecian," Keats's favorite, bestows "on *fluent* operations a *fixed* shape" (727), these cultural combinations of stasis and kinesis become formulaic. What the Babylonians and Chaldeans achieved through mythical science, the Greeks attained in mythopoetic art:

> emanations were perceived; and acts
> Of immortality, in Nature's course,
> Exemplified by *mysteries, that were felt*
> *As bonds* . . .   [738–41, italics added]

The mysteries' function is to control the release of vision, the same role played by hermitic discipline in "The Tuft of Primroses," and a need deeply felt by Wordsworth in similar language describing his efforts to compose *The Recluse*: "Ascending or descending, I construct / A scale to measure, or appoint a zone / To circumscribe, some philosophic Hymn / In praise of nature sung & Natures God."[9]

Unfortunately, the Solitary is unmoved by this sort of spiritual analogizing. Like Wordsworth in the early 1790s, he is a disillusioned rational idealist, not a Hartleyan, a Unitarian, or even a Berkeleyan—any one of which might have been more sympathetic to the Wanderer's illustrations.[10] Naturally he objects: "Is it well to trust / Imagination's light when reason's fails, / The unguarded taper when the guarded faints?" (771–73).[11] As Lamb said in his review of *The Excursion*, the operation of imagination "in producing the several fictions of . . . idolatry, is described with such suggestive power, that the Solitary, in good earnest, seems alarmed at the tendency of [the Wanderer's] argument."[12] But the Wanderer cannot be stopped; the accumulating force of Wordsworth's rhetoric has generalized beyond the Solitary's particular situation, and he laments the demise of mythopoeic power in a passage directly parallel to the lament of "Home at Grasmere" for paradisal fictions and the dirge of "The Tuft of Primroses" for the passing of spiritual institutions. What, the Wanderer demands scornfully, has been the historical development of these first explanations of natural mystery? Modern science sees more powerfully, but sees less:

> Oh! there is laughter at their work in heaven!
> Enquire of ancient Wisdom; go, demand
> Of mighty Nature, if 'twas ever meant
> That we should pry far off yet be unraised;
> That we should pore, and dwindle as we pore,
> Viewing all objects unremittingly
> In disconnection dead and spiritless;
> And still dividing, and dividing still,
> Break down all grandeur, still unsatisfied
> With the perverse attempt, while littleness
> May yet become more little; waging thus
> An impious warfare with the very life
> Of our own souls!   [956–68]

This rhetoric of scientific divisions and separations is the opposite of the blending, unifying imagery that runs through all *The Recluse* fragments. Phenomenologically, the Wanderer is recommending meditation on the *joining* function of boundaries, whereas the joylessness of modern science lies exactly in its failure, or reluctance, to synthesize and unify. The Solitary "affronts the eye of Solitude" when he thinks this way and earns the melancholy revenge held in store for self-pitying escapists, a kind of self-conscious insanity: "[Solitude's] mild nature can be terrible" (1032). A more "blest seclusion" is one where "the mind admits / The law of duty; and can *therefore* move / Through each vicissitude of loss and gain" (1035–37; italics added). For a conclusive image of the folly of modern rationalism, the Wanderer mockingly pictures a nation's celebration of its laureate in the capital: "the laughing Sage of France.— / Crowned was he . . . / With laurel planted upon hoary hairs" (996–98). The image recalls the Solitary's abused copy of *Candide* in Book II; but more important to an overall reading of *The Recluse* is our recognition of Wordsworth's own motive for national honor, antithetically projected, as in *Prelude* I's introduction/rejection of meditative avengers who descend from northern exile to purge the corrupted capital. The Wanderer clinches his lesson with the image of the "ample moon" of imagination transforming the "dusky veil" of the human condition into "contingencies of pomp." And this emblem, at last, moves the Solitary out of his cynicism.

Ghostlier Demarcations, Keener Sounds

"But how begin? and whence?" he cries (1080). The Solitary's condition remains critical, a debilitating self-consciousness. He stands at the beginning of a century of a peculiar form of personal and religious doubt, notably commented on by Carlyle and Mill, Newman and Kierkegaard, and studied systematically in M. H. Abrams's *Natural Supernaturalism*. It is one thing to be intellectually or rationally convinced, but how can belief lead to committed action? "Alas! such wisdom bids a creature fly / Whose very sorrow is, that time hath shorn / His natural wings!" (1083–85). Just as the Wanderer recognized the Solitary's special situation regarding belief, he appreciates how hard it is to live and move and act one's being in the dawn of tragic knowledge. Rather than give "unbending . . . counsel" (1104), he follows Wordsworth's advice to "Mathetes" and makes even greater allowances for character, pushing still further into the possible influences of imaginative activity upon purely natural forms. Beyond tragedy himself, his "discriminating sympathy" gives him authority to waive the entire theological foundation on which Book IV opened. "Manifold and various are the ways / Of restoration" (1112–13), and he suggests that the Solitary is already following one path, though very different from the one he would choose:

> I have seen
> A curious child, who dwelt upon a tract
> Of inland ground, applying to his ear
> The convolutions of smooth-lipped shell;
> . . . .
> . . . whereby the monitor expressed
> Mysterious union with its native sea.   [1132–35, 1139–40]

Again the imagery and conviction of the Intimations Ode work their way into *The Recluse*. The Wanderer offers the Solitary regeneration through radical innocence: "you stand, / Adore, and worship, when you know it not; . . . you have felt, and may not cease to feel" (1147–48, 1151). The phenomenology of the Solitary's character at this point removes the necessity for any conscious ground of belief. Feeling is as certain as knowing, and here imperceptibly replaces it. The Solitary may save himself with his own two eyes, if he links them to his imagination, with never a thought of placing their mutuality in a higher dispensation. He needs no excuse; he need only become conscious of the value of his feelings, the grandest and simplest of Wordsworth's myths.

Indeed, he is already conscious of something. The Wanderer asks if his soul "received a shock of awful consciousness" (1157) when he heard a "solitary raven" flying out of sight above the twilit valley:

> Athwart the concave of the dark blue dome,
> Unseen, perchance above all power of sight—
> An iron knell! with echoes from afar
> Faint—and still fainter—as the cry, with which
> The wanderer accompanies her flight
> Through the calm region, fades upon the ear,
> Diminishing by distance till it seemed
> To expire; yet from the abyss is caught again,
> And yet again recovered! [1179–87]

The passage is another emblem, both of the "possible sublimity" the Solitary knows and the challenge he represents to it: "from the abyss is caught again, / And yet again recovered!" Wordsworth drafted two passages for this climactic moment of Book IV, the rejected one a visual parallel to the aural image of the raven's cry, showing that the Solitary's "awful consciousness" is indeed a mode of veiled vision, of silent vision rather than of invisible sound:

> Lo in the west a solemn sight, behold
> Upon yon craggy barrier's lofty ridge
> A Pageantry of darksome trees that stand
> Single in their aerial solitude,
> Stand motionless in solitary calm
> Yet greeted gently by the moving clouds
> That pass and pass, and ever are to come
> Varying their colours slowly in the light
> Of an invisible moon. Cloud follows cloud
> As thought [?succeeds] to thought, but now ensues
> A pause—the long procession seems to end,
> The breeze that was in heaven hath died away
> And all things are immoveably composed
> Save here and there an uncomplying Star
> That twinkles in its station self-disturbed. [*PW*, V.429–30]

This scene parallels the effect of "diminishing by distance" in the raven passage—expiring yet recovering—as much as sight can parallel sound. But its special visionary quality, especially the clouds that "pass and pass, and ever are to come," does not really manifest itself without glossing from other, similar visionary paradigms in *The Recluse* like "A Night-Piece," the Snowdon vision, and "St. Paul's." The visionary quality lies in the unity of nature's still solitude with heaven's multitudinous motion. The trees are slightly blurred by the clouds, which in turn blur the moon, but only to alter, not obliterate, its light. Visual overlay dominates visual contrast. The "solemn sight" is a cinematic veiled vision, but its special effect comes with the sudden still shot: "Immoveably composed." All motion ceases, the light is unchanging, and stillness is marked by the random twinkle of one or more stars, whose movement, "self-disturbed," certainly suggests the Solitary's human condition. Both these passages are indeed "imaginative heights," as the Wanderer says. They bring to a dramatic climax the stage of work on *The Recluse* devoted to the Solitary. As emblems, they are offered to the Solitary for whatever interpretation he may attach to them. Even interpretation is unnecessary, for on the grounds of simple visual faith which the Wanderer elucidated earlier, their meaning is simply intuited: you either see it or you don't.

Indistinct Conclusions

None of the three characters construes the implications of the Wanderer's address as I have, yet the possibility of such an interpretation is definitely present in what may be called the subconscious structure of Book IV. Wordsworth was aware of this possible drift, or was made aware of it by readers' reactions to *The Excursion*. In replying to the criticisms of a Unitarian lady reported to him by his correspondents (always the forum of his bluntest and most personal literary criticism), he rested his case on the orthodoxy of the Wanderer's opening speech. To the charge of nature-worship he replied:

> Unless I am mistaken [there is nothing?] of this kind in the Excursion—There is indeed a passage towards the end of the 4th Book where the Wanderer introduces the Simile of the Boy & the Shell and what follows—That has something ordinarily but absurdly called Spinosistic—but the intelligent reader will easily see the *dramatic* propriety of the passage. The Wanderer in the beginning of the book had given vent to his own devotional feelings and announced in some degree his own creed. He is here preparing the way for more distinct conceptions of the Deity by reminding the Solitary of such religious feelings as cannot but exist in the minds of those who affect Atheism.[13]

But the images which prepare the way are *in*distinct in a special way. Speaking simply in terms of visual imagery, the question raised in some readers' minds might be, how far do indistinct conceptions of deity based on imagination lead toward distinct conceptions based on faith? Images of the Solitary's restoration from "false conclusions of the reasoning power" are repeated from the end of Book III, where he had complained, "How languidly I look / Upon this visible fabric of the world" (III.962–63). Now the Wanderer promises that "within the circuit of this fabric huge" (1177) the Solitary will see life infinitely multiplied "above all power of sight / ... yet from the abyss ... recovered!" (1180, 1186–87). These are offered as *true* conclusions of the *feeling* power.

The Solitary's imminent redemption (which, however, is never fully completed in *The Excursion*) is generalized into a hope for mankind, with similar imagery. The man who "communes with the Forms / Of nature ... contemplating these Forms / In the relations which they bear to man" (1208–09, 1230–31) shall "clothe / The naked spirit" with the "spiritual presences of absent things" (1249–50, 1234), just as natural objects speak in a process unvaried since the Pedlar's experiences of 1797, "to social reason's inner sense, / With inarticulate language" (1206–07). The dull eye of Science,

> taught with patient interest to watch
> The processes of things, and serve the cause
> Of order and distinctness . . .
> Shall [find] . . .
> Its most illustrious province . . .
> In furnishing clear guidance, a support
> Not treacherous, to the mind's *excursive* power.   [1257–63]

Wordsworth's italics emphasize the poem's thematic excursion, unfortunately buried under an unmanageable narrative plot.[14] The last two hundred lines of Book IV are replete with images not of "order and dinstinctness" but of nature clothed and veiled, or clothing and veiling, the visual manifestations of the mind's excursive power. Like Wordsworth's Grasmere, the Solitary's valley seems to the undespondent eye a "fixed centre of a troubled world" (V.16). But there is a tension in this veiled vision of imagination which contrasts usefully not only with apocalyptic self-consciousness but also with Christian orthodoxy; the remainder of *The Excursion* removes that tension utterly. In Book IX, the Wanderer rejoices that "throughout the world of sense" every object is "laid open to the view / Without reserve or veil" (IX.214–17); and in the final sunset scene of *The Excursion*, where Wordsworth pulls out all the stops to describe a "local transitory type / Of God's paternal splendors," the tenuous subtlety of Book IV's sunset is gone. Having gone as far as he dared as a "Prophet of Nature" giving himself up to the influx of her spirit on his feelings, Wordsworth turned in the last five books to a sacramental, priestly style of natural interpretation which enabled him to complete *The Excursion*—but it finished *The Recluse*.

9

The Graveyard Recluse
(*The Excursion,* Books V–IX)

> Along the mazes of this song I go
> As inward motions of the wandering thought
> Lead me, or outward circumstance impels.
> Thus do I urge a never-ending way
> Year after year, with many a sleep between,
> Through joy and sorrow; if my lot be joy
> More joyful if it be with sorrow sooth'd.
>
> PW, V.347

The history of *The Recluse* is one of repeated new beginnings; it is no surprise that Wordsworth's final and most extended period of work on it should start all over again, with a new character, the Pastor, and a new cast to whom he gives voice, the rural folk buried in his churchyard. The manuscript history of Books V–IX is so tangled that it may never be known exactly;[1] nevertheless, it is generally clear their composition commenced about 1811, after the basic completion of the Solitary's story, and that the poem proceeded "under conceptions of principal characters and main themes similar to those of the poem as published [though] final organization . . . was fixed during the period of intense work commencing 3 January, 1813" (CMY, 675). More exact dates are not critically important, as it is abundantly evident that these five books are motivated by a single imaginative impulse.

If, however, we ask what poetic logic informs this "philosophical pastoral,"[2] the answer is less sure. As Lamb observed in his review, "Those who hate *Paradise Lost* will not love this poem,"[3] and these books of the poem that was to supplant Milton's epic have suffered the corollary of the fate Dr. Johnson ascribed to it: everyone has wished them shorter. Some commentators have suggested that *The Excursion* is incomplete even at nine books and nine thousand lines, because Wordsworth intended it to include the Solitary's "renovation," which could not have been dramatically portrayed in either the first or third proposed parts of *The Recluse* (*The Excursion* is the second part), because they were to be "chiefly meditations

285

in the Author's own person."[4] Early reviewers were much exercised, not to say alarmed, by the question of *The Excursion*'s length in relation to Wordsworth's prefatory announcement that it was only one-third of a much longer work, which, furthermore, was preceded by still another poem, finished but unpublished (*The Prelude*). Francis Jeffrey made a hasty or willful conflation of the two poems' autobiographical character, related them to *The Excursion*'s time span of barely three days, and concluded "that, by the use of a very powerful *calculus,* some estimate may be formed of the probable extent of the entire biography."[5] Charles Lamb loyally defended *The Excursion* as not a "branch . . . prematurely plucked . . . but . . . in itself, a complete and legitimate production," resting his case on the unity of the second half (Books V–IX) "as being almost a continued cluster of narration . . . not wanting in stories of the most interesting kind."[6] Yet Books V–IX create so massive a delay in the imaginative redemption offered the Solitary in Book IV that they must be seen as a revisionary corrective to IV's wide-open possibilities. The Pastor's voicing of his parishioners' lives shifts the focus from suffering (Margaret's or the Solitary's) to death and a plan of salvation. However, this scheme is only nominally Christian—pious evangelicals were fiercely indignant about the poem's lax representation of faith—and many of its most orthodox touches were not added until 1845.[7] The Pastor's flock certainly led lives based on Christian assumptions, but their author stresses their paramount virtue as strength of mind, the sheer mental effort with which they met—or failed to meet—the conditions of their lives. This primacy of mind over faith makes *The Excursion* a meditative rather than a devotional work and accounts for its extremely tough, relentlessly cold comfort, so different from (though no more attractive than) the sentimentally pietistic way in which it is regarded by people who have not read it.[8] When Lamb speaks of its "liberal Quakerism" and "Natural Methodism," his adjectives underscore by redundancy a paradox that is lost if we fasten on his denominations, since nothing Christian (in 1814) could be more liberal than the ethics of Quakers or more natural than the emotions of Methodists.[9]

Mental fortitude is also the basis of a second new theme in Books V–IX: the imaginative vigor of everyday life, or what Wordsworth conceived of as the genius of nonvisionary existence. These stories complete one of the deepest intentions of *The Recluse,* the *decentralization of imagination* from its traditional location in privileged classes in capital cities. But—and here's the rub—they also entail a displacement from the mind of the poet who proposes such decentralization as his mode of triumph over established imaginations. These stories contain "no visionary experi-

ences whose power arises from their personal significance for the narrator" (M. II.181). The true, blind sublimity of Wordsworth's egotistical
genius in *The Recluse* was its wish to ignore its own prerogatives in order
to write the redemptive poem he felt modern man needed: democratic,
necessarily unheroic, lost to the admirations of traditional genius. As
Frances Ferguson has demonstrated, this results in *The Excursion*'s "repeated questioning of the poeticalness of poetry itself."[10] As characters, the
Pastor's buried minds lived somewhere between Margaret's inarticulate fi-
delity and the Solitary's loquacious skepticism. Some were village intellectuals. In their mental strength and fortitude, combined with their middling
quotient of self-knowledge, lies a basis for tragic knowledge. They see their
fate, they complain, they compromise, and they finally accept. Although
they are dead, the concentration of their stories is not upon death as such,
but on death as the final shaper of our ends, the last touch which completes the form of our lives. Like Wordsworth's contemporaneous "Essay
upon Epitaphs," these stories dwell less upon death than on what might be
said about it; each of them is in effect an epitaph, the smallest compression
of the fullest story, a direction in which *The Recluse* was always tending
once it began its dialectical relations with *The Prelude,* the fullest expansion of the most individual story.

The theme of nonvisionary lives entails a third emphasis, which is not
new but familiar in *The Recluse*'s history: Wordsworth's swing away from
concentration on the individual mind (in his Solitary-surrogate) to characters other than himself. As usual, his success in this operation is relative,
because his characteristic voice always speaks "as if there were nothing but
himself and the universe."[11] But the graveyard villagers are the first *Recluse* characters since the solitaries of 1798 and the Grasmere creatures of
1800 who are not Wordsworth or idealized versions of himself. Their stories are for the most part based on actual Lake District facts, and to a degree the evident normality of their lives balances the uniquely inarticulate
sufferings of the first *Recluse* protagonists—Margaret, the old Cumberland beggar, and the Discharged Veteran. Since most lives are failures from
the perspective Wordsworth established for his life and master-poem, these
stories concentrate largely on the paradox of success-through-failure, as
Wordsworth charts the movement of his characters' minds through the re-
calcitrant matter of their lives. They are ordinary, but selectively so. Their
mental energy resists accommodation to the ordinary; they acquiesce, but
not always gracefully; their life-expectations are defeated or heavily com-
promised, but the real significance of their lives lies in the vigor with which
they maintain their illusions, causing them further pain but making them

in a sense triumphant. As such, they are conscious embodiments of the theme of the extraordinary-in-the-ordinary which Coleridge, many years after the *Lyrical Ballads* had been published but only shortly after *The Excursion*, said had been Wordsworth's intention from the first.[12]

Criticism is provoked by *The Excursion*; Jeffrey may have been rude, but he was not wrong, when he said, "This will never do!" Wordsworth spoke smoothly in his preface of "the attentive Reader" who would find the unifying connections between his "minor Pieces" and "the main Work," and would have "no difficulty in extracting the system" from the author's "clear thoughts, lively images, and strong feelings" (*PW*, V.2). But these coolly confident expressions are, in the history of *The Recluse* as we can now see it, rather the result of confirmed wishful thinking. *The Excursion* presents, in Jeffrey's harsh half-truths, "innumerable changes . . . upon a few very simple and familiar ideas . . . [in] such a hubbub of strained raptures and fantastical sublimities, that it is often difficult for the most skillful and attentive student to obtain a glimpse of the author's meaning."[13] Especially in the last five books, Wordsworth asks too much if he expects us to read poetically. Nevertheless, this is what I have tried to do, looking round for poetry, as Wordsworth said we might in *Lyrical Ballads*, inquiring "by what species of courtesy these attempts can be permitted to assume that title."[14] The evident moral and philosophic burdens of *The Excursion* have led most commentators to the sensible expedient of abstracting its lessons and arguments. This clarifies much of its obscurity and prolixity, but at the expense of its object: we are left with a set of consoling maxims about human life so general as to be, if not useless, at most uninteresting. These are the truisms Coleridge complained about, saying that Wordsworth had "*himself* convinced *himself* of Truths, which the generality of persons have . . . taken for granted from their Infancy" (*LSTC*, IV.554). Coleridge also remarked that Wordsworth's convictions were so firmly "self-established" that they give "to certain Thoughts and Expressions a depth and force which they had not for readers in general" (*LSTC*, IV.573).

Between these truisms and neosophisms *The Excursion* will languish forever: words that speak of nothing more than what we are, but with an emphatic uniqueness of expression that often escapes us altogether. But the language of *The Excursion* is only intermittently its focal point of interest. Rather, the last five books are a monument to Wordsworth's massive architectonic powers, encrusted with a "relentlessly Miltonic"[15] language that drags down rather than highlights its structure. We are often, in *The Recluse*, in the presence of structures we cannot see because they are so much larger than what we had imagined. Interpretation is most valuably employed in uncovering the imaginative value of *The Excursion*'s buried foundations, since, as Hazlitt prophetically concluded, "this very original and powerful performance may . . . remain like one of those stupendous but half-finished structures, which have been suffered to moulder into decay, because the cost and labour attending them exceeded their use or beauty."[16]

Telling, compulsive tale-telling, motivates these books.[17] The compulsion arises in response to the Solitary's objection that human life is by nature fragmented, has no significant shape or form, no essentially meaningful "image," in the terms he and the Wanderer argued in Books II–IV. The artistic problem of significant form is thrust back upon the life-problem of meaning, as though the shape of one's life (fully evident only after death) could answer the problematics of its content. The idea that anything incomplete is by definition fragmented thus links these stories to the motivation of *The Recluse*, as complicated by the existence of *The Prelude*. Could *The Prelude* ever be finished; was it ever finished? If so, where was *The Recluse*? If the life story was satisfactory, should not the lifework follow? How could the former become the latter without some prior differentiation between them? The obscurely fruitful relation for Wordsworth of these two poems—neither, in the common sense of the word, complete—attaches in *Excursion* V–IX to the metacritical question, for writers, of the "good" of any storytelling whatever.

The deep complexity of Wordsworth's narrative theory, combined with the democratic commonness of his subjects, may help to explain why *The Excursion* grew slowly, if steadily, in serious reputation, until by the 1840s it "had become almost the Bible of the poetry-reading public" (M. II.183). For all their occasional dullness, these stories were ahead of their time; Wordsworth's handling of them anticipates and prepares the way for the coming era of social seriousness. He manages to make all the hilarious jibes of Hazlitt, Jeffrey, Shelley, and Byron at prosy parsons and dusty pedlars look decidedly retrograde and old-fashioned in historical comparison. Lamb's simple, generous suggestion that we "substitute silently the word *Palmer*, or *Pilgrim*" for Pedlar if it offends us, is easily accepted by twentieth-century readers, whatever their reservations about other aspects of the poem, as is his comparison of the Wanderer to Piers Plowman, whereby "the lowness of the teacher seems to add a simple dignity to the doctrine."[18] In marked contrast to the Solitary's Romantic *Weltschmerz*, which is accurately represented as a dated fashion, the last five books of *The Excursion* are about the importance, perhaps the glory, of being earnest. The ideal of democratized imagination to which Wordsworth here sacrificed his egotistical genius gradually became, in the decades after 1815, the goal of enlightened social thought, the spirit of reform.[19] In part it represents Wordsworth's "unchanging concern with man as a 'moral being,'" and Mary Moorman's estimate of its social significance chastens facile cynicism: "it is the poetic charter of the poor, the ignorant, and the underprivileged in a way that no English poem has been before or since" (M. II.182). Moreover, there are signs in Wordsworth's drive to finish it, coupled with his other activities in 1813–14, that suggest he foresaw the coming of a new era, interpreted it partly as a justification of his long-scorned opinions on life and literature, and strove to publish *The Excursion* as the necessary *"instructive* book" for the times (M. II.260).

All during the last year of intense organizational work on the poem, the final defeat of Napoleon was clearly imminent; his unconditional abdication on 11 April 1814 must have given Wordsworth a special satisfaction as he put the final touches in May (*CMY*, 25) to Book IX's suggestion that reformed national education systems are the best guarantee against future tyrannies. Other things seemed to be falling into place for Wordsworth as the poem and the Napoleonic Wars drew to a close together, somewhat recapitulating the life-settling atmosphere of December 1800, when Book I, Part I of *The Recluse* was undertaken. In April 1813 his commission as Stamp Distributor for Westmorland was confirmed; in May the family removed to Rydal Mount, the impressive seat where he would receive visitors' homage for the rest of his life; in June they were visited by the recently freed French prisoner Eustace Baudouin, soon to become Caroline Wordsworth-Vallon's brother-in-law in a wedding Dorothy hoped fervently to be able to attend (*CMY*, 491, 521, 554). During these months, Wordsworth instructed his brother to be ready to sell his stocks at an expected new postwar high (*CMY*, 551). On 4 November 1813, the day Napoleon's decisive defeat in the "Battle of Nations" at Leipzig was reported in the *Times,* Wordsworth's friend Southey took his oath as poet laureate after his friend Scott had declined the honor (*CMY*, 545). Wordsworth's sonnet on the military occasion ("November, 1813") rather oddly celebrates George III's opposition to Napoleon, wishing that God might send a ray of recognition into the monarch's deep insanity (*PW*, III.143). While I do not say he wished that the king might also have recognized a better laureate, this turn of sentiment parallels the conclusion of his later "Thanksgiving Ode" on Waterloo: that "I, or some more favoured Bard" might arise to rightly hail British valor, with "A corresponding virtue to beguile / The hostile purposes of wide-wasting Time" (*PW*, III.143–48).

Needless to say, Wordsworth's hopes saw too far into the future; England did not soon rise to its new opportunities for social virtue, but the fact remains that *The Excursion,* not *The Prelude,* was the major *"instructive* book" read by precocious children like Mary Ann Evans (George Eliot) growing up in the literary wasteland of the 1820s and 1830s. How different would the course of this period of English literary history look, had Wordsworth published *The Prelude* in 1814 and reserved *The Excursion* for posterity! As it was, he gave his Victorian epic to the Romantics; his Romantic one, to the Victorians. The literary world was not ready for *The Excursion*'s seriousness in 1814 but had had too much of *The Prelude*'s individualism by 1850. Wordsworth's own pleasure at receiving an honorary Oxford degree in 1839 illustrates the difference. Though satisfied with Keble's oration praising *The Excursion* for setting the condition of the poor in "a celestial light," he cherished far more the information that the undergraduates' applause for him was greater than any they had bestowed on anyone except that other conqueror of the times, the Duke of Wellington (M. II.542–43).

These associations are integral to Wordsworth's conception of himself as author of *The Recluse,* and are confirmed by his peroration in an extremely long letter of 1811, at the beginning of *The Excursion*'s final period of composition, to Captain C. W. Pasley, author of *The Military Policy and Institutions of the British Empire,* a book arguing for the defeat of Napoleon by counteradoption of his policy of imperial conquest. Wordsworth deeply admired Pasley's book, read it several times (*CMY,* 471), and offered his help on several occasions to advance Pasley's military career (*LMY,* II.20, 663). After a perspicacious statement of the need for a "remodelling of Europe" into a system of unified nations, and an intellectual's plea for "a new course of education, a higher tone of moral feeling, and more of the grandeur of the imaginative faculties" in national policy, Wordsworth's letter concludes with an image that clearly reflects his sense of himself and the spirit informing his poetry:

> Now a State ought to be governed (at least in these times) . . . upon calculations and from impulses similar to those which give motion to the hand of a great artist when he is preparing a picture, or of a mighty Poet when he is determining the proportions and march of a Poem. Much is to be done by rule; the great outline is previously to be conceived in distinctness, but the consummation of the work must be trusted to resources that are not tangible, though known to exist. [*LMY,* I.481–82]

In a people, he told Pasley, these hidden resources are the character and freedom with which they develop "civil arts and habits"; in a mighty

Poem, as we know from studying the "proportions and march" of *The Recluse,* they were "the grandeur of the imaginative faculties" that would arise to fill what it had never had, a distinct outline. The peroration of *The Excursion,* "Your Country must complete / Her glorious destiny" (IX.407–08), composed contemporaneously with the letter to Pasley (*CMY,* 679) and the gathering of *La Grande Armée,* the largest Europe had ever seen, for its final disastrous march into Russia, stands at the beginning of a nineteenth-century tradition of intellectuals placing themselves in imagined antagonism to Napoleon, in which Tolstoy's Pierre Bezukhov stands near the end.[20] Wordsworth's international gestures may in part have been capitalizing on the success of the first two cantos of *Childe Harold's Pilgrimage* (1812),[21] but in viewing the conclusion of *The Excursion* as Wordsworth's imagined contribution to the end of Napoleon's imperial adventure, we may also look for evidence in the internal development of *The Recluse,* where the effective end of *The Prelude*'s narrative story had been achieved by Wordsworth's imagined triumph over Robespierre for the championship of the Revolution's republican phase.

The last five books of Wordsworth's proposed epic are difficult to read, yet their difficulty can be conceived as equal-but-opposite to that other obscure Romantic epic of similarly universal scope, Blake's *Jerusalem.* Blake places the reader in a privately constructed visionary world where he is easily lost; Wordsworth places him in what looks to be the dullest, most ordinary setting imaginable, but his opaque emphasis on the power of the unusual in the ordinary loses us among his buried assumptions as easily as we are lost among Blake's visionary forms. Blake's mythos tells us that achieving the extraordinary is not impossible, whereas Wordsworth's graveyard stories insist repeatedly that maintaining the ordinary is not easy, and that any human norm is established only after many victories over life's randomness without and all the temptations of the *eccentric* ego within. To preserve mental equilibrium is therefore a heroic endeavor, and one worth voicing in song by the poet who had achieved it in his masterpiece and wanted to offer it as a model to others.

BOOK V: "THE PASTOR"

An enormous shifting of gears begins in the fifth book of *The Excursion* from a naturalistic, individualistic view of imagination to a social, institutional one. It is not a shift in Wordsworth's valuation of imagination but in the perspective from which it can be most profitably observed: its presence in all "hopes divine / Of pure imagination" (V.909–10). The new character, the Pastor, is thus radically subordinated to his institutional role, in responding to the Solitary's skepticism about the value of all established forms of culture whatsoever. Since the Solitary casts his questions in the traditional metaphor of human life as "an ill-constructed tale" (432), the philosophic issue of ultimate good is transmuted into the aesthetic one of significant form, leading to the Pastor's function as narrator of his flock's lives. Telling the story of a life is not sufficient to give it meaning; the Pastor's telling shapes these lives within the institutional context he represents, his tales are legitimized by his author-ity. Their volume and variety are necessary because multiplication of instances is Wordsworth's usual mode of generalization, and the Solitary, as his antagonistic alter ego, will doubt the validity of any single example; his mind operates by binary exclusions, an analytic rationalism that forces itself to apocalyptic negatives: "Not for a happy land do I enquire, / Island or grove, that hides a blessed few / . . . / But whom, I ask, of individual Souls, / Have [philosophy and religion] withdrawn from passion's crooked ways?" (349–50, 354–55). This states Wordsworth's central hope as a contrary doubt. Instead of the "Paradise, and groves Elysian" which the "Prospectus" promised would be the "simple·produce of the common day," the Solitary rejects all fantasy projects ("happy land," "blessed few") to emphasize his doubt of any real satisfactions whatsoever. Wordsworth invests an Aeschylean pessimism in the Solitary's taunt, aiming it perilously near to his own paradisal dreams of what "a blessed few" might accomplish, and to the intimately sensitive relation of *The Recluse* to *The Prelude*: How call any man happy before he is dead? How determine the full significance of a life, or a poem, before it is finished? By means of "solemn institutions," the Pastor will answer, established by "the care prospective of our wise / Forefathers . . . to guard against the shocks, / The fluctuations and decay of things" (997–99).

In this context, Book V's departure from the Solitary's valley becomes Wordsworth's farewell to the special, isolated retreats which he had constructed in all the major *Recluse* fragments, usually at fatal cost to their conclusions. But whereas in "Home at Grasmere" and "The Tuft of Primroses" problematic questions had arisen externally (who killed the swans? who cut down the trees?), in the Solitary's valley the "pale Recluse" himself infects the place. Book V's opening lines date from the 1809–10 period of composition on Books II–IV (*CMY*, 24), indicating Wordsworth's recognition of the need to bid adieu to his deeply symbolic valleys, his "retreat within retreat" (II.446). The Poet considers himself one of the lucky few who can still live properly in such places, even as the poem turns away from them: "Sheltered, but not to social duties lost, / Secluded, but not buried" (V.54–55). The negatives are crucial, implying Wordsworth's uncertainty about the value of his strategic retreat from society, anticipating the buried lives of Books VI and VII which assert that no life, no matter how remote or ordinary, is "buried" from social significance, and looking far ahead to the conclusion of *The Excursion*'s establishmentarian argument: "Even till the smallest habitable rock / . . . hear the songs / Of humanised society; and bloom / With civil arts . . . / . . . From culture, unexclusively bestowed" (IX.387–92).

Both the Solitary and the Poet hang back, each for his own reasons, from this necessary advance toward a new social perspective on imagination. But the Wanderer urges them forward into another valley, with a "grey church-tower" at its center. Memorial matters immediately grasp the attention of these intellectual tourists: the "foot-worn epitaphs . . . faded narrative . . . silent language" of the county nobility's tombs (169, 207, 189). The Solitary blends right into this melancholy scene ("gracefully he stood, / The semblance bearing of a sculptured form / That leans upon a monumental urn," 214–16), and his Hamlet-like characteristics are provoked by that "easy-hearted churl," the gravedigger, who fails to be appropriately depressed by his surroundings. Like Hamlet's, the Solitary's mind moves by either/or exclusions, and he expects, if "every grave were as a volume," they would tell stories illustrating that human life *does not work out* according to the patterns which philosophy and religion present in sacramental form (baptism) or symbol (star, anchor, or Cross). He demands, like Hamlet and most artists, a sense of unity in life. If "the poetry of common speech" (392) pictures human life as a single year, why aren't glowing summer and bounteous autumn justly proportioned to the "resemblance not to be denied / . . . Foretelling aged Winter's desolate sway" (405, 410)? Such unities as we foist upon ourselves are "fashioned like an ill-constructed tale / . . . for the sequel leaving / Old things repeated with diminished grace; / And all the laboured novelties at best / Imperfect substitutes" (432–38). Since the timid Poet cautiously seconds this literary criticism of life, the Pastor must account for the lack of organic connection between life's content and its form, to answer the Solitary's "languageless ideal."[22] His certain faith must meet the Solitary's certain doubt in man's "illusive power, / That finds and *cannot fasten down*" (322–23; italics added).

The Solitary's exclusionary mode of argument is met in the Pastor's reply by an inclusive, both/and logic. Between them, they represent the apocalyptic discontinuity and the naturalistic continuities which are the

fundamental poles of Wordsworth's imagination, the latter working massively everywhere in his best poetry to resist the former.[23] The Wanderer's
report of the previous day's conversation faithfully recapitulates the Solitary's insistent dichotomies: is man preponderantly a creature of good or
evil, is virtue real or "no better than a name," "Do generations press / On
generations, without progress made?" (466–67). The Pastor replies that final answers are for angels, "the good *and* evil are our own" (490; italics
added). This announces the pairing principle, or complementarity, that
will govern the graveyard stories to come. The Pastor's first homely attention to the grave mounds as they appear in early April anticipates every
moral he will later draw from them: they are snowy on the north side,
green on the south, their unified significance is not absolute but a matter
of perspective—"we see, then, as we feel" (558). Human life is not an argument invalidated by inconsistency, as the Solitary argues; when the Solitary "buoyantly" endorses manual labor—"body and mind in one captivity," nervous hands blessedly dissevered "from a too busy commerce with
the heart" (605, 610)—his own images prefigure his potential agreement
with the Pastor. They emblematize the central philosophic argument that
Coleridge wanted *The Recluse* to make: thought integrally connected with
feeling. Such connections are not mechanical but vital, not the sum or answer of a problem but a process of continuous creation, not a text as a
finally-shaped artifact but the ongoing life of its writing and readings.

   This pairing principle of form and content, which will govern the
structure of Books VI and VII, begins to operate in the Pastor's preliminary exemplum of the "sequestered pair" of old folks living on a nearby
mountainside. On the one hand, they are as low "in powers of mind, / In
scale of culture" (716–17) as any the Pastor knows. On the other, their
cottage's "lofty site" is an ideal *Recluse*-spot: such as "a hermit might
have chosen / . . . [to] look down upon the works, / The habitations, and
the ways of men, / Himself unseen!" (681, 684–86). "No such visionary
views" (689) are theirs; rather, like the graveyard heroes to follow, their
wedded strength is undergirded by their shadowy affinity to that which
they are not: visionary seers. The Wanderer muses that they are descended
from "a race illustrious for heroic deeds" to their present condition,
"Humble, but not degraded" (792–93). Like the Poet's earlier self-defense
of his life ("Secluded, but not buried"), the Wanderer's reflections place
the old couple's decline into an overall cyclical pattern, "fall from high to
low, ascent from low to high" (796), in which we recognize "Home at
Grasmere"'s visionary ideal extended onto a historical grid. There is a
sublime banality in Wordsworth's insistence on the heroism of ordinary

lives beneath the veil of custom. Whatever the old couple might have wished to do with their lives is set aside in honor of what they did in fact achieve: steadiness, symbolized in their "rough abode . . . / Such as in unsafe times of border-war / Might have been wished for and contrived" (697–99). Of course, in "these our unimaginative days" (II.24) there are no more border wars, but the subjunctive heroic reference sticks, and makes of this old couple the firm foot of a long scale of examples that will culminate with the history of Sir Alfred Irthing at the end of Book VII, an ascending scale that supports the Wanderer's exordium on the whole pattern of history, "ascent and progress in the main" (VII.1005).

Internally, the stories will introduce the offspring that "proceed from the conjunction" of another old couple, that most "mysteriously-united pair / . . . Death and Life" (903–04)—namely, Faith, Hope, Reason, Charity, and Love. Externally, the significance of the villagers' deaths is equated with the wildest, most catastrophic, death scenes imaginable (i.e., the most exciting to read stories about): battlefield slaughter, the "dismal prospect" of a "wild shore strewn / With wrecks," "Tyrants who utter the destroying word, / And slaves who will consent to be destroyed" (930–31, 941–42). Wordsworth's excitement over what these little lives and deaths could mean is clearly evident in a rejected manuscript passage in which, as in similar crucial moments in *The Prelude,* his metaphors spin out to imperial Eastern cities, at the precise moment of highest apocalyptic interest: "a City to the flames / Of war delivered . . . / Till irresistibly the storm break in" (*PW,* V.183, *app. crit.*). He wants to make very sure we get the point of what is coming, yet his prolixity indicates his own doubt that he can convey it effectively. If the tales seem monotonous, this oblique introduction seems to warn us, it is because of our excessive expectations for both life and literature; ultimately, all poetry is called into question "as a possibly spurious sublimity."[24] The stories will seem moving only if we are sympathetic to absences, to the sense of otherness which can be discovered in these nonvisionary lives as the road *not* taken—the high road toward the extraordinary—rather than the beaten path of ordinariness.

BOOKS VI AND VII: "THE CHURCHYARD AMONG THE MOUNTAINS"

The sixteen short stories that make up Books VI and VII constitute Wordsworth's largest projection of his peculiar genius onto other lives. In a sense miniature *Preludes,* they are also postludes, for in them the final temper of mentality can be gauged. Books VI and VII correspond to the social or public sections of *The Prelude*; they respond to the Solitary's skepticism with an unsentimental conservatism set in the enabling context of the "solemn institutions" of Church and State; their power is manifested not in theological or political doctrine but in images of the little institutions or structures which their heroes built up to support their best idea of themselves, as Wordsworth constructed *The Prelude* to shore up his claim to be the bard of *The Recluse*. Neither saints' lives nor lives of poets, they are nonetheless conceived as representations of truth in biographical form. But they are lives without "spots of time." Instead of arresting visionary moments expanded into lifetime significance, these stories represent whole lifetimes compressed into a single summary account, or epitaph, in Wordsworth's new idiom.[25]

Their meaning is conveyed by the structural principles according to which they are presented. They progress through a vague sociohistorical hierarchy, from the old couple on the mountainside to the Elizabethan knight, Sir Alfred Irthing. An informal chronological sequence is also observed, from the most recently dead, the Unrequited Lover whose open grave awaits him, to Sir Alfred's ancient gravesite. The stories are further divided into two books on the basis of the source of the characters' sufferings. Book VI deals with mental stress brought on by the characters themselves and endured inwardly, while Book VII concerns physical disabilities or disasters suffered silently and their reflective effects upon others. But their most important structural element is the pairing principle by which Wordsworth divided them into four quartets: there are four sequences of four stories each, two sequences in each book, divided in the middle of each book by a digressive interlude on method. Within each sequence, each story is paired by complement or contrast to its fellow, especially the first to the second and the third to the fourth (the Deaf and Blind Dalesmen in Book VII are the signaling example), so that the second story in each pair rounds out the exemplum of the first. All of these people were defeated by life in regard to their hopes or talents, but by deprivations or excesses that are represented in nearly polar opposition. Wordsworth as "modernizer" of Chaucer (*PW*, IV.209) was a close student of *The Canterbury Tales*' structural principles, and since his philosophic poem was coming to depend more on the arrangement of humanistic tales within enabling religious contexts than on systematic argument, it may well be that he had Chaucer's example in mind in constructing a modern sequence that ended rather than began with a Knight's Tale, and framing the whole in a contemporary Parson's tale. This kind of densely intricate organization is characteristic of Wordsworth's supposed simplicity, and Dorothy was at about this time carefully reading Chaucer's "General Prologue" and "The Knight's Tale" (*CMY*, 457–58).

Book VI: Mental Suffering, Personal Effects
   1. The Unrequited Lover (95–211)
   2. The Persevering Miner (212–75)
   3. The Wastrel Talent (275–391)
   4. The Old Jacobite and the Old Whig (392–521)
First Interlude: Upon Inscriptions, Epitaphs, Myths, and Stories (522–674)
   5. The Tall Intellectual Woman (675–777)
   6. Ellen, the Village Magdalene (778–1069)
   7. Wilfred Armathwaite, Adulterous Husband (1069–1114)
   8. The Happy Widower (1115–1267)

Book VII: Physical Suffering, Social Effects
   1. The Ruined Cottage of the Sympson Family (31–310)
   2. The Priest called "Wonderful" (310–95)
   3. The Deaf Dalesman (395–481)
   4. The Blind Dalesman (482–536)
Second Interlude: The Jolly Old Woodcutter (537–86)
   5. The Personified Trees the Woodcutter Kills, and His Own Coming "Fall" (587–631)
   6. Little Margaret Green of Gold-rill Side (632–714)
   7. Young Oswald, Village Opponent of Napoleon (714–890)
   8. Sir Alfred Irthing of "Eliza's Golden Days" (891–1057)

The range of human experience is sufficiently representative, and though a certain amount of selectivity is evident, they are not all sad stories. Book VI has more negative factors—loss of love, lack of success, wasted talents, betrayal and fraud—but like Book VII's physical infirmities, these are portrayed to show how they were—more or less—surmounted. The Pastor's only proviso is that he will tell no tales of crime or disaster and recite no lives of obviously pointed significance. Thus, unlike sensational lives about which all or nothing is to be said, these graveyard recluses *require* telling to come alive, to be noticed. As one of the earliest insightful observers of modern mass journalism, Wordsworth was alert to the ways in which its "human interest" stories depend precisely on the uncommon rather than the usual, and in these stories he undertakes the thankless task of exposing the extravagance of the ordinary. One element notable by its absence is the fact that none of these people was unhappy simply because of being poor, though there are suggestions of economic factors at work in the stories of the Tall Intellectual Woman and Wilfrid Armathwaite. This oversight is consistent with the special quality of unoppressive poverty that Wordsworth, as a material and spiritual "rentier" in Grasmere, believed existed there.[26]

The operation of the stories' sequential pairing principle is most obvious in the first group of four, where Wordsworth draws our attention to it by a set of binary oppositions that would please a structural anthropologist. The Unrequited Lover, nearly crazed by what he failed to win, is followed by the persevering miner, who struck it rich so late in life that his mind "proved all unable to support the weight / Of prosperous fortune" (237–38). They are followed in turn by the young musician who started out with great natural gifts but squandered them, and the whole sequence of pairs is wrapped up with an internal pairing, the "sullen" old Whig and the "flaming" old Jacobite, who wasted their considerable material wealth in vain pursuit of political ends. Like all the characters in Book VI, their respective obsessions—love, wealth, fame, power—kept them apart from the common rout, and they are pointed opposites of the rags-to-riches staple of mass journalism, more resembling traditional religious exempla of riches-to-rags, in a new dispensation. To expose their failure is not Wordsworth's intention, but to reveal the special nature of their success, narrowly mental and wholly moral: the lover finally did triumph over his sense of loss, the miner's perseverance paid off, the musician kept his energy through repeated shocks and shames, and the two old activists achieved tranquility beyond politics.

The Unrequited Lover, like many of the figures to follow, is abstracted by nouns that suggest a more general plight; not only "Lover," he is also "Sufferer" and, after his breakdown, "Intruder" upon the common scene. His real story is not lost love but the heroism of his efforts to triumph over his crippling sense of loss. Like Wordsworth and Coleridge in their dejection, he turns "to books, and . . . science . . . to quell his pain" (149–52). But mental discipline is effective only when placed in "Nature's care," so he becomes a naturalist, and his deathbed gift to his now-married beloved—flowers pressed into a book—is not simply a sentimental end to a sentimental story, but a sign of "faithful love / Conquered and in tranquility retained!" (210–11). The typically obscure Wordsworth exclamation mark forces us to look closely to see the paradox compressed into this concluding formula, where *conquering* carries the opposite of its usual meaning in love stories, and *retaining* also signifies a tranquil contrary to conventional wisdom regarding lost love (i.e., forget it or you will be tormented). Like his creator, he has achieved the blessed condition of recollecting emotion in tranquility, and his book of pressed flowers is the first of many crafted items or structures in these stories in which, instead of in poems, these heroes memorialize the meaning of their lives. Such recompense as they achieve is not "invariably askew"[27] but is transmuted by their minds' necessary, even unwilling, cooperation with natural and social facts into a creation that is not what they wanted but what they got.

The miner persevered in his hopes till old age (the lover died young), when luck comes too late. All his life, the "counsel of his own clear thoughts" (219) maintained his confidence against others' scoffs, but when he gained what he wanted ("precious ore"), he lost what he had in "an unsettled liberty of thought" (239). He dies of insane joy, and all that remains is the thing that kept him on track all his life, going from his house to his mine, "named, in memory of the event, / The PATH OF PERSEVERANCE" (253–54). His perseverance paid off in a different monument from what he had imagined, the sign of his victory in defeat. The Wanderer quotes from *Paradise Lost* to honor such mental strength ("'Unshaken, unseduced, unterrified,'" 260; *PL*, V.896), and the Pastor's immediate assent that such heroism would not be misplaced in Westminster Abbey reminds us not only of the main topic, everyday heroism, but also, on top of the reference to Milton, of Poet's Corner and the motive of personal glory within Wordsworth's reclusive celebration of mute, inglorious folk.

The heroism of the Wastrel Talent is less obvious, since he frittered away his artistic gifts, but he struggled with more difficulty than the Lover and the Miner because "two several souls alternately had lodged" within him (288), in contrast to their pure singlemindedness. Wordsworth, master of double consciousness, empathizes deeply with this "zealous actor" whose music could range from mimicking a wild Indian bird to a mute swan. In a lightsome career, this Talent lost himself in his art's excitement (emotion without tranquility), sinking rapidly from the "proud saloons" of the rich through the city's "guilty bowers" down to the "hovels . . . rifted barns . . . and bare haunts" of the countryside. Rising and sinking three times like a drowning man, this "ghost of beauty" and "wreck of gaiety" (330–31) achieves a perversely heroic stature by seeming to incarnate "the very presence of the Fiend" (349) with his "freaks" among the astonished "merry-making beggars." His manic-depressive nature long supports him even as it finally defeats him; destined by his family for respectable art, he became the "Hired minstrel of voluptuous blandishment" (a sexy expression of an awful fate, for Wordsworth), and the changeling nature of his

life ("beneath one mother hatched, / Though from another sprung,"
367–68) can only be resolved in death: "One with himself, and one with
them that sleep" (375).

The Wastrel Talent's internal split is externalized in the two characters of the last story in the first quartet: the veteran Jacobite of Culloden's
great lost cause, and "the vanquished Whig" ruined by his efforts to win a
seat in Parliament. They retreated to the Pastor's valley (which is, of
course, Grasmere) to shun the human fellowship that the Wastrel Talent
desperately sought. Their stories are too long in background, since, as in
all Book VI's psychodramas, what they did after their life-crisis is more interesting than their earlier, undifferentiated normal lives. Having failed
by violent revolution or political faction to affect their country's destiny,
these polar antagonists daily filled the "bowling-green with harmless
strife" (466), until their "bickerings" become the spice that make their
yoked disappointments bearable. Failures on a national scale, they finally
achieve, together, a public service: to memorialize "an old yew, their
favourite resting-place" (493),

> They, with joint care, determined to erect,
> Upon its site, a dial, that might stand
> For public use preserved, and thus survive
> As their own private monument.   [496–99]

Like the lover's book of pressed flowers and the miner's path of perseverance, this sundial preserves in public, quasi-artistic form the private meaning of their lives. Such crafted memorials are, in their strange way, everyday versions of the hopes Wordsworth had for his poetry when he stood
before the decayed or threatened remnants of Christian civilization at
Tintern Abbey and the Grand Chartreuse. But such parallels, though apt,
also serve to expose the potential silliness of such symbols, and it is to
Wordsworth's credit that he can employ the Solitary's skepticism to question the sundial's conventional inscription ("*Time flies*," etc.) with an inquiry into all the many lives that are never memorialized, generalized to
the doubtful usefulness of all stories and myths, thus by a natural reflex
introducing the topic of the graveyard colloquy's first interlude.

The mild difference of opinion on which the first interlude turns is
whether there are fit epitaphs "for those among our fellow-men" who, unlike the reconciled Whig and Jacobite, "Are yet made desperate by 'too
quick a sense / Of constant infelicity'" (530, 532–33). The Solitary's apt
quotation from Taylor's *Holy Dying* makes him a devil's advocate for the

existence of irremediable tragedy in all times and places, while the Pastor
must insist that there are no Christian tragedies, strictly speaking, only
positive or negative illustrations of faith. In this old debate, the Solitary
has our sympathy and Wordsworth's too:

> The generations are prepared; the pangs,
> The internal pangs, are ready; the dread strife
> Of poor humanity's afflicted will
> Struggling in vain with ruthless destiny.   [554–57]

Wordsworth will not ease away that stern "in vain," and by the interlude's
end the Pastor has come round to a compromise, agreeing "we should not
leave / Wholly untraced a more forbidding way / . . . [to] declare / The native grandeur of the human soul" (661–62, 665–66). The methodological
impact of this interlude is to raise the humanizing function of all human stories by their connection to myth. The stories of Prometheus, Tantalus, and
Thebes are "Fictions in form, but in their substance truths, / Tremendous
truths" (545–46). What the Pastor's stories lack in form they will make
up for with a new kind of imaginatively informed, substantial realism.
Agreeing with the Solitary's proposed "exchange [of] shepherd's frock of
native grey / For robes with regal purple tinged" (548–49), he determinedly enunciates Wordsworth's intention to reveal the visionary force of
nonvisionary lives, "lifting up a veil, / . . . so that ye shall have / Clear images . . . / Of nature's unambitious underwood" (649–53). This is apocalyptic self-consciousness lowered to a socially acceptable pitch,[28] a crucial
part of *The Recluse*'s remorseless logic of imaginative decentralization,
Wordsworth turning his democratic will upon his aristocratic genius.

Reflecting the generalizing impact of the interlude, the last two pairs
of stories in Book VI allude more directly to major themes of Western civilization. But they continue the symmetrical organization of the first four:
two women disappointed early in love, one by unhappy marriage, the
other by broken betrothal; two men whose romantic disappointments
come late, one by betraying his good wife, the other reconciled to his
wife's death by the love of his daughters.

Mental travail is more palpable in the Tall Intellectual Woman's story
than in any other. "Surpassed by few / In power of mind" (676–77), it
shows on her face, "wrinkled and furrowed with habitual thought" (683).
Her wrinkles deepen when her youthful "desire of knowledge" is shunted
aside by an unluckily necessary marriage that perverts her intellect into a
stingy, scrimping household genius. When she finally establishes some fi-

nancial security for her family, it is "a pile / Constructed, that sufficed for every end, / Save the contentment of the builder's mind" (727–29). Thus her monument is flawed like her, and Wordsworth leaves her story open to the question of whether frustration of intellect or intellect itself caused her sorrow. Her bitterness has a quality of daring that is not palliated by Wordsworth's very late addition of some lines about her devout resignation. The Pastor fears he has gone too far toward portraying actual viciousness, but the woman is a splendid expression of the mind's strength to bear threats to its native enjoyments by persevering even as it is perverted from its ends: "A mind intolerant of lasting peace, / And cherishing the pang her heart deplored" (732–33). Although formally intended as a lead-in to the story of Ellen's long-suffering forbearance which follows, the Tall Woman's tale has its own integrity and approaches tragic status in its turn from a natural "flowering" of mind to the mechanical construction of a "pile" (her financial independence), which breaks the integral human connection between the woman's head and heart.

The story of Ellen, the "rueful, weeping Magdalene" of the village, is the centerpiece of Book VI and the most satisfactorily developed of the entire graveyard sequence. A tragedy of feeling rather than of intellect, Ellen's motherhood is as transcendent as the Tall Intellectual Woman's was neglectful. But Ellen's truly sisterly affinities, directly stressed by Wordsworth, are with Margaret of Book I: "sinking on the lonely heath / With the neglected house to which she clung" (1060–61). Like Margaret, Ellen is abandoned and left with a child whose death, like those of Margaret's children, is not the tragedy itself but a mark of the heroine's fate. Ellen's is one of Wordsworth's great maternal tragedies, in which the temper of human spirit is tested by enormous strains put upon humanity's most basic natural bond. Alone with her illegitimate child, Ellen is forced to hire herself out as a "Foster-mother" to ease the increased domestic burdens on *her* mother, but in her foster role she is forbidden to see her own baby lest it divide her attention. This cruel touch is hammered down hard at the end: she is not with her baby when it dies, arrives late for its funeral, and only there does her dignity peremptorily assert itself, forcing the gathered mourners to remain and watch her "weeping and looking, looking on and weeping, / . . . / Until at length her soul was satisfied" (980–82).

As in all these stories, the causes of suffering are less important than the effects they produce. Ellen, who had been queen of the valley on May Days and Twelfth Nights, an "Oread or Dryad . . . such as might have quickened and inspired / A Titian's hand" (827–29)—or a Wordsworth's pen—becomes after the birth of her child a more reflective person, finding "in lonely reading . . . a meek recompense," making of cottage-barn and garden "a secret oratory . . . [to] pore upon her book" (896, 899, 901). But such compensatory strength is not enough when her child dies; the "nest . . . her fond maternal heart had built . . . all too near the river's edge" (1019–20) is swept away. The fate of her reading "oratory" and metaphorical "nest" parallel the reflexive decay of Margaret's cottage and the Tall Woman's discontented "pile," inadequate structures symbolizing the builders' failure to impress their minds upon nature as forcefully as nature has pressed upon them (for example, Ellen's "secret burden" in her last dance round the maypole). But, like the lover's book of flowers, the miner's Path of Perseverance, and the old politicians' sundial, another image remains, her grave mound and her infant's, "screened by its parent." The idea of a parent-grave ushers us into Wordsworth's surreal elegiac world, in which there is point to the Pastor's weird observation that it still rains upon the child's grave even though Ellen's tears are no longer falling upon it. He is, in fact, echoing the substance of Ellen's own lament, which he found written in "the blank margin of a Valentine" (892), on the inconstancy of human words in lovers' vows. In this large marginal discourse, Ellen's asking why the verbal pledges of humanity cannot "prevail for human life" (874) echoes the poet's question of all language ("Oh! why hath not the Mind / Some element to stamp her image on / In nature somewhat nearer to her own?" *Prelude*, V.45–47). The Pastor wishes "any spot of earth" could "render back an echo / . . . an image of the pangs / Which it hath witnessed" (807–09), but nature still requires tongued intermediaries.[29] What mind cannot do by itself it can do in response to a more impressive power, as Ellen attests in one of *The Excursion*'s few overtly Christian moments: " 'He who afflicts me knows what I can bear' " (1046). Speaking like Job, her words are recounted in the presence of *The Recluse*'s permanently unreconstructed Job-figure, the Solitary.

Ellen's mind could not sufficiently impress itself upon mortal conditions of wrong, but it could bear immortal pressures aright. Much worse is the condition of Wilfrid Armathwaite, who wronged another and whose mind "could [not] endure the weight of his own shame" (1114). His story, and the Happy Widower's which follows it, were both lifted from "Home at Grasmere" and clearly bear the stamp of that poem's fantastic equations of mind and matter. The sheer mental power of his remorse over his adultery gives his spirit its wished-for release from its earthly "clog." He finds no forgiveness in himself, though pitied by men and absolved by God; the one is not enough, the other, too much. So he dies on his own terms, a suicide by force of moral strength—a twist suggested in more than one of these stories.

In final contrast to this efficient moral self-immolation, the Happy Widower's gaily bedecked cottage stands opposite Wilfrid's neglected flock and fields. The Pastor's attention turns immediately from the wife's grave to "the Cottage where she dwelt" (1119), preferring as usual to meditate upon the structures built by man's mental bias toward immortality. The cottage seems "self-raised from earth, or grown / Out of the living rock" but is in fact "a studious work / Of many fancies" (1144–48), garlanded by the widower's six daughters. Its honeysuckle seems "a plant no longer wild" (1151) and is but one of many subtle changes working there: one daughter does more work than a boy could, the rill "attunes his voice / To the pure course of human life" (1171–72), and the eldest daughter spins "amain, as if to overtake / The never-halting time" (1180–81). All are witnesses "in mind" of how the mother's "Spirit yet survives on earth" (1190–91). This last line of the story (an unbalancing third domestic tragedy was wisely cut after 1820; *PW*, V.227–29, *app. crit.*) sharply contrasts with the last line of Wilfrid Armathwaite's—"Nor could endure the weight of his own shame"—but the evidences which support it cannot be dismissed as any more sentimental (though surely no less so) than the mental power by which he killed himself.

Book VII is doomed by definition to be less interesting than Book VI, because it deals primarily with physical sufferings which befall the characters independent of their wills. In poetry as in life, there is much less to be said about such ills. But it is just for this reason, to be rigorously honest, that Wordsworth included them, though he made many of them representative types in order to generalize situations whose particular meaning is beyond words. These stories show the strength of human mind under pathos, as Book VI's more particular tales showed the dawning of tragic knowledge. The great temptation to be overcome in Book VII is self-pity, as remorse and regret were in VI.

The difference between silent suffering and active resistance is immediately apparent in the story of the Sympson family, whose deaths have left nature free to undo the imaginative discipline which they imposed on the trees, shrubs, and flowers surrounding their cottage. The Sympsons' cottage, also imported from "Home at Grasmere," is thus an admonitory mirror image to the Happy Widower's house, garlanded by his six daughters, making the pattern of dialectical commentary a transitional device between the two books. The five Sympson graves testify to the departure of something like a traveling troupe of mental energy. They brought lively intelligence into the sleepy valley, not unlike the Wastrel Talent or the more sober Wordsworths. When they arrived, singing and jesting in their wagon, the astonished villagers thought they were "Strollers . . . of the fortune-telling tribe" come to enact "Fair Rosamond, and the Children of the Wood [and] The lucky venture of the sage of Whittington" (90–92) —all themes expressing the triumph of naive native imaginations over the superpowers of nature and culture. Their conspicuously *embowered* cottage is the symbol of their artistic spirit. Sympson, a priest of "active, ardent mind," gave up a career of cultivating the favors of the nobility for the healthy independence, but "doubtful choice," of "this secluded chapelry" (134), thus constituting, like the Solitary and the Pastor, another version of Wordsworth's dream biography. Finding the place and the parsonage "bleak and bare . . . naked without, and rude within" (136, 138), he and his family proceed energetically to give it human significance, with an almost baroque attention to fine details of interior decoration and landscape gardening. Their deaths thus cancel out their vital signs, the cottage "all unembowered" (54), and Reverend Sympson, dying last, "deprived and bare" (263). But though what they gave to the valley is now lost, they also gained something from it while alive: a necessary chastisement and gentling of their imaginations in response to its harsher natural realities. Sympson's mind had been too active in his former life, "irregular, I might say, wild; / By books unsteadied" (114–15), and the beautifying of the cottage reciprocates a calming process in his character that makes explicit the graveyard stories' linkage of internal frames of mind to externally created structures:

> Time, which had thus afforded willing help
> To beautify with nature's fairest growths
> This rustic tenement, had gently shed,
> Upon its Master's frame, a wintry grace;
> The comeliness of unenfeebled age.   [204–08]

This balanced strength of mind and nature stays with the old man as his family dies before him, "still . . . still . . . still" keeping a "thousand schemes" alive in his head. But how can he keep it up and what should we call a man who can? Everyone wonders, " 'What titles will he keep? will he remain / Musician, gardener, builder, mechanist, / A planter, and a rearer from the seed?' " (273–75). The Wanderer finally bestows upon him *The Recluse*'s most honorific title, in lines of cutting brilliance: "The hermit, lodged / Amid the untrodden desert," has a "smooth task" compared to old Sympson, "whose mind could string, / Not scantily, bright minutes on the thread / Of keen domestic anguish; and beguile / A solitude, *un*chosen, *un*professed; / Till gentlest death released him" (302–10; italics added).

The power of Sympson's mind, channeled by his life in the valley, is so strong that its source is moot: is it the "blind result" of genetic factors or from "higher powers"? With the next story, Wordsworth adjusts the balance in favor of the latter. The priest called "WONDERFUL" is more devout than Sympson, and his story also turns upon his unique title as contrasted to more traditional public adjectives: "The great, the good, / The well-beloved, the fortunate, the wise,— / These titles emperors and chiefs have held" (341–43). It will finally become his epitaph (he is still alive); but though it may keep his name alive for a century, it will ultimately "dissolve." This inevitability provokes the Pastor to an outburst against poets' fascination with stories of love and war, and the whole world's fixation on greatness—Wordsworth glancing at Byron by way of stressing the secondary, reflexive theme of all the graveyard stories: significant life forms among the lowly. The noise of war and the pangs of love are sufficiently piercing by themselves, whereas spreading the word of a "good man's purposes and deeds" (376) might actually do some good. Wordsworth's wish to do good through poetry plots the conclusions of both *The Prelude* and *The Excursion,* whether to extend "the mind's *excursive* power" to the "smallest habitable rock" in the world (IX.387), or simply, as here, "o'er field, / Hamlet, and town . . . hall or bower" (382–84). The "wonderful" priest thus bears the *Recluse*-ideal of poetry as a mass medium counteractive to the public's "craving for extraordinary incident which the rapid communication of intelligence hourly gratifies" (Preface to *Lyrical Ballads*).

The next pairing, the Deaf and Blind Dalesmen, is the paradigm of the structure of Books VI and VII and of their theme of compensatory virtue. These two, who (unlike Sympson) never knew what they missed, develop respectively a wealth of book knowledge and of natural lore testifying to the mind's superiority over bodily defect and expressive of the traditional moral hope that one man's deficiencies may be another's powers.[30] The deaf man's books supplied the "familiar voice" that nature could not: the "solace of his own pure thoughts" (417) and the essence of his epitaph, "pure contentedness of mind" (475). The blind man's "industrious mind" transferred power to his "enlightened . . . ear" (503, 495). More than mental compensation for sensory deprivation, this is "type and shadow . . . to the imagination" of the "awful truth" beyond death (526–27). Wordsworth tries to raise this power to sublimity by referring to blind poets like

Homer and Milton (534–36) with Shakespearean overtones: "What terror doth it strike into the mind / To think of one, blind and alone, advancing / Straight toward some precipice's airy brink!" (491–93). But, as almost always in *The Excursion*, the literary symbolism is too heavy; he would have done better to make use of Coleridge's comments on the real-life model of the deaf man: "Why his face sees all over! It is all one eye! . . . it is the mere stamp, the undisturbed *ectypon* [outward type] of his own soul!" (*PW*, V.465). This impress of soul upon face, like the "visionary dreariness" of mind-full sight in *The Prelude*'s "spots of times," puts more strongly the dominant intention of all the graveyard stories.

An image like Coleridge's would also have made Book VII's interlude arrive less arbitrarily, because the Old Woodcutter who noisily interrupts the conversation is preeminently an instance of mindlessness. An emptily echoing mind in a full if aging body, his existence requires no effort, being as natural as the trees he topples without compunction. His curls are "like [the] ivy" of his oak victims, and his only worship, "of the kind which beasts and birds present" (581; added 1827). A low-level paradox is intended in his being the "keen Destroyer" of the natural beings he so closely resembles. The trees are listed without definite articles, generic labels that produce an effect like proper nouns of actual missing persons: "Tall ash-tree . . . Light birch . . . and oak." He would if he could kill even the most personal trees in the valley, "Yon household fir . . . the JOYFUL ELM . . . and the LORD'S OAK" (612, 620, 622). Is this a joke? In its heavy Wordsworthian way, it is, a "fond half-smile" on the inhumanity of natural man, and not without its social thrust, since the woodcutter unwittingly feeds the motors of civilization, "the enormous axle-tree" of the spinning factory and "the vast engine labouring in the mine" (606–08). Completely without "the obligation of an anxious mind" (571), the woodcutter's death will in effect be a humanizing consolation, or recompense in reverse, because his longevity has put him "in rivalship with . . . the forest's more enduring growth" (627–28). Man's triumph depends on something far different from long life: death is the mother of beauty only where mind informs the still unequal contest. This stress upon the woodcutter's death, in relation to the trees he "kills," shifts the interlude back into the paired sequences of memento mori.

The hope that our minds fondly invest in nature links the woodcutter's interlude to the pathetic tale of little Margaret Green of Gold-rill side. Born the only daughter after "seven lusty sons," the "crowning bounty of

the whole," she brings her mother "heavenly calm," lifts her father to
"bolder transport," and becomes to her grandfather the reincarnation of
his own dead wife: "'Another Margaret Green,' / Oft did he say, 'was
come to Gold-rill side'" (672–73). Margaret is not a character but the emblem of her family's excessive hope. The emblem of their compensatory
mental fortitude is, however, less the "due resignation" they learned than
the "tears [that] fail not to spring" when they hear of other infant deaths.
The idea that continuing, if displaced, grief may be the proper counter to
their loss is suggested by the balanced account Wordsworth gives of its
coming and going: "pang unthought of, as the precious boon / Itself had
been unlooked-for" (674–75). If this is the low point of Wordsworth's invention in the churchyard, it is because he has not flinched from address-
ing the death of which least can be said, that of a child, in direct juxtaposition to the one least requiring comment, the passing of an old, healthy,
happy, careless man.

The combination of young and old deaths also helps unite the final
pair of stories, young Oswald and Sir Alfred Irthing, bringing the entire series to a fitting close with historically resonant meditations upon the spirit
of England, present and past. No comparison is spared in bestowing heroic
stature on Oswald ("Pan, or Apollo, veiled in human form," 730; "No
braver Youth [marched] with righteous Joshua," 811–13), nor in giving
scope to the meaning of his death: a denunciation of the Napoleonic des-
pots whose military adventures make it necessary to conscript such fine
young men. Though he actually died from a chill after swimming, he was
still entitled to the military funeral his fellows gave him, for he was their
"gallant teacher," leading these indigenous recluses out of "their shy solitude, to face the world" (774) by bringing the map of Europe alive before
their eyes: "'Here flows,' / Thus would he say, 'the Rhine, that famous
stream! / . . . / Here reigns the Russian, there the Turk; observe / His capital city!'" (787–88, 793–94). Knowing observation of capital cities from
country vantage points is *The Recluse*'s essential perspective on Human
Life. Oswald is the natural king of a natural realm, yet his death by pneu-
monia may suggest the difficulty of transferring natural man into the
realms of civilization and politics, especially as Wordsworth's adherence to
the literal facts of his case makes him eschew the obvious fictional benefits
of giving him a hero's death in, say, Wellington's victory at Salamanca (22
July 1812). Yet his lordship over the eagle ("subject to young Oswald's
steady aim, / And lived by his forebearance," 756–57), appearing in the
same lines with the "boastful Tyrant" of France, makes comparison with
Napoleon inevitable, on the same fantasy scale of values implied by *Pre-*

lude X's linking Wordsworth and Robespierre as antagonists and Wordsworth's comparing the authorship of a great poem to generalship of a state "at least in these times."

Since the name Oswald is Wordsworth's pseudonym for an actual Grasmere Volunteer, the choice is rife with ambivalent richness for the deep structure of *The Recluse*. At the time these lines were written, the Wordsworths were living in the rectory of Grasmere church, dedicated to Saint Oswald, the Northumbrian king who brought Christianity to the Lakes and was martyred in the politicized ecclesiastical warfare of medieval Britain. But Oswald is also the name of one of Wordsworth's most dangerous characters, the intellectual radical of *The Borderers* (set in the same era), a rationalizing seducer rather than educative leader of credulous border youth. None of this is apparent to any common reader of *The Excursion*, and might represent only Wordsworth's private balancing of poetic accounts. Yet Oswald, soldiery, and poetry are still more strangely mixed in his experience. David Erdman's researches into "The Man Who Was Not Napoleon," Colonel John Oswald, strongly suggest that Wordsworth may have known this fanatical English radical in Paris, who schemed to assassinate George III and died leading a company of *piquiers* in the suppression of counterrevolutionary Vendée.[31] If this French connection influenced Wordsworth's renaming of his first Oswald from 1795, its reappearance in the naming of his second may have been stimulated by recollection of another of his tangential involvements in provincial antirevolutionary activism, his own enlistment in the Grasmere Volunteers of 1803 (*CMY*, 237–38; M. II.64). All these associations buried deep beneath the surface of Book VII's graveyard tale bring back to mind the *Recluse*'s pattern of philosophic poets-at-arms, initiated in *Prelude* I's epic catalog of right-minded dictatorial avengers, and connect Wordsworth's master-project with the Romantic trope of poet-activist that extends from Byron, Stendhal, Lamartine, and DeVigny to remote literary echoes in Yeats's Cuchulain and Stevens's ironic statued generals.

Appropriately, it is the Poet's voice that interrupts the Pastor to lament yet praise the "Power to the Oppressors of the world given . . . To be the awakener of divinest thoughts" in idealistic youth (821, 823). Though Napoleon still threatens, the divine opposition-thinking of Oswald and his ilk makes their "capacities / More than heroic!" (826–27), and their final victory symbolically inevitable: "England, the ancient and the free, appeared / In him to stand before my swimming eyes, / Unconquerably virtuous and secure" (856–58). Thus Oswald's death is transmuted from a fact of blighted promise to a sign of constant hope, by returning *The Excursion* to its major theme, "prolongation of . . . Spirit" (895–97), or victory-via-symbolic-forms, in individuals and in history, to be summarized in the final story of Sir Alfred Irthing.

Coming last where Chaucer's Knight had come first, Sir Alfred anchors the historical and hierarchical scales of the graveyard sequence with his experience in both English Reformation and English Revolution, times "conspicuous as our own / For strife and ferment in the minds of men" (1009–10), the only life buried in the churchyard whose significance was felt outside the valley. He is the Wordsworthian hero par excellence, because he is the hero-come-home, active in the great world but retired to this "sequestered vale." His career parallels the Solitary's and the Pastor's, and Wordsworth's reclusive vocation. Typically, Wordsworth locates the power of Irthing's example not in his person or deeds, but in the nobility of mind with which he bore the decline of his knightly order and of "Eliza's golden days." Even his memorials have all but vanished; only an indecipherable tomb, a broken archway, a cluster of cottages, and a set of church bells inscribed with his name remain. But they testify to that prolongation of spirit in Oswald's story, and the ancient story thus pairs off its modern partner. Some of Irthing's lines are lifted directly from the great dirge passage of "The Tuft of Primroses," making the "decay / Restless, and restless generation" (1001–02) of human mental orders part of an eternal process. "All that this world is proud of" (978) decays—houses, families, "Degrees and ranks, / Fraternities and orders" (988–89)—but with a purpose and direction: "functions dying and produced at need / . . . With an ascent and progress in the main" (1003–05). This is the same phrasing Wordsworth used to reassure himself of the value of nonvisionary human-heartedness in "Home at Grasmere": "Alternate progress and impediment, / And yet a growing prospect in the main."

Wordsworth's special faith in his special place is put forward in Sir Alfred's story as a general human condition, or at least an English one. The knight's vanished "stately lodge" is less important now than "the last remains / Of that foundation" which are the spiritual source of the cottages "that sprang / From out the ruins" like shoots from "a tree / That falls" (963–64, 968–69, 957–58). This suggests that culture has its reviving second growths like nature, though in different forms than we expect, as in the progression from Saint Oswald to young Oswald, and running parallel to Wordsworth's hope, in "Michael," that by telling the full meaning of the ruined sheepfold he might inspire the foundation of a new, Wordsworthian school of poetry.[32] In just this way, the poet's faith that mental transformations work progressively through time is finally symbolized in the continued sounding-out of the knight's name, "Sir Alfred Irthing, with appropriate words / Accompanied, still extant, in a wreath / Or posy" round the church bells, "clear-sounding and harmonious" (971–74). The function of the Knight's tale is pointed by his name, totally Wordsworth's invention, spelled "Erthing" by some editors, a heavily symbolic combination of the name of England's first great king with a pun that asks whether man is more or less than an earth-thing.[33] Wordsworth was as personally implicated in his knight's name and history as he was in Oswald's; when these lines were written, he was negotiating the rental of Rydal Mount, in which the actual knight's descendants had lived for nearly a century. Irthing, like his creator, left several fragments of his works scattered about Grasmere, but the fact that the clearest of these is his own name, in a "posy" of "appropriate words . . . still extant," suggests that the final imaginative artifact found in the Grasmere churchyard is the one that comes closest to the hopes of the poet who was moving from its rectory to its gentry seat when he wrote these stories. Wordsworth's Knight's memorial thus completes the pattern of identification that began in *The Prelude* between reclusive poets and single heroes, an earth-thing immortalized by his words' worth.

The Wanderer closes the churchyard colloquy by generalizing from the knight's experience to present times, and from the knight's tale to the present state of literature. Irthing had really seen what Wordsworth thought he saw at the Grand Chartreuse: "that violent commotion, which o'erthrew . . . old religious house[s]—pile after pile; / And shook their tenants out into the fields, / Like wild beasts without home!" (1022, 1025–27). The casting-out of spirit from its abiding places, whether in the established order or the stable mind, is the permanent threat *The Recluse* constantly reengages. No matter what people's religious or political persuasions are, such vast "alteration in the forms of things" (1011) should at least make them stop and think, the Wanderer supposes, anticipating Arnold's *Culture and Anarchy*. But no—"Festive songs / Break from the maddened nations at the sight / Of sudden overthrow"—while "cold neglect / Is the sure consequence of slow decay" (1037–40). Like the Pastor's earlier attack on poets for tuning their songs to the loud noise of war and the sharp pangs of love, this complaint points to a constitutional sensationalism in human nature that Wordsworth, in the Preface to *Lyrical Ballads*, set himself to reform. As a comment about subject matter, the Wanderer is voicing Wordsworth's fear that his contemporaries were missing the massive changes occurring all around them, principally industrialization, in consequence of their mesmerized fascination with the French

Revolution and its Napoleonic aftermath. Philosophically, his glum sense of disproportion between man's "airy hopes" and "Those meditations of the soul that feed / The retrospective virtues" (1036–37) raises the question of *The Recluse*'s chances of gaining an audience for poetry of redemptive long views. Nervously, he questions the mind's ability to speak at large in face of possible changes in the very nature of mind. All who most resembled Irthing "in the mind" are gone, a ferment "in the minds of men" having wrought a fundamental "alteration in the forms of things," frustrating the "expectations of self-flattering minds" in the English Revolution as now again in the French (986, 1010–11, 1007). This redaction of the Renaissance theme of constant mutability thus challenges any poetry or text which would embody it.

But when the Wanderer offers the decline of his own "errantry," peddling, as an analogue to make the excursionists "linger 'mid the last" (1014) memorials of great English civilization, his reasons shift our attention from subject to author: "If I may venture of myself to speak, / Trusting that not incongruously I blend / Low things with lofty . . ." (1045–47). Where have we heard before that cadence of assured diffidence? Surely from all of *The Prelude,* and most particularly from the concluding lines of *The Recluse*'s great "Prospectus": "And if with this / I mix more lowly matter; with the thing / Contemplated, describe the Mind and Man / Contemplating; and who, and what he was / . . . Be not this labour useless." The parallels should not be taken too literally; Wordsworth does not think a decline in poetry is inevitably linked to society's failure to support pedlars and beggars. Yet the "philosophic song" was never abstractly intended but was squarely addressed to the proposition that the mental energy released by the French Revolution should not dissipate in cynicism. The crucial element for Wordsworth was a poetry that could mediate convincingly between the lowly individual and lofty general themes of Human Life. It is perfectly expectable that the personality of the teller should reflex into the tale at this point, for this is *The Recluse*'s basic dialectic between private and public modes, and the question occurs in some form near the end of all the *Recluse* fragments, always, as here, too difficult to answer: "But enough; / —Thoughts crowd upon me—and 'twere seemlier now / To stop" (1050–52).

BOOK VIII: "THE PARSONAGE"

As Book VIII of *The Prelude* corrects Book VII's hellish city image of Bartholomew Fair with the peaceful "retrospect" of Helvellyn Fair, so the eighth book of *The Excursion* shores up the frail memorials of Human

Life constructed in Books VI and VII with a solid image of living tranquility, the parsonage. Some present-tense image of comfort is needed thematically to assuage the Wanderer's desperate realization that modern man's lust for tales of "sudden overthrow" makes it highly unlikely that a large audience will ever listen to the morals he attaches to the Knight's mute grave. The counterbalance provided by the parsonage is dramatic as well as thematic, since the Pastor invites everyone home to tea to break up an impasse that develops between the Wanderer and the Solitary, bringing *The Excursion* close to bad words. Their argument is actually an interruption, nearly four hundred lines long, of the Pastor's first invitation, a summary speech that seems to be bringing the poem to a benign close:

> Life, death, eternity! momentous themes
> Are they—and might demand a seraph's tongue,
> Were they not equal to their own support;
> And therefore no incompetence of mine
> Could do them wrong.   [10–14]

The psychological defense of *The Prelude*—that Wordsworth cannot err if he sticks to talking about himself—here becomes a theological defense based on the teller's faith. The language resembles the invocation in the "Prospectus" for a Muse greater than Milton's to sing of Man, Nature, and Human Life, but even angels are rendered superfluous by the grandeur of still higher themes, Life, Death, and Eternity. Between *The Prelude* and this point in *The Excursion* Wordsworth has tried several times to achieve the humanistic ideal of *The Recluse,* poetry addressed to all men and women on the subject of all men and women in the language of all men and women. His failure to do so is, of course, not unique but merely an early episode in a pattern of similar failures in Western culture since the Romantic revolutionary era.

Yet Wordsworth is hard on himself for his failure, since the Solitary's interruption of the Pastor's invitation is very much based on the inadequacy of modern images of man. He teases the Wanderer for the resemblance between his peddling "errantry" and Irthing's vanished knightly ideal, but in reflecting that modern lives and occupations seem intrinsically less significant than traditional ones, the Solitary is content to make the best of diminished things. Indeed, he feels that such "exiles and wanderers" (46) are "apt agents" for the gradual improvement of civilization, "Raising, through just gradation, savage life / To rustic, and the rustic to urbane" (70–71). But the Wanderer will have none of it. He interprets any such historical parallels quite differently and turns the Solitary's pleasant tea-time joke into a diatribe against the present immense "alteration in the forms of things" (VII.1011), which ends by angering the Solitary and makes the Pastor's renewed invitation to the parsonage a civilizing gesture that saves the argument, and the poem, from outrage. Even in this published part of *The Recluse*, as in its unpublished fragments, Wordsworth's honest turns of argument upon himself threaten, or heighten, the interest of their structure.

What specifically enrages the Wanderer is, of course, the Industrial Revolution—"Industrious to destroy!" (95). Wordsworth's attack is not surprising; he was among the enlightened conservatives who feared that "the vast expansion of the manufacturing system" might lead to "social war" between rich and poor.[34] What is noteworthy, rather, is its surreally diagrammatic symbolism. "A new and unforeseen creation" has arisen in the land, altering the natural form of things. Ancient villages and familiar paths have been bypassed or obliterated by the new high roads, the very water and air are harnessed to machines, and hamlets have erupted from "germ" to "huge town" with the virulence of a pox upon its victim: "hiding the face of earth for leagues" (95–121). Composing these lines circa 1812, Wordsworth is of the first generation to recognize a new face on the world, and his description of "perpetual, multitudinous" crowds (142) pressing in from or spilling out upon solitude is underwritten by the powerful signature of his own experience of coming, solitary, into the hubbub of Cambridge, London, and Paris. An infection is spreading; even the "soothing . . . undisturbing" peace of darkness is disrupted by the "unnatural light" of factory night-shifts. Candles that burned "of old" in religious vigil are now made part of the "perpetual sacrifice" offered up in these new temples "To Gain, the master-idol of the realm" (184–85). The "still domain[s]" of nighttime vision and religious meditation have become, in the progress of *The Recluse*, imaginative regions, their common enemy being, here as in the Grand Chartreuse lines, the glare, noise, and bustle of modern political and industrial movement. That these "profaner rites" could be redeemed "by the thinking mind" (206) is a possibility the Wanderer regards with a withering dubiety. Lacking "due proportion" (213), these new temples are more likely to repeat the fate of Thebes, Tyre, and Palmyra—more famous as ruins than as civilizations: "the Arts died by which they had been raised" (219). Even Archimedes, one of Wordsworth's favorite images of a philosophic world-mover, is presented in admonitory terms, the adjectives in, "his buried tomb / Upon the grave of vanished Syracuse" (220–21) effecting a double remove from real effect. The "vaunted Arts" of the new civilization will come to nothing without the gold standard or earnest money of the natural life of the mind, "That made the very thought of country-life / A thought of refuge, for a mind

detained / Reluctantly amid the bustling crowd" (243–45). With that
"fled, fled utterly!" a wild mental inflation sets in, and the Wanderer's vision of the future rises to heights of insane apocalypticism. No one is at
home anywhere—"habitations empty!" Life no longer progresses by
"each day's little growth" (270) but is everywhere emptied of significance:
"Nothing to speed the day, or cheer the mind; / Nothing to praise, to
teach, or to command!" (274–75). A lifetime becomes a synecdoche for a
prison term (303); the "organic frame [is] to the joy of her own motions
dead" (322–24). What hope can there be for "a manhood raised / On
such foundations" (333–34)?

Wordsworth is trying to breathe life into metaphors of social organization, and though such subjects do not inspire lyricism, his stiffness cannot be attributed to declining powers, since many of these lines come from
manuscripts of 1798–99 devoted to "The Ruined Cottage" and the Salisbury Plain poems (*PW*, V.470–71). The depth of his effort is gauged by
the frequency with which he echoes his greatest poetry in the Wanderer's
peroration. The sociological destruction of the tie between mothers and
"infant Being" by "premature necessity" (287)—in itself a striking metaphorical compression of physiological stillbirth—recalls the "Blest infant
Babe" of *The Prelude* only to spoil its positive psychology with a negative
social vision. This new civilization will fall and crush the genial powers of
the individual beneath it, because it is impervious to Nature's kindly influences:

> The boy, where'er he turns,
> Is still a prisoner; when the wind is up
> Among the clouds, and roars through the ancient woods;
> . . . .
> Behold him—in the school
> Of his attainments? no; but . . .
> . . . .
> His raiment, whitened o'er with cotton-flakes
> Or locks of wool, announces whence he comes.
> Creeping his gait and cowering, his lip pale,
> His respiration quick and audible;
> . . . .
> Is this the form,
> Is that the countenance, and such the port,
> Of no mean Being?   [302–04, 306–07, 309–12, 315–17]

The heavenly child of the Intimations Ode may pass into the light of common day, but the glare of uncommon night is another thing altogether; instead of trailing clouds of glory, this mean Being trails clouds of factory

dust, and the brave individual stoicism of the Ode is wiped out by an industrial pollution of man's immortal spirit.[35]

These echoes make it impossible to overestimate Wordsworth's vehemence; self-quotation is the strongest form of authority this poet knows. His intensity continues into the rejoinder of the Solitary (334–433), who is driven by the Wanderer's hysteria to the opposite side of the debate, and whose genius for contrariness is all that saves the poem from breaking down, a further aspect of Wordsworth's genius for making poetry out of arguments with himself. He flings down a countervision to the Wanderer's wastelandscape, turning the blame for "these [modern] structures" away from "those arts" which raised them back to their historical foundations in earlier "multitudes" who, though they breathed "unimprisoned" air, were yet "in human shape, / As abject, as degraded" (343–45). His vision of miserable Olde England is less an attack upon past brutalities than an imagistic answer to the Wanderer's horror at "straggling burgh" and "habitations empty!" (101, 266):

> At this day,
> Who shall enumerate the crazy huts
> And tottering hovels, whence do issue forth
> A ragged Offspring, with their upright hair
> Crowned like the image of fantastic Fear?   [345–49]

"Ill-adjusted" human beings, their tenuous connection to human life was marked by the tangential quality of their residences, on "darksome heaths," "some natural cave," or "the green margin of the public way" (362–72), whole segments of the nation's population appearing "like the vagrants of the gipsy tribe," Wordsworth's consistent image of irremediable social alienation, and the structural corollary of his deep-seeing hermits. Continuing the thrust of *The Excursion*'s argument into social theory, the Solitary escalates his rhetoric as wildly as the Wanderer, stretching to include those "Britons born and bred within the pale / Of civil polity" (392–93) in his sarcastic conclusion that massive failures of political democracy cannot be laid to "modern ingenuity" or the viciousness of "town [or] crowded city" (421–22). He indicts both the vaunted British constitution and English Nature ("This Boy the fields produce," 425), taking issue directly with that authenticating link between rural peace and peace of mind the Wanderer had proposed: "his country's name, / Her equal rights, her churches and her schools— / What have they done for him?" (429–31). The Solitary is, of course, not progressive in his social views, but he is determined not to let the old man get away with the simplistic logic of proving civilization's decline by reference to past glories.

The moment of actual impasse is stark—"In brief, what liberty of *mind* is here?" (433; Wordsworth's italics)—returning *The Recluse* to its primary theme of mental growth in nature and society. This final over-statement has the breaking force of similar moments in earlier parts of *The Recluse,* such as the "Farewell to the Warrior's schemes" in "Home at Grasmere" 's realization that "something must be done." Just when the ba-sic terms of modern cultural debate have been set down, the progress or decline of human civilization in relation to technological and political re-finements, the Pastor invites everyone to tea. What a proper British re-sponse to such a contretemps! Yet Wordsworth cannot easily be faulted for being reluctant to enter into a debate that became the intellectual par-lor game of the next century, through Nietzsche and Spengler to writers who were willing to date the actual year of Western civilization's decline, fall, or rebirth: Woolf (1910), Yeats (1919), or Willa Cather (1923). Wordsworth was ready to say "1812" before the Century of Progress had well begun, but stopped himself and presented another kind of answer—an emblem—in the Parsonage that gave Book VIII its title.

Wordsworth tries to make it a high tea indeed by his description of the parsonage, though he embeds his meaning too deep for ready compre-hension. More than a residence, more even than a home, the parson-age—where Wordsworth was living at the time he wrote about it (*CMY,* 475)—is a home with an institutional, professional dimension. It will not decline with the departure of its inmates, like the Sympsons' ruined cottage, and is full of peaceable life, unlike the Wanderer's "habitations empty!" and the Solitary's "crazy huts and tottering hovels." Preeminently, this parsonage is an image of blended opposites intended to convey the healing force of tradition (construed as systematic reconciliation of contraries) that is missing from the polemical visions of the Wanderer and the Solitary. An "image of solemnity, conjoined / With feminine allurements soft and fair" (459–60), thus embodying its master and mistress, it has "bold projec-tions and recesses deep; / Shadowy, yet gay and lightsome" (462–63). Ev-ery aspect bears the impress of mental activity, past or present, making the parsonage the culmination of the churchyard tales' pattern of symbolic structures upon which departed minds have left their "stamp." The clinch-ing detail is the last one—"the picture else were incomplete"—

> a relique of old times
> Happily spared, a little Gothic niche
> Of nicest workmanship; that once had held

> The sculptured image of some patron-saint,
> Or of the blessed Virgin, looking down
> On all who entered those religious doors. [485–90]

Though empty, the niche "happily" remains, to be filled by the reflections of the Poet now entering the parsonage, who has stood in many ruined abbeys and wondered wildly if he might not somehow fill such empty religious spaces under threat of modernist destructions with a contemporary "gothic" masterpiece. Ostensibly representing the via media of Anglican Protestantism—progress with respect for tradition—this architectural detail symbolizes within the sequence of *Recluse* texts a final vision of imagination preserving departed stages of human faith and consciousness, memorially linking one to another and thus overcoming the impasse of radically discontinuous historical visions to which the Wanderer and the Solitary had brought *The Excursion*. The parsonage is in effect the institutional renovation of all *The Recluse*'s ruined cottages and completes a frame around the graveyard stories by presenting an idealized place to match Book V's ideal person, the Pastor. It is internally significant in *The Recluse*'s image system because a residence is here coterminous with its resident, a parson*age,* an official public form of the unity intended by the poem's unusual hero-figure, the Recluse, whose title, function, and location would all be one and the same, with reference to the rest of Human Life.

Looking out from this specially constructed residence, the Solitary sees a vision of landscape as shaped by it, a moment as close as the poem comes to representing his mental renovation:

> He gazed, with admiration unsuppressed,
> Upon the landscape of the sun-bright vale,
> Seen, from the shady room in which we sate,
> In softened pérspective; and more than once
> Praised the consummate harmony serene
> Of gravity and elegance, diffused
> Around the mansion and its whole domain. [534–40]

Such a moment is brother to similar conclusive moments in *The Recluse*, in which a close circle of family or friends look out upon the world from beneath a "humble Roof embowered among the trees" ("Home at Grasmere"), safe within a "lowly Edifice / Embraced by grounds that did not aim / To overshadow but to screen and hide" ("The Tuft of Primroses"). These conclusions are all landscape prospects containing an implied poetic prospectus, in which the poet and his "happy band" dedicate themselves to a cottage industry whose influence will be felt at circumferences far removed from their imaginative center. *The Excursion,* however, has already begun to shift to more institutional forms of outreach, articulated in Book IX as the province not of poetry but of public education.

BOOK IX: "DISCOURSE OF THE WANDERER AND AN EVENING VISIT TO THE LAKE"

Book IX has the same structure as Book VIII: an agrument clinched by a set of emblems, the two-part division indicated by its title. The unifying emblems, a "snow-white ram," a rowboat trip, and the "unity sublime!" of the final sunset, are not as recondite as Wordsworth's presentation of the parsonage, but their connection to the Wanderer's discourse on education is, if anything, more problematic. The relation is intended to be that of visual blendings (e.g., the ram and his reflection, "Blended in perfect stillness") to historical and psychological continuities: the growth of individuals and the progress of nations through the systems of mental discipline (education) needed to foster the former and assure the latter. Past is joined to present, saith the Wanderer, by education—as we are joined to God, saith the Pastor, by typological evidence like clouds reflecting glory from the setting sun. This is not very promising logic, but it is the final form of *The Recluse* and may represent a realistic compromise. Wordsworth's vision of a national or imperial education system is not a tacked-on digression reflecting his passing enthusiasm for Dr. Andrew Bell's "Madras system" of pupil-tutors, but an integral culmination of his wish to generalize and decentralize imagination. Pupils teaching each other are not very far removed from poets speaking as men to men.

The Wanderer's discourse actually begins in Book VIII's last lines, where he is figured "as One / Who from truth's *central* point serenely views / The *compass* of his argument" (VIII.598–600; italics added), thus transmuting into human form the parsonage's architectural version of Wordsworth's center-to-circumference myth. The power of his argument derives from Hope, our "*active* Principle" (Wordsworth's italics), that is similarly expansive: "Spirit that knows no insulated spot, / No chasm, no solitude; from link to link / It circulates, the Soul of all the worlds" (IX.13–15). But this benevolent centrifugal force is "least respected in the human Mind, / Its most apparent home" (19–20), a flaw that Wordsworth recognizes but can only gloss over in trying to raise individual hopefulness to metaphysical dimensions.[36] We are again at the critical point for *The Recluse* where the lesson of *The Prelude*—that mind grows well in this world—must be generalized to other minds than Wordsworth's.

The topic in which this thesis is imbedded is the indefatigably interesting, interminably boring one of progress or decline in human history, given new currency as Wordsworth was finishing *The Excursion* by the signs of Napoleon's defeat. Given such enormously hopeful opportunities for rebuilding civilization and overcoming postrevolutionary despair, human hopelessness seems almost wilfully perverse. The arguments for hope are everywhere, says the Wanderer, looking down upon "the VALE of years" from "Age, / As a final EMINENCE" (49, 51–52). This self-validating metaphor for his vantage point will be actualized in Book IX's concluding mountain sunset and is already massively predetermined by Wordsworth's adaptation of it from the Snowdon vision. From such high perspective, "the gross and visible frame of things" gives up its hold on the senses, "Yea almost on the Mind herself," and yet, "how loud the voice / Of waters, with invigorated peal / From the full river in the vale below, / Ascending!" (65–69). Local and immediate distractions fall away, revealing "the mighty stream of tendency" (87), which figures, in *The Recluse*'s image system, as a consolation for creative risk-taking (Hope), more generally available than Snowdon's "roar of waters" in its "fixed, abysmal, gloomy, breathing-place." Any self-quotation or self-allusion within *The Recluse* is important and tends to generate others, for the ongoing poem increasingly becomes the source of its own authoritative precedents. In such confident moments the Wanderer is sure that "Country, society, and time itself" (107) contribute to the stream of tendency, a triad that sounds like a version of Man, Nature, and Human Life, and for which the Wanderer counsels obedience to "the law / Of life, and hope, and action" (127–28). But since all these triads begin to sound interchangeable, we soon tire of Wordsworth validating himself with his own words, and, rightfully suspicious of concepts like "the law of life," we demand to know what exactly the Wanderer is talking about.

Wordsworth checks his own murky extravagance by allowing the Solitary to interrupt with hard questions about the "multitude" that reaps sickness and death from the seeds the Wanderer says are so generously sown. Taken straight on, this objection would lead back to Book VIII's impasse, so the Wanderer makes an important limitation in "the mighty stream of tendency," fundamentally compromising *The Excursion*'s philosophical pretensions but allowing Wordsworth to get to an endpoint. He is not talking about the millions whose minds are "starved by absolute neglect" (97), but the specifically English situation of supposed improvements in civilization that are in fact perversions: "Little-one[s] subjected to the arts / Of modern ingenuity" (157–58), "victims, which the merciful can see / Nor think that they are victims" (191–92). He is alluding to Book VIII's attack on child labor, and we also recognize the language of *Prelude* V's educational satire. Wordsworth, however, glossed these lines by reference to the Chartists, deploring the irresponsibility of the liberal intellectuals who encouraged them, "which nothing but wiser and more brotherly feeling towards the many, on the part of the wealthy few, can moderate or remove" (*PW*, V.473). The smugness of such views goes without saying, yet Wordsworth is specifically attacking the arrogance of social engineers who turn the individual into "a tool / Or implement, a passive thing" (115–16). Rather than address any worse exploitation, he is simply deploring the sheer differentiation of man from man, which interferes with the spreading of Hope's "*active* principle," arguing as he had since the *Lyrical Ballads,* and in the same language ("for the injustice grieving, that hath made / So wide a difference between man and man," 253–54), for a democracy of imagination. Tampering with children's mental and moral development was one topic—landscape gardening was another—that could provoke Wordsworth to outright sarcasm, nor can his romantic view that the mysteries of mental growth should be left well enough alone ever be entirely dismissed. His view of the Pastor's son and comrades as "thriving prisoners of their village-school" (260) expresses an ambivalent optimism based on the pedagogy of indirection he used for his own children and Basil Montagu's. It seemed to find systematic form in Bell's *Experiment in Education Made at the Asylum of Madras* (1797), leading to Dr. Bell's being invited to the Lake Country, the adoption of his methods in a local school, and, for a brief period in the fall of 1811, to Wordsworth himself serving as a practice teacher, though he soon resigned such chores to his "female Votaries" (M. II.178–79).

Thus the peroration of the Wanderer's discourse (290–415), however didactic, is a direct, organic outgrowth of Wordsworth's deepest convictions and is consistent to the point of inevitability with *The Recluse*'s development. The Wanderer envisions education as a process of blending diffusion, countering exclusive traditional views, on the one hand, and revolutionary breaks with the past, on the other. His views seem utterly natural now but still seemed against human nature in Wordsworth's time, and one would have to review the harsh polemical milieu of antidisestablishmentarianism to recapture a sense of the mountains educational reformers were trying to move. England's obligation to her children is construed as "parental," in contrast to the "dark discontent, or loud commotion" which now *rends* and *splits* Europe "from Calpe's sunburnt cliffs / To the flat margin of the Baltic Sea" (348, 336–37). Seen from Grasmere's "Unity entire" (*HG*, 151), England "remains entire and indivisible" (345), and what can spill over from Grasmere to all England can—as the metaphor moves—fly, flow, wash, literally *sail* to the rest of the world as the "deserved reward" of enlightened colonial policy. People less favored than the graveyard heroes "with moral and religious truth / . . . However destitute [will not] be left to droop / By timely culture unsustained" (302–05). Without such culture, the organic metaphor continues, mere drooping will "run into a wild disorder" of either "savage horde" or "servile band" within the social fabric. Wordsworth fully appreciates that antisocial behavior can be "by process indirect" a legitimate declaration of need, hence the Wanderer's plea is directed to "the State's parental ear" because individual parents worn down by lack of "timely culture" cannot see that their children need what they themselves do not have. Generalized to a national level, England's "discipline of virtue" is contrasted to Europe's "discipline of slavery" as a means of permanent nonrevolution, allowing "genuine piety" to descend "Like an inheritance, from age to age" (362).

Wordsworth is certainly a Tory humanist in these views, but there are worse social philosophies, and his linking of his new friend Bell's educational reform with the abolition of the slave trade effected by his old friend Clarkson as "the most happy event of our times" (M. II.179) indicates a more than orthodox subtlety.[37] In language outstripping revolutionary ideologies, he imagines the spread of virtuous empire as the fulfillment of Adam's uncertain vision of human history at the end of *Paradise Lost* ("Change wide, and deep . . . / This Land shall witness; and as days roll on, / Earth's universal frame shall feel the effect," 384–86). In *The Recluse*'s central metaphor of power radiating from a core, "Even . . . the smallest habitable rock [will] hear the songs / Of humanised society" (387–89). Centers of power seemed bypassed in this extraordinary sweep of ordinariness, from provincial Grasmere to colonial Madras, Port-au-Prince, and other remote rocks "beaten by lonely billows," *blooming* "with civil arts . . . From culture, unexclusively bestowed" (390, 392). Yet in a dramatic shift of centers, he acknowledges that poetry alone cannot make it happen: "—Vast the circumference of hope—and ye / Are at its centre, British Lawgivers; / Ah! sleep not there in shame!" (398–400). The barely acknowledged poet substitutes real legislators for himself at the crucial moment of wishing his visions real, and one's general bemusement at his jingoism should not blur the fact that something like this vision is essentially what happened, after all allowances for better and for worse, in the next century and a half in India, Australia, New Zealand, Canada, America, and parts of Africa. Wordsworth presses his characteristic tropes of organic feeling and growth into active political service, yet their awkwardness is not the result of hardening poetic arteries so much as expecting too much from imagination or becoming impatient with its ineffectuality.

Though Wordsworth has reestablished the universal "philosophic" scope of his argument by recasting logical generalization into the form of a world education system, thus recouping the Wanderer's earlier concession that he was only talking about English matters, he has again paid a high price: the substitution of politics for poetry. Perhaps, fifteen years after the Preface to *Lyrical Ballads* had imagined the same wide scope of renovation as an entirely spiritual process, he was more ready for action; Jeffrey shrewdly observed the costs of twenty years of imaginative capital stubbornly sunk in the same concern.[38] It is all but impossible to keep on writing literature at such a juncture, and "Abruptly here, but with a graceful air, / The Sage broke off" (416–17). In the 1814 edition, this break was underscored in Book IX's headnote—"Wanderer breaks off"—as was the similar impasse in Book VIII: "Conversation broken off by a renewed Invitation from the Pastor." Each impasse is equally serious: Book VIII's, between irreconcilable views of the ends of human history; Book IX's, between radically different means of ameliorating it. These clean breaks in *The Excursion*'s structure indicate Wordsworth's shifts from topics he wants to address but doesn't know how to—history and politics (Human Life)—to topics he loves and knows very well—the interpenetrative play of mind with nature—as surrogates or sublimates of the former. Thus the remainder of Book IX, "An Evening Visit to the Lake," constructs three emblems (as Book VIII had erected the emblematic parsonage) that present the mutuality of all forms of life, in support of the Wanderer's discourse, which has been *The Recluse*'s most explicit statement of the mental renovation of Human Life.

The first of these is the "snow-white ram" and his reflection, "a two-fold image":

> Each had his glowing mountains, each his sky,
> And each seemed centre of his own fair world:
> Antipodes unconscious of each other,
> Yet, in partition, with their several spheres,
> Blended in perfect stillness, to our sight!   [447–51]

This picture could stand as a frontispiece to all of *The Recluse,* though close reading of several texts is required to appreciate the many ways in which its paradox of "blended partition" between levels of being or consciousness is a holographic cross-section of the entire Grasmerian myth. In such images, Wordsworth's meaning turns upon the dividing *yet* that blends two different foci into one in the awareness of the informed observer. He even admits that understanding such processes of unifying division is difficult when the Pastor's wife's comments about "that eloquent old Man": "'While he is speaking, I have power to see / Even as he sees; but when his voice hath ceased, / Then, with a sigh, sometimes I feel, as now, / That combinations so serene and bright / Cannot be lasting in a world like ours'" (465–69). There are other little moments of tension in the needlework apocalypse that closes *The Excursion,* such as the Solitary's grumpy observation that the dying picnic fire shows "the common course of human gratitude," but they are not developed dramatically, nor could they be without breaking down the poem's motion toward some sense of an ending.

"More had she said"—but another emblem comes in aid of common doubt. Rowing across the lake, the Poet observes that, "Turn where we may . . . we cannot err / In this delicious region" (503–04). It is the Poet speaking, because he is now very much the Wordsworth who said, "I cannot miss my way," in setting out for this "chosen Vale" at the beginning of *The Prelude,* and whose alter ego's "delicious Pontic solitude" was a thinly veiled metaphor for the same place. He seems to acknowledge the private nature of his observations in saying that such visions of unity cannot be reproduced "by words, nor by the pencil's silent skill," even as the possession of it seems to depend on a literal process of composition-of-place: "But is the property of him alone / Who hath beheld it, *noted* it with care, / And in his mind *recorded* it with love!" (514–17; italics added). No more pictorially descriptive than ever ("Cultured slopes, / Wild tracts . . . scattered groves, / And mountains bare," 504–06), the vision simply outlines a sphere of continuous process: "They ceased not to surround us; change of place, / From kindred features diversely combined, / Producing change of beauty ever new" (509–11).

The concluding sunset emblem must, however, be made more available to public interpretation, and no one could miss the thrust of the "prodigal communion . . . / Which from the unapparent fount of glory / . . . the heavens displayed, the liquid deep / Repeated; but with unity sublime!" (604–08). More subtle is the way in which Wordsworth anticipates the sunset's sacramental image by careful attention to its effect on the com-

pany seeing it. This last vision of *The Recluse* is the first group vision in
Wordsworth's poetry; at least eight persons are present! They had set out,
"a broken company" (435) like the straggling climbers of Snowdon,
"each / Not seldom over anxious to make known / His own discoveries"
(583–85), and what Wordsworth emphasizes as unforgettable in the sunset is not the vision itself but its unifying effect upon the beholders: "never
shall I forget / When these particular interests were effaced / From every
mind!" (588–90). Though hardly a striking redemption, its tiny social
thrust is consonant with the direction in which Wordsworth is now trying
to push his imagination, and represents the last appearance of the "happy
band" of fellow spirits who manifest themselves at the end of every *Recluse* fragment. As usual, the small size of the group calls attention to itself
by contrast to the prospect in sight, whether *The Prelude*'s promised redemption of the sinking nations or the "courts of highest heaven" the Pastor sees here. But the disproportion always occurs by Wordsworth's literal
projection of his intention. The Pastor's interpretation of the sunset is of
course Christian, yet the terms are specifically Wordsworthian. The "nations" who "linger still" unredeemed (654) are parallel to the "nations
sink[ing] together" at *The Prelude*'s end, and the "thoughtful few" who lament "this dire perverseness" are religious types of *The Recluse*'s small
bands of imaginative activists. Indeed, they are more Wordsworthian than
Christian in the terms in which they imagine redemption arriving:

> Shall that blest day arrive
> When they, whose choice or lot it is to dwell
> In crowded cities, without fear shall live
> Studious of mutual benefit; and he,
> Whom Morn awakes, among dews and flowers
> Of every clime, to till the lonely field,
> Be happy in himself?   [666–72]

These are hopefully rhetorical questions about love of God leading to love
of man *and* nature, and in their dual focus on urban crowd and rural solitude they speak directly to the "Prospectus" lines first published in the
preface to this poem: "the fierce confederate storm / Of sorrow, barricadoed evermore / Within the walls of cities," and "Humanity in fields and
groves / Pip[ing] solitary anguish." That Wordsworth should have this
much good (however little) to say about living in cities, and this much bad
(however little) to imply about rural loneliness shows his own attentive-
ness to the arguments he has put in his Solitary's mouth throughout. These
questions about the best places to read or write poetry, though we now

treat them as ephemeral, were important to Wordsworth and to his reviewers; Wordsworth may be said to anticipate here a host of objections like Jeffrey's to his apparent escapism: "all the greater poets lived, or had lived, in the full current of society."[39]

Equally critical rhetorical questions continue to be raised, until we begin to doubt the grounds of the Pastor's thanksgiving, but he answers them, with suddenly "wild demeanor," in a vision of inevitable progress, returning *The Recluse* to its theme of historical optimism by reference to the ground on which it stands. On these very mountains, "the savage nations" once made human sacrifice to Celtic idols, where now, kneeling "devoutly in yon reverend Pile [are] worshippers how innocent and blest!" (725, 714):

> So wide the difference, a *willing* mind
> Might *almost* think, at this *affecting* hour,
> That paradise, the lost abode of man,
> Was raised again: and to *a happy few*,
> In its original beauty, here restored.   [715–19; italics added]

There it is: the earthly paradise of the "Prospectus" realized for a sunset moment by the "happy few" who can balance its elements properly, part local church, part mental abode, part the "gothic church" to which Wordsworth compared his entire poetic canon in *The Excursion*'s preface. This "little band" (729) and "thoughtful few" (658) comprise a picnic party of intellectuals who see a vision of modern redemption as they look at a beautiful landscape, on an excursion that will often be repeated in the next hundred and fifty years, with hopes as high and as tenuously connected to the world they live in. The Pastor's benediction makes a blessing out of the mental condition in which Wordsworth always felt himself with reference to *The Recluse*, "with scantiest knowledge, master of all truth / Which the salvation of his soul requires" (736–37), accompanied by his tabernacle choir, "Woods waving in the wind their lofty heads, / Or hushed; the roaring waters, and the still— / They see the offering of my lifted hands" (746–48), echoing the paeans to the "workings of one mind" in the "Characters of the great Apocalypse" in the Ravine of Gondo, as he tries to establish the workings of imagination outside himself in the very language of doxology,

> For, though in whispers speaking, the full heart
> Will find a vent; and thought is praise to him,
> Audible praise, to thee, omniscient Mind,
> From whom all gifts descend, all blessings flow!   [751–54]

The descent from these peaks, rhetorical and real, at the fall of darkness, is precipitous, suggesting thematic as well as practical dangers: "No trace remained / Of those celestial splendours . . . too faint almost for sight" (759–60, 763). To hear an echo here of the Intimations Ode's "celestial light," "thoughts that do often lie too deep for tears," and weight of Custom "heavy as frost, and deep almost as life" were to hear too finely, were it not for the Solitary's almost direct allusion, reminding us that *The Excursion* is a narrative expansion of the same themes: " 'Another sun,' / Said he, 'shall shine upon us, ere we part; / Another sun, and peradventure more' " (779–81). (Cf. "Another race hath been, and other palms are won," *Ode*, 200.) *The Excursion* begins the process of self-reference to many of his poems, but especially to the *Ode*, which Wordsworth used increasingly in his later works to shore up weaker poems; besides these echoes, his notes to the 1814 edition cite the *Ode* in reference to Book IV.205–06. He speaks the last fourteen lines himself, in propria persona, beyond such allusions and outside his thinly disguised character-role as the Poet. Yet they, too, speak as from another poem that he could not cite because it was slated for posthumous publication, echoing the last verse paragraph of *The Prelude* as if from beyond the grave:

> To enfeebled Power,
> From this communion with uninjured Minds,
> What renovation hath been brought; and what
> Degree of healing to a wounded spirit,
> Dejected, and habitually disposed
> To seek, in degradation of the Kind,
> Excuse and solace for her own defects;
> How far those erring notions were reformed;
> And whether aught, of tendency as good
> And pure, from further intercourse ensued;
> This—if delightful hopes, as heretofore,
> Inspire the serious song, and gentle Hearts
> Cherish, and lofty Minds approve the past—
> My future labours may not leave untold.   [783–96]

The Solitary's habits of mind are the corollary opposite of Wordsworth's, and thus a large part of the motive of his writing. If the Solitary extends his own unease to all "the Kind," Wordsworth's avowed mission is to go from the healthy growth of his own mind to the Mind of Man. Its difficulty is expressed in the same kind of sentence that ends *The Prelude*, where honest qualifications and doubts intervene between subject and predicate almost to the loss of grammatical direction (chap. 4). The poem's last verb, *may*, can be either a conditional or an imperative, and depends on the same set of conditions that obtain at the end of all *Recluse* efforts: (1) "delightful hopes"; (2) the "gentle Hearts" of Mary, Dorothy, and Sara; and (3) Coleridge's "lofty Mind" approving past efforts. This little band is needed for the continuation of the poem as critically as the "little band" to which the Pastor addressed his vision of Paradise Regained. But the third condition was already in default, dissipating the first, in no small measure complicated by their competition, real or subconscious, for the favor of those "gentle Hearts."

If *The Excursion,* in the private messages of this ending, was partly intended as a peace offering and last earnest to Coleridge that *The Recluse* yet lived, we may see *The Excursion,* no less than *The Prelude,* as a poem to Coleridge, who is addressed in its preface as "a dear Friend, most distinguished for his knowledge and genius, and to whom the Author's Intellect is deeply indebted." Like the other parts of *The Recluse,* it is one man's inspiration seeking to fulfill the other's idea, a compensatory arrangement not unlike that of the Deaf and Blind Dalesmen. In default of Coleridge's aid, the burden is thrown upon the reader: "the Reader will have no difficulty in extracting a system for himself." But the Friend was already deep in composition of his version of the literary biography they had shared together, a book quite as visionary in both scope and execution as either *The Prelude* or *The Excursion,* and worthy to be called Coleridge's contribution to the *Recluse* project. Wordsworth, for his part, was already well into the new arrangement of his poems for his comprehensive 1815 edition by the time *The Excursion* appeared. His new categorization abandoned the gothic church metaphor which he had used to figure *The Recluse* and incorporate all his poems into it. Instead, he now adopted an organizational metaphor keyed to his own life and body; the cathedral became the man. These new Coleridgean texts and Wordsworthian textual strategies ended the further growth of *The Recluse,* and our attention must turn briefly to them in order to complete its history.

Epilogue

10

The Recluse and *Biographia Literaria,* 1814–1815

Of unknown modes of being which on earth,
Or in the heavens, or in the heavens and earth
Exist by mighty combinations, bound
Together by a link, and with a soul
Which makes all one.

PW, V.340–41

Wordsworth's *Recluse* project came to an end as soon as part of it saw the light of public day. The storm of critical abuse provoked by *The Excursion,* swirling round its near-vacuum in sales, effectively halted his efforts to finish, let alone publish, any more of his definitive genius-work. The idea lived on briefly before it disappeared into the limbo of family talk, in his efforts to redress the outrages perpetrated on *The Excursion* by Francis Jeffrey, not by defending that poem, but by asserting the consistency of his oeuvre and the stature of his genius within the "philosophical" context offered by *The Recluse.* And the idea transmigrated to literary immorality by another route, as *The Excursion* and Wordsworth's preface and "Essay, Supplementary" to his *Poems* of 1815 provided some of the occasion, much of the matter, and above all the motive of Coleridge's *Biographia Literaria.* After nearly twenty years of poetical hospitality within Wordsworth's genius, hard work, friendship, and misunderstanding, *The Recluse* came home to rest in the mind of its progenitor, reappropriated by Coleridge to help define his own account of mental growth. One conclusion of the *Biographia* is that "[Wordsworth] is capable of producing . . . the FIRST GENUINE PHILOSOPHIC POEM" (chap. XXII); another, slightly prior conclusion is that Coleridge was the first genuinely philosophical critic able to recognize such a poem when and if it appeared.[1] Scholars have long recognized that Wordsworth's 1814–15 publications influenced

Coleridge's composition of the *Biographia*;[2] in these concluding pages I wish to display more of the complexities of this influence, as revealed by understanding the sway of the *Recluse* ideal over both men.

WORDSWORTH'S REACTION TO ATTACKS ON *THE EXCURSION*

Throughout the fall and winter of 1814, the Wordsworth household anxiously awaited the world's response to *The Excursion*. As with each of his published volumes since 1800, they hoped this one would finally establish his national reputation on an unimpeachable basis, turn the tide of abuse that had sprung up after *Poems, in Two Volumes* seven years earlier (*Prose*, iii.55), and help set the cultural agenda for the coming postrevolutionary era.[3] But instead of accomplishing any of these things, *The Excursion* produced the sharpest intensification of public opinion against Wordsworth, enshrined in the stinging words of Francis Jeffrey's lead sentence, "This will never do!" which has become posterity's favorite excuse for not reading the poem.

Very late in 1814 or early in 1815 (*Prose*, iii.23), Wordsworth suddenly decided to respond to his critics by affixing a preface and appending an "Essay, Supplementary to the Preface" to his forthcoming *Poems*. This delayed by several months the appearance of this collection, which had been in preparation since before the completion of *The Excursion* and intended to appear more or less simultaneously with it, to fulfill Wordsworth's promise of "properly arranged . . . minor Pieces," that would clarify the total, "gothic" form of *The Recluse*. The vehement, radical nature of Wordsworth's arguments in the preface and essay of 1815 very closely reflects his most intimate thoughts about the stature of his work, as indicated by Dorothy's comment to Sara Hutchinson in February: "You would almost feel as if you were nearer to us [when you receive the *Poems* from the publisher], especially the preface and the essay will have this effect" (*LMY*, ii.202).

Wordsworth's principal strategy was to defend the coherence of his works, first by direct reference to the "philosophical" context of *The Recluse*, then by gradually expanding to still larger systems of justification, idealized versions of the past history of English culture and, via posterity, to its implied future. These strategies mark a decisive and terminal shift in *The Recluse*'s development, both in composition and in its usefulness as an inspirational idea. Until this point, the importance of the masterwork had been defended extrinsically, in terms of its useful applicability to Human

Life; but now, aspects of human life (particularly literary history and reader-psychology) are invoked inward to defend *The Recluse* as symbol of the philosophic consistency of Wordsworth's genius. Wordsworth's period of retrenchment and consolidation of his reputation begins here; it was time to save the poet, not the world, and the defense of the poet proceeds largely in terms that had been used to defend the poem which was to have guaranteed his reputation.

Wordsworth evidently felt that the construction of a permanent "Wordsworth" was the necessary task before him. One does not criticize his decision to begin cutting his losses, in light of the rough treatment *The Excursion* received from the reviewers, but his tactics are illuminating, casting the last days of *The Recluse* into bold relief. Though the preface to *The Excursion* had indeed been somewhat "pompous" (*Prose,* iii.3), it is demure by comparison with the preface and supplementary essay of the 1815 *Poems,* whose full eccentricity becomes apparent only when we grasp the peculiar polemical context existing between Wordsworth and Coleridge in 1814–15, wherein they addressed each other in published prose full of veiled private references only they could understand. Unraveling these complications is like uncoiling the intellectual DNA of their organic relationship and yields the separated strands of their once-fecund "symbiosis" (McFarland).

The Excursion's preface, invoking the authority of "a dear Friend, most distinguished for his knowledge and genius," had referred to an easily extractable "system" of thought and to an analogously transparent organization of texts: "minor Pieces, which have long been before the Public, when they shall be properly arranged, will be found by the attentive Reader to have such connection with the main Work [the "gothic church" of *The Recluse,* and its "ante-chapel," *The Prelude*] as may give them claim to be likened to the little cells, oratories, and sepulchral recesses, ordinarily included in those edifices." The preface to the first edition of the 1815 *Poems* picks up at this point, referring to "the Preface of that part of 'The Recluse,' lately published under the title of 'The Excursion,'" directing the same "attentive Reader" to Wordsworth's "meditated arrangement" of his minor poems, and offering to explain "their connection with each other, and also their subordination to that Work [*The Recluse*] . . . as carried into effect in the present Volumes" (*Prose,* iii.26n.). He also states that his "guiding wish" for his new categorical arrangement of his poems is to cause them to be "regarded under a twofold view; as composing an entire work within themselves, and as adjuncts to the philosophical Poem, 'The Recluse'" (*Prose,* iii.28). The primary assumption of the 1815 preface is that a coherent arrangement of texts implies a coherent system of thought, in order that a collection of "poems, apparently miscellaneous" may be seen to exemplify the philosophical basis of their author's genius. The preface seeks to demonstrate this coherence internally or synchronically; the "Essay, Supplementary" advances toward the same goal by means of external, historical evidence. Though the image of the "gothic church" is invoked only by cross-reference to *The Excursion,* the relation proposed between major and minor works is manifestly a free, organic, and "gothic" one, and appears, in the actual categories of the 1815 volume, as a highly various set of organizing principles, which Wordsworth followed (with constant expansion and revision) in all subsequent collected editions of his work, retaining this same prefatory announcement until 1836, after which the opening paragraph and its pointers toward *The Recluse* were dropped.

This is not the place to rehearse the strengths and weaknesses of Wordsworth's categorization of his poems. Posterity has for the most part found his rhetorical fail-safe device irresistible: "if, by the plan adopted, any thing material would be taken from the natural effect of the pieces, individually, on the mind of the unreflecting Reader . . . [the author] should have preferred to scatter the contents of these volumes at random." Instead, we can observe the strain to which the very concept of organizational coherence is subjected when, by the end of the preface, no less than six overlapping principles have been proposed, only some of which (and those only partially) actually appear in the table of contents: (1) the "meditated arrangement," referring explicitly to *The Recluse* and imagistically to the main body and side-recesses of a gothic church; (2) an arrangement according to the "powers of mind *predominant*" in the creation of the poems (Fancy, Imagination, Sentiment, Reflection); (3) a generic arrangement, according to the "mould in which they are cast" (Sonnets, Epitaphs, Inscriptions); (4) an arrangement by subject matter (Naming of Places, Liberty, Immortality); (5) a biochronological arrangement, "that the works may more obviously correspond with the course of human life" (Childhood, Juvenile Pieces, Old Age), necessitated by (6) "the three requisites of a legitimate whole, a beginning, a middle, and an end." There are several transfers possible among the categories, but, taken all together, they continue the dominant strain of all composition on *The Recluse*: the need for a "philosophical" (i.e., systematic) structure to support Wordsworth's "views" "on Man, on Nature, and on Human Life." Wordsworth had proposed a sociobiographical arrangement of his poems to Coleridge in 1809,[4] when *The Excursion* was just beginning to take shape, and one based on "the psychology of literary creation" to Crabb Robinson in

1812, when it was beginning to head toward a conclusion (*Prose,* iii.23); but now that it was published, and suffering mightily for its pretensions, he concocted the richest possible mixture of schemes to defend the coherence of his genius.

By his references to *The Recluse,* we can see that the categorization of 1815 supplants an architectural model by an autobiographical one: the cathedral becomes the man, as Wordsworth's tactics shift from applying his poetry to life, to applying his life to his poetry and making the "system" of his works coterminous with his life. This possibility was always imminent in *The Recluse*'s unstable relation to *The Prelude,* and indeed may be said to point the way toward the posthumous publication of the latter. Setting aside the preface's references to *The Recluse,* the 1815 volumes' dominant impression is that of a biographical plan wrapped around conventional genre and subject arrangements, complicated by what has always been the most controversial part of Wordsworth's categorization, his arrangement according to the "powers of mind *predominant*" in the creation of poems. This necessitated his defining the various powers, to demonstrate the dominance of one over the other, and, since Imagination is valorized over all, to present a working definition of that central Romantic faculty by way of distinguishing it from the more comprehensible and traditional Fancy, "or, as my friend Mr. Coleridge has styled it, 'the aggregative and associative power,'" to which definition he adds, "my objection is only that [it] is too general" (*Prose,* iii.36). Much hangs upon that slight emendation. In the larger context of the 1815 preface—its insistent reinvoking of *The Recluse* or "philosophical" context once shared by Wordsworth and Coleridge—it implies that a Wordsworthian system has corrected a Coleridgean one, or supplanted one that Coleridge had failed to supply.[5] This implication is pointed by the farewell which ended the preface in all editions until after Coleridge's death:

> It remains that I should express my regret at the necessity of separating my compositions from some beautiful Poems of Mr. Coleridge, with which they have long been associated in publication. The feelings, with which that joint publication was made, have been gratified; its end is answered, and the time is come when considerations of general propriety dictate the separation. [*Prose,* iii.39n.]

Unexceptionable in itself, though somewhat gratuitous,[6] this is another in a series of baits Wordsworth threw out consciously or unconsciously in his 1814–15 prefaces, directing the attention of his most "attentive Reader" to considerations of "propriety"—considerations to which, in the end, Coleridge could hardly fail to reply.

The "Essay, Supplementary to the Preface" of 1815 (hereafter Essay) invokes more comprehensive systems to support still larger claims. The preface argues for a coherent organization of poems as subordinate adjuncts to a projected philosophical poem; the Essay argues that William Wordsworth's literary experience is homologous with that of the greatest figures of English literary history. If in the preface we witness the "gothic church" in process of transmutation into its human architect, in the Essay we observe the canonization of the poet into the sainted company of English genius, as Wordsworth writes a specialized history of English literature from Spenser to Samuel Johnson, demonstrating that his published works have shared the same fate as those of the truly great, especially Shakespeare and Milton. They are all

> select Spirits for whom it is ordained that their fame shall be in the world an existence like that of Virtue, which owes its being to the struggles it makes, and its vigour to the enemies whom it provokes;—a vivacious quality, ever doomed to meet with opposition, and still triumphing over it; and, from the nature of its dominion, incapable of being brought to the sad conclusion of Alexander, when he wept that there were no more worlds for him to conquer. [*Prose*, iii.67]

The allusion to Alexander at the beginning of this historical sketch is balanced by one to Hannibal at the end, so that there is, metaphorically, no mistaking the stature of the company of world-conquerors to which Wordsworth here admits himself, like Napoleon crowning himself emperor. Consistent with his overall shift in argumentative tactics, Wordsworth's allusions now move from military heroes toward literary ones, rather than in the other direction as they did earlier in *The Recluse*'s history; 'victory' is now the firm establishment of this poet's "fame . . . in the world," rather than of the philosophy his works may be said to contain. But, amazing as this performance is, it demands neither criticism nor ridicule so much as the recognition that it is, finally, right: the next great figure in the "lives" of English poetry is certainly William Wordsworth. From a popular American perspective, the Essay looks like Babe Ruth pointing out the exact spot where he will hit his next home run; overriding squeamish considerations of taste, Wordsworth aims at the niche he will occupy in the pantheon of posterity.

Naturally, this is the kind of argument one can hardly abide without damaging one's self-respect, and Wordsworth's critics continued to have field days with the large targets he offered them. (James Hogg published three effective parodies in 1816, under the general title *The Recluse*, indicating the extent to which Wordsworth could be recognizably identified with his master project.)[7] But the Essay is both serious and rhetorically astute, once we grant its awkward posture of an author arguing himself into his nation's history of genius.

Wordsworth frames his historical system's premise (that no great writers were immediately popular, and no immediately popular ones were great) with three subsidiary schemes, all of which are meant to demonstrate how difficult it is for great, original writers to be properly understood: (*a*) a psychological hypothesis of readers' development, showing that old age tends to repeat the delusions of youthful enthusiasm (*Prose*, iii.62–64); (*b*) a quasi-sociological scheme distinguishing religious readers from truly philosophic ones—the former close in spirit to the latter, but because of their doctrinal prejudices, "no lovers of art have gone farther astray than the pious and the devout" (64–66); and (*c*) a distinction, familiar to the eighteenth century, between "the PUBLIC ("that small though loud portion of the community, ever governed by factitious influence") and "the People, *philosophically characterised,*" on whose "accord of sublimated humanity" (*Prose*, iii.83–84; italics added) he rests his ultimate vindication. Each of these subsidiary systems refers to segments of Wordsworth's contemporary audience: readers raised on neoclassical tastes, religious readers shocked by *The Excursion*'s liberal theology, and readers influenced by opinions expressed in journals like the *Edinburgh Review*. The correction of all these sources of systematic misunderstanding, and the recognition of Wordsworth's genius in which a correct understanding would eventuate, depends upon the criticism of "a mind at once poetical and philosophical," which appears at the end of his historical survey to clinch it with real life authority: "every author, as far as he is great and at the same time *original*, has had the task of *creating* the taste by which he is to be enjoyed: so it has been, so it will continue to be. This remark was long since made to me by the philosophical Friend for the separation of whose poems from my own I have previously expressed my regret" (*Prose*, iii.80). This reference to Coleridge is simultaneously back-handed and highly charged; does it apportion philosophical knowledge to him at the expense of appropriating poetical power to Wordsworth? It is followed immediately by the allusion to the artist-as-Hannibal, clearing and shaping the road "for what is peculiarly his own," for recognition of which in his poetry Wordsworth had gratefully thanked Coleridge in *The Prelude* (XII.354–79). The importance of this philosophical criticism is in direct ratio to its rarity; in the general category of critics, "meet together the two extremes of best and worst," and what is best (their "trust-worthy" judgment) is overbalanced by what is worst, their "palsied imaginations and indurated hearts" (*Prose*, iii.66).

Such references form another pattern throughout the Essay, corollary to the heroic allusions to Alexander and Hannibal, of sickly, stupid, insane critics ("the orb of my genius (for genius none of them seem to deny me) acts upon these [critics] like the moon upon a certain description of patients," 62n.) and luxuriously passive, self-indulgent readers ("like an Indian prince or general—stretched on his palanquin, and borne by his slaves," 82), who also have a real historical embodiment in the Essay: "Dr. Johnson, 'mid the little senate to which he gave laws" (75; alluding to Pope's pitying portrayal of Addison in decline). This leitmotif of sarcastic references to conservative, oligarchic critics whose enervated *taste* unfits them to exert the active reading habits required by a radically imperial poetry of *imagination* is an important foil to the psychological, sociological, and historical systems which form the Essay's argumentative backbone. Wordsworth's attitude toward Johnson is the most important part of this pattern, especially as it relates to Coleridge's criticism. On the one hand, Johnson's *Lives of the Poets* (1779) is Wordsworth's primary source for the historical data which he contorts to his own purposes. On the other, Johnson's authority must be torn down as much as possible, so that another form of genius that what he valued may be admitted.[8] Wordsworth certainly has *The Recluse* in mind when, by way of disagreeing with Johnson on the reception of *Paradise Lost*, with reference to Milton's prayer for a "fit audience though few," he adds, "I have said elsewhere that he gained more than he asked" (alluding to "Prospectus," ll. 23–24), even though this internal self-reference puts him in the awkward position of having to correct his own implication (i.e., Milton did not gain more than he asked *immediately*, only with posterity). Even when he agrees with Johnson, as on the fradulence of Ossian, he does so with as little grace as possible, merely by way of leading into his final denigration of the *Lives'* standards of judgment, in which Johnson's omissions are glaringly exaggerated, ignoring his prefatory explanation of the circumstances of the *Lives'* publication: "Where is the ever-to-be-honored Chaucer? where is Spenser? where Sidney? . . . where Shakespeare?" And Johnson's most minor inclusions are scrupulously accumulated: "Roscommon, and Stepney, and Phillips, and Walsh, and Smith, and Duke, and King, and Spratt—Halifax, Granville, Sheffield, Congreve, Broome, and other reputed Magnates" (79).[9] The purpose of this slanted rhetoric becomes clear when, closing sardonically on "the distinguished event" of Johnson's *Lives*, Wordsworth protests that he does "not mean to bring down this retrospect to our own times." But the inference is as inescapable as the fact: another master critic is needed to replace Dr. Johnson as the expert arbiter of English genius, one who will base his judgments on the active, informing, creative power of Imagination rather than on the passive, reactive, artificial quality of Taste, and who will recognize and exemplify these qualities in the poetry of William Wordsworth.

These rhetorical gestures also have sociopolitical overtones, referring to French decadence in the context of the failing Napoleonic adventure with the same imagery that Wordsworth used in the conclusions of the two-part and thirteen-book *Preludes,* which derived from Coleridge's letter to Wordsworth linking the French Revolution to the aims of *The Recluse*: "the pathetic and the sublime;—are neither of them, accurately speaking, objects of a faculty which could ever without *a sinking in the spirit of Nations* have been designated by the metaphor—*Taste*" (81, italics added; cf. *1799*.ii.478–89; *1805*.XIII 431–35).[10] He also makes convenient use of the poor literary judgment of Napoleon's brother, Lucien Bonaparte, who had praised Ossian and devalued Milton in the preface to his own massive epic effort, *Charlemagne; ou l'Eglise deliverée,* a topic close to *The Recluse*'s theme of redeemed religious institutions, published in London the year before, when Lucien's imprisonment in England was coming to an end, carefully read in part by Wordsworth (*Prose,* iii.100), and now scoffingly triumphed over: "These opinions are of ill omen for the Epic ambition of him who has given them to the world" (78). Since Napoleon's own fondness for Ossian was well known, there is in Wordsworth's scorn a light suggestion of preferring his own "Epic ambitions" over those of Lucien's brother, and, insofar as these references call up the entire history of *The Recluse*'s development, the Essay's reference to the artist-as-Hannibal can be seen without undue exaggeration as a historic type of the two most important Alp-crossers in Wordsworth's contemporary experience, Napoleon and himself.

COLERIDGE RESPONDS TO WORDSWORTH

Wordsworth's references to Coleridge and his allusions to the philosophical ideal of *The Recluse* can be read as declarations of independence or cries for help, and probably partake of both. All of this took a personal turn in April 1815, when Coleridge wrote Lady Beaumont asking for her fair copy of the poem now known as "To William Wordsworth; Composed on the Night After His Recitation of a Poem on the Growth of an Individual Mind" (*LSTC,* iv.564–65). Coleridge was collecting his scattered verses for publication, the first stage of a heroic self-rehabilitation effort which he had begun by placing himself under the care of a person (John Morgan) who could effectively regulate his intake of laudanum. In passing, he opined to Lady Beaumont that, "comparing Wordsworth with himself" (i.e., with Wordsworth), *The Excursion* was not "equal to the Work on the Growth of his own spirit" because he labored too hard to present truths that were already truisms to "the generality of persons." This apt but comparatively mild criticism Lady Beaumont relayed to Wordsworth (along with Coleridge's stout denunciation of "the infamous Edinburgh Review") and did not send Coleridge the poem he had requested. On May 22, Wordsworth wrote to Coleridge, their first correspondence in over two and a half years, begging him not to publish "To William Wordsworth" because of the "great disadvantage . . . such a precursorship of Praise" would have upon "my work when it appears," and asking for Coleridge's "remarks on the Poems [1815], and also upon the Excursion, only begging that whenever it is possible references be made to some passages which have given rise to the opinion whether favourable or otherwise," for lack of which he had been unable to comprehend Coleridge's "*comparative* censure" to Lady Beaumont, since his aim in *The Excursion* had been precisely to make "commonplace truths . . . interesting . . . and rather to remind men of their knowledge . . . than to attempt to convey recondite or refined truths" (*LMY*, ii.238).

Coleridge responded immediately, on May 30, for once throwing off his "habit of procrastination." His reply is a long and rhetorically complicated document, as it could hardly be otherwise, given his situation of struggling "between sincerity and diffidence" in offering criticism "to an absent friend, to whom for the more substantial Third of a Life we have been habituated to look up." It contains the description of *The Recluse* which has been cited more than any other as containing the essence of that poem, but it is a postmortem statement, with intricate and confusing references not only to Wordsworth's other *Recluse* works, but also to Coleridge's works. Coleridge was just then composing an autobiographical sketch to preface his collection of miscellaneous pieces and impose some unity upon their appearance, a relation very similar to that proposed between *The Prelude* and *The Recluse* in the preface to *The Excursion,* and between "poems, apparently miscellaneous" and larger systems of imaginative unity set forth in the Preface of 1815. Coleridge's reassurance that he would not publish "To William Wordsworth" without permission makes a distinction between poetry and biography which indicates that he, too, had the critical authority of Samuel Johnson in mind at the time: "It is for the Biographer, not the Poet, to give the *accidents* of *individual* Life. Whatever is not representative, generic, may be indeed most poetically exprest, but it is not Poetry" (*LSTC*, iv.572). This paraphrases the famous pronouncement from *Rasselas*, implicitly substituting Wordsworth for Johnson's idiosyncratic tulip.[11]

These two letters leap like bolts across the void left in each man's life by the breach of misunderstanding in 1810, bridged only superficially by their legalistic "understandings" in 1812.[12] Only intimately and ultimately important concerns could have prompted Wordsworth to write and Coleridge to respond. Wordsworth's desire to know Coleridge's opinion of *The Excursion* and the *Poems* of 1815 was probably greater than his wish not to have "To William Wordsworth" published, but since that poem in turn evoked *The Prelude,* the two issues cannot be separated. Wordsworth's extreme claims for his poems and his masterwork in the preface and Essay of 1815 would have benefited enormously from modulation by Coleridge, but this is tantamount to assuming that Coleridge could have provided at long last his "notes" for *The Recluse.* In the event, Coleridge's response established the circuit by which the electricity of *The Recluse* was transformed back to him, connecting Wordsworth's prefaces of 1814–15 to Coleridge's "preface" (the *Biographia* as it then was) and to his subsequent career.

After repeating to Wordsworth the substance of his valuation of *The Excursion* to Lady Beaumont, Coleridge makes two elaborate conjectures of the *Prelude–Recluse* relation which effectively exclude *The Excursion* and obviate his need to say anything directly about it. His disappointment was relative to his expectations: "the Poem on the growth of your own mind was as the ground-plat and the Roots, out of which the Recluse was to have sprung up as the Tree—as far as the same Sap in both, I expected them doubtless to have formed one compleat Whole, but in matter, form, and product to be different, each not only a distinct but a different Work" (*LSTC*, iv.573). This organic expression parallels the terms Wordsworth had been using to unite his minor poems to, yet distinguish them from, "the philosophical poem, 'The Recluse,'" in the Preface of 1815, which Coleridge had received and read in April. But when Coleridge quotes the lines from "To William Wordsworth" (ll. 12–47) that synopsize the plot of *The Prelude,* and concludes, "*This* I considered as 'the EXCURSION,'" he leaves both us and Wordsworth in confusion, unless we infer, dubiously, that he has conflated *The Excursion*'s prefatory reference to "passing events, and to an existing state of things" with the sociohistorical portions of *The Prelude.* Since he says *The Prelude* has already accomplished the task of *The Excursion,* Coleridge's statement about the second poem, *The Recluse,* must be quoted in full to see how it distinguishes it from the other two, and also to notice how, though ostensibly originating in "what I had at various times gathered from your conversation" (just the obverse of most extant evidence as to who was describing what to whom), it returns by degrees to the mind of its creator.

'THE RECLUSE' I had . . . anticipated as commencing with you set down and settled in an abiding Home, and that with the Description of that Home ["Home at Grasmere"] you were to begin a *Philosophical Poem,* the result and fruits of a Spirit so fram'd & so disciplin'd, as had been told in the former [*The Prelude,* in itself, or "considered as" *The Excursion*]. Whatever in Lucretius is Poetry is not philosophical, whatever is philosophical is not Poetry [cf. the similarly exclusive formulation between poetry and biography earlier in the letter]: and in the very Pride of confident Hope I looked forward to the Recluse, as the *first* and *only* true Phil. Poem in existence. Of course, I expected the Colors, Music, imaginative Life, and Passion of *Poetry*; but the matter and arrangement of *Philosophy*—not doubting from the advantages of the Subject that the Totality of a System was not only capable of being harmonized with, but even calculated to aid, the unity (Beginning, Middle, and End) of a *Poem* [Subject/Poem and System/Philosophy come near tautological collapse here, perhaps with a glance at the 1815 Preface's "three requisites of a legitimate whole, a beginning, a middle, and an end"]. Thus, whatever the Length of the Work might be, still it was a *determinate* Length: of the subjects announced each would have its own appointed place, and excluding repetitions each would relieve & rise in interest above the other. I supposed you first ["Beginning"] to have meditated the faculties of Man in the abstract, in their correspondence with his Sphere of action, and first, in the Feeling, Touch, and Taste, then in the Eye, & last in the Ear, to have laid a solid and immoveable foundation for the Edifice by removing the sandy Sophisms of Locke, and the Mechanic Dogmatists, and demonstrating that the Senses were living growths and developements [*sic*] of the Mind & Spirit in a much juster as well as higher sense, than the mind can be said to be formed by the Senses—. Next ["Middle"], I understood that you would take the Human Race in the concrete ["Human Life"], have exploded the absurd notion of Pope's Essay on Man, Darwin, and all the countless Believers—even (strange to say) among Xtians of Man's having progressed from an Ouran Outang state—so contrary to all History, to all Religion, nay, to all Possibility—to have affirmed a Fall in some sense, as a fact, the possibility of which cannot be understood from the nature of the Will, but the reality of which is attested by Experience & Conscience—Fallen man contemplated in the different ages of the

World, and in the different states—Savage—Barbarous—Civilized
["ages"]—the lonely Cot, or Borderer's Wigwam—the Village—the
Manufacturing Town—Sea-port—City—Universities ["states"]—and
not disguising the sore evils, under which the whole Creation groans, to
point out however a manifest Scheme of Redemption from this Slavery, of
Reconciliation from this Enmity with Nature—what are the Obstacles,
the *Antichrist* that must be & already is—and to conclude ["End"] by a
grand didactic swell on the necessary identity of a true Philosophy with
true Religion, agreeing in the results and differing only as the analytic and
synthetic process, as discursive from intuitive, the former chiefly useful as
perfecting the latter—in short, the necessity of a general revolution in the
modes of developing & disciplining the human mind by the substitution
of Life, and Intelligence (considered in its different powers from the Plant
up to that state in which the difference of Degree becomes a new kind
(man, self-consciousness) but yet not by essential opposition) for the philosophy of mechanism which in everything that is most worthy of the human Intellect strikes *Death,* and cheats itself by mistaking clear Images
for distinct conceptions, and which idly demands Conceptions where Intuitions alone are possible or adequate to the majesty of the Truth. —In
short, Facts elevated into Theory—Theory into Laws—& Laws into living & intelligent Powers—true Idealism necessarily perfecting itself in Realism, & Realism refining itself into Idealism.—(*LSTC,* iv.574–75)[13]

Of this tall order, we may say on the one hand that we know what he
means, or that something like this was what Coleridge *always meant*
whenever he tried to free himself from associationism and Unitarianism.
But, on the other hand, to try to state his meaning exactly would contradict his own insistence on conclusions "where Intuitions alone are possible." This was to be the essence of Coleridge's problem in *Biographia
Literaria,* which launched out from this precise moment. Setting aside the
only partial aptness of his description to *The Recluse*'s themes of Man,
Nature, and Human Life (since it reintroduces the all-comprehending
fourth term, God),[14] its movement from (1) "Senses [as] living growths
and developments of the Mind & Spirit," to (2) "the Human Race in the
concrete," to (3) "a grand didactic swell on the necessary identity of a true
Philosophy with true Religion," resembles nothing so much as the sequence of lines about *The Prelude* he has just quoted from "To William
Wordsworth," which moved from (1) "Tides obedient to external force, /
And Currents self-determined . . . When Power stream'd from thee, and
thy Soul received / The Light reflected as a Light bestow'd!," to (2)
"the *social sense* / Distending wide and man beloved as man," to (3) "A
SONG DIVINE OF HIGH AND PASSIONATE TRUTHS / TO THEIR OWN MUSIC

CHAUNTED!" Particularly close are the poem's tropes of self-reflexive vision ("man's absolute Self . . . herself a Glory to behold, / The Angel of the Vision!") and the letter's paradoxes (or conundrums) of Real Idealism and Ideal Realism. These self-canceling parallels between what Coleridge says *The Recluse* was to have done and what he says *The Prelude* has already done (complicated by his insertion that "*This* I considered as 'the EXCURSION'") are underscored by the developmental metaphors that creep into his description of *The Recluse*'s central theme, of *in*nate, organic, *non*-developmental powers of mind, urged against all systems of psychology, history, or theology (associationism, necessarianism, mechanism) which pretend to trace things from beginnings to ends. Thus, the faculties of man do "correspond" to his "Sphere of action"; the different "ages" and "states" of fallen man do seem to progress (from savage to civilized, from cottage to city); and the methodological coda to his "grand didactic swell" sets the relation between the analytic and synthetic, or discursive and intuitive, powers of mind so close ("the former chiefly useful as perfecting the latter") that his final organic metaphor for the development of intelligence terminates in a gap so small as to be incomprehensible, which he closes the instant it opens: "that state in which the difference of Degree becomes a new kind (man, self-consciousness) but yet not by essential opposition." In such small, evanescent spaces lie the epistemological verifications of all philosophical definitions of free will, imagination, or God. Or, to compare small matters of form with large matters of substance, the kind of *life* with which Coleridge here seeks to invest human intelligence (against the *death* of developmental mechanism) partakes of the same definitional strategy by which both he and Wordsworth tried to connect the ideal *Recluse* with the extant *Prelude*: "one compleat Whole, but in matter, form, and product to be different, each not only a distinct but a different Work." As intelligence to matter, so philosophy to autobiography.

On the internal evidence of this important letter, *The Prelude* has already accomplished what *The Recluse* was supposed to,[15] without using any other system than the chronology of a human life—an idea that had occurred to Coleridge long before ("to write my metaphysical works, as *my Life,* & *in* my Life," *NBSTC,* i.1515 [September-October 1803]), and which now was brought forcibly home to him as a lively possibility by the strengths and weaknesses of Wordsworth's achievement in the same genre. The *Biographia Literaria* will be rushed to completion partly to realize what Wordsworth had only alluded to in the preface to *The Excursion*—the relation of autobiographical experience to philosophic truth—but it will also be heavily determined by Coleridge's conceptions of what *The Recluse* should have been. How much would be philosophy and how much mere biography? In the case of Wordsworth, which lay open before him, the question was, how much was philosophy and how much mere poetry? He undertook to adjudicate these relations with reference to Wordsworth's complaint that his "object 'was not to convey recondite or refined truths but to place commonplace Truths in an interesting point of View'" (576). Again he excludes *The Excursion* from consideration, this time by referring to the *Poems* of 1815:

> Now this [object] I supposed to have been in your two Volumes of Poems, as far as was desirable, or p[ossible,] without an insight into the whole Truth—. How can common [tru]ths be made permanently interesting but by being *bottomed* in our common nature—it is only by the profoundest Insight into Numbers and Quantity that a sublimity & even religious Wonder become attached to the simplest operations of Arithmetic, the most evident properties of the Circle or the Triangle—. [576]

If Wordsworth had accomplished his object of conveying commonplace truths in his *Poems* of 1815, what remained, implicitly, was the need to connect the commonplace to the recondite or, mutatis mutandis, the natural to the supernatural. Having blocked off consideration of *The Excursion*'s failure in this effort by citing *The Prelude* on the one hand and the *Poems* on the other, Coleridge proceeds immediately to talk about his own work in progress, a preface to his collected poems which will blossom into the full-blown *Biographia* precisely at the point (chap. XIV) where he uses his famous statement about the natural-supernatural "plan" of *Lyrical Ballads* as the introductory link between his autobiographical and philosophical reflections (vol. I) and his lengthy critique of Wordsworth's poetry (vol. II).[16]

> I have only to finish a Preface which I shall have done in two or at farthest three days—and I will then, dismissing all comparison either with the Poem on the Growth of your own Support [*sic*], or with the imagined Plan of the Recluse, state fairly my main Objections to the Excursion as it is—But it would have been alike unjust both to you and to myself, if I had led you to suppose that any disappointment, I may have felt, arose wholly or chiefly from the Passages, I do not like—or from the Poem considered irrelatively. [*LSTC*, iv.576]

In short, *The Excursion* cannot be considered "irrelatively," but only within the larger context of *The Recluse*, which is to say, the context of the particular genius of William Wordsworth, which will require a prior general definition of genius and imagination, which the *Biographia Liter-*

aria undertakes to supply. Coleridge never did supply Wordsworth with an account of his objections to *The Excursion*; instead, they formed the conclusion or terminus ad quem (chaps. XXI–XXII) of the single most important work of his life, which he now launched into, stimulated by the *Recluse*-ideals of a philosophically informed poetry and a philosophically based literary criticism which Wordsworth's published prefaces, essay, and private letter had helped to revive in him.

FROM *THE RECLUSE* TO *BIOGRAPHIA LITERARIA*

The *Biographia*'s growth out of the demise of *The Recluse* can be understood further in light of a recently established chronology of its composition.[17] We are not certain how much, if any, of his "preface" Coleridge had written when he received and responded to Wordsworth's letter in late May 1815. His estimate to Wordsworth on May 30 that he would finish it "in two or at the farthest three days" coincides almost exactly with his estimate to Byron on March 30 that his collection and preface would be ready "by the first week in June" (*LSTC*, iv.561). But as to the length and contents of said preface, we have only Coleridge's description to Byron: "A general Preface will be pre-fixed, on the Principles of philosophic and genial criticism relatively to the Fine Arts in general; but especially to Poetry." We do know, however, that in June and July Coleridge abandoned his timetable, suddenly accelerating the intensity and quantity of his work on the preface until, by the end of July, he had drafted the bulk of what are now chapters I–V and XIV–XXII of what is now the *Biographia*. If any of the preface existed, in draft or in Coleridge's mind, before late May, it most likely consisted of large chunks of what are now chapters I–V and smaller bits from the more general portions of chapters XIV–XXII (especially XV and XVI), since these are the sections which conform closest to the description he gave Byron. But in late July he found himself with some autobiographical and critical material (chaps. I–V) that could have formed a plausible preface to a new collection of his poems, were it not completely overbalanced by a mass of material (chaps. XIV–XXII) devoted largely to analytical criticism of Wordsworth's poems and prefaces.

 Though the catalyzing stimulus of Wordsworth's letter and prefaces, reinvoking the once-shared *Recluse* ideals, is suggestively obvious here, we should beware of identifying Wordsworth as the "cause" of the *Biographia* in any simple sense. References to a work like the *Biographia* can be traced in Coleridge's notebooks and correspondence as early as 1802–04, and were very probably entertained even earlier.[18] But he did not have such a work foremost in mind when he began collecting his poems in March of 1815. His intentions did, however, include a desire to reestablish his reputation by separating his works from their association with Wordsworth's in the public mind, which they had had since the joint publication of *Lyrical Ballads* and its several subsequent editions. Also, his early work on his preface went forward with the model of Wordsworth's 1815 preface very much before him (he received the *Poems* in April); he refers in scrupulous detail to the format and even the typography of Wordsworth's preface during the course of composing his own.[19] And when the *Biographia* and the collected poems were finally published in 1817, they appeared as complementary though separate works, as *The Excursion* and the *Poems* had been intended to, and Coleridge's title for his poems, *Sibylline Leaves,* may be said to translate the Wordsworthian plain style ("Miscellaneous Pieces") into esoteric Coleridgese.[20]

But in late July Coleridge's short autobiographical-critical sketch and long critique of Wordsworth constituted a proportion unsuited not only to a preface of his collected poems but even to an autobiographical work, strictly speaking. Though parts of the 1800 preface are indeed beside the points at issue as they had come to be understood by both Wordsworth and Coleridge in 1815, particularly the existence, nature, and workings of Imagination,[21] Coleridge could not address the "philosophical" *Recluse*-context invoked by Wordsworth in his 1815 preface and essay since it was not public knowledge, and even as private knowledge was more a shared aspiration than a coherent plan open to dispute. Though Coleridge indicates in a progress report to R. H. Brabant that his preface was finished, it manifestly was not, and his next sentence suggests why:

> One long passage—a disquisition on the powers of association, with the History of the Opinions on this subject from Aristotle to Hartley, and on the generic difference between the faculties of Fancy and Imagination—I did not indeed altogether insert, but I certainly extended and elaborated, with a view to your perusal—as laying the foundation Stones of the Constructive or Dynamic Philosophy in opposition to the merely mechanic—. [*LSTC*, iv. 579]

This refers to chapter V, which, as it stood at this point in July, was a very long loose thread stretching between the autobiographical sketch of chapters I–IV and the criticism of Wordsworth that became chapters XIV–XXII; indeed, it dangled a clue from *The Excursion* to anticipate the labyrinth to follow, as Coleridge prays for readers' patience "while I thus go 'sounding on my dim and perilous way'" (quoting, without noting, *Excursion*, III.701, which derives in turn from *The Borderers*, l. 1775).[22]

From the beginning of August until the middle of September, he composed what are now chapters VI–XIII, the philosophical disquisition
against associationism, ending with the famous abrupt definition of imagination, or "esemplastic power," in chapter XIII, which he finished "at
white heat" along with chapter XII before delivering the completed manuscript to the printer on 19 September 1815.[23] In early August the first
three chapters had been sent off to the printers by John Morgan and might
well have become the preface to a collection of poems:[24] but, although the
more succinct chapters on Wordsworth and philosophy (IV and V) were
already completed then, Coleridge's holding them back for further revision
clearly suggests that it was the connections between himself (i.e., his own
life or autobiography), Wordsworth, and philosophy that needed clarification. In the event, the last term, philosophy, became the mediator between
the other two. Coleridge had been having thoughts for years on the essential questions covered in chapters VI–XIII: how to dismantle associationist
or mechanist theories of mind with a definite proof of man's innately creative faculties. But his immediate compositional problem was to find a
connection between the autobiographical chapters he had already composed and his long, close analysis of Wordsworth. With the benefit of
hindsight, the solution seems inevitable: a philosophic survey of material
versus creative theories of mind that, at one end, raises the autobiographical issues of Coleridge's literary life to philosophic importance, and, at the
other, devolves into a pointed *demonstration* of the validity of his argument upon the body of Wordsworth's works, distinguishing the truly creative from the mechanically adventitious.[25] Thus volume II of the *Biographia* appears not simply as Samuel Taylor Coleridge appreciating and
correcting the works of his old friend and long-time associate William
Wordsworth, but presents Coleridge as the inheritor, understander, and
corrector of philosophic traditions from Aristotle through Descartes and
Hartley to Kant, Fichte, and Schelling, exercising and proving his claim to
be the newest part of this tradition by demonstrating what was and what
was not genius in the poet whom he "could pronounce with the liveliest
convictions . . . capable of producing . . . the FIRST GENUINE PHILOSOPHIC
POEM" (chap. XXII), and, at the same time, directly answering Wordsworth's call for "a mind at once poetical and philosophical" with his own
desideratum: "long have I wished to see a fair and philosophical disquisition into the character of Wordsworth as a poet" (chap. XXI). Or, as
Jerome Christensen has said, coming to similar conclusions by a different
interpretive route: "[*The Recluse*] will be both monument to Wordsworth's genius and fulfillment of Coleridge's criticism . . . the move which

substitutes Coleridge's principled preface, his literary life and opinions, for Wordsworth's erroneous sentiments has as its corollary the substitution of Wordsworth's philosophical poem for Coleridge's own volume of poems, the pretext for the preface of the *Biographia*."[26]

Coleridge's insuring the coherent dignity of his *Biographia* by connecting autobiography to literary criticism via a specialized philosophical history also parallels, rhetorically, Wordsworth's specialized history of English literature in the Essay of 1815, which admitted him into its company of tutelary geniuses by referring to his "philosophical" friend for empowering authority. Coleridge may have felt forestalled by Wordsworth in his literary history as well, since he says that he had intended to organize his literary lectures in a much neater sequence than they were delivered, but he changed his plans for much the same reason Wordsworth had introduced his survey. He had planned to trace English literature through its three different eras (Chaucer to Milton, Dryden to Thomson, and "from Cowper to the present day"), but dropped the last lest his words be misconstrued "as current coin in the marts of garrulity or detraction." Thus he would have completed the entire range that Wordsworth stopped just short of ("I do not mean to bring down this retrospect to our own times"), and both his intention and his desisting from it are motivated by reasons nearly identical to Wordsworth's, to solve the mystery of how he *"could offend any member of the republic of letters"* (I.53). Wordsworth had generalized such antagonisms as the very badge of fame ("which owes its being to the struggles it makes, and its vigour to the enemies it provokes"; *Prose*, iii.67), but Coleridge discovers them in his case to have had a rather more particular cause: [the fact that] *"I was in habits of intimacy with Mr. Wordsworth and Mr. Southey"* (I.55). In part, their interchanges continue a long English tradition of distinguishing naive, native genius from self-conscious, sophisticated talent, as in Dryden's comparisons of Shakespeare and Ben Jonson, or Samuel Johnson's comparisons of Dryden and Pope, or, for that matter, Wordsworth's comparisons of Shakespeare-Milton-Wordsworth and Pope-Thomson-Johnson. A signal facet of this polarizing tradition is the increasing self-consciousness of even the "naive" pole, Wordsworth's Essay being a particularly blatant example.

As many commentators have noted, chapter IV of the *Biographia* is the natural, topical antecedent of chapter XIV, each having essentially the same subtitle (respectively, "The *Lyrical Ballads* with the Preface," and "Occasion of the *Lyrical Ballads,* and the objects originally proposed—Preface to the second edition"). In between comes philosophy, devolving upon chapter XIII's definition of Imagination in the same or-

ganic figures, regarding the differences between his distinction of Fancy
and Imagination and Wordsworth's, that Coleridge had used in his May
30 letter to describe the relation of *The Prelude* to *The Recluse*:

> But it was Mr. Wordsworth's purpose [in the Preface of 1815] to consider
> the influences of fancy and imagination as they are manifested in poetry,
> and from the different effects to conclude their diversity in kind; while it
> is my object to investigate the seminal principle, and then from the kind
> to deduce the degree. My friend has drawn a masterly sketch of the
> branches with their *poetic* fruitage. I wish to add the trunk, and even the
> roots as far as they lift themselves above ground, and are visible to the
> naked eye of our common consciousness. [chap. IV; *BL*, I.87–88]

The all-but-invisible origins of the power which Coleridge here pictures as
above-ground roots, are in chapter XIII figured at a contrary extreme, in
the lofty arches of a ruined Gothic cathedral, barely visible against a
moonlit sky.

IMAGINATION, THE ESEMPLASTIC POWER

To the extent that chapter XIII was substantially the last-composed portion of the *Biographia*, we see in it *The Recluse*'s final transmigration from
a Wordsworthian project back into a Coleridgean idea. The chapter is
framed as a rhetorical response to a dual challenge Coleridge lays down
for himself and for Wordsworth at the end of chapter XII, directly ad-
dressing Wordsworth's slight objection to Coleridge's distinction between
Imagination and Fancy, pointing out that it will be "necessary to go back
much further ["in the next chapter"] than Mr. Wordsworth's subject required or permitted": "He will judge. Would to heaven, I might meet with
many such readers. I will conclude with the words of Bishop Jeremy
Taylor: 'he to whom all things are one, who draweth all things to one, and
seeth all things in one, may enjoy true peace and rest of spirit.'" These last
words of chapter XII recapitulate almost exactly, in their reference to
Wordsworth and the need to go further into the subject of Imagination
and Fancy, the rhetorical situation at the end of chapter IV, from which
the entire philosophical section of the *Biographia* was launched. Coleridge's invocation of Wordsworth's judgment is both challenge and prayer,
a doubling of motives that reflects the double aspect we have noted in
Wordsworth's prefaces and essay of 1814–15 — that they are simultaneously declarations of independence and pleas for help. Jeremy Taylor's
prayer is already an anticipatory definition of the workings of Imagination

and applies as much to Coleridge-as-author as it does to Wordsworth-as-reader. When Coleridge wishes "to heaven, I might meet with many such readers," he colloquially paraphrases Milton's invocation of a "fit audience though few," which Wordsworth quoted in the "Prospectus" to *The Recluse* and alluded to in his "Essay, Supplementary" by way of disputing Dr. Johnson's estimate of *Paradise Lost*.

This accumulation of connective rhetorical tissue continues in Coleridge's epigraph to chapter XIII, from Book V of *Paradise Lost,* where Taylor's unification benediction is repeated in a higher key: the "one Almighty . . . from whom / All things proceed, and up to him return." Chapter XIII is the only chapter in the entire *Biographia* with an epigraph, and it has three: from Milton, Leibniz, and the neoplatonic Christian poet-bishop, Synesius. The latter two assert the reality of mental phenomena, but Milton comes first because his description of God evokes the more important aspect of Imagination for Coleridge and the tradition he represents: not simply its existence, but its godlike, unifying, opposite-reconciling force, its *esemplasm* (to make or force into one).[27] Coming at the beginning of chapter XIII of the *Biographia,* Milton's thoroughly developmental "gradual scale sublim'd . . . whence the soul / Reason receives" nicely parallels, perhaps not coincidentally, Wordsworth's "perfect image of a mighty Mind" at the beginning of Book XIII of *The Prelude*. Like the vision from Snowdon, with its "express resemblance" between the creative Power in Nature and "the glorious faculty / Which higher minds bear with them as their own," chapter XIII of the *Biographia* also climbs toward a visionary peak that will intuit rather than demonstrate the workings of Imagination, and also points for validation to a subsequent Coleridgean work. In *The Prelude,* it is "*Thy* monument of glory" (*Prel.* XIII.430); in the *Biographia,* it is "your great book on the CONSTRUCTIVE PHILOSOPHY" (*BL,* I.302).

From behind this sequence of allusive buffers, Coleridge leaps into his metaphysical argument by means of Schelling's analogy between Descartes and "the transcendental philosopher" that shuts its eyes to all the many ways in which these two philosophers, as materialism and idealism, simply cannot be analogized. The *Recluse*-ideal of a philosophically informed poetry manifests itself throughout chapter XIII's three-part structure, moving from an opening logical-metaphysical thesis, to a closing religious-supernatural synthesis, by means of a middle antithesis based on personal, practical considerations of tact and sensibility—Coleridge's self-composed letter from a "friend" urging him to abandon his project as he has "thus far" carried it out.

Although almost all of the first part is cribbed or summarized from Schelling, Fichte, and Kant (*BL*, I.296n–300n.), Coleridge's selection of his plagiarized material is, as usual, apt and to the point not only of his general philosophic argument but also the specific intertextual context existing between him and Wordsworth. He first uses Schelling's polarities of nature's infinite expansion and man's infinite efforts at self-comprehension to recapitulate *The Prelude* on a philosophic scale: "and as it were represent its [Intelligence's] history to the mind from its birth to its maturity" (I.297). Though the logic is nearly impenetrable because of Schelling-Coleridge's failure to keep clear the identities of the two polarities, Coleridge's controlling figure for Kant, "an effective pioneer," is appropriately military—"establishing and pacifying the unsettled, warring and embroiled domain of philosophy"—for a specialized history of philosophy that will devolve from Aristotle into a Coleridgean definition of Imagination, as Wordsworth's specialized literary history used military figures (Alexander, Hannibal, and the Bonapartes) to get from Shakespeare to a definition of Wordsworthian genius. At the end of this march of mind, we get a glimpse of the partly personal identity of his two opposing forces when he concludes his awfully obscure discussion with the defensive statement that not everyone will be able to understand his conclusion because "There is a philosophic, no less than a poetic genius, which is differenced from the highest perfection of talent, not by degree but by kind." Or, to paraphrase freely from the intimate rhetorical situation which obtains here: I understand this by my philosophic genius as intuitively and irrefutably as Wordsworth understands his poetical genius in the "Essay, Supplementary." Talent and genius were the personal traits commonly attributed by eighteenth-century aestheticians (*BL*, I.31n.5) to the faculties of Fancy and Imagination, respectively; Wordsworth had once discriminated pointedly between himself and Coleridge on these same grounds: "[He] observed of himself that he [unlike Coleridge] has comparatively but little talent; genius is his characteristic quality" (*Prose*, iii.85). Coleridge doubtless agreed with such distinctions insofar as they distinguished between him and Wordsworth as poets. But when it came to philosophy the shoe was on the other foot, or was here thrust upon it, as an assertion of his fitness to understand his own argument, relative to "he [who] will judge."

Their terminological hair-splitting over whether the words *evoke, combine, associate,* and *aggregate* could describe Imagination in *kind,* or only *degrees* of Fancy, had deep personal roots. Assessments of degrees versus kinds of difference form a dialectical pattern throughout Wordsworth's prefaces and essays of 1814–15, and while such distinctions are of

course the very staple of philosophic discourse, reference to a private polemical context here is more apt than casual, since it is just as this point,
when we come to the "tertium aliquid [which] can be no other than an
inter-penetration of the counteracting powers, partaking of both," that the
ellipses cross the page, and we enter the second part of chapter XIII, the
letter "from a friend whose practical judgment I have had ample reason to
estimate and revere, and whose taste and sensibility preclude all the ex-
cuses" which Coleridge might make against his advice. Just at the point,
that is, of naming the "third something" resultant from his two great
counteracting powers, the names of which it has been the boast of his
"philosophic genius" to know, he writes a letter to himself recommending
that he cease and desist.[28] Imagination as valued by Coleridge cannot be
defined further by the method he has adopted,[29] for he is at the point of
originary knowing/creating within the system of human representations of
which the conception of God is the originary point of knowing/creating
without. It can be believed in, and its works pointed out and praised, but
its mysterious workings can hardly be demonstrated—leaving it, like the
notion of God, open to the charge of nonexistence or irrelevance by persons who insist on other ways of knowing, and who are capable of living
and understanding human life valuably without it. So, whether considered
as a literal failure of nerve or as the ultimate refinement in ironically self-
conscious artistry,[30] Coleridge's epistolary device (like most of his plagia-
risms) certainly comes at the right place in his argument, extricating him
from an impasse.

The device's usefulness is not exploded when we know that the letter
was written by Coleridge himself, any more than the person from Porlock
invalidates the unity of "Kubla Khan."[31] As a letter to himself, in what
persona does he write? The "friend" need have no referent at all, other
than Coleridge's own measure of the qualities attributed to him (practical
judgment, taste, sensibility, tact, and feeling), but since several of these not
even Coleridge would have laid large claim to in 1815, who else might be
his persona? One candidate stood right at his elbow while these words
were being written (John Morgan), but in light of the letter's dominant imagery and specific arguments, coupled with Coleridge's suddenly accelerated composition beginning after his May 30 letter to Wordsworth, I believe that Coleridge is writing to himself as he had written to Wordsworth,
and as if Wordsworth were now writing to him—albeit a Wordsworth
who speaks in playful Coleridgean ironies. In his May 30 letter, Coleridge
had spoken discouragingly about what Wordsworth had produced (*The
Excursion*) by reference to another work *(The Recluse)* that he had not

produced; in his letter to himself, he discourages himself in the work that
he is producing (the *Biographia*) by reference to another much larger work
"your great book on the CONSTRUCTIVE PHILOSOPHY") that he has not yet
produced. Furthermore, his objection to his own philosophizing as an im-
position on readers who from his title page would be led to expect an autobiographical work, "published too as introductory to a volume of miscellaneous poems," juggles elements of philosophy, autobiography, and
poetry in ratios similar to his May 30 objections to Wordsworth's first in-
stallment on his "philosophical poem," relative to his autobiographical
work (*The Prelude*), on the one hand, and his poetry of "commonplace
Truths" (*Poems . . . Miscellaneous Pieces*), on the other. Finally, the May
30 letter set forth the same philosophy of creative mind which Coleridge,
after his self-interrupting letter, goes on to adumbrate, pretending self-
protectively (as in "Kubla Khan") that he has not made himself clear. Although the letter twits Coleridge at Wordsworth's expense, the difficulty
of conceiving what it means to twit oneself *at another's expense* is perfectly appropriate to the density of cross-reference, or cross-fire, with
which we are here confronted.

The letter divides into two parts: the friend's personal reaction to the
progress of chapter XIII "thus far," and his estimate of its effect upon the
public. Throughout, the controlling question is, What follows (or should
follow) from what? and applies equally to stages of philosophical argument and sequences of forthcoming publications. Intellectually, the friend's
reaction is that his understanding has been placed in the state of "*bull*,"
which he defines by reference to Coleridge's footnote in chapter IV explaining reviewers' "unexampled opposition" to Wordsworth's theories,
relative to their recognition of his genius. (A *bull* "consists in the bringing
together two incompatible thoughts, with the *sensation*, but without the
sense, of their connection . . . 'I was a fine child, but they changed me'";
I.72.) This imbalance between recognition of genius and misapprehension
of its theoretical definition is the same one Wordsworth had established in
the original opening paragraph of the "Essay, Supplementary" (*Prose*,
iii.62n.). Thus the friend has the sensation, but not the sense, of this connection, just as reviewers' had the sensation (poetical) of Wordsworth's
genius but not the sense (philosophical) of it—at least not as Wordsworth
had argued it in his 1800 Preface to *Lyrical Ballads*.

The friend's elaboration of chapter XIII's effect on his *feelings* draws
still closer to the *Recluse* context of 1814–15. Its controlling image is the
sensation of having been transported "and left alone, in one of our largest

Gothic cathedrals in a gusty moonlight night of autumn," a Coleridgean complement to the "gothic church" in the preface to *The Excursion,* from which Wordsworth had spun out all his organic analogies for the unity of his poems and the coherence of his genius. Coleridge's cathedral is more palpable—set to verse, it would do well in "Christabel," to which he alludes—and its purpose clearer than Wordsworth's. Wordsworth's gothic image suggested unity-in-diversity; Coleridge's, transvaluation of the familiar into the strange, and vice versa. As a metaphor for his *chapter* on Imagination, its main external characteristic is its distinction from "light airy modern chapels of ease," and its main internal feature is its revaluation of human intellect: "Those whom I had been taught to venerate as almost superhuman in magnitude of intellect, I found perched in little fretwork niches, as grotesque dwarfs; while the grotesques, in my hitherto belief, stood guarding the high altar with all the characters of Apotheosis" (*BL,* I.301). In self-deprecatory joking, he nonetheless accurately distinguishes his argument from the clear and light, but easy and airy, philosophical arguments of prevailing Cartesian empirical modes and defends the primacy he has given to obscure thinkers (Plotinus, Boehme, Bruno, Schelling) relative to the famous ones he has criticized (Aristotle, Descartes, Bacon, Hartley) by a free adaptation of the gothic image which has been the archetype of spiritual transformation throughout *The Recluse.* This cathedral of human genius is also an architectural complement to Wordsworth's history of English genius in the "Essay, Supplementary." Coleridge's transformation of superhuman intellects into dwarfs, and apotheosis of ostensible dwarfs into giants, visually complements Wordsworth's image of great writers struggling against initial ignorant rejection to create the taste by which they are to be enjoyed, as contrasted with the immediately popular non-great (Pope, Thomson), who would certainly be found, were the two images conflated, in "our light airy modern chapels of ease." As a visionary scene, Coleridge's high altar recasts *The Prelude*'s "Characters of the great Apocalypse" into comic "characters of Apotheosis," but with irony directed only at the difficulty of expressing and apprehending the vision, not at its object.

These deep cross-references are clinched in the friend's backhandedly generous concession, "Yet after all, I could not but repeat the lines which you had quoted from a MS. poem of your own in *The Friend* and applied to a work of Mr. Wordsworth's, though with a few words altered." This is Coleridge-as-Wordsworth citing Coleridge-on-Wordsworth, for the lines, though they indeed appeared in *The Friend* in 1809, are the same ones

with which Coleridge had ended his quotation from "To William Wordsworth" in his letter of May 30, now repeated to express rueful admiration
for the extravagance of Coleridge's genius, in comparison to Wordsworth's:

May 30, 1815	Chap. XIII (ca. Sept. 15, 1815)
—AN ORPHIC SONG INDEED,	—An orphic tale indeed,
A SONG DIVINE OF HIGH AND PASSION- ATE TRUTHS	A Tale *obscure* of high and passionate thoughts
TO THEIR OWN MUSIC CHAUNTED!	To *a strange* music chaunted!

Although Wordsworth's autobiographical song is divinely self-sufficient
("to *their own music* chaunted"), Coleridge's strange obscurities are by no
means entirely humiliated in the comparison, nor by the other words he al-
ters but does not italicize, as Wordsworth's *song* becomes Coleridge's *tale*,
and the former's *truths* the latter's *thoughts*. As a self-quoting, self-substi-
tuting piece of literary criticism, Coleridge's citation of these lines is perfectly insightful and has the effect of elevating, by appearing to ridicule, his
thirteenth chapter on Imagination into company with the thirteenth book
of Wordsworth's "MS. poem" on the same subject. We recall that
Coleridge's manuscript poem on Wordsworth's manuscript poem had been
the immediate occasion of their briefly but intensely renewed correspondence in late May. At such points of contact in the *Biographia* we are
reading not so much a published book as a privately coded communication
between two friends; to cite his manuscript poem on Wordsworth's manuscript poem is to make "the poem to Coleridge" a gloss on Coleridge's literary biography by the intermediation of Coleridge's poem "To William
Wordsworth."

The friend's estimate of the effect of Coleridge's chapter on the *public*,
though apt for the *Biographia*, also draws from objections that had been
raised against *The Recluse*, Wordsworth's public and private reactions to
them, and Coleridge's knowledge of both. Indeed, when the friend introduces his objections by saying, "if I may recur to my former illustration,"
and images the faulty chapter as being "like the fragments of the winding
steps of an old ruined tower" (*BL*, I.303), he sounds so much like Wordsworth "continuing this allusion" (of the "gothic church") into the image
of his minor poems as "the little cells, oratories, and sepulchral recesses,
ordinarily included in those edifices" (Preface to *The Excursion*) that it is
easier to imagine Coleridge writing this friend's letter with Wordsworth's
preface open before him than any other way. This is as far from plagiarism
as criticism is from creation: a very negotiable distance. In both texts, ex-

pectations of a balance between poetry and autobiography are upset by the intervention of philosophy; Coleridge's "friend" assures him that his chapter will find its "proper place" in his "greater work," as guaranteed by "your prospectus [which] will have described and announced both its contents and their nature." A similarly futuristic placing of things in proper order closes *The Excursion*'s preface, with "a kind of *Prospectus* of the design and scope of the whole Poem."

Though Coleridge never published any such prospectus, his immediately subsequent statement of "the main result" of his chapter (the famous definitions of imagination) has sufficiently established "a philosophical vestibule" to his creative ideal for subsequent generations (in the excellent formulation of Engell and Bate; *BL*, I.lvi), as Wordsworth's autobiographical "ante-chapel" and "Prospectus" do for his *Recluse*-ideal. The definitions of imagination are the third part of chapter XIII, transmuting its opening logical-metaphysical deductions into theological-supernatural analogies, the secondary or creative imagination being the "echo" of the power (primary imagination) of "all human perception," which in turn is "a repetition in the finite mind of the eternal act of creation in the infinite I AM." The analogy is one of self-validating self-consciousness, simultaneously product and process. These analogies proceed by linear connections, and are thus markedly different in their relationship from the chapter's opening logical deductions, in which a *tertium aliquid* was to to have been the "product" of two infinite, polar, "*counter*acting powers." The secondary imagination stands in a much different subsidiary relation to the primary imagination and to God than the *tertium aliquid* does to its constitutive contraries, evidently weaker (as an "echo" of a "repetition"),[32] but perhaps more certain and certainly more human, as "it dissolves, diffuses, dissipates, in order to re-create; or where this process is rendered impossible, yet still, at all events, it struggles to idealize and to unify." The secondary imagination can do something that the *tertium aliquid* cannot: it can fail and start over.[33]

This tactful distancing of creative imagination from both philosophic certainty and divine creativity has its own parallel in the text, in the horizons Coleridge casts up between himself and any further definition of it, mirroring the allusive buffers he set up at the chapter's beginning. Between "the main result" just stated of the *proposed* chapter and Coleridge's narration at this moment in chapter XIII we find: (1) the chapter as "reserved" for, (2) "that future publication," (3) "a detailed prospectus of which the reader will find at the close of the second volume," (4) supplemented by "whatever more than this I shall think it fit to declare concern-

ing the powers and privileges of the imagination in the present work," (5)
to be "found in the critical essay on the uses of the supernatural in poetry
and the principles that regulate its introduction," (6) "which the reader
will find prefixed to the poem of *The Ancient Mariner.*" These are the last
words of chapter XIII and of volume I of the *Biographia Literaria.* That
only one of the texts referred to existed, or ever came into existence, is perhaps less important than the imprimatur of authority suggested by Coleridge's citing the title of that one, his most famous poem and a work of
"pure imagination," as his last word, so that we may feel indisposed to argue definitions of imagination with the man who could write this poem.
But Coleridge gave as good as he got. As a self-conscious, self-destructing
fragment, exploding itself with ammunition that he took from and used
against Wordsworth—part logic, part metaphysics, part literary criticism,
part confession, part theology, and part prospectus—chapter XIII's true
generic character is not that of chapter, still less of a conclusion, but of a
set of notes or jottings, providing in public form what the May 30 letter
had conveyed privately, the explanation Coleridge had been promising
Wordsworth on and off for twenty years: of a philosophical poem containing "pictures of Nature, Man, and Society . . . [whose] title will be *The
Recluse*" (*LEY,* 212, 214).

What follows is the already written critique of Wordsworth's
strengths and weaknesses, chapters XIV–XXII, volume II of the *Biographia,* in which Coleridge accepts for purposes of public discussion the
"Wordsworth" created by Wordsworth's turning the *Recluse*-ideal into a
defense of his own life and existing works. But what also follows, in a
larger sense, is the second half of Coleridge's career, arguably the more important half. Beginning with the huge effort of composing his *Biographia*
in 1815, Coleridge produced during the remaining nineteen years of his life
the major works of cultural criticism on which his general intellectual
value to Western civilization (as distinct from his specific artistic reputation) is founded. The *Biographia* was for Coleridge as important a point of
self-origination as *The Prelude* was for Wordsworth, and the most intense
point in the process was Coleridge's reappropriation of the *Recluse*-ideal
of a philosophically informed poetry requiring a philosophically informed
criticism. Though *The Prelude* and the *Biographia* are, as often noted, the
true companion pieces of these two geniuses, *The Recluse* was for both the
very name and form of their genius. It was the poetic reflection of Coleridge's magnum opus, which, like Wordsworth's *Recluse,* we have grown
accustomed to regarding as a phantom or a failure, but which, like *The Re-*

cluse, we are now rediscovering amid the voluminous unpublished fragments of its author's literary remains.

The power of this transfer is also indicated by what happened in
Wordsworth's career after 1815, having exposed *The Recluse* to the world
and to Coleridge and, disappointed from both quarters, abandoning it forever. Though I have never felt any strong need to defend or deny Wordsworth's "decline," it can certainly be dated from 1815, and its main cause
claimed to be the separation of Wordsworth's imaginative motivation
from *The Recluse,* which occurred then.[34] After 1815, Wordsworth's major imaginative activity became the refinement and republication of his collected works in the order first adopted then as complementary to *The Recluse.*[35] Wordsworth had made good use of the idea of poetic or artistic
truth represented by *The Recluse.* Not only did he write far more of the
poem itself than we have heretofore recognized, a fragment large enough
and good enough to stand with *The Canterbury Tales* and *The Faerie
Queene,* but it also provided a motivational context for almost all of his
greatest poetry, as he clearly indicated in his 1815 Preface, by linking the
order of his poems to the system of *The Recluse.*

It is fitting in the deep imaginative economy of supply and demand
between these two men that the ideal should now return to its primogeni-
tor and similarly provide a motivational context for his most important
legacy to us. For it is via Coleridge's criticism—or more accurately the
ideal informing his criticism—that *The Recluse* is with us today: all literature regarded as "views of Man, Nature, and Human Life," explained as
the workings of a real human power (Imagination), the defense and pro-
mulgation of which provides the institutional charter for organized study
of art in modern democratic societies. This is our own "philosophical
poem," attempting to humanize the progress of civilization on a much
wider scale than Coleridge imagined in his definition of the "clerisy,"
which gave a real social form to Wordsworth's world-vision of "culture
unexclusively bestowed" at the end of *The Excursion:*

> The Clerisy of the nation, or national church, in its primary acceptation
> and original intention comprehended the learned of all denomina-
> tions;—the sages and professors of the law and jurisprudence; of medi-
> cine and physiology; of music; of military and civil architecture; of the
> physical sciences; with the mathematical as the common *organ* of the pre-
> ceding; in short, all the so called liberal arts and sciences, the possession
> and application of which constitute the civilization of a country, as well
> as the Theological. The last was, indeed, placed at the head of all; and of
> good right did it claim the precedence. But why? Because under the name

of Theology, or Divinity, were contained the interpretation of languages; the conservation and tradition of past events; the momentous epochs, and revolutions of the race and nation; the continuation of the records; logic, ethics, and the determination of ethical science, in application to the rights and duties of men in all their various relations, social and civil; and lastly, the ground-knowledge, the prima scientia as it was named, —PHILOSOPHY, or the doctrine and discipline of *ideas*.[36]

Yet the ideal is, if anything, now more vulnerable than Coleridge's definition in chapter XIII of the *Biographia*, far more comprehensively established but no more certainly influencing the realm of "Human Life," to connect with which was the glory and the doom of *The Recluse*. We are still trying to demonstrate, or enact, the aptness of imagination to social reality, but as our definitions of its enabling power are refined scientifically, they seem evermore to retreat defensively into academia—protected but ineffectual, like endangered species on a game preserve, as Jürgen Habermas has suggested: "Perhaps the process of petrification of our administered consciousness has progressed so far that insensitivity to what in more naive times philosophers called 'the good life' can only be broken through today under the sociopsychologically exceptional conditions of university study."[37] But if this view of modern university culture sounds uncannily like Wordsworth's ideal university ("a domain for quiet things to wander in," *Prelude* III.449–50), its defense has also been anticipated by the *The Recluse*'s ideal: imaginative power held in philosophical reserve.

Notes

CHAPTER 1

1 *LEY*, 76, 113, 118–20, 123–28, 134–36; Wordsworth's summary of *The Philanthropist*'s contents gives an idea of the large scope it shared with *The Recluse*, which was contributory to its similar reasons for failing to appear: (1) general political news and comment; (2) essays on morals and manners and "institutions whether social or political"; (3) essays for instruction and amusement, particularly biographical sketches of libertarian heroes like Milton and Sidney, arranged "as much as possible [to] form a series exhibiting the advancement of the human mind in moral knowledge"; (4) essays on taste and criticism, works of imagination and fiction; (5) reviews; (6) "some poetry," but no original compositions, to avoid the "trash" infesting most journals; and (7) reports of parliamentary debates and selected state papers (*LEY*, 125–26).

2 Alexander Pope, *An Essay on Man*, ed. Maynard Mack (London: Methuen, 1947), xi-xii, 7. The subjects of the *Essay*'s four epistles are closely comparable to *The Recluse*'s: man in relation to the universe, to his own personality, to society, and to happiness.

3 E. P. Thompson, "Disenchantment or Default?," in *Power and Consciousness*, ed. O'Brien and Vanech (New York: NYU Press, 1969), 169.

4 Butler's account (x–xi) suggests the addition of from 300 to 600 lines, double or triple the length of the 1797 version, the estimate varying according to how many lines describing the Pedlar are considered to be part of the poem at any given time.

5 Finch, "On the Dating of *Home at Grasmere*," in *Bicentenary Wordsworth Studies*, ed. Jonathan Wordsworth and Beth Darlington (Ithaca, N.Y.: Cornell University Press, 1970), 14–15; Reed, *CEY*, 223n.–224n.; De Selincourt, *Prelude*, xiv–xvi. All authorities stress that the identification of the 1,300 lines cannot be certain, but no other poems have been plausibly suggested, except the "Prospectus," which is now authoritatively dated somewhat later.

6 Butler, 14–22.

7   R. L. Brett and A. R. Jones estimate that the poem was "probably begun as
    early as 1795" (*Lyrical Ballads* [London: Methuen, 1968], 294–95).

8   In his evidence for including "A Night-Piece" in the 1,300 *Recluse* lines, Finch
    stresses the similarity of its narrative situation to "The Discharged Soldier"
    (45–47).

9   The definitive account of the text is Darlington's, "Two Early Texts: *A Night-
    Piece* and *The Discharged Soldier*," in *BWS*, 425–48.

10 By the time he became a captain, in 1800, John Wordsworth was, like all the
    company's commanders, more than an employee, an entrepreneurial investor
    in his own right (M. I.32–33; Frank Rand, *Wordsworth's Mariner Brother*
    (Amherst, Mass.: The Jones Library, 1966), 13–47).

11 Fawcett was the main model for the Pedlar-Wanderer. For the influence of his
    poetic and political style on Wordsworth, see G. M. Harper, *William Words-
    worth* (New York: Scribner's, 1916), 261–64.

12 Bad harvests in 1794 were followed by one of the worst winters on record,
    which destroyed much of the seed-grain in the ground, resulting in a doubling
    of the price of wheat and leading to bread riots in Nottingham, Coventry, and
    Sussex in 1795 (Butler, 4).

13 Sheats, 91; "If we could erect a little cottage and call it *our own* we should be
    the happiest of human beings. I see my Brother fired with the idea of leading
    his sister to such a retreat as Fancy ever ready at our call hastens to assist us in
    painting" (*LEY*, 97; 10 July 1793); Bateson notes at the end of *An Evening
    Walk* "precisely the prospect" of the next logical step for Wordsworth's life in
    1793: a country curacy, with Dorothy as his housekeeper. *Wordsworth: A Re-
    Interpretation* (London: Longmans, 1954), 80.

14 "To be attached to the subdivision, to love the little platoon we belong to in
    society, is the first principle (the germ as it were) of public affections. It is the
    first link in the series by which we proceed towards a love to our country and
    to mankind." *Reflections on the Revolution in France*, ed. Conor Cruise
    O'Brien (London: Penguin, 1968), 135; Burke set this little platoon in oppo-
    sition to "the unnatural universals" of revolutionary ideology (Friedman, 92).

15 Finch, 12.

16 M. I.293; citing Coleridge's report to Thelwall (*LSTC*, I.216).

17 Finch notes the subtitle's similarities and cites other late eighteenth-century
    uses of the main title, such as Charlotte Smith's *Ethelinde, or the Recluse of
    the Lake* (21–23); Thelwall's favor among intellectual radicals like Coleridge
    and Southey derived from his having been one of the three principals in the
    1794 Treason Trials; he had been for a time the most effective radical orator
    in London (Donald Reiman, "Introduction," *Ode to Science, John Gilpin's
    Ghost,* and *Poems Written Chiefly in Retirement* (New York: Garland, 1978),
    v–vii; Albert Goodwin, *The Friends of Liberty* (Cambridge, Mass.: Harvard
    University Press, 1979), 318–22, 472–67).

18 The standard work on the subject is Brian Wilkie, *Romantic Poets and Epic
    Tradition* (Madison: University of Wisconsin Press, 1965).

19 Finch, 17.

20 Ibid., 15.

21 Ibid., 23.

22 Lewis Patton, "Editor's Introduction," *The Watchman, The Collected Works*

of Samuel Taylor Coleridge (Princeton: Princeton University Press, 1970), 2: xxxix.

23 John Thelwall, *The Peripatetic,* ed. Donald H. Reiman (New York: Garland, 1978), 1:49–50.

24 Ibid., 127. Cf. "A captive greets thee, coming from a house / Of bondage, from yon City's walls set free, / A prison where he hath been long immured" (*Prelude* I.6–8).

25 "Wordsworth on Man, on Nature, and on Human Life," *Studies in Romanticism* 21 (1982): 601–18.

26 Jonathan Wordsworth indicates some of the millenarian and pantheistic *assumptions* that were to have informed *The Recluse* but similarly concludes that "there is no evidence that [Coleridge's] influence in the early period led to positive definitions, or to a system that could have formed a basis for *The Recluse*" (*Borders,* 340–55); cf. *MH,* 108, 195n.

27 *The Philosophic Mind* (Columbus: Ohio State University Press, 1973), 70–71.

28 For my more particular statements about Coleridge's philosophical views, I am indebted, here and throughout, primarily to the following works: W. J. Bate, *Coleridge* (New York: Collier, 1968); Thomas McFarland, *Coleridge and the Pantheist Tradition* (Oxford: Clarendon Press, 1969); J. A. Appleyard, *Coleridge's Philosophy of Literature* (Cambridge, Mass.: Harvard University Press, 1965); Jerome Christensen, *Coleridge's Blessed Machine of Language* (Ithaca, N.Y.: Cornell University Press, 1981).

29 A century of scholarly work has been devoted to this effort, largely to answer Matthew Arnold's charge that the Romantic poets "did not know enough . . . [that] Wordsworth even, profound as he is, [is] yet so wanting in completeness and variety" ("The Function of Criticism at the Present Time," 1865). The line of scholarly response runs mainly from A. C. Bradley's lectures in the 1890s, through the work of Arthur Beatty, R. D. Havens, and Melvin Rader on the primary intellectual foundations of Wordsworth's thought, to an effective conclusion in Newton Stallknecht's *Strange Seas of Thought* (1945), which demonstrated the presence in Wordsworth's poetry of knowledge more various than Arnold dreamed of. The value of philosophical approaches to Wordsworth has been revived for the present generation by Alan Grob and Jonathan Wordsworth, and most recently by John Hodgson, *Wordsworth's Philosophical Poetry, 1797–1814* (Lincoln: University of Nebraska Press, 1980).

30 Finch, 15, 27.

31 Butler, 392, 394. I quote MS E for clarity; the same passage occurs in MS B, app. crit. (Butler, 151), identified as from early 1798 (17, 131). All references to "The Ruined Cottage" in this section are from Butler's transcriptions of MS B, the likeliest version of 1798; references to MS D, the state of the poem in 1799, will be noted as such.

32 Butler, 17, citing the Fenwick note (1843) from the Dove Cottage Papers.

33 H. W. Piper, *The Active Universe* (London: Athlone Press, 1962), 73n. Jonathan Wordsworth strongly qualifies Piper, pointing out that between 1794 and 1798 Wordsworth wrote no more about the "One Life," that at most he held only a vague general belief in animated matter, and that he had neither a

fullness of belief in such things nor any "total scheme of things" into which he could fit his social observations about human suffering and happiness (*MH*, 185–87, 108, 202).

34 Butler (21) excludes some of these lines from the early March 1798 version of the poem, but states (19–20) that there is "no way of knowing" whether these additions to MS B are closer in time to the March 1798 version or the 1799 version (MS D); cf. *MH*, 162.

35 In this form, the lines probably date from 1799 (Butler, 282, 372n.); ultimately, they became part of Book IV of *The Excursion*.

36 *Wordsworth and the Poetry of Human Suffering*, Ithaca, N.Y.: Cornell University Press, 1980. Friedman interprets the narrators' encounters with ravaged, marginal beings as the meeting of Wordsworth's "princely" self with his weak, insecure alter ego (19, 30–32); Onorato notes the poet's tendency to approach social realism via scenes of passionate distress and his own involvement in them (324).

37 Cf. Sheats, 85, 93.

38 Hartman interprets the young man's lack of motive as the necessary but unconscious "murder" of innocent, "nature-involved," unselfconsciousness in a progress toward "the enlightened pain of self-consciousness" (*WP*, 133–34).

39 Sheats, 133–34.

40 De Selincourt, *PW*, I.375.

41 This question will arise explicitly at the end of "Home at Grasmere": "Why does this inward lustre [his genius] fondly seek / And gladly blend with outward fellowship? / Why shine they round me thus, whom thus I love? / Why do they teach me, whom I thus revere? / Strange question, yet it answers not itself" (cf. chap. 6).

42 Butler, 468–69. Reed (*CEY*, 193) dates it March-June 1797, when Wordsworth was completing "The Ruined Cottage" as the "new poem" to read to Coleridge; Butler suggests the lines were originally part of "The Ruined Cottage" (461).

43 Butler, 461.

44 Butler's transcription shows that some of these lines—the physical action without the mental valuation—originally described the Pedlar (84–87).

45 1850 *Prelude*, IV.359.

46 Jacques Lacan, "Of Structure as an Inmixing of an Otherness Prerequisite to Any Subject Whatever," in *The Languages of Criticism and the Sciences of Man: The Structuralist Controversy*, ed. Macksey and Donato (Baltimore: Johns Hopkins University Press, 1970), 186–200. Cf. Leslie Brisman, *Romantic Origins* (Ithaca, N.Y.: Cornell University Press, 1978), for an extension of some of these insights to the reading of English Romantic poetry.

47 "A Night-Piece" has come to be accepted by many critics as a laboratory sample of Wordsworth's visionary elements in their essential purity. Cf. Karl Kroeber, *Romantic Narrative Art* (Madison: University of Wisconsin Press, 1960), 51–53; Frederick Garber, *The Poetry of Encounter* (Urbana: University of Illinois Press, 1971), 80–85; K. R. Johnston, "The Idiom of Vision," in *New Perspectives on Coleridge and Wordsworth*, ed. Geoffrey Hartman (New York: Columbia University Press, 1972), 10–25; Jonathan Wordsworth,

"The Climbing of Snowdon," in *BWS*, 454–56; Robert Barth, *The Symbolic Imagination* (Princeton, N.J.: Princeton University Press, 1977), 52–54; James Kissane, "'A Night-Piece': Wordsworth's Emblem of the Mind," *Modern Language Notes* 81 (1956): 183–86; David Ferry, *The Limits of Mortality* (Middletown, Conn.: Wesleyan University Press, 1960), 30–31.

48 Wordsworth's principal revision of the poem for inclusion in *The Prelude* cut 28 lines describing the helpless, pathetic qualities of the Soldier, "Thus stressing the power to endure suffering rather than the suffering itself" (Darlington, *BWS*, 429–30).

49 Cf. Hartman's use of the "Halted Traveler" motif (*Siste, viator*) as the emblem of his argument for the radically human, antinatural impulses of Wordsworth's imagination (*WP*, 1–30).

50 Phillip Cohen, "Narrative and Persuasion in *The Ruined Cottage*," *Journal of Narrative Technique* 8 (1978): 185–99, summarizes the critical tradition on both sides, arguing in favor of the balanced focus Wordsworth achieves in the version of *The Excursion*, Book I. Cleanth Brooks states the two critical choices the poem offers for consolation, one based on a distanced view of natural process, the other on the aesthetic vision of tragedy ("Wordsworth and Human Suffering: Notes on Two Early Poems," in *From Sensibility to Romanticism*, ed. Hilles and Bloom (Oxford, 1965), 373–87).

51 All references to "The Ruined Cottage" in this section are to the Reading Text of MS B in Butler's edition (42–72), unless otherwise noted.

52 The text and relevance of the Goethe fragments are presented in *MH*, 261–68; Butler restates the connections with Lamb's *Tale of Rosamund Gray* and *Old Blind Margaret* (1798) and Southey's *Joan of Arc* (1796), 5–6; Averill analyzes its place in the eighteenth-century tradition of sentimental drama (56–61, 116–41).

53 *MH*, 92.

54 Mary Jacobus, *Tradition and Experiment in "Lyrical Ballads"* (Oxford, 1976), 176–77.

55 Charles Patterson, "The Still Sad Music of Humanity in *The Excursion*: Wordsworth's Tragic View of Man," *Milton and the Romantics*, 4 (1980): 35–36.

56 *WP*, 135–40.

57 Cited in *MH*, 134n.

58 Reeve Parker, "'Finer Distance': The Narrative Art of Wordsworth's 'The Wanderer,'" *ELH* 29 (March 1972): 87–111.

59 Averill, 58.

CHAPTER 2

1 "There is in fact a sense in which *1799* shows Wordsworth moving *away* from Coleridge." Jonathan Wordsworth and Stephen Gill, "The Two-Part *Prelude* of 1798–99," *JEGP* 72, (1973), 512.

2 Douglas, 43–45.

3 De Selincourt, xliii–viii; M. I.418–21; Douglas, 52–55; Wordsworth and Gill, 510; Hartman discusses this aspect of *The Prelude* as "the Puritan quest

for evidences of election [in] the most ordinary emotional contexts" (*WP*, 5–6).

4 James Averill, "Wordsworth and 'Natural Science': The Poetry of 1798," *JEGP* 77 (1978): 232–46.

5 Stephen Parrish, "The Growth of the Two-Part *Prelude*," in *The Prelude, 1798–1799* (Ithaca, N.Y.: Cornell University Press, 1977), 3–36; cf. also Wordsworth, Abrams, and Gill, 510–15. All line references to the 1799 *Prelude* are to the "Reading Text" established by Parrish (41–67), unless otherwise indicated. I have used the numerals "i" and "ii" for convenience in distinguishing the First Part and the Second Part and to avoid confusion with the books of the 1805 and 1850 *Prelude*, which are identified by large Roman numerals.

6 Douglas develops at length the "errant and profitless" character of Wordsworth's life in the 1790s (23–26, 37–39, 56).

7 Douglas argues persuasively that by 1799 unenthusiastic book reviewers and inept friends (Cottle, Southey) had replaced unsympathetic uncles in Wordsworth's image of the "harsh world" that was preventing him from realizing his needs (57–58).

8 Cited by Wordsworth and Gill, "The Two-Part *Prelude* of 1798–99," 513.

9 Hayden White, "Foucault Decoded," in *Tropics of Discourse* (Baltimore: Johns Hopkins University Press, 1978), 243.

10 Parrish, viii; J. R. MacGillivray, "The Three Forms of *The Prelude*, 1798–1805," in *Essays Presented to A. S. P. Woodhouse* (Toronto: University of Toronto Press, 1964), 236.

11 Abbie F. Potts, *Wordsworth's Prelude* (Ithaca, N.Y.: Cornell University Press, 1953), 68–76, 99–106; WAG, 513.

12 Wordsworth, Abrams, and Gill, x.

13. Bishop C. Hunt, in a review of Parrish's edition, *TWC* 8 (Summer 1977): 217–19; Wordsworth and Gill interpret *1799*'s allusions to "Frost at Midnight" as Wordsworth's acknowledgment "that this too had been a Conversation Poem" ("The Two-Part *Prelude*," *JEGP*, 518).

14 Cf. Michael Cooke, "The Mode of Argument in Wordsworth's Poetry," in *Acts of Inclusion: Studies Bearing on an Elementary Theory of Romanticism* (New Haven: Yale University Press, 1979), 186–215, for an extended discussion of "the fact that the romantics candidly acknowledged, confronted, and perhaps actually created an uncertain and 'problematical' situation" (187).

15 The first line begins with a lower case *w* in both early manuscripts, which suggests that Wordsworth meant to provide a clearer antecedent to his opening question (Wordsworth, Abrams, and Gill 513). His failure to do so until 1804–05, and subsequent capitalizations of *was* in fair-copy manuscripts, are constitutive acts that give the text what might be called "aperture" (as opposed to closure), making it more available to interpretation.

16 Pope, "Epistle to Arbuthnot," ll. 1–2; "Frost at Midnight" is quoted directly at i.8 and ii.496–97 (Wordsworth, Abrams, and Gill, 513); *Borders* cites several eighteenth-century precedents for the exact form of Wordsworth's question (420n.3).

17 John T. Ogden develops these implications of the question for pedagogical ap-

plication ("'Was It For This?'" *TWC* 9 (1978): 371–72); Finch (41) attributes the trouble implied by "this" primarily to Wordsworth's doubts that he really had the major poetic vocation implied by *The Recluse,* warning also that this doubt should not be connected (in reading the 1799 text) with the discontents specified in the 1805 version; Parrish (6) interprets some of Wordsworth's revisions as suggesting that "the tone of 'was it for this' may not, in fact, be ironic, or regretful, but wondering, perhaps confused, even perhaps quietly exultant"; Ogden similarly sees the *expressive* power of the question turning despair into joy ("The Structure of Imaginative Experience in Wordsworth's *Prelude,*" *TWC* 6 (1975): 296).

18 Finch (138–39); Parrish (6).

19 J. R. Watson, "Wordsworth's Card Games," *TWC* 6 (1975): 299–302; James Holt McGavran, Jr., "The 'Home-Amusements' Scene in *The Prelude* and the Speaker's 'Residences,'" *ELN* 16 (1978): 94–103.

20 Wordsworth states his thesis explicitly in a deleted draft version: "unusual was the power / Of that strange spectacle" (Parrish, 91; transcript of MS JJ).

21 The Boy of Winander passage ("There was a Boy") was once part of this sequence in MS JJ (Finch, 145, n.27); it matches identically the natural-to-supernatural pattern established by the other four episodes.

22 Finch, 142.

23 I do not mean to suggest that critics who have sought such connections are misguided; the passages are set up to *require* an effort of connection-making: this is what they are "about." Fittingly, they have stimulated some of the best close readings of any Wordsworthian texts, most notably Jonathan Bishop, "Wordsworth and the 'Spots of Time,'" *ELH* 26 (March 1959): 45–64.

24 Douglas, 51; M. I.443, citing *Memoirs,* I.159.

25 Finch, 143.

26 These touches are also examples of what Michael Friedman sees as Wordsworth's wish to attach older, precapitalist associations to the Lake District, despite changes in its economy already well underway (*The Making of a Tory Humanist,* 171–81 and passim).

27 Averill shows how this passage connects with the classifying vocabulary and specimen cabinets of eighteenth-century collector-scientists like Linnaeus ("Wordsworth and 'Natural Science,'" 235–36).

CHAPTER 3

1 Friedman, 191; cf. Fred V. Randel, "Wordsworth's Homecoming," *SEL* 17 (1977): 575–91, for incisive analysis of dialectical patterns of desire and frustration throughout Wordsworth's early poetic representations of homes.

2 A letter of 31 March 1799 from Dorothy's "Aunt" Rawson laments William's "spending his youth in so unprofitable a way" (*LEY,* 245n.).

3 Charles Lloyd and his new wife and baby arrived to reinforce the spreading domesticity, and within the year young Christopher Wordsworth was engaged to Lloyd's sister, Priscilla (M. I.520).

4 The Wordsworths also evinced a nascent anthropological interest in the

Lakes; Dorothy took considerable pains to describe the local dialects to
worldly friends like Lady Beaumont and Catherine Clarkson.

5 Finch, 182.

6 A still closer resemblance obtains between "Home at Grasmere" and the
"glad Preamble" to the 1805 *Prelude,* composed in November 1799 (Finch,
195); it could easily be inserted in "Home at Grasmere" without any noticeable disruption of tone or intention. Wordsworth and Gill (519) associate the
"glad Preamble's" mood of confidence with Wordsworth's hopes for *The Recluse;* M. H. Abrams attributes it to Wordsworth's choice of a place to live,
noting that the vale toward which he sets out in the Preamble is the Grasmere
of 1800 ("The Design of *The Prelude,*" in WAG, 595).

7 "Wordsworth's Unfinished Gothic Cathedral," *University of Toronto Quarterly* 32 (1963): 179; Stevenson's essay is a playfully suggestive extension of
Wordsworth's "gothic church" metaphor to the entirety of his collected works
(the Immortality Ode as the "high altar," and so on).

8 All line references, unless otherwise indicated, are to the Reading Text of MS
B, the earliest full text of the poem, in *"Home at Grasmere": Part First, Book
First, of "The Recluse,"* ed. Beth Darlington (Ithaca, N.Y.: Cornell University
Press, 1977), 38–106. This is not the same text printed in *PW,* V.313–39,
which is MS D, a considerably later reworked version. Darlington prints MS
D on pages facing MS B, while De Selincourt and Darbishire reproduce much
of MS B in their *apparatus criticus.*

9 "'Home at Grasmere': Reclusive Song," *Studies in Romanticism* 14 (1975):
1–28.

10 Darlington identifies lines 1–457 and 859–74 of MS B as belonging certainly
to 1800, and lines 875–958, a somewhat miscellaneous transition between
the narrative portions of the poem and its "Prospectus" conclusion
(959–1048), as also likely to have been constructed from lines composed in
1800 or earlier. Jonathan Wordsworth dates almost all of the poem's *composition* from 1800, while allowing its rounding off and consolidation into a coherent whole to be the product of 1806 (*RES,* n.s. 31 [1980]: 17–29), basing
his argument on qualities of tone, style, and preoccupation which he feels unlikely to have been possible in 1806 (i.e., after the death of John Wordsworth). He believes this dating receives "a great deal of support" from his
critical account in *The Borders of Vision* (98–148, 425–30). While I must respectfully refrain from entering into these differences between textual experts,
I continue to follow Darlington's division because I find her evidence more
persuasive, and believe that my critical reading of the poem gives added support to it. As with other textual cruxes in *The Recluse,* what is at issue is less
our understanding of a given text than of the bearing and sequence of such
understandings in larger discussions of Wordsworth's development; thus Jonathan Wordsworth's account of the poem is, like mine, divided into two
markedly different movements, which he calls "Paradise Regained" (ll.
1–667) and "The Serpent in Eden" (ll. 667–1048). All discussion of the two
dates for the poem derives from Finch, "On the Dating of *Home at Grasmere*:
A New Approach," *BWS,* 14–28, which demonstrated that the traditional

dating of its composition from its initial moments of inspiration (Spring 1800) was not supported by physical manuscript evidence.

11 I am indebted to Eva Gold for this observation. Wordsworth's inability to accept fully his rural retreat indicates his divergence from such possible literary models as Habington's *Castara* (Potts, 203–17) or Crevecoeur's *Letters from an American Farmer,* first published in England in 1782.

12 Cf. identical rhetoric from the contemporaneous "glad Preamble": "The earth is all before me . . . I cannot miss my way" (*Prel.* I.15, 19). "Braving" is Jonathan Wordsworth's apt term for much of Wordsworth's adaptation of Milton's style; he notes that Wordsworth moved rapidly from "playful" echoes of Milton in the Preamble to a thoroughgoing Miltonic *style* in the "Prospectus" ("Secession at Grasmere," *TLS* [26 March 1976], 355). Finch makes similar observations, also pointing out that Wordsworth himself anticipated these uses of Milton in some of his revisions of the Pedlar's "prophetic" character (198–99).

13 Lindenberger cites the poem's present-centered quality as unique in Wordsworth's works (163–66); Jonathan Wordsworth calls it "a poem of the present if there ever was" ("Secession," 354). Cf. also Karl Kroeber, "'Home at Grasmere': Ecological Holiness," *PMLA* 89 (1974): 132–41; William Heath, *Wordsworth and Coleridge: A Study of Their Literary Relations in 1801–1802* (Oxford, 1970), 11–16; Hartman, *WP*, 171–74; M. H. Abrams, *NS*, 288–92.

14 Muriel Mellown, "The Development of Imagery in 'Home at Grasmere,'" *TWC* 5 (1974): 23–27; Stephen Spector, "Wordsworth's Mirror Imagery and the Picturesque Tradition," *ELH* 44 (1977): 85–107.

15 Finch, 199.

16 Bruce Clarke interprets Wordsworth's intense language describing the swans as evidence of his sublimation of sexual feelings for Dorothy—one pair displacing the other in the destined home ("Wordsworth's Departed Swans: Sublimation and Sublimity in *Home at Grasmere,*" *SIR* 19 (1980): 355–74). While I would not want to underestimate the depths of feeling (conscious and unconscious) existing between this brother and sister, Clarke's analysis does not seem to me explanatory enough and fails to take into account the sociopolitical nature of the language Wordsworth used to correct his descriptive "error." Clark seeks to account for the "characteristic elision of sexual themes" in Wordsworth's poetry (357), but this may not be a relevant problem. However, if we are to imagine that Wordsworth's return to the Lakes, to a redefined conception of poetic vocation, and to a renewed commitment to a philosophic masterwork was also complicated by ambivalent sexual feelings for Dorothy, then Clarke's analysis has a bearing upon a history of *The Recluse*'s development.

17 These two lines are from MS D (269–70).

18 J. L. Austin, *How To Do Things with Words* (Cambridge, Mass.: Harvard University Press, 1962).

19 Friedman, 163–203.

20 MS A runs on for two more lines that show Wordsworth marking time until a

fitting closure of the simile might occur to him: "Or so it seems to be for it be-
fits it yet / Newcomer as I am to speak in doubt" (Darlington, 16).

21 Butler, 25 (citing DW, *Journals*, 96).

22 Cf. *MH*, passim., esp. 164–66.

23 Butler, 30.

24 Ibid., 329–31.

25 Moorman, I.367–68; cf. Owen and Smyser, *Prose*, III.11–12.

26 The dating of the "Prospectus" lines is perhaps the most vexed of *The Recluse*'s many textual cruxes. Darlington identifies "the period between spring,
1800, and early spring, 1802" as the likeliest time, while cautioning that exact
pinpointing is not possible (22). However, she assigns a version of it to quite
early in 1800, contemporaneous with the composition of "Home at Grasmere": ll. 959–1001 and 1015–1048—i.e., all but 13 lines of the final version (13). (Those 13 lines, everyone agrees, are an addition of ca. 1805–06.)
Scholars have long sought to establish an early date for the lines, as Reed explains: "no evidence . . . absolutely precludes composition—and such a speculation remains persistently appealing on the basis of content—between 1798
and 1800" (*CEY*, 665). Jonathan Wordsworth has argued for a ca. January
1800 date, *before* the composition of "Home at Grasmere," on the basis of its
very close similarities in spirit to the "glad Preamble" of November 1799
(*RES* [1980], 26–28). Such a date would affect the symmetry of my argument
but not its substance—i.e., that the "Prospectus" lines recapitulate the structure of "Home at Grasmere" in a high mythopoeic key.

27 This meaning is clarified in a later revision of reduced power: "Of madding
passions mutually inflamed" (MS D, line 828).

28 This reading of the "Prospectus," stressing internal tensions, should be contrasted and complemented with that of M. H. Abrams, who uses the stated intentions of the "Prospectus" as an interpretive device to open up an enormous
range of Romantic texts, under the rubric of their displacement or extension
of traditional religious topoi into modern secular forms (*NS*, passim, especially 19–32, 463–79).

29 Wordsworth and Gill, 521.

30 "Stanzas in Memory of the Author of 'Obermann,'" ll. 53–54.

31 Finch notes the parallel to Milton (229–30).

32 Ibid., 219.

CHAPTER 4

1 Lindenberger , 233–70; Jonathan Grandine, *The Problem of Shape in "The
Prelude": The Conflict of Private and Public Speech* (Cambridge, Mass.: Harvard University Press, 1968).

2 Reported by Orville Dewey, in *The Old World and the New*, cited by Lindenberger, 205; cf. Carl Woodring's authoritative summation: "During his sixty
years of contemplating the nature of the poetic office, William Wordsworth
spent very few moments questioning the degree of a poet's responsibility to
society. To the contrary, he increased from time to time his sense of that responsibility, sometimes by intensifying it, sometimes by enlarging its objec-

tives." *Politics in English Romantic Poetry* (Cambridge, Mass.: Harvard University Press, 1970), 85.

3   The relations between the two are further complicated by references in 1804–05 to a third major poem, "a narrative Poem of the Epic kind" (*LEY*, 594), usually taken to mean *The Excursion*, even though such an identification strains the definition of both genres; cf. Jonathan Wordsworth, "That Wordsworth 'Epic,'" *TWC* 11 (1980): 34–35.

4   The principal addition during these years was III.1–167 (*WAG*, 514–15). I am indebted to Jonathan Wordsworth, M. H. Abrams, and Stephen Gill for most of my statements of textual and chronological fact about the 1805 *Prelude*, especially 510–26 ("The Texts: History and Presentation"); unless otherwise noted, inferences and interpretations drawn from these facts are my own.

5   Finch, 252–53.

6   Cf. "I cannot say how much I was affected at this unthought-of sight in such a place" (*LMY*, 209; 8 April 1808), upon reflecting that "the imagery of London has . . . been more present to my mind than that of this noble vale [Grasmere]."

7   *WAG*, 513.

8   Ibid., 8n., 428n.

9   Potts, 63–85, 120–48; Everard King, "Beattie's *The Minstrel* and the Scottish Connection," *TWC* 13 (1982): 20–26; cf. Paul Fry, *The Poet's Calling in the English Ode* (New Haven: Yale University Press, 1980).

10 *WAG*, 516–17, based on Jonathan Wordsworth, "The Five-Book *Prelude* of Early Spring 1804," *JEGP* 76 (1977): 1–25.

11 *WAG*, 499–500; brackets and queries are the editors'.

12 Jonathan Wordsworth, "The Five-Book *Prelude*," 18.

13 *WAG*, 498–99; the passages are also printed in De Selincourt, 623–28.

14 Jonathan Wordsworth, "The Five-Book *Prelude*," 20, 24.

15 Joseph Kishel notes "a strong thematic resemblance" between this passage and the "upheaval of the French Revolution and Wordsworth's own spiritual crisis in the second half of the 1805 *Prelude*" ("The 'Analogy Passage' from Wordsworth's Five-Book *Prelude*," *SIR* 18 (1979): 270–85).

16 Sara Suleri, "'Once Out of Nature': The Uses of System in Wordsworth, Arnold, Yeats" (Ph.D. diss., Indiana University, 1983). I am indebted at several points to Professor Suleri's thesis that the *Recluse*-as-system was a heuristic device used by Wordsworth to lend philosophical universality to *The Prelude* while at the same time insuring—by its obvious incompleteness—that the reader (especially as Coleridge) would sympathetically supply the missing connections.

17 "There is also the interesting possibility that the two and a half French Books were composed in a single manuscript, now lost" (*WAG*, 519); cf. also M. II.14–16.

18 The original beginning of Book VIII became the beginning of VII, while the original beginning of VII was incorporated into VIII at lines 711–51 (*WAG*, 519).

19 Ibid., 520; M. II. 46–48.

20 WAG, 520.
21 Abrams, *NS*, passim.; especially 19–70.
22 J. T. Ogden, "The Structure of Imaginative Experience in *The Prelude*," *TWC* 6 (1975): 290–98.
23 MacGillivray, 243.
24 *WP* (1971 edition), xvi.
25 Though some of this same material appears in *Descriptive Sketches* (1793), neither complicating theme, Revolution or Imagination, emerges explicitly or with originality there.

CHAPTER 5

1   Jones, *The Egotistical Sublime* (London: Chatto & Windus, 1954), 126; Lindenberger, 111.
2   1850 *Prelude*, IV.469–71; first printed in WAG, 151. Except for this reference, all line citations to *The Prelude* are to the 1805 version first established by Ernest de Selincourt in 1926 (Oxford, 1959). I use this edition with misgivings, for it is now superseded in particular readings and notes on the chronology of the poem's composition by that of Jonathan Wordsworth, M. H. Abrams, and Stephen Gill (Norton, 1979), but I presume it is still the most generally available standard edition. New scholarly editions of the 1805 and 1850 versions are forthcoming from Cornell University Press, edited by Mark Reed and W. J. B. Owen, respectively.
3   Cf. McFarland, *Romanticism and the Forms of Ruin*; D. F. Rauber, "The Fragment as Romantic Form," *MLQ* 30 (1969): 212–21; and, for modern variations (principally *Finnegans Wake*), Umberto Eco, *Opera aperta: Forma e indeterminazione nelle poetiche contemporanee* (Milan: Bompiani, 1962).
4   Paul Sheats, "Wordsworth's 'Retrogrades' and the Shaping of *The Prelude*," *JEGP* 71 (1973): 473–90.
5   "In due course [the] poem develops corrections to such unrestrained sentiments" (Edward Said, *Beginnings: Intention and Method* [New York: Basic Books, 1975], 44–45); Said finds *The Prelude* philosophically radical insofar as (like *Paradise Lost*) it "imagines human life as having a 'beginning'" which the author recapitulates in starting to write. I am also indebted to Karl Johnson for several ideas about the poem/place pattern in *The Prelude*'s beginning. *The Written Spirit: Thematic and Rhetorical Structure in Wordsworth's "The Prelude"* (Salzburg: Institute für Englische Sprache und Literatur, 1978).
6   De Selincourt, *Prelude*, 511; WAG, 28n.2; *WS*, 6.
7   M. H. Abrams, "The Correspondent Breeze: A Romantic Metaphor," *The Kenyon Review* 19 (1957): 113–30; revised version in *English Romantic Poets*, ed. Abrams (New York: Oxford University Press, 1960), 37–54.
8   Cf. the contemporaneous "Unity entire" of "Home at Grasmere," l. 170.
9   *WS*, 48–49.
10 Cf. Parrish, *"The Prelude," 1798–1799*, 6.
11 These lines conclude an insertion between lines 206 and 207 of *1799* (*1805*, I.510–34) which strengthens the thematic point of the "home amusements" lines following.

12   WAG, 515, 100n.3.
13   WS, 94; Johnson usefully notes positive, contented movements in Books II,
     IV, and VI, answering negative, alienated feelings in I, III, V.
14   Johnson compares Book III's ideal universities and heroic scholars to Book I's
     ideal homes and heroic epic subjects (WS, 106–09).
15   Potts, 235; Potts develops other parallels between Bunyan and Wordsworth
     throughout his "Pilgrim" chapter, 218–43.
16   WS, 94.
17   David Ferry has pursued this negative view of Wordsworth's personality fur-
     ther, with more positive results for our understanding of the poetry, than any
     other critic (The Limits of Mortality, Middletown, Conn.: Wesleyan Univer-
     sity Press, 1959).
18   John Nabholtz, "The Journey Homeward: Drama and Rhetoric in Book IV of
     The Prelude," SIR 2 (1971): 81, 91.
19   Ibid., 90.
20   WS, 147–48, citing Lindenberger, 146.
21   Ibid.; Hartman, 223; cf. LEY, 136: "I begin to wish much to be in town; cat-
     aracts and mountains are good occasional society, but they will not do for
     constant companions."
22   Onorato rightly stresses the veteran's "almost hallucinatory challenge" to the
     Dawn Dedication, yet overestimates the young Wordsworth's assurance in
     dealing with him (249); Jonathan Wordsworth underestimates the contrastive
     relationship between the two scenes (MH, 225).
23   Nabholtz, 93.
24   Nabholtz further establishes the Dawn Dedication and the Discharged Vet-
     eran as internal "journeys" balancing the two external journeys of Book IV's
     opening narrative sections: the return to Hawkshead and Wordsworth's po-
     etry-composing walks there.
25   There have been several persuasive readings of Book V's special unities, but
     none which places the book's problems in the larger context of The Recluse;
     cf. W. G. Stobie, "A Reading of The Prelude, Book V," MLQ 24 (1963):
     365–73; Joel Morkan, "Structure and Meaning in The Prelude, Book V,"
     PMLA 87 (1972): 246–54; David Wiener, "Wordsworth, Books, and the
     Growth of a Poet's Mind," JEGP 74 (1975): 209–20; Michael Jaye, "The Ar-
     tifice of Disjunction: Book 5, The Prelude," Papers on Language and Litera-
     ture 14 (1978): 32–50; Kurt Heinzelman has developed the labor theory of
     value with respect to reading and writing literature and criticism in an inter-
     esting extension of Romantic arguments like Wordsworth's (The Econom-
     ics of the Imagination, Amherst: University of Massachusetts Press, 1980);
     Alan G. Hill finds Wordsworth's experiential theories of education closest
     to those of Comenius (1592–1670), whose Orbis Pictur was in his library
     ("Wordsworth, Comenius, and the Meaning of Education," RES 26 [1975]:
     301–12).
26   Frank McConnell, The Confessional Imagination (Baltimore: Johns Hopkins
     University Press, 1974), 133.
27   Onorato, 376; M. I.250.
28   Hartman, 228–31; for qualifications and extensions of Hartman's interpreta-

tion, cf. Cynthia Chase, "The Accidents of Disfiguration: Limits to Literal and Rhetorical Reading in Book V of *The Prelude*," *Studies in Romanticism* 18 (1979): 547–65; Timothy Bahti, "Figures of Interpretation, The Interpretation of Figures: A Reading of Wordsworth's 'Dream of the Arab,' " *Studies in Romanticism* 18 (1979): 601–27.

29   Jane Worthington Smyser, "Wordsworth's Dream of Poetry and Science," *PMLA* 71 (1956): 269–75. Descartes actually had three dreams, the third of which Smyser finds relevant for *Prelude* V; but all three interweave apocalyptic images and vocational crisis. The dreams occurred at the turning point of Descartes's life, with many associations that suggest Wordsworth's reasons for knowing them well: Descartes's tribute to the poetical imagination over philosophic rationality, his taking himself as a proper object of study, and his dedication to "an *opus infinitum* . . . not to be achieved by any one man . . . how incredibly ambitious!" (N. K. Smith, *New Studies in the Philosophy of Descartes* [New York: Russell & Russell, 1963] 7–16, 33–39). Descartes went on pilgrimage to Loreto to give thanks for his dreams' having chastised him into dedication to a sinless life of the mind. Mary Jacobus makes excellent use of Descartes's dreams in an argument for Book V's importance in larger issues of the ontological status of fictive language ("Wordsworth and the Language of the Dream," *ELH* 46 (1979): 618–44).

30   *WS*, 199.

31   II.266 ("An inmate of this *active* universe"); VI.524 (*"that we had cross'd the Alps*; not italicized by WAG, 216); VIII.701 ("That aught *external* to the living mind"); IX.301 ("Injuries / Made *him* more gracious"); IX.518–19 (" 'Tis against *that* / Which we are fighting' "); X.18 ("A race of victims, so they seem'd, *themselves*"); X.536 ("That, *Robespierre was dead*"); X.640 ("To turn *all* judgments out of their right course"); X.897 ("And what the sanction, till, demanding *proof*").

32   Wordsworth alludes to Thomson's *The Castle of Indolence*, I.xv; cf. Potts, 86–131, for extended discussion of Wordsworth's echoes of Thomson.

33   *LEY*, 32–41; *LMY* (1812–20), 2:615–47; Dorothy Wordsworth, *Journal of a Tour on the Continent*, in *Journals of Dorothy Wordsworth*, ed. E. De Selincourt (New York: Macmillan, 1941), 1–336.

34   A. C. Bradley, "Wordsworth," in *Oxford Lectures on Poetry* (London: Macmillan, 1909), 99–145, esp. 138–41).

35   "The Speaker of *The Prelude*," in *BWS*, 283–89; also J. T. Ogden, "Structure of Imaginative Experience," 295–96.

36   Johnson strikingly interprets Wordsworth's missing the "top" of the Alps as a simultaneous decapitation of his narrative progress (*WS*, 253).

37   Reed agrees with De Selincourt that the lines on Imagination were composed in 1804 (*CMY*, 12–13, 641–42, 652).

38   *WS*, 244 and 221–72 passim.

39   WAG, 217n.4.

40   Cf. the parallel drawn above between the conclusion of Book V and the lines in Book II about "the ghostly language of the ancient earth," where natural or poetic language processes are also imaged as homes or abodes. Alec King has persuasively developed the idea that Wordsworth's visionary passages enact

verbally the process they representationally describe. *Wordsworth and the Artist's Vision* (London: Athlone Press, 1966), 1–10, 62–79.

41 Hartman, "Retrospect 1971," xvi, in fourth printing of *WP*.
42 Dorothy Wordsworth, *Journals*, 257.
43 *WS*, 235–37.
44 WAG, 515–16, 518–19.
45 Ibid., 519.
46 De Selincourt, *Prelude*, 563–64; WAG, 244, nn. 7, 8.
47 Wordsworth's attitude toward London and individuals living there is complicated and obscurely expressed, but it is not a simple constitutional dislike of other people, nor a country boy's distaste for city-dwellers, nor (a more complicated, because anachronistic, judgment) a failure of liberal social sympathies for the modern urban underclass; cf. Ferry, "his genius was his enmity to man, which he mistook for love" (173); Lindenberger, "Wordsworth's portraits of society must stand or fall by one's degree of assent to his theories" (211); Raymond Williams, "Prelude to Alienation," *Dissent* 11 (1964): 303–15. Lindenberger is closer to the mark when he interprets Wordsworth's detachment not as impersonality but "the detachment of the private self fighting to preserve its identity" (239)—to which I would add, apropos *The Recluse*, that the private self is fighting because it is also determined to write publicly responsible poetry.
48 Onorato is excellently suggestive on the psychoanalytic dimensions of Wordsworth's Good Mother and Bad Mother images in Book VII (200–05).
49 W. J. B. Owen, "Two Wordsworthian Ambivalences," *TWC* 11 (1980): 2–9; E. A. Horsman sees nearly diagrammatic "overt contrast between Book VII—man in London—and Book VIII—man in the Lake District." "The Design of Wordsworth's *Prelude*," in *Wordsworth's Mind and Art*, ed. A. W. Thomson (Edinburgh: Oliver & Boyd, 1969), 100.
50 De Selincourt, *PW*, V.415; WAG, 519.
51 Onorato speculates that the "bad poetry" of such sentimental stories as the Matron's Tale derives from Wordsworth's touching "upon matters that unconsciously appealed to repressed infantile feelings in him" (204n.20).
52 Keats, *Letters*, ed. Hyder Rollins (Cambridge, Mass.: Harvard University Press, 1958), I.224 (February 1818).
53 Owen, "Two Wordsworthian Ambivalences," 8–9.
54 A very important note in WAG (304n.7) indicates that VIII.711–27 ("The grotto of Antiparos") was first drafted as part of Wordsworth's effort to describe or explain his "sense of anticlimax at having unknowingly crossed the Alps in August 1790." Besides supporting my point about Wordsworth's egotistical sublimation of London in Book VIII, such a cross-reference further illuminates a subtle leitmotif in *The Prelude*—Wordsworth's tendency in moments of imaginative ecstasy to employ grandiloquent urban or imperial imagery, observable in the Simplon Pass lines themselves ("The mind beneath such banners militant," VI.543), but often ignored because of the presumption that Wordsworth the nature poet did not like cities.
55 De Selincourt, *Prelude*, liii; Finch, 221–23, 252–65; Jonathan Wordsworth, "The Five-Book *Prelude*," 18; Hartman, 242–47.

56 Ogden, "Structure of Imaginative Experience," 291.

57 I am indebted to Stanley Cavell for this observation, adumbrated in *The Claim of Reason: Wittgenstein, Skepticism, Morality, and Tragedy* (New York: Oxford University Press, 1979), especially part 4, addressed to the dangers of viewing human life as an intellectual problem susceptible to solution.

58 M. I.191–95; De Selincourt, *Prelude*, 588 (citing Legouis, *The Early Life of Wordsworth*, and Legouis and Bussiere, *Le Général Michel Beaupuy*); cf. Matlak, "The Men in Wordsworth's Life," *TWC* 9 (1978): 392, for interpretation of elements of frustration that entered into Wordsworth's early male friendships, linked to his conscious and unconscious emotions at the early death of his father.

59 *Letters from France*, ed. Janet M. Todd, 2 vols. (Delmar, N.Y.: Scholars' Facsimiles and Reprints, 1975); the original eight volumes run to over two thousand pages; Wordsworth's source seems to be the first volume, Williams's first detailed account of "the history of my friends" (1:123–223). De Selincourt, writing close to the time of Legouis's *William Wordsworth and Annette Vallon* (1922), is surprisingly hard on Wordsworth's tale: "a climax of absurdity difficult to parallel in our literature" (*Prelude*, 591–93); M. II.15; F. M. Todd, "William Wordsworth, Helen Maria Williams, and France," *MLR* 43 (1948): 456–64; M. Ray Adams, "Helen Maria Williams and the French Revolution," in *Wordsworth and Coleridge*, ed. Earl Leslie Griggs (New York: Russell & Russell, 1962), 87–117.

60 "Sonnet, On Seeing Miss Helen Maria Williams Weep at a Tale of Distress" (*PW*, I.529; first published March 1787 in *The European Magazine*).

61 Onorato draws interesting parallels (from Freud and Erikson) to the similar psychological biographies of Brutus and Luther (323–30).

62 WAG, 391n.4, 519–20.

63 Bateson, 123; M. I.308; Friedman, 109. The psychological presence of Robespierre in Wordsworth's mind is not in question—he was an element in the consciousness of almost every contemporary European—though I imagine that his moralistic temper and provincial severity of dress and speech might initially have appealed strongly to Wordsworth; the important question is, rather, what effect Robespierre's psychological presence had on Wordsworth's poetry (see note 64 below).

64 Onorato, 339–51; I interpret Onorato as referring to Wordsworth's "repressed desires" for *authoritative power,* hence his feeling of psychic threat as the Revolution—the social form in which he had invested such desires as they pertained to his sense of creative power—came under Robespierre's control, and seemed to turn inhumane and evil.

65 Abrams, *NS,* passim, gives the fullest and most sympathetic account of the theodical pattern in Wordsworth's work and Romantic tradition, an account I demur from only to stress its dramatic uncertainties and their effects on the formal structure of *The Prelude.*

66 Susan Luther anticipates some of these points in "Wordsworth's *Prelude,* VI.592–616 (1850)," *TWC* 13 (1981): 253–61.

67 De Selincourt and WAG both italicize the phrase only in the 1805 version, not in 1850.

68 *The Borderers,* III. 1495–96; the influence of Robespierre on Wordsworth's

creation of Oswald is well recognized; in Book X, we may see the influence of Oswald on Wordsworth's re-creation of Robespierre as a character in his poem.

69 Bate, 118–19; I agree with Bate's opinion that Coleridge "later exaggerated, possibly invented" his place on Napoleon's blacklist for articles he had written for the Morning Chronicle (BL, X.216–17) and see them as of a piece with Wordsworth's similar imaginative-fantasy uses of Robespierre and Napoleon—usages by no means limited to these two Romantic writers.

70 De Selincourt, Prelude, 608.

71 The Spirit of the Age, in Complete Works, ed. P. P. Howe (London: Dent, 1932), 11:37. Hazlitt makes the statement in his essay on Coleridge, but versions of the same formulation are implicit in nearly every essay in the collection.

72 Hartman, "Romanticism and 'Anti-Self-Consciousness,'" The Centennial Review 6 (1962): 553–65; its main proponent was, of course, Carlyle.

73 Helen Darbishire persuasively corrects De Selincourt's view that the lines refer to Dorothy (Prelude, 611–12).

74 WAG, 8n.4, 428n.2, and 510, where the different adjectives are called "the most notable textual change" between their edition of 1805 and De Selincourt's.

75 "She dwelt among th'untrodden ways," ll. 11–12; cf. Walter J. Ong, The Presence of the Word (New Haven: Yale University Press, 1967), 253–54, and "Romantic Difference and the Poetics of Technology," in Rhetoric, Romance, and Technology (Ithaca, N.Y.: Cornell University Press, 1971), 255–83.

76 Friedman gives a good summary of Wordsworth's reasons for studying the lower classes: to show more clearly the invariables of human nature (as we now study primates and primitives), thereby to educate the privileged classes in the universal rudiments of human nature, and thus to demonstrate that violent revolution is neither necessary nor inevitable, since the lower classes are already fully developed human beings (200–02).

77 WAG, 442n.2.

78 Excursion, III.538; cf. "Home at Grasmere," l. 85: "unappropriated bliss"; I allude to these similar phrases here because their extravagant, unguarded quality is of a piece with Wordsworth's rhetoric in Book XII, on essentially the same topic: defining the well-being of the sensitive individual intellect in socially responsible terms.

79 Bateson stresses the incident's importance for Wordsworth's creative development more appropriately, to my mind, than almost anyone else (109–19); cf. M. I.232–37; Hartman, 252–54; Sheats makes several excellent observations about the incident itself in the course of analyzing the poem (Salisbury Plain) that it immediately provoked (83–94, 108–18).

80 "A philosopher may have done a great deal if he has made us think even a little differently . . . by inducing us to shift the emphasis and orientation of some of the basic notions we use in everyday life" (W. B. Gallie, "Is The Prelude a Philosophical Poem?" Philosophy 22 (1947): 124–38; reprinted in WAG, 663–78).

81 Cf. William Empson's similar rhetorical analysis of "Sense in The Prelude," in

The Structure of Complex Words (London: Chatto & Windus, 1951), 289–305.

82 WAG, 434n.9.

83 Ibid., 482n.7.

CHAPTER 6

1 Although Wordsworth became owner of the Broad How estate in 1807, he never built on it (M. II.59–62).

2 Darlington, 13–19; cf. chap. 3, n. 10.

3 Finch, 194–97.

4 Darlington , 30–32.

5 Darlington, 81; *PW,* V.329.

6 MS D approaches one, cautiously: "How pleased he is, where thin and thinner grows / The veil or where it parts at once, to spy / The dark pines . . ." (478–80); Darlington, 81.

7 *PW,* V.320, *app. crit.,* reads "receding"; Darlington's photocopy and transcript (298–99) make clear the true—and much more apt—reading; cf. Jonathan Wordsworth, "Secession at Grasmere," *Times Literary Supplement,* 26 March 1976, 354–55.

8 Kurt Heinzelman notes Wordsworth's echo of the Latin political slogan in his excellent chapter on "Wordsworth's Labor Theory: An Economics of Compensation," in *The Economics of Imagination* (Amherst: University of Massachusetts Press, 1980), 231–32.

9 *Review of English Studies,* n.s. 31 (1980): 25–27.

10 *The Anxiety of Influence* (New York: Oxford University Press, 1973), 125; Bloom also notes that Thomas Mann recorded Goethe's question in his diary upon receiving a copy of Herman Hesse's *Glasperlenspiel* while at work on *Dr. Faustus:* "To be reminded that one is not alone in the world—always unpleasant" (49).

11 Jonathan Wordsworth cites the early (ca. 1800) flavor of these lines and notes the poet's habit of switching blank-verse passages from poem to poem (*Review of English Studies,* n.s. 31 [1980]: 26).

12 John Wordsworth also had legitimate public claims to naval heroism, having received five hundred guineas and a sword like the other officers of his merchant fleet for their "famous victory" in early 1804, when they repelled a fleet of French warships off the Straits of Malacca (Rand, *Wordsworth's Mariner Brother,* 27–28). Wordsworth was not personally affected by Nelson's death, as he regarded his "public life [as] stained with one great crime" (crushing the patriotic Neapolitan revolt), and had a shrewd view of the effects of the manner of Nelson's death: "Considering the matter coolly there was little to regret. . . . Few men have ever died under circumstances so likely to make their death of benefit to their country; it is not easy to see what his life could have done comparable to it" (*LMY,* i.7; Feb. 11, 1806). Dorothy's letter to Lady Beaumont of Christmas Day, 1805, in which she notes that her brother is "very anxious to get forward with The Recluse," follows this news immediately with references to their mutual fascination with the newspaper

accounts of Nelson's death: "I was exceedingly interested in your Extract from the Newspaper concerning Lord Nelson's last moments—how very affecting the noble Creature's thoughts of his early pleasures, and the happy Fair-day at [his] home! My Brother was at Park House when I received it—he had [seen] the same account at Penrith" (*LEY*, 664–65).

13 Darlington, 18.

14 Ibid., 22.

CHAPTER 7

1 Coleridge later said that he had sent his notes for *The Recluse* from Malta with one Major Adye, who died en route of the plague and whose papers were burned as a quarantine measure (M. II.19; *LEY*, 573). Darlington (6) expresses doubt whether these notes ever existed; my examination of the *Recluse* project makes me equally dubious. Almost anything Coleridge said or wrote could be considered a "note" for *The Recluse,* since his fuller statements about it in 1815 and 1832 do not differ in philosophic essentials from other things he had been saying for years on the key points of the relation of consciousness to sense experience and an imaginative scheme of progressive human redemption. Though Major Adye was a real person, the possibly ambiguous pronunciation of his name and the circumstances of his death are so rife with ironic possibilities that Coleridge might almost have made him up.

2 The statement of *LMY*, I.64n., that the "700 additional lines" Wordsworth refers to on 1 August 1806 probably became part of *Excursion* IV, is now superseded by Reed's estimate that "most of these are probably now found in 'Home at Grasmere'" (*CMY*, 328), except for some lines corresponding to *Excursion* II.725–895, which Reed dates September 1807 or possibly as late as summer of 1808 (*CMY*, 362).

3 See chap. 8, n. 1, for dates of *The Excursion*'s composition; also, *CMY*, appendix 6, 675–85.

4 Jared Curtis, ed., *"Poems, in Two Volumes," and Other Poems, 1800–1807* (Ithaca, N.Y.: Cornell University Press, 1983), 527.

5 Joseph Kishel, ed., *Late Poems for "The Recluse"* (Ithaca, N.Y.: Cornell University Press, forthcoming), MS pp. 1–2. I am very grateful to Professor Kishel for making his introduction and reading texts available to me in advance of their publication.

6 *LMY*, I.269 (to Samuel Rogers, 29 September 1808); Kishel MS, 8.

7 Kishel MS, 22.

8 *PW* II.316–20. Line references are to this edition except where I have made reference to Joseph Kishel's Early Reading Text of 1808 (see n. 5 above); such references are indicated by "1808" before the line numbers. Kishel presents the essential textual evidence in "Wordsworth's 'To the Clouds,'" *TWC* 14 (Spring 1983): 92–94.

9 Kishel MS, 21.

10 Darlington, 22.

11 For ideas about the emblematizing tendency of Wordsworth's imagination, I am indebted to James Heffernan, *Wordsworth's Theory of Poetry: The Trans-*

forming Imagination (Ithaca, N.Y.: Cornell University Press, 1969), 193–225.

12   *PW,* V.348–62; all line citations are to this edition.

13   The ecclesiastical coincidences surrounding Wordsworth's use of Basil's letters are worth noting. While nursing Coleridge in London, he visited his brother Christopher, who was then domestic chaplain to the archbishop of Canterbury (M. II.32). In the library of the episcopal palace at Lambeth, with his vision of Saint Paul's fresh in mind and having just completed two poems on legends of Bolton Priory, he was attracted to a Latin edition of the works of Gregory of Nazianzen, which included some of Basil's replies. His adaptation of their correspondence is their first translation into English; the edition remained important to him, for another copy was in the Rydal Mount library at the time of his death. Chester L. and Alice C. Shaver, *Wordsworth's Library: A Catalog* (New York: Garland, 1979), 109.

14   Newman's translation of Basil's letter 14, the letter which Wordsworth followed very closely in writing lines 332–431, shows that Basil's feelings about imperial capitals were congenial to Wordsworth's: "Does it not strike you what a foolish mistake I was near making when I was eager to change this spot for your Tiberine, the very pit of the whole earth?" *The Church of the Fathers,* trans. J. H. Newman (Dublin, 1839), 60; cited in Kishel MS, 34.

15   James Joyce, *A Portrait of the Artist as a Young Man,* ed. Chester Anderson (New York: Viking, 1968), 243.

16   Half a century later, Matthew Arnold would stand in the unharmed monastery and feel himself "Wandering between two worlds, one dead / The other powerless to be born" ("Stanzas from the Grand Chartreuse," 85–86). The difference is accounted for by the history of revolutionary expectations. As a Romantic imaginative disability, this persisted at least to the time of Yeats's diagnosis: "The best lack all conviction, while the worst / Are full of passionate intensity."

17   For example, Naciens, the Divine Hermit of Carbonek Castle (whose name may have echoed Nazianzen's for Wordsworth), had sinned against Joseph of Arimathea and was released from his earthly penance only with the arrival of Sir Galahad, whose shield bore a red cross marked in Joseph's blood.

18   Northrop Frye, "The Drunken Boat: The Revolutionary Element in Romanticism," in *Romanticism Reconsidered* (New York: Columbia University Press, 1963), 1–25.

19   "The Waggoner," canto 4, l. 212 (*PW,* II.204).

20   *The Letters of Charles Lamb,* ed. E. V. Lucas (New York, 1935), 1:246 (February 15, 1801).

21   For further parallels between the two, see my essay, "The Idiom of Vision," in *New Perspectives on Coleridge and Wordsworth,* ed. Geoffrey Hartman (New York: Columbia University Press, 1972), pp. 1–28; also, J. Robert Barth, *The Symbolic Imagination* (Princeton: Princeton University Press, 1977), 52–55; Karl Kroeber, *Romantic Narrative Art* (Madison: University of Wisconsin Press, 1960), 51–53.

CHAPTER 8

1   The date of *Excursion* II–IV is, after the date of the "Prospectus" and "Home
    at Grasmere," the third major textual crux in the history of *The Recluse*. I fol-
    low Reed's carefully phrased conclusions: "A great amount of continuous or
    methodical composition toward a poem similar to the present *Excursion* can-
    not have taken place before late 1809 or early 1810" (*CMY*, 666); he also
    identifies some months in 1811–12 as probable periods of additional compo-
    sition (*CMY*, 22–23). These dates are important for the sequence of my argu-
    ment because they indicate that coherent composition of a poem like *The Ex-
    cursion* most probably follows the *Recluse* poems of 1808 rather than
    beginning, as formerly thought, in 1806–07 (*PW*, V.370–71, 415–19; M.
    II.77–79; *LMY*, I.64n.). However, the dates are not positively established, es-
    pecially for Book II. Reed acknowledges that the 1806 date is "remotely possi-
    ble" for the major portion of Book II; Jonathan Wordsworth continues to
    date the origin of the Solitary's story from 1806, while allowing that it was
    "revised, reordered, and expanded" in 1809–10, and that it is no longer pos-
    sible to determine how much of the story existed, or in what shape, in 1806
    (*Borders*, 364, 449n.40). Given the protean nature of *The Recluse*, both as
    text and as idea, these uncertainties are inevitable and often derive from two
    different kinds of textual observation: first, manuscript evidence which shows
    the poet working with certain themes, images, or narrative lines that appear in
    other poems; second, manuscript evidence which shows him working toward
    establishment of a text that we know in a subsequently published form.
    Though Wordsworth doubtless entertained some ideas for a story like the Sol-
    itary's earlier (especially insofar as it is a fictionalized abstract of his own life
    story), I find the 1809–10 date persuasive on internal grounds as well, be-
    cause Books II–IV are clearly determined by a single structural impulse, dif-
    ferent from that for Book I or Books V–IX. Thus I interpret Dorothy's com-
    ment of 28 February 1810, that William is hard at work on "3 books of the
    Recluse" (*LMY*, I.392), as referring to Books II–IV, in light of Reed's conclu-
    sions, rather than Books V–VII, as stated by De Selincourt and Moorman
    (*LMY*, I.390n.). Considerations of space prevent me from interpreting differ-
    ences between Book I and its 1797–98 version, "The Ruined Cottage" (see
    chap. 1, n. 53); this has been done by William Galperin, "'Then . . . the voice
    was silent': 'The Wanderer' *vs. The Ruined Cottage*," *ELH* 51 (1984).
2   *PW*, V.40–41. All line references for *The Excursion* are to this edition, which
    I have checked against the original edition of 1814; all lines cited exist in the
    original version unless otherwise noted.
3   Wordsworth said the character was based upon Joseph Fawcett, a radical
    London preacher whom he often heard in the mid-1790s (M. II.79) and au-
    thor of *The Art of War* (1795), which may have exerted some influences on
    the first *Recluse* poems (chap. 1). John Thelwall's life and personality also in-
    fluenced the creation of the Solitary, in addition to Wordsworth's direct bor-
    rowing of the character of the Wanderer from Thelwall's *Peripatetic*. Alan C.
    Hill has persuasively demonstrated similarities between the characters and
    plan of *The Excursion* and those of the *Octavius* of Minucius Felix (2d–3d

century A.D.), which features a dialogue between a skeptical pagan and a Christian lawyer ("New Light on *The Excursion*," *Ariel* 5, no. 2 (1974): 37–47).

4 Lindenberger, 267; cf. Gordon K. Thomas, *Wordsworth's Dirge and Promise: Napoleon, Wellington, and the Convention of Cintra* (Lincoln: University of Nebraska Press, 1971).

5 *PW*, V.418–19; *CMY*, 23.

6 *WP*, 312.

7 In the most complete scholarly account of *The Excursion*, Judson S. Lyon anticipates this view of Book IV: "It seems almost a matter of indifference whether or not the faith at the end of the process is achieved. The emphasis is all on the intermediate steps . . . and they seem to be important as ends in themselves, as well as means to the ultimate faith in God" (*The Excursion: A Study* [New Haven: Yale University Press, 1950], 80). However, Lyon is not prepared to take this poetic seeming as the real structure of Book IV. Hartman also notes that in Book IV "other traditional supports against despair are invoked" without being clearly distinguished from the Wanderer's orthodoxy (*WP*, 316). Enid Welsford anticipates some of my reading of Book IV, though specific interpretations and the conclusions she draws from them are different; she accepts the Wanderer's opening harangue as the essence of the entire book, allowing the rest to stand as rhetorical hyperbole. *Salisbury Plain: A Study of the Development of Wordsworth's Mind and Art* (New York: Barnes and Noble, 1966), 77–91.

8 *PW*, V.131, *app. crit.* (MS 58, dated July–August, 1806).

9 Michael Jaye, "*The Prelude, The Excursion,* and *The Recluse*: An Unpublished *Prelude* Variant," *Philological Quarterly* 54 (1975): 484–93.

10 *MH*, 184–201.

11 These lines are probably a late addition from 1813, put in to check the "Spinosistic" tendency of the argument to this point.

12 *The Works of Charles and Mary Lamb,* ed. E. V. Lucas (London: Methuen, 1903), 1:167.

13 *The Correspondence of Crabb Robinson with the Wordsworth Circle,* ed. Edith J. Morley (1927), 1:79–80.

14 Welsford, 90.

CHAPTER 9

1 Drafts and revisions reached heights of confusion remarkable even for the Wordsworth workshop (*CMY*, appendix 6, pp. 660–63, 666–67, 675–85). The authoritative account will be Michael Jaye, ed., *The Excursion* (Ithaca, N.Y.: Cornell University Press, forthcoming). By 1814, Dorothy was desperate about the mess, and publication seems to have been in part a means of escaping from it: "We are all most thankful that William has brought his mind to consent to printing so much of this work; for the MSS. were in such a state that, if it had pleased Heaven to take him from this world, they would have been almost useless" (*LMY*, II.140).

2 *The Complete Works of William Hazlitt,* ed. P. P. Howe (London: Dent, 1930), 4:112.

3 Lamb, I.161.

4 *PW,* V.2; Carl Woodring, *Wordsworth* (Cambridge, Mass.: Harvard University Press, 1968), 182; Hartman, *WP,* 290–91.

5 *Contributions to the Edinburgh Review* (London: Longman, 1844), 235.

6 Lamb, I.162.

7 M. II.264–65; *PW,* V.372 and *app. crit.* passim. Hazlitt leaped upon the religious pretensions of the poem, closely scrutinizing Wordsworth's calling it "only a portion of a poem": "Why is the word *portion* here used, as if it were a portion of Scripture? . . . Now, Mr. Wordsworth's poems, though not profane, yet neither are they sacred, to deserve this solemn style, though some of his admirers have gone so far as to compare them for primitive, patriarchal simplicity, to the historical parts of the Bible" (17:59n.).

8 A scholarly symposium on *The Excursion* was remarkable for the uniformly stern conclusions drawn by its contributors (*TWC* 9 [Spring 1978]: 131–99). In this respect, modern interpreters have read the poem more accurately than its original critics; Jeffrey, Byron, Hazlitt, and others, for all their criticisms, were generally disposed to assign it a character of benign moral uplift. Only Shelley, whose *Peter Bell the Third* is inspired by the genius of disappointed expectations, cut close to *The Excursion*'s tough existentialism: "To Peter's view, all seemed one hue; / He was no Whig, he was no Tory; / No Deist and no Christian he; — / He got so subtle, that to be / Nothing, was all his glory. / One single point in his belief / From his organization sprung, / The heart-enrooted faith, the chief / Ear in his doctrines' blighted sheaf, / That 'Happiness is wrong' " (canto 6).

9 Lamb, I.166; cf. Hazlitt's paradoxical phrase, "scholastic romance," pointing to a formal quality of the poem akin to what Lamb addressed in its doctrinal content (4:112). Richard E. Brantley's *Wordsworth's "Natural Methodism"* (New Haven: Yale University Press, 1975) is a theologically sophisticated study of the pervasiveness of Evangelical idiom in Wordsworth's poetry, with some reference to *The Excursion* (110–24).

10 Frances Ferguson, *Wordsworth: Language as Counter-Spirit* (New Haven: Yale University Press, 1977), 197.

11 Hazlitt, 4:113.

12 *Biographia Literaria,* chap. 14; cf. Mark L. Reed, "Wordsworth, Coleridge, and the 'Plan' of the *Lyrical Ballads,*" *University of Toronto Quarterly* 34 (1965): 238–53.

13 Jeffrey, 238.

14 "Advertisement," *Lyrical Ballads,* 1798.

15 Lindenberger, 259.

16 IV.125.

17 Ferguson, 195–241.

18 Lamb, I.171.

19 Patrick Brantlinger, *The Spirit of Reform: British Literature and Politics, 1832–1867* (Cambridge, Mass.: Harvard University Press, 1977).

20 Wordsworth believed that England should maintain a large standing army as

an unfortunate necessity for the preservation of civilized life (*LMY*, II.312); his militarism was not professional but part of his imaginative critique of the mean commercial circumstances of modern industrial society; just wars in relief of oppressed nations were regarded as legitimate extensions of policies of social justice. Nancy Rosenblum, "Romantic Militarism," *Journal of the History of Ideas*, 43 (1982): 249.

21 Such hints were, of course, taken much more forcefully by Byron himself, in canto III's conflation of military and creative conquerors ("the greatest, nor the worst of men, / Whose spirit antithetically mixed . . . Conqueror and captive of the earth art thou!" III.36, 37).

22 Ferguson, 231; Wordsworth underscores the heroic dimension of the Solitary's critical skepticism by alluding to Milton's "lost Angel" (319).

23 Hartman's *Wordsworth's Poetry 1787–1814* (1964) is the definitive statement of the apocalyptic tendency of Wordsworth's imagination. Philosophically sophisticated statements of Wordsworth's both/and logic are: E. D. Hirsch, *Wordsworth and Schelling: A Typological Study* (New Haven: Yale University Press, 1960); Jonathan Wordsworth, *The Music of Humanity*; and Alan Grob, *The Philosophic Mind* (Columbus: Ohio State University Press, 1973). Since the appearance of Hartman's study, several efforts have been made to balance the apocalyptic and naturalistic strains in Wordsworth's oeuvre; among the most persuasive of these are Charles Altieri, "Wordsworth's Wavering Balance: The Thematic Rhythm of *The Prelude*," *TWC* 4 (Autumn 1973): 226–40; Charles Sherry, *Wordsworth's Poetry of Imagination* (Oxford: Clarendon Press, 1980); M. H. Abrams, *Natural Supernaturalism;* David Pirie, *Wordsworth: The Poetry of Grandeur and of Tenderness* (London: Methuen, 1981).

24 Ferguson, 207.

25 He composed the three "Essays on Epitaphs" in 1810 (*CMY*, 49) and appended the first of them (reprinted from Coleridge's *The Friend*) as a note to V.978: "And whence that tribute? wherefore these regards?"

26. Friedman, 144–46.

27 Ferguson, 239.

28 I am playing with Hartman's key phrase, *"consciousness of self raised to apocalyptic pitch"* (*WP*,17).

29 Cf. Ferguson's conclusion: "silence occurs only within . . . poems; it never takes the form of thoroughgoing misology . . . individuals must be repeatedly humbled by the recognition that humans and natural objects and language are inescapably binding" (241).

30 Ibid., 240.

31 "The Man Who Was Not Napoleon," *TWC* 12 (Winter 1981): 92–96; "Wordsworth as Heartsworth," in *The Evidence of Imagination*, ed. Reiman, Jaye, and Bennett (New York: New York University Press, 1978), 12–41.

32 ". . . for the sake / Of youthful Poets, who among these Hills / Will be my second self when I am gone" (ll. 37–39); I am grateful to Anthony J. Harding for pointing out this parallel.

33 "Two or three cottages still remain, which are called Knott-houses from the name of the gentleman (I have called him a knight) concerning whom these traditions survive. He was the ancestor of the Knott family, formerly consider-

able proprietors in the district" (Wordsworth's note; *PW*, V.468); for "Erth-ing," see *The Poetical Works*, ed. T. Hutchinson, rev. E. De Selincourt (Ox-ford Standard Authors, 1904, 1936, 1960), p. 680, l. 971.

34 *Diary, Reminiscences, and Correspondence of Henry Crabb Robinson*, ed. Thomas Sadler (London: Macmillan, 1869), 1:389. Wordsworth's comment, made in 1812, seemed prophetic to Robinson in 1848, when he observed that two new words had been coined to describe the contending parties in France, *propriétaires* and *prolétaires*.

35 The lines on the factory boy date from 1798–99 and are related to similar concerns in "The Old Cumberland Beggar," "The Last of the Flock," and the *Salisbury Plain* poems. Since Wordsworth had no direct experience of factory life, it is likely he derived the description from Thelwall's "On Leaving the Bottoms of Gloucestershire": "the unwieldy pride / Of Factory overgrown, when Opulence, / Dispeopling the neat cottage, crowds his walls / . . . with a race / Of infant slaves, brok'n timely to the yoke / Of unremitting drudgery" (M. II.175–76; *PW*, V.471).

36 David Q. Smith, "The Wanderer's Silence: A Strange Reticence in Book IX of *The Excursion*," *TWC* 9 (Spring 1978): 163–67.

37 He could also feel he was close to centers of power which might turn such po-etic ideas into reality, given the importance of Bell's work in developing the British system of education in India and Clarkson's similar influence in Haiti, where he had persuaded Henri Christophe to adopt the Lancastrian system. The Wordsworths were later much interested in the Clarksons' reception of Christophe's widow, "the Sable Queen," following his suicide in the revolu-tions of 1820 (*LMY*, II.655n; *LLY*, I.87–88).

38 Jeffrey, 236.

39 Ibid., 236–37

CHAPTER 10

1 Jerome Christensen, *Coleridge's Blessed Machine of Language* (Ithaca, N.Y.: Cornell University Press, 1981), 148.

2 "Evidently it was influenced by Coleridge's study of *The Excursion*" (E. K. Chambers, *Coleridge* [Oxford: Clarendon Press, 1938], p. 270); "Among the influences contributing to this change [in the *Biographia*, from preface to in-dependent work] were his recent unsatisfactory exchange of letters with Wordsworth and his reading of *The Excursion, The White Doe*, and particu-larly the 1815 edition of Wordsworth's Poems and the prefaces to them" (E. L. Griggs, *LSTC*, ii.579n.); "The effective cause of the *Biographia* is Wordsworth's 1815 Preface . . . Wordsworth had suddenly done exactly what Coleridge himself had been planning to do . . . he was . . . thinking of his work—both the Preface and the poems—as a rival twin to Wordsworth's edi-tion" (Engell and Bate, *BL*, pp. cxxxv, L).

3 "Refer to the 4th Book of the Excursion and you will find an admirable com-ment upon the Conduct of the Allies from beginning to end" (DW to Cather-ine Clarkson; *LMY*, II.229).

4 He proposed six groups: (1) poems relating to childhood, (2) to friendship

and other emotions of youth and early manhood, (3) to natural objects and their influence on the mind, (4) on the naming of places, (5a) on human life ("the understanding affected through the imagination"), (5b) on social and civic duties ("interesting to the imagination through the understanding"), and (6) poems relating to old age (*LMY*, i.334–46). This division, besides being the clearest Wordsworth ever proposed, is also the closest to *The Recluse's* equal emphases on Man, Nature, and Human Life.

5   Engell and Bate stress that the distinction between Fancy and Imagination was probably the single most important intellectual issue stimulating Coleridge's "desire to correct [Wordsworth] gently" (p. liii), since "Wordsworth, he could fairly argue, would never have heard of this important 'distinction'—certainly would never have been able to make a large issue of it—had it not been for Coleridge" (l).

6   Coleridge told Byron the separation had been "agreed on mutually" (*LSTC*, iv.560; March 30, 1815).

7   James Hogg, *The Poetic Mirror, or The Living Bards of Britain* (London: Longman, 1816), 131–87. Hogg uses the salient quality of *The Recluse* in 1816—incompleteness—to connect his three parodies: "The Stranger" is "A Farther Portion of *The Recluse*, A Poem"; "The Flying Tailor," a "Further Extract"; and "James Rigg," a "Still Further Extract." The last is, appropriately, presented as a fragment; the *Quarterly Review*, by way of criticizing Hogg's parodies, said that "with the exception of one or two lines, Mr. Wordsworth would not disclaim" it (July 1816; p. 472). Hogg's parodies are not very good as poetry, being mere pastiche of Wordsworth's habits of minute description. But they are humorous intellectual parodies of Wordsworth's philosophic bent, as each poem loses itself in strings of speculation upon some common or uncommon occurrence. In "The Stranger," a horse breaks wind with a noise like thunder, and its keeper is "stunn'd—for on similitude / In dissimilitude, man's sole delight, / And all the sexual intercourse of things, / Do most supremely hang." James Rigg's sensory compensation for his blindness (cf. The Blind Dalesman in *Excursion* VII) comes from "gracious Nature [who] doth not pine / And fret away her mystic energies / In fainting inanition . . . even as if th' external world / Were one great wet-nurse of the human race." And the conclusion of "The Flying Tailor" shows that Wordsworth's Preface and Essay had had their popular effect: "Reader . . . mark my words,—eternally my name /Shall last on earth, conspicuous like a star / 'Mid that bright galaxy of favour'd spirits / Who, laugh'd at constantly whene'er they publish'd, / Surviv'd the impotent scorn of base Reviews." These sharp thrusts notwithstanding, Wordsworth's dirge upon the occasion of their author's death nineteen years later is his last great poem, lamenting the passing of his entire Romantic generation ("Extempore Effusion upon the Death of James Hogg," 1835).

8   Wordsworth's arguments against Johnson are extremely awkward, unable to rest a conclusion without a qualification. The entire Essay is shot through with the strong-sounding rhetoric but weakly persuasive logic of its final sentence: if Wordsworth "were not persuaded that the contents of these Volumes, and the Work [The Recluse] to which they are subsidiary, evince some-

thing of the 'Vision and the Faculty divine' . . . [for] the benefit of human nature . . . he would not, if a wish could do it, save them from immediate destruction;—from becoming at this moment, to the world, as a thing that had never been" (84). This grandly negative apocalyptic vision clinches his *argument,* strictly speaking, by saying; 'If you don't believe me [or even: If I don't believe myself], forget that I ever said it.'

9   Prominent among the poets Johnson included, whom Wordsworth omits to mention, are: Cowley, Milton, Butler, Rochester, Dryden, Addison, Prior, Gay, Swift, Pope, Thomson, Collins, and Gray. Johnson's "Advertisement" is typically forthright: "The Booksellers having determined to publish a Body of English Poetry, I was persuaded to promise them a Preface to the Works of each Author; an undertaking, as it was then presented to my mind, not very extensive or difficult. My purpose was only to have allotted to every Poet an Advertisement, like those we find in the French Miscellanies, containing a few dates and a general character; but I have been led beyond my intention, I hope, by the honest desire of giving useful pleasure. . . . As this undertaking was occasional and unforeseen, I must be supposed to have engaged in it with less provision of materials than might have been accumulated by longer pre-meditation" (*The Lives of the Most Eminent English Poets* [London: Bathurst, Buckland, et al., 1781], pp. iii, v).

10 Given Johnson's evident presence in the background of Wordsworth's arguments, there may be an echo here of "The Vanity of Human Wishes": "How nations sink, by darling schemes oppress'd" (l. 13).

11 "The business of a poet . . . is to examine, not the individual, but the species; to remark the general properties and large appearances: he does not number the streaks of the tulip, or describe the different shades in the verdure of the forest" (chapter X, "A dissertation upon poetry"). Coleridge also may have been echoing Wordsworth's scorn for Johnson as an archetype of sickly, luxurious, impotent critics when, discussing the cultural decline from learned to candid to merely popular readers, he refers to the power of these "invisible ministers, whose intellectual claims to the guardianship of the muses seem, for the greater part, analogous to the physical qualifications which adapt their oriental brethren for the superintendence of the Harem" (*BL*, I.59). Such imagery has, however, been constant in the internecine strife of authors and critics.

12 The two years empty of extant correspondence or contact before the exchange of May 1815 is deepened by even longer stretches of silence and absence afterward. No letters of Coleridge to Wordsworth are preserved between May 30, 1815, and April 12, 1824—when, ironically, the former responded with disappointment to another request for his opinion on another literary production, Wordsworth's translation of the *Aeneid* (*LSTC,* v.353–54). No letters of Wordsworth to Coleridge are preserved between the exchange of May 1815 and July 1820. The two men did not meet personally for six years after the formal settling of their differences in 1812, and then very coolly (M. II.313–14).

13 Coleridge's late redaction of this statement in 1832 makes the extent of his participation much more explicit: "The plan laid out, and, I believe, partly

suggested by me, was [there follows the same tri-partite division: (1) the senses informed from the mind, (2) "the pastoral and other states of society, assuming something of the Juvenalian spirit as he approached the high civilization of cities and towns," (3) "thence he was to infer and reveal the proof of . . . a redemptive process in operation"]. . . . Something of this sort was, I think, agreed on" (*TT*, ii.770–71). Finch sees a congruence between the plan outlined in Coleridge's letter of 1815 and that of Wordsworth's "Prospectus" (270–73); though I find this parallel strained, it is certainly of the type characteristic of every stage of their "symbiosis": what one man gave would sooner or later be returned by the other.

14 McFarland, "Wordsworth on Man, on Nature, and on Human Life," *SIR* 21 (1982): 601–18.

15 Coleridge's conclusion has often been reached by other critics following different lines of argument, notably Karl Kroeber, Geoffrey Hartman, Thomas McFarland, and most recently Jonathan Wordsworth, who aptly observes that "Coleridge in his 1815 letter is thinking of *The Recluse* in terms of *Biographia*" (*Borders*, 353). My conclusion is somewhat different: *The Prelude* accomplishes some, but not all, of what *The Recluse* was intended to; likewise the *Biographia*.

16 Reed's argument that this plan is more the product of seventeen years' hindsight from 1815 than a literal representation of the two authors' ideas in 1798 supports the context I am describing ("The 'Plan' of *Lyrical Ballads*").

17 D. M. Fogel, "A Compositional History of the *Biographia Literaria*," *Studies in Bibliography* 30, (1977); 219–34; Fogel's dates are largely corroborated by Engell and Bate (*BL*, I.xlv–lxvii); inferences from these facts are my own unless otherwise indicated; Engell and Bate anticipate some of my particular conclusions in their general statements about the influence of Wordsworth's 1815 preface (see above, n.2).

18 Kathleen Wheeler, *Sources, Processes and Methods in Coleridge's "Biographia Literaria"* (New York: Cambridge University Press, 1980), 8–26.

19 Fogel, 225, 229–30; "Your old friend Coleridge is very hard at work on a preface to a new edition which he is going to publish in the same form as Mr. Wordsworth's" (*Letters of Charles and Mary Lamb*, II.172); *BL*, I.l–li.

20 The full title of Wordsworth's 1815 *Poems* is: *Poems by William Wordsworth: Including Lyrical Ballads, and the Miscellaneous Pieces of the Author. With Additional Poems, A New Preface, and a Supplementary Essay.*

21 *BL*, I.xlvi–li; Don Bialostosky, "Coleridge's Interpretation of Wordsworth's Preface to *Lyrical Ballads*," *PMLA* 93 (1978): 912–24.

22 Christensen analyses this allusion, 118–19.

23 Fogel, 232.

24 Ibid., 221.

25 Engell and Bate make this point more generally, with reference to Coleridge's philosophic development: "An impartial and solid 'philosophic reason, independent of all foreseen application to particular works and authors,' was making his *actual* applications of the greatest possible worth when finally they came, as they do come profusely in the second volume" (*BL*, I.lxix).

26 Christensen, 132, 148.

27 An authoritative modern history of the development of this idea is James Engell's *The Creative Imagination* (Cambridge, Mass.: Harvard University Press, 1981).

28 ". . . that letter addressed to myself as from a friend, at the close of the first volume of the Literary Life, which was written without taking my pen off the paper except to dip it in the inkstand" (*LSTC*, iv.728).

29 See J. A. Appleyard, *Coleridge's Philosophy of Literature* (Cambridge, Mass.: Harvard University Press, 1965), 197–208, for a succinct statement of Coleridge's alternative possible meanings.

30 Wheeler, 88, 111–12.

31 Ibid., 150–53; Leslie Brisman, *Romantic Origins* (Ithaca, N.Y.: Cornell University Press, 1978), 30–37. Gaiatreya C. Spivack has analyzed some aspects of Coleridge's letter from the perspective of Lacanian psychoanalytic criticism; my analysis fits into some of her conclusions, though considerably reducing the mysterious absences in Coleridge's rhetorical gaps from which she derives interpretive power. "The Letter as Cutting Edge," *Yale French Studies* 55/56 (1977): 208–26.

32 But cf. W. J. Bate, "Coleridge on the Function of Art," in *Perspectives of Criticism,* ed. Harry Levin (Cambridge, Mass.: Harvard University Press, 1950), 145 ff.

33 Cf. similar statements by Jacques Derrida on the function of metaphor ("White Mythology," *New Literary History* 6 [1974]: 41–46, 70–71).

34 McFarland makes the point more generally, noting gains and losses for both men in their collaborations and in the cessation of it (97–100).

35 Wordsworth published six complete and three partial collections of his poetry between 1815 and 1850. Of his remaining post-1815 books, two had been composed much earlier (*Peter Bell* and *The Waggoner,* both published in 1819), three were occasional (*Letter to a Friend of Burns* and *Thanksgiving Ode,* 1816; *Two Addresses to the Freeholders of Westmorland,* 1818), and four were volumes of new poetry, each worked into the subsequent collected edition (*The River Duddon,* 1820; *Memorials of a Tour on the Continent, 1820* and *Ecclesiastical Sketches,* both 1822; *Yarrow Revisited, Itinerary Sonnets, Evening Voluntaries,* 1835). The concentration of publications between 1819 and 1822 is noteworthy: these were supposed to have been the last gatherings of "miscellaneous" poems, clearing the decks for concentration on *The Recluse,* but the note of doubt in Sara's voice at the time ("He says . . . he will work only on the Recluse") was a suspicion increasingly confirmed as the years went by. There is a kind of poetic justice in the fact that Wordsworth's first admission that *The Recluse* would never be finished came in terms of a comparison with Thomas Gray, whose works had provided the test cases (in the Preface to *Lyrical Ballads*) whereby he distinguished his new poetry from the bad examples of the preceding age. When the American publisher George Ticknor visited Rydal Mount in 1838, Mrs. Wordsworth set him (as she did many visitors) to prod the poet about *The Recluse.* "On my asking him why he does not finish it, he turned to me very decidedly, and said, 'Why did not Gray finish the long poem he began on a similar subject [the projected series of odes of which only "The Bard" and "The Progress of Poetry" were com-

pleted]? Because he found he had undertaken something beyond his powers to accomplish. And that is my case'" (*LLY*, III.583).

36 *On the Constitution of the Church and State,* ed. John Colmer (Princeton: Princeton University Press, 1976), 46–47.

37 *Toward a Rational Society,* trans. Jeremy J. Shapiro (Boston: Beacon Press, 1970), 30.

Index

Abrams, M. H.: *Natural Supernaturalism*,
    280
Adams, Henry, 92
Aeneas, 130
Akenside, Mark, 254
Alexander the Great, 338, 340, 354
Antidisestablishmentarianism, 322
Arnold, Matthew, xv, 98
Averill, James, 27

Basil of Caesarea, 244
Bate, W. J., 359
Beattie, James, 57; *The Minstrel*, 107
Beaumont, George, 237, 239
Beaumont, Lady, 341
Beaupuy, Michel, 175–78
Bell, Andrew: *An Experiment in Education
    Made at the Asylum of Madras*, 266, 320,
    322–23
Berkeley, Bishop George, 17
Blair, Alexander, 266–67
Blake, William, 35, 46, 97, 247, 292;
    Milton, 107
Bloom, Harold, xxv, 230
Bonaparte, Napoleon, 191–92, 218, 266,
    290, 292, 309, 313, 321
Bradley, A. C., 150
Burke, Edmund, 8, 194
Burns, Robert, 55
Byron, Lord George Gordon, xiii, 12, 265,
    267, 307, 310, 348; *Childe Harold's
    Pilgrimage*, 292

Calvert, Raisley, 212–13
Carlyle, Thomas, 280
Chartism, 322
Chaucer, 340; *The Canterbury Tales*,
    297–98, 361

Christensen, Jerome, 350
Christianity: as stage in the evolution of
    human consciousness, 254–58
Clarkson, Thomas, 323
Coleridge, Samuel Taylor, 8, 9–19, 70, 188,
    191; clerisy, his definition of, xxiv, 361;
    complained about Wordsworth's con-
    victions, 288; his critique of Wordsworth's
    poetry, 360; illness, 237, 240; his
    definition of imagination, 354; lived in
    Lake District, 265; philosophical poem,
    dream of, 10; philosophic traditions, 350;
    second half of career, 360; university
    career, 148
—*The Recluse*, C's contributions to:
    definition of, 208; form of, 10–14; idea
    of, 343–47, 360–61; notes on, 103;
    philosophy of, 15–19; response to *The
    Excursion*, 341–48
—*Sicily and Malta*: departure for, 102, 110;
    residence in, 192–94; return from,
    214, 218–19
—"The Ancient Mariner," 360
—*Biographia Literaria*, 18; Chapter *13*,
    352–60; chronology of composition,
    348–50; as epistolary device, 355–58;
    grew out of *Recluse*, 348; relation of
    autobiography to philosophy, 346
—*The Brook*, 11–12
—"Dejection: An Ode," 188, 197, 211
—"Kubla Khan," 356
—*Sibylline Leaves*, 349
—"To William Wordsworth," 237,
    341–43, 358
Collins, William, 82; "Ode on the Poetical
    Character," 107
Columbus, Christopher, 109

393

Cowper, xxii, 7, 13, 82, 254; *The Task*, 12, 113

Crabbe, George, 6

Daedalus, Stephen, 254
Darwin, Erasmus: *Zoonomia*, 20
De Man, Paul, xx
DeQuincey, Thomas, 50
Descartes, René, 17–20, 140, 353, 357
Dewey, John, xiv

Eliot, George, 291
Emerson, Ralph Waldo, 202
Engell, James, 359
Epic poems, 11–12
Erdman, David, 184, 310
Evans, Mary Ann. *See* Eliot, George

Fawcett, Joseph, 7
Ferguson, Frances, 287
Finch, John Alban, xxvi, 98
Fish, Stanley, 122
Formalist methods, xix
French Revolution, 6, 108, 110, 112–16, 232, 253, 312–13; and legal reforms, 178; September Massacres, 181
Freud, Sigmund, 56, 118, 230

Gill, Stephen, 98, 108
Girondism, 177
God: as necessary to philosophic poems, 15
Godwin, William, 7, 13, 26, 189, 201, 218
Goethe, Johann Wolfgang von, xviii, xxiii, 45, 197, 230, 265; *Dichtung und Warheit*, 101; *Faust*, xiii, xxiii
Goldsmith, Oliver, 6
Gothic image, xxii–xxiv, 352, 357
Grand Chartreuse, the, 244, 255–58, 301
Grasmere, 81–82, 221
Gray, Thomas, "Ode on a Distant Prospect of Eton College," 167
Gregory of Nazianzen, 244
Grob, Alan, 16

Habermas, Jurgen, 362
Hannibal, 338, 340, 354
Hartley, David, 16–17
Hartman, Geoffrey, xxv, 114, 140, 150, 154, 158, 275
Hazlitt, William, 194, 289
Hercules, labors of, 187
Hogg, James, 338
Hunt, Leigh, 274
Hutchinson, Mary, 197
Hutchinson, Sara, 197
Hutchinson family, 82

Imagination, xv, 17, 352–60
Imperialism, 6
Industrialism, 6
Industrial Revolution, 17–18, 315

Jacobins, 218
Jeffrey, Francis, 286, 288, 324, 327, 334
Johnson, Samuel, 146, 285, 338, 342–43, 351; *Lives of the Poets*, 340–41
Jones, John, 119
Jones, Robert, 151
Juvenal, 113

Kant, Immanuel, 17, 174
Keats, John, 170, 267, 274, 278; "Ode to Melancholy," 86
Kierkegaard, Søren, 118, 280
Kishel, Joseph, 241

Lake District, 81–84, 130, 159, 166, 287
Lamb, Charles, 285–86, 289
Langhorne, John, 6
Lindenberger, Herbert, 119
Long poems, xiii
Losh, James, 4

McFarland, Thomas, 15, 335
MacGillivray, J. R., 57
Malthus, Thomas, 7
Marx, Karl, 118, 230
Mathews, William, 4
Milton, John, xii, xxvi, 12, 45, 86–87, 90, 98, 211, 308, 338; "Nativity Hymn," 256; *Paradise Lost*, 11, 75, 86–87, 121, 125, 233–34, 285, 300, 340, 353
Miltonic language, 288
Minto, William, xx–xxi
Moorman, Mary, 84, 290

Nelson, Horatio, 218
New Testament, 191
Nietzsche, Friedrich, 118, 318

Odysseus, 130
Old Testament, 184, 191
Onorato, Richard, 180, 182
Ossian, 340–41
Oswald, Colonel John, 310
Owen, W. J. B., 171

Pantheism, 20
Parrish, Stephen, 57
Pasley, C. W.: *The Military Policy and Institutions of the British Empire*, 291–92
Pirie, David, xxii
Plato, 274

Pope, Alexander, 4, 340, 357; *Essay on Criticism,* 107
Potts, Abbie F., 57
Prometheus, 302

Quine, W. V., xiv

Reed, Mark, 150
Robespierre, Maximilian: in *Prelude,* 174–75, 180–87
Robin Hood, 254
Robinson, Mary, *The Beauty of Buttermere,* 159–62, 169
Romantic epic, xiii
Romantic primitivism, 204
Rorty, Richard, xiv
Rousseau, Jean-Jacques, 146

Schelling, Friedrich, 17, 353–54, 357
Scott, Sir Walter, 218
Self-consciousness, xiv, 73
Shaffer, Elinor, xxiii
Shakespeare, William, 338
Shelley, Percy Bysshe, 267; *Prometheus Unbound,* 198
Smith, Charlotte: *Ethelinde, or the Recluse of the Lake,* 13
Spenser, Edmund, 169, 338, 340; *The Faerie Queene,* 361
Sublime and the Beautiful, 150, 155, 166

Taylor, William, 186
Thelwall, John: *The Peripatetic,* 11–14
Thompson, E. P., 184
Thomson, James, 254, 357
Tillich, Paul, 195
Tobin, James, 3
Tolstoy, Leo Nikolaevich, 292

Vallon, Annette, 179
Valmy, Battle of, 181
Voltaire, 146; *Candide,* 268, 279

Wallace, William, 129–30, 213
Whitman, Walt, 4; *Leaves of Grass,* 121
Williams, Helen Maria: *Letters from France,* 179–80
Wilson, John, 266–67
Woodring, Carl, xxi
Wordsworth, Dorothy, 8, 188, 191, 225
Wordsworth, John, 83; death of, 111, 244
Wordsworth, Jonathan, xxii, 98, 108
Wordsworth, William: career after *1815,* 361; categorization of poems, 336; childhood memories, 83; decline, 361; and egotistical sublime, 54–55; enlistment in the Grasmere Volunteers, 310;

identification with Nelson, 231–33; in Germany, 53–54; love of wandering, 149; reaction to attacks on *The Excursion,* 334–41; sense of himself, xx; stamp distributor for Westmorland, 290; Tory humanist, 323; university career of, 148; walking tour of *1790,* 149, 157, 193
—*Adventures upon Salisbury Plain,* 8, 27, 44, 205, 316
—"Argument for Suicide," 31–33
—*The Borderers,* 3, 8, 29–31, 190, 310, 349
—"Character of a Happy Warrior," 231
—"Composed When a Probability Existed of Our Being Obliged to Quit Rydal Mount as a Residence," xix, 82
—*The Convention of Cintra,* 266
—*Descriptive Sketches,* 20, 255, 258
—"The Discharged Veteran," 37–39
—*Ecclesiastical Sonnets,* 244
—"Essay, Supplementary to the Preface" (*1815*), 338–41, 356–57
—*The Excursion*: as Bible of the poetry-reading public, 289; breaks in structure of, 324; critical abuse of, 333–34; mythology, 276–78; as narrative project, 238; only nominally Christian, 286; the Pastor, 293; philosophical pretensions of, 321; as poem to Coleridge, 330; preface, 335, 358; social theory, 317; the Solitary, like Hamlet, 294; Victorian epic, 291
     Book II, 268–72; Books II–IV, 263–68; Book III, 268, 270–72; Book IV, 272–84; Book V, 292–96; Books V–IX, 285–92; Book VI, 299–305, the story of Ellen, 303–04; Books VI and VII, 296–99, outline, 298, pairing principle, 295, 299, theme of compensatory virtue, 307; Book VII, 305–13, Sir Alfred Irthing, 311–12, young Oswald, 309–10; Book VIII, 313–20, the Parsonage, as emblem, 318–19; Book IX, 320–29, the Wanderer's discourse on education, 320
—"The Force of Prayer, or, The Founding of Bolton Priory: A Tradition," 240
—"Fragment of a Gothic Tale," 29
—"Hart-Leap Well," 85–86
—"Home at Grasmere," 88–91; portion composed in *1800,* 87–94: linguistic peculiarities of, 88; portions composed in *1806,* 219–32: animal stories, 225–26, bridge passage, 228–32, compared to Simplon and Snowdon visions, 224, outline, 220, political language, 227
—"Incipient Madness," 33–34
—*Lyrical Ballads,* xxi, 45, 139, 200, 202, 214, 223, 288, 307, 312, 322, 324

Wordsworth, William (*continued*)
—"Michael," 311
—"A Night-Piece," 5, 36–37, 260
—"Ode: Intimations of Immortality from Recollections of Early Childhood," 115, 316, 328
—"Ode to Duty," 232
—"The Old Cumberland Beggar," 5, 19, 39–43
—"On the Power of Sound," xix
—"The Pedlar," character of, 19–27, 34, 68, 95, 99
—"Peele Castle," 232
—*The Philanthropist*, 3, 13
—*Poems, in Two Volumes*, 238
—*Poems, 1815*, preface, 335–37
—"Poems on the Naming of Places," 83–84
—*The Prelude*: five-book version (*1804*), 106–10; ideal images in, 177; lesson of, 321; relation to *The Recluse*, 100–04; residences of, 100; as Romantic epic, 291; self-reflection in, xvi

Version of *1799*, 53–78; addresses to Coleridge, 60–61; conclusion, 77, 131; Coniston Hall lines, 105–06; decon-struction of, 104–06; endings, 63–65; first part, 66–70; inside-out rhetoric, 61–65; love poem, 60; opening question, 62–63; outline, 58–59; second part, 70–77; two-part movement, 65–77

Version of *1805*, 72; address to Coleridge, 133; beginning, structure of, 123–31; Cambridge University, 146–49; causes of imaginative impair-ment, 200; completion, 217; composition, 110–12, 168; false endings, 211; French Revolution, 151–52, 172–87; introduction, 127–31; Italy, 155–57; last judgment, scene of, 190; looseness of, 122; Lost Sons, 162, 169, 172, 180; plan of, 112–18; postlude, 214–16; post-preamble, 126–27; preamble, 124–25; pre-postlude, 214; preliminary conclusion, 212–14; residential crises, 167; residential structure, 72, 108, 120–21, 146–49, 183; Simplon Pass, 153–55, 248; Snowdon, 207–09, 216, 224, 248, 321, 353; "spots of time," 105, 112, 150, 174, 207; Switzerland, 152–53; theme of avengers, 128–30, 178, 182; theme of human life, 184, 212–14; theme of imagination, 113–16, 175, 188, 194–95, 203–05, 210; urban theme in, 158–60

Book III, 132–36, ideal university, 134–36; Book IV, 136–38, Dawn Dedication, 137, Discharged Veteran, 137–38; Book V, 139–45, Boy of Winander, 141–42, dream of the Arab-Quixote, 140–41, theory of education, 141; Book VI, 146–58; Book VII, 159–65, Bartholomew Fair, 164–65, London satire, 163–65, Matron's Tale, 169; Books VII and VIII, placement of, 111; Book VIII, 165–73, outline, 166–67, London, 171–72; Book IX, 175–80, custom and revolution, 177, Vandracour, 175–80, 194; Book X, 180–94, Death of Robespierre, 185–87; Book XI, 195–99, "spots of time," 197–99, Waiting for the Horses, 198–99; Books XI–XIII, made up from material written earlier, 174; Book XII, 199–206, Salisbury Plain visionary experience, 203–04; Book XIII, 206–16
—"Prospectus," 95–99, 189, 232–34, 244, 257, 259, 313, 314, 326–27, 353; biblical imagery in, 96–99
—*The Recluse*, 13–14, 15–19; beginnings, 3–5; *Biographia Literaria*, 333–62; characteristic paradoxes, 250; as Coleridge's idea, 352; community, 211; decentralization of imagination in, 286–87; first four poems, 5–9, 36–51; fragmentary form, 260; fragments, xix; generalization by story-telling, 220; group vision, 326; human suffering, 27–35; image of avenging band, 231; image of happy band, 8, 147–48, 228, 319–20, 329; imaginative regions, 315; narrative, 27, 74; objections to, 358; organization, 13; parallels to two-part *Prelude* of *1799*, 221; philosophical poem, xiv, 21–27, 54; philosophy, xii, 9–10, 14, 15–19, 188, 295; plot, 6–8; presence of death, 248; primary theme, 318; prospective endings, 242–43, 244; recurrent patterns, xiii; relation to new homes, 82–84; resumption in *1800*, 84–85; self-creating fiction, xxi; self-quotation, 321; sensationalism, 43–44, 47; society and history, xiv; themes: implied sequence, 57, historical optimism, 327, human life, xxi, 18, 233, 309, 362; three-part poem, xi, xiv, xviii; title, connotations of, 13; veiled visions, 245, 261, 281–82
—"Reply to 'Mathetes,' " 267
—"Resolution and Independence," 238
—"The Ruined Cottage," 5, 19–20, 25, 32–33, 43–51, 263–65, 316
—The Solitary, character of: like Job, 304; like Vaudracour, 269; parallels with Wordsworth, 264, 271
—"St. Paul's," 240, 260–62

—"The Tables Turned, 18
—"Thanksgiving Ode," 290
—"Tintern Abbey," 92, 104, 188, 210, 211, 220, 241–43, 244, 245, 253–54, 257, 301
—"To the Clouds," 241–43

—"The Tuft of Primroses," 207, 243–60; Basil of Caesarea, 249–52
—"Upon Westminster Bridge," 261

Yeats, William Butler, 205, 310, 318